W9-AJM-528

PRESIDENTIAL LEADERSHIP
Politics and Policy Making

Fifth Edition

PRESIDENTIAL LEADERSHIP
Politics and Policy Making

Fifth Edition

George C. Edwards III
Texas A & M University

Stephen J. Wayne
Georgetown University

St. Martin's / WORTH

Presidential Leadership:
Politics and Policy Making, Fifth Edition

Copyright © 1999 by Worth Publishers, Inc.
All rights reserved.
Manufactured in the United States of America.
Library of Congress Catalog Card Number: 98-85403
ISBN 0-312-16739-3
Printing: 3   4   5
Year: 02   01   00

Executive Editor: James R. Headley
Project Director: Scott E. Hitchcock
Editorial Assistant: Brian Nobile
Design Director: Jennie R. Nichols
Production Editor: Douglas Bell
Production Manager: Barbara Anne Seixas
Project Coordination: Publisher's Studio
Text and Cover Design: Paul Lacy
Cover Photo: Jefferson Memorial. Len Holsborg/Photonica
Cover Printer: Phoenix Color Corporation
Composition: Stratford Publishing Services, Inc.
Printing and Binding: R.R. Donnelley & Sons Company

Worth Publishers
33 Irving Place
New York, NY 10003

www.worthpublishers.com

Acknowledgments
Acknowledgments and copyrights appear at the back of the book on page 532, which constitutes an
extension of the copyright page.

About the Authors

George C. Edwards III (Ph.D., University of Wisconsin) is Distinguished Professor of Political Science at Texas A&M University and director of the Center for Presidential Studies in the Bush School. He also holds the Jordan Professorship in Liberal Arts, and has held visiting appointments at the U.S. Military Academy at West Point, Peking University in Beijing, Hebrew University in Jerusalem, and the University of Wisconsin in Madison. One of the country's leading scholars of the presidency, he has authored dozens of articles and has written or edited fifteen books on American politics and public policy making, including *At the Margins: Presidential Leadership of Congress*; *Presidential Approval*; *Presidential Leadership*; *National Security and the U.S. Constitution*; *Implementing Public Policy*; and *Researching the Presidency*. He is also editor of *Presidential Studies Quarterly* and the *PRG Report*. Edwards has served as president of the Presidency Research Section of the American Political Science Association, and is frequently interviewed by journalists representing the national and international press.

Stephen J. Wayne (Ph.D., Columbia University) is a professor of government and head of the American Government Section at Georgetown University. An author of numerous professional articles, book chapters, and reviews, he has also written multiple editions of several well-known college texts, including *The Road to the White House* (soon to be published in its sixth edition) and *The Politics of American Government* (St. Martin's/Worth Publishers, 1999). Professor Wayne is an advisory editor for several publishers. He has testified before Congress on the presidency; he is frequently interviewed by the news media on American politics and government and is widely quoted by print journalists as well. A popular lecturer, he regularly speaks to executives in the public and private sectors, international journalists and governmental officials, and students at colleges and universities in the United States and abroad. He is currently writing a book on democracy and U.S. elections.

To Carmella and Cheryl

CONTENTS

Contents

PROLOGUE

THE SCANDALOUS PRESIDENCY

Most presidents have had their share of scandals. Harry Truman had to contend with the underhanded tactics of some of the Missouri cronies he brought into the White House. Dwight Eisenhower's chief of staff, Sherman Adams, was accused of exercising improper influence on behalf of a New England businessman who was also his friend and benefactor. Lyndon Johnson was embarrassed when long-time aide, Walter Jenkins, was arrested by the FBI for propositioning another man in the basement of a YMCA. Richard Nixon had his plumbers, Watergate burglars, dirty tricksters, and political henchmen who shook down wealthy executives for political contributions. Ronald Reagan had a secretary of urban affairs, whose name he couldn't even remember, whose department awarded contracts as political rewards; an attorney general whose behavior bordered on the unethical; and two National Security Council aides who diverted public money to one of the president's favorite causes, the Nicaraguan Contras. George Bush had a chief of staff who used government transportation for visits to his dentist and to add to his stamp collection. Bill Clinton had five cabinet secretaries who at one time or another were under investigation for illegal activities and unethical behavior before or during their government service; a senior White House aide who fired career travel office employees and then invited the FBI to investigate their financial irregularities; and a lower-level aide who collected FBI files on principal Republican opponents. The list goes on!

For the most part, however, the scandals that have embarrassed presidents have involved aides and executive branch appointees. Occasionally, a federal judge has also been the source of unfavorable publicity, such as when Judge Alcee Hastings (currently a member of Congress) was accused of accepting bribes and was later impeached for corrupt behavior, or when Judge Harold Baer Jr., after a huge public outcry, had to reverse a ruling in a drug case that the evidence seized was inadmissible in court because police did not have probable cause.

Although embarrassed by the behavior of their appointees, presidents have usually stayed above the fray. It was not their personal behavior, per se, that was at issue; instead it was their supervisory skills or political judgments that were called into question. During the Nixon and Clinton administrations, however, presidential behavior was *the* issue. Public attention during the Watergate scandal, the Senate investigation of the 1972 presidential campaign, and the House impeachment proceedings focused on the president himself: What did he order? What did he know? And when did he know it? Three of "the high Crimes and Misdemeanors" with which the House Judiciary Committee charged the president—obstruction of justice, abuse of power, and contempt of Congress—were directed at Nixon himself.

Bill Clinton has also been subjected to attacks for his judgments, decisions, and personal behavior. These attacks have concerned some of his appointees like Zoe Baird and Kimba Wood for attorney general, Lani Guinier for assistant attorney general for civil rights, Jocelyn Elders and Henry Foster for surgeon general, Anthony Lake for head of the CIA . . . to name but a few of the most controversial. The president's judgment on issues, such as gays in the military and universal health care, and a host of activities involving campaign fund-raising and expenditures have also been subject to considerable scrutiny and negative commentary. But all of this has paled in comparison to the media frenzy surrounding the independent counsel's investigation of Clinton's sexual relationships, particularly with a 21-year-old White House intern, Monica Lewinsky.

The president initially denied a sexual relationship with Ms. Lewinsky during a deposition in a case charging Clinton with sexual harassment while governor of Arkansas. Subsequent investigation by independent counsel Kenneth Starr provided evidence that a relationship did exist and that the president had not been candid about it when questioned under oath by federal investigators (see Appendix D). The president's judgment, his integrity, his candor, and his moral turpitude were all at issue. His presidency was threatened.

The investigation of Bill Clinton's behavior as president has had and will continue to have a profound effect on the institution of the presidency, on the power of the president (not only Bill Clinton's but that of his successors), on contemporary politics and policy, and on the legacy of the Clinton administration. Moreover, the scandal is bound to affect media coverage of the presidency, public expectations of the president and the office, and evaluations of job performance, both now and in the future.

No person, especially the president, is above the law. That was the basis of the Supreme Court's decision in *United States v. Nixon* when the Court compelled the president to provide tape recordings of White House conversations to the Congress which was investigating his actions in the Watergate affair. That is also the basis of the Court's decision in *Clinton v. Jones,* where it held that a sitting president could be subjected to a civil suit. Although federal judge Susan Wright Weber later dismissed the sexual harassment case against Clinton, the principle that the president is subject to civil law like anyone else is firmly established.

The independent counsel's inquiry into the Whitewater land development deal, the testimony taken during the Jones deposition, and subsequent questioning of the president, his aides and acquaintances, and government

Secret Service employees about Clinton's relationship with other women aimed a legal spotlight at heretofore behind-the-scenes White House activities.

The administration responded to information requests by stonewalling the investigator and impeding his investigation with various appendages of the institutional presidency. *Executive privilege*—the term used to describe conversations between the president and his advisers that are not subject to public revelation or part of the official record—was asserted to prevent two senior aides from being forced to answer questions before a grand jury. When the courts ruled that executive privilege could not be invoked to deny information sought in a criminal inquiry, the White House resorted to a claim of lawyer-client relations to prevent Bruce Lindsay, a presidential counselor and a lawyer, from testifying. But again, the courts held that an attorney employed by the government does not have the same privileged status and relationship as one employed by the president to advise and defend him on personal legal matters. An attempt to prevent current and former Secret Service agents from testifying about the president's activities was also thwarted by judicial decision. Together, these court rulings have narrowed the scope of the presidency's authority: They have reduced the president's claim of executive privilege to discussions of public matters between presidents and their advisers in which there is no alleged criminal activity involved, narrowed the president's claim of attorney-client relationship to that involving private matters between the president and his personal counsel, and removed the claim that forcing Secret Service agents to reveal information might undermine their protective mission. Morever, the president himself was forced to answer questions before a grand jury, although he gave his testimony at the White House while the grand jury watched from another location.

Not only has the scandal shrunk the presidency's legal authority, it has also weakened presidential influence in policy and politics. It reduced the president's ability to set a policy agenda and build support for it; it made the president more dependent on his partisan supporters in Congress whose backing would be needed in any impeachment proceeding. At the same time, it initially encouraged congressional supporters to distance themselves from the president, put them on the defensive for the next election, and opened the party to a potentially divisive fight for its forthcoming presidential nomination.

Naturally, the scandal has conversely benefited opposition party members. It has unified them and their constituency, provided an incentive and rationale for voting in the next election, and enabled them to place Clinton's behavior as the lead item on their campaign agenda. However, their perceived partisanship on the Clinton matter engendered a backlash from those who thought the Republicans too harsh.

The scandal has also accelerated the "lame duck" effect that afflicts incumbents in their second term. It has forced the president to assume more of a ceremonial, head-of-state role. Since the investigation began, public relations has replaced domestic policy making as the preeminent White House activity, and the president has been traveling more than ever before.

One of the more interesting aspects of the Clinton presidency has been the president's continued high standing in presidential approval polls despite his personal behavior and Americans' conclusions that he is not trustworthy. Most citizens have compartmentalized their evaluations of the president, emphasizing the performance of the economy while viewing the independent counsel's charges as dealing with purely private behavior. Many have criticized the intrusiveness of the independent counsel and questioned his motivations as political vendetta. At the same time, the opinions of elites in the media and in and around government have been considerably more negative about the president. Those in the Washington establishment and the media have viewed the president's behavior as a betrayal of the public trust and a failure to "take care that the laws be faithfully executed." The divergence of opinion between elite and mass attitudes toward the president has also made it more difficult for the president's critics in Congress to pursue impeachment as vigorously as they might like.

President Clinton has repeatedly complained about the intrusiveness of the investigation into his private life. It is clear, however, that the distinction between the public and private lives of presidents has become blurred. There may be little left to a president's "private" life. One of the implications of this blurring may be to discourage people from running for president. Even those with blameless lives may resist the loss of privacy and being subjected to continuous investigation.

President Clinton's problems also raise the question of whether a president who has been found to be engaging in immoral behavior in the Oval Office can exercise moral leadership. For example, President Clinton declared that he wanted to precipitate a great national debate on overhauling the financing of Social Security, the federal government's largest program. The options include higher taxes, lower benefits, working longer before receiving benefits, and investing funds in the stock market. Each option requires the American people to make sacrifices or take risks. Can a president whom the people do not trust successfully make such requests and can his statements about the consequences of his policy proposals be believed?

Naturally, the role of the media has been questioned, especially by the White House. When allegations of the president's affair with Monica Lewinsky first surfaced in January 1998, there was a media frenzy such as the nation had seldom seen. Attention to the issue drove out virtually all other news. This frenzy temporarily subsided when the president made a dramatic denial of the affair. Media attention rose dramatically in August, however, when Ms. Lewinsky reached an immunity agreement with Kenneth Starr and testified before a grand jury. Soon the president also testified and then admitted to the American people that he had misled them in January. Polls showed that people felt that the media and Congress were devoting too much attention to the scandal, even while news shows focusing on the scandal enjoyed record ratings.

Both the Nixon and Clinton presidencies suffered from scandal-related fallouts. Both were forced to curtail their policy agendas, retrench their political bases, broaden their ceremonial and public activities, and devote more time and attention to foreign affairs as their domestic options shrunk. Nixon left the institution weaker than when he entered it. Clinton probably will do so as well. In trying to exert leadership, both fell victim to the vicissitudes of the office: unreasonably high expectations of their public, and now private, performance, multiple and often conflicting political forces and policy agendas, deep-seated and complex economic and social issues, and a public with an ambivalent view of government as untrustworthy but essential.

Under such circumstances, it was difficult for them, as it would be for any president, to exert strong leadership. Yet that is precisely what we demand of our presidents and it is often the criteria by which we evaluate their performance in office. This book is about that leadership dilemma.

PREFACE

The presidency is a much praised, much damned institution. During the early 1960s, it was seen as the major innovative force within the government. People looked to the president to satisfy an increasing number of their demands. Presidential power was thought to be the key to political change.

By the late 1960s and early 1970s, this power was seen as a serious problem. Scholars blamed presidents and their excesses for involvement in the war in Southeast Asia and for Watergate and other scandals. Restrain the "imperial" presidency became the cry.

Presidents Ford and Carter responded to this plea by attempting to deimperialize the office. Ford opened the White House to opposing views; Carter initially reduced the size, status, and perquisites of presidential aides. Both were careful not to exceed their constitutional and statutory powers.

Growing institutional conflict between Congress and the presidency and within the executive branch raised questions about the possibility of effective governance. Worsening economic conditions, increasingly scarce resources, and a series of foreign policy crises produced a desire for more assertive, more directive leadership. The presidency was seen as imperiled; weakness, not strength, its problem. Disappointment in presidential performance replaced fear of presidential abuses.

The Reagan presidency led scholars once again to reevaluate the workings of the system and the role of the president within it. Reagan's ability to achieve some of his major policy goals at the beginning of his administration indicated that stalemate need not paralyze the government. But it also gave rise to fears, particularly after the Iran-Contra affair, of the dangers that improperly exercised power can produce.

During the Bush and Clinton presidencies, the need for change, accompanied by the difficulty of achieving it within a divided government, reemerged. Both presidents were frustrated in their attempts to govern, particularly within the domestic arena, and the public expressed its own disillusionment—first in defeating Bush and then in putting the Republicans in power in both houses of Congress for the first time in forty years. Yet, in the midst of defeat, Clinton rejuvenated himself, his presidency, and his party, winning the 1996 presidential election but lacking a clear policy mandate and a governing majority.

And then, amidst a scandal involving Democratic fund-raising during the Clinton-Gore reelection campaign, the president and Congress reached agreement on a balanced budget, proving once again that divided government works quite well during periods of economic prosperity, social tranquility, and world peace—when the government does not face increased demands, and especially when $250 billion of unexpected revenues are predicted over a five-year period.

As he began his second term, the president was popular but not necessarily powerful. Clinton's popularity seemed to be a product of several factors: prosperous economic conditions, successful White House public relations, and good role-playing by a president who had finally learned how to take advantage of the prestige and status of his office. But the president's popularity was soon to be tested again, this time by charges of sexual improprieties. Although Clinton's popularity may have survived this test, his presidency was weakened by it and the president's own credibility was undermined.

There has always been some tension between the personal and the institutional presidency. Presidents are elected in part on their personal leadership experience and potential, on who they are, what they have done, what they promise to do, and whether their promises are believable and seem to address the nation's problems. But once they get into office, the institutional dimension plays a larger role in influencing whether they are able to achieve their policy and political goals. Environmental conditions—economic, social, and political—as well as events and decisions over which they have little or no control also affect their leadership.

This is a book about that leadership, the obstacles to it and the skills necessary to overcome those obstacles. We posit two models of leadership: the president as director of change and the president as facilitator. In the director of change model, presidents lead the nation by dominating other political players; in the facilitator model, they work, bargaining and pleading, at coalition building, to further the attainment of their goals and the goals of their constituencies. These models provide the framework within which we assess leadership in the modern presidency and evaluate the performance of individual presidents.

We offer no simple formula for success, but we do assess the costs and consequences of presidential leadership in a pluralistic system in which separate institutions are forced to share powers. We believe that effective, responsible presidential leadership can play a vital role in providing the coherence, direction, and support necessary to articulate and achieve national policy and political goals.

We wish to thank our friends at St. Martin's/WORTH for the help they have provided us in the development, editing, and marketing of the fifth edition of this book. Most importantly, we want to acknowledge and thank our respective wives, Carmella Edwards and Cheryl Beil, for their patience, encouragement, and help. It is to them we dedicate this book.

George C. Edwards III
Stephen J. Wayne

1

PRESIDENTIAL LEADERSHIP: AN INTRODUCTION

NO OFFICE WITHIN AMERICAN GOVERNMENT or, for that matter, within most other systems has commanded the attention, stirred the imagination, and generated the emotions as has the presidency. Considered the first among equals, it has become the dominant institution in a system designed for balanced government, the prime initiator and coordinator among separate and independent institutions sharing power, the foremost mobilizer among disparate and, often, competing interests, and the principal communications link from, and to, a multitude of groups and individuals. It is a many-faceted, dynamic office—with a plethora of responsibilities, a variety of roles, and a large range of powers.

Within the presidency, the president is clearly the chief. Executive officials look to the office for direction, coordination, and general guidance in the implementation of policy; members of Congress look to it for establishing priorities, exerting influence, and providing services; the heads of foreign governments look to it for articulating positions, conducting diplomacy, and flexing muscle; the general public looks to it for enhancing security, solving problems, and exercising symbolic and moral leadership—a big order, to be sure.

Unfortunately for most presidents, these expectations often exceed their abilities to meet them. It is not simply a question of skill or personality, although both contribute to the capacity to do the job and do it well. The problem is the system, particularly its constitutional, institutional, and political structures. The Constitution divides authority; institutions share power; and parties usually lack cohesion and a sustained policy thrust.

Despite the president's position and status, these constraints are difficult to overcome. Expectations cannot easily be ignored or reduced. As a consequence, disappointment is frequent, regardless of who occupies the Oval Office.

To some extent this has always been the case, but since the 1970s, the gap between expectations and performance seems to have widened. Disenchantment has increased; confidence has declined; the popularity of many presidents has

1

plummeted during the course of their administrations. Exercising effective presidential leadership has thus become more difficult, but no less vital if the American system is to work.

This book addresses these problems and the ability of presidents to surmount them. First and foremost, this is a book about presidential leadership and the capacity of chief executives to fulfill their tasks, exercise their powers, and utilize their organizational structures. It is a book about political leadership—about public opinion, group pressures, media coverage, and presidential salesmanship before, during, and after elections. It is also a book about policy leadership, about institutions and processes, and about priority setting, coalition building, and governmental implementation. Finally, it is a book about personal leadership, incumbents in office and their goals, national needs, and the formal and informal ways of accomplishing presidential objectives.

In order to understand the problems of contemporary presidential leadership, it is necessary to gain perspective on the institution and its development. The first two sections of this chapter provide that perspective. There we present an overview of the creation of the office and its evolution. We place particular emphasis on the growth of presidential policy-making roles, advisory and administrative structures, and the office's political and public dimensions. In the third section we examine recent changes in the political and policy environment and the impact of those changes on the president's job performance. We assess the sources of the institution's problems and present the dilemmas involved in exercising contemporary leadership. In the final section we discuss how to explore these dilemmas.

THE ORIGINAL PRESIDENCY

In 1787, the framers of the Constitution faced a challenge in designing the world's first popularly elected national chief executive. There were few precedents to guide them, and their experience under a king had made them cautious about centralizing power in one individual.

The Creation of the Institution

Although the Constitution's framers saw the need for an independent executive empowered with its own authority, they did not begin with a consensus on the form this executive should take or the powers it should possess. At the outset of their deliberations, two basic questions had to be answered: (1) Should the office be entrusted to one person or to several individuals? and (2) What combination of functions, responsibilities, and powers would yield an energetic, yet safe, executive?

The first of these questions was resolved early in the convention after a short, but pointed, discussion. James Wilson, delegate from Pennsylvania, had proposed that only a single individual could combine the characteristics of "energy, dispatch, and responsibility." Critics immediately charged that such an executive would be dangerous—"the foetus of monarchy," in the words of Edmund Randolph of Virginia.

In denying the allegation that what they really wanted was a king, Wilson and James Madison sought to contrast the powers of their more limited executive with those of a king. As the debate intensified, Madison proposed that the institution's authority be established before the number of executives was decided, a proposal that constituted one of the most astute parliamentary moves of the Constitutional Convention. Wilson had previously declared that the prerogatives of the British monarch were not a proper guide for determining the executive's domain as they were too extensive. The American executive, he argued, should possess only executive authority—the power to execute laws and make those appointments that had not otherwise been provided for. The convention accepted Wilson's delineation, which made it safe to entrust the office to a single individual. This was was promptly done, and only later were the executive powers elaborated.

Wilson was primarily responsible for this elaboration as well. As a member of the committee charged with taking propositions approved by the convention and shaping them into a constitution, he detailed the executive's powers with language taken from the New York and Massachusetts constitutions. Surprisingly, his enumeration engendered little debate. The powers were not particularly controversial, and couching them in the language of two state constitutions made them even more more palatable to the delegates. Thus, most of the powers were quickly and quietly adopted.

Achieving agreement on the checks to secure and restrain the executive was a little more difficult. Abuses by past executives—particularly British monarchs and colonial governors—combined with the excesses of contemporary legislatures made the maintenance of an institutional balance essential. The problem was how to preserve the balance without jeopardizing the independence of the separate branches or impeding the lawful exercise of their authority.

In the end, the framers resolved this problem by checking those powers that they believed to be most dangerous (the ones that had been subject to greatest abuse during the colonial era, such as appointments, treaty making, and declarations of war), while protecting the general spheres of authority from encroachment (in the executive's case, by a qualified veto). Presidential responsibility was also encouraged by the provisions for reeligibility and a short term of office. Reappointment was the principal motive to good behavior. For those executives who flagrantly abused their authority, impeachment was the ultimate recourse.

The traditional weapon used to defend executive authority was the veto. Theoretically, it could function to protect those executive prerogatives that were threatened by the legislature, but in practice, it had frequently been employed to preclude the enactment of laws that the executive opposed. Herein lay its danger. The compromise was to give the president the veto but allow two-thirds of both houses to override it.

In summary, the relative ease with which the presidency was empowered indicates that a consensus had developed on the bounds and substance of executive authority. Not only had certain traditional prerogatives been rejected, but others had been readily accepted. In deciding which of these powers should be given to the new institution, the framers turned to the tenets of balanced government, as articulated by the French theorist Charles de Montesquieu in his often-quoted treatise, *The Spirit of the Laws*, and practiced to some extent in the states of Massachusetts and New York.[1] Those powers that conformed to the basic division of authority were accepted; those that, actually or potentially, threatened the institutional balance were rejected.

Fears of potential abuse led to differing opinions on how best to constrain the branches without violating the principle of separate spheres of authority. The majority of the delegates opted for sharing powers, particularly in foreign affairs and principally with the Senate. Their decision, which was reached toward the end of the convention when the pressures to compromise were greatest, exacerbated the fears of those who believed that the Senate would come to dominate the president and control the government.

Many of the opponents of the Constitution saw the sharing of powers as far more dangerous than the general grant of executive authority that was specified in Article II. Although each of the president's powers engendered some objection during the ratification debate, the most sustained criticism was directed at the president's relationship with the upper chamber. In the end, the proponents of the Constitution prevailed, but the debate over the efficacy of shared powers between the executive and legislative branches has continued through the years.

The Scope of Article II

In one sense, what the framers did is obvious: It is written in Article II. In another sense, however, their deliberations and decisions have been subject to constant interpretation. Unlike Article I, where the Constitution detailed the legislative powers that were given to Congress, Article II described executive authority in a more general way: "The executive power shall be vested in a President of the United States of America." For years scholars have debated whether this designation provides presidents with an undefined grant of authority or simply confers on them the title of the office.

Although the answer to this question remains in doubt, the executive portion of the president's responsibilities is relatively clear. The framers charged the executive with the administration of government, the task of faithfully executing the law, and the capacity to do so by overseeing the executive departments. The departments were not designated by the Constitution. Rather, they were established by legislation during the first and later Congresses. The president, however, was to have a hand in choosing the people who ran them.

The need to provide the executive with some discretion to respond to emergency or extraordinary situations was also considered essential. Heading the only institution with continuous tenure—and the only one with a national perspective—the president was thought to be able to respond to events more quickly and decisively than the Congress. Traditionally, this type of emergency power resided in the executive.

In his *Second Treatise of Civil Government,* the British philosopher John Locke had written of the need for such a power, which he termed a prerogative.[2] The framers agreed. Having themselves experienced a legislature unable to respond to emergencies under the Articles of Confederation, they desired to provide such a capacity in their constitutional arrangement, and they gave it to the president.

The debate over the war powers illustrates the framers' dilemma as well as their solution. Initially, the Congress was given the authority to "make war." However, fearing that the word "make" might preclude the executive from responding to an attack if Congress were not in session, the framers agreed to substitute the word "declare." This provided the president with flexibility but did not alter the basic intent—to have the Congress decide whether to go to war. Even after making that decision, it retained powers that affected the conduct of hostilities. These powers serve to limit the president's discretion as commander in chief.

In foreign affairs, the president was similarly limited in what could be done alone without the approval of the Senate or both houses. The executive did, however, share the treaty-making role with the upper chamber and exercised the initiative. But even here, the wording of the Constitution suggested that the Senate was to have a role in the negotiation of treaties as well as in their ratification.

Although executive powers were expected to expand during emergencies, they were never without limits. The exercise of discretionary powers by the executive was always tied to legislation. Presidents could summon Congress into special session, but they were obligated to report to it on the state of the union; they could recommend necessary and expedient legislation, but it was Congress that, in the end, had to decide what laws, if any, to enact. Even in the case of the veto, two-thirds of both houses would have the last word.

In short, the relatively general grant of executive authority gave the office broad discretion in the exercise of its principal responsibility—the execution of the law. Some of its powers were exclusive, but others were shared. Some powers were enumerated, but their enumeration was not exhaustive. Presidents had considerable freedom to oversee subordinates of their own choosing in their administration of government. On the other hand, their discretion in formulating policy was extremely limited. In the normal course of events, Congress, not the executive, was expected to assume that role.

THE EVOLUTION OF THE PRESIDENCY

The contemporary presidency bears little resemblance to that which the framers of the Constitution had artfully designed in 1787 in Philadelphia. Their executive had less authority, less functional responsibility, and no explicit institutional structure or operating procedures. Of course, these were different times.

Policy-Making Roles

Although the president's constitutionally designated authority has not been formally amended, the scope of that authority has been expanded by law and precedent. Over the years, the president's policy-making powers have grown dramatically. Chief executives, starting with George Washington, set the contours of foreign policy. Beginning with Thomas Jefferson, they shaped it to the point of actually defining what the war policy would be. There were other early examples of presidential initiatives in foreign affairs, notably James Monroe's famous doctrine pledging U.S. protection of the independent states on this side of the Atlantic.

Crisis situations expanded the president's powers still further, as Abraham Lincoln's actions during the Civil War demonstrated. Lincoln justified his exercise of power by the gravity of the situation. "Was it possible to lose the nation and yet preserve the Constitution?" he asked. To his own question he replied, "I felt that measures otherwise unconstitutional might become lawful by becoming indispensable to the preservation of the Constitution through the preservation of the nation."[3]

Lincoln's assertion of power was not checked by Congress during the war, but that body was to reassert its authority after the war ended. Throughout the remainder of the nineteenth century, Congress, not the president, dominated the relationship between the branches. In fact, when

Woodrow Wilson, then a professor of politics, wrote his perceptive study on the American political system in the mid-1880s, he titled it, *Congressional Government.*

Wilson wrote at the end of an era. By the time he became chief executive, the president's roles in both foreign and domestic affairs had expanded (and Wilson revised his book). Demands for a more activist government had encouraged Presidents William McKinley and, especially, Theodore Roosevelt to work more closely and harmoniously with Congress in fashioning major policy initiatives.

Assuming an assertive posture in both foreign and domestic affairs, Roosevelt expanded the president's policy-making roles. He sent the navy halfway around the world (and then requested appropriations from Congress to return it home); he announced a corollary to the Monroe Doctrine, further involving the United States in hemispheric activities; he helped instigate a revolution in Colombia; and he quickly recognized the independence of insurgents on the Isthmus of Panama and entered into an agreement with them to build a canal. He was the first president to travel outside the United States (to Mexico and Panama) and the first to help settle a war, for which he won the Nobel Peace Prize. Within the domestic sphere, Roosevelt busted trusts, crusaded for conservation, and mediated a major coal strike. He was also instrumental in getting Congress to enact important legislation, including the Pure Food and Drug Act, the Meat Inspection Act, and the Hepburn Act (regarding railroads).

Roosevelt's theory of the presidency justified and accommodated his activism. Writing in his autobiography after his political career had ended, Roosevelt stated: "My view was that every executive officer . . . was a steward of the people bound actively and affirmatively to do all he could for the people."[4]

In contrast, William Howard Taft, Roosevelt's successor, expressed a much more restrained conception: "The president can exercise no power which cannot be fairly and reasonably traced to some specific grant of power. . . . There is no undefined residuum of power which he can exercise because it seems to him to be in the public interest.[5]

Roosevelt's *stewardship* theory has prevailed. With the exception of the three Republican presidents of the 1920s, occupants of the Oval Office in the twentieth century have assumed active political and policy-making roles. Woodrow Wilson and Franklin Roosevelt, in particular, expanded Theodore Roosevelt's initiatives in international and domestic matters.

Wilson was the first president to propose a comprehensive legislative program and the first to be involved in summitry. He was also the architect of the proposal to establish a League of Nations, although he was unable to persuade the Senate to accept his plan.

Franklin Roosevelt enlarged the president's role in economic affairs. On coming into office (in the midst of the Great Depression), he initiated a series of measures to deal with the domestic crisis and succeeded in getting Congress to enact them. He also maintained the posture of an international leader, maneuvering the country's entrance into World War II and participating in summit conferences to win the war and plan the peace. In addition, he made the critical decision to develop the atomic bomb.

The modern presidency is said to have begun in the era of Franklin Roosevelt. It is characterized by presidential activism in a variety of policy-making roles. Many of the practices that Roosevelt initiated or continued have been institutionalized by his successors or required by Congress.

Organizational Structure

The structure of the modern presidency also developed during the Franklin Roosevelt period. In 1939, the Executive Office of the President was created. Prior to that time, presidents had depended largely on their department heads for administration and advice.

The Constitution did not explicitly provide for an administrative structure. It did, however, contain an oblique reference to one through a provision in Article II stating that the president could demand, in writing, the opinions of subordinate officials. It was up to the first Congress to establish the executive departments as the principal administrative units of government. It created three departments (Foreign Affairs, Treasury, and War) and appointed an attorney general and a postmaster general. Since then, ten more departments and more than 150 agencies have been established.

Throughout most of the nineteenth century, it was Congress, not the president, who dominated the administration of government. Statutes specified many organizational details of the departments, including their jurisdiction, staffing levels, and even operating procedures. For the most part, there was little oversight from the president.

The autonomy of the departments contributed to the influence of the secretaries who headed them. Since the department heads were the president's principal advisers, they exercised considerable leverage in helping to design administration goals and in mobilizing congressional support. With the exception of the Jefferson, Andrew Jackson, and Lincoln administrations, strong department secretaries and weak presidents characterized executive advisory relationships.

This began to change at the outset of the twentieth century as a consequence of the president's growing influence in Congress. As that influence increased, the potency of the department secretaries, individually and collectively, began to decline. They lost their privileged position between president and Congress, and their support of administration proposals became less critical to the president's legislative success.

The concern that Theodore Roosevelt and, particularly, William Howard Taft evidenced toward the organization of government also contributed eventually to the president's enhanced status and power within the executive branch. Taft appointed a Committee on Economy and Efficiency to recommend improvements. Reporting in 1913, the committee urged the creation of a more hierarchical structure, with the president assuming a larger administrative role.

Initially, Congress was reluctant to comply. However, sizable budget deficits, inflated by U.S. involvement in World War I, provided the legislature with a financial (and political) incentive to do so. Unable to control the deficits, Congress turned to the president for help. In particular, it enacted the Budget and Accounting Act of 1921, which made it a presidential responsibility to estimate the financial needs of the individual departments and agencies on a yearly basis and provided the president with an institutional mechanism to do so: the Bureau of the Budget.

When Franklin Roosevelt took office and expanded the president's domestic policy role, he needed more information, more expertise, and more staff. At first he depended on personnel provided by the executive departments, but when that did not prove satisfactory, he turned to a small group of experts to advise him on how to make the organizational structure of the executive more responsive to his needs. The group, headed by Louis Brownlow, issued a report that urged the creation of a separate presidential office.[6] In 1939 Congress approved the act that established the Executive Office of the President. Initially the office consisted of five units: the White House, the Bureau of the Budget, and three World War II agencies (the National Resources Planning Board, the Liaison Office for Personnel Management, and the Office of Government Reports). Eventually, over forty different councils, boards, and offices were housed, at one time or another, in this office.

The creation of the Executive Office provided the president with a structure directly responsive to his interests, and the White House became his personal office. Presidential aides performed political tasks that were dictated by the president's immediate needs, actions, and goals. Having no constitutional or statutory authority of their own and no political base other than the president's, their influence was dependent on their access to him. Thus, they did his calling.

Whereas the White House functioned as a personal extension of the president, the Bureau of the Budget became an institutional extension of the presidency. It coordinated the policy-making functions of the departments and agencies, imposing a presidential perspective on the executive branch in the process.

During subsequent administrations, the duties of the Executive Office have been expanded and its organizational structure redesigned. Staffed by civil servants and run by political appointees, it continues to perform a variety of critical tasks. It is considered essential for an activist presidency, but its large size, many roles, and organizational autonomy make it difficult for the president to oversee on a continuing basis, much less to control.

Public Dimensions

In addition to the development of the presidency as an institution and the growth of its policy-making roles, the public dimension of the office has expanded as well. This, too, has been a relatively recent phenomenon. Franklin Roosevelt was the first to use the mass media (radio) to communicate directly with the American people on a regular basis. His successors have used television to the same end.

For most of the nineteenth century the presidency was not a particularly visible office, although the president received his share of critical commentary. Jefferson was the first to claim a partisan mandate, and Jackson the first to claim a public one.[7]

A variety of factors contributed to the adoption of a more active public posture by presidents toward the beginning of the twentieth century. The growth of news-gathering organizations and newspaper chains made it possible to communicate faster and with more people. The advent of yellow journalism, combined with the increased activism of government, generated more interest in the opinions and behavior of public officials, particularly the president.

Theodore Roosevelt, more than any of his predecessors, took advantage of these developments to focus attention on himself, his policies, and his activities. He was the first president to give reporters a room in the White House and the first to hold regular meetings with the press. Using his position as "a bully pulpit," Roosevelt rallied public support for his positions and proposals.

Roosevelt's presidency prompted Professor Woodrow Wilson to revise his view that the governmental system was dominated by Congress. The president could have as big a role as he wanted, Wilson asserted in 1908. He could use his position as party and national leader to enhance his political power, and thereby exert influence on Congress:

> His capacity will set the limit; and if Congress be overborne by him, it will be no fault of the makers of the Constitution—it will be from no lack of constitutional powers on its part, but only because the President has the nation behind him, and Congress has not. He has no means of compelling Congress except through public opinion.[8]

Wilson clearly attempted to heed his own words, and the enactment of his legislative program can be attributed in large part to his political leadership and public oratory. His greatest disappointment, however—his inability to persuade the Senate to ratify the Treaty of Versailles, ending World War I—stemmed from his failure to exercise these skills successfully. Wilson, who went on a public-speaking tour to build support for his position, overestimated his ability to lead public opinion and underestimated his opponents' capacity to do so.

Although Theodore Roosevelt and Woodrow Wilson used the presidency as a podium, neither of them was as skillful at manipulating the press as was Franklin Roosevelt. In his first term, Franklin Roosevelt held more press conferences than any of his predecessors. Meeting frequently with small groups of reporters in the Oval Office, he used these sessions to articulate his views and float trial balloons. He also made extensive and productive use of radio, especially in his famous "fireside chats."

By the end of the Roosevelt era, the presidency had been permanently altered by the news media. It had become the most visible national office. Coverage of the White House was constant, and the president was always in the news.

The intensive and extensive media focus on the president had three principal effects. First, it permanently added a new role to the president's job, that of communicator in chief, and required that skills commensurate with this role be exercised. Second, it heightened public expectations of presidential performance. Advances in communications have enabled organized groups to promote the desires of their membership more effectively, and the president has become the focal point for many of these increased demands on government. Third, media coverage linked public approval more closely to the exercise of presidential power. Now, more than ever, presidents need to build support outside of government to gain support within it. Taken together, these factors indicate why increased public exposure for the president has, at best, been a mixed blessing.

PROBLEMS OF CONTEMPORARY LEADERSHIP

The changes that evolved during the twentieth century have created new demands on presidents that, as a consequence, have generated new roles and obligations for them and new criteria by which they are judged. These new roles and criteria have, in turn, affected perceptions of leadership. In the past, the people did not look to the president to solve most national economic, social, and political problems. Today, however, they do. The president is expected to be a chief policy maker and to exercise a wide range of powers. Ancillary coordination, communication, and co-optation functions have followed from these expanded roles and powers.

Institutional growth has been another consequence of a more activist presidency. Indeed, the size of the office has increased enormously. Prior to 1939 the president was assisted by a few aides, most of whom were detailed from executive departments and agencies. The total budget for the salaries and expenses of those working for the president was $125,804.98 in 1925, and in 1939, when the Executive Office was created, it was about $250,000. Today, however, it is approximately $200 million. The first Executive Office of the President consisted of five agencies, including the White House; today it has twelve agencies, two residences, and a combined staff of approximately 1,500.

The larger staff has increased the president's capacity to perform added responsibilities and to do so with less dependence on executive departments and agencies. However, the staff's enlargement has also worked to extend the very functions and responsibilities it was designed to serve. This expansion has limited the president's personal influence over what functions are performed and, to a lesser extent, how the administration is organized to perform them.

Not only has the presidential office grown in size and solidified in organization, but its policy processes have become institutionalized. Mechanisms for preparing the budget, formulating a program, building support in Congress, and advising the president whether to sign or veto legislation have been developed and continued from administration to administration. These routines have also worked to shape the functions and processes they serve.

There have been significant changes in the public dimensions of the office as well. For one, the selection process has become more individualized. Parties do not organize and mediate between candidates and the voters as they did in the past. Performance expectations have increased as a consequence of longer campaigns, more personalized appeals, and many specific promises made to organized groups. However, the electoral coalition that is needed to win today no longer provides the basis for governing. New coalitions have to be formed on an issue-by-issue basis.

The national media are more critical of the president than in the past. Communications from, and to, the public are more direct and immediate. Such communications enable the White House to measure the pulse of public opinion more accurately, but they can also condition responses, shorten the response time frame, and, ultimately, constrain the president's options.

Interest groups have proliferated and become professionalized. They have also become more sophisticated at influencing their members and mobilizing them behind specific policy positions. No institution or individual—not the Executive Office of the President, the White House, or even the president—is immune from these pressures.

'Okay, bring in the new guy . . .'

Source: AUTH Copyright © 1976, *Philadelphia Inquirer.* Reprinted with permission of Universal Press Syndicate. All rights reserved.

Lobbying increases the political impact of many presidential decisions. It can force the president's hand, necessitating a compromise for political reasons when an alternative may be preferred for policy reasons. The proliferation of professionalized interest groups makes the redistribution of resources more difficult. Over time, it increases levels of dissatisfaction among different sectors of the public. It adversely affects presidential relations with Congress and, ultimately, the president's capacity to lead.

Changes within the legislature have reinforced this organized pluralism. Over the past generation, Congress has decentralized lawmaking by shifting power to a large number of members. Ironically, more members of Congress must now be consulted, coordinated, and cajoled at the very time when that body has involved itself in more issues of executive policy making and policy implementation. Presidents must work harder than in the past to achieve their legislative goals. Whether the current efforts of Republican Newt Gingrich to centralize power in the Speakership can be maintained remains to be seen. What is not in question is that centralized power in the hands of a Republican Speaker is unlikely to be a boon for a Democratic president—or possibly even a Republican one.

Similar constraints are found within the executive branch. The continuing orientation of the bureaucracy to outside groups, plus its ongoing relationships with Congress, work to limit presidential influence. Most presidential appointees in the departments and agencies soon find themselves with divided loyalties.

There are other constraints as well. External factors within the environment have enlarged policy expectations of the president yet, at the same time, made meeting those expectations less subject to presidential control than in the past. Presidents are expected to manage the economy, but the increasing interdependence of nations limits their ability to do so; similarly, the scarcity of some natural resources no longer permits unlimited development and forces decisions that have important political consequences. Finally, vulnerability of the United States to terrorist attack shortens the president's reaction time and broadens the effect of national security decisions. It also contributes to the public's psychological dependence on the president and the security needs that the office serves.

Finally, events from the late 1960s to the present—U.S. involvement in Vietnam, the Watergate cover-up, the Iran-Contra affair, the Monica Lewinsky scandal, and various departmental and congressional scandals—have impugned the motives and integrity of high officials, including the president. Occupants of the Oval Office no longer enjoy the benefit of the doubt, making it more difficult for them to rally and maintain public support despite the expectation that they do so.

ORIENTATION AND ORGANIZATION OF THIS BOOK

This book is titled *Presidential Leadership* because it focuses on just that— leadership. The exercise of influence is central to our concept of leadership, as it is for most political scientists. We want to know whether the president can influence the actions and attitudes of others and affect the output of government. It is important to distinguish between attempts to lead and leadership itself. Both concepts are of primary interest in this book, and we devote much of our effort to exploring the relationship between the two.

Presidential leadership typically involves obtaining or maintaining the support of other political actors for the chief executive's political and policy stances. In the U.S. political system, most political actors, with the exception of those in uniform, are free to choose whether to follow the chief executive's lead; the president cannot force them to act, which presents a challenge to his political leadership. Harry Truman, writing to his sister, made this comment about the presidency:

> Aside from the impossible administrative burden, he has to take all sorts of abuse from liars and demagogues. . . . The people can never understand why the President does not use his supposedly great power to make 'em behave.

Well, all the President is, is a glorified public relations man who spends his time flattering, kissing and kicking people to get them to do what they are supposed to do anyway.[9]

Thinking about Leadership: Two Perspectives

Although thinking of leadership in terms of influence is useful for the study of the presidency, the concept remains somewhat nebulous. To guide our examination, we consider it useful to refine the concept of leadership by contrasting two broad perspectives on the presidency. In the first, the president is seen as the *director* of change, who creates opportunities to move in new directions and leads others where they otherwise would not go. In the role of director, the president is out in front, establishing goals and encouraging others inside and outside of government to follow. Accordingly, the president is the moving force of the system and the initiator of change.

A second perspective is less heroic, but nonetheless, important. Here the president is seen primarily as a *facilitator* of change, who exploits opportunities to help others go where they want to go anyway or, at a minimum, do not object to going. In the role of facilitator, the president reflects, and perhaps intensifies, widely held views, and uses available resources to achieve his constituency's aspirations. Thus, the president prods and pushes the government, in which roles, responsibilities, and powers are shared.

The director creates a constituency to follow his lead, whereas the facilitator endows his constituency's views with shape and purpose by interpreting and translating them into legislation. The director shapes the contours of the political landscape to pave the way for change, whereas the facilitator exploits opportunities presented by a favorable configuration of political forces.

The director moves mountains and influences many independent actors. This is the more formidable task—establishing the agenda and persuading a (perhaps reluctant) public or Congress to support administration policies. In contrast, the facilitator works at the margins, influencing a few critical actors and taking advantage of the opportunities for change already present in the environment. In both cases the president exercises leadership, yet the scale of the leadership clearly differs. The range and scope of the director's influence are broad, whereas those of the facilitator are more narrow.

The two perspectives are not neat categories; we employ them simply to aid our understanding of the concept of leadership and its application to the president. They reflect, but do not precisely mirror, different thrusts in the scholarly literature on the presidency. On the one hand, Richard Neustadt's *Presidential Power,* the most influential book on the presidency, focuses on the president as center of government, and the one who must lead if leading is to be done.[10] Similarly, Theodore Lowi argues that the president has eclipsed the Congress and political parties and become the center of the political system.[11]

Other scholars see the presidency differently. Charles O. Jones, for example, argued: "The president is not the presidency. The presidency is not the government. Ours is not a presidential system."[12] One of the authors of this book has argued that presidential influence is "at the margins" of American politics and emphasized the importance of the political environment in which the president operates.[13] Stephen Skowronek found presidents constrained in important ways by the historical context in which they serve, but he also saw them as the major force in causing fundamental political change.[14]

The issue is not whether leadership matters, but rather how much it does matter and under what conditions. It is not sufficient to conclude, however, that the environment is sometimes receptive to change and at other times not. This viewpoint simply begs the question of whether presidents are able to influence the environment to create the opportunity for change. Understanding the possibilities of leadership permits an assessment of presidential performance.

The notion of a dominant president who moves the country and the government by means of strong, effective leadership has deep roots in our political culture. Those chief executives whom Americans revere— particularly Washington, Jefferson, Jackson, Lincoln, Wilson, and both Roosevelts—have taken on mythical proportions as leaders. Even though the public is frequently disillusioned with presidential performance and recognizes that stalemate is common, Americans eagerly accept what appears to be effective presidential leadership, as in the case of Ronald Reagan in 1981, as evidence on which to renew their faith in the potential of the presidency. After all, if presidential leadership works some of the time, why not all the time?

This perception directly influences the expectations and evaluations of presidents. If it is reasonable to expect successful leadership from the White House, then failures of leadership must be due to personal deficiencies. If problems arise because leaders lack the proper will, skills, or understanding, then the solution to the need for leadership is straightforward and simple: Elect presidents who are willing and able to lead. Because the system is responsive to appropriate leadership, it will function smoothly with the right leaders in the Oval Office. The public and the media can indulge in high expectations of chief executives and freely criticize them if they fail— for example, at swaying Congress or the public to their point of view. The blame lies clearly in the leader rather than the environment. Americans need not concern themselves with broader forces in U.S. society that may influence presidential leadership. Because these forces are complex, and perhaps even intractable, to focus on the individual as leader simplifies the analysis and evaluation of the problems of governing.

On the other hand, what if presidential leadership is not preeminent in American government? What if presidential leadership has less potential than holders of the conventional wisdom believe, and the president actually operates at the margins in leading the country? What if the national preoccupation with the chief executive is misplaced and belief in the impact of the individual leader is largely a myth—a product of a search for simple solutions in an extremely complex, purposefully inefficient system in which the founders' handiwork in decentralizing power defeats even the most capable leaders?

If this is the case, the public should expect less of its presidents and be less disappointed when they are not successful in leading. In addition, the focus should be less exclusively on the president and more on the context in which the president seeks to lead. Major changes in public policy may then require more than just the "right" person in the job and may not turn on a president's leadership qualities. It does not follow, of course, that failures of presidential leadership may never be attributed to the White House or that presidents have no control over the outcome of their relations with other political actors. However, it does mean that a better understanding of presidential leadership is necessary in order to think sensibly about the role of the chief executive within the nation's political system.

Conceptual Focus

This book will explore the president's leadership problems and the attempts by recent chief executives to overcome them. It will do so by examining multiple facets of the presidency within the context of its political and policy-making roles. Our orientation is eclectic. Instead of adopting a particular perspective, the book will present several. Instead of imposing a single thesis, it will discuss many of the hypotheses, generalizations, and conclusions that have been advanced by students of the presidency.

The reason for utilizing a variety of approaches and presenting a broad body of research findings is that there is no one generally accepted theory of the presidency or single conceptual framework within which to study the office (other than, perhaps, Richard Neustadt's volume on presidential power) that has commanded the attention and acceptance of most presidency scholars.[15]

Despite an abundance of literature on the presidency, our understanding of how that institution works is not nearly as sophisticated as our understanding of Congress or even the Supreme Court. Much of the presidency still operates behind closed doors.

What factors have conditioned the methodology, shaped the content, and limited the findings of so much of the presidency literature? Three stand out: (1) the view that each president (and administration) is relatively unique; (2) the difficulty of obtaining firsthand information on the internal operation of the institution; and (3) the absence of a comprehensive theory of presidential behavior. Together these factors have impeded the ability of scholars to do rigorous, analytic, empirical research on the presidency.

The personalities of individual presidents and their staffs, the particular events and circumstances of their times in office, and the specific problems and actions of their administrations have led scholars to treat each presidency as if it were unique. Emphasizing the differences, rather than the similarities, between presidencies makes the identification of patterns and relations more difficult and, in turn, makes it harder to generalize. Description rather than analysis, and speculation rather than generalization, have become the standard fare.

The relatively closed character of the institution has contributed to the problem. The presidency is not easy to observe from a distance. Public pronouncements and actions tell only part of what happens and why—and usually only the part that the people in power wish to convey. Inside information is difficult to obtain. Decision makers, particularly those at the top of the executive bureaucracy, are not readily accessible. Their busy schedules, combined with their natural reluctance to reveal information that may be embarrassing, sensitive, or in other ways controversial, often make them unwilling and unresponsive sources.

Nor is dependence on journalistic accounts usually satisfactory. Journalists tend to be event oriented. They do not usually employ a time frame or perspective that is sufficiently broad or historical to permit generalizations, particularly on the institutional and behavioral aspects of the office.

The third factor that contributes to the problem is the absence of an overall theory that explains presidential behavior. Unlike other areas in political science—such as individual voting behavior, in which there is a body of theory that explains and predicts who votes and why—the presidency literature has not produced a comprehensive explanation of why presidents do what they do or the consequences of their actions. Nor have we been able to predict what they will do or the consequences of their actions in the future. There are, however, many prescriptions of what presidents should do.

The nature of these problems suggests that when examining the institution and exploring the president's leadership opportunities and problems, we should cast our net as broadly as possible. This is why we decided not to focus on a single theme (which might exclude important information) but rather to examine a set of critical relationships—the relationships between the president and those whose support he needs to do his job.

To function effectively, a chief executive must be elected, build and maintain popular support, make decisions, and present, promote, and implement policies. Each of these requirements involves reciprocal relationships in which presidents influence, and are influenced by, others. That is why we must examine both sides of these relationships rather than focus exclusively on the president.

Relationships provide a conceptual framework for studying presidential leadership as they enable us to explain the behavioral causes and consequences of presidential activities. By stressing relationships, however, we do not suggest that legal powers, informal roles, institutional structures, or psychological factors are unimportant. Indeed, we firmly believe that we cannot understand the presidency without an extensive knowledge of these matters. This is the background that we provide here. Our point of departure is a discussion of these matters within the context of presidential relationships, rather than vice versa. Powers, roles, structures, and personality should not be viewed as ends in themselves. Rather, they are important for what they contribute to the president's ability to formulate, establish, and implement policies.

A Preview

This book focuses on four broad areas: (1) politics and public relations, (2) the person in the presidency, (3) the interaction between that institution and the rest of the government, and (4) the policy-making process.

The next four chapters concern the relationship between the president and the public. In Chapters 2 and 3 we discuss nomination politics and the general election. Here the focus is on the interaction between presidential candidates, the electorate, and the implications of this interaction for governing—what an administration tries to do, when, and to what effect. In Chapter 4 we turn to presidents in office and their relations with the general public, and in Chapter 5 we examine the communications link between the incumbent and the news media. In each of these chapters we explore leadership problems. Obviously, winning electoral support, gaining public approval, and obtaining favorable media coverage are critical to a president's success.

In Chapters 6, 7, and 8 we analyze the relationship between the institution and the people in it—specifically, interactions among the president, senior White House advisers, and others who wish to affect presidential decisions. Here attention is directed toward decision making at the presidential level. The institutional environment combined with the incumbent's personal style condition presidential discretion and ultimately presidential choices.

In Chapters 9 through 11, we turn to the interactions that the president must have with the executive branch, Congress, and the judiciary, respectively, to achieve policy objectives. Promoting programs in Congress, implementing them in the bureaucracy, and adjudicating them in the courts are necessary if presidential leadership is to be effective.

After scrutinizing presidential relations, we then discuss the formulation of public policy in and by the presidency. Chapters 12 through 14 concern domestic, budgetary and economic, and foreign and defense policy making, respectively. In each chapter we identify and assess expectations of presidential leadership, the resources available for meeting them, and the policies that presidents have pursued and, to some extent, achieved.

Having explored the critical relationships between the president and the public, the president and the presidency, the president and the other branches, and the president and the policy-making process, we end with appendixes, one of which discuss another important, but different, kind of relationship—that of the president and political science. Two other appendixes provide background on succession, tenure, and removal and list relevant provisions of the Constitution. Finally, we include material relevant to the issue of impeaching President Clinton. Our objective is to demonstrate how various perspectives on the office and methods of studying it can affect what we know about the president. Thus, we conclude where we began. If the presidency is a multifaceted institution (as we claim it is), then it can best be understood only by adopting a variety of approaches and techniques. That is why our orientation is eclectic, why we have introduced a number of themes, and why we have chosen critical presidential relationships as the conceptual framework for this book.

SELECTED READING

Cronin, Thomas E., ed. *Inventing the American Presidency*. Lawrence: University Press of Kansas, 1989.

Ellis, Richard, and Aaron Wildavsky. *Dilemmas of Presidential Leadership: From Washington through Lincoln*. New Brunswick, N.J.: Transaction Publishers, 1989.

Hamilton, Alexander, James Madison, and John Jay. "Federalist Papers Nos. 67–77." In *The Federalist Papers*. New York: New American Library, 1961.

McDonald, Forrest. *The American Presidency: An Intellectual History*. Lawrence: University Press of Kansas, 1994.

Neustadt, Richard E. *Presidential Power*. New York: Free Press, 1990.

Pika, Joseph, and Norman Thomas. "The Presidency since Mid-Century." *Congress and the Presidency* 19 (Spring 1992): 29–49.

Riccards, Michael P. *A Republic, If You Can Keep It*. New York: Greenwood, 1987.

Robinson, Donald L. *"To the Best of My Ability."* New York: Norton, 1987.
Skowronek, Stephen. *The Politics Presidents Make.* Cambridge: Harvard University Press, 1993.

Notes

1. Charles de Montesquieu, *The Spirit of the Laws,* vol. 1 (New York: Hafner, 1949).
2. Locke wrote:

   > Where the legislative and executive power are in distinct hands, as they are in all moderated monarchies and well-framed governments, there the good of the society requires that several things should be left to the discretion of him that has the executive power. For the legislators not being able to foresee and provide by laws for all that may be useful to the community, the executor of the laws, having the power in his hands, has by the common law of Nature a right to make use of it for the good of the society, in many cases where the municipal law has given no direction, till the legislative can conveniently be assembled to provide for it. (John Locke, "Second Treatise of Civil Government," in Thomas I. Cook, ed., *Two Treatises of Government* [New York: Hafner, 1956], p. 203).

3. Abraham Lincoln, letter dated April 8, 1964, reprinted in Harry A. Bailey, Jr., ed., *Classics of the American Presidency* (Oak Park, Ill.: Moore Publishing, 1980), p. 34.
4. Theodore Roosevelt, *The Autobiography of Theodore Roosevelt* (New York: Scribner's, 1913), p. 197.
5. William Howard Taft, *Our Chief Magistrate and His Powers* (New York: Columbia University Press, 1916), p. 138.
6. President's Committee on Administrative Management, *Report with Special Studies* (Washington, D.C.: Government Printing Office, 1937), p. 5.
7. It was during the 1820s that the electorate began to choose presidential electors directly rather than have them selected by state legislatures. This increased the value of obtaining and maintaining public support for the president. Tradition, however, required that this be done in a manner that befitted the dignity of the office. Public addresses were permitted, but personal campaigning was discouraged. Instead, the party was expected to shoulder the electoral burden for its candidates. Not until William Jennings Bryan's quest for the nation's highest office in 1896 did candidates take to the stump themselves.
8. Woodrow Wilson, *Constitutional Government* (New York: Columbia University Press, 1908), pp. 70–71.
9. Quoted in David McCullough, *Truman* (New York: Simon and Schuster, 1992), pp. 584–585.
10. Richard E. Neustadt, *Presidential Power* (New York: Free Press, 1990).
11. Theodore J. Lowi, *The Personal President* (Ithaca, N.Y.: Cornell University Press, 1985).
12. Charles O. Jones, *The Presidency in a Separated System* (Washington, D.C.: Brookings Institution, 1994), p. 1.
13. George C. Edwards III, *At the Margins: Presidential Leadership of Congress* (New Haven: Yale University Press, 1989). See also Mark A. Peterson, *Legislating Together* (Cambridge: Harvard University Press, 1990); Jon R. Bond and Richard Fleisher, *The President in the Legislative Arena* (Chicago: University of Chicago Press, 1990).
14. Stephen Skowronek, *The Politics Presidents Make* (Cambridge: Harvard University Press, 1993).
15. Neustadt, *Presidential Power.*

2

THE NOMINATION PROCESS

EVERY FOUR YEARS THERE ARE TWO PRESIDENTIAL selection processes: The first is to nominate candidates, and the second, to choose between them. Both require considerable time, money, and effort.

The nominating system has evolved significantly in recent years. Rules governing delegate selection, laws regulating contributions and expenditures, and communications (whether controlled or uncontrolled by the candidates) have all changed dramatically since the 1970s. These changes have literally revolutionized the nomination process. They have affected the types of candidates who seek their party's nomination, the qualifications they have, the policies they pursue, and the leadership they exert on their party and, ultimately, as president. Today, aspirants for a party's nomination are more on their own. They have greater opportunities to articulate their own priorities and shape their own issue agenda, to develop their own style, and to build their own political coalitions. In this sense, should they prove successful, they will be in a good position to bring new ideas, people, and leadership to the presidency; however, they will also have to confront experienced Washingtonians with different perspectives, needs, and interests, who preceded them in attaining national office and may very well be there after they leave.

The nomination process, however, contributes to the difficulty that presidential aspirants encounter in exercising such leadership. The process heightens public expectations but weakens partisan support, usually accentuating divisions within the party. It encourages personality politics by focusing on personal characteristics, a theatrical style, and a "sound-bite mentality" rather than on a more substantive debate of the nation's critical goals and the issues that lie ahead. It also produces negative campaigning, which highlights the less desirable qualities of candidates and parties. This negativism leaves a residue of cynicism, which must be overcome by the winning candidate and party if they are to successfully exercise personal and policy leadership.

In this chapter we will discuss the changes in the nominating system and their impact on individuals seeking the presidency. The chapter is organized into four sections. In the first we present a historical overview of the nomination process, describing its evolution from congressional caucus to brokered national conventions and then popular selection of the delegates through primaries and caucuses. In the second part we examine the factors that condition the selection: party rules, campaign finance, and public relations as exercised through the prism of the mass media. In emphasizing the changes that have occurred within each of these areas, we describe their impact on the parties and their standard-bearers. Next, we turn to the strategy and tactics of seeking the nomination. Here we discuss the principal strategic components for both front-runners and non–front-runners and illustrate the discussion with examples from Bill Clinton's 1992 and 1996 nomination strategies. In the last section of the chapter, we follow this quest to the national convention and describe the unofficial and official business of these large, semipublic extravaganzas: drama and staging; rules, credentials, and platforms; and the nominations themselves. We also present a brief characterization of the successful candidate. In conclusion, we summarize changes in the nomination process and note their implications for winning the general election and governing the country.

THE EVOLUTION OF THE SYSTEM

The nominating system began to evolve after the writing of the Constitution and the holding of the first two presidential elections. The framers had not concerned themselves with nominations because there were no parties to nominate. Because they assumed that well-qualified individuals would comprise the pool from which the president and vice president would be selected, the convention delegates instead directed their efforts toward encouraging an independent judgment by the electors. They considered such a judgment to be essential if the two most qualified persons were to be chosen.

Once political parties emerged, however, the notion of making an independent decision was constrained by the party's desire to choose an individual whose views were consistent with its own. This required a mechanism by which the parties could designate their nominees.

In 1796, party leaders gathered together informally to agree on their tickets. Four years later partisan congressional caucuses met for the purposes of recommending candidates. "King Caucus," as it came to be known, became the principal mode of nomination until the 1820s, when factions developed within Jefferson's Democratic-Republican party, the only viable national party at the time. These factions eventually led to the demise of the caucus and the development of a more decentralized mode of nomination, which was consistent with the increasingly sectional composition of the parties. By the 1830s, national nominating conventions became the principal means for brokering those interests and uniting the party for a national campaign.

The first convention was held in 1831 by the Anti-Masons, a small, but relatively active, third party. Having virtually no congressional representation of its own, this party could not use a caucus of its members of Congress to decide on its candidates. Instead, it organized a general meeting in which delegates from the state parties could choose the nominees as well as determine the party's positions on the important issues of the day. The Democratic party—they had dropped "Republican" from their title—followed suit with a nominating convention of its own in 1832, and thereafter, conventions became the standard method for selecting nominees and articulating policy positions.

These early conventions were informal and rowdy by contemporary standards. In fact, the delegates themselves decided on the procedures for conducting the meetings. The method for choosing the delegates was left to the state parties and, more specifically, to its party leadership. In most cases, public participation was minimal.

Nineteenth-century conventions served a number of purposes. They provided a forum for party bosses and constituted a mechanism by which agreements could be negotiated and support could be mobilized. By brokering interests, they helped unite disparate elements within the party, thereby converting a conglomeration of state organizations into a national coalition created for the purpose of electing a president and vice president. The nominating system buttressed the position of party officials, but it did so at the expense of the rank-and-file party members. The influence of the leadership depended in large part on its ability to deliver the votes. To ensure loyalty, the bosses handpicked their delegations.

Demands for reform began to be heard at the beginning of the twentieth century, when a number of states changed their mode of selection to primary elections in order to permit greater public participation. This movement, however, was short-lived. Low voter turnout in the primaries, the costs of holding such elections, and the opposition of party leaders to rank-and-file involvement persuaded several state legislatures to make their primaries advisory only or even discontinue them entirely. As a consequence, the number of primaries declined after World War I, as did the percentage of delegates selected in them (see Table 2–1).

Strong candidates avoided the primaries. Running in too many of them was interpreted as a sign of weakness, and indicated a lack of national recognition or a failure to obtain the support of party leaders. Those who did enter these public contests did so mainly to test their popularity rather than to win convention votes. Dwight D. Eisenhower (in 1952), John F. Kennedy (in 1960), and Richard M. Nixon (in 1968) had to demonstrate that being a general, a Catholic, or a once-defeated presidential (and later, gubernatorial) candidate, respectively, would not be fatal to their chances.

TABLE 2–1. **Number of Presidential Primaries and Percentage of Convention Delegates from Primary States, by Party, since 1912**

	Democratic[†]		Republican	
Year	Number of Primaries	Percentage of Delegates from Primary States*	Number of Primaries	Percentage of Delegates
1912	12	32.9	13	41.7
1916	20	53.5	20	58.9
1920	16	44.6	20	57.8
1924	14	35.5	17	45.3
1928	17	42.2	16	44.9
1932	16	40.0	14	37.7
1936	14	36.5	12	37.5
1940	13	35.8	13	38.8
1944	14	36.7	13	38.7
1948	14	36.3	12	36.0
1952	15	38.7	13	39.0
1956	19	42.7	19	44.8
1960	16	38.3	15	38.6
1964	17	45.7	17	45.6
1968	17	37.5	16	34.3
1972	23	60.5	22	52.7
1976	29*	72.6	28*	67.9
1980	31*	74.7	35*	74.3
1984	26	62.9	30	68.2
1988	34	66.6	35	76.9
1992	39	78.8	38	80.4
1996[‡]	36	67.0	43	90.0

*Does not include Vermont, which holds nonbinding presidential preference votes but chooses delegates in state caucuses and conventions.

[†]Includes party leaders and elected officials chosen from primary states.

[‡]Two of the Democratic primaries in 1996 were not binding.

Sources: 1912–1964: F. Christopher Arterton, "Campaign Organizations Face the Mass Media in the 1976 Presidential Nomination Process" (paper delivered at the annual meeting of the American Political Science Association, Washington, D.C., September 1–4, 1977); 1968–1976: Austin Ranney, *Participation in American Presidential Nominations, 1976* (Washington, D.C., American Enterprise Institute, 1977), Table 1, p. 6. The figures for 1980 were compiled by Austin Ranney from materials distributed by the Democratic National Committee and the Republican National Committee; figures for elections since 1980 were compiled by the authors from data supplied by the Democratic and Republican National Committee and by the Federal Election Commission.

In other words, they needed to prove that they could win the general election by doing well in the electoral arena.

With the possible exception of Kennedy's victories in Wisconsin and West Virginia in 1960 and Barry Goldwater's win in California in 1964, the primaries were neither crucial nor decisive for winning the nomination until the 1970s.[1] Until that time, if there was a consensus within the party on a single candidate, the primaries helped confirm it; when there was not, the primaries were not able to produce it. Thus, they had little to do with whether a party was united or divided at the time of the convention.

CHANGES IN THE POLITICAL ARENA

Party Reforms

By the end of the 1960s, the situation had altered dramatically, largely as a result of the tumultuous Democratic convention of 1968. That year, the Democratic Party nominee, Hubert Humphrey, had not actively competed in the primaries, and demands for a larger voice for the party's rank and file increased.[2] The party responded by appointing a series of commissions to examine its rules for delegate selection and propose changes in the process. The commissions had two basic goals: encourage greater participation in party activities and make the convention more representative of typical Democratic voters.

To achieve these objectives, in the 1970s the party attempted to ensure that delegate selection more closely reflected popular sentiment. Primaries thus became the preferred method of choosing delegates, and the popular vote was more closely tied to the allocation of delegates to the convention. These changes made the nomination process more open and participatory, but also more divisive.

In 1988 and 1992, voter turnout exceeded 33 million, a sizable gain over the 12 million who participated in 1968. However, it declined in 1996 to 25 million (14 million in the Republican primaries and 11 million in the Democratic contests), a consequence of Bob Dole's early win and Bill Clinton's lack of opposition.

Conventions became more representative of rank-and-file party voters. However, the delegates to them were also more activist, more ideological, and as a consequence, less compromising than were the former delegates, who had been handpicked by party leaders. Democratic delegates tended to be more liberal, and Republicans more conservative, than the average Democratic and Republican voters, respectively.

Nominees were often disadvantaged. Indeed, the more divisive the process, the greater was the disadvantage. The eventual winners were subjected to much more criticism than they would have received had they been handpicked by the party leaders. This critical scrutiny damaged the image they wished to convey in the presidential campaign. They also entered the general election with a plateful of promises in addition to the platforms on which they had to run. Because many of the promises made during the nomination period were to groups that had clout, being comprised of party activists, the agenda of candidates selected after a divisive nomination struggle tended to be more ideological than it would have been otherwise. The party's nominee either had to run away from these promises, as Bob Dole did on the social issues of abortion, prayer in schools, and homosexuality, or to embrace them, as George Bush had appeared to do four years earlier. During much of the 1970s and 1980s, it was the Democratic candidates who had to deal with an ideological agenda that cast their nominees in a disadvantageous "liberal" glow.

To offset these unintended and, from the party's perspective, undesirable consequences, the Democrats, and to a much lesser extent, the Republicans, have continued to tinker with the rules of their nomination processes in the hopes of putting their nominees in a stronger position at the onset of the presidential campaign.

The Democrats now require straight proportional voting for the allocation of delegates within states and a minimum threshold of 15 percent in order to be eligible to win delegates. The threshold was designed to discourage frivolous candidates from running and siphoning off votes. They also created a new category of delegates, known as "superdelegates," to ensure that state and national party leaders and elected officials are represented at the party's nominating convention and enable them to broker a compromise should the convention become hopelessly divided.

In an effort to counter the increasing front-loading of the nomination process, the Republicans instituted a bonus system, to become effective in 2000, that rewards states that hold their primary or caucus later in the nomination cycle with extra delegates.[3] They were unsuccessful, however, as states continued to schedule their primaries earlier. What the Republicans wanted to avoid by this change was a situation like the one in which Dole found himself in spring 1996: he had effectively wrapped up the Republican nomination by mid-March, yet the convention was not scheduled until mid-August. What was he to do in the interim? Unable to focus public attention, low on funds, and not in a position to lay the foundations for his presidential campaign, Dole and his Republican colleagues were in limbo, which made them a target for criticism but deprived them of the podium and resources needed to respond.

Another development in the nomination cycle, which may not be harmful to the parties and their nominees, has been the progressive regionalization of primary elections. Beginning in 1988 with the southern regional primaries, neighboring states throughout the country have begun to act in concert with one another by scheduling their nomination contests on the same day or during the same week. They do so in order to capture the attention of the candidates, get them to campaign in the region (and, of course, spend money while doing so), encourage them to address regional issues and concerns, and give the region more clout in determining the successful nominee.

The party's reforms and their impact on the nomination process have affected how presidential aspirants seek the nomination and which ones are most likely to win. Initially, when the Democrats first reformed their delegate selection process in the 1970s, the changes seem to benefit candidates who were outsiders and who appealed to party activists. Since the 1980s, however, they have given the advantage to candidates who are insiders and who have greater financial and political resources available. These individuals tend to have a national reputation and are seen as having the best chance of winning for the party.

The reason why the best known, organized, and funded candidates enter the contest in an advantageous position has to do with the front-loading of the process, the need for extensive mass media exposure, and the importance of gaining the support of state party leaders and their organizations. The choosing of so many delegates so early in the multistate contests requires that candidates raise money, develop their own organization and ties to others, and begin to design their partisan appeal and media strategy early, often in the year before the election. In 1998, even before the midterm congressional elections, many of the aspirants for their party's 2000 nomination had formed precandidacy organizations, leadership political action committees (PACs) in most cases, and were actively campaigning in the early caucus and early primary states.[4]

Campaign Finance

While the reforms in party rules have had a profound effect on American electoral politics, they are not the only major change to affect the nomination process. New finance laws have had a major impact as well by altering the way in which money is raised and spent and the amount that is available.

Throughout most of American history, candidates of both parties have depended almost exclusively on large contributions from private donors to finance their campaigns. This dependence, combined with spiraling costs, secret and sometimes illegal contributions, and little public information about who gave how much and what they received in return, raises serious questions about the conduct of elections in a democratic society. Can officials be responsive to national needs as well as those of their individual benefactors? Has the presidency become an office that only the wealthy or those with wealthy "friends" can seek?

In the 1970s, Congress began to address these issues. In particular, it enacted legislation to limit skyrocketing expenses (especially in the mass media), reduce the influence of large contributors, and reveal contributors' identities. The amount of money that presidential and vice presidential candidates and their families could contribute to their own campaigns was also limited. Other legislation established a fund to subsidize the presidential nomination process and support the general election.[5]

The Federal Election Campaign Act (FECA), enacted in 1974, provided for public disclosure, contribution ceilings, campaign spending limits, and federal subsidies for the nomination process. Some of its provisions were highly controversial. Opponents of the legislation challenged the limits on contributions and spending as a violation of the First Amendment right to freedom of speech. In the landmark case of *Buckley v. Valeo* (424 U.S. 1, 1976), the Supreme Court upheld the right of Congress to regulate the contributions and expenditures of campaign organizations, but not the independent spending of individuals and groups during the campaign.

The Court's decision forced Congress to pass new legislation in 1976, which it subsequently amended in 1979. The major provisions of this legislation provide for public disclosure of all contributions and expenditures over a certain amount (now $200), limits on individual and group contributions to candidates (summarized in Table 2–2), federal subsidies for the

TABLE 2–2. Contribution Limits

	To Each Candidate or Candidate Committee per Election	To National Party Committee per Calendar Year	To Any Other Political Committee per Calendar Year	Total per Calendar Year
Individual may give	$1,000	$20,000	$5,000	$25,000
Multicandidate committee* may give	5,000	15,000	5,000	No limit
Party committees may give	1,000 or 5,000†	No limit	5,000	No limit
Other political committees may give†	1,000	20,000	5,000	No limit

*A multicandidate committee is a political action committee with more than fifty contributors which has been registered for at least six months and, with the exception of state party committees, has made contributions to five or more federal candidates.

†Limit depends on whether or not the party committee is a multicandidate committee.

Source: Federal Election Commission, *The FEC and the Federal Campaign Finance Law* (Washington: Government Printing Office, 1978), p. 4.

nomination process, and outright grants for the general election. These federal subsidies and grants amounted to almost $175 million in 1992 and $234 million in 1996. The Federal Election Commission estimates that they will be about $287 million in 2000 (approximately $100 million for matching funds to the candidates for their party's nomination; $26.6 million to the Democratic and Republican parties and $2.5 million to the Reform party for their conventions; and $136 million to the Democratic and Republican nominees and $12.7 million to the Reform party candidate in the general election).[6]

Candidates who accept public funding are also limited in the amount they can spend. During the preconvention period, they are subject to an overall ceiling as well as individual state limits. In 1996 the ceiling was $31 million plus an additional 20 percent for fund-raising; in 2000, it will be about $34 million. There are also state limits, which are based on the size of the voting-age population plus a cost-of-living adjustment. Candidates who accept federal funds can spend only $50,000 of their own money in the prenomination process, but those who refuse federal funds can spend as much as they want. Thus, millionaire Steve Forbes spent an estimated $37.5 million of his own money in his quest for the 1996 Republican nomination.

The 1979 amendments to the FECA, however, do provide a huge loophole to the revenue and spending limits imposed on the presidential election. To encourage voting, the amendments permit an unlimited amount of money to be spent on voluntary efforts by state and local parties to get people out to vote. These expenditures are referred to as "soft money," and since 1980, political parties have raised substantial amounts by soliciting large donations in return for access to powerful elected party leaders. Large contributors are offered VIP treatment, including briefings, visits, and other occasions to interact with elected party officials. For example, President Clinton went to great lengths to extend White House hospitality to Democratic donors in his first term. Major contributors were invited to sleep in the Lincoln bedroom, drink coffee with the president, and even ride on *Air Force I*, the president's plane. The Republicans were not to be outdone. They, too, hosted, fed, and informed party donors, who were also given access to the congressional leadership and committee chairs. Giving donors these perquisites raises questions about the use of public facilities for private political gain, as do fund-raising calls made by public officials from government buildings.[7] It also raises questions about the adequacy of the law itself. Does it need fixing?

Congress had a number of objectives in enacting campaign finance legislation in the 1970s: to reduce the dependence on large donors, discourage illicit and unreported contributions, broaden the base of public giving, and curtail spiraling costs at the presidential level. Clearly, the law has not achieved all these objectives, although it has had a major impact on electoral politics. Secret contributors and unexplained expenses have been reduced, although violations, overpayments, and improper reporting procedures have persisted. Individual and group contributions to candidates are limited, but soft money contributions to political parties are not. The law has even encouraged electoral activities of nonparty groups known as political action committees (PACs), which compete with political parties for influence with the public. PACs operate telephone banks, distribute promotional material, hold newsworthy events, and mobilize their membership and sympathizers in get-out-the-vote-campaigns. All these activities can influence the election. Their influence tends to be greatest in the early primaries and caucuses when the candidates are not well known and lack large organizations.

The law also shapes the candidates' strategy and tactics. It is considered essential to have a solid financial base at the beginning of the nomination process. Early money is important for several reasons:

1. It buys recognition for those who need it. Steve Forbes bought that recognition in 1995–1996 with his expenditures of millions of dollars of his own money.

2. It buys legitimacy. The press evaluates the credibility of candidates in part on the basis of how much money they can raise and how willing people are to contribute to their campaign. Candidates who cannot raise much money are not usually taken seriously by the news media and by other potential contributors. It requires money to raise money—which is why nationally recognized candidates are advantaged.

3. The most important reason for having early money is that it gives a candidate maximum flexibility in deciding where and how to campaign. The early expenditure of funds can build support, win delegates, generate momentum, and result in an early knockout of one's opponents.

There are two drawbacks to spending campaign funds quickly, however. With limits placed on expenditures for candidates who accept federal funds (which is usually everyone but multimillionaires), money can run out even if the competition stays in. This is a particular problem when not all the primaries and caucuses are clustered at the beginning of the nomination process, as was the case in the 1970s. Today's clustered primaries require that every candidate spend the bulk of their funds early. For example, Dole spent one-third of his expenditures before any of the primaries and caucuses had been held. Dole's early expenditure of funds helped ensure his victory, but it also left him with very little money to reply to an advertising barrage that his Democratic opponent aired after Dole had effectively won the nomination but before he was officially anointed as the Republican candidate, in mid-August (see Figure 2-1).

Dole

WHERE THE MONEY CAME FROM*

Receipts for the primary campaign
through August 1996, in millions

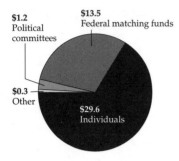

$1.2
Political
committees

$13.5
Federal matching funds

$0.3
Other

$29.6
Individuals

TOTAL: $44.6 million

WHERE THE MONEY WENT*

Campaign expenses by category,
January 1995 through July 1996,
in millions

$5.0
Other campaign
activity

$0.7
Polling

$12.1
Overhead

$10.1
Fund-
raising

$6.5
Advertising

TOTAL: $34.5 million

Clinton

WHERE THE MONEY CAME FROM*

Receipts for the primary campaign
through August 1996, in millions

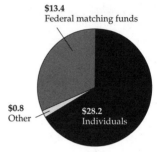

$13.4
Federal matching funds

$0.8
Other

$28.2
Individuals

TOTAL: $42.4 million

WHERE THE MONEY WENT*

Campaign expenses by category,
January 1995 through July 1996,
in millions

$1.8
Other campaign
activity

$1.0
Polling

$8.8
Advertising

$14.1
Overhead

$4.6
Fund-
raising

TOTAL: $30.4 million

Figure 2–1. The Costs of Politics: The 1996 Presidential Nomination
*Numbers may not add up to totals due to rounding.
Sources: Revenues: Federal Election Commission, October 1996. Expenditures: *Washington Post*,
April 18, 1996, p. A3, and August 24, 1996, p. A11, respectively.

Two principal consequences follow from the need for early money. First,
campaigns start earlier to raise the needed funds. For example, the Republican contenders for the party's 2000 presidential nomination will doubtless
engage in a furious competition in 1999 to raise the $20+ million considered
essential to compete. Second, since 1980, the candidate who has been in the

strongest financial position at the beginning of the process has usually won the nomination, so raising a large amount of money confers a psychological advantage as well.

In short, money *contributes to* success, but it does not guarantee it. Moreover, potential success also attracts money. This creates a vicious cycle, which candidates without a national reputation or much outside support have difficulty entering.

Public Relations

The third major change in the nomination process has been the enlargement of its public dimension and the use of new communication channels to reach the voters. Throughout most of American history, the quest for the nomination was a relatively private, party affair. Candidates made their case primarily to state party leaders, so there was little need to discern public attitudes, project public appeals, or build public support. Now, of course, that need has grown. Had Republican party leaders had their druthers, Robert Dole would have been selected the Republican nominee by acclamation in 1996. However, to win the nomination, Dole had to enter the primaries and caucuses (and had to struggle in the early contests).

The cast of characters has also changed. In the past, a preconvention campaign organization consisted of a relatively small group of party regulars, but today that organization numbers in the hundreds at its headquarters and the thousands in the field. Moreover, most of the senior campaign advisers do not hold important party positions; instead, they are professional campaign consultants—pollsters, media gurus, grassroots organizers, direct mailers, accountants, and attorneys—all of whom specialize in electoral politics. No candidate can afford to be without these wizards of modern campaign technology.

Even the demands on today's candidates are different. They must be willing to campaign continuously in the public eye through the mass media (primarily on radio and television), often for more than a year. They need to be well versed on a range of issues, with relatively well-defined messages that generate strong appeal within the party's electoral coalition without alienating other partisans, whose support is necessary in the general election. Steve Forbes, who promoted the flat-rate income tax in 1996, was not adequately familiar with social issues. He seemed inconsistent and unsure of himself when he talked with the Christian Coalition and other fundamentalist religious groups. Forbes learned his lesson, however, and during the next four years, he spoke out and addressed the religious right on a range of social issues on which he was both knowledgable and opinionated.

The pulse of the voters conditions the message that is presented and the images that candidates try to create. Thus a critical early step for any serious candidate is to have that pulse taken. A pollster must be hired and a private poll commissioned.

Polls John F. Kennedy was the first candidate to engage a pollster in his quest for the nomination. Preconvention surveys conducted by Louis Harris in 1960 indicated that Hubert Humphrey, Kennedy's principal rival, was vulnerable in Wisconsin and West Virginia. On the basis of that information, the Kennedy campaign wisely decided to concentrate time, effort, and money in these states. Victories in both helped demonstrate Kennedy's popularity, thereby enormously improving his chances for the nomination.

Another device that is frequently used to explore the public mood and how to respond effectively to it is the focus group—a collection of individuals who are brought together and are asked to discuss and respond to a variety of real and hypothetical situations involving candidates, issues, and ideology. Information gleaned from focus groups is often extremely helpful in creating and adjusting a campaign appeal. Focus groups were used extensively and successfully by Bill Clinton in 1992 to gauge voter reaction to the allegations about his character and his response to those allegations. He continued to use them in 1996 to decide which ads to run, where, and for how long. The entire Clinton advertising campaign in 1996 was developed and monitored through careful and constant White House polling, combined with the use of focus groups, to determine which words and pictures seemed to have the greatest impact. The Dole campaign also used focus groups to develop and test its ads.

Polls and focus groups are important for several reasons. They provide information about the opinions, beliefs, and attitudes of voters; they identify people's perceptions of the candidates and their positions; and they suggest the kinds of appeals that are apt to be most persuasive, the groups to whom these appeals should be made, and even the words and expressions that should be used to elicit the maximum impact. Armed with this information, media campaigns can be designed, targeted, and continually tested.

Polls are important for another reason: they affect news media coverage. During the nomination process, when the outcome is in doubt, the candidates' standings in the polls influence the amount of coverage they receive. In general, those who are deemed by the public to be most electable get the most coverage. The coverage, in turn, increases the candidates' ability to raise money, gain volunteers, and extend their appeal. This produces a situation in which those who cannot gain media attention have great difficulty improving their public standing, while those who cannot do so also cannot gain media attention. Frequently this situation encourages bizarre behavior by candidates, who may desperately seek the limelight through their strident rhetoric or unconventional actions or both.

Media When party leaders exercised the dominant influence on the nominations, personal contact with party regulars was the most effective
method of campaigning. Appearances at rallies, speeches before clubs, and
press conferences held for local news media energized rank-and-file supporters. Before the advent of the electronic media, people received most of
their information from newspapers and from campaign literature designed
and distributed by the party.

All this has changed, however. For almost forty years now, television has
been the primary source of election news for most people. Along with radio, it
has become the major vehicle for getting a candidate's message across. With
the primaries concentrated at the beginning of the nomination process (many
of them even on the same day), candidates have little choice but to depend on
the mass media to reach potential voters. The only way for candidates to
reduce their media dependency is to have a strong army of activists—as did
Pat Buchanan in 1992 and 1996 and Jesse Jackson in 1984 and 1988—to
ring doorbells and make phone calls. However, having such volunteers alone
is not sufficient. Candidates must also get television airtime.

The use of visual and audio media has revolutionized campaigning. It
has made image creation more important, brought public relations specialists into candidate organizations, and siphoned off a relatively large proportion of the campaign budget for television and radio. Due to the glare of the
news media, candidates have also become less spontaneous. Fearful that
their words and actions might be misinterpreted or misconstrued, they now
tend to play it safe, ad-libbing less and following scripts more. When they
fail to follow a script, they can get into trouble with offhanded comments,
as Robert Dole did in 1996, when he said in a television interview that
tobacco may not be addictive, or Clinton did when he suggested that he had
made a mistake by raising taxes too much in 1993.

In debates, press conferences, and interviews, candidates tend to repeat
their stump speeches and to sound increasingly like their commercials.
Events are staged for consumption by home viewers. Candidates also try to
obtain as much free media coverage as possible. Take a typical day in 1996
in the life of Pat Buchanan, a long-shot candidate who was seeking to gain
public attention at the beginning of the nomination cycle. Terence Jeffrey,
Buchanan's campaign manager, describes this day as follows:

> Pat would get up at about five in the morning, get some coffee, get in the mini-
> van, and go from one TV station to the other, in the local market, wherever they
> had morning shows[,] and . . . would do a live segment on every morning televi-
> sion show.
>
> Then they [Buchanan and his press secretary] would come back to the
> hotel, read through the newspapers[,] and at 10 A.M. we'd go out and do our

theme event for the day—hopefully, with an excellent photo—drive whatever our message was, get out a press release, which we faxed out everywhere[,] and let that, hopefully[,] resonate into the newspapers.

At noon, we'd go back to the television stations, if they would have us, or else we'd drive to a new market. . . . Buchanan would literally go from one station to the other to the other, go back to the hotel, maybe take a nap in the afternoon, then . . . go out at 5:00 P.M. and . . . do the evening TV stations.[8]

The news media, particularly television, influence the nomination process in several other respects. The early contests have become more important because of the attention they are given. Iowa, which traditionally is the first state to hold a caucus and New Hampshire, the first to hold a primary, get the bulk of media coverage. These states usually rank first in the amount of attention they receive. More than half the campaign coverage of the 1996 Republican nomination on the three major networks' evening news shows focused on Iowa and New Hampshire.[9]

Naturally, candidates who do surprisingly well benefit from this coverage enormously. Eugene McCarthy in 1968, George McGovern in 1972, Jimmy Carter in 1976, Gary Hart in 1984, George Bush in 1988, and Pat Buchanan in 1996 all gained visibility and credibility from their New Hampshire performances, even though none had a majority of the vote. Bill Clinton's strong second-place finish in New Hampshire in 1992 against favorite son Paul Tsongas, a former senator from neighboring Massachusetts, enhanced Clinton's candidacy, particularly in light of the personal allegations that had been directed against him prior to the primary. Doing more poorly than expected has the opposite effect, as Robert Dole found, much to his dismay, when he came in second to George Bush in New Hampshire in 1988 and to Pat Buchanan in 1996, in both cases after Dole had won the previously held Iowa caucuses.

Early victories help establish a candidate's credibility as a potential nominee. For one thing, they can provide an important psychological boost. Being declared a winner improves a candidate's standing in the polls, makes fund-raising easier, and aids in attracting backers to contribute to a later primary success. Buchanan and Forbes benefited from their early showings in 1996 but simply could not sustain them. Currently, the rapid onset of other caucuses and primaries makes it more difficult for a lesser-known candidate to take advantage of an early win. There is simply not enough time to do so.

The news media also affect delegate selection in their interpretation of the results. The winners are not necessarily those who do best but those who do better than expected. When performance exceeds expectations or else fails to meet them, that is news. However, when performance meets expectations, it is less newsworthy. Given the media's bias for the unexpected, candidates tend to underestimate their vote in public in order to be able to claim satisfaction with the results. Eugene McCarthy's ability to do this was a key factor in his primary challenges, first of Lyndon Johnson, and then of Robert Kennedy, in 1968. McCarthy contested nine primaries and won two, but he minimized the impact of his seven losses by using this low-prediction posture. Similarly, in 1976 Jimmy Carter purposely kept his predictions low. Likewise, after Dole's initial difficulty in New Hampshire, he kept expectations low in the elections that followed to discourage calls for him to drop out of the race. Preventing the front-runner from being embarrassed is a key goal.

Not only is the outcome of the primaries subject to interpretation, but so is the importance attached to particular contests. Generally speaking, the news media give more attention to primaries than caucuses, big states than small ones, and winner-take-all contests than proportional votes. Similarly, close elections receive more emphasis than one-sided ones, and statewide contests get better coverage than district elections.

Candidates can affect the coverage they receive through their timing and staging of events, their release of information, and even the access they provide to candidates and their senior aides. Major announcements are made in sufficient time to get coverage on the evening news; speeches are scheduled to maximize the viewing audience; quiet periods, such as Saturday, are considered a good time to hold a press conference or schedule interviews. In addition to receiving same-day coverage by television, a Saturday event usually gets prominent treatment in the Sunday papers and may be mentioned on the Sunday morning TV talk shows.

Access is another valuable commodity. At the beginning of the nomination process, access is cheap, especially for lesser-known candidates, who need media attention. However, as the campaign progresses, access becomes more important and, at the same time, more difficult to obtain. There is more competition among journalists, the candidates have a more strenuous schedule, and a larger public relations staff stands between the correspondents and the nominees. Granting interviews under these circumstances can do much to affect the quantity and quality of coverage received. To a large extent, those who report the news are dependent on this information. Many news stories about the candidates come directly from the candidates themselves and their campaigns. Additionally, they are the source of much of the negative news about their opponents.

Advertising is another way to shape and, if need be, change public perceptions. Its principal advantage is the great degree to which it can be controlled by candidates and their advisers. The messages can be designed to create a desired effect. They can also be aired as often as funds permit and much money is devoted to this effort.

Political ads are not without their limitations, however. Like all commercials, they are blatantly partial, usually expensive, and require the services of skilled personnel to buy time, produce the spot, and act in it. Although they can be used to discredit an opponent, the discrediting process itself can take its toll on the candidate sponsoring the ads. This happened to Steve Forbes in Iowa and New Hampshire in 1996. The more negative ads he ran, the more negative were the responses from his opponents, and the more his popularity fell among Republican voters.

The increasing importance of the media has had a profound effect on the conduct of campaigns. It has made radio and television the principal communication links between the candidates and the voters, and it has encouraged candidates to spend a sizable portion of their money on advertising and to orient their campaigns to the camera. In 1996, Clinton spent $8.8 million (29 percent of his funds) and Dole $6.5 million (almost 19 percent of his) on advertising; the Democrats supplemented Clinton's effort by spending $40 million on generic advertising and the Republicans supplemented Dole with $28 million.

Fieldwork   Despite the importance of the media, candidates still need to organize at the grass roots. They need advance people to arrange for their appearances and assemble the crowds, other politicians, and the media. They need schedulers to plan their days and decide which invitations to accept. They need local organizers to run phone banks to identify voters, and they need volunteers to ring doorbells, circulate literature, and get would-be supporters to the polls. Eugene McCarthy and Robert Kennedy recruited thousands of college students to help them in their primary efforts in 1968, as did George McGovern in 1972. Armies of volunteers were also organized by Jimmy Carter in 1976, Jesse Jackson in 1984 and 1988, Pat Robertson in 1988, and Pat Buchanan in 1996. Steve Forbes did not have such an army and was compelled to buy one. In fact, he paid $1 million simply for field organizers to get him on the ballot in New York's thirty-one legislative districts. In caucus states, field organizations can make a difference, often overwhelming the less effectively organized efforts of those who lack grassroots support. Getting people out to vote is a problem made more difficult today by public indifference (see the Hot-Button Issue box).

THE QUEST FOR THE NOMINATION

Greater public involvement in the nomination process has changed the strategy and tactics of those seeking the nomination. Campaigns begin much earlier than in the past. They require more money up front, an in-place organization, and a game plan that targets an appeal and constructs a

☼ HOT-BUTTON ISSUE

Public Indifference

In a democracy, government is supposed to rest on the consent of the governed. Elections are the principal mechanisms for registering that consent, as well as for choosing the people and, indirectly, the policies they will pursue. However, in the last presidential election, only about 25 million people (around 13 percent of the adult population) voted in the primaries and about 96 million people (49 percent) voted in the general election. Why do so few vote, and what can be done about this lack of participation?

The problem is complex. It stems from feelings of cynicism and mistrust about government which have been growing in the United States for the last thirty years, from lack of knowledge and interest in political affairs, from the weakening of partisan allegiances which for some were a motivation for voting, from the requirement to register in order to vote, and from the negativism that is generated by critical media coverage and campaign advertising, which discourages many people from voting. Yet another factor is the very length of the campaigns themselves—over two years.

Congress tackled the registration requirement in 1993 by enacting legislation that made it easier for people to obtain and submit the necessary forms to register to vote. Today, some groups, such as Rock-The-Vote, now even have on-line registration. Nonetheless, one year after the new law went into effect, voting turnout declined.

What else can be done by Congress or public interest groups, such as Common Cause and the League of Women Voters? Congress could require U.S. citizens to vote. Countries such as Australia, Belgium, and Chile do, and they exact fines on those who fail to comply. We could make voting easier, by allowing people to vote by mail or, eventually, on-line. Oregon tried a mail ballot for a special Senate election in 1994, and the concept seemed to work. Most states permit absentee ballots to be filed. However, is it desirable to force, or even encourage, people who are uninformed, uninvolved, and unconcerned to vote? Would they make an intelligent judgment in the country's interest or even their own or simply cancel out the votes of those who are informed, involved, and concerned?

Having a national primary would probably generate a substantially larger turnout than the current system of caucuses and primaries, which now are held over a period of almost four months, but which tend to determine the likely nominees much earlier. What incentive for voting is there for residents of states that hold May and June primaries?

Perhaps the finance laws should be changed to allow more spending to "get the word out" or less to "equalize the playing field." Providing free television time, more public debates, more campaign events, or even more emphasis on grassroots activities might increase the number of voters, but then again it might not.

The issue is one of great concern, not only because low turnout can affect election outcomes, but because it can also have an impact on governance and how legitimately the policies of that government are viewed by the population. President Clinton received the support of only 43 percent of the 55 percent of citizens who voted in 1992, which amounts to only 23.65 percent of the adult population; similarly, he received only 49 percent support from the 49 percent of citizens who voted in 1996, which, again, is only 24 percent of the adult population, hardly a mandate for pursuing his campaign promises and party platform in either election. Is it any wonder that he had difficulty or that he felt compelled to use the status, visibility, and respect of his office to improve his public image and try to enhance his political power?

winning coalition from the ground up. The game plan is, in turn, predicated on certain fundamental assumptions about the nomination:

1. Sufficient time and energy must be devoted to personal campaigning in the preprimary and early preconvention periods, in which candidates interact with the general public. Even an incumbent cannot take renomination for granted and instead must use the presidential office to deter opponents.

2. A strong field organization must be built for the initial caucuses and primaries. But television advertising is also an important component of multistate campaigns if the primaries are front loaded as they will be in 2000.

3. A firm financial base must be established early and a spending strategy must be devised. All caucuses and primaries are not equally important; the first ones, which receive the most attention, require the allocation of greater resources. However, allocating too many resources to too few states early in the process can also be dangerous if it depletes a campaign's treasury for the later contests, approaches the legal limit on future expenditures, or leaves a victor without enough

money to respond to accusations by the other party and its probable nominee.

4. The order of caucuses and primaries and their rules and procedures must be understood and, if possible, manipulated to the candidate's advantage. Magnifying victories and minimizing defeats usually requires that strong states be isolated and weak ones paired with strong ones.

5. Groups within the party must be targeted and appeals must be made to them. Over the course of the campaign, however, these appeals must be broadened, and often moderated, without necessarily contradicting previously taken stands or negating earlier promises. If the overall constituency is too narrow, it will be difficult to gain the nomination and even more difficult to win the general election.

The actual strategy that candidates adopt depends on their status at the beginning of the campaign. If they are not well known, their initial goal must be to establish their credentials as viable contenders. Publicly announcing their intentions, creating a campaign headquarters, qualifying for matching funds, and obtaining political endorsements are critical steps to this end. At the outset, the key is recognition, whereas over the long haul, it lies in momentum and the acquisition of delegates.

Recognition is bestowed by the news media on candidates who do better than expected in the early primaries and caucuses; momentum can be achieved by winning a series of prenomination victories, which increases the amount of delegate support. Together, recognition and momentum compensate for what the non–front-runners lack in reputation and appeal. That is why they concentrate their time, efforts, and resources on the first few contests. They have no choice. Winning will provide them with opportunities later on; whereas losing will confirm their secondary status.

Jimmy Carter's 1976 quest for the Democratic nomination is a good example of a successful non–front-runner strategy. Carter began his campaign as a relatively unknown southern governor with limited financial resources and organizational support. He concentrated his efforts in Iowa and New Hampshire, with the aim of doing well in these early contests. By attracting the attention of the press, he hoped to establish his credibility as a viable candidate. Early success, he anticipated, would facilitate fundraising, organization building, and continued media coverage—and he was proved right.

The Carter strategy has become the model for most non–front-runners in both parties. In 2000, all the Republican contenders are expected to emphasize the early contests in Iowa and New Hampshire. Even those who stand little realistic chance of winning run in the early contests so as to take advantage of the media coverage. Pat Buchanan's challenge to George Bush in 1992 is a case in point. In the words of Bay Buchanan, the candidate's sister and campaign manager, "Winning New Hampshire was never in the cards, but New Hampshire would give us momentum maybe to carry it through Georgia and then possibly an outside chance, in our wildest dreams, to make it through Super Tuesday."[10] Lamar Alexander had a similar strategy in 1996. In the words of Lanny Griffith, his senior strategist:

> As much as you'd like to think you're running a unique campaign, or have a unique strategy, the look of the Alexander campaign really wasn't unlike the Carter strategy of 1976 or the Bush strategy of 1980. . . . [It was] to organize for a long period of time, raise sufficient money, and get hot in Iowa and then let the campaign sort of ride on the momentum coming out of an early victory. . . . [Griffith added,] We heard our candidate say, . . . "The strategy is money, message, Iowa, New Hampshire and Florida."[11]

Jesse Jackson's campaigns in 1984 and 1988 and, to a lesser extent, Pat Robertson's runs in 1988 and Pat Buchanan's 1992 and 1996 attempts do not fit the typical non–front-runner's strategic model. Lacking a large financial base, these candidates mobilized an army of volunteers in grassroots efforts, which were most effective in states with caucus-type elections and those in which their supporters constituted a significant portion of the electorate. All three candidates also attracted considerable press coverage by virtue of their extreme perspectives, their passionate supporters and detractors, their effectiveness as speakers and campaigners, and the perennial desire of the news media to add color and excitement to the race. In each case, these nontraditional candidates used the campaign as a "bully pulpit" to articulate their views, maintain their bases of support, and legitimize their candidacies.

Steve Forbes used a variant of this nontraditional approach in 1996. Instead of mobilizing an army of volunteers, he launched an avalanche of television ads to introduce himself, promote his positions, and criticize his opponents. Lacking a cadre of true believers but possessed of a great deal of money, Forbes was able to use his millions to pay for grassroots operations to support his candidacy.

For the front-runners—such as Democrats Walter Mondale in 1984 and Al Gore in 2000 and Republicans George Bush in 1988 and Robert Dole in 1996—the task is different. They have to maintain credibility, not establish it. At the outset they have a little more flexibility, which derives from having greater name recognition, a larger resource base, and more political endorsements. Status and position make it easier for them to raise money and build an organization, thereby enhancing their potential, but also creating expectations that may be difficult to meet and easier for the press to deflate. A front-runner can overcome a single defeat but will find it more difficult to survive a string of setbacks.

Ronald Reagan's preconvention campaign in 1980 is a good example of the front-runner approach. Reagan raised, and spent, much of his money in the early primaries and caucuses. He built in-depth organizations in many states, obtained the support of many state officials, and benefited from a large staff of professionals and volunteers. George Bush and Robert Dole followed similar strategies in 1988 and 1996 and were equally successful. By the beginning of the election year, both had raised the most money, built the largest field organizations, gained the most political endorsements, and also put their media operations in place. They were ready to run for, and as, their party's nominee.

Bill Clinton used variants of both the non–front-runner and front-runner strategies in his two successful nomination campaigns (see box: The Clinton Presidency: Contrasting Strategies in 1992 and 1996.)

THE NATIONAL CONVENTIONS

In theory, a party chooses its standard-bearers at its national convention in the summer preceding the presidential election, but in practice, the nominees have usually been determined well before the convention meets. Since most of the delegates are publicly committed, their decisions are readily predictable. Television networks and wire services provide a running total of the number of delegates pledged to individual candidates throughout the nomination period, so the convention's choice is no surprise.

Theoretically, the delegates make policy decisions when formulating their party's platform, but in practice, platform decisions are hammered out by representatives of the principal candidates in the weeks prior to the convention. Occasionally, however, there remains a point of contention in the form of disappointed delegates whose positions were not incorporated into the draft platform.

Theoretically, conventions try to unify the delegates for the forthcoming election. If the divisions within the party are not too great, if no ill will exists among the principal candidates, and, particularly, if the leading candidate has a large delegate advantage, unity may be achieved. However, party leaders often face another problem in achieving this objective: negative information and sensational coverage. Indeed, the press often deems policy and personal disagreements within the party to be more newsworthy than consensus.[12]

As a consequence, controversy is highlighted. To offset the emphasis placed on controversy and on people, issues, and events that detract from

THE CLINTON PRESIDENCY

Contrasting Strategies in 1992 and 1996

Although Bill Clinton did not begin his quest for the 1992 Democratic nomination as a front-runner, he became one after other would-be contenders, such as Governor Mario Cuomo of New York, decided not to seek their party's nomination. With superior financial resources and organizational support, Clinton was in a stronger position than any of his declared rivals—Senator Tom Harkin (Iowa), Senator Bob Kerrey (Nebraska), former Senator Paul Tsongas (Massachusetts), and former Governor Jerry Brown (California). Clinton's centrist policy positions also worked to his advantage.

The first primary in New Hampshire was expected to be tough for the Arkansas governor. Not only was he not well known in the state, but he faced a neighboring senator, Tsongas, and a war hero, Kerrey. To add to Clinton's woes, allegations about his martial infidelity and draft dodging exploded in the weeks before the primary, threatening to end his campaign before it even began.

Clinton's campaign decided to tackle the infidelity issue head-on. Appearing with his wife on the CBS news program *60 Minutes,* Clinton admitted that he and his wife had marital problems, but indicated that they were a thing of the past. His quick response to a potentially fatal issue limited its political fallout, raised his stature, and enabled him to return to substantive policy issues, primarily the state of the economy. The draft-dodging issue was not handled nearly as well and plagued him throughout the campaign. Nonetheless, the skill with which his campaign handled the fidelity issue allowed Clinton to persevere; in fact, after his second place finish in New Hampshire, which his campaign described as a moral victory, Clinton referred to himself as "the comeback kid." The campaign had survived its first and most difficult hurdle.

The next objective of the campaign was to prevent the New Hampshire winner, Tsongas, from gaining momentum as a result of his early win. With three primaries the following week in Georgia, Colorado, and Maryland, the Clinton forces needed at the very least a mixed verdict to carry them into the Southern regional primaries in which Clinton could be expected to do well. Clinton concentrated successfully on Georgia with the support of Democratic governor Zell Miller. The Georgia primary had been moved up a week to accommodate the Clinton campaign. Tsongas won Maryland, but Clinton raised issues which helped Jerry Brown in Colorado. Thus the Clinton campaign achieved its second goal, to blunt Tsongas's momentum and put Clinton in a position to win big in the southern regional primaries, thereby building a large delegate.

The campaign then moved to the Midwest. The Clinton plan was to concentrate resources on Michigan and Illinois. It was Clinton's victory in these states that eliminated Tsongas and relegated Brown to the role of critic rather than formidable opponent. Although Brown did not threaten to take the nomination from Clinton, he did damage Clinton's image in the eyes of the public.

Following the end of the primaries, the Clinton campaign concentrated on restoring the candidate's image by designing and airing a series of biographical advertisements that presented the hardships and struggles that this poor boy from Arkansas had to overcome in his rise to political prominence. The success of this campaign combined with Ross Perot's entrance as an independent candidate and the Bush campaign's attack against Perot enabled Clinton to get back on his feet, resurrect his image, and use a well-orchestrated Democratic convention to launch his campaign against President George Bush.

The situation Clinton faced in 1996 was entirely different. As the incumbent, he did not have to worry about being renominated, although he did have to worry about being embarrassed as his last two Democratic predecessors, Lyndon Johnson and Jimmy Carter, had been. Clinton's objective was to avoid a primary challenge by pursuing a strategy that his renomination and reelection were inevitable.

The strategy was designed to raise as much money as quickly as possible in order to dry up funds for would-be challengers and provide the president with maximum flexibility to rebut any criticism, regardless of the source or subject. The White House, under the direction of Deputy Chief of Staff Harold Ickes, made sure that there were be no straw polls which could embarrass the president and mended ties to those who were unhappy with Clinton's self-proclaimed moderation, especially organized labor and minority groups.

The Clinton campaign also made a conscious decision *not* to establish a fully staffed and operational reelection committee so as to save money and more importantly, maintain the appearance of Clinton as president rather than presidential candidate.

The strategy worked. There was no challenger. Clinton emerged from the 1996 nomination process with his image intact, his campaign in full gear, and his message of good times, incremental gains, and smaller government echoing across the country.

the public image that the party wishes to present, the convention's organizers orchestrate the proceedings.

Public Dimensions

From the perspective of the party, the real function of the convention is to show off its nominees and its policy positions; from the perspective of the candidates, it is a place to start building a broad-based electoral coalition; from the perspective of organized groups, it is a tool to gain visibility and support for their positions and causes; and from the perspective of the news media, it is a chance to capture the excitement and ritual of an extravaganza and spotlight whatever drama and suspense are produced.

Television broadcasting of national conventions began in 1952, and almost immediately, a sizable audience was attracted. According to the Nielsen ratings, 20 to 30 percent of the potential audience watched the conventions between 1952 and 1968, with the number swelling during the most significant events. In 1996 it was estimated that between 23 and 25 million people, less than 10 percent, saw each of the acceptance speeches of the presidential nominees on the last nights of the conventions: this was a substantial decline from previous years.[13]

The number of people who tune into conventions is important because of the conventions' potential effect: they heighten interest, thereby potentially increasing turnout; they arouse latent feelings, thereby raising partisan awareness; and they color perceptions, thereby affecting the public's evaluation of the candidates and their stands.[14]

Party leaders assume that the more unified the convention, the more favorable will be its impact on the electorate. That is why they take the news media, particularly television, into account when planning, staging, and scheduling their national meetings.

Convention planners try to capture a television audience by providing entertainment and conducting a fast-paced meeting. They also contrive to put their candidates and party in the most favorable light by scripting the meetings and by placing the major unifying events, such as major addresses and movies, during prime viewing hours and potentially discordant situations, such as debates on controversial issues or speeches by people who may be discredited in the eyes of the public or party, before or after prime time. Both the 1996 nominating conventions were major media extravaganzas, designed especially for the television audience. The Republicans featured short, upbeat speeches, which were moderate in tone and given by a cross-section of elected Grand Old Party (GOP) officials. The Democrats, not to be outdone, gave their elected officials and party leaders prime-time appearances and staged a presidential whistle-stop train whereby they beamed the president's enthusiastic reception by small-town America into their convention and, at the same time, into the homes of millions of viewers.

Although party officials try to present a united front favoring their nominee and platform, the television networks do not. They try to generate interest by emphasizing variety, maximizing suspense, and exaggerating conflict. This attempt often requires them to focus less on the official proceedings and more on other activities, such as disputes between the delegates or demonstrations occurring outside the convention hall. The vice presidential selection frequently receives much attention, although in recent years the likely nominee has been identified before the convention has gotten underway. Still, in 1988 Bush's choice of Senator Dan Quayle attracted considerable scrutiny from the press during the convention period, much of it negative.

Official Business

Conventions still make, or at least ratify, major decisions. They adopt rules, accept credentials, determine platforms, and choose the party's standard-bearers. Of these functions, approving the platform has been the most controversial in recent years. The reforms in the delegate selection process have produced more issue-oriented delegates who tend to gravitate to the platform committee and, specifically, to the subcommittee considering "their" issues. They are less prone to compromise and more prone to try to raise public consciousness for their position. Television also magnifies party divisions by providing publicity for platform challenges such as those on the abortion plank at the 1992 and 1996 Republican conventions.

While platforms contain much partisan rhetoric and self-praise, they also consist of goals and proposals that differentiate the parties and their beliefs from one another. Moreover, and contrary to popular mythology, elected public officials do try to redeem their own promises and those of their party.[15]

Finally, the convention must select the nominees, a decision that is usually predictable and generally occurs on the first ballot. Since 1924, when it took the Democrats 103 votes to agree on John W. Davis, there have been only four conventions (two in each party) in which more than one ballot was needed. For the Republicans, this last occurred in 1948; for the Democrats, in 1952.

Characteristics of the Nominees

The nomination of small-state governors by the Democrats in 1976, 1988, and 1992 and of a former movie actor and big-state governor by the Republicans in 1980 indicates that changes in the preconvention process have affected the kind of people chosen by the parties. In theory, many are qualified, but in practice, a number of informal qualifications limit the pool of potential nominees. Successful candidates have usually been well known prior to the delegate selection process. Most have had promising political careers and held high government positions. Of all the positions from which to seek the presidential nomination, the presidency is clearly the best. Only five incumbent presidents (three of whom were vice presidents who succeeded to the office) failed in their quest for the nomination, although it should be noted that several others, including Harry Truman and Lyndon Johnson, were persuaded to retire rather than face tough challenges.

Other informal criteria have less to do with qualifications for office than with public prejudices and prescriptions of the most desirable presidential traits. Only white males have ever been nominated for president by the two major parties. However, the support that General Colin Powell received in 1995 when he considered running for president indicates that race may no longer be the barrier it once was. Until 1960, no Catholic had ever been elected, although Governor Al Smith of New York was nominated by the Democrats in 1928.[16] Michael Dukakis, who is of Greek ancestry, was the first candidate to lack a northern European heritage—a surprising commentary on a country that has regarded itself as a melting pot.

Personal matters, such as health, age, finance, and family life, can also be factors. After George Wallace was crippled by a would-be assassin's bullet in 1972, people including his own supporters began to question his ability to withstand the rigors of the office. Even the stamina of a healthy, but seventy-three-year-old Robert Dole became an issue in 1996 which he attempted to counter by staging a ninety-six–hour, marathon campaign in the final four days.[17] Today, presidential candidates are expected to release medical reports, financial statements, and to respond to potentially damaging personal allegations.[18]

Family ties have affected nominations and elections. For example, only two bachelors have been elected president: James Buchanan and Grover Cleveland. During the 1884 campaign, Cleveland was accused of fathering an illegitimate child for which he admitted responsibility even though he was not certain the child was his. Although the dissolution of Nelson Rockefeller's marriage and his subsequent remarriage in 1964, Senator Edward Kennedy's marital problems and the Chappaquiddick incident in 1980, and Gary Hart's alleged affair in 1984 seriously damaged the presidential aspirations of these three candidates, Bill Clinton has shown that those type of personal allegations need not be fatal. In recent years, two divorced candidates, Ronald Reagan and Robert Dole, were nominated by their party.

Most of the characteristics of the presidential nominee apply to the vice presidential candidate as well. However, that choice has also been affected by the perceived need for geographic, ideological, and political balance. Robert Dole's selection of Jack Kemp provided this type of balance to the ticket, but Bill Clinton's selection of Senator Albert Gore did not. Clinton chose Gore to reinforce, rather than balance, his own moderate policy perspective, southern political base, and relative youth.

Presidential aspirants have tended to select vice presidential candidates primarily as running mates, and only secondarily as governing mates. Despite statements to the contrary, most attention is given to how the prospective nominee may help the ticket. Like the presidential nominee, the parties, too, have insisted that the vice presidential aspirant should articulate basic values, possess all-American traits, and have led an exemplary life. In 1972, Senator Thomas Eagleton was forced to withdraw as the Democratic vice presidential nominee when his past psychological illness became public. Similarly, in 1988, Republican vice presidential nominee Senator Dan Quayle was hounded by charges that his father, a wealthy Indiana newspaper publisher, had used his influence to get young Quayle into the National Guard and thus reduce his chances of serving on active duty in the Vietnam War.

CONCLUSION

The nominating process has evolved significantly over the years. Although it was developed initially to enable the parties to influence electoral selection, it now permits the public to affect that selection as well. Moreover, with broader rank-and-file participation have come expanded appeals and activities by candidates and expanded coverage by the news media.

When the presidency was created, the nomination of candidates for the office was not considered apart from the election of the president. The development of political parties at the beginning of the nineteenth century led to an informal modification of the electoral system. At first, congressional caucuses performed the nominating function, but as the parties acquired a broader, more decentralized base, the caucus system broke down and was replaced by national nominating conventions. These conventions have continued to operate, although within these meetings the power has shifted from political leadership within states to the party activists and members of the general public who participate in caucuses and primaries. The growth of primaries, the increasing impact of the news media, and, eventually, the changes in party rules, finance laws, and campaign technology accelerated the movement toward a more participatory nominating politics, in which public support has become the key element.

On balance, these changes have made the nomination process more democratic. In particular, they have encouraged greater rank-and-file participation in the selection of the party's nominees. Moreover, they have also generated greater sensitivity on the part of the candidates to the desires of groups within the party and the opinions and attitudes of the general electorate.

However, the costs of democracy have been high. The more contentious is the quest for the nomination, the more difficult it is for the successful nominee to win the general election. The more promises are made to different groups within the party, the more difficult it may be for the nominee to appeal to independents and to partisans of other parties (much less govern, if elected). The parties as institutions have also suffered. They have become more fractionalized, and now exercise less control over who their nominees will be and how they will perform if elected.

Campaigns have become more onerous and expensive, and candidates have to spend years in seeking the nomination. Even worse, the public is subjected to a barrage of appeals, images, promises, and positions for a relatively long period of time—so long in fact that people may become numbed by the campaign, and consequently indifferent.

Not only is it more difficult to win the nomination, today, it is also more difficult to govern. Contemporary campaigns hype expectations; they make agendas more expansive and priorities more difficult to define; they contribute to fragile and more personal alliances; and they dispense, and ultimately decrease, the president's political power while increasing the demands of the job. All this has made strong presidential leadership more difficult to achieve and sustain.

Clinton encountered this situation firsthand at the beginning of his presidency. On seeking to fulfill campaign promises to a variety of constituency groups such as the middle class, homosexuals, small businesses, and urban mayors and their inner-city populations, he found himself unable to do so and consequently had to alter or abandon many of his initial campaign pledges. The process of publicly making promises and then being forced to back off damaged his reputation, adversely affected his public image, and decreased the political capital he had to achieve his goals. Clinton learned his lesson, however, and in his reelection campaign he made fewer promises on which he ultimately could not deliver. Moreover, his principal pledge, to eliminate the budget deficit, was achieved.

DISCUSSION QUESTIONS

1. Construct likely strategies for three Republican candidates (one front-runner, one non–front-runner, and one "bully pulpit" candidate) who are likely to seek their party's nomination in 2000. In your strategy indicate what you think should be their basic appeal, to whom that appeal should be directed, how it should be directed, what image they should try to create, and whether you think the strategy you have designed is likely to be successful.

2. Look at the principal promises of the 1996 Democratic platform and indicate which of these promises has been proposed or implemented by President Clinton.

3. Explain how George Bush and Bill Clinton used their incumbency to enhance renomination by their parties.

WEB EXERCISES

1. Access the Web sites of the Republican and Democratic National Committees at <http://www.rnc.org> and <http://www.democrats.org>. Download and compare the latest party platforms. Indicate the principal issues on which the Republicans and Democrats took differing positions, and then explain which of these positions have become public policy. From your analysis, answer the question of whether party platforms really matter.
2. Compare the levels of funding for the various candidates who are currently seeking their party's nomination by accessing the Federal Election Commission Web site at <http://www.fec.gov>. Note the amounts the candidates have reported received and spent, the matching funds they have received, and whether their contributions have come primarily from individuals or groups. Does their funding appear to come from any particular sector (such as business groups, trade associations, or advocacy groups)?
3. If candidate Web sites are available, access them by going to the Web White and Blue site at <http://www.webwhiteblue.org>, and then describe their principal campaign strategies and tactics.

SELECTED READING

Bartels, Larry M. *Presidential Primaries and the Dynamics of Public Choice.* Princeton, N.J.: Princeton University Press, 1988.

Corrado, Anthony. *Paying for Presidents: Public Financing in National Elections.* New York: Twentieth Century Fund Press, 1993.

Kennedy Institute of Politics, Harvard University. *Campaign for President: The Managers Look at '96.* Hollis, N.H.: Hollis Publishing, 1997.

Maisel, L. Sandy. "The Platform-Writing Process." *Political Science Quarterly* 108 (Winter 1993–1994).

Mayer, William G., ed. *In Pursuit of the White House: How We Choose Our Presidential Nominees.* Chatham, N.J.: Chatham House, 1995.

Morris, Dick. *Behind the Oval Office.* New York: Random House, 1997.

Shafer, Byron E. *Bifurcated Politics: Evolution and Reform in the National Party Convention.* Cambridge: Harvard University Press, 1988.

Smith, Larry David, and Dan Nimmo. *Cordial Concurrence: Orchestrating National Party Conventions in the Telepolitical Age.* Westport, Conn.: Praeger, 1991.

Sorauf, Frank J. *Inside Campaign Finance: Myths and Realities.* New Haven: Yale University Press, 1992.

Teixeira, Ruy A. *The Disappearing American Voter.* Washington, D.C.: Brookings Institution, 1992.

Thomas, Evan, et al. *Back from the Dead.* New York: Atlantic Monthly Press, 1997.

Wayne, Stephen J. *The Road to the White House, 2000.* New York: St. Martin's/Worth, 2000.

Woodward, Bob. *The Choice.* New York: Simon and Schuster, 1996.

Notes

1. In 1968, however, the primaries did provide incentive for Lyndon Johnson to withdraw. In that year, dissent within the Democratic party, as evidenced by Senator Eugene McCarthy's surprisingly strong showing in the New Hampshire primary, indicated that incumbent Lyndon Johnson would have difficulty securing renomination, much less reelection. Johnson chose to step aside and not seek reelection soon after the New Hampshire vote.

2. Humphrey was listed on the ballot in the District of Columbia, and he did win its Democratic primary.

3. The system works as follows: States that hold their primary or caucus between March 15 and April 14 are entitled to 5 percent more delegates to represent them; those who hold their contests between April 15 and May 14 receive 7.5 percent more; and those who hold theirs after May 15th get 10 percent more delegates added to their convention delegation.

4. Reforms in the delegate selection process have affected both parties, although the Republicans have not mandated national guidelines on their state parties as the Democrats have. Nonetheless, state legislatures have continually adjusted their election process in accord with party rules and popular preferences, as well as to maximize their state's influence. They have had little choice. Two Supreme Court decisions, *Cousins v. Wigoda* (419 U.S. 477, 1975) and *Democratic Party of the U.S. v. La Follette* (449 U.S. 897, 1981), give the party the right to reject delegates to its national convention who have not been selected in conformity with its rules.

5. According to the terms of the original legislation, individuals could designate that $1 of their taxes be placed in the Presidential Election Campaign Fund. Initially, more than 25 percent of taxpayers made such a designation. Increased campaign expenditures, combined with a decreasing percent of the population designating money for the fund—only 17.7 percent did so in 1992—threatened to deplete the fund to the point that there would not be sufficient money to meet expenses. Congress responded by raising the amount of money that individuals could designate to the fund to $3, an increase equal to the inflation that had occurred over the twenty-year period. Nonetheless, there was still an initial shortfall in funds in 1996, when entitlements for matching grants reached an all-time high of $37.3 million on January 1 (compared to $6 million four years earlier), but the money available for primary candidates was only $22 million. Candidates were initially paid only 60 percent of what they were entitled to receive, although they eventually got the full amount when the Treasury had sufficient funds in the election account. Another more extensive shortfall is likely in 2000 when both parties are expected to have multiple candidates seeking their nominations.

6. Federal Election Commission, "Record," July 1998, pp. 1, 5.

7. A particularly contentious fund-raising issue involved contributions by foreign nationals, companies, and even countries. These contributions were investigated by Senate and House committees and by the Department of Justice to determine whether they were legal and whether the contributors received tangible benefits for their money. There were even accusations that foreign policy was affected by the contributions.

8. Quoted in Kennedy Institute of Politics, *Campaign for President: The Managers Look at '96* (Hollis, N.H.: Hollis Publishing Co., 1997), p. 7.

9. In 1988, with both parties involved in contested nominations, there were a total of 601 campaign stories on the three major networks' evening news shows between January 1 and the

middle of March; in 1992, there were 424. In 1996, approximately 55 percent of all the prenomination election stories on the evening news occurred before the New Hampshire primary. See "The Bad News Campaign," *Media Monitor,* March/April 1996, pp. 1–3.

10. Buchanan actually received 34 percent of the New Hampshire vote in 1992; he received 28 percent four years later, although he was running against six other candidates at that time.

11. Quoted in Kennedy Institute, *Campaign for President*, p. 3.

12. The exception was the 1992 Democratic convention. Compared to previous Democratic conventions, it was a love feast. The press reported it as one in contrast to its reporting of the 1992 Republican convention in which the conservative rhetoric and policy demands on the incumbent president were stressed.

13. "Edge for Democrats in TV Audiences." *New York Times,* August 31, 1996, p. 9.

14. Thomas E. Patterson, *The Mass Media Election* (New York: Praeger, 1980), pp. 72, 274.

15. Gerald M. Pomper, "Control and Influence in American Politics," *American Behavioral Scientist* 13 (1969): 223, 228; Gerald M. Pomper, with Susan S. Lederman, *Elections in America* (New York: Longman, 1980), p. 161.

16. Pat Buchanan's Catholicism did not seem to be an issue in his two quests for the Republican nomination in 1992 and 1996, although some of his political views were.

17. About one-third of the population questioned whether a person of that age could withstand the rigors of the office and generate enough "new" ideas to solve the nation's problems.

18. To help mitigate the age issue and the fact that he had had an operation for prostate cancer, Dole released a comprehensive medical report about his health at the very beginning of his quest for the 1996 Republican nomination.

3

THE PRESIDENTIAL ELECTION

WINNING THE NOMINATION IS ONLY HALF THE BATTLE: The real prize comes from being elected. For most candidates, the general election campaign is at least as arduous as the nomination struggle. Shorter in length, but with a larger and more heterogeneous electorate, it requires similar organizational skills but different strategic plans and public appeals to build a majority coalition. For the party, the quest for the presidency is only one election among many, although perhaps the most important. Like the other elections, however, the campaign is subject to the party's influence but not its control. For the voter, the effective choice is narrower but the criteria for judgment are more extensive. Personal evaluation alone is not the only factor that affects the decision of whether to vote and, if so, for whom.

For the presidency, the campaign has significant implications. Not only does it designate which team and party will direct activities for the next four years, but it highlights the key policy issues at the beginning of the president's term and the priorities attached to each. It provides the contours of the administration's initial agenda and contributes to the components of its governing coalition. Moreover, it sets the tone and indicates the kind of leadership that the public expects and wants. In this sense, the campaign defines the president's initial leadership tasks and opportunities, whether they be to direct change or simply facilitate it by pointing the machinery of government in the appropriate direction and keeping it running as smoothly as possible.

In this chapter we will explore these factors and their implications for the U.S. electoral and governing systems. We will do so by examining the strategic environment in which presidential elections occur, the critical factors that must be considered when planning and conducting campaigns, and the meaning of elections for the voters and new administration.

The chapter is organized into three sections. In the first we focus on the strategic environment and its impact on the election: the constitutional features, notably the Electoral College; the political climate, particularly the partisanship of the electorate; legal issues such as public financing; and press coverage. We then turn to the strategy and tactics of the campaign itself. Here we discuss how organizations are constructed; how appeals are designed, projected, and targeted; and how coalitions are built. In the third section we evaluate the election outcome from two perspectives: what it suggests about the moods, opinions, and attitudes of the electorate, and what it portends for the president and the capacity of the new administration to govern.

THE STRATEGIC ENVIRONMENT

Every election occurs within an environment that shapes its activity and affects its outcome. For the presidency, the Electoral College provides the legal framework for this environment, while public attitudes and group loyalties condition the political climate. Money and media constitute the principal resources and instruments by which campaign objectives may be achieved. Each of these factors must be considered in the design and conduct of a presidential campaign and the assessment of its impact on the election.

The Electoral College

Creation   Of all the elements that affect presidential campaigns, only the Electoral College is truly unique. It was designed by the framers of the Constitution to solve one of their most difficult problems: how to protect the president's independence and, at the same time, have a technically sound, politically efficacious electoral system that would be consistent with a republican form of government. Most of the delegates at the Philadelphia convention were sympathetic to a government based on consent, but not to direct democracy. They wanted a mechanism that would choose the most qualified person, but not necessarily the most popular. Moreover, they had no precise model to follow.

Two methods had been proposed originally: selection by the legislature and election by the voters. Each, however, had its drawbacks. Legislative selection posed a potential threat to the independence of the presidency. How could the executive's independence be preserved if election and reelection hinged on the president's popularity with Congress?[1] However, popular election was seen as undesirable and impractical. Not only did most of the delegates lack faith in the public's ability to choose the best-qualified candidate, but they also feared that the size of the country and the poor state of its communication and transportation systems would preclude holding a national campaign. Sectional distrust and rivalry aggravated this problem, since the states were obligated to oversee the conduct of such an election. A third alternative, consisting of some type of indirect election, was proposed a number of times but not seriously considered until near the end of the convention.

According to the terms of the Electoral College compromise, presidential electors were to be chosen by the states in a manner designated by their legislatures. In order to ensure their independence, the electors could not simultaneously hold a federal government position. The number of electors was to equal the number of senators and representatives from each state (see Appendix C). Each elector had two votes but could not cast them both for inhabitants of his or her own state.[2] At a designated time, the electors would vote and send the results to Congress, where they were to be announced to a joint session by the president of the Senate, the nation's vice president. The person who received a majority of votes cast by the Electoral College would be elected president, and the one with the second highest total would be vice president. In the event that no one received a majority, the House of Representatives would choose from among the five candidates with the most electoral votes, with each state delegation casting one vote. The Senate was to determine the vice president should there be a tie for second place.

The new mode of selection was defended on two grounds: (1) it allowed state legislatures to establish the procedures for choosing electors but, if there were no Electoral College majority, it permitted the House of Representatives to decide; and (2) it gave the larger states an advantage in the initial voting for president (in accordance with the principle of majority rule) but provided the smaller states with an equal voice if the electoral vote were not decisive (in accordance with the principle of equal representation for each of the states). These compromises placated sufficient interests to get the proposal adopted and subsequently ratified as part of the Constitution.

Evolution   Only in the first two elections, when Washington was the unanimous choice, did the electors exercise a nonpartisan and, presumably, independent judgment. Within ten years from the time the federal government began to operate, a party system had emerged, and the electors became its political captives. They were nominated by their party and expected to vote for its candidates, which they did. In 1800, all the Republican electors voted for Thomas Jefferson and Aaron Burr. Since the procedure for casting ballots did not permit electors to distinguish between their presidential and vice presidential choices, the election ended in a tie, which the House of Representatives, controlled by the Federalist party, resolved by choosing Jefferson. To avoid creating such problems in the future, the Constitution was amended in 1804 to provide for separate balloting for the president and vice president.

The next nondecisive presidential election occurred in 1824, when four candidates received votes for president: Andrew Jackson (99 votes), John Q. Adams (84), William Crawford (41), and Henry Clay (37). The new amendment required the House of Representatives to choose from among the top three choices, not the top five as the Constitution had originally prescribed. Eliminated from the competition was Henry Clay, the most powerful member of the House and its Speaker. Clay then threw his support to Adams, who won. It was alleged that Clay did so in exchange for an appointment as secretary of state, a charge that he vigorously denied. After Adams became president, however, Clay did accept appointment as the secretary of state, a position that in those days was considered the stepping stone to the presidency.

Jackson, who was the winner of the popular vote, was outraged at the turn of events and urged the abolition of the Electoral College. Although his 1824 claim of a popular mandate is open to question, opposition to the system mounted and a gradual democratization of the election process occurred.[3] Increasing numbers of states began to elect their electors directly, on the basis of their partisan leanings, and by 1832, only South Carolina retained the practice of having its legislature make the selection.

There was also a trend toward statewide election of the entire slate of electors. In the past, some states had chosen their electors within legislative districts. Choosing the entire slate of electors on the basis of the popular vote produced a bloc of electoral votes. Whichever candidate received the most popular votes in a state got all the electoral votes of that state. This had two principal effects: It maximized the state's voting power, but it also created the possibility of a disparity between the popular and electoral votes in the nation as a whole. Thus, it became possible for the candidate with the most popular votes to lose in the Electoral College (if that candidate lost the big states by small margins and won the smaller states by large margins).

This occurred in 1876, the next disputed election, when Democrat Samuel J. Tilden received 250,000 more popular votes and nineteen more electoral votes than his Republican rival, Rutherford B. Hayes. However, Tilden was one short of a majority in the Electoral College. Moreover, twenty electoral votes were in dispute as dual returns had been received from three southern states. Charges of fraud and voting irregularities were made by both parties.

Three days before the Electoral College vote was to be officially counted, Congress established a commission to resolve the dilemma. Consisting of eight Republicans and seven Democrats, the commission, in a strictly partisan division, validated all the Republican claims, thereby giving Hayes a one-vote victory. Tilden could have challenged the results in court but chose not to do so.

The only other election in which the popular vote winner was beaten in the Electoral College occurred in 1888, when Democrat Grover Cleveland won a plurality of 95,096 popular votes but only 168 electoral votes, compared with 233 for the Republican candidate, Benjamin Harrison.

Although all other popular vote leaders have won a majority of electoral votes, shifts of just a few thousand popular votes in a few states could have altered the results in the elections of 1948, 1960, and 1976.[4] Clearly, the potential for the popular will to be thwarted remains a real possibility.

Additionally, in 1948, 1960, 1968, and 1992, there arose the further possibility that the Electoral College itself would not be able to choose a winner. In each of these elections, third-party candidates or independent electoral slates threatened to secure enough votes to prevent either of the major candidates from obtaining a majority.[5] The combination of close competition between the major-party candidates and a strong third-party or independent candidacy presents the greatest potential for a nondecisive outcome in the Electoral College vote.

The Electoral College is not neutral: No system of election can be. In general, it works to the benefit of the very largest states (those with more than fourteen electoral votes) and the very smallest (those with less than four). It helps the largest states, not only because of the larger number of electoral votes they cast but also because the votes are normally cast in a bloc. The smallest states are aided because they are overrepresented in the Electoral College. Because states have a minimum of three electoral votes regardless of size, people in a sparsely populated state such as Alaska will have more influence than they would otherwise have in a direct election.

The winner-take-all system also gives an edge to pivotal groups within the larger and more competitive states, groups that are geographically concentrated and have cohesive voting patterns seem to derive the most benefit. Part of the opposition to changing the system has been the reluctance of such pivotal groups to give up what they perceive as their competitive edge.

The Electoral College works to the detriment of third and independent parties. The winner-take-all system within states, combined with the need for a majority within the college, make it difficult for third parties or independent candidates to accumulate enough votes to win an election. To have any effect, their support must be geographically concentrated, as George Wallace's was in 1968 and Strom Thurmond's in 1948, rather than evenly distributed across the country, as Ross Perot's was in 1992.

Periodically, proposals to alter or abolish the Electoral College have been advanced. Most of these plans would eliminate the office of elector but retain the college in some form. One would allocate a state's electoral vote in proportion to its popular vote; another would determine the state's electoral vote on the basis of separate district and statewide elections. A third, direct election, would abolish the Electoral College entirely and simply rely on the popular vote.

The Polity

As the constitutional framework structures presidential elections, so partisan attitudes and group loyalties affect the conduct of campaigns. Voters do not come to the election with completely open minds, but rather with preexisting views. They do not see and hear the campaign in isolation, they observe and absorb it as part of their daily lives. In other words, their attitudes and associations affect their perceptions and influence their behavior. This is why it is important for students of presidential elections to examine public political attitudes and patterns of social interaction.

Research conducted on these subjects suggests that people develop political attitudes early in life.[6] Over time these attitudes tend to become more intense and more resistant to change, and therefore exert an important influence on voting behavior. Attitudes affect perceptions of the campaign and evaluations of the parties, the candidates, and the issues.

Partisanship   Of all the factors that contribute to the development of a political attitude, identification with a political party has been the most important. For most people, party identification operates as a conceptual filter, providing them with clues for interpreting the issues, for judging the candidates, and deciding if, and how, to vote. The stronger this identification, the more compelling the cues. Conversely, the weaker the identification, the less likely it is to affect perceptions during the campaign and influence voting on Election Day.

The amount of information that is known about the candidates also affects the influence of partisanship on voting behavior. In general, the less people know about the candidates and the issues, the more likely they are to follow their partisan inclinations when voting. Since presidential campaigns normally convey more information than do other elections, the influence of party is apt to be weaker in these higher-visibility contests than in congressional and state elections, but it is certainly not absent.

When identification with a party is weak or nonexistent, other factors, such as the personalities of the candidates and their issue positions, will be, correspondingly, more important. In contrast to party identification, which is a long-term, stabilizing factor, candidate and issue orientations are short-term, variable influences that change from election to election. Of the two, the image of the candidate has been more significant in recent elections.

Candidate images turn on personality and policy dimensions. People tend to form general impressions about candidates on the basis of what is known about their leadership potential, decision-making capabilities, and personal traits. For an incumbent president seeking reelection, accomplishments in office provide many of the criteria for evaluation. People make a retrospective judgment, deciding whether or not to vote for a candidate seeking reelection on the basis of how well they believe that candidate and party have performed during the candidate's term of office and how well they will continue to do so. In a retrospective judgment, the past is prologue to the future.

For the challenger, the criteria are slightly different: Experience, knowledge, confidence, and assertiveness must substitute for performance and provide a basis for anticipating how well the candidate might do in office. For both, character issues, such as trustworthiness, integrity, empathy, and candor, also shape people's perceptions, which in turn can affect voting.

The policy positions of the incumbent and challenger are obviously important as well. Knowing how the candidates stand on the issues permits voters to make a judgment on the consequences of electing either of them. However, the complexity of many issues, the low level of information and awareness that much of the electorate have about them, and the fact that a candidate's policy stands may be inconsistent or may change after the election reduce the salience of issues for many people.

To be important, issues must stand out from the campaign rhetoric. They must attract attention; indeed, they must resonate with the voters. Without personal impact, they are unlikely to be primary motivating factors in voting. To the extent that positions on issues are not discernible, personality considerations become more critical.

Ironically, that portion of the electorate that can be more easily persuaded—weak partisans and independents—tends to have the least information. Conversely, the most committed voters tend to be the most informed and to use their information to support their partisanship.

Since the 1960s, the percentage of the population identifying with a party has declined, as has the intensity of their identification. This has resulted in a more volatile electorate which usually decides later in the campaign whether and how to vote. In 1996, about two-thirds of the electorate identified with one or the other of the major parties, compared with three-fourths of the electorate forty years earlier.

Turnout   The weakening of party identification has also contributed to a decline in turnout. In 1996, only 49 percent of those who were eligible voted. In the midterm elections of 1994 and 1998, that number was about 36 percent (see Table 3–1).

Turnout depends on the legal and political environment in which elections occur. In 1993 Congress enacted a law known as the "motor-voter" bill, which was designed to make it easier for people to register to vote. The

TABLE 3–1. Suffrage and Turnout

Year	Total Adult Population (including aliens)*	Total Presidential Vote	Percentage of Adult Population Voting
1824	3,964,000	363,017	9.0
1840	7,381,000	2,412,698	33.0
1860	14,676,000	4,692,710	32.0
1880	25,012,000	9,219,467	37.0
1900	40,753,000	13,974,188	35.0
1920	60,581,000	26,768,613	44.0
1932	75,768,000	39,732,000	52.4
1940	84,728,000	49,900,000	58.9
1952	99,929,000	61,551,000	61.6
1960	109,672,000	68,838,000	62.8
1964	114,090,000	70,645,000	61.9
1968	120,285,000	73,212,000	60.9
1972	140,777,000	77,719,000	55.5
1976	152,308,000	81,556,000	53.5
1980	164,595,000	86,515,000	52.6
1984	174,447,000	92,653,000	53.1
1988	182,600,000	91,602,291	50.2
1992	189,044,000	104,426,659	55.2
1996	196,507,000	96,277,564	49.0

*Restrictions based on sex, age, race, religion, and property ownership prevented a significant portion of the adult population from voting in the nineteenth and early twentieth centuries. Of those who were eligible, however, the percentage casting ballots was often quite high, particularly during the last half of the nineteenth century.

Sources: Population figures for 1824 to 1920 are based on estimates and early census figures that appear in Neal R. Pierce, *The People's President* (New York: Simon and Schuster, 1968), p. 206. Population figures from 1932 to 1984 are from the U.S. Department of Commerce, Bureau of the Census, *Statistical Abstract of the United States* (Washington, D.C.: Government Printing Office, 1987), p. 250. Figures for 1988 and 1992 were compiled from official election returns supplied by the Federal Election Commission. Data for 1996 based on official elections returns from the Federal Election Commission, revised October 1997.

legislation permits registration by mail and requires states to make registration forms available at many statewide offices, including the Department of Motor Vehicles. By facilitating registration, Congress hoped that a larger proportion of the eligible electorate would vote, but so far, that hope has not been realized.

Longer-term trends, such as citizen satisfaction with, and trust of, government; feelings of political efficacy (the belief of citizens that they can make a difference and their vote really matters); and partisan identification are additional factors that affect turnout. Additionally, interest in the election, concern over the outcome, and feelings of civic responsibility also affect voting. Naturally, a person who feels strongly about the election and its consequences is more likely to vote than someone who does not care or feels voting will make no difference.

In addition to attitudinal factors, demographic characteristics that relate to turnout include age, education, income, and occupational status. People who are older, more educated, farther up the socioeconomic ladder, or in higher-status jobs are more likely to vote than people who are younger, less educated, and have less income. Education is the most important of these variables (i.e., it has the greatest bearing on whether people vote).[7]

Turnout has partisan implications. Republican partisans, who are generally better educated and have a higher income than Democrats, tend to vote with greater regularity than do their Democratic counterparts. Higher Republican turnout has helped that party counter an advantage in the number of registered voters held by the Democrats since the 1930s. In 1992 and 1996, however, turnout among Republicans was lower than among Democrats, thereby negating the GOP's usual partisan advantage in those elections.

Candidates and their advisers must take the voting behavior of the electorate into account when planning their campaign. They must also be conscious of the social basis of contemporary American politics: the racial, ethnic, religious, and even gender groupings that comprise each party's electoral coalition.

Electoral Coalitions   It was during the Depression that the Democrats became the majority party. They built their coalition primarily along economic lines, with the bulk of their supporters coming from those in the lower socioeconomic strata. In addition, the party maintained the backing of white southerners, who had voted Democratic since the Civil War.

Today the Democrats no longer constitute the majority. The major parties are at rough parity with one another. Moreover, the Democrats' electoral coalition has shifted. White southern support has eroded since the 1960s, the labor vote has also declined as a proportion of the total electorate, and Italian and Irish Catholics are not as loyal to the Democratic party as they once were; however, the increasing numbers of Hispanic voters and their loyalty to the Democratic ticket have helped the party retain the Catholic vote (see Table 3–2).

The Democratic electoral coalition has also benefited from continuing support from African-American and Jewish voters. In recent years the Democrats have also been the beneficiaries of a strong women's vote, particularly among unmarried working women and young voters. Democratic support is frequently concentrated in the cities of the large industrial states in the Northeast, the Midatlantic, and the Pacific coast.

The Republicans were the majority party before the 1930s. During the Depression, however, the GOP lost the support of much of the working

TABLE 3–2. Portrait of the American Electorate, 1984–1996 (in percentages)

Percentage of 1996 Total		1984 Reagan	Mondale	1988 Bush	Dukakis	1992 Clinton	Bush	Perot	1996† Clinton	Dole	Perot
	Total Vote	59	40	53	45	43	38	19	49	41	8
48	Men	62	37	57	41	41	38	21	43	44	10
52	Women	56	44	50	49	46	37	17	54	38	7
83	Whites	64	35	59	40	39	41	20	43	46	9
10	Blacks	9	90	12	86	82	11	7	84	12	4
05	Hispanics	37	62	30	69	62	25	14	72	21	6
01	Asians	—	—	—	—	29	55	16	43	48	8
66	Married	62	38	57	42	40	40	20	44	46	9
34	Unmarried	52	47	46	53	49	33	18	57	31	9
17	18–29 years old	59	40	52	47	44	34	22	53	34	10
33	30–44 years old	57	42	54	45	42	38	20	48	41	9
26	45–59 years old	60	40	57	42	41	40	19	48	41	9
24	60 and older	60	40	50	49	50	38	12	48	44	7
06	Not high school graduate	50	50	43	56	55	28	17	59	28	11
24	High school graduate	60	39	50	49	43	36	20	51	35	13
27	Some college education	61	38	57	42	42	37	21	48	40	10
43	College graduate or more	58	41	56	43	44	39	18	47	44	7
26	College graduate	—	—	62	37	40	41	19	44	46	8
17	Postgraduate education	—	—	50	48	49	36	15	52	40	5

continued

TABLE 3–2. Portrait of the American Electorate, 1984–1996 (in percentages) *continued from previous page*

Percentage of 1996 Total		1984 Reagan	Mondale	1988 Bush	Dukakis	1992 Clinton	Bush	Perot	1996† Clinton	Dole	Perot
46	White Protestant	72	27	66	33	33	46	21	36	53	10
29	Catholic	54	45	52	47	44	36	20	53	37	9
03	Jewish	31	67	35	64	78	12	10	78	16	3
17	White born-again Christian	78	22	81	18	23	61	15	26	65	8
23	Union household	46	53	42	57	55	24	21	59	30	9
11	Family income under $15,000	45	55	37	62	59	23	18	59	28	11
23	$15,000–$29,999	57	42	49	50	45	35	20	53	36	9
27	$30,000–$49,999	59	40	56	44	41	38	21	48	40	10
39	over $50,000	66	33	56	42	40	42	18	44	48	7
18	over $75,000	69	30	62	37	36	48	16	41	51	7
9	over $100,000	—	—	65	32	—	—	—	38	54	6
	Family's financial situation is										
33	Better today	86	14	—	—	24	62	14	66	26	6
45	Same today	50	50	—	—	41	41	18	46	45	8
20	Worse today	15	85	—	—	61	14	25	27	57	13
23	From the East	53	47	50	49	47	35	18	55	34	9
26	From the Midwest	58	41	52	47	42	37	21	48	41	10
30	From the South	64	36	58	41	42	43	16	46	46	7
20	From the West	61	38	52	46	44	34	22	48	40	8

continued

TABLE 3–2. Portrait of the American Electorate, 1984–1996 (in percentages) *continued*

Percentage of 1996 Total		1984		1988		1992			1996†		
		Reagan	Mondale	Bush	Dukakis	Clinton	Bush	Perot	Clinton	Dole	Perot
35	Republicans	92	7	91	8	10	73	17	13	80	6
26	Independents	63	36	55	43	38	32	30	43	35	17
39	Democrats	25	74	17	82	77	10	13	84	10	5
20	Liberals	28	70	18	81	68	14	18	78	11	7
47	Moderates	53	47	49	50	48	31	21	57	33	9
33	Conservatives	82	17	80	19	18	65	17	20	71	8
64	Employed*	60	39	56	43	42	38	20	48	40	9
—	Full-time student	52	47	44	54	50	35	15	—	—	—
36	Unemployed*	32	67	37	62	56	24	20	49	42	8
—	Homemaker	62	38	58	41	36	45	19	—	—	—
—	Retired	60	40	50	49	51	36	13	—	—	—
9	First-time voters	61	38	51	47	48	30	22	54	34	11

†Based on unofficial results.

*In 1996 poll, the question was: Are you employed full time? "Yes" answers are listd as employed; "No" answers are listed as unemployed.

Notes: Data for 1992 were collected by Voter Research and Surveys based on questionnaires completed by 15,490 voters leaving 300 polling places around the nation on Election Day. Data based on surveys of voters conducted by the *New York Times* and CBS News: 9,174 in 1984 and 11,645 in 1988. Those who gave no answer are not shown. Dashes indicate that a question was not asked or a category was not provided in a particular year. Family income categories were, in 1984, under $12,500, $12,500–$24,999, $25,000–$34,999, $35,000–$50,000, and over $50,000; in 1988, under $12,500, $12,500–$24,999, $25,000–$34,999, $35,000–$49,999, $50,000, and over. "Born-again Christian" was labeled "born-again Christian/fundamentalist" in 1992 and "fundamentalist and evangelical Christian" in 1988. Family financial situation is compared to four years ago in 1984 and 1988; 1984 numbers from NBC News.

Source: Voter News Service based on interviews with 16,627 randomly selected voters leaving 300 polling sites throughout the United States, as reported in "Portrait of the Electorate," *New York Times*, November 10, 1996, p. 28.

class and was unable to attract new immigrant groups to its coalition. Business and professional people did maintain their Republican affiliation, as did nonsouthern white Protestants. Today, the Republican party receives much of its support from white-collar workers (professionals and managers) and those in the upper-middle and upper classes. The party has increased its popularity in the Sunbelt and the West, particularly in the more sparsely populated Rocky Mountain states. Republicans have maintained much of their traditional support from Protestants and gained adherents from Christian fundamentalist groups, which have now become a powerful force in the party's electoral coalition. In addition, since 1980 male voters have given GOP candidates at the national level more support than have female voters.

What conclusions can we draw about the social and attitudinal bases of politics today? It is clear that the party coalitions have shifted and, in the Democrats' case, weakened. In particular, there has been a realignment of voters in the South. It is also clear that more people identify themselves as independent than in the past. The growing number of self-declared independents has contributed to more split-ticket voting (that is, splitting one's vote among candidates of different parties). This partisan dealignment has resulted in more fluid electoral coalitions, which fluctuate with the public mood and contemporary political environment.

Financial Considerations

A third factor that affects the strategic environment of presidential campaigns is money. The high costs of campaigning (which began to escalate in the 1960s with the advent of television advertising), the dependence on large donors, and the inequities in the amounts of money candidates received and could spend prompted a Democratically controlled Congress to enact legislation in the 1970s that provides for the public funding of presidential elections. The funding provision went into effect in 1976. At that time, the federal contribution to the major-party candidates was set at $10 million each plus a cost-of-living adjustment. In 1996, with that adjustment taken into account, each of the major candidates received $61.8 million; in 2000, that amount should be about $65 million.

The nominees of the major parties are automatically eligible for funds. Third-party and independent candidates do not qualify unless they receive a minimum of 5 percent of the presidential vote. Thereafter, they are eligible to receive funds equal to their proportion of the popular vote unless that figure drops below 5 percent. Although billionaire H. Ross Perot chose not to accept federal funds in 1992, he received 19 percent of the popular vote, making him eligible to receive $29 million in 1996, which he accepted. Perot's receipt of 7.5 percent of the 1996 vote will make his Reform party eligible for funding in 2000, about $12.7 million, whether or not he runs as that party's candidate.

The law permits the national parties to spend $.02 for each citizen of voting age in support of their presidential nominees. (In 1996 this amounted to almost $12 million each.) In addition, a 1979 amendment to the Federal Election Campaign Act (FECA) also allows state and local political parties to spend an unlimited amount of funds on voluntary efforts to turn out the vote. This funding is referred to as "soft money." The printing and distribution of literature, the operation of phone banks, generic advertising on radio and television, and the coordination of registration and get-out-the-vote drives are all included, thereby creating a huge loophole around the contribution and spending limits. During the 1996 election cycle, both parties exploited this loophole; the Republicans raised and spent $141 million in soft money and the Democrats, $122 million. Moreover, the money race is continuing as the election of 2000 approaches.[8]

Federal finance laws have had a profound effect on the conduct of presidential elections. Theoretically, they have equalized spending between the major-party candidates, but when soft money and independent expenditures are included, the appearance of equality quickly breaks down. Even though Bill Clinton and the Democrats have utilized their control of the White House to gain large donations, the Republicans continue to raise even more. Thus, it is no wonder that the Republican party leadership opposes changes in the Federal Election Campaign Act.

The law may help the parties raise more money, but it has also undercut them by encouraging political action committees (PACs) to organize and become involved in the electoral process, thereby competing with the parties as a principal link between the electorate and the elected (see the Hot-Button Issue box). The role and impact of the PACs, however, is less at the presidential level than at the state and congressional levels; moreover, it is greater in the precandidacy and preconvention nomination periods than in the presidential election.

News Coverage

News coverage is another factor that shapes the strategic environment. Today most people follow presidential campaigns on television. As an action-oriented, visual medium, television reports the drama and excitement of the campaign by emphasizing the horse race. Who is ahead? How are the candidates doing? Is the leader slipping?

The need to stress the contest affects which issues are covered and when. Television tends to focus on those issues that provide clear-cut differences between the candidates, provoke controversy, and can be presented in a simple, straightforward manner. These are not necessarily the issues that

☀ HOT- BUTTON ISSUE

Campaign Finance Reform

In 1996, both major parties were accused of accepting millions of dollars in illegal contributions from noncitizens, foreign companies, and even other governments, and with abusing their official positions in the White House and Congress to solicit donations on a continuing basis. Moreover, they admitted circumventing the spirit and intent of the campaign finance laws by raising hundreds of millions of dollars of "soft money" and spending it on generic advertising for Clinton and Dole as well as their other candidates for national office. Since that time, the financial race has continued.

In 1997, an off year following the most expensive election in the nation's history, the Democrats raised almost $65 million with the help of vigorous fund-raising activities by President Clinton and Vice President Al Gore, who attended many of the Democrats' "big bucks" events. However, the Republicans were not to be outdone. They raised even more (almost $109 million), thanks in part to the efforts of Speaker Newt Gingrich, a favorite on the Republican money trail. As the 2000 presidential election approaches, even more time will be spent raising even more money, with no end in sight.

Is the system broken? Does it need fixing? Many people say it does and point to the huge amounts of funds, which now dwarf the official and controlled contributions and expenditures for presidential elections.

Congress has been forced to consider the issue. Indeed, various proposals to prohibit "soft money," ban state parties from using it for federal elections, increase the amounts individuals can contribute to the parties and candidates for their nomination, make it more difficult for the parties to encourage and coordinate the spending of individuals and groups on the party candidates, prohibit PACs, and require the television broadcast media to provide candidates with free airtime have all been advanced, but to no avail. Why is there such opposition?

Part of the difficulty in reaching a consensus lies in the needs and desires of the parties to adequately support their own nominees; they feel that the amount of federal funds is insufficient in an age of television advertising. Part of the problem lies in partisan politics, resulting in the financial advantages that the Republicans have enjoyed under the present system.

There are also serious constitutional issues. The Supreme Court has held that the constitutional protection of freedom of speech prevents

Congress from placing limits on the amounts that individuals and groups spend on their own behalf in the electoral process. Freedom of association may also be involved where groups such as PACs are prevented from contributing or spending money.

Finally, there are those who say that, regardless of what the law intends, there will be unintended consequences. In particular, people will find legal ways to circumvent the law. Therefore, Congress should do nothing or, better yet, some argue, eliminate all campaign finance laws except for the reporting requirements. What do you think should be done?

the candidates wish to stress during their campaigns. In general, substantive policy questions of what the government should do tend to receive less coverage than events surrounding the campaign itself and the strategies, controversies, and activities of the candidates.

Moreover, much of the "spin" is negative: It includes more critical comments than favorable ones. According to one analysis of the evening news on the three major television networks, good news is hard to find (see Figure 3–1). In 1992, only 31 percent of Bush's coverage was positive, compared to 37 percent for Clinton and 46 percent for Perot.[9] The bad news continued for the Republicans in 1996, when Bill Clinton was again more favorably evaluated than his Republican challenger, Robert Dole.[10]

Why is there so much bad press? The answer relates in large part to the definition of what is newsworthy to the media. A fresh face winning and an experienced candidate losing are news; an experienced candidate winning and new one losing are not. Similarly, the first time a candidate states a position, it is news, but the second time, it is not. Since candidates cannot give new speeches every time they address a group, the news media that cover the candidate look for other things to report. These include slips of the tongue, inconsistent policy statements, mistakes, and even past private behavior, which may have little relevance to contemporary issues and job performance. The penchant of the press for reporting these topics as news discourages candidates from being spontaneous, candid, or reckless. In effect, it forces them to orchestrate their words and actions during the campaign.

To make matters worse, today the candidates are usually not given the opportunity to tell their own story in their own words, at least not on the evening news. The average length of a quotation from the candidates on national news in 1968 was 42.3 seconds. However, in 1992 it had fallen to

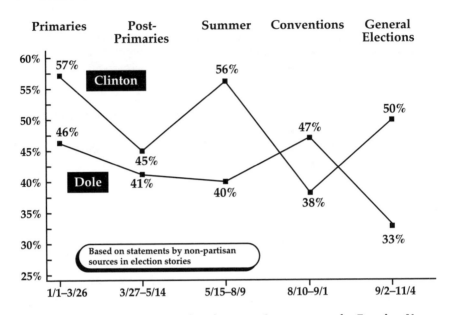

FIGURE 3–1. Good Press over Time in 1996: Coverage on the Evening News
Sources: "Take This Campaign—Please," *Media Monitor,* September/October 1996, p. 5; "Campaign '96 Final," *Media Monitor,* November/December 1996, p. 3.

8.4 seconds and in 1996 it was even less (8.2 seconds).[11] It is the television network anchors, correspondents, and commentators who tell the story of the election, not the candidates—at least not on the evening news.

In addition to the presumption about the nature of news and the format in which it is presented, there is also a framework into which that news is fitted. According to Thomas E. Patterson, a dominant story line emerges, and much of the campaign is explained in terms of it.[12]

The press does not create new stories for new events; more often than not, it fits those events into a preexisting campaign story. Naturally this story affects the electorate's perceptions of what is occurring. Candidates try, however, to influence the coverage by choosing the events which they create and the issues which they stress and by entering into an ongoing debate with other candidates.

Given the ability of the news media to control the campaign agenda, fit events into a storyline, and assess the qualities of the candidates, their impact on the election is considerable; however, the media's influence also varies with the strength of the voters' partisan identity. The news media tend to reinforce the feelings and loyalties of the party faithful, for whom the campaign is too short to change their beliefs or attitudes, but long enough to affect their perceptions of the candidates, and thus influence their vote. The effect on independents is different. In this group, the media can excite interest, arouse concern, improve knowledge, and, in the end, affect their judgment of whether to vote, and if so, for whom.

THE PRESIDENTIAL CAMPAIGN

Campaigning by presidential candidates is a relatively recent phenomenon. For much of American history, personal solicitation by the party nominees was viewed as demeaning and unbecoming of the dignity and status of the presidency. It was not until 1840 that this tradition of nonparticipation by the candidates was broken: that year, candidate General William Henry Harrison made twenty-three speeches in his home state of Ohio.[13] His precedent was not quickly followed, however. It was twenty years before another presidential candidate, Senator Stephen A. Douglas of Illinois, spoke out on the slavery issue as the Democratic nominee. In so doing, he denied his own presidential ambitions.

Presidential candidates remained on the sidelines until the 1880s, when Republican James Garfield broke tradition by receiving visitors at his Ohio home. Four years later, in 1884, Republican James Blaine made hundreds of campaign speeches in an unsuccessful effort to offset public accusations that he had profited from a fraudulent railroad deal. Benjamin Harrison, the Republican candidate in 1888, resumed the practice of front-porch campaigning. William McKinley saw even more visitors than did Harrison but his front-porch campaign paled in comparison to William Jennings Bryan's traveling road show in 1896. Bryan, who gained the Democratic nomination after making his famous "cross of gold" speech at his party's convention, traveled more than 18,000 miles, made more than 600 speeches and (according to press estimates) spoke to almost 5 million people.[14] In 1900, Republican vice presidential candidate Theodore Roosevelt challenged Bryan, "making 673 speeches, visiting 567 towns in 24 states, and traveling 21,209 miles."[15] Campaigning across the country was fast becoming the rule; in fact, the last of the front-porch campaigns was staged in 1920 by Warren G. Harding.

Herbert Hoover was the first incumbent to actively campaign for reelection. He did so to counter his opponent, Franklin Roosevelt, who crisscrossed the country by railroad, thereby making it possible for thousands of people to see him.[16] Roosevelt's skillful use of radio also reinforced the impact that a personal appeal can have for winning and leading.

Television accelerated personal campaigning by creating the possibility that a candidate could appeal directly to millions of voters. However, the medium also created new obstacles for the nominees and their parties. For one thing the physical appearance of the candidates became more important as public attention was directed to their personal images. New game plans had to be designed to contain broad public appeals that were candidate oriented, projected by sophisticated marketing techniques, and carefully targeted to specific groups within the electorate. Additionally, large, multitiered, functionally differentiated campaign organizations had to be set up.

Creating an Organization

A large, specialized political organization is essential to coordinate the myriad activities that must be performed in any presidential campaign. These include advance work, scheduling, press arrangements, issue and candidate research, speech writing, polling, advertising, grassroots organizing, accounting, budgeting, legal activities, and liaison with state and local party committees and other "friendly" groups.

Until recently, Democratic campaign organizations tended to be looser in structure and more decentralized in operation than those of the Republicans. For many years, the Democrats had stronger state parties and a weaker national base, with the consequence that their presidential candidates tended to rely most on state party organizations. The national party structure has been strengthened in recent years, and the Democratic candidates, like their Republican counterparts, have established separate organizations to run their presidential campaigns. Nonetheless, both depend on the state parties to turn out the vote.

In 1984 and 1988, the organizations of Walter Mondale and Michael Dukakis, respectively, experienced difficulty in carrying out coordinated campaign efforts, problems from which the Clinton organizations of 1992 and 1996 did not suffer. Tightly run operations, the Clinton campaign organizations had carefully designed strategic plans and a "war room" for tactical operations. Although the principals were different in the two campaigns, the structures and operating styles were almost identical. They were highly centralized, dependent on pollsters, engaged in targeted television advertising, and capable of rapidly responding to any criticisms of their candidate.

In contrast, the Dole operation was not nearly as well run or as organized. Plagued by considerable staff turmoil and turnover, the Dole campaign continually changed its messages, shifted its resources, and moved its geographic emphasis. A conflict over the control of advertising led to the resignation of Dole's principal media consultants as the fall campaign was just getting underway, which doubtless contributed to the disorganization. (Figure 3–2 depicts the 1996 campaign organizations for Clinton and Dole.)

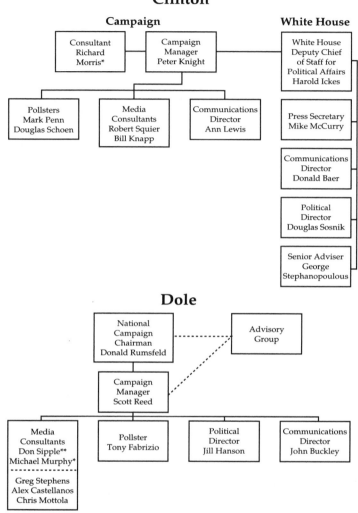

FIGURE 3–2. The Clinton and Dole Campaign Organizations in 1996

*Resigned in August 1996.

**Resigned in September 1996.

Campaign organizations are important, not only for winning the election, but also for making the transition to government and providing a preview of the new administration. They indicate the likely management style of the winner: Is there a willingness to take advice, delegate to others, make decisions, and either adhere to or adjust them if the situation changes, new information comes to light, or the desired objective remains unachieved? Ronald Reagan's reliance on his campaign organization and his reluctance to second-guess his advisers augured his White House staffing arrangement and passive administrative style. In contrast, Clinton's penchant for details, involvement in campaign strategic and tactical decisions, and apparently constant desire to assess the public mood were also reflected in how he has operated as president.

Campaign personnel are frequently recruited for key administration positions, particularly for those in the White House. Many of the senior aides in the Carter, Reagan, and Clinton White Houses also served in the inner circles of their presidential campaigns, as have many junior aides. However, the success with which these campaign personnel have made the adjustment to White House staff has been mixed at best.

Designing an Image

To become president, a candidate must act presidential by displaying the traits of an ideal president. Strength, boldness, and decisiveness are intrinsic to the public's image of the office. During times of crisis or periods of social anxiety, these leadership characteristics are considered absolutely essential. The strength that Franklin Roosevelt was able to convey by virtue of his successful bout with polio and that Eisenhower imparted by his military command in World War II contrasted sharply with the perceptions of Adlai Stevenson (in 1956), McGovern (in 1972), and Carter (in 1980) as weak, indecisive, and vacillating. Mondale (in 1984) and Bush (in 1988 and 1992) also suffered from the general perception that they lacked key leadership traits.

In addition to projecting an image of strength, a candidate must also appear competent by exhibiting sufficient knowledge and skills for the job. Although Ross Perot's prowess as a successful business executive was commonly cited as a strength of his candidacy, particularly in the light of the country's economic woes in 1992, his lack of experience in government raised questions about his ability to be its top public official.

Honesty, integrity, and trustworthiness are also essential attributes for the presidency. Clinton's lack of candor about his personal life, his draft status, and his campaign finance activities, and his equivocation on controversial issues were factors in both the 1992 and 1996 elections and have continued throughout his presidency, as revealed in his admission of an improper relationship with a White House intern which was later detailed by the report of the independent counsel charged with investigating the affair.

Incumbency contributes to a perception of leadership but does not guarantee it, as the defeats of Gerald Ford, Jimmy Carter, and George Bush attest. If there are national problems that the government is unable to address successfully, the president will usually be blamed. On the other hand, presidents often receive more credit for good times than they deserve, provided they successfully make the case that their policies have worked. Most of their campaigns are directed to making this claim and to raising doubts about their opponent's capabilities and actions.

Challengers usually face the more difficult task. Not only must they make a case against the incumbent but they must appear presidential when doing so, even without a presidential podium. Dole found that his position as Senate majority leader was a liability rather than an asset. The Senate's sparse record of legislative accomplishments hurt Dole's own claim that he was "a doer not a talker," and eventually forced him to resign from that body.

Being president produces recognition, esteem, and status. It also gives incumbents the ability to affect events (or at least influence their timing), help certain individuals, groups, and areas of the country, and promote various policies and programs that have political benefit. As president, Bill Clinton used his presidential podium and perquisites masterfully in 1995 and 1996 to promote his reelection.

Projecting a Partisan Appeal

Presidential images are usually set within a partisan context. Since the 1930s, Democratic candidates have traditionally clothed themselves in the garb of their party by stressing the "bread and butter" economic issues—jobs, wages, and benefits—that lay at the core of their New Deal electoral coalition. As long as the Republicans were the smaller of the two major parties, their candidates for the presidency did not emphasize partisanship, preferring instead to emphasize their own personal qualifications and foreign policy and national security issues. Since 1980, however, Republican candidates have not shied away from their partisan affiliation. They have also emphasized "family values," code words for conservative social positions such as allowing prayer in schools and prohibiting abortion and enacting special laws to protect the rights of homosexuals.

In 1992 and 1996, the Clinton campaign effectively countered this Republican imagery by taking policy positions that promoted family and community values, personal safety, and a less intrusive role for government. Occupying the middle ground, the Democrats successfully denied the Republicans some of their most successful policy issues. Only in the areas of abortion and school prayer have the major-party candidates and their parties offered clear-cut differences.

Naturally, candidates can be expected to raise questions about their opponents. These questions assume particular importance if the public's initial impression of a candidate is fuzzy, as it may be with outsiders who win their party's nomination. When Republican polls revealed Dukakis's imprecise image in 1988, senior Bush advisers devised a strategy to take advantage of this situation and define Dukakis in ways that would discredit him. Clinton did the same thing to Bush in 1992 and Dole in 1996.

Emphasizing the negative is a strategy based on the premise that the higher the negative perceptions of a candidate, the less likely that candidate will be to win. Lee Atwater, architect of this strategy, put it this way: "When I first got into politics, I just stumbled across the fact that candidates who went into an election with negatives higher than 30 or 40 points just inevitably lost."[17]

Clinton put a new twist on this strategy in 1996. Rather than putting a negative spin on Dole's personal traits, which might bring attention to his own character weaknesses, his ads stressed issues. They painted his Republican opponent as "Mr. No," opposed to practically every popular program including Medicare, family leave, and education. Dole countered with character ads of his own that emphasized the contrast between Clinton's promises and his performance. Clinton's focus on issues made his ads seem informational, whereas, in contrast, Dole's ads were perceived by voters as negative. This perception worked to reinforce Clinton's depiction of Dole as mean-spirited (see The Clinton Presidency box).

Building a Winning Coalition

In addition to creating a presidential image, designing a basic appeal, and criticizing the opponent's image and party, candidates need to pull together a winning coalition and target appeals and messages to potentially receptive voters. In the process, they must consider their political bases of support as well as the geographic foundations of the Electoral College. The goal is to build a coalition that results in winning a majority of the electoral votes, not necessarily a huge popular victory.

For both parties this translates into three basic strategic objectives: rekindle partisan loyalty, generate an appeal to independents, and turn out a sizable vote.

During the nomination process, candidates tend to aim their message at activists in order to win their party's nomination, but they have to broaden and moderate that appeal in the general election in order to reach out to other voters. Increasingly, contemporary presidential campaigns have been directed toward independents and weak party identifiers. In the 1980s, the Republicans were more successful in appealing to these groups, using symbols and slogans to reinforce their positions and stereotype their opponents. In 1992 and 1996, the Democrats used similar rhetoric and symbols to preempt the Republican advantage and make their case to independent, and even Republican, voters.

THE CLINTON PRESIDENCY

Running for Reelection

President Clinton began planning his reelection strategy in 1995. Designed by political consultant Dick Morris, the strategy was calculated to take advantage of Clinton's presidency, the country's prosperity, and the Republicans' opposition to popular domestic programs.

Clinton campaigned as the president, not as a presidential candidate. He used the perquisites of the office to great advantage, not only for fund-raising but to act as the people's president. From natural disasters and military base closings to town meetings on racial, social, and economic issues, issues that spanned the gamut from the health and welfare of children to the viability of the Medicare and Social Security systems for the elderly, Clinton was seen meeting with average Americans, listening to their problems, commiserating with their hardships, and proposing mainstream, Main Street policy solutions.

Since 1995, Clinton had become a "born-again" moderate, a New Democrat, preempting the Republicans on their issues and taking consistently centrist policy positions, which appealed to a majority of Americans (and which he had discerned through careful and continuous public opinion polling). In doing so, he emphasized his skills of compromise, reconciliation, and pragmatism. In contrast, Clinton and his aides presented the Republicans as extremists who were more concerned with their wealthy and religious constituencies than the needs and desires of the general public.

To promote the image that he wanted to convey, Clinton hired a new consulting team to poll the public, test his ideas and the "sound bites" in his speeches, develop appropriate advertisements, and target the ads to Democratic and independent voters. Underlying the entire renomination strategy was the assumption that the election would be decided before the national nominating conventions *not after* them. The key was to create the impression that the president's reelection was inevitable.

To achieve this objective, an advertising campaign was designed and commercials were aired beginning in summer 1995. Concentrated in key swing states in the Midwest, the Midatlantic, the South, and the Pacific Coast, but not in the major media markets, the advertising was aired on the cheaper, local affiliates and was issue oriented.

When it became clear that Robert Dole would be the Republican nominee, the focus of the advertising shifted to Dole, his tie to Speaker Newt Gingrich, and his opposition to popular programs such as family leave, educational spending, and tobacco advertising. The ads almost always pictured Dole standing with Gingrich as if they had become inextricably bound together into a single opponent.

Initially, Dole did not reply, as he had little money left after his primary campaign. By the time the Republicans did respond, it was too late. Even Morris's embarrassing resignation from the campaign during the Democratic convention (due to revelation of his affair with a Washington prostitute) made no difference. The die had been cast, and Clinton's election was seen as inevitable. The strategy had worked even *before* the official campaign had begun.

In addition to group appeals, campaigns also have a geographic thrust, which must be consistent with the composition of the Electoral College. Consequently, the large states always receive attention, as do the middle-sized, competitive ones. In the last three decades the Democrats have been forced to focus on certain Northeast and Midwest states because of their party's declining competitiveness in the South and the Rocky Mountain states. This gave the Republicans the advantage of concentrating their efforts and resources on a few of the key states that the Democrats needed to win. To overcome the Republican advantage, the Democrats have to be competitive in the South and strong in the largest states. They succeeded in 1992 and 1996, forcing the Republicans to spread their resources more thinly than in previous elections.

The Republican problem in 1996 was magnified by constant shifts in Dole's resource allocation. Initially, his campaign planned to focus on the Midwest. However, when polls indicated that he was far behind in all the key states in this region except Indiana and Ohio, he shifted his attention east to New Jersey, Pennsylvania, and Connecticut. But again when polls indicated that he was not making progress in these states, his focus shifted once again, this time to California, a state which his strategists had previously written off. Approximately $4 million was spent in California by the Dole campaign in the last three weeks before the election. Additionally, considerable resources were also put into Florida, a state that had voted for the Republican presidential candidate in the previous seven presidential elections. Despite his efforts, Dole ended up losing both of these large states.

Media Tactics

News Coverage Campaign organizations work very hard to influence the coverage they receive. Speeches are now scripted to produce sound bites, and events are staged with television in mind. Satellite broadcasting has made it possible for campaign press secretaries to give local newspaper reporters and television stations more direct access to the candidates. Interviews conducted by the local press are apt to be less hostile and more favorable than those conducted by the national reporters covering the campaign.

Although contemporary campaigns lack spontaneity, they are designed for maximum public impact. Symbols are used to convey images; themes are presented on a weekly or biweekly basis. Press releases, advertisements, and speeches are carefully synchronized to strengthen a candidate's appeal. Even seemingly off-the-cuff remarks are usually prepared and timed to contribute to the overall thematic effect.

The Clinton campaigns of 1992 and 1996 were fairly successful in maintaining their focus and themes. In 1992 Clinton constantly talked about the economy and the need for change; in 1996, he reiterated his priorities: the economy, education, health, and the environment. In contrast, Bush and Dole struggled to find themes that resonated with the American people.

One of the reasons why candidates go to great length to organize their campaign is to exercise maximum influence over its coverage by the news media. They wish that coverage to be on their agenda, issues, and policy positions, not the items that the media designated for the entertainment or interest of their audience.

Presidents may face difficulties in controlling the pace and tone of the campaign for several reasons:

1. Unexpected actions and events frequently take center stage, preempting their activity. In this case, candidates have but no choice to react.

2. Their motives for whatever they say and do will be scrutinized and, in all likelihood, dismissed as political by the news media. In other words, the news media assume self-interest to be a prime motivating factor of the candidates (but certainly not the press).

3. They may have trouble getting their message across. Remarks may be edited for the sake of the story. Moreover, candidates can be interrupted, their comments interpreted, and their policies evaluated. The national press corps is usually confrontational. Thus, whenever possible, candidates like to avoid tough interviews and press conferences and favor questions from average citizens or folksy talk-show hosts.

The advantage of a talk/entertainment format is that questions posed by ordinary people tend to be less hostile than the confrontational kind of journalism practiced by the national news correspondents. Moreover, the audience tends to be different. Those who watch talk and entertainment shows are, on the whole, less oriented toward politics, particularly partisan politics, and thus may be more amenable to influence by the candidates who appear on these programs. Bill Clinton has been particularly effective in this setting; George Bush and Robert Dole were not.

Debates Another news/entertainment format that has become part of the American political tradition is the presidential debate. More than any other single campaign activity, presidential debates have gained public attention. It is estimated that more than half the adult population in the United States watched all the 1960 Kennedy-Nixon debates, the first debate between presidential candidates, and almost 90 percent saw one of them.[18] Although less attention has been riveted on a single debate since then, millions still watch all or parts of them. Approximately 40 million people saw one or more of the presidential debates in 1996, a figure that was approximately one-third less than in 1992.

With so many people watching, meticulous planning goes into each debate. Representatives of the candidates study the locations, try to anticipate questions, and brief and rehearse the candidates. Mock studios are built and the debate environment simulated. In 1980 this elaborate preparation took a bizarre twist when the staff readying Ronald Reagan for his debate with President Carter obtained briefing material prepared for Carter by his aides. Knowing the questions that Carter anticipated and the answers he had been advised to give helped Reagan counter Carter's responses. The debate cast the Republican challenger in a favorable light..

Candidates have viewed these debates as vehicles for improving their images and damaging their opponents. They seek to establish their leadership credentials and critique those of their opponents. In 1992 Clinton took a traditional challenger's approach by criticizing the incumbent's record and talking about the need for change. In 1996, however, as the incumbent, he sounded the litany of his administration's accomplishments and his goals for the next four years.

Dole was in a far more difficult position in 1996. Not only was he the challenger, but he was trailing the president badly in the polls. Thus, he had to make the case for himself and against the president, and to do so in a manner that did not seem "mean-spirited." How can one harshly criticize a sitting president without sounding mean and nasty?

In the first debate, Dole tried to achieve this objective by focusing on the substantive policy issues: reiterating the arguments he had made on the campaign trail about slow economic growth, the rise in drug usage, and Clinton's liberal, big-government policies. These positions appealed to Republicans far more than they did to the general electorate. In the second debate, still lagging far behind in the polls, Dole raised the issue of trust and character, presenting himself as a person who keeps his word and suggesting that the president did not. Clinton anticipated the attack, however. While Dole was talking, Clinton stepped closer to his opponent and looked directly at him, but he did not respond to his attacks. Instead, he continued to talk about substantive issues, and remained dignified on his "presidential" pedestal.

Once the debate ends, the news media are preoccupied with evaluating it. They use the winner/loser format when doing so, fitting the debate results into the dominant story. Knowing this, the campaigns try to affect their press evaluation through the use of "spin doctors," luminaries who are made available to speak to the media following the debate.

The conventional wisdom is that debates help challengers more than incumbents if they help anyone at all. Because challengers are less well known to the electorate, the debates give them an opportunity to define themselves, articulate their positions, and demonstrate their competence and capacity to be president by appearing at least the equal of the incumbent. But few voters admit that the debates actually changed their vote.

More often than not, debates reinforce the views and perceptions that those in the viewing and listening audience bring to the debate. People who are inclined toward a particular candidate tend to see that candidate in a more favorable light in the debate. Even a weak performance, such as Reagan's in his first debate with Walter Mondale in 1984, did not seem to change many voting decisions.

Debates tend to be decisive only in very close elections in which influencing the perceptions of a relatively small proportion of voters can make a difference. In 1960 and again in 1976, the debates may have affected who won and who lost. In 1980, the single presidential debate probably contributed to Reagan's margin of victory. In 1992 they may have elevated Perot's vote, but in 1984, 1988, and 1996, debates had a less discernible impact on the results.

Despite the attempts to script and orchestrate their campaigns to influence the press, candidates are never content with the news coverage they receive and generally complain about being shortchanged and misinterpreted. Naturally, they prefer to present their case directly to the electorate without mediation. They can do this through advertising.

Ads   To be effective, ads must seem truthful, convey relevant information, and be interesting. Ads must engage the audience to exert influence. For television advertising especially, this means action: The ad must move. In 1980, Reagan faced a different need. Fearful that a slick presentation would bring attention to his background as a professional actor, Reagan's media advisers designed commercials containing as few gimmicks and diversions as possible. Reagan appeared as a talking head.

Radio and television advertising tends to be targeted to different sections of the country and different groups within the electorate. The objective of targeting is to bring the campaign home by influencing specific groups of voters who share many of the same concerns. This requires that issues and positions must appeal to the particular audience to which they are targeted. Media buyers will normally code stations by their viewers and program format so that the messages fit the audience both demographically and regionally.

As mentioned previously, candidates work as hard to destroy their opponent's image as they do to build their own. Negative advertising has been used with regularity since 1964, when perhaps the most famous (or infamous) negative ad was created for the Democrats. Called "Daisy Girl," it was designed to reinforce the impression that Republican candidate Barry Goldwater was a trigger-happy zealot who would not hesitate to use nuclear weapons against a Communist foe.

The advertisement began with a little girl standing in a meadow and plucking petals from a daisy. She counted to herself in a soft voice. When she reached eleven, her voice faded and a stern-sounding male voice began counting down from nine. At zero, there was an explosion, the little girl disappeared, and a mushroom-shaped cloud covered the screen. President Johnson was then heard saying: "These are the stakes, to make a world in which all of God's children can live or go into the dark. The stakes are too high for you to stay at home." The ad ended with a plea to vote for Lyndon Johnson on election day.

The commercial was run only once. Goldwater supporters were outraged and protested vigorously. Their protest kept the issue alive. In fact, the ad itself became news, and parts of it were shown on television newscasts, thereby conveying the impression the Democrats wished to leave in the voters' minds.

The emphasis given negative advertising has increased in recent years. In 1988 the ads themselves became a campaign issue when a PAC that was supporting Bush showed a picture of Willie Horton, a convicted murderer, who stabbed a man and raped his female companion after escaping while on a furlough from a Massachusetts prison. Amid gruesome commentary about Horton's criminal acts, the ad contrasted the positions of Dukakis and Bush on crime, much to Dukakis's disadvantage. This ad was particularly controversial because it had racial overtones with Horton an African American and his victims white. Dukakis countered Bush's negative advertising with anti-negative ads about Bush's negative advertising.[19]

Negative advertising is designed to raise questions about the candidate targeted in the ads. However, it can also have an adverse impact on the candidate who sponsors them. Because Bush ran so many negative ads in 1988, his ads in 1992 were not believed by a majority of the electorate; even worse, Dole's negative ads four years later reinforced the image that Clinton and the Democrats had painted of him as "mean-spirited."

Dukakis failed to respond quickly and effectively to Bush's negative portrayal of him in 1988. Instead, he allowed the message of Bush's ad to sink in. The Clinton campaign profited from this lesson, and both in 1992 and 1996 it operated a "war room" to help anticipate and react rapidly to Republican charges. Running against Bush in 1992, Clinton's media consultants went so far as to obtain copies of the opponent's advertisements even before they were aired and crafted responses that could be shown within hours of Bush's. The Clinton campaign continued to stay a step ahead of the Republicans four years later. For example, the Clinton campaign drafted and distributed its response to Dole's economic plan *before* Dole even formally presented it, and they faxed a response to each of Dole's charges in the first debate to the networks even before the debates had ended.

The need for quick response is based on the premise that political advertising can be very effective in shaping voter perceptions, reinforcing attitudes and opinions, and affecting the judgment of whether to vote and, if so, for whom. Consequently, much time and effort are devoted to them.

THE MEANING OF THE ELECTION

Polling the People

From the candidate's perspective, the name of the game is to win. From the voter's perspective, it is to decide who will govern for the next four years. Naturally, throughout the campaign there is considerable interest in what the probable results will be.

Prior to the election, pollsters take the pulse of the electorate. Those who work for the candidates do so to help their campaigns adjust and target appeals. Those who work for the media do so to provide "entertaining" news on the race and to forecast the likely winner.

Since 1916 there have been nationwide surveys of public sentiment during the campaign. However, some of the early polls did not accurately forecast the results. The most notable gaffes occurred in 1936 and 1948, when major surveys predicted that Alfred M. Landon and Thomas E. Dewey, respectively, would win. The principal errors in these surveys were that their selection of people to be interviewed was not random and that they concluded polling too early before Election Day. These problems have been corrected with the consequence that public opinion surveys are more accurate. Nonetheless, they only measure opinion at the time they are taken, although the nearer to the election they are conducted, the more likely they are to reflect the final results of the vote. Table 3–3 lists the final polls and actual results in the most recent three elections.

TABLE 3–3. **Final Preelection Polls and Results, 1988–1996 (in percentages)**

Year/Candidates	Gallup Poll	CBS/NYT Polls (1988 and 1992), NBC (1996)	Harris Poll	Actual Results
1988				
Bush	53	48	51	53.4
Dukakis	42	40	47	45.6
Others/Undecided	5	12	2	1.0
1992				
Clinton	44	44	44	43.0
Bush	37	35	38	37.5
Perot	14	15	17	18.9
Others/Undecided	5	6	1	1.6
1996				
Clinton	52	49	51	49.2
Dole	41	37	39	40.8
Perot	7	9	9	8.5

The most accurate poll is one taken after people vote and as they leave the voting booths. Called an exit poll, it surveys over 10,000 voters across the country to determine for whom they voted and why.[20]

One of the problems with exit polls lies in their accuracy (rather than inaccuracy): They give the press access to sufficient data to predict the outcome before the elections have been concluded. The problem is that such predictions might affect voters who have not yet voted. In 1980, for example, President Carter conceded defeat in a nationally televised statement at 8:30 P.M. Eastern Standard Time (EST), 5:30 P.M. Pacific Standard Time (PST). West Coast Democratic candidates complained that Carter's early concession, reinforced by exit polling results, cost them their elections. Although the evidence is not conclusive, it suggests that early predictions may depress later turnout but do not appreciably affect the vote of those do go to the polls.

Nonetheless, criticism of these early concessions and forecasts persuaded the television networks not to broadcast exit poll results from a state until the polls in that state had closed; they also promised not to make national predictions until West Coast voting has been completed (a promise that was abandoned in 1996).

Analyzing the Results

What does the election mean? Obviously, it indicates who wins and who loses—who will control the White House and Congress. With the help of exit polls and other surveys, it also provides a demographic snapshot of the electorate on Election Day: which groups voted for which candidates? More than this information, however, in-depth surveys can indicate public expectations for the new president. Is the president expected to change policy, like Reagan was in 1980 and Clinton in 1992, or to continue the policy as Bush was in 1988 and Clinton in 1996? Moreover, what are the perceptions of the new president? What policies should be pursued, and what is the likelihood of their success?

Let us take Carter's election in 1976. Why did he beat Ford? According to analyses of the exit poll and other surveys, Carter won because he was unconnected to the Watergate scandals, whereas Ford, by virtue of his party and his pardon of predecessor Richard Nixon, was not. That Carter was the candidate of the majority party, came from the South, and was viewed as a highly religious and moral man certainly helped. However, none of these qualities provided much direction for the new administration, nor did Carter's electoral coalition adhere for very long.

Carter pursued policy that divided his Democratic supporters. Adverse economic conditions, embarrassments in U.S. foreign policy (particularly the Iranian hostage crisis), and Carter's inability to provide strong leadership combined to doom the administration. In the 1980 election, voters looked back to evaluate Carter's record and found it wanting.

Reagan won in 1980 for the same reason Carter had won four years earlier: The voters did not believe that the incumbent president deserved another four years in office. Reagan did not win because of his ideology, policy positions, or personal appeal, but in spite of these factors. In fact, he was less popular among both his supporters and opponents than any other winner in recent times, yet nonetheless he was seen as having a greater potential for leadership than Carter.

Four years later it was another story. The voters rewarded Reagan for a job well done. The 1984 election was a referendum on Reagan's performance in office. The electorate voted for him then just as they had voted against Carter in 1980. The American people approved of Reagan's leadership and wanted his tenure in office to continue.

The 1988 election constituted still another referendum on the Reagan presidency, although obviously not on President Reagan. Vice President Bush benefited from the public's perception of good times and greater national security. Bush had promised to pursue the policies of the still popular Reagan administration but to do so in a "kinder and gentler" way. The electorate divided accordingly. Most of those who had cast ballots for Reagan in 1984 voted for Bush in 1988: Republicans and conservatives did so overwhelmingly, while independents gave him a solid 12 percent lead; Democrats and liberals stayed with Dukakis. In addition to partisan and ideological divisions, the 1988 vote also evidenced class, race, and gender differences, with the Republicans doing better among voters who were wealthier, white, and male and the Democrats doing better among the lower socioeconomic groups, ethnic and racial minorities, and women. These trends continued in 1992 and 1996.

Like the vote four years earlier, the electorate in 1992 made a retrospective judgment; in doing so, however, it rejected the incumbent. George Bush who was not perceived to have done a good job with the economy, the nation's number one issue in that year and for that election. Bush's vote in 1992 fell among every population group, including Republicans, conservatives, and even born-again Christians. For the first time in three presidential elections, Republican defections topped Democratic defections.

Clinton was the principal beneficiary of this anti-incumbency vote, aided by Ross Perot, who siphoned votes from Bush by appealing to independents and, to a lesser extent, some Republicans who would normally have voted for the GOP ticket but instead protested economic conditions by voting for Perot. Bush received less than one-third of the independent vote.

Clinton did reasonably well among independents, gaining 38 percent of their vote. In addition, he maintained the traditional Democratic support. Although Clinton received 69 percent of the electoral vote, he won only 43 percent of the popular vote, which amounted to a very thin mandate for the policy changes he had promised. When combined with the slow and unsteady start of his administration, this fragile mandate proved to be an insurmountable barrier to achieving many of his policy objectives. Moreover, by 1994 voters had indicated their displeasure by electing the first Republican Congress in forty years.

What followed in the next two years was a remarkable recovery as Clinton repositioned himself in the mainstream of public opinion, preempted the Republicans on their issues, and successfully defined their "Contract with America," ten principles and policy positions that all Republican candidates for the House of Representatives pledged to support, as an extremist doctrine. By 1996, with the economy was stronger, the crime rate down, and the nation remaining at peace, he won a significant election victory.

Clinton's popular and electoral vote exceeded his 1992 totals, although the regional composition remained essentially the same as four years earlier. Democrats and liberals stayed with the president and Republicans and conservatives supported their own candidates. Clinton, however, did better among moderates and independent voters than his Republican challenger.

The groups that shifted most in their support of the president from 1992 to 1996 were women and younger voters. In fact, the gender gap (17 percent) was the largest in the nation's history. Moreover, for the first time, a majority of women voted for one candidate and a plurality of men for another. In addition, despite the Democrats' support among the elderly, it was the youth who gave the president greater support than any other age cohort (see Table 3–2).[21]

The 1996 election was a referendum on the Clinton presidency, and Clinton won (see Figure 3–3 and Table 3–4). Not only did the electorate evaluate his first term favorably in 1996, voters saw the president as more capable of understanding and handling the challenges of the 1990s and, in his own words, "building a bridge to the twenty-first century," than either Dole or Perot; the latter ran a distant third. This assessment suggested that moderate, incremental policy was the order of the day. Clinton proceeded accordingly.

Assessing the Mandate

Despite the many postelection analyses conducted by political scientists, journalists, and politicians, the election results often raise more questions than they answer. The reasons that people vote for a candidate vary. Presidents are rarely given a clear mandate for governing, even though they may try to claim one.

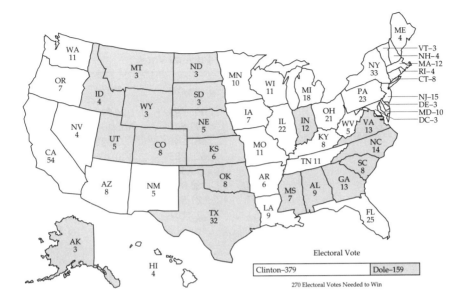

Electoral Vote

| Clinton–379 | Dole–159 |

270 Electoral Votes Needed to Win

FIGURE 3–3. The 1996 Presidential Electoral Vote

TABLE 3–4. The 1996 Presidential Vote: Electoral and Popular Vote Summary

State	Electoral Vote		Popular Vote			Total Popular Vote
	Clinton	Dole	Clinton	Dole	Perot	
AL		9	662,165	769,044	92,149	1,534,349
AK		3	80,380	122,746	26,333	241,620
AZ	8		653,288	622,073	112,072	1,404,405
AR	6		475,171	325,416	69,884	884,262
CA	54		5,119,835	3,828,380	697,847	10,019,484
CO		8	671,152	691,848	99,629	1,510,704
CT	8		735,740	483,109	139,523	1,392,614
DE	3		140,355	99,062	28,719	270,845
DC	3		158,220	17,339	3,611	185,726
FL	25		2,546,870	2,244,536	483,870	5,303,794
GA		13	1,053,849	1,080,843	146,337	2,299,071
HI	4		205,012	113,943	27,358	360,120
ID		4	165,443	256,595	62,518	491,719
IL	22		2,341,744	1,587,021	346,408	4,311,391

continued

TABLE 3–4. The 1996 Presidential Vote: Electoral and Popular Vote Summary *continued from previous page*

State	Electoral Vote		Popular Vote			Total Popular Vote
	Clinton	Dole	Clinton	Dole	Perot	
IN		12	887,424	1,006,693	224,299	2,135,842
IA	7		620,258	492,644	105,159	1,234,075
KS		6	387,659	583,245	92,639	1,074,300
KY	8		636,614	623,283	120,396	1,388,708
LA	9		927,837	712,586	123,293	1,783,959
ME	4		312,788	186,378	85,970	605,897
MD	10		966,207	681,530	115,812	1,780,870
MA	12		1,571,763	718,107	227,217	2,556,786
MI	18		1,989,653	1,481,212	336,670	3,848,844
MN	10		1,120,438	766,476	257,704	2,192,640
MS		7	394,022	439,838	52,222	893,857
MO	11		1,025,935	890,016	217,188	2,158,065
MT		3	167,922	179,652	55,229	407,261
NE		5	236,761	363,467	71,278	677,415
NV	4		203,974	199,244	43,986	464,279
NH	4		246,214	196,532	48,390	499,175
NJ	15		1,652,329	1,103,078	262,134	3,075,807
NM	5		273,495	232,751	32,257	556,074
NY	33		3,756,177	1,933,492	503,458	6,316,129
NC		14	1,107,849	1,225,938	168,059	2,515,807
ND		3	106,905	125,050	32,515	266,411
OH	21		2,148,222	1,859,883	483,207	4,534,434
OK		8	488,105	582,315	130,788	1,206,713
OR	7		649,641	538,152	121,221	1,377,760
PA	23		2,215,819	1,801,169	430,984	4,506,118
RI	4		233,050	104,683	43,723	390,284
SC		8	506,283	573,458	64,386	1,151,689
SD		3	139,333	150,543	31,250	323,826
TN	11		909,146	863,530	105,918	1,894,105
TX		32	2,459,683	2,736,167	378,537	5,611,644
UT		5	221,633	361,911	66,461	665,629
VT	3		137,894	80,352	31,024	258,449
VA		13	1,091,060	1,138,350	159,861	2,416,642
WA	11		1,123,323	840,712	201,003	2,253,837
WV	5		327,812	233,946	71,639	636,459
WI	11		1,071,971	845,029	227,339	2,196,169
WY		3	77,934	105,388	25,928	211,571
Total:	379	159	47,402,357	39,198,755	8,085,402	96,277,634

Source: Federal Election Commission, October 1997.

For a mandate to exist, the party's candidates must take discernible and compatible policy positions, and the electorate must vote for them because of those positions. Moreover, the results of the national election must be consistent. If one party wins the White House and another the Congress, it is difficult for the president to claim a mandate. Few elections meet these criteria. Obviously, the election of 1996 did not.

Presidential candidates usually take a range of policy positions, often waffle on a few highly divisive issues, may differ from their party and its other candidates for national office in their priorities and their stands, and rarely have coattails long enough to sweep others in with them. In fact, they may run behind their congressional candidates, as Bush did in 1988 and Clinton did in 1992.

Nonetheless, the promises candidates make during the campaign create the expectations that they have to try to meet. Kennedy pledged to get the country moving again in 1960; Johnson, to continue the momentum and create a Great Society in 1964; Nixon, to bring a divided nation together in 1968 and keep it together (in 1972); and Carter, to provide a more honest, open, and responsive presidency in contrast to the imperial style of the office that had involved the United States in Vietnam and Watergate. Four years later, Reagan pledged to return America to its traditional roots of economic individualism and its position as leader of the free world, and in 1984, he promised to continue his strong leadership at home and abroad. His vice president, George Bush, said he would continue the policies of less government, lower taxes, and a stronger military force in 1988. In response to the economic recession in 1991–1992, Clinton pledged to stimulate it, reduce the deficit, lower middle-class taxes, reform health care, and change welfare "as we know it" in 1992. Four years later, he promised to balance the budget by 2002 without hurting education, the environment, or the Medicare and Social Security systems.

Achieving their mandates has proved difficult for many presidents. Nonetheless, the promises do become the agenda for the winning administration as well as the criteria by which that administration will initially be judged. What candidates promise matters, and as a result, which one wins does make a difference.

Converting the Electoral Coalition for Governance

Not only does the selection process inflate performance expectations and create a set of diverse policy goals, but it also lessens the presidents' power to achieve them. The transition from a winning electoral coalition to a successful governing coalition has become much more difficult. The declining power of party leaders, the growth of autonomous state and congressional electoral systems, and the personalization of the election process, has left presidents with fewer dependable allies.

In the aftermath of Watergate, Jimmy Carter made much of the fact that he did not owe his nomination to the power brokers within his party or his election to them or to members of Congress. But the same can be said for members of Congress and, for that matter, governors and state legislators. Presidents were not indebted to them nor were they indebted to presidents. The increasing independence of Congress from the presidency decreases legislators' political incentives to follow the president's lead.

Bill Clinton found this out the hard way. He ran away from fellow Democrats in Congress during the 1992 election, not wanting to be tainted by the anti-incumbent, anti-Congress, anti-Washington attitude of voters at that time. But he soon found that he needed the support of Democratic members of Congress to obtain his legislative objectives. Nor could he easily or effectively go over their heads to the voters. His inability to obtain congressional support for health care and other priority programs led to the Democratic debacle of 1994, when that party lost control of Congress to the Republicans.

What can presidents do to prevent the electorate from being disappointed in their leadership? How can they meet public expectations in light of the weakening of partisanship and the increased sharing of policy-making powers? How can they lead, achieve, and satisfy diverse pluralistic interests at the same time? Obviously, there is no set formula for success. Forces beyond the president's control may affect the course of events. Nonetheless, presidents must exercise strong political leadership as soon as possible. They must establish their own priorities and thereby shape public expectations of what they hope to do. These priorities need to be consistent with their election campaign and in accord with the public mood. If that mood changes and/or if conditions change, presidents must recast their priorities as well. Bush was unable to do so. Clinton was slow to establish his leadership credentials. The ability of both to implement change suffered as a result. Clinton recovered; Bush did not.

To be successful, presidents must take advantage of *their* opportunities, particularly in the period following the election. They must construct their own policy alliances; they must mobilize their own supporters. Presidents who fail to do so, who do not focus their appeal and articulate it clearly and effectively to the general and specialized publics, will have difficulty building the coalitions they need to govern.

With fewer natural allies, presidents face a decline in their popularity over time, which can detract from their ability to accomplish their goals. The growing influence of personality on people and events makes the president's job much tougher. As a consequence, during ordinary times presidents are forced to be facilitators even though they might prefer to be directors of change.

CONCLUSION

The system of election designed by the framers of the Constitution has been substantially modified over the years. Theoretically, the Electoral College continues to select the president, but in practice the popular vote, aggregated by states, decides the outcome.

During much of America's electoral history, political parties were the principal link between candidates and voters. They chose the nominees, organized their campaigns, mobilized their support, and stood to gain if they were elected. Moreover, partisan attitudes conditioned the perceptions and voting behavior of much of the electorate.

Times have changed. Today there are more mediators and more mediums. Party professionals are less important than they were, and campaign professionals more important. Pollsters, grassroots organizers, and media experts now plan and run the general election campaigns. These handlers discern attitudes, design and project appeals, target voters, and mobilize what they hope will be a winning coalition. They utilize the techniques of market research and the vehicles of the modern electronic age. Radio and television (including satellite hookups and entertainment and talk shows) plus direct mail and phone banks are the principal communications vehicles to reach voters. The Internet is also being used and will figure more prominently in future elections. The campaigns have become more candidate oriented. It is the candidates who now create their organizations, receive federal funds, and mount highly personalized appeals. Moreover, the electorate's personal evaluation of the candidates plays an increasingly important role in its voting decisions.

This personalization of the presidential selection process has serious implications for the exercise of presidential leadership. It tends to inflate public expectations yet reduces the capacity to achieve them. Presidents are more on their own. Their electoral coalition is not easily converted into a governing coalition, forcing presidents to devote more time, energy, and resources to mobilizing and maintaining outside support, to controlling the focus of the national news media, and to worrying about reelection. *In short, presidential candidates campaign as if they are going to be directors but when they get into office, they usually find that the best they can do, barring a crisis, is to facilitate the operation of government.*

DISCUSSION QUESTIONS

1. Explain some of the ways in which advances in communication technology have changed the conduct of presidential elections, the candidates and campaigns of political parties, and the relationship between elections and government.

2. For many years political scientists have debated the merits and liabilities of the Electoral College, and in particular whether the college should be reformed and, if so, how. Is this still an important and relevant debate today? Is the Electoral College undemocratic in theory? Has it been so in practice? For which groups, geographic areas, or institutional entities has the Electoral College been most problematic in recent elections? Explain.

3. Design a campaign strategy for the likely Republican and Democratic nominees in 2000. In your strategy discuss the substance and targets of the candidates' basic appeals, how they should project these appeals in paid and unpaid media, the geographic/Electoral College emphases they should employ, and whether and how each candidate should treat the issue of the incumbent administration. Which of these strategies do you think will be most successful, and why?

WEB EXERCISES

1. See if you can find a simulation for the next presidential campaign. Two good link sites are the Kennedy School at Harvard <http://www.ksg.harvard.edu> and one at <http://www.webwhiteblue.org>. If you can find a simulation, access it and participate. How realistic do you think the simulation was? What were its principal strengths and weaknesses?

2. Try to ascertain how effective the candidates were in 1996 by analyzing exit poll data currently available on the *New York Times* Web site at <http://www.nytimes.com>.

   Look at the appeals of the candidates, the groups to which they were targeted, and how those groups voted in 1996. Using material from Table 3–2 (pages 63–65), compare that group's vote to that of previous elections.

SELECTED READING

Abramson, Paul R., John H. Aldrich, and David W. Rhode. *Change and Continuity in the 1996 Elections.* Washington, D.C.: Congressional Quarterly, 1998.

Campbell, Angus, Philip E. Converse, Warren E. Miller, and Donald E. Stokes. *The American Voter.* New York: Wiley, 1960.

Jamieson, Kathleen Hall. *Packaging the Presidency: A History and Criticism of Presidential Campaign Advertising.* 3rd ed. New York: Oxford University Press, 1996.

Kennedy Institute of Politics. Harvard University. *Campaign for President: The Managers Look at '96.* Hollis, N.H.: Hollis Publishing, 1997.

Ladd, Everett Carll. "1996 Vote: The 'No Majority' Realignment Continues," *Political Science Quarterly* 112 (1997): 1–28.

McCubbins, Mathew D., ed. *Under the Watchful Eye*. Washington, D.C.: Congressional Quarterly, 1992.

Nelson, Michael, ed. *The Elections of 1996*. Washington, D.C.: Congressional Quarterly, 1997.

Patterson, Thomas E. *Out of Order*. New York: Knopf, 1993.

Pomper, Gerald M., et al. *The Election of 1996: Reports and Interpretations*. Chatham, N.J.: Chatham House, 1997.

Tenpas, Kathryn Dunn. *Presidents as Candidates*. New York: Garland Publishing, 1997.

Thomas, Evan, et al. *Back From the Dead*. New York: Atlantic Monthly Press, 1997.

Troy, Gil. *See How They Ran: The Changing Role of the Presidential Candidate*. New York: Free Press, 1991.

Wayne, Stephen J. *The Road to the White House, 2000*. New York: St. Martin's/ Worth, 2000.

Wolfinger, Raymond E., and Steven J. Rosenstone. *Who Votes?* New Haven: Yale University Press, 1980.

Notes

1. The initial solution to this problem was to have a long term of office but make the president ineligible for reelection. This, however, created additional dilemmas: It provided little incentive for the president to perform well and denied the country the possibility of reelecting a person whose experience and success in office might make the incumbent better qualified than anyone else. Reflecting on these concerns, delegate Gouverneur Morris urged the removal of the ineligibility clause on the grounds that it "intended to destroy the great motive to good behavior, the hope of being rewarded by a re-appointment" (Gouverneur Morris, *Records of the Federal Convention*, ed. Max Farrand [New Haven: Yale University Press, 1921], pp. 2, 33).

2. So great was the sectional rivalry, so parochial the country, and so limited the number of people with national reputations that it was feared that electors would tend to vote primarily for candidates from their own states. To prevent the same states, particularly the largest ones, from exercising undue influence in the selection of both the president and vice president, this provision was included. It remains in effect today.

3. The most populous state at the time, New York, did not permit its electorate to participate in the selection of electors. Moreover, in three of the states in which Jackson won the electoral vote but lost in the House of Representatives, he had fewer popular votes than Adams. He captured the majority of electoral votes in two of these states because the electors were chosen on a district, rather than a statewide basis.

4. Thomas E. Dewey could have denied Harry S Truman a majority in the Electoral College in 1948 with 12,487 more California votes, and in 1960, a change of fewer than 9,000 votes in Illinois and Missouri would have meant that John F. Kennedy lacked an Electoral College majority. In 1968, a shift of only 55,000 votes from Richard M. Nixon to Hubert H. Humphrey in three states (New Jersey, Missouri, and New Hampshire) would have thrown the election into a Democratic House of Representatives, and in 1976, a shift of only 3,687 votes in Hawaii and 5,559 in Ohio would have cost Jimmy Carter the election.

5. In 1948, Henry Wallace (Progressive party) and Strom Thurmond (States' Rights party) received almost 5 percent of the total popular vote, and Thurmond won thirty-nine electoral votes. In 1960, fourteen unpledged electors were chosen in Alabama and Mississippi. In 1968,

Governor George Wallace of Alabama, running on the American Independent party ticket, received almost 10 million popular votes (13.5 percent of the total) and forty-six electoral votes. In 1992, H. Ross Perot received 19.7 million votes (19 percent of the total) but no electoral votes.

6. Much of this research has been conducted by the Center for Political Studies at the University of Michigan. Starting in 1952, the center began conducting national surveys, known as American National Election studies, during the presidential elections. The object of these surveys is to identify the major influences on voting behavior. A random sample of the electorate is interviewed before and after the election. Data from these surveys are made available to political scientists, who analyze American voting behavior following each presidential election.

7. Raymond E. Wolfinger and Steven J. Rosenstone, *Who Votes?* (New Haven: Yale University Press, 1980), pp. 13, 226.

8. In 1997, a nonelection year, the Republicans raised $40.4 million, compared to the Democrats' $27.0 million (Ruth Marcus, "Common Cause Lists 'Soft' Donors," *Washington Post*, March 13, 1998, p. A23).

9. "Clinton's the One," *Media Monitor*, November 1992, p. 2.

10. "The Bad News Campaign," *Media Monitor*, March/April 1996, pp. 2–4; "Dole's Summer Doldrums," *Media Monitor*, July/August 1996, p. 3.

11. "The Bad News Campaign," p. 2.

12. Thomas E. Patterson, *Out of Order* (New York, Knopf, 1993), pp. 106–121.

13. Keith Melder, *Hail to the Candidate: Presidential Campaigns from Banners to Broadcasts* (Washington, D.C.: Smithsonian Institution Press, 1992), pp. 70–74.

14. William J. Bryan, *The First Battle* (Port Washington, N.Y.: Kennikat Press, 1971), p. 618.

15. Melder, *Hail to the Candidate*, p. 129.

16. One reason why Roosevelt initiated the whistle-stop tour in 1932 was to overcome the whispering campaign about his physical condition (the result of having been crippled by polio). To demonstrate that he was not confined to a wheelchair, he appeared standing while he addressed groups from the rear platform of his train. However, Roosevelt could not get up or sit down without aid, so before the train arrived and again after it left the station, Roosevelt's aides would assist him, out of public view.

17. Atwater's point is that if 30 to 40 percent of the electorate evaluate a candidate more negatively than positively, that candidate is in trouble. Atwater's quote appears in Thomas B. Edsall, "Why Bush Accentuates the Negative," *Washington Post*, October 2, 1988, p. C4.

18. Elihu Katz and Jacob J. Feldman, "The Debates in the Light of Research: A Survey of Surveys," in Sidney Kraus, ed., *The Great Debates* (Bloomington: Indiana University Press, 1962), p. 190.

19. In one, the governor was seen sitting in front of a television set showing a Bush commercial that accused Dukakis of being against virtually every new weapons system for the military. An angry Dukakis turns off the set and says: "I'm fed up with it. Haven't seen anything like it in twenty-five years of public life, George Bush's negative TV ads: distorting my record, full of lies, and he knows it."

20. Here's how exit polls work: A large number of precincts across the country are randomly selected. Representatives of the media, often college students, interview voters as they leave the polls. The interview is intended to measure the beliefs and attitudes of the electorate. In the course of the interview, each voter is asked to complete a printed ballot and deposit it into a sealed box. Throughout the day, these ballots are collected and tabulated and the results are telephoned to a central computer bank. After the election in a state has been completed, the findings of the poll are broadcast.

21. In other respects, the vote reflected patterns evident in recent presidential elections, with racial and religious minorities strongly favoring the Democrats and white Protestants, particularly religious fundamentalists, voting heavily Republican.

4

THE PRESIDENT AND THE PUBLIC

"PUBLIC SENTIMENT IS EVERYTHING. With public sentiment nothing can fail, without it nothing can succeed."[1] These words, spoken by Abraham Lincoln, pose what is perhaps the greatest challenge to any president: to obtain and maintain public support. As every student of the presidency quickly learns, presidents are rarely in a position to command others to comply with their wishes. Instead, they must rely on persuasion. A principal source of influence for presidents is public approval of their performance and their policies.

Presidents have generally not been content to follow public opinion on issues or let their approval ratings reach some "natural" level. Instead, they usually have engaged in substantial efforts to lead the public. Sometimes their goals have been to gain long-term personal support, while at other times they have been more interested in obtaining support for a specific program. Often, of course, both goals are present.

Success at moving the public provides one of the clearest tests of presidential leadership. Presidents who direct change impose their priorities on the national agenda and create and mobilize a constituency to follow their lead. Presidents who facilitate, on the other hand, reflect and, perhaps, intensify widely held views. Their challenge is to convert these views into political capital to achieve specific, more incremental programmatic goals.

In this chapter we explore presidential attempts to understand public opinion and the public's expectations and evaluations of the chief executive. We are interested in both the nature of the public's attitudes and (even more important) why it holds them. Such study will deepen our understanding, not only of expectations and evaluations, but of the obstacles the White House faces in measuring public opinion. We also examine presidential efforts to influence public opinion. We do not assume, of course, that presidents are always successful in influencing the public, and thus we are also concerned with the effectiveness of the various techniques of opinion leadership that presidents use.

UNDERSTANDING PUBLIC OPINION

Presidents need public support, and understanding public opinion can be a considerable advantage to them in gaining and maintaining it. At the very least, presidents want to avoid needlessly antagonizing the public. Thus, they need reliable estimates of public reactions to the actions they are contemplating. They also need to know what actions and policies, either symbolic or substantive, the public wants. By knowing what the public desires, presidents may use their discretion to gain public favor whenever they feel the relevant actions or policies are justified.

In addition, presidents often want to lead public opinion in support of themselves and their policies. To do so, they need to know the views of various segments of the public, whom they need to influence and on what issues, and how far people can be moved. Presidents usually want to avoid expending their limited resources on hopeless ventures. Nor do they want to be too far ahead of the public, lest they risk losing their followers and alienating segments of the population.

Americans' Opinions

Before a president can understand what opinions the public holds, individual citizens must form opinions. Although Americans are usually willing to express opinions on a wide variety of issues, these responses cannot be interpreted as reflecting crystallized and coherent views. Opinions are often rife with contradictions; this is because the public often fails to give views much thought or consider the implications of policy stands for other issues.[2] For example, national polls show consistently that the American people place a very high priority on balancing the budget. At the same time, however, majorities favor maintaining or increasing spending on most components of domestic policy, even as they oppose increasing taxes sufficiently to cover the costs of the policies.

Policy making is a very complex enterprise, and most voters do not have the time, expertise, or inclination to think extensively about most issues (especially those as distant from their everyday experiences as, perhaps, federal regulations, nuclear weapons, and bureaucratic organization). Even closer to home, after more than two decades of political controversy, nearly half of Americans fail to realize that the nation must import oil.[3] Similarly, the major domestic policy initiative of Ronald Reagan's second term was tax reform, yet as the bill was nearing the end of its legislative path in the Senate, only 40 percent of the public had heard or read even "some" about it.[4] Likewise, Bill Clinton was, understandably, disappointed that even after three years of his administration, nearly half the American people thought the U.S. annual budget deficit had been going up during his administration, while only one-fifth (correctly) knew it had gone down.[5]

On the other hand, *collective* public opinion has properties quite different from those of individual citizens. There is evidence that the general public holds real, stable, and sensible opinions about public policy, which develop and change in a reasonable fashion in response to changing circumstances and new information. Any changes that occur are usually at the margin and represent the result of different trade-offs among constant values.[6]

In short, as the White House attempts to understand American public opinion, it is handicapped by the fact that many people have no opinion on issues of significance to the president and, moreover, that many of the opinions the public does express are neither crystallized, coherent, nor informed. On the other hand, it is possible to grasp the essential contours of public opinion, especially where opinions are widely held—for example, on issues, such as economic conditions and civil rights, that touch the public directly. Moreover, the president may desire to know the distribution of whatever opinions that do exist. Under these circumstances, what means can be relied on to measure public opinion?

Public Opinion Polls

A common tool for measuring public attitudes is the public opinion poll. Whether commissioned on behalf of the White House or by various components of the mass media, it allows the president to learn how a cross section of the population feels about a specific policy, general living conditions, or the administration's performance.

In an attempt to understand public opinion on matters of special concern to them, recent presidents have commissioned their own polls. Franklin D. Roosevelt was the first to pay close attention to polls, which were just being made scientific during his tenure in office. All presidents since John F. Kennedy have retained private polling firms to provide them with soundings of American public opinion, and in the last four administrations, pollsters have also played a significant role as high-level political advisers.

Despite their widespread use in the contemporary White House, public opinion polls are not completely dependable instruments for measuring public opinion. An important limitation of polls is that the questions they contain usually do not attempt to measure the intensity with which opinions are held. In reality, however, people with intense views will probably be more likely to act on those views to reward or punish politicians than people whose preference for the issue is a matter of indifference.

A related problem with polls is that the questions asked of the public seldom mesh with the decisions that presidents face. In fact, the executive rarely considers issues in the "yes/no" terms presented by most polls. Moreover, evidence of widespread support for a program does not indicate how the public stands on most of the specific provisions under consideration. Such details do not lend themselves to mass polling because they require specialized knowledge of the issues, which few Americans possess.

Another problem is that responses may reflect the particular wording of the choices that are presented, which is a problem especially for people who lack crystallized opinions on issues. Moreover, if questions are of the "agree/disagree" variety, there may be a bias toward the "agree" alternative. Similarly, if the "official" government position is indicated in a question, this often elicits a bias toward that position, especially on foreign policy issues. For example, public attitudes toward the People's Republic of China softened considerably after President Nixon began making overtures toward establishing relations with that nation.

On policies that are very controversial, it may be impossible to ascertain public attitudes without some contamination caused by the use of "loaded" symbols in the questions. For example, in one poll, when people were asked to evaluate the amount government spends on "welfare," only 13 percent replied that it was "too little." When asked about expenditures for "assistance to the poor," however, 57 percent replied that government did not spend enough.[7]

Questions that inevitably arise when discussing presidents and polls include: How should presidents use public opinion data? Does the use of these data constrain presidents rather than indicate where their persuasive efforts should be focused? By using polls, do presidents, in effect, substitute followship for leadership?

Presidents ritually deny that their decisions are influenced by polls. According to President Carter's chief media adviser, Gerald Rafshoon, "If we ever went into the president's office and said, 'We think you ought to do this or that to increase your standing in the polls,' he'd throw us out."[8] Polls *do* indeed influence White House political strategy, however.

More than any previous administration, the Reagan White House used polling in its decision-making process. Reagan's pollster, Richard Wirthlin, took polls for the president every three or four weeks (more often during a crisis) and met regularly with Reagan and his top aides. Wirthlin's goal was to determine when the nation's mood was amenable to the president's proposals and gauge public reactions to the president's actions. The White House wanted the timing of the president's proposals to be compatible with the political climate so as to maximize the probabilities of achieving its objectives; thus, polls were used to help set the presidential agenda.[9]

Presidents Bush and Clinton used their pollsters to perform similar functions, although Bush commissioned only a small number of polls. President Clinton, on the other hand, has been very attentive to polls, and his administration has the most comprehensive White House polling operation in history. Within a week of taking office, Clinton directed his aides to begin regular polling on issues, and pollsters have been thoroughly integrated into the Clinton White House planning and strategy sessions on legislation. They assess public support for various policy options (such as how to fund health care) and test market phrases for describing proposals ("anticrime" was found to be preferable to "gun control," for example). Whenever the president gives a speech, pollsters gather groups of people to watch and register their reactions on a handheld device called a dial-a-meter.[10]

Much of this effort is designed to frame the president's message most effectively in order to win public support for his policies. At other times, the White House may be trying to identify possible pitfalls in its path or to clarify the administration's policies. When polls revealed that the public was ignorant about an issue such as President Reagan's education policy or President Clinton's cooperation with the Whitewater investigation, the White House went to great lengths to talk about them.

Presidential Election Results

Although presidents cannot always rely on polls to inform them about public opinion, they can, theoretically, gain valuable insights through the interpretation of their own electoral support in the period following the election. In other words, they may be able to learn what voters are thinking when they cast their ballots for president. For such an approach to be useful for a president seeking to understand public opinion, the following conditions must be met:

1. Voters must have opinions about the policies.

2. Voters must know the candidates' stands on the issues.

3. The candidates that voters support must offer them the alternatives they desire.

4. There must be a large voter turnout.

5. Voters must vote on the basis of issues.

6. The president must be able to correlate voter support with voters' policy views.

As we saw in Chapter 3, these conditions rarely occur, thus making presidential election results a tenuous basis for interpreting public opinion.

Mail from the Public

The mail, including both letters and E-mail, is another potential means for the president to learn about public opinion. Although estimates vary and record keeping is inconsistent, there can be no doubt that the White House receives several million communications from the public each year, including more than 25,000 letters, phone calls, and electronic mail messages daily. (The president's E-mail address is <President@whitehouse.gov>.) The White House staff screens the mail and keeps a log summarizing opinion on critical issues. Correspondence that requires a response is forwarded to the relevant agencies.

The president usually reads only a few items from a day's mail, primarily communications from personal friends, prominent and influential citizens, and interest group leaders. Although a few letters from ordinary citizens may be answered by the president, primarily as a public relations ploy, mail from important individuals and organizations is usually answered by top White House aides. The rest is answered by lower-level officials and volunteers using computer-designated responses.

Even if the president could read more mail, this would not necessarily provide a useful guide to what the public is thinking about policy issues since little of it focuses on the issues with which the president must deal. In addition, those who communicate with the White House are not a cross section of the American people. Instead, they overrepresent the middle and upper classes and people who agree with the president.

Acting Contrary to Public Opinion

Presidents find it difficult to understand public opinion, and there is no lack of examples of the White House being surprised by public reaction to events and presidential actions. These range from President Nixon's decision to invade Cambodia in 1970 and Ronald Reagan's efforts to halt increases in Social Security benefits in 1981 to President Clinton's nomination of Zoe Baird as attorney general and his proposal to lift the ban against homosexuals in the military in 1993.[11]

Even if presidents believe (or, at least, claim to believe) that they understand public opinion on a particular issue, they do not necessarily follow it.[12] Throughout most of Ronald Reagan's tenure in office, polls showed that the public wanted him to lower the federal deficit but not to cut social programs. Moreover, people were willing to decrease planned military spending to accomplish these goals. However, the president refused to act accordingly.

Presidents offer several rationales for not following public opinion. President Nixon claimed that he was not really acting contrary to public opinion at all; instead he represented the "silent majority," which did not express its opinion in activist politics. Similarly, presidents may argue that their actions are carried out on behalf of underrepresented groups, such as the poor or an ethnic minority, or of a future generation. This kind of rationale is used today on behalf of budget-balancing efforts designed to decrease the burden of debt for future generations and environmental protection policies designed to preserve a healthy and rich natural environment for others to share.

Presidents have also wrapped themselves in the mantle of the courageous statesman following his principles and fighting the tides of public opinion. For example, in a speech on the invasion of Cambodia in 1970, President Nixon stated, "I would rather be a one-term president and do what I believe is right than to be a two-term president at the cost of seeing America become a second-rate power and to see this nation accept the first defeat in its proud 190–year history."[13] Similarly, President Bush told his staff that if the United States had to fight Iraqi leader Saddam Hussein to liberate Kuwait, "it's not going to matter to me if there isn't one congressman who supports this, or what happens to public opinion. If it's right, it's gotta be done."[14]

Presidents often feel (and with good reason) that they know more about policy than most members of the public and that they sometimes must lead public opinion instead of merely follow it. In the words of Gerald Ford:

> I do not think a President should run the country on the basis of the polls. The public in so many cases does not have a full comprehension of a problem. A President ought to listen to the people, but he cannot make hard decisions just by reading the polls once a week. It just does not work, and what the President ought to do is make the hard decisions and then go out and educate the people on why a decision that was necessarily unpopular was made.[15]

PUBLIC EXPECTATIONS OF THE PRESIDENT

When new presidents assume the responsibilities of their office, they enter into a set of relationships, the contours of which are largely beyond their control. The nations with which they will negotiate, the Congress they must persuade, and the bureaucracy they are to manage, for example, have well-established routines and boundaries within which they function, and which set the context of the president's relationships with them.

Public evaluations of the president also occur within an established environment: that of public expectations. The president is in the limelight of American politics. Although this provides the potential for presidential leadership of the public, it is purchased at a high cost. The public has demanding expectations of what presidents should be, how they should act, and what their policies should accomplish. It is up to the chief executive to live up to these expectations.

Although some presidents may, over time, succeed in educating the public to alter its expectations, views change slowly, and the changes that do take place usually create additional burdens for the president. In addition, the static nature of the president's personal characteristics and leadership style and the American political system's inherent constraints on executive power and capacity to choose the most effective policies limit the executive's ability to meet the public's expectations. Frustration, on the part of both the president and the public, is inevitable in such a situation.

High Expectations

The public's expectations of the president in the area of policy are substantial and include the assurance of peace, security, and prosperity. Table 4–1 shows the results of polls taken in December 1976 and 1980 following the elections of Presidents Carter and Reagan, respectively. Performance expectations of each president are quite high and cover a broad range of policy areas. Clearly, citizens want the good life and look to the president to provide it.

In addition, there is a substantial gap between the public's expectations of what presidents should accomplish (and for which it will hold them accountable) and the degree of success it expects presidents to have in meeting such expectations. For example, at the time of Bill Clinton's election, most people expected him to be an "outstanding" or "above average" president and were optimistic about the next four years of his administration (almost exactly the same results found in 1977, 1981, and 1989 for Carter, Reagan, and Bush, respectively).[16] At the same time, over 70 percent of respondents did not expect Clinton to keep his campaign promise not to raise taxes, and clear majorities did not expect him to reduce the deficit or control federal spending (see Table 4–2). Clearly, the fact that such a juxta-

TABLE 4–1. Early Expectations of Presidents Carter and Reagan

Policy	Precent Who Felt They Could Expect:	
	Carter	Reagan
Reduced unemployment	72	69
Reduced inflation	*	66
Reduced cost of government	59	70
Increased government efficiency	81	89
Effective dealings with foreign policy	79	77
Strengthened national defense	81	76

*Not available.

Sources: "Early Expectations: Comparing Chief Executives," *Public Opinion*, February/March 1981, p. 39.

TABLE 4–2. Expectations of the Clinton Administration

Do you think the Clinton administration will or will not be able to do the following?

	Will	Will Not
Improve education	69%	25%
Help minorities and the poor	68	27
Improve health care	64	30
Improve the environment	64	29
Keep the nation out of war	60	27
Impove the economy	59	35
Reduce unemployment	58	37
Increase respect for the United States abroad	50	40
Control spending	40	54
Reduce the federal budget deficit	38	54
Avoid raising taxes	20	74

Source: Gallup poll, November 10–11, 1992.

position of views might be unfair to the president seems irrelevant to many of his constituents.

Later in this book we will show how the president's influence on public policy and its consequences is often limited. Nevertheless, the public holds the president responsible. To quote President Carter: "When things go bad you [the president] get entirely too much blame. And I have to admit that when things go good, you get entirely too much credit."[17] Since conditions emphasized in the press seem to be bad more than good, the attention presidents receive is usually negative.

In addition to expecting successful policies from the White House, Americans expect their presidents to be extraordinary individuals.[18] (This, of course, buttresses the public's policy expectations.) The public desires the president to be honest, intelligent, cool in a crisis, caring, competent, and possessed of a sense of humor. Substantial percentages also want the nation's leader to have imagination and charisma. Obviously, it is not easy to meet these diverse and somewhat unrealistic expectations.

The public not only has high expectations for the president's official performance but also lofty expectations for their leader's private behavior.[19] Substantial percentages of the population strongly object if a president engages in bad behaviors that are nonetheless very common in American society. For example, when the Watergate tapes revealed that President Nixon frequently used profane and obscene language in his private conversations, many Americans were outraged. Similarly, revelations regarding President Clinton's extramarital affairs have diminished the public's regard for him as a person.

The Sources of High Expectations   The tenacity with which Americans maintain high expectations of the president may be due in large part to the encouragement they receive from presidential candidates to do so. As noted in Chapter 3, the lengthy process by which Americans select their presidents lends itself to political hyperbole. For one year out of every four, the public is encouraged to expect more from the president than it is currently receiving. Evidently, it takes this rhetoric to heart and holds presidents to high standards of performance, independent of the reasonableness of these expectations.

High expectations of presidents are also supported by political socialization; for example, schoolchildren are often taught American history organized by presidential eras. Implicit in much of this teaching is the view that great presidents were largely responsible for the freedom and prosperity that Americans enjoy. From such lessons it is a short step to presuming that contemporary presidents can be wise and effective leaders and, therefore, that the public should expect them to be so. Furthermore, commentators may compare contemporary presidents to an ideal president—a composite created out of the strongest attributes (but none of the liabilities) of their predecessors.

Another factor encouraging high expectations is the prominence of the president. As the nation's spokesperson and the personification of the nation, the chief executive is the closest thing Americans have to a royal sovereign. At election time, presidents and their families—even their pets—dominate the news in America. Their great visibility naturally induces people to focus attention, and thus demands and expectations, on them.

Related to the president's prominence is the tendency to personalize. Issues of public policy are often extremely complex. To simplify them, Americans tend to think of issues in terms of personalities, especially the president's. It is easier to blame a specific person for personal and societal problems than it is to analyze and comprehend the complicated mix of factors that really forms the cause. Similarly, it is easier to project frustrations onto a single individual than it is to deal with the contradictions and selfishness in people's own policy demands. At the midpoint of his term in office, President Carter reflected: "I can see why it is difficult for a President to serve two terms. You are the personification of problems and when you address a problem even successfully you become identified with it."[20]

Part of the explanation for the public's high expectations of the president probably lies in its lack of understanding of the context in which the president functions. We shall see in later chapters that the president's basic power situation in the nation's constitutional system is one of weakness rather than strength. However, this fact is widely misperceived by the public, most of whom do not feel that the president has too little power.[21]

Consequences of High Expectations   Do high expectations of our presidents affect the public's evaluations of their performance? Although we lack sufficient data to reach a definitive conclusion, there is reason to believe that they do.[22] Sometimes the negative impact of high expectations in the public's support for the president is of the chief executive's own making. Jimmy Carter provides a good example of a president who was his own worst enemy in this regard. Both before and after taking office, he set very high standards for himself and his administration and assured the public that he would live up to them. Unfortunately, he was unable to keep many of his promises, such as balancing the budget or keeping his administration free from scandal.

Similarly, George Bush promised, in dramatic fashion, not to raise taxes and to create millions of jobs. When he agreed to a tax increase as part of a budget agreement with Congress and the jobs failed to materialize, his opponents, and even his friends, wasted no time in criticizing him. Bill Clinton began his administration on a sour note when he announced that he would not be able to provide a tax cut for the middle class as he had promised during the campaign.

We have, of course, no way to calculate precisely the influence of such unkept promises on the president's standing with the public, and many of them may be of little significance in isolation. However, their collective impact, particularly during periods of some domestic distress, undoubtedly depresses the president's approval ratings because they help to undermine the aura of statesmanship and competence that attracted support in the election campaign. According to Richard Wirthlin, President Reagan's pollster, expectations are the ultimate source of public frustration.[23] Perhaps presidents should lower expectations, especially at the beginning of their terms, so they will not have to mortgage their reputations and prestige to nuances of governing that they have yet to learn.

Contradictory Expectations

The contradictions in the public's expectations present an additional obstacle to presidents in their efforts to gain public support. As the focus of contradictory expectations, it is very difficult to escape criticism and loss of approval—no matter what they do. Contradictory expectations of presidents deal with either the content of policy or their style of performance. The public's expectations of policy are confused and seemingly unlimited. We want low taxes and efficient government, yet we do not want a decrease in most public services. We expect plentiful gasoline, but not at a higher price. We want economic inflation to be controlled, but not at the expense of higher unemployment or interest rates. We want a clean environment, yet we support industrial development.

It is true, of course, that the public is not entirely to blame for holding these contradictory expectations. Presidential candidates often enthusiastically encourage voters to believe that they will produce the proverbial situation in which the people can have their cake and eat it, too. In the 1980 presidential campaign, Ronald Reagan promised, among other things, to slash government expenditures, substantially reduce taxes, increase military spending, balance the budget, and maintain government services. Similarly, in 1992 Bill Clinton promised to increase social services while lowering taxes on most Americans—a feat he was not able to accomplish.

Our expectations of presidential leadership style are also crucial in our evaluation of the president. The public wants a president who embodies a variety of traits, some of which are contradictory.

1. We expect the president to be a *leader*—an independent figure who speaks out and takes stands on the issues, even if the views are unpopular. We also expect the president to preempt problems by anticipating them before they arise. Similarly, we count on the president to provide novel solutions to the country's problems. To meet these expectations, the president must stay ahead of public opinion, acting on problems that may be obscure to the general populace and contributing ideas that are different from those currently in vogue in policy discussions.

   In sharp contrast to our expectations for presidential leadership are our expectations that chief executives be *responsive* to public opinion and that they be constrained by majority rule, as represented in Congress. The public overwhelmingly wants Congress to have final authority in policy disagreements with the president, and it does not want the president to be able to act against majority opinion.[24]

   These contradictory expectations of leadership versus responsiveness place presidents in a no-win situation. If they attempt to lead, they may be criticized for losing contact with their constituents, being unrepresentative, and, at worst, acting like demagogues. Conversely, if they try to reflect the views of the populace, they may be reproached for failing to lead and settling for the easiest, rather than the optimal, solution to a problem.

2. We expect our presidents to be openminded politicians in the American tradition, and thus exhibit *flexibility* and willingness to compromise on policy differences. At the same time, we expect presidents to be *decisive* and to take firm and consistent stands on the issues. These expectations are also incompatible, and presidents can therefore expect to be criticized for being rigid and inflexible when they are standing firm on

an issue. Presidents will also be disparaged for being weak and indecisive when they do compromise.

3. We want the president to be a *statesman*—to place the country's interests ahead of politics—yet we also want a skilled *politician* who exercises loyalty to his or her political party. A president who acts in a statesmanlike manner may be criticized for being an ineffective idealist who is too far above the political fray and insufficiently solicitous of party supporters. Jimmy Carter began his term on such a note when he attempted to cut back on "pork barrel" water projects. A president who emphasizes a party program, however, may be criticized for being a crass politician who lacks concern for the broader national interest; this happened to Bill Clinton when he proposed an economic stimulus plan in his first year in office that contained billions of dollars for projects designed to please Democratic constituents around the country.

4. We like our presidents to run *open* administrations. We expect a free flow of ideas within the governing circles in Washington, and we want the workings of government to be visible, not sheltered behind closed doors. At the same time we want to feel that the president is *in control* of things and is providing a rudder for government. If presidents allow internal dissent among their aides and this becomes visible to the public, critics will complain that the White House is in disarray. However, if presidents should attempt either to stifle dissent or to conceal it from the public, they will be accused of being isolated, undemocratic, unable to accept criticism, and desirous of muzzling opposition.

5. Finally, we want our presidents to be able to *relate* to the average person in order to inspire confidence in the White House and promote compassion and concern for the typical citizen. However, we also expect the president to be above the crowd—to possess characteristics far *different* from our own and to act in ways that are beyond the capabilities of most of us. To confuse the matter further, we also expect the president to act with a special dignity, befitting the leader of the country (and the free world) and to live and entertain royally, with much pomp and circumstance. In other words, presidents are not supposed to resemble the average person at all.

   If presidents seem too common, they may be disparaged for being just that. One only has to think of the many political cartoons of Harry Truman and Gerald Ford that implied they were really not up to the job of president. On the other hand, if presidents seem too different, appear too cerebral, or engage in too much pomp, they will likely be denounced as snobbish and isolated from the people and as too regal for Americans' tastes. The Nixon White House evoked such criticisms about the president and his aides.

PUBLIC APPROVAL OF THE PRESIDENT

The most visible and significant aspect of presidents' relations with the public is their level of approval. Presidents' efforts to understand and lead public opinion and their efforts to influence the media's portrayal of them are aimed at achieving public support. This support is related to their success in dealing with others, especially the Congress. The higher the public's level of approval of the president, the more support Congress will give administration programs.[25]

Whether they are based on perceptions encouraged by the White House, the media, or other political actors or based on detached and careful study, opinions about presidents and their policies are constantly being formed and reformed. Opinions are also affected, sometimes quite directly, by the impact of foreign and domestic policies. In this section we examine issues, the president's personality and personal characteristics, and dramatic international events as possible influences on presidential approval. In addition, there are certain less-dynamic factors in the form of predispositions that citizens hold, such as political party identification and the positivity bias, that may strongly influence their evaluations of the president. Political party identification, in particular, not only directly affects opinions of the president, but also mediates the impact of other influences. Thus, it is important to examine predispositions as well as more specific opinions about presidents and their policies.

Party Identification

Evaluations of the president's performance reflect the underlying partisan loyalties of the public. Members of the president's party are predisposed to approve of his performance, whereas members of the opposition party are predisposed to be less approving. Independents (those without explicit partisan attachments) fall between the Democrats and Republicans in their levels of approval. The average difference in support between Democrats and Republicans over the past forty years has been nearly 40 percentage points, a very substantial figure. Independents fall in between, averaging a difference of about 20 percentage points from both the Democrats and the Republicans. The public was especially polarized along party lines during Ronald Reagan's tenure, when the gap between Democrats and Republicans widened to 52 percentage points. A similar partisan gap has characterized the Clinton presidency, as shown in Table 4–3.

The impact of partisanship on evaluations of the president can also be seen by examining presidential approval at a cross section of time. For example, in July 1974, shortly before he resigned, Richard Nixon registered overall support of 25 percent. Approval among Democrats had diminished

TABLE 4–3. Partisan Support for President Clinton

	Approval (percent)		
Year	Republican	Independent	Democrat
1993	23	45	73
1994	21	45	74
1995	21	45	75
1996	23	50	83
1997	31	54	84

Source: Gallup Poll.

to a meager 13 percent, and among Independents he received only a 23 percent approval rating. Nonetheless, even at the height of the Watergate crisis, 52 percent of Republicans gave the president their approval. Five years later, at the end of July 1979, Jimmy Carter, a Democratic president, saw his approval fall to an overall 29 percent, with Republican approval at only 18 percent. Democrats, on the other hand, were more than twice as likely to support Carter, giving him 37 percent approval. Independents were in the middle, at 27 percent.

Positivity Bias

Another predisposing factor is the "positivity bias," which one authority defined as the tendency "to show evaluation of public figures and institutions in a generally positive direction."[26] Americans have a general disposition to prefer, to learn, and to expect positive relationships more than negative ones and to perceive stimuli as positive rather than negative. Thus, they tend to have favorable opinions of people.

The causes of the positivity bias are not well known but it seems to have the greatest potential for influence in ambiguous situations, such as the beginning of a president's term, when the new occupant of the Oval Office is unknown to the public as chief executive. There tends to be a national consensus following a presidential campaign: People want their new president to succeed and usually give him the benefit of the doubt.

Although the positivity bias should encourage presidential approval throughout a president's tenure, it is likely to be especially important at the beginning, when no record exists. One way to perceive the impact of positivity bias is to compare the electoral percentage by which presidents first won election with their approval level in the first Gallup poll after inauguration. Table 4–4 presents such a comparison. (President Ford is excluded because he never won an election for the presidency.)

TABLE 4–4. Comparison of Electoral Percentages and Postinaugural Approval

President	Popular Vote in First Election (percent)	Approval in First Postinaugural Poll (percent)
Eisenhower	55	69
Kennedy	50	72
Johnson	61	71
Nixon	43	60
Carter	50	66
Reagan	51	51
Bush	53	51
Clinton	43	58

Source: Gallup Poll.

The figures in Table 4–4 clearly show that, with the exception of Ronald Reagan and George Bush, a substantially larger percentage of the people are willing to give new presidents their approval at the beginning of their terms than were willing to vote for them two months earlier.

As presidents perform their duties they become better known to the citizens, who thus develop a greater basis for judging them. Moreover, as time passes, people may begin to perceive greater implications of presidential policies for their own lives. If these implications are viewed unfavorably, the public may be more open to, and pay more attention to, negative information about the president.

A related factor may affect public approval early in a president's term. As people have little basis on which to evaluate the president, they may turn elsewhere for cues. A new chief executive is generally treated favorably in the press. Moreover, there is excitement and symbolism inherent in the peaceful transfer of power, the inaugural festivities, and the prevalent sense of "new beginnings." All this creates a positive environment in which initial evaluations of elected presidents take place, buttressing any tendency toward the positivity bias.

Several studies have found evidence of what some authors term a *fait accompli* or bandwagon effect, which occurs after an election when people, especially those who voted for the loser, tend to view the winner more favorably than they did before the election. The depolarization of politics following an election and the positivity bias itself probably help to create an environment that is conducive to attitude change.[27]

The Persistence of Approval

We have seen that presidents typically begin their initial terms with the benefit of substantial support from the public, but how long does this honeymoon last? Conventional wisdom indicates that it does not last long. The thrust of the argument is that the president will soon have to begin making hard choices, which will inevitably alienate segments of the population. Additional support for this view comes from a revealing response by President Carter in 1979 to a reporter's question concerning whether it was reasonable to expect the president to rate very highly with the American people. The president answered:

> In this present political environment, it is almost impossible. There are times of euphoria that sweep the Nation immediately after an election or after an inauguration day or maybe after a notable success, like the Camp David Accords, when there is a surge of popularity for a President. But most of the decisions that have to be made by a President are inherently not popular ones. They are contentious.[28]

Despite the reasonableness of these expectations, presidential honeymoons are not always shortlived. Examining shifts in presidents' approval ratings reveals that although declines certainly do take place, they are neither inevitable nor swift. Eisenhower maintained his standing in the public very well for two complete terms. Kennedy and Nixon held their public support for two years, as did Ford (after a sharp initial decline). Johnson and Carter's approval losses were steeper, although Johnson's initial ratings were inflated by the unique emotional climate at the time he assumed office. (The same was true, of course, for Ford.) Reagan's approval ratings were volatile, but he stood at 64 percent approval at the time of his second inauguration, 13 percentage points higher than when he began. Bush maintained very high levels of public support until about the last year of his tenure. Clinton sank in the polls soon after taking office but enjoyed higher average levels of approval in his fourth, fifth, and sixth years than for any of his first three years.

Thus honeymoons are not necessarily fleeting times during which the new occupant of the White House receives a breathing period from the public. Instead, the president's constituents seem to be willing to give a new chief executive the benefit of the doubt for some time. It is up to each president to exploit this goodwill and build solid support for his administration in the public. This is why the first few months are often critical for setting the tone of the administration and shaping the president's reputation. In particular, President Clinton's rocky early months in office made it more difficult for him to obtain the public's support.

Long-Term Decline

In addition to examining approval levels within presidential terms, we also need to look for trends in public support across presidents. As shown in Figure 4–1, from 1953 through 1965, with the single exception of 1958, at least 60 percent of the public, on average, approved of the president. At that time, support from two out of three Americans was not unusual. Starting in 1966, however, approval levels changed dramatically. Since that time, presidents have obtained support from even a bare majority of the public only about half the time.

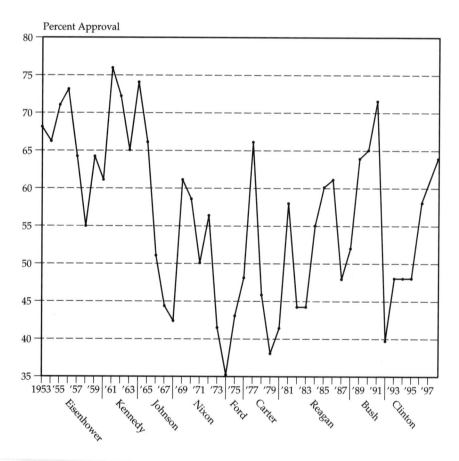

FIGURE 4–1. Average Yearly Presidential Approval, 1953–1998
Source: Gallup Poll.

We cannot provide a definitive answer to what effected the change, but it is reasonable to argue that the war in Vietnam, which proved to be a highly divisive policy following an era of peace, had a destructive effect on President Johnson's approval levels. Although Richard Nixon rebounded somewhat from his predecessor's low standing in the polls from 1966 to 1968, he failed to rise back to pre-1966 levels and Watergate sent his approval levels to new lows.

Just how much residual effect the factors of Vietnam and Watergate have had on the approval levels of subsequent presidents is impossible to determine with certainty. We do know that President Ford's pardon of Nixon tied the former irrevocably to the Watergate scandal and that his public support plunged immediately thereafter. Moreover, there is survey evidence that Watergate had reduced the confidence of many people in the office of president.[29]

We also know that President Carter did not enjoy high levels of approval and Ronald Reagan's approval varied considerably over the course of his presidency. Contrary to accounts in the popular media, Reagan sustained high levels of approval only for a two-year period, beginning near the end of his first term. President Bush rose to great heights of public support, but his ratings fell to less than 40 percent approval during his last year in office and he was defeated for reelection. Bill Clinton had the lowest approval ratings of any modern president in his first months in office—less than 40 percent in June 1993—and failed to average even 50 percent approval for any of his first three years in office. Although the generally low level of support for some presidents may be purely a product of their individual actions and characteristics, it is difficult not to conclude that the events of the late 1960s and early 1970s weakened the predispositions of many Americans to support the president. This conclusion is consistent with findings of a decline in the enthusiasm of voters for winning presidential candidates over the same period.[30]

Personality or Policy?

One factor commonly associated with approval of a president is personality. In common usage, the term *personality* refers to personal characteristics, such as warmth, charm, and humor that may influence responses to an individual on a personal level. It is not unusual for observers to conclude that the public evaluates presidents based more on style than substance, especially in an era in which the media and sophisticated public relations campaigns play such a prominent role in presidential politics. The fact that Americans pay relatively little detailed attention to politics and policy adds further support to the view that the president's personality plays a large role in the public's approval or disapproval. In other words, some argue that members of the public evaluate the president by how much they like him as a person.

Dwight Eisenhower was unique among modern presidents in that his public standing preceded, and was independent of, his involvement in partisan politics. He was a likable war hero who had recently been a principal leader in the highly consensual policy of defeating Germany in World War II. His image following the war was so apolitical that both parties approached him about running for president. Nevertheless, Eisenhower was evaluated by the public as a partisan figure. Republicans were much more likely to approve his handling of the presidency than were Democrats. Moreover, the differences between the approval levels of the two groups of party identifiers are typical of those for other presidents. Thus, the personal component of Eisenhower's public support may have kept his overall level of approval high, but it did not protect him from evaluations as a partisan figure or from fluctuations in approval related to other conditions and events in the public's environment.

Personality may buttress presidential approval, but it is not a dynamic factor. In other words, it cannot explain shifts in the president's standing with the public. Sharp changes in approval have occurred for presidents whose public manners have remained unaltered. Although the impressions the public holds of the president's personality form early and change slowly, factors such as what the public feels ought to be and the way people evaluate what they see can change more rapidly. "Cleverness" can also be viewed as "deceit," "reaching down for details" as "a penchant for the trivial," "evaluating all the alternatives" as "indecisiveness," "charm" as "acting common" (or, even worse, "vulgar"), and "staying above politics" as "naivete." The contradictory expectations that people hold about the president help to set the scene for these changing interpretations of presidential behavior, allowing the public to switch emphasis in what it looks for in a president and how it evaluates what it sees.

In addition, Americans appear to compartmentalize their attitudes toward the president and seem to have little difficulty in separating the person from the performance. Thus, the public may "like" a president but still disapprove of the way he is handling his job. For example, a poll taken near the middle of President Carter's term found that almost twice as many people liked the president as approved of the manner in which he was handling the presidency.[31] Similarly, several years later a Gallup poll found that while 74 percent of the public approved of President Reagan as a person, only 49 percent approved of his performance as president.[32] In Bill Clinton's case, compartmentalization has also occurred—but in reverse. Most Americans believe that he has engaged in behavior of which they disapprove, both before and after entering the White House, yet a clear majority has approved of the president's performance in office throughout his second term (see the Hot-Button Issue box).[33]

Thus, although we cannot specify the contribution of personality to presidential approval, we can say that changes in presidential approval are, in large part, a response to what people see happening in the world, and not merely a reaction to a particular personality. Clearly, *policy matters play a large role in evaluations of presidents.*

Personal Characteristics

Much of the commentary on presidents in the press and other forums focuses on their personal characteristics, especially integrity, intelligence, and leadership abilities. When the public is asked about such job-related

---

☀ HOT- BUTTON ISSUE

Why Is Bill Clinton So Popular (When No One Seems to Like Him)?

One of the more interesting phenomena of contemporary politics is President Clinton's high standing in the presidential approval polls in light of a wide range of allegations concerning his personal behavior, both before and after entering the White House. Moreover, most Americans believe that at least the essence of the charges is true and that the president is not peculiarly trustworthy. In Bill Clinton's case, compartmentalization has indeed occurred—but in reverse. Most Americans believe that he has engaged in behavior of which they disapprove, yet a clear majority has approved of the president's performance in office throughout his second term.

Bill Clinton received a lucky break when he was scheduled to deliver his State of the Union message the week after the Monica Lewinsky story broke. While ignoring the latter, he spoke to a huge audience and reminded people why they had elected him president: to achieve peace and prosperity. He was able to emphasize job performance, making it salient in the public's evaluations of him. Thus, he switched the debate on his presidency from character to leadership and performance. Since then, he has been able to portray himself as a victim of an intrusive and irresponsible press and an undisciplined special prosecutor. As a result, he has benefited from a backlash by asking the public to evaluate not his character, but rather that of his critics and those who report on them.

characteristics, its responses are clearly related to its evaluations of the president. Assessments of characteristics such as the president's integrity, reliability, and leadership ability may change as new problems arise or in relation to the president's past performance. Certain characteristics may become more salient in response to changing conditions. For example, when the Iran-Contra affair became news, President Reagan's decision-making style became a prominent issue. Many people came to evaluate his focus on the "big picture" and detachment from the details of governing in a less positive light.

Issues

Ultimately, the public cares about presidents because of issues of public policy. For an issue to have a significant influence on presidential evaluation, it must be salient to people, they must hold the president responsible for it, and they must make their evaluation in terms of the president's performance regarding the issue. Obviously, perceptions of reality mediate each of these components of assessment.

Salience of Issues   For most of his tenure in office, George Bush stood high in the polls despite the public's low rating of his performance on a wide variety of issues, ranging from abortion to the economy. How could the public approve of a president who was considered to be doing a poor job on so many issues? The answer is that it evaluated the president primarily in terms of other issues, especially foreign policy, on which it approved of his performance.

If a matter is not salient to people, it will be unlikely to play a major role in their evaluations of the president. Understanding presidential approval, then, requires identifying what is on the minds of Americans. One cannot assume that people always judge the president by the same benchmarks. In fact, people generally have only a few issues that are particularly important to them and to which they pay attention.[34] The importance of specific issues to the public varies over time and is closely tied to objective conditions such as unemployment, inflation, international tensions, and racial conflict. In addition, different issues are likely to be salient to different groups in the population at any given time. For example, some groups may be concerned about inflation, others about unemployment, and yet others about a particular aspect of foreign policy or race relations.[35]

The relative weights of values and issues in evaluations of the president also vary over time. Valence or style issues are values, such as patriotism, morality, or a strong national defense, on which there is a broad consensus in the public and that are more basic than a position on a specific policy. The president's articulation of valence issues, directly and in the symbols the White House employs in speech and actions, can affirm the values and beliefs that define citizens' political identities. Valence issues can be powerful instruments for obtaining public support because presidents often prefer to be judged on the basis of consensual criteria with which they can associate themselves.

The relative weights given to values and issues is not the only factor that varies over time—so do the trade-offs made among competing values and among individuals at any given time. Research has found that values are relatively constant over time and that policy debates are rarely single valued. Some values become more salient and some less so in making such trade-offs.[36] For example, antigovernment and antiwelfare attitudes give way to concerns for health and compassion if it is discovered that children are going hungry. Similarly, in the debate over abortion, the salience of values represented by "life" and "choice" varies substantially among citizens.

Finally, within an issue area, the bad news may outweigh the good in capturing the public's attention. Several scholars have found that people weigh negative information more heavily than positive—that is, bad news is more salient to them.[37] If the economy slumps, for example, this may be more salient to the public than if it continues to grow at a moderate rate. Thus, it is possible that presidents may be punished in the polls if the economy is not doing well yet not be comparably rewarded for prosperity.[38] It may be that an issue comes to the public's attention only when it reaches a certain threshold level, which usually means that there is a problem.[39] This, in turn, may provide the basis for more vocal, and thus more salient, opposition to the president.

Responsibility   Even if a matter such as the economy is salient to the public, it is not likely to affect people's evaluations of the president unless they hold him responsible for it.[40] Furthermore, the more the public attributes responsibility for an issue to the president, the more the issue is likely to affect evaluations of his performance.[41]

Despite the prominence of the chief executive, there are several reasons why people may not hold the president responsible for all the problems they face personally or for some problems that they perceive to be confronting the country. Most people do not politicize their personal problems, and most of those who are concerned about personal economic problems do not believe the government should come to their assistance.[42] There is also evidence that people do not necessarily exaggerate the importance of the president or ignore contextual and institutional factors beyond his control.[43] In addition, some people may feel that those who preceded the president or who share power with him are to blame for important problems.

Presidential Performance on an Issue For an issue that is salient to the public and for which it holds the president accountable, the quality of the president's performance on that issue should become a factor in presidential approval. Many observers assume that, for example, if unemployment is rising, the president will be seen as doing a poor job. Perhaps this is true, but perceptions may not follow directly from objective indicators of the economy's performance.

The unemployment level was virtually the same in summer 1984 as it was in summer 1992, yet the public evaluated the economic performance of Presidents Reagan and Bush (respectively), quite differently. Reagan was rewarded for bringing the level down, whereas Bush suffered the consequences of economic stagnation.

The public may be less harsh in its evaluations of presidents who are struggling with difficult situations, even if they are not meeting with short-term success. Franklin D. Roosevelt may have enjoyed the public's tolerance in 1933 and 1934 not only because he could not be held responsible for the Great Depression, but also because he was seen as doing the best that could be done under trying circumstances. Jimmy Carter's standing in the public benefited for several months from favorable public perceptions of his handling of the Iranian hostage crisis, despite the fact the hostages were not freed during this period.

In addition, a substantial and growing body of evidence supports the argument that the political attitudes of Americans are more influenced by what they see as important national issues than by their personal experience. Focusing on the most often discussed issue area, the economy, will clarify the point.

The conventional view is that people's evaluations of the president are affected strongly by their personal economic circumstances. That is, they are more likely to approve of the president if they feel they are prospering personally. In recent years, an impressive number of studies have found that when people evaluate government performance or individual candidates, personal economic circumstances are typically subordinated to other, broader considerations.[44] More specifically, it appears that citizens evaluate the president on the basis of broader views of the economy rather than simply their narrow self-interests. In other words, rather than asking what the president has done for them lately, citizens ask what the president has done for the *nation*.[45]

Furthermore, people typically differentiate their own circumstances from those of the country as a whole. For example, polls regularly report that only small percentages of the population are satisfied with the way things are going in the nation, yet about 80 percent are satisfied with the way things are going in their personal lives.[46]

Source: Drawing by Ziegler. Copyright © 1989 The New Yorker Magazine, Inc.

Rally Events

To this point we have examined factors that may affect presidential approval systematically over time, yet sometimes public opinion takes sudden jumps, as in the case of the 18 percentage point increase George Bush received in the polls after the Persian Gulf War began, in January 1991. One popular explanation for these surges of support involves "rally events." John Mueller, in his seminal definition, explained the concept as an event that is international, directly involves the United States (and particularly the president), and is specific, dramatic, and sharply focused. Such events confront the nation as a whole, are salient to the public, and gain public attention and interest.[47]

The theory behind attributing significance to rally events is that the public will increase its support of presidents in times of crisis or during major international events, at least in the short run, because at such times they are the symbol of the country and the primary focus of attention. Moreover, people do not want to hurt the country's chances of success by opposing the president. The president, meanwhile, has an opportunity to look masterful and evoke patriotic reactions among the people. Conversely, there is also reason to expect the potential to have the public "rally around the flag" to be limited. Studies of American public opinion regarding national security have found little inherent deference to the president.[48] More than patriotic fervor is involved in rallies, as those involved are those who were most disposed to support the president in the first place.[49]

The preponderance of evidence indicates that the rally phenomenon rarely appears and that the events that generate it are highly idiosyncratic and do not seem to differ significantly from other events that were not followed by surges in presidential approval. Moreover, the events that cause sudden increases in public support are not restricted to international affairs, and most international events that would seem to be potential rally events fail to generate much additional approval of the president. Rather than being a distinctive phenomenon, a rally event seems to be simply an additional force that pushes potential supporters over the threshold of approval.

LEADING THE PUBLIC

If public support can be a useful leadership resource for presidents, are they in a position to call on it when needed? Commentators on the presidency often assume that the White House can persuade, or even mobilize, the public provided the president is a skilled enough communicator, and various presidents have agreed. In the words of Franklin Roosevelt, "All our great Presidents were *leaders* of thought at times when certain historic ideas in the life of the nation had to be clarified." His cousin, Theodore Roosevelt, had earlier observed: "People used to say of me that I . . . divined what the people were going to think. I did not 'divine.' I simply made up my mind what they ought to think, and then did my best to get them to think it."[50] Just how useful is the "bully pulpit"?

Direct Opinion Leadership

The most visible and obvious technique employed by presidents to lead public opinion is to seek the public's support directly. Presidents frequently attempt to do so with speeches over television or radio or made in person to large groups. Recent presidents have averaged one public appearance every day (George Bush and Bill Clinton have been especially active). Not all presidents are effective speakers, however, and not all look good under the glare of hot lights and the unflattering gaze of television cameras. Moreover, the public is not always receptive to a president's message.

All presidents since Truman have sought media advice from experts on lighting, makeup, stage settings, camera angles, clothing, pacing of delivery, and other facets of speech making. Despite this aid and the experience that politicians inevitably gain in public speaking, presidential speeches aimed at leading public opinion directly have typically been less than impressive. Only Kennedy, Reagan, and Clinton mastered the art of speaking to the camera.

No matter how effective presidents may be as speakers, they still must contend with the predispositions of their audience. As noted in the discussion of presidential election campaigns in Chapter 3, members of the public screen the president's messages through their own views and values, which poses a formidable challenge to persuasion. Moreover, the president cannot depend on an attentive audience. Most people are not very interested in politics.

The relative importance the typical person attaches to a president's address is illustrated by the attention presidential staffs give to setting the date for the president's annual State of the Union message. They have to be careful to avoid preempting prime time on the night that offers the current season's most popular shows while at the same time trying to maximize their national viewing audience. In general, the size of the audience for televised presidential speeches has declined over time. For example, only a minority of those watching television tuned in to see President Bush's triumphal speech to a joint session of Congress following the success of the Gulf war.[51]

The public's general lack of interest in politics constrains the president's leadership of public opinion in the long run as well as on any given day. Although they have unparalleled access to the American people, presidents cannot make much use of it. If they do, their speeches will become commonplace and lose their drama and interest. That is why they do not make appeals to the public, particularly on television, very often—only four or five times a year, on average.[52] Some presidents, such as Clinton, Reagan, and Nixon, have turned to radio and midday addresses in order to reserve primetime televised addresses for more important issues.

Television is a medium in which visual interest, action, and conflict are most effective. Unfortunately, presidential speeches are unlikely to contain these characteristics. Although some addresses to the nation—such as President Johnson's televised demand for a voting rights act, made before a joint session of Congress in 1965—occur at moments of high drama, they do not typically do so.

Presidents not only have to contend with the medium, they also must concern themselves with their messages. It is not clear what approach works best. Many of the most effective speeches seem to be those whose goals are gaining general support and image building rather than gaining specific support. They focus on simple themes rather than complex details. Calvin Coolidge used this method successfully in his radio speeches, as did Franklin Roosevelt in his famous "fireside chats."[53] The limitation of such an approach, of course, is that general support cannot always be translated into public backing for specific policies.

In addition, presidential efforts at persuading the public usually involve more than one speech. Most observers argue that to be effective, the president must focus the public's attention on his policies for a sustained period of time. For example, the Reagan White House was successful in maintaining a focus on its top-priority economic policies in 1981. It molded its communication strategy around its legislative priorities and focused the administration's agenda and statements on economic policy to ensure that the president's message was not diffused by discussing a wide range of topics.[54] In contrast, the Clinton administration blurred its focus by raising a wide range of issues in its first two years in office.

Sustaining such a focus is very difficult to do, however, as there are many competing demands on the president to act and speak, which divert attention from his or her priorities. After 1981, President Reagan had to deal with a wide range of noneconomic policies, and Clinton encountered similar problems. As Clinton aide George Stephanopolous put it:

> On the campaign trail, you can just change the subject. But you can't just change the subject as President. You can't wish Bosnia away. You can't wish David Koresh [the leader of the Branch Davidian sect in Waco, Texas] away. You can't just ignore them and change the subject.[55]

Success of Appeals   Given the obstacles to moving the public, it is not surprising that appeals to the public often fail. Ronald Reagan was certainly interested in policy change and went to unprecedented lengths to influence public opinion. Moreover, he had a receptive audience. The conservative winds of the 1980s were fully in place even *before* his election.[56] Thus, Reagan arrived at the White House on the crest of a preexisting tide of conservatism, which he helped to articulate, but not to create. What happened after he took office? Was the "Great Communicator" able to use the "bully pulpit" to move the public to support his policies?

Reagan knew better. In his memoirs he reflected on his efforts to ignite concern among the American people regarding the threat of communism in Central America and mobilize them behind his program of support for the Contras.

> For eight years the press called me the "Great Communicator." Well, one of my greatest frustrations during those eight years was my inability to communicate to the American people and to Congress the seriousness of the threat we faced in Central America.[57]
>
> Time and again, I would speak on television, to a joint session of Congress, or to other audiences about the problems in Central America, and I would hope that the outcome would be an outpouring of support from Americans. . . .

But the polls usually found that large numbers of Americans cared little or not at all about what happened in Central America—in fact, a surprisingly large proportion didn't even know where Nicaragua and El Salvador were located—and, among those who did care, too few cared enough about a Communist penetration of the Americas to apply the kind of pressure I needed on Congress.[58]

Numerous national surveys of public opinion have found that support for regulatory programs and spending on health care, welfare, urban problems, education, environmental protection, and aid to minorities increased, rather than decreased, during Reagan's tenure.[59] On the other hand, support for increased defense expenditures was decidedly lower at the end of his administration than when he took office.[60] In each case, the public was moving in the *opposite* direction to that of the president.

In the realm of foreign policy, Reagan was frustrated in his goal of obtaining public support for aid to the contras in Nicaragua.[61] However, his problem was even broader. Whether the issue was military spending, arms control, military aid and arms sales, or cooperation with the Soviet Union, by the early 1980s public opinion had turned to the left—and *ahead of* Reagan.[62]

Finally, Americans did not move their general ideological preferences to the right.[63] Indeed, rather than conservative support swelling once Reagan was in the White House, there was a movement away from conservative views almost as soon as he took office.[64] According to one scholar, "Whatever Ronald Reagan's skills as a communicator, one ability he clearly did not possess was the capacity to induce lasting changes in American policy preferences."[65] As press secretary Marlin Fitzwater put it, "Reagan would go out on the stump, draw huge throngs and convert no one at all."[66] President Clinton's similar frustrations at moving public opinion are described in The Clinton Presidency box.

Despite the limitations of their abilities to exercise direct opinion leadership over the public, presidents are aided by the willingness of Americans to *follow* their lead, especially on foreign policy. Foreign policy is more distant from the lives of most Americans than domestic policy, and is therefore seen as more complex and based on more specialized knowledge. Thus people tend to defer more to the president on foreign issues than on domestic problems, which they can relate more easily and directly to their own experience. Studies have shown public opinion to have undergone changes in line with presidents' policies on the liberation of Kuwait, the invasion of Grenada, the testing of nuclear weapons, relations with the People's Republic of China, isolationism, and both the escalation and the deescalation of the Vietnam War.[67]

One scholar ascertained public opinion on six potential responses to the 1979–1980 hostage crisis in Iran. He then asked those who opposed each

THE CLINTON PRESIDENCY

Bill Clinton and the Public Presidency

The Clinton administration is the ultimate example of the public presidency, one based on a perpetual campaign to obtain the support of the American people and fed by public opinion polls, focus groups, and public relations memos. It is ironic, then, that the Clinton White House has found it difficult to move the public to support its policies. When the president's first major economic proposal, the 1989 fiscal stimulus plan, was introduced, it ran into strong Republican opposition. Counting on a groundswell of public opinion to pressure moderate Republicans into ending the filibuster on the bill, Clinton stepped up his rhetoric, but the expected public response never materialized.

The president's next major legislative battle was over the budget. On August 3, 1993, he spoke on national television on behalf of his budget proposal, after which Senate Republican leader Robert Dole spoke against the plan. A Cable News Network (CNN) overnight poll following the president's speech found that, in fact, support for his budget plan had *dropped*. Calls to Congress overwhelmingly opposed the president's plan.

The White House had more success on the North American Free Trade Agreement (NAFTA) when Vice President Al Gore debated Ross Perot on the *Larry King Live* television show. Among those who watched the debate, support for NAFTA increased and opposition decreased. Even here, however, the White House's ability to move public opinion was limited: Gallup polls taken before the House vote showed that only 38 percent of the public favored the trade agreement.

When the House rule on the 1994 crime bill was voted down, the president again went public. Speaking to police officers with American flags in the background, he blamed special interests (like the National Rifle Association) and Republicans for a "procedural trick," but his appeal failed to catch fire. Meanwhile, the Republicans were tapping public resentment by talking about pork.

Most important of all, despite substantial efforts, the president was unable to sustain public support for health care reform. Once again, the White House hoped for a groundswell of public support, but there was no response. Indeed, by mid-August 1994, only 39 percent of the public favored the president's proposals, while 48 percent opposed them.

In late 1995, the president gave a nationally televised address seeking the public's support for deploying U.S. peacekeeping troops to Bosnia. Nonetheless, as the troops landed in Eastern Europe, less than 40 percent of the public supported their deployment.

Given his experience, it is no wonder that the president often declared that he needed to do a better job of *communicating*: "What I've got to do is to spend more time communicating with the American people about what we've done and where we're going."[68]

Beginning in mid-1995, the president fashioned a new communications strategy, in which he switched from offense to defense. The White House ran an unprecedented public relations campaign to show that Clinton shared the basic values of the American people and to defend the *status quo* against changes advocated by the new Republican majorities in Congress.

Seeking public support by becoming a more moderate version of the Republicans was apparently quite good for campaigning. It also lifted the president in the public opinion polls. Yet, campaigning, posturing, and pronouncing is not governance—certainly not in the usual sense of precipitating great national debates on important questions of public policy or of driving legislation through Congress. Although the president benefited from standing in counterpoint to the Republicans, he was also forced to embrace some their more appealing images in his rhetoric. Declaring the era of big government to be over, he changed his focus from programs and dollars to inspiration and values and defused a host of Republican cultural and values issues with his symbolic stands on family values. He also co-opted many of the Republicans' issues, such as the need for welfare reform and balancing the budget. As a result of his defensive communications strategy, the president allowed much of his agenda to be determined by the opposition party.[69]

option whether they would change their view "if President Carter considered this action necessary." The policy options and the public's responses to them are shown in Table 4–5.[70] In each case a substantial percentage of respondents changed their opinions in deference to the supposed opinion of the president. Similarly, a poll of Utah residents found that although two-thirds of them opposed deploying MX missiles in Utah and Nevada, an equal number said they would either "definitely" or "probably" support

TABLE 4–5. Reconsidering Iran Hostage Crisis Policy Opinions in Response to the President

Policy	Original Approval (percent)	Approval after Reconsideration (percent)	Change Due to President (percent)
Wait and see	58	83	25
Return shah to Iran	21	53	32
Send shah elsewhere	74	87	13
Naval blockade	62	85	23
Threaten to send troops	43	73	30
Send troops	29	62	33

Source: Lee Sigelman, "Gauging the Public Response to Presidential Leadership," *Presidential Studies Quarterly* 10 (Summer 1980): 431.

President Reagan if he decided to go ahead and base the missiles in those states.[71]

Not all results are as positive, however. In one study, different sample groups were asked whether they supported two proposals, a domestic policy proposal dealing with welfare and a proposal dealing with foreign aid. One of the groups was told that President Carter supported the proposals, while the president was not mentioned to the other group. The authors found that attaching the president's name to either proposal not only failed to increase support for it, but actually had a negative effect because those who disapproved of Carter reacted very strongly against proposals they thought were his.[72]

The public generally does not have crystallized opinions on issues and is therefore often easy to sway in the short run. However, this volatility also means that any opinion change is subject to slippage. As issues fade into the background or positions on issues are confronted with the realities of daily life, opinions that were altered in response to presidential leadership may quickly be forgotten. This is especially likely to occur in the area where the president's influence on public opinion seems to be greatest: foreign policy.

A balanced view of the president's ability to lead public opinion directly must take into consideration both the potential for, and the obstacles to, leadership. The limited evidence indicates that presidents are much more likely to be successful in influencing public opinion when they themselves have high approval ratings.[73] As in so many other presidential relationships, the direct leadership of public opinion provides opportunities, especially in foreign policy, but no guarantees of success. It is for this reason that presidents often rely on more subtle methods of opinion leadership.

Information Control

Information control is a less direct technique for influencing public opinion than appeals to the public. The goal is to influence public opinion by controlling the information on which the public bases its evaluations of chief executives and their policies and which it analyzes to determine if there is cause for concern. If the public is unaware of a situation or has a distorted view of it, then presidents may have more flexibility in achieving what they desire—which often is public passivity as much as public support.

Withholding Information   The classification of information under the rubric of "national security" is a frequently used means of withholding information. Most people support secrecy in handling national security affairs, especially in such matters as defense plans and strategy, weapons technology, troop movements, the details of current diplomatic negotiations, the methods and sources of covert intelligence gathering, and similar information about the defense, negotiations, and intelligence gathering of other nations. However, there has been controversy over the amount of information classified and whether classification is used by the president and other high officials to influence public opinion. When officials withhold information that might aid the public in evaluating their performance in office and answering general questions of public policy but that might embarrass them if made public, they may provide a distorted view of reality in an attempt to increase or maintain support for themselves.

There are other means of withholding information. For example many critics charged that President Clinton's desire to invoke executive and attorney-client privileges regarding the Whitewater scandal and related controversies represented an attempt to prevent harmful information from becoming public.

Deemphasis of Information   Presidents can also employ more subtle methods of manipulating information in an effort to influence public opinion. They can, for example, order that information collected by the government be deemphasized. When the economy was not doing well in 1971, the White House ordered the Bureau of Labor Statistics to discontinue its monthly briefing of the press on prices and unemployment. Similarly, during the Vietnam War, the Defense Department gave much more attention in its public announcements to deserters from enemy forces than to deserters from the armed forces of our South Vietnamese allies. In each case the government possessed information that might negatively influence public perceptions of the president and his administration, which it chose not to emphasize.

Timing of the Release of Information   Sometimes information is indeed provided but the timing of its release is used to try to influence public opinion. For example, on November 2, 1970, the White House announced the most recent casualty figures from Vietnam. They were at a five-year low and their announcement was made on Monday instead of the usual Thursday, presumably because the 1970 congressional elections were being held the next day. Similarly, the Carter administration revealed that the Pentagon had developed a new technology that made aircraft virtually invisible to enemy detection devices. This disclosure coincided with an administration effort during the 1980 presidential election campaign to show that it was working to strengthen national defense. Taking the opposite tack, the Ford administration announced that the country was in a recession one week *after* the 1974 congressional elections. The Reagan administration knew that its economic forecasts had been too optimistic, but it did not change them until after the crucial vote on the president's tax cut proposal in 1981.

Obfuscation   Presidents and their aides may also attempt to obscure or distort the truth in order to confuse or mislead the public. President Eisenhower regularly gave purposefully ambiguous answers at his press conferences.[74] When George Bush agreed to accept "tax revenue increases" as part of the 1990 budget agreement with Congress, his announcement was so confusing that it took officials in Washington several days to determine whether he meant increases resulting from increased economic growth, a cut in capital gains taxes, or an increase in tax rates—and his press secretary refused to define the president's terms, in large part because of Bush's campaign promise not to raise taxes. Bill Clinton carried semantic hairsplitting to new heights with his arguments regarding smoking marijuana (he claimed he did not inhale), dodging the draft, raising campaign funds within the White House, and, of course, the nature of his relationship with White House intern Monica Lewinsky.[75]

Distortion   Distortion comes in many forms. One of the most common is to provide impressive statistics without going into the details of how they were compiled. For example, Reagan's budget director, David Stockman, admitted "rigging the [budget] numbers to the point that even we couldn't understand them."[76] In 1982 President Reagan told the American people that more than half the stores investigated by the government were accepting food stamps for items that were prohibited. However, the president omitted the fact that the stores that were investigated were ones already suspected of abuse.

In March 1993, Secretary of Labor Robert Reich called a special news conference to argue that the figures his department was releasing—showing that during February 1993 the nation had experienced a large gain in jobs—were misleading because 90 percent of the jobs were just part-time. He wanted to show that the Clinton administration's economic stimulus program was still necessary, but he arrived at his figures through spurious inferences that were later widely criticized in the economics community. That same year, Bill Clinton proposed to increase the percentage of taxable income of certain Social Security recipients. This proposal would increase the taxes paid by these people, yet his administration listed the proposal as a spending cut![77]

It is not only what goes into compiling a "fact" that is important for public evaluation but also the context of events in which the so-called fact occurs. For example, in 1964 Lyndon Johnson went before Congress to ask for a resolution supporting retaliation against North Vietnam for two "unprovoked" attacks on U.S. ships in the Gulf of Tonkin. The Gulf of Tonkin Resolution was subsequently passed, marking a watershed in the nation's military actions in Vietnam. The public might have been less enthusiastic in its backing of military reprisals, however, if it had known that the United States had been supporting covert South Vietnamese operations against North Vietnam for several years and that, moreover, there was considerable reason to doubt that the second attack had ever occurred! As President Johnson later said privately, "For all I know, our Navy was shooting whales out there."[78]

Attempts to distort information are not always successful. For example, by 1967 two-thirds of the American people felt that the Johnson administration was not telling them the whole truth about the Vietnam War, and in 1971, a similar percentage felt the same way about the Nixon administration.[79] Out of such attitudes emerged a credibility gap and low levels of popular standing for these presidents.

Prevarication   The most extreme form of information control is lying. The range of subjects about which presidents have lied is great, ranging from U-2 spy plane flights over the Soviet Union and the nation's attempts to prevent the election of Marxist Salvador Allende as president of Chile to the U.S. military situation in Vietnam and the Watergate cover-up.[80] Bill Clinton lied about his relationship with Monica Lewinsky.[81] White House press secretaries have often misled the press regarding imminent U.S. military actions.[82]

In his press conference on September 28, 1982, President Reagan responded to questions on the economy with descriptions of the growth of the gross national product, the rate of increase in the unemployment rate under his predecessor, the proportion of the population in the workforce, and the increase in the purchasing power of the average family. All of these assertions described the economy's performance, and all were motivated by a desire to depict the performance in the best possible light. Unfortunately, however, all these statements were also untrue![83] Whether the president's responses were carefully planned to deceive or the result of a misunderstanding of the statistics is unclear.

One thing is clear: The American people resent being lied to. Most feel it is unacceptable for the government to lie—even to achieve foreign policy goals (although it is acceptable to confuse an enemy).[84] When an administration is seen as being untruthful, it loses credibility—a precious resource in White House efforts to lead the public.[85]

Information Control and National Security   Information control is most common in the national security area because it is difficult for the public to challenge official statements about events in other countries, especially military activities, which often are shrouded in secrecy. It is much easier to be skeptical about domestic activities that American reporters can scrutinize and to which they can provide alternative views. In addition, people can relate many domestic policies to their own experiences more easily than they can relate most foreign and military policies. When official statements fail to correspond to people's experiences, the stage is set for skepticism.

Information control is employed to deny information, not only to a foreign adversary, but also to the American public. In virtually all the examples involving national security policy, from the U-2 flight over the Soviet Union to the secret bombing of Cambodia, the "foreign adversary" knew the truth. Only the American public was left in the dark.

The Use of Symbols

The language used in political discourse may have an influence on public opinion independent of the particular subject under discussion. One important aspect of political language is the use of symbols: things that are simple or familiar that stand for things that are more complex or unfamiliar. Symbols are frequently used to describe politicians, events, issues, or some other aspect of the political world. Naturally, symbols are not synonyms for what they describe. The choice of symbols inevitably highlights certain aspects of an issue or event and conceals others. Thus, if presidents can persuade a substantial segment of the public to adopt symbols that are favorable to them, they will be in a better position to influence public opinion.

Because of the potential power of symbols in shaping public opinion, presidents have encouraged the public to adopt certain symbols as representative of their administrations. Franklin Roosevelt dubbed his administration the "New Deal," and Harry Truman termed his the "Fair Deal." Each symbol was an oversimplification for new and extremely complex policies, but each served to reassure many Americans that these policies were for their good. Similarly, John Kennedy's "New Frontier" and Lyndon Johnson's "Great Society" served as attractive symbols of their administrations.

Many observers feel that a president's failure to lead the public to adopt broad symbols for his administration can cause severe problems in relations with the public. Presidents Carter, Bush, and Clinton received substantial criticism for lacking unifying themes and cohesion in their programs and for failing to inspire the public with a sense of purpose or idea to follow.[86] Instead of providing the country with a sense of their vision and priorities, they emphasized discrete problem solving.

On the other hand, Ronald Reagan understood instinctually that his popular support was linked to his ability to embody the values of an idealized America. He projected a simple, coherent vision for his presidency that served him well in attracting adherents and countering criticism when the inevitable contradictions in policy arose. He continually invoked symbols of his vision of America and its past—an optimistic view that did not closely correspond to reality but did sustain public support. For example, he maintained his identification with balanced budgets even though he never submitted a budget that was even close to balanced and his administration was responsible for more deficit spending than all previous administrations combined.

According to Pat Buchanan, who served as the White House director of communications: "For Ronald Reagan the world of legend and myth is a real world. He visits it regularly and he's a happy man there."[87] In his 1965 autobiography, Reagan described his feelings about leaving the military at the end of World War II: "All I wanted to do . . . was to rest up awhile, make love to my wife, and come up refreshed to a better job in an ideal world."[88] The reader would never realize from this that Reagan never left Hollywood while serving in the military during the war! However, in politics, perceptions are as important as reality; consequently, many people responded positively to the president's vision of history and his place therein.

Symbols are also used to describe specific policies. President Johnson declared a "War on Poverty" despite the fact that many saw the "war" as more of a skirmish. Similarly, President Nixon went to considerable efforts to have the public view the January 1973 peace agreement ending the involvement of American troops in Vietnam as "peace with honor," which was clearly a controversial conclusion.

Symbols can be manipulated in attempts, not only to lead public opinion, but also deliberately to mislead it. Perhaps the most important and effective televised address President Reagan made to the nation in 1981 was his July 27 speech seeking the public's support for his tax-cut bill. In it he went to great lengths to present his plan as "bipartisan." It was crucial that he convince the public that this controversial legislation was supported by members of both parties and therefore was, by implication, fair. Despite the fact that House Democrats voted overwhelmingly against the president's proposal two days later, Reagan described it as "bipartisan" eleven times in the span of a few minutes! No one could miss the point.

Symbols can be used by the White House to label opponents as well as policies. For example, President Clinton referred to conservative talk-show hosts as "purveyors of hatred and division" following the 1995 Oklahoma City bombing.

The presidency uniquely lends itself to symbolic manipulation. As chief of state, the president personifies the government and the nation's heritage. Presidents use this status to enhance their public standing. They are frequently seen on television welcoming heads of state or other dignitaries to the White House, dedicating federal projects, speaking before national groups, or performing ceremonial functions, such as laying a wreath at the Tomb of the Unknowns in Arlington National Cemetery.

Foreign travels provide even greater opportunities for the president to be viewed as the representative of America and a statesman operating above partisan politics. When dealing with the leaders of other nations on

The ceremonal role of the presidency lends itself to associating the president with symbols that represent widely shared values. Here, President Clinton places a wreath at the Tomb of the Unknowns at Arlington National Ceremony. Source: AP/Wide World Photos.

matters of international importance and being greeted by cheering crowds of Egyptians, Poles, or Chinese, the president is a source of pride as the representative of the country, the embodiment of its goals, and the bearer of its goodwill. Presidents and their staffs are aware of the power of these symbols and try to schedule activities so they will be covered on primetime television.

The president also participates in many ceremonial roles dealing with domestic matters. These include having pictures taken with the U.S. Olympic team, the winner of the national spelling bee, the Teacher of the Year, the March of Dimes poster child, or championship college or professional sports teams; lighting the national Christmas tree; and issuing proclamations celebrating national holidays, such as Thanksgiving and Veterans Day, as well as lesser-known celebrations such as National Pickle Week.

All of this activity as chief of state, the president hopes, will help foster the view that he is a fitting leader who is competent to run the country and make important and difficult decisions. Presidents want to try to relieve some of the fears and anxieties of the public and provide hope for, and confidence in, the future. If they are successful in projecting an image of dignity and ability (which may or may not be accurate), they will make it easier for members of the public to vest their allegiance in them as visible, human sources of authority and accept decisions they might otherwise oppose.

While engaging in these and other functions, presidents often make appeals to patriotism, traditions, and U.S. history (and its greatness) to move the public to support them, thus reminding people of their common interests. They also frequently invoke the names of revered leaders of the past who made difficult decisions on the basis of high principles, such as Lincoln or Truman, and then relate themselves or their decisions to these paragons.

Presidents also make gestures to show that they are really "one of the people." President Carter made considerable use of this technique in his desire to be seen as a people's president. At his inauguration, he chose to walk (instead of ride) down Pennsylvania Avenue from the Capitol to the White House after taking the oath of office. He conducted a "fireside chat" over national television, seated before a blazing fire and dressed casually in a sweater instead of a suit. He also staged a press conference in which private individuals could call in from around the country and directly ask him questions, and he held many town meetings where he could be questioned directly by local citizens. Bill Clinton has followed in the same vein, holding a variety of televised town meetings and devoting time to meeting with average citizens.

Public Relations

In its efforts to mold public opinion, the White House employs public relations techniques modeled after those of commercial advertising firms. One indicator of the importance of public relations to contemporary presidents is the presence of advertising specialists in the White House. Michael Deaver, one of the three aides forming the "troika" at the top of the White House hierarchy in Ronald Reagan's first term, was a public relations specialist. His role was that of a general adviser with special responsibilities for developing and coordinating public relations. These responsibilities included orchestrating the president's public appearances and scheduling and coordinating public appearances by other administration officials. His intent was to help ensure that they publicized the president's policies, had maximum impact, and exhibited public postures that were consistent and not distracting.

The use of public relations specialists has become customary. One of President Johnson's closest aides, Jack Valenti, came to the White House from the advertising business and went into the motion picture industry when he left. Richard Nixon carried the hiring of public relations experts even further. His chief of staff, H. R. Haldeman; his press secretary and later close adviser, Ron Ziegler; and several other aides came to the White House from advertising firms. President Carter put Gerald Rafshoon, the advertising director for his 1976 campaign, on the White House staff. Soon after Bill Clinton's election, the Democratic National Committee negotiated contracts with the political and communication consultants who had run the president's campaign and hired them to sell his legislative program.

Aside from serving as an indicator of the importance presidents place on public relations, the presence of these aides may influence the substance and, especially, the timing of policy. Being human, all presidents are subject to the temptation to do the most popular thing.[89] The potential for subordinating substance to style is clearly present. This is especially evident when presidents hire public relations aides to promote their image, like Michael Deaver, who freely admitted that he had little interest in matters of public policy and argued that "image is sometimes as useful as substance."[90]

There is also the potential for running the White House like an advertising agency. A close observer of the Reagan administration found that a single focus permeated staff meetings of top White House officials: how the topic under discussion would play in the media.[91] In addition, since an advertising specialist's orientation is to stress a uniform image, the power of such persons can be a centralizing force in an administration. Emphasis on "team play" inevitably leads to the discouragement of dissent and irregularity because it blunts the impact of the president's image. The parallels between this description and the Nixon White House are especially striking.

Spreading the Word   The primary goal of White House public relations efforts is to build support for the president and his policies. Part of this job is "getting the word out" about the president, his views, and his accomplishments. The president, of course, carries much of this burden and appears in many venues. Bill Clinton even appeared on the MTV television network within six weeks of taking office in an attempt to reach a more youthful audience. The White House also places representatives of the administration on television programs such as the Sunday interview shows (*Issues and Answers, Meet the Press,* and *Face the Nation), Nightline, The News Hour with Jim Lehrer,* and the morning news shows. Similarly, the White House provides or clears speeches for officials to give at university commencement ceremonies and in other visible settings. It also disperses information to editors, commentators, and reporters and to ethnic, religious, geographic, professional, and other types of groups interested in particular policies.

The president's aides may also try to stimulate favorable articles on the First Family and is happy to provide photographs portraying the president as family oriented, a pet owner, or the like. For example, Reagan White

House aides ghostwrote, under the president's name, a story on keeping physically fit and had it published in a popular Sunday newspaper magazine supplement. The idea was to make the point subtly that Ronald Reagan was not too old for the job. Likewise, the White House paid close attention to the president's image, trying to portray him as busy and engaged in important decision making rather than remote and passive, as critics charged.

Reaching the enormous television audience of about 50 million viewers of the evening news is especially important to the White House, and the president's staff builds his schedule around efforts to do so. As one press aide put it: "Whenever possible, everything was done to take into account the need for coverage. After all, most of the events are done for coverage. Why else are you doing them?"[92]

Presidents and their aides tailor the messages they wish to transmit to the public to the needs of the press. The Reagan White House was especially skilled at providing sound bites for the television news. Similarly, announcements are timed so that reporters can meet their papers' deadlines. Those made too late in the evening will not appear in the next morning's newspapers.

If the White House wants to decrease the coverage of an event, it can wait until after the evening news programs or weekends to announce it. Then it might be buried among the next day's occurrences. It can also pass the word to administration officials to avoid appearing on interview programs or holding press conferences. Alternately, the president might take another newsworthy action at the same time. President Clinton timed his firing of Federal Bureau of Investigation (FBI) director William Sessions so that it would cut into the news coverage of a speech on his policy on homosexuals in the military and vetoed a ban on late-term abortions on a heavy news day dominated by the funeral of Commerce Secretary Ron Brown.

The White House tries to avoid associating the president with bad news. When the United States pulled the marines out of Lebanon, it was announced after President Reagan flew to his California ranch for a vacation and was not available for questions.[93] It was preferable to let a subordinate serve as the lightning rod.[94] Similarly, the highest-priority domestic policy legislation in Reagan's second term was reform of the federal income tax. It was originally presented as Treasury Secretary Donald Regan's plan rather than the president's, thus diverting criticism to the secretary.

Presidents may also try to avoid being caught up in controversies. Presidents Reagan and Bush addressed the annual Washington antiabortion rally by phone, even though it was held only a short distance from the White House. They wanted to avoid being seen with the leaders of the movement on the evening news. Similarly, President Clinton left a recorded message for those participating in a 1993 gay rights rally in the capital.

Conversely, the White House loves good news, which it tries to distribute over time so that each incident receives full coverage. What the president does not want is for bad news to drive out the good, yet this does happen. The first major piece of legislation that President Clinton signed was the popular Family Leave Act. Coverage of the signing ceremony was diluted, however, by media attention focused on Kimba Wood's withdrawal from consideration as attorney general.

Media Events   In addition to general efforts to publicize the president, the White House often stages "media events" in hope of obtaining additional public support. When President Bush unveiled his proposal for a constitutional amendment to prohibit burning the American flag, he chose to do it at the Iwo Jima Memorial in Arlington National Cemetery. Similarly, he announced his support for renewal of the Clean Air Act in Jackson Hole, Wyoming, with the Grand Tetons as the backdrop.

No administration was more attentive to the potential of media events than Ronald Reagan's. His press secretary, Larry Speakes, kept a sign on his desk that read, "You don't tell us how to stage the news, and we don't tell you how to cover it." Michael Deaver carefully scripted every second of the president's public appearances, right down to placing tape on the floor to show Reagan where to stand for the best camera angles.[95] Deaver was very clear about the importance of appealing to television: "You get only forty to eighty seconds on a given night on the network news, and unless you can find a visual that explains your message you can't make it stick."[96]

At times, media events can be used quite cynically. When President Reagan was under fire for not supporting civil rights, he paid a visit to a black family who had had a cross burned in its front yard. However, the White House did not mention that the cross burning had occurred five years earlier. When the president's pollster found that the public overwhelmingly disapproved of the administration's reductions in aid to education, Michael Deaver arranged for Reagan to make a series of speeches emphasizing quality education. As Deaver later gloated, public approval of the president regarding education "flip-flopped" without any change in policy at all.[97]

Sometimes, media events backfire on the White House. George Bush's first nationally televised address featured him displaying a bag of crack cocaine purchased across the street from the White House. The president was embarrassed, however, when the press learned that the administration had lured a drug dealer to Lafayette Park (not an area known for heavy drug trafficking), in order to buy drugs "across from the White House."

Some of the emphasis on media events is the White House's response to the nature of the media (which we will examine in Chapter 5). According to Larry Speakes, the White House press spokesman during most of Ronald Reagan's tenure in the White House:

We knew that television had to have pictures to present its story. . . . So when Reagan was pushing education, the visual was of him sitting at a little desk and talking to a group of students, or with the football team and some cheerleaders, or in a science lab. Then we would have an educators' forum where the president would make a noteworthy statement. We learned very quickly that the rule was no picture, no television piece, no matter how important our news was.[98]

Operating on similar assumptions, President Clinton twice hosted signings of Arab-Israeli peace accords in full view of the press on the White House lawn. The president also traveled to Oklahoma City in 1995 to attend the funeral services for those killed in the bombing of the federal building. Pictures of the president as First Mourner made the story, which was covered much more extensively than if the White House had simply released a press statement.

CONCLUSION

A president's relations with the public are complex. All chief executives need the support of the people in order to play an effective leadership role, yet they have a difficult time obtaining it. Expectations are high and contradictory, and the public's desires are frequently difficult to ascertain. Although the public appears to award or withhold its support of the chief executive based largely on job performance, its perceptions of issues and the president's actions may be hazy. Just how the public reaches its conclusions about the president's performance is not well understood. In theory, however, there is ample opportunity for the president, directly and through the press, to influence public perceptions.

Given this environment, presidents are not content to follow public opinion. In their search for public support, they invest substantial amounts of time, energy, ingenuity, and personnel in techniques that include direct appeals to the public, the use of symbols, information control, and public relations. Some of this activity is quite legitimate. Some is not, instead following Richard Nixon's view that "It's not *what* Presidents do but how they do it that matters."[99]

There is no guarantee of success in these efforts, however, and presidents often fail to achieve their desired effects. Even those who are considered "great communicators" are not able to move the public much on their own. Chief executives are not directors who lead the public where it otherwise refuses to go, thus reshaping the contours of the political landscape. Instead, they are facilitators who reflect, and may intensify, widely held views and who endow the views of their constituencies with structure and purpose through their interpretations.

DISCUSSION QUESTIONS

1. Private public opinion polls, commissioned by the White House, have become common. Should presidents take so many polls? How should they use the results?
2. Do presidents suffer politically from public expectations that are contradictory and unreasonably high? If so, how would you advise a president to deal with this problem?
3. Leading the public is difficult to do, and presidents employ many techniques to influence public opinion. What is the most useful approach to obtaining the public's support?

WEB EXERCISES

1. Listen to the president's weekly radio address and read the text along with the president. Why is the address so short? Go to <http://www.whitehouse.gov/WH/html/briefroom.html>.
2. Check the latest Gallup Poll on the president's public approval. Given our discussion in this chapter, why does the president have this level of public support? Go to <http://www.gallup.com/polltrends/jobapp.htm>.

SELECTED READING

Brody, Richard A. *Assessing the President: The Media, Elite Opinion, and Public Support*. Palo Alto, Calif.: Stanford University Press, 1991.

Cohen, Jeffrey E. *Presidential Responsiveness and Public Policy-Making*. Ann Arbor: University of Michigan Press, 1997.

Cronin, Thomas E. "The Presidency and Its Paradoxes." In Thomas E. Cronin and Rexford G. Tugwell, eds., *The Presidency Reappraised*. 2nd ed. New York: Praeger, 1977.

Cronin, Thomas E. "The Presidency Public Relations Script." In Rexford G. Tugwell and Thomas E. Cronin, eds., *The Presidency Reappraised*. New York: Praeger, 1974.

Edwards, George C., III. *Presidential Approval*. Baltimore: Johns Hopkins University Press, 1990.

Edwards, George C., III. *The Public Presidency*. New York: St. Martin's, 1983.

Edwards, George C., III, William Mitchell, and Reed Welch. "Explaining Presidential Approval: The Significance of Issue Salience." *American Journal of Political Science* 39 (February 1995): 108–134.

Jacobs, Lawrence R., and Robert Y. Shapiro. "The Rise of Presidential Polling: The Nixon White House in Historical Perspective." *Public Opinion Quarterly* 59 (Summer 1995): 163–195.

Kernell, Samuel. *Going Public*. 3rd ed. Washington, D.C.: Congressional Quarterly, 1997.

Kinder, Donald R. "Presidents, Prosperity, and Public Opinion." *Public Opinion Quarterly* 45 (Spring 1981): 1–21.

Krosnick, Jon A., and Donald R. Kinder. "Altering the Foundations of Support for the President through Priming." *American Political Science Review* 84 (June 1990): 497–512.

Lau, Richard, and David O. Sears. "Cognitive Links between Economic Grievances and Political Responses." *Political Behavior* 3, no. 4 (1981): 279–302.

Miroff, Bruce. "The Presidency and the Public: Leadership as Spectacle." In Michael Nelson, ed., *The Presidency and the Political System*, 4th ed. Washington, D.C.: Congressional Quarterly, 1995.

Sigelman, Lee. "Gauging the Public Response to Presidential Leadership." *Presidential Studies Quarterly* 10 (summer 1980): 427–433.

Sigelman, Lee, and Carol K. Sigelman. "Presidential Leadership of Public Opinion: From 'Benevolent Leader' to Kiss of Death?" *Experimental Study of Politics* 7, no. 3 (1981): 1–22.

Tulis, Jeffrey K. *The Rhetorical Presidency*. Princeton: Princeton University Press, 1987.

Wayne, Stephen J. "Great Expectations: What People Want from Presidents." In Thomas E. Cronin, ed., *Rethinking the Presidency*. Boston: Little, Brown, 1982.

Notes

1. "First Debate with Stephen A. Douglas," August 21, 1858, in Roy P. Asler, ed., *The Collected Works of Abraham Lincoln* (New Brunswick, N.J.: Rutgers University Press, 1953), p. 27.
2. See Stanley Feldman and John Zaller, "The Political Culture of Ambivalence: Ideological Responses to the Welfare State," *American Journal of Political Science* 36 (February 1992): 268–307.
3. "U.S. Dependence on Foreign Oil," *Gallup Poll Monthly*, February 1991, p. 35.
4. CBS News/*New York Times* Poll, June 24, 1986, Table 9.
5. CBS News/*New York Times* Poll, October 22–24, 1995.
6. Benjamin I. Page and Robert Y. Shapiro, *The Rational Public* (Chicago: University of Chicago Press, 1992); James A. Stimson, *Public Opinion in America: Moods, Cycles, and Swings* (Boulder, Colo.: Westview, 1991).
7. R. Kent Weaver, Robert Y. Shapiro, and Lawrence R. Jacobs, "The Polls–Trends: Welfare," *Public Opinion Quarterly* 59 (Winter 1995): 607, 618, 619.
8. Quoted in Dom Bonafede, "Carter and the Polls—If You Live by Them, You May Die by Them," *National Journal*, August 19, 1978, pp. 1312–1313.
9. Interview by author with Richard Wirthlin, West Point, N.Y., April 19, 1988; John Anthony Maltese, *Spin Control* (Chapel Hill, NC: University of North Carolina Press, 1992), p. 185.
10. Dick Morris, *Behind the Oval Office* (New York: Random House, 1997), pp. 10–11, 83, 338; James A. Barnes, "The Endless Campaign," *National Journal*, February 20, 1993, p. 461; James A. Barnes, "Polls Apart," *National Journal*, July 10, 1993, 1750–1752; Richard L. Berke, "Clinton Adviser Says Polls Had a Role in Health Plan," *New York Times*, December 2, 1993, p. A17; James Carney, "Playing by the Numbers," *Time*, April 11, 1994, p. 40; James M. Perry,

"Clinton Relies Heavily on White House Pollster to Take Words Right Out of the Public's Mouth," *Wall Street Journal*, March 23, 1994, p. A16.

11. See, for example, Saul Pett, "Interview Draws Rare Portrait of Carter," *New Orleans Times-Picayune*, October 23, 1977, sect. 1, p. 13; Richard M. Nixon, *RN: The Memoirs of Richard Nixon* (New York: Grosset and Dunlap, 1978), pp. 935, 945; and Herbert G. Klein, *Making It Perfectly Clear* (Garden City, N.Y.: Doubleday, 1980), p. 341.

12. Jeffrey E. Cohen, *Presidential Responsiveness and Public Policy-Making* (Ann Arbor: University of Michigan Press, 1997).

13. Richard M. Nixon, "Address to the Nation on the Situation in Southeast Asia," *Public Papers of the President of the United States: Richard Nixon, 1970* (Washington, D.C.: Government Printing Office, 1971), p. 410.

14. Quoted in Tom Matthews, "The Road to War," *Newsweek*, January 28, 1991, p. 65.

15. Gerald R. Ford, "Imperiled, Not Imperial," *Time*, November 10, 1980, p. 31.

16. See *The Polling Report* 5 (January 30, 1989): 2–4.

17. President Carter, quoted in Godfrey Hodgson, *All Things to All Men: The False Promise of the Modern American Presidency* (New York: Simon and Schuster, 1980), p. 25.

18. George C. Edwards III, *The Public Presidency* (New York: St. Martin's, 1983), pp. 189–190. See also Times Mirror Center for the People and the Press, public opinion survey, October 25–30, 1995.

19. Edwards, *The Public Presidency*, pp. 189–191.

20. "Carter Interview," *Congressional Quarterly Weekly Report*, November 25, 1978, p. 3354.

21. See, for example, Gallup poll, *Attitudes toward the Presidency*, January 1980, p. 21.

22. Edwards, *The Public Presidency*, pp. 193–195.

23. Wirthlin interview.

24. See, for example, *The Gallup Poll Monthly*, May 1993, p. 13; *The Gallup Poll Monthly*, September 1994, pp. 17, 39, 44; George Gallup, Jr., and Frank Newport, "Wary Americans Favor Wait and See Posture in Persian Gulf," *The Gallup Monthly Report*, November 1990, p. 14; Jack Dennis, "Dimensions of Public Support for the Presidency" (paper presented at the Annual Meeting of the Midwest Political Science Association, Chicago, April 1975), Tables 4, 8; Hazel Erskine, "The Polls: Presidential Power," *Public Opinion Quarterly* 37 (Fall 1973): 492, 495.

25. George C. Edwards III, *At the Margins* (New Haven: Yale University Press, 1989), chap. 6; "Aligning Tests with Theory: Presidential Approval as a Source of Influence in Congress," *Congress and the Presidency* 24 (Fall 1997): 113–130.

26. David O. Sears, "Political Socialization," in Fred I. Greenstein and Nelson Polsby, eds., *Micropolitical Theory*, Vol. 2 of *Handbook of Political Science* (Reading, Mass.: Addison-Wesley, 1975), p. 177.

27. See Edwards, *The Public Presidency*, p. 261, n. 13.

28. "Remarks of the President at a Meeting with Non-Washington Editors and Broadcasters," White House Transcript, pp. 11–12.

29. "Institutions: Confidence Even in Difficult Times," *Public Opinion*, June/July 1981, p. 33.

30. Martin P. Wattenberg, "The Reagan Polarization and the Continual Downward Slide in Presidential Candidate Popularity," *American Politics Quarterly* 14 (July 1986): 219–245.

31. *Gallup Opinion Index*, November 1978, pp. 8–9.

32. "Reagan: A Likeable Guy," *Public Opinion*, December/January 1981, p. 24.

33. See, for example, The Pew Research Center survey of January 30–February 2, 1998.

34. Philip E. Converse, "The Nature of Belief Systems in Mass Publics," in David Apter, ed., *Ideology and Discontent* (New York: Free Press, 1964), pp. 206–261.

35. Charles W. Ostrom, Jr., and Dennis M. Simon, "The President's Public," *American Journal of Political Science* 32 (November 1988): 1096–1119.

36. Stimson, *Public Opinion in America*, pp. 24–25.

37. David J. Lanoue, *From Camelot to the Teflon President* (New York: Greenwood Press, 1988); Howard S. Bloom and H. Douglas Price, "Voter Response to Short-Run Economic Conditions: The Asymmetric Effect of Prosperity and Recession," *American Political Science Review* 69 (December 1975): 1240–1254; Samuel Kernell, "Presidential Popularity and Negative Voting: An Alternative Explanation of the Midterm Congressional Decline of the President's Party," *American Political Science Review* 71 (March 1977): 44–66; Richard R. Lau, "Two Explanations

for Negativity Effect in Political Behavior," *American Journal of Political Science* 29 (February 1985): 119–138; Clyde Wilcox and Dee Allsop, "Economic and Foreign Policy as Sources of Reagan Support," *Western Political Quarterly* 44 (December 1991): 941–958. However, compare Morris P. Fiorina and Kenneth A. Shepsle, "Is Negative Voting an Artifact?" *American Journal of Political Science* 33 (May 1989): 423–439.

38. Lanoue, *From Camelot to the Teflon President*; George C. Edwards III, "Comparing Chief Executives," *Public Opinion*, June/July 1985, p. 54. However, compare Michael S. Lewis-Beck, *Economics and Elections* (Ann Arbor: University of Michigan Press, 1988).

39. Ostrom and Simon, "The President's Public."

40. See, for example, Jon Hurwitz and Mark Peffley, "The Means and Ends of Foreign Policy as Determinants of Presidential Support," *American Journal of Political Science* 31 (May 1987): 236–258.

41. Shanto Iyengar, *Is Anyone Responsible?* (Chicago: University of Chicago Press, 1992), chap. 8; Shanto Iyengar, "Television News and Citizens' Explanations of National Affairs," *American Political Science Review* 81 (September 1987): 815–831.

42. Richard A. Brody and Paul Sniderman, "From Life Space to Polling Place," *British Journal of Political Science* 7 (July 1977): 337–360; Paul Sniderman and Richard A. Brody, "Coping: The Ethic of Self-Reliance," *American Journal of Political Science* 21 (August 1977): 501–522. See also Stanley Feldman, "Economic Self-Interest and Political Behavior," *American Journal of Political Science* 26 (August 1982): 449–452; and Kay L. Schlozman and Sidney Verba, *Injury to Insult: Unemployment, Class, and Political Response* (Cambridge: Harvard University Press, 1979).

43. K. Jill Kiecolt, "Group Consciousness and the Attribution of Blame for National Economic Problems," *American Politics Quarterly* 15 (April 1987): 203–222; Iyengar, *Is Anyone Responsible?* p. 80.

44. See Edwards, *The Public Presidency*, chap. 6; George C. Edwards III, *Presidential Approval* (Baltimore: Johns Hopkins University Press, 1990); and sources cited therein.

45. See, for example, Michael B. MacKuen, Robert S. Erikson, and James A. Stimson, "Peasants or Bankers? The American Electorate and the U.S. Economy," *American Political Science Review* 86 (September 1992): 597–611; Donald R. Kinder, "Presidents, Prosperity, and Public Opinion," *Public Opinion Quarterly* 45 (Spring 1981): 1–21; Richard Lau and David O. Sears, "Cognitive Links between Economic Grievances and Political Responses," *Political Behavior* 3, no. 4 (1981): 279–302; Diana C. Mutz, "Mass Media and Depoliticization of Personal Experience," *American Journal of Political Science* 36 (May 1992): 495–496.

46. See, for example, *Gallup Poll Monthly*, March 1966, pp. 48–49.

47. John E. Mueller, *War, Presidents, and Public Opinion* (New York: Wiley, 1970), pp. 208–213.

48. See, for example, Market Opinion Research, *Americans Talk Security*, no. 12 (January 1989): 31–32, 106.

49. George C. Edwards III and Tami Swenson, "Who Rallies? The Anatomy of a Rally Event," *Journal of Politics* 59 (February 1997): 200–212.

50. Franklin Roosevelt and Theodore Roosevelt, quoted in Emmett John Hughes, "Presidency vs. Jimmy Carter," *Fortune*, December 4, 1978, pp. 62, 64; our italics.

51. Samuel Kernell, *Going Public*, 3rd ed. (Washington, D.C.: Congressional Quarterly, 1997), p. 131–132.

52. Paul Brace and Barbara Hinckley, "Presidential Activities from Truman through Reagan: Timing and Impact," *Journal of Politics* 55 (May 1993): 387.

53. One scholar counted only four times when Roosevelt used a fireside chat to discuss legislation under consideration in Congress. See Elmer E. Cornwell, Jr., *Presidential Leadership of Public Opinion* (Bloomington: Indiana University Press, 1965), p. 263.

54. Mark Hertsgaard, *On Bended Knee: The Press and the Reagan Presidency* (New York: Farrar, Straus, and Giroux, 1988), pp. 107–108; Larry Speakes, *Speaking Out* (New York: Scribner's, 1988), p. 301.

55. Quoted in Thomas L. Friedman and Maureen Dowd, "Amid Setbacks, Clinton Team Seeks to Shake Off the Blues," *New York Times*, April 25, 1993, sect. 1, p. 12.

56. Stimson, *Public Opinion in America*, pp. 64, 126–127; Page and Shapiro, *The Rational Public*, pp. 127, 136; James A. Davis, "Changeable Weather in a Cooling Climate," *Public Opinion Quarterly* 56 (Fall 1992): 261–306; William G. Mayer, *The Changing American Mind* (Ann Arbor: Uni-

versity of Michigan Press, 1992), p. 123; Tom W. Smith, "Liberal and Conservative Trends in the United States since World War II," *Public Opinion Quarterly* 54 (Winter 1990): 479–507.

57. Ronald Reagan, *An American Life* (New York: Simon and Schuster, 1990), p. 471.

58. Reagan, *An American Life*, p. 479.

59. Seymour Martin Lipset, "Beyond 1984: The Anomalies of American Politics," *PS* 19 (1986), pp. 228–229; Mayer, *The Changing American Mind*, chaps. 5, 6; Page and Shapiro, *The Rational Public*, pp. 133, 136, 159; William Schneider, "The Voters' Mood 1986: The Six-Year Itch," *National Journal*, December 7, 1985, p. 2758. See also "Supporting a Greater Federal Role," *National Journal*, April 18, 1987, p. 924; "Opinion Outlook," *National Journal*, April 18, 1987, p. 964; "Federal Budget Deficit," *Gallup Report*, August 1987, pp. 25, 27; Davis, "Changeable Weather in a Cooling Climate"; CBS News/*The New York Times* Poll, October 27, 1987, Tables 16, 20.

60. This may have been the result of the military buildup that did occur, but the point remains that while Reagan wanted to continue to increase defense spending, the public was unresponsive to his wishes. Larry M. Bartels, "The American Public's Defense Spending Preferences in the Post–Cold War Era," *Public Opinion Quarterly* 58 (Winter 1994): 479–508; Lipset, "Beyond 1984," p. 229; Mayer, *The Changing American Mind*, pp. 51, 62, 133. See also "Defense," Gallup Report, May 1987, pp. 2–3; "Opinion Outlook," *National Journal*, June 13, 1987, p. 1550; CBS News/*The New York Times* Poll, October 27, 1987, Table 15.

61. Reagan, *An American Life*, pp. 471, 479; Richard Sobel, ed., *Public Opinion in U.S. Foreign Policy* (Lanham, Md.: Rowman and Littlefield, 1993); Page and Shapiro, *The Rational Public*, p. 276. See also CBS News/*The New York Times* Poll, December 1, 1986, Table 5; CBS News/*The New York Times* Poll [news release], (October 27, 1987), Table 17; "Americans on Contra Aid: Broad Opposition," *New York Times*, January 31, 1988, sec. 4, p. 1.

62. Page and Shapiro, *The Rational Public*, pp. 271–281; John E. Reilly, ed., *American Public Opinion and U.S. Foreign Policy 1987* (Chicago: Chicago Council on Foreign Relations, 1987), chaps. 5, 6; Mayer, *The Changing American Mind*, chaps. 4, 6.

63. See, for example, John A. Fleishman, "Trends in Self-identified Ideology from 1972 to 1982: No Support for the Salience Hypothesis," *American Journal of Political Science* 30 (1986): 517–541; Martin P. Wattenberg, "From a Partisan to a Candidate-Centered Electorate," in Anthony King, ed., *The New American Political System* (Washington, D.C.: American Enterprise Institute, 1990), pp. 169–171; Wattenberg, *The Rise of Candidate-Centered Politics*, pp. 95–101.

64. Stimson, *Public Opinion in America*, pp. 64, 127.

65. Mayer, *The Changing American Mind*, p. 127.

66. Quoted in R. W. Apple, "Bush Sure-Footed on Trail of Money," *New York Times*, September 29, 1990, p. 8.

67. Eugene J. Rossi, "Mass and Attentive Opinion on Nuclear Weapons Test and Fallout, 1954–1963," *Public Opinion Quarterly* 29 (Summer 1965): 280–297; Robert S. Erikson, Norman R. Luttbeg, and Kent L. Tedin, *American Public Opinion: Its Origins, Content, and Impact*, 2nd ed. (New York: Wiley, 1980), p. 144; Mueller, *War, Presidents, and Public Opinion*, pp. 69–74; CBS News/*The New York Times* Poll, October 28, 1983, p. 2; Page and Shapiro, *The Rational Public*, p. 182; Barry Sussman, "Reagan's Talk Gains Support for Policies," *Washington Post*, October 30, 1983, sec. A, pp. 1, 18. However, compare Page and Shapiro, *The Rational Public*, pp. 242, 250.

68. White House transcript of interview of President Clinton by WWWE Radio, Cleveland, October 24, 1994.

69. George C. Edwards III, "Frustration and Folly: Bill Clinton and the Public Presidency," in Colin Campbell and Bert A. Rockman, eds., *The Clinton Presidency: First Appraisals* (Chatham, N.J.: Chatham House, 1995).

70. Lee Sigelman, "Gauging the Public Response to Presidential Leadership," *Presidential Studies Quarterly* 10 (Summer 1980): 427–433. See also Pamela Johnston Conover and Lee Sigelman, "Presidential Influence and Public Opinion: The Case of the Iranian Hostage Crisis," *Social Science Quarterly* 63 (June 1982): 249–264.

71. "Most Utah Residents Say 'No' to MX Missile Deployment," *Bryan-College Station Eagle*, September 15, 1981, p. 5A.

72. Lee Sigelman and Carol K. Sigelman, "Presidential Leadership of Public Opinion: From 'Benevolent Leader' to Kiss of Death?" *Experimental Study of Politics* 7, no. 3 (1981): 1–22.

73. Benjamin I. Page and Robert Y. Shapiro, "Presidential Leadership through Public Opinion," in George C. Edwards III, Steven A. Shull, and Norman C. Thomas, eds., *The Presidency and Public Policy Making* (Pittsburgh: University of Pittsburgh Press, 1985), pp. 22–36.

74. Fred I. Greenstein, "Eisenhower as an Activist President: A Look at New Evidence," *Political Science Quarterly* 94 (Winter 1979–1980): 588–590.

75. See, for example, Howard Kurtz, *Spin Cycle* (New York: Free Press, 1998), pp. 300–301.

76. David Stockman, *The Triumph of Politics* (New York: Harper and Row, 1986), p. 173; see also pp. 132, 353.

77. For other budgetary distortions, see Tim Muris, "Budget Manipulations," *The American Enterprise,* May/June 1993, pp. 24–28.

78. Quoted in Joseph C. Goulden, *Truth Is the First Casualty* (Chicago: Rand McNally, 1969), p. 160.

79. Mueller, *War, Presidents, and Public Opinion,* pp. 112–113.

80. For a more complete discussion, see Edwards, *The Public Presidency,* pp. 60–64. See also Speakes, *Speaking Out,* pp. 141, 160–162, 172.

81. The Pew Research Center for the People and the Press, poll of January 30–February 2, 1998. See also Gallup Poll of March 20–22, 1998.

82. Kurtz, *Spin Cycle,* pp. xxi–xxii.

83. Dick Kirschten, "Reagan and Reality," *National Journal,* October 16, 1982, p. 1765.

84. See, for example, CBS News/*The New York Times* Poll, October 30, 1986, Table 29.

85. See, for example, William Schneider, "Opinion Outlook," *National Journal,* November 29, 1986, pp. 2908–2909.

86. See, for example, Dan Quayle, *Standing Firm* (New York: HarperCollins, 1994), p. 94; Charles Kolb, *White House Daze* (New York: Free Press, 1994).

87. Quoted in Steven V. Roberts, "Return to the Land of the Gipper," *New York Times,* March 9, 1988, p. A28.

88. Ronald Reagan, *Where's the Rest of Me? The Autobiography of Ronald Reagan* (New York: Karz, 1965), p. 138.

89. An analysis of President Johnson's public statements on Vietnam shows that he varied their content—that is, their "hawkishness"—depending on the audience he was addressing. Lawrence C. Miller and Lee Sigelman, "Is the Audience the Message? A Note on LBJ's Vietnam Statements," *Public Opinion Quarterly* 42 (Spring 1978): 71–80. See also Malcolm Goggin, "The Ideological Content of Presidential Communications," *American Politics Quarterly* 12 (July 1984): 361–384.

90. Michael K. Deaver, *Behind the Scenes* (New York: William Morrow, 1987), p. 73; see also pp. 126–127, 135.

91. Laurence I. Barrett, *Gambling with History* (New York: Penguin, 1983), p. 442.

92. Quoted in Michael Baruch Grossman and Martha Joynt Kumar, *Portraying the President: The White House and the News Media* (Baltimore: Johns Hopkins University Press, 1981), p. 29.

93. Lou Cannon, *President Reagan: The Role of a Lifetime* (New York: Simon and Schuster, 1991), p. 453.

94. See Richard Ellis, *Presidential Lightning Rods: The Politics of Blame Avoidance* (Lawrence: University Press of Kansas, 1994); Fred I. Greenstein, *The Hidden-Hand Presidency: Eisenhower as Leader* (New York: Basic Books, 1982), pp. 90–92.

95. See Donald T. Regan, *For the Record* (San Diego: Harcourt Brace Jovanovich, 1988), pp. 247–249.

96. Deaver, *Behind the Scenes,* p. 141.

97. Quoted in Rich Jaroslovsky, "Manipulating the Media Is a Specialty for the White House's Michael Deaver," *Wall Street Journal,* January 5, 1984, p. 44.

98. Speakes, *Speaking Out,* p. 220.

99. Quoted in John Ehrlichman, *Witness to Power: The Nixon Years* (New York: Simon and Schuster, 1982), p. 267.

5

THE PRESIDENT AND THE MEDIA

DESPITE ALL THEIR EFFORTS TO LEAD PUBLIC OPINION, presidents do not directly reach the American people on a day-to-day basis. It is the news media, or press, that provide people with most of what they know about chief executives, their policies, and their policies' consequences. The media also interpret and analyze presidential activities, including even the president's direct appeals to the public.

The media is the principal intermediary between the president and the public, and relations with the press are an important aspect of the president's efforts to lead public opinion. Presidents who are portrayed in a favorable light will face fewer obstacles in obtaining public support than those who are treated harshly by the media.

In this chapter we examine the nature and structure of presidential relationships with the press, emphasizing both the context of these relationships and the White House's attempts to obtain favorable coverage through holding press conferences and providing services for the press. We also focus on the substance of the news media's coverage of the president, discussing the controversial issues of leaks to the press and of superficiality and bias in the news. Finally, we consider the evidence regarding the important, but generally overlooked, question of the effects of press coverage of the White House on public opinion.

If presidents fit the director model, they will tend to receive favorable press coverage of their administration and reliably use the press to advance their interests. In contrast, if presidents are facilitators, they will tend to experience a more adversarial relationship, which will be characterized by more negative coverage and a constant struggle by the White House to obtain both space and sympathetic treatment in the media.

THE EVOLUTION OF MEDIA COVERAGE

Today we are accustomed to turning to our newspapers or television sets to learn almost immediately about what the president has said or done. Things have not always been this way: Before the Civil War, newspapers were generally small, heavily partisan, and limited in circulation. Between 1860 and 1920, however, a number of changes occurred that permanently altered the relationship between the president and the press.

Several technological innovations—from the electric printing press, the telegraph, the typewriter, and the telephone, to Linotype and woodpulp paper—made it both possible and economical to produce mass-circulation newspapers carrying recent national news. Aside from the sales efforts of the newspapers themselves, the increasing literacy of the population helped to create a market for these papers.

The growing interest in national affairs as a result of the Civil War and the new importance of the national government also fostered the newspapers. The government began to regulate the economy with the Interstate Commerce Commission and its antitrust efforts. Moreover, it expanded its role in world affairs during the Spanish-American War and World War I. These events kindled support for, and great interest in, the activities of the government in Washington. The increased interest in national affairs was also caused by the renewed prominence of the presidency following an era of congressional ascendancy.

Reporters first obtained space in the White House in 1896,[1] but it was Theodore Roosevelt who made the greatest strides in exploiting the new opportunities to reach the public provided by the mass-circulation press. He took an activist view of the presidency and used the White House as a "bully pulpit" to dramatize himself and the issues in which he was interested. He sought and gained extensive access to the press in order to forge a more personal relationship with the American people. Establishing a casual and candid relationship with journalists, he floated trial balloons, leaked stories, and held informal press conferences (some while he was receiving his daily shave). Since that time, news about the president has played an increasingly prominent role in the printed press, both in absolute terms and relative to coverage of Congress or the national government as a whole.[2]

Presidents have found that they need the press because it is their primary link to the people. The press, in turn, finds coverage of the president indispensable in satisfying its audience and reporting on the most significant political events. The advent of radio and television has only heightened these mutual needs.

The history of relations between the president and the press has not been characterized by unlimited goodwill. President George Washington complained that the "calumnies" against his administration were "outrages of common decency" motivated by the desire to destroy confidence in the new government.[3] John Adams was so upset at criticism in the press that he supported the Sedition Act and jailed some opposition journalists under its authority.

Thomas Jefferson, certainly one of our greatest defenders of freedom, became so exasperated with the press as president that he argued that "even the least informed of the people have learned that nothing in a newspaper is to be believed." He also felt that "newspapers, for the most part, present only the caricature of disaffected minds. Indeed, the abuses of freedom of the press have been carried to a length never before known or borne by any civilized nation." These observations, it should be noted, come from the man who earlier had written that "were it left to me to decide whether we should have a government without newspapers or newspapers without a government, I should not hesitate to prefer the latter."[4]

Almost two centuries later, things have changed very little. Although all presidents have supported the abstract right of the press to criticize them freely, while in office, most have found this criticism uncomfortable. They have viewed some of the press as misrepresenting (perhaps maliciously) their views and actions, failing to perceive the correctness of their policies, and dedicated to impeding their goals. For example, as the Iran-Contra scandal unfolded, Ronald Reagan complained of the press circling the White House like "sharks." A quarter century earlier, John F. Kennedy, a favorite of the press, exulted in the potential of television for going directly to the people when he told journalist Ben Bradlee that "when we don't have to go through you bastards, we can really get our story to the American people."[5] President Clinton, who expressed a desire to punch columnist William Safire in the nose for calling Hillary Clinton a "congenital liar," has had his own frustrations with the press, as shown in The Clinton Presidency box.

THE CLINTON PRESIDENCY

The President Assesses the Press

Near the end of his first year in office, President Bill Clinton was interviewed by Jann Wenner and William Greider for *Rolling Stone* magazine. During the interview, Greider told the president of complaints about his willingness to stand up for his beliefs. As the journalist described it, President Clinton "turned and glared at him." Then, "his face reddened, and his voice rose to a furious pitch as he delivered a scalding rebuke":

> But that is the press's fault, too, damn it. I have fought more damn battles here for more things than any president has in 20 years . . . and not gotten one damn bit of credit from the knee-jerk liberal press, and I am sick and tired of it. . . .
>
> I have fought my guts out. . . . And you get no credit around here for fighting and bleeding. And that's why the know-nothings and the do-nothings and the negative people and the right-wingers always win. Because of the way people like you put questions to people like me. . . .
>
> That's why they always win. And they're going to keep winning until somebody tells the truth.[6]

No matter who is in the White House or who does the reporting, presidents and the press always struggle for dominance. Presidents are inherently policy advocates and want to be able to define a situation and receive favorable coverage. They will naturally assess the press in terms of how it aids or hinders their goals. The press, on the other hand, has the responsibility for presenting and assessing what is really going on. Although the press may fail in its efforts, it will assess itself on those criteria. Presidents want to control the amount and timing of information about their administrations, while the press wants all the information that exists without delay. As long as their goals are different, presidents and the press are likely to be adversaries.

RELATIONS BETWEEN THE PRESIDENT AND THE PRESS

To understand presidential relations with the press, we must understand the journalists with whom the White House deals and the ways in which the president's staff tries to influence them. Because of the importance of the press to the president, the White House goes to great lengths to encourage the media to project a positive image of the president and the administration's policies. These efforts include coordinating the news, holding press conferences, and providing a range of services such as formal briefings, interviews, photo opportunities, background sessions, travel accommodations, and daily handouts.

The White House Press Corps

Who are the reporters that regularly cover the White House? This elite contingent represents diverse media constituencies, including daily newspapers like the *Washington Post* and *New York Times*; weekly newsmagazines like *Time* and *Newsweek*; wire services like the Associated Press (AP) and United Press International (UPI); newspaper chains like Hearst, Gannett, Scripps-Howard, Newhouse, and Knight-Ridder; the television and radio networks; the foreign press; and "opinion" magazines like the *New Republic* and the *National Review*.

In addition, photographers, columnists, television commentators, and magazine writers are regularly involved in White House–press interactions. More than 1,800 journalists have White House press credentials. Fortunately, not everyone shows up at once (there are only forty-eight seats in the White House briefing room). Fewer than seventy reporters and fifteen photographers regularly cover the White House, although the total increases to more than one hundred when an important announcement is expected.

Attendance at a presidential press conference may number about three hundred.

The great majority of daily newspapers in America have no Washington correspondents, much less someone assigned to cover the White House. The same can be said for almost all of the country's individual television and radio stations. Unless they are part of a network, these papers and stations rely heavily on the AP and UPI wire services, each of which covers the White House continuously and in detail with several full-time reporters.

The Presidential Press Operation

White House relations with the media occupy a substantial portion of the time of a large number of aides. About one-third of the high-level White House staff is directly involved in media relations and policy of one type or another, and most staff members are involved at some time in influencing the media's portrayal of the president.

Press Secretary The person in the White House who daily deals directly with the press is the president's press secretary. According to Marlin Fitzwater, press secretary to Presidents Reagan and Bush, "The press secretary stands between the opposing forces, explaining, cajoling, begging, sometimes pushing both sides toward a better understanding of each other."[7]

The central function of press secretaries is to serve as conduits of information from the White House to the press. They must be sure that clear statements of administration policies have been prepared on important policy matters. The press secretaries usually conduct the daily press briefings, giving prepared announcements and answering questions. In forming their answers, they often do not have specific orders on what to say or not say. Instead, they must be able to think on their feet to ensure that they accurately reflect the president's views. Sometimes these views may be unclear, however, or they may be views that the president may not wish to articulate. Therefore, press secretaries may seem to be evasive or unimaginative in public settings. They also hold private meetings with individual reporters, where the information that is provided may be more candid and speculative.

To be effective in the conduit role, the press secretary must maintain credibility with reporters. Credibility rests on at least two important pillars: (1) truth and (2) access to (and respect of) the president and senior White House officials. Press secretaries viewed as not telling the truth or (like President Clinton's first press secretary, Dee Dee Myers) as being too distant from the top decision makers (and therefore not well informed) will not be effective presidential spokespersons because the press will give less credence to what they say. Credibility problems have arisen for several press secretaries as a result of these perceived deficiencies.

Press secretaries also serve as conduits from the press, sometimes explaining the needs of the press to the president. For example, all Lyndon Johnson's press secretaries tried to persuade the president to issue the press advance information on his travel plans. When he refused, they provided the information anyway (and then had it expunged from the briefing transcript so the president would not see it). Press secretaries also try to inform the White House staff of the press's needs and the rules of the game, and they help reporters gain access to staff members.

Press secretaries typically are not involved in substantive decisions, but they do give the president advice—usually on what information should be released, by whom, in what form, and to what audience. They also advise the president on rehearsals for press conferences and on how to project the proper image and use it to political advantage.

Coordinating the News Since the time of William McKinley and Theodore Roosevelt, the White House has attempted to coordinate executive branch news. Presidents have assigned aides to clear the appointments of departmental public affairs officials, to keep in touch with the officials to learn what news is forthcoming from the departments, and to meet with them to explain the president's policy views and try to prevent conflicting statements from emanating from the White House and other units of the executive branch. Specialists have had responsibility for coordinating national security news.

Of course, such tactics do not always work. President Ford wanted to announce from the White House the results of the successful effort to rescue seamen from the *Mayaguez,* but he found, to his disappointment, that the Pentagon had already done so, making any presidential announcement anticlimactic. Similarly, at the beginning of his second year in office, President Reagan issued an order that required advance White House approval of television appearances by cabinet members and other top officials, but it soon lapsed.

Coordinating the news from the White House itself has also been a presidential goal. Presidents have sometimes monitored and attempted to limit the press contacts of White House aides, who have annoyed their bosses by using the media for their own purposes. President Reagan, for example, instituted a policy midway through his administration that required his assistant for communications to approve any interview with any White House official requested by a member of the media. All requests were monitored and entered on a computer so the White House could keep tabs on whom reporters wanted to see. Since even the White House press cannot wander through the East or West Wings on their own, the only way to speak to aides without administration approval was to call them at home, a practice discouraged by presidential assistants and generally avoided by reporters. Such efforts to limit press access are exceptional, however, and have proved to be largely fruitless.

Recent administrations have also made an effort to coordinate publicity functions within the White House and to attempt to present the news in the most favorable light, such as preventing two major stories from breaking on the same day, smothering bad news with more positive news, and timing announcements for maximum or minimum effect (discussed in Chapter 4).

Attending to the News   All recent presidents have read several newspapers each day, especially the *New York Times* and the *Washington Post*, and most have also been very attentive to television news programs. Johnson had a television cabinet with three screens in order to watch all three commercial networks at once. However, even this was not enough to satisfy his thirst for news. He also had Teletypes that carried the latest reports from the AP and UPI wire services installed in the Oval Office, which he monitored regularly.

President Nixon rarely watched television news and did not peruse large numbers of newspapers or magazines, but he was extremely interested in the press coverage of his administration. He had his staff prepare a daily news summary of newspapers, magazines, television news, and the AP and UPI news wires. Often this summary triggered ideas for the president, who gave orders to aides to follow up on something he read. The news summary also went to White House assistants. Subsequent presidents have continued the news summary, altering it to meet their individual needs, and have circulated it to top officials in their administrations. The Carter White House instituted a separate magazine survey and even began producing a weekly summary of Jewish publications after it became concerned about a possible backlash within the American Jewish community against the administration's Middle East policy.

The Presidential Press Conference

The best-known direct interaction between the president and the press is the formal presidential press conference. The large number of reporters covering these press conferences and the setting in which they take place (such as the East Room in the White House) have inevitably made them more formal than in the days when Franklin D. Roosevelt held forth from his desk in the Oval Office. Transcripts of the press conferences were first made during Eisenhower's tenure, and the conferences were televised live beginning in the Kennedy administration. Presidents since Truman frequently have begun their press conferences with carefully prepared opening statements that give them an opportunity to reach the public on their own terms.

Presidents have taken other steps that contributed to the formalization of press conferences. Beginning with Truman, they have undergone formal briefings and dry runs in preparation for questions that might be asked, in which aides are asked to submit possible questions and suggested answers. In 1982 President Reagan began holding full-scale mock news conferences. Guessing the media's questions is not too difficult. There are obvious areas of concern, and questions raised at White House and departmental briefings and other meetings with reporters provide useful cues. The president can also anticipate the interests of individual reporters and can exercise some discretion over whom to recognize. (Once Ronald Reagan, using a seating chart of reporters, called on a reporter only to discover that this individual was not even attending the conference. He was, however, watching the conference at home and did stand up when his name was called.)

From the press's perspective, the change in the nature of presidential press conferences from semiprivate to public events diminished their utility in transmitting information from the president to the press. Since every word they say is transmitted verbatim to millions of people, modern-day presidents cannot speak as candidly as, say, Franklin D. Roosevelt could. Nor can they speculate freely about their potential actions or evaluations of persons, events, or circumstances. Instead, they must choose their words carefully and, as a result, their responses to questions are often not very enlightening. In addition, the increased number of reporters attending press conferences has meant a wider range of questions, and thus less likelihood of covering any one subject in depth.

The White House has seen things differently, however. As President Kennedy's press secretary, Pierre Salinger, put it: "The idea of going to television . . . was to jump over the press and go directly to the people."[8] Thus, the White House has tried to use the press as a prop with which to speak to the public. In response, the networks have become more reluctant to cover presidential news conferences.

Until the end of George Bush's tenure, the networks would preempt programs for a live, primetime televised presidential press conference almost without question. In June 1992, however, all three networks refused to run one of President Bush's press conferences on the grounds that it was mostly a campaign event. Only one network covered President Clinton's first primetime press conference, and then only for thirty minutes. Since that time, the major television networks have continued the pattern of frequently carrying their regular entertainment programming instead of the president. The CNN and C-Span cable networks do cover the president's addresses and press conferences, however.

Presidents may employ a range of techniques to be firmly in control of their press conferences. They may declare that they will not entertain questions on certain topics, and they may also evade questions with clever rhetoric or a simple "no comment." Alternately, they can use a question as a vehicle to say something that they had planned ahead of time. If necessary, they can reverse the attack and focus on the questioner, or conversely, they can call on a friendly reporter for a "soft" question.

The trend is clearly in the direction of holding fewer formal press conferences: Franklin Roosevelt held about seven a month, whereas Ronald Reagan held only about one press conference every two months. Naturally, as more time elapses between press conferences, more events and governmental actions will have transpired since the last press conference, and as more events and actions have transpired, the questions are likely to be more far-ranging. As a result, the coverage of any one topic is likely to be superficial.

In a break with precedent, President Bush virtually abandoned formal, primetime press conferences in favor of frequent, brief, informal morning sessions with reporters, which he often called on short notice. It was difficult for the commercial networks to provide live broadcasts without costly interruptions of scheduled programs, and many reporters were absent. Oddly, in an age of television, Bush's format was aimed at the newspapers.

Bush made little connection between his public relations and his policy initiatives. He held more press conferences in a year than Ronald Reagan did in eight years, and met frequently with reporters in informal ways as well. However, he used these sessions to respond to journalists' inquiries rather than as part of an effort to advance his own policies. He talked *to* the press, not *over* it.

Bill Clinton took office with an antagonistic attitude toward the national media, which he planned to bypass rather than use it as part of his political strategy. He waited two months before holding his first formal news conference and five months before he held one in primetime viewing hours. As he told an audience of journalists shortly after taking office: "You know why I can stiff you on press conferences? Because [talk-show host] Larry King liberated me by giving me to the American people directly."

After a rocky start in his press relations, Clinton's orientation changed. He found that he could not avoid the national press, which remains the primary source of news about the federal government. "I did not realize the importance of communications," he confessed, "and the overriding importance of what is on the evening television news. If I am not on there with a message, someone else is, with their message."[9] Clinton hired David Gergen, who had been a communications adviser in Republican administrations, as a top aide. He also made himself somewhat more accessible to the national press, appearing frequently in the White House briefing room to make prepared statements (but often leaving without answering more than a question or two).

Services for the Press

In order to get their messages across to the American people and to influence the tone and content of press presentation of those messages, presidents have provided services for the press.

Briefings   Briefings are held each weekday morning and afternoon for the White House press, and at other times as the situation requires. In the daily briefings, reporters are provided with information about appointments and resignations, decisions of the president to sign or not to sign routine bills and explanations for these actions, and the president's schedule (appointments, meetings, future travel plans, and availability to the press). More significant from the standpoint of the press, the briefing provides presidential reactions to events, the White House "line" on issues and whether it has changed, and a reading of the president's moods and ideas. This information is obtained through prepared statements or answers to reporters' queries. (Responses to the latter are often prepared ahead of time by the White House staff.) The daily briefings, of course, also provide the press with an opportunity to have the president's views placed on the public record, which eases the burdens of reporting.

Usually the president's press secretary or the press secretary's deputy presides over these briefings, although sometimes the president participates. White House staff members and executive branch officials with substantial expertise in specific policy areas, such as the budget or foreign affairs, sometimes brief the press and answer questions at the daily briefing or at special briefings, especially if the White House is launching a major publicity campaign.

Backgrounders   One of the most important services for the press is the backgrounder. The president's comments to reporters may be "on the record" (remarks may be attributed to the speaker); "on background" (a specific source cannot be identified but the source's position and status can, such as a "White House source"); "deep background" (no attribution); or "off the record" (the information reporters receive may not be used in a story). For purposes of convenience we shall term all sessions between White House officials (including the president) and the press that are not "on the record" as "backgrounders." All recent presidents, especially Johnson and Ford, have engaged in background discussion with reporters, although President Nixon's involvement was rare. Some presidents, especially Eisenhower and Nixon, have relied heavily upon their principal foreign policy advisers to brief reporters on foreign affairs.

The most common type of White House discussion with reporters on a background basis is a briefing. In a typical background briefing, a senior presidential aide, such as the director of the Office of Management and Budget or the president's national security assistant, explains a policy's development and what it is expected to accomplish. Interestingly, the White House does not appear to stress the substance of policy and seldom makes "hard" news statements in background briefings because this would irritate absent members of the press. The briefings do play an important role in preparing the news media for legislative and administrative initiatives, presidential trips, and important speeches, however. Special background sessions are held for the weekly newsmagazines at the end of the week.

Backgrounders have a number of advantages for the White House. Avoiding direct quotation allows officials to speak on sensitive foreign policy and domestic policy matters candidly and in depth, something domestic politics and international diplomacy would not tolerate if speakers were held directly accountable for their words. The White House hopes such discussions will help it communicate its point of view more clearly and serve to educate journalists and make them more sympathetic to the president's position in their reporting. Moreover, background sessions can be used to scotch rumors and limit undesirable speculation about presidential plans and internal White House affairs.

In these briefings, reporters carefully watch the president or senior aides perform. Since the White House controls the conditions of these briefings, the chances of making a favorable impression are good. An impressive performance in a background session can display the administration's competence and perhaps elicit the benefit of the doubt in future stories.

Backgrounders may be also be aimed at the public (in the form of trial balloons that the White House can disclaim if they meet with disapproval) or at policy makers in Washington. They may also be directed at other countries. For example, to discourage the Soviet Union's support of India in its war with Pakistan, Henry Kissinger told reporters in a backgrounder that the Soviet policy might lead to the cancellation of President Nixon's trip to Moscow. Since the statement was not officially attributed to Kissinger, it constituted less of a public threat to the Soviet Union, while it simultaneously communicated the president's message.[10]

Reporters have generally been happy to go along with protecting the identities of "spokespersons" and "sources" (although an experienced observer can identify most of them), because the system provides them more information than they would have without it. This increase of information available to reporters adds to the information available to the public and probably helps advance journalistic careers as well.

In addition to official backgrounders, White House aides may provide reporters information "on background." Reporters tend to view middle-level aides as the best sources of such information because they have in-depth knowledge about the substance of programs and are generally free from the constraints of high visibility. Most interviews with White House staff are made on this basis because presidents are generally intolerant of staff members who seek publicity for themselves. Sometimes an aide will say more than his or her superiors would like in order to prod the president in a particular policy direction or cast doubt on a rival in the administration. Self-serving propaganda is a common feature of these sessions.

Interviews   Interviews with the president and top White House staff members are a valuable commodity to the press, and sometimes the White House uses them for its own purposes. For example, President Nixon traded an exclusive interview to Hugh Sidey of *Time* for a *Time* cover story on him. Similarly, in order to obtain an interview with President Ford, even the venerable Walter Cronkite agreed to use only questions the president could handle easily. At other times the White House may give exclusives to a paper like the *New York Times* in return for getting a story in which it is interested located in a prominent place in the paper.[11]

Cultivation   Recent presidents, with the exceptions of Richard Nixon and Jimmy Carter, have regularly cultivated elite reporters and columnists, the editors and publishers of leading newspapers, and network news producers and executives with small favors, social flattery, and small background dinners at the White House. (Nixon turned these chores over to top aides and Carter was neither interested in, nor skilled at, cultivation.)[12] President Clinton invited the television network anchors to lunch at the White House before delivering his first primetime address to the nation. The first call ABC network anchorperson Peter Jennings received after winning his job was from Ronald Reagan.[13] Since the 1960s, the White House has had, first, a designated person, and then an office, for media liaison to deal directly with the representatives of news organizations, such as editors, publishers, and producers, in addition to the press office that deals with reporters' routine needs.

Additional Services   There are many additional services that the White House provides for the press. It gives reporters transcripts of briefings and presidential speeches and daily handouts containing a variety of information about the president and his policies, including advance notice of travel plans and upcoming stories. (These items are also available to the general public at the White House's Internet site.) Major announcements are timed to accommodate the deadlines of newspapers, magazines, and television networks.

Photographers covering the president are highly dependent on the White House press office, which provides facilities for photographers on presidential trips and arranges photo opportunities to make sure they will produce the most flattering shots of the president (for Johnson, his left profile). President Reagan even prohibited impromptu questions from reporters at photographing sessions. Moreover, the official White House photographers provide many of the photographs of the president that the media use. Naturally, these are screened favorably to feature the president's "warm," "human," or "family" side. These photos please editors and the public alike.

When the president goes on trips, whether at home or abroad, extensive preparations are made for the press by the White House travel and press offices (perhaps explaining why the press was so critical of Bill Clinton when he summarily fired travel office employees in 1993). These preparations include arranging transportation and lodging for the press, installing equipment for radio and television broadcasting, obtaining telephones for reporters, erecting platforms for photographers, preparing a detailed account of where and with whom the president will be at particular times, providing elaborate information about the countries the president is visiting, forming pools of press members to cover the president closely (as in a motorcade), and scheduling the press plane to arrive early so the press can cover the president's arrival.

As many of these services suggest, the press is especially dependent on the White House staff in covering presidential trips, particularly abroad. The number of sources of information is generally reduced on such trips, as is the access of the press to the principal figures it wishes to cover. Thus, the president's aides are in a good position to manipulate press coverage to their advantage. Coverage of foreign trips is generally favorable, although less so than in the past now that reporters with expertise in foreign affairs have started to accompany the president, and the press will point out the relationship of the trip and its goals and accomplishments to the president's domestic political problems. (It is interesting that foreign travel does not seem to increase a president's approval ratings.)[14]

Even in Washington, however, reporters are very much in a controlled environment. Reagan aides went so far as to have the motor of the president's helicopter revved to prevent him from hearing questions shouted by the press as he left for a weekend at Camp David. Similarly, when Reagan wanted to avoid the press during the 1984 presidential campaign, he simply held no formal press conferences at all. Bill Clinton did the same thing in 1996.

Managing the News

Reporters may not freely roam the halls of the White House, interviewing whomever they please. In one of its first acts, the Clinton White House even barred reporters from the area behind the press room, where the offices of the press secretary and communications director are located (this policy was changed after a few months). Reporters are highly dependent on the press office for access to officials, and about half their interviews are with the press secretary and his or her staff. Much of their time is spent waiting for something to happen or watching the president at formal or ceremonial events. Since most news stories about such occurrences show the president in a favorable light, the press office does everything possible to help reporters record these activities.

Briefings, press releases, and the like can be used to divert the media's attention from embarrassing matters. The Reagan White House adopted a strategy of blitzing the media with information to divert its attention after the press raised questions about the president's sleeping through Libyan attacks on United States forces off the coast of Africa. To avoid publicity about illegal transfers of arms to Nicaragua, the Reagan White House spear-headed a drive for an "Economic Bill of Rights."[16]

More frequently, the White House, by adopting an active approach to the press, gains an opportunity to shape the media's agenda for the day. Through announcements and press releases, it attempts to focus attention on what will reflect positively on the president. Such information frequently generates questions from reporters and subsequent news stories. Representatives of the smaller papers, who have few resources, are more heavily dependent on White House–provided news than are the larger news bureaus, including the major networks. Thus, the former are the most likely to follow the White House's agenda. Moreover, since White House reporters, especially the wire services, are under pressure to file daily "hard news" reports, the White House is in a strong position to help by providing information—much of it trivial, some of it personal, and all of it designed to reflect positively on the president. As a Ford official put it: "You can predict what the press is going to do with a story. It is almost by formula. Because of this they are usable."[17]

Many observers, including journalists, feel that, especially early in a president's term, the press tends to parrot the White House line, which is conveniently provided at a briefing or in a press release. The pressure among journalists to be first with a story increases the potential for White House manipulation inherent in this deferential approach, as concerns for accuracy give way to career interests.

Presidents have undoubtedly hoped that the handouts, briefings, and other services they and their staffs provide for reporters will gain them some goodwill. They may also hope that these services will keep the White House press from digging too deeply into presidential affairs. In addition, they want to keep reporters interested in the president's agenda because bored journalists are more negative in their reporting and may base their stories on trivial, embarrassing incidents like the president stumbling while getting off a plane.

In addition, the White House controls a commodity of considerable value to the press: information on the president's personal life. Most reporters are under pressure to provide stories on the minutiae of presidents' lives, no matter what they do. Some White House aides have found that the provision of such information can co-opt journalists or sidetrack them from producing critical stories. Some reporters will exploit the opportunity to please their editors instead of digging into more significant subjects; others reciprocate their favorable treatment by the White House with positive stories about the president.

Servicing the Local Press   Once the Washington press reports an issue, it tends to drop it and move on to the next one; however, repetition is necessary to convey the president's views to the generally inattentive public. Moreover, the Washington press tends to place more emphasis on the support of, or opposition to, a program than on its substance, although the White House wants to communicate the latter. The Washington- and New York–based national media also have substantial resources to challenge White House versions of events and policies and to investigate areas of government not covered by briefings or press releases. As a result, the White House provides services for the local as well as the national media.

The White House invites local editors, reporters, and news executives to Washington for exclusive interviews and briefings by the president and senior administration officials. Recent presidents have also arranged to be interviewed from the White House by television and radio stations through satellite hookups, and the White House provides briefings for the local press using the same technology. It also sends administration briefing teams around the country to discuss the president's policies with local media representatives and provides press releases, speeches, other documents, and audio clips for local media. President Clinton meets frequently with journalists representing local media during his trips around the country. These efforts enable the White House to tailor unedited messages for specific groups and reach directly into the constituencies of members of Congress while reinforcing its policy message. Naturally, presidents hope to create goodwill and to receive a sympathetic hearing from journalists who are grateful for contact with the White House and, perhaps, susceptible to presidential charm.

PRESS COVERAGE OF THE PRESIDENT

In addition to the chief executive's efforts to influence the media, there is another side of this relationship we must examine: the content of the news. Ultimately, it is the written and spoken word that concerns the president. Leaks of confidential information and what is seen in the White House as superficial or biased reporting exacerbate the tensions inherent in relations between the president and the press. Presidents commonly view the press as a major obstacle to their obtaining and maintaining public support. Criticism of media coverage as being trivial and distorted and as violating confidences is a standard feature of most administrations. The White House feels that this type of reporting hinders its efforts to develop public appreciation for the president and his policies.

Leaks

After some time in office, Bill Clinton made it a rule not to say anything sensitive in a room with more than one aide. If he did, he felt, he might as well speak directly to the Associated Press.[18] Leaks bedevil most presidents. Sometimes they are potentially quite serious, as when the U.S. negotiating strategy for nuclear disarmament talks was disclosed during the Nixon administration. When the Pentagon Papers (on decision making on the war in Vietnam) were leaked to the public, President Nixon felt that there was a danger that other countries would lose confidence in our ability to keep secrets and that information on the delicate negotiations then in progress with China might also be leaked, endangering the possibility of rapprochement.[19] At other times leaks are just embarrassing—for example, when internal dissent in the administration is revealed to the public. President Johnson feared that leaks would signal what he was thinking and he would lose his freedom of action as a result.

Who leaks information? The best answer is "everybody." Presidents themselves do so, sometimes inadvertently. As Lyndon Johnson once put it: "I have enough trouble with myself. I ought not to have to put up with everybody else too."[20] Once John F. Kennedy ordered Secretary of State Dean Rusk to find out who had leaked a story on foreign policy only to discover that the culprit was the president himself.[21]

Top presidential aides may also reveal more than they intend. When a leak regarding President Reagan's willingness to compromise on his 1981 tax bill appeared in the New York Times, White House aides tracked down the source of the story and found it to be budget director David Stockman.[22] A year earlier, a leak revealing secret Central Intelligence Agency (CIA) arms shipments to Afghan rebels was attributed to the office of the president's chief national security adviser.[23] Lt. Col. Oliver North charged that members of Congress had leaked the fact that the United States had intercepted Libyan radio messages, which in turn enabled it to capture the hijackers of the *Achille Lauro* cruise liner. However, *Newsweek* reported that the source of the leak had been none other than Oliver North himself.

Most leaks, however, are deliberately planted. As one close presidential aide put it, "99 percent of all significant secrets are spilled by the principals or at their direction."[24] Presidents are included in those who purposefully leak. For example, *Newsweek* used to hold space open for the items John Kennedy would phone to his friend Benjamin Bradlee right before the magazine's deadline.[25]

There are many reasons for leaks. In particular, they may be used as trial balloons to test public or congressional reaction to ideas and proposals or to stimulate public concern about an issue. Both the Ford and Carter White Houses used this technique to test reaction to a tax surcharge on gasoline. When the reaction to these proposals turned out to be negative, both administrations denied ever contemplating such a policy. President Clinton's task force on health care reform engaged in a series of leaks regarding a wide range of health policy options.

" I HAD TO SWITCH YOUR LIE DETECTOR TEST THIS AFTERNOON FROM 3 TO 1 BECAUSE YOU'RE SCHEDULED TO LEAK SOME INFORMATION AT 2 ! "

Source: Cartoon by Wayne Stayskal (1983). From the *Chicago Tribune*. Reprinted by permission, Tribune Media Services.

At other times information is leaked to reporters who will use it to write favorable articles on a policy. Alternately, as the Clinton White House has often done, the administration may leak an exclusive story on relatively modest proposals, such as plans to renovate schools or to crack down on truants, to one news organization, thus encouraging that organization to give it added coverage as an exclusive story and forcing the competition to play catch-up and give the president two days of favorable publicity instead of only one.[26]

Diplomacy is an area in which delicate communications play an important role. Leaks are often used to send other nations nuanced signals of friendship, anger, or willingness to compromise. While sending messages to other nations, leaks provide the president with the opportunity to disavow publicly or to reinterpret what some might view as, for example, an overly "tough" stance or an unexpected change in policy. This makes it easier for these countries to respond to U.S. wishes. For example, during negotiations with the Japanese regarding restricting imports, the Reagan administration leaked a story that the talks were going badly so as to pressure Japan into moderating its position. President Clinton's national security assistant regularly leaked stories to CNN for diplomatic purposes, including using a leak to warn Iraqi leader Saddam Hussein to move his troops away from the Kuwaiti border in 1994.[27] Diplomatic leaks also have the advantage of speed. When President Bush wanted to send a message of U.S. support for Soviet President Mikhail Gorbachev during the attempted coup to remove him, he wanted to use the fastest source available for getting a message to Moscow, so he chose to leak the message to CNN.[28]

Leaks may also be used to influence personnel matters. The release of information letting a stubborn official know that the official's superiors wish him or her to leave may force a resignation and thus save the problem of firing the official, or, conversely, make the official's position a public issue, increasing the costs of such a firing. Similarly, the release of information on an appointment before it is made places presidents in an awkward position and can help ensure that they follow through on it or else prematurely deny they have such plans.

Some leaks are designed to force the president's hand on policy decisions. Officials in the Clinton administration who were hostile to welfare reform regularly leaked stories critical of the plan the administration was formulating. They also tried to tie the president's hands by leaking false stories that the president had made a decision, thus hoping to encourage him to actually make that decision to avoid being viewed as flip-flopping.[29] During the Indian-Pakistani War, President Nixon maintained a publicly neutral stance but really favored Pakistan. When this fact was leaked, there was inevitably pressure to be neutral in action as well as in rhetoric. Conversely, in the case of Lyndon Johnson, a leak that he was thinking about a decision would generally ensure that he would take no such action.

Leaks may serve a number of other functions. They may make some individuals feel important or help them gain favor with reporters. Leaks may also be used to criticize and intimidate personal or political adversaries in the White House itself or to protect and enhance reputations. In the Ford administration, White House counsel Robert Hartmann and Chief of Staff Richard Cheney often attacked each other anonymously in the press. Several members of the White House staff attacked Press Secretary Ron Nessen in an effort to persuade the president to replace him. When negotiations with North Vietnam broke down in late 1972, White House aides employed leaks to dissociate the president from Henry Kissinger, his national security assistant.

Presidents sometimes leak information for their own political purposes. The Reagan White House was able to influence the first reports on the study done on the deaths of 241 marines in Beirut in 1983. By leaking findings about lax security measures, presidential aides were able to focus press attention on security lapses rather than the criticism of the ill-defined nature of the marines' mission in Lebanon.[30]

In all these cases, government officials were using the press for their purposes, not vice versa. Although reporters may well be aware of being used, the competitive pressure of the news business makes it difficult for them to pass up an exclusive story. Nevertheless, most good reporting, even investigative reporting, does not rely heavily on leaks. Instead, reporters put together stories by bits and pieces.

It is generally fruitless to try to discover the source of a leak. The Reagan administration tried everything from lie detector tests to logging every journalist's interview on a computer, but nothing stopped the leaking it experienced. According to White House Chief of Staff Donald Regan: "In the Reagan Administration the leak was raised to the status of an art form. Everything, or nearly everything, the President and his close associates did or knew appeared in the newspapers and on the networks with the least possible delay."[31]

The Clinton White House made some progress in discouraging leaks when chief of staff Leon Panetta began trying to identify who had leaked and then retaliating by leaking a critical story to a major news outlet about the suspect.[32] Nevertheless, leaks remain common in press coverage of the president, and the incentives to leak remain as strong as ever.

Superficiality

Early in this century Woodrow Wilson complained that most reporters were "interested in the personal and trivial rather than in principles of policies."[33] Things have only gotten worse in the ensuing generations. In a background briefing in 1979, President Carter complained to reporters, "I would really like for you all as people who relay Washington events to the world to take a look at the substantive questions I have to face as a president and quit dealing almost exclusively with personalities."[34] In this section we examine the question of the superficiality of the coverage of the presidency and the reasons for it.

Today media coverage of national news in mainline media such as most newspapers and broadcast networks is characterized by brevity and simplicity. Editors do not want to bore or confuse their viewers, listeners, or readers. They often resort to the use of themes ("another example of rivalries within the White House"), symbols (a supermarket checkout line may represent inflation or an expensive haircut, losing one's democratic roots), and personification (an unemployed single mother of five) to simplify issues. Moreover, most reporting is about events, actions taken or words spoken by public figures, especially if the events are dramatic and colorful, such as ceremonies and parades. Conflicts between clearly identifiable antagonists (President Clinton versus Speaker of the House Newt Gingrich or independent counsel Kenneth Starr) are highly prized, particularly if there is something tangible at stake such as the passage of a bill or criminal charges against the president.

The amount of information transmitted under such conditions is limited. This type of news coverage is ill-equipped to deal with the ambiguities and uncertainties of most complex events and issues. Moreover, it provides little in the way of the background and contextual information that is essential for understanding political events. Although the electronic media, especially television, are the most typical source of news for Americans, they do a relatively poor job of providing information to the public. According to CBS network anchorperson Dan Rather, "You simply cannot be a well-informed citizen by just watching the news on television."[35]

Human interest stories, especially those about presidents and their families, are novel and easier for the public to relate to than are complex matters of public policy. They are always in high demand because the public likes them. Socks, the Clintons' cat, and Buddy, their dog, became overnight celebrities. Disasters and incidents of violence (shootings in schools, for example) make for excellent film presentations; they are novel, contain human drama and ample action, and can be portrayed in easily understood terms. However, the intricacies of, for example, a presidential tax proposal are not so intriguing.

Scandals involving public persons, but especially the president, receive high-priority coverage in the media, often driving out coverage of news on the president's policies. For example, on April 22, 1994, President Clinton held a press conference on imminent air strikes in Bosnia, which only CNN carried live. On the same day, First Lady Hillary Rodham Clinton held a press conference on the Whitewater investigation, which all the networks

Even the president's cat becomes the object of media attention.
Source: Copyright © 1992 Agence France-Presse Photo. Reproduced with permission.

carried. When Paula Jones charged President Clinton with sexual harass-ment (while he was governor of Arkansas), the media devoted extensive coverage to the case, yet even this attention paled in comparison to the frenzy of coverage devoted to the president's sexual relationship with a White House intern, Monica Lewinsky. No policy issue has received as much attention, especially on television, since the charges were made public.[36]

As explained in Chapters 2 and 3, coverage of presidential election cam-paigns is typically superficial, especially on television. Coverage of issues is spotty and substantive issues are usually reported in terms of their impact on politics rather than their merits. What does receive extensive coverage is the "horse race"—the campaign, as opposed to what the campaign is osten-sibly about. Stories feature conflict, make brief points, are easily under-stood (often in either/or terms), and, especially on television, have film value.[37]

Superficial news coverage is not limited to elections. Most of the White House press activity comes under the heading of the "body watch." In other words, reporters focus on the most visible layer of the president's personal and official activities and provide the public with a step-by-step account. They are interested in what the president is going to do, how his actions will affect others, how he views policies and individuals, how he presents himself, and whose stars are rising and falling, rather than in the substance of policies or the fundamental operations of the executive branch. Coverage of the consideration of President Clinton's massive health care proposal in 1993–1994 focused much more on strategy and legislative battles than on the issues of health care.[38]

Editors expect this type of coverage (which they believe will please their readers), and reporters do not want to risk missing a story. As the Washington bureau chief of *Newsweek* said: "The worst thing in the world that could happen to you is for the President of the United States to choke on a piece of meat, and for you not to be there."[39] When President Bush vomited at a state dinner in Japan, television networks had a field day, and ran the tape of the president's illness again and again.

Journalists are generally not allowed at Camp David, the presidential retreat. However, about twenty minutes before the president's helicopter lands or departs, a few photographers are allowed to sit in something akin to a duck blind about 150 yards from the helicopter pad and observe the landing and departure. They leave immediately after, without ever speaking to the president. Why do they bother? They are there for the "death watch"—to be on hand in case the president's helicopter crashes.

The emphasis of news coverage is on short-run, "instant history." Perspective on the events of the day is secondary. Thus, embarrassing items such as blunders and contradictions made by presidents and their staff are widely reported, especially if the president is low in the polls (providing a consistent theme). Similarly, major presidential addresses are often reported in terms of how the president looked and spoke, as well as the number of times the speech was interrupted by applause, as much as in terms of what was said. In the case of President Clinton, how long he spoke is also frequently mentioned because he tends to deliver long addresses.

Presidential slips of the tongue or gaffes are often blown out of all proportion. For example, in the second debate between Gerald Ford and Jimmy Carter during the 1976 presidential campaign, Ford made a slip and said that Eastern Europe was "free from Soviet domination." Everyone, including the president, knew he had misspoken. Unfortunately for Ford, however, he refused to admit his error for several days while the press had a field day speculating about his basic understanding of world politics. Similarly, when Richard Nixon described the persons "blowing up the campuses" as "bums," the press extended the category to all students, something the president had not meant. The uproar following this report can well be imagined.

In its constant search for "news," the press, especially the electronic media, is reluctant to devote repeated attention to an issue even though this might be necessary to explain it adequately to the public. As a deputy press secretary in the Carter administration said: "We have to keep sending out our message if we expect people to understand. The Washington Press corps will explain a policy once and then it will feature the politics of the issue."[40] This is one incentive for the president to meet with the non-Washington press and to address the nation directly on television or radio.

One of the causes of superficial press coverage of the presidency is the demand of news organizations for information that is new and different, personal and intimate, or revealing and unexpected. According to former ABC White House correspondent Sam Donaldson, "A clip of a convalescent Reagan waving from his window at some circus elephants is going to push an analytical piece about tax cuts off the air every time."[41] Given the emphasis on the short run and the demand for details of the president's activities, reporters face continual deadlines. There is little time for reflection, analysis, or comprehensive coverage.

A related factor contributing to the trivialization of the news is the great deal of money and personnel needed to cover presidents, including following them around the globe on official business and vacations. Because of this investment and the public's interest in the president, reporters must come up with something every day. Newsworthy happenings do not necessarily occur every day, however, so reporters either emphasize the trivial or blow events out of proportion. While covering a meeting of Western leaders on the island of Guadeloupe, Sam Donaldson faced the prospect of having nothing to report on a slow news day. Undaunted, he reported on the roasting of the pig the leaders would be eating that evening, including "an exclusive look at the oven in which the pig would be roasted."[42] Similarly, the White House press often focuses on the exact wording of an announcement in an effort to detect a change in policy, frequently finding significance where none really exists.

There are more than organizational imperatives at work in influencing coverage of the president, however. Reporters' backgrounds and personal interests also underlie the trivialization of the news. Reporters are often ill at ease with abstractions, and when they talk to each other about politics, they emphasize the specifics of the game—who will be elected, what bills will pass, what personalities the principal actors have, and who has power. The typical White House reporter lacks special background on the presidency. Moreover, the White House press frequently lacks policy expertise relevant to understanding the issues with which the president deals. Thus, its focus on politics and personalities rather than issues is not surprising.

To delve more deeply into the presidency and policy requires, not only substantial expertise, but also certain technical skills. Washington reporters in general, and White House reporters in particular, do little documentary research. They are trained to conduct interviews and transmit handouts from press secretaries and public information officials rather than to conduct research. Moreover, in-depth research demands a slower

pace and advance planning, and journalists tend to be comfortable with neither requirement.

Sometimes several factors influence coverage of the presidency at the
same time. Despite the glamour attached to investigative reporting since
the Watergate scandal, not much of it takes place. Most news organizations
are unwilling or unable to devote the time and resources necessary for
investigative work or the coordination required with other reporters and
news bureau staff to cover all leads successfully. The maxim of journalism is
to go it alone, and the incentives are generally to get the news out fast—and
first. Similarly, the slowness of the process of using the Freedom of Information Act to force the release of documents inhibits its use.

Not only does the press provide superficial coverage of the stories it
reports, but many important stories about the presidency are missed altogether because of the media's emphasis. The implementation of policy,
which is the predominant activity of the executive branch, is very poorly
covered because it is not fast-breaking news; it takes place mostly in the
field, away from the reporters' natural territory, and it requires documentary analysis and interaction with civil servants who are neither famous nor
experts at public relations. Similarly, the White House press misses most of
the flow of information and options made available to the president from
the rest of the executive branch unless a scandal is involved.

Bias

Bias is the most politically charged issue in press relations with the president. It is also an elusive concept with many dimensions. Although we typically envision bias as news coverage favoring identifiable persons, parties,
or points of view, there are more subtle and more pervasive forms of bias
that are not motivated by the goal of furthering careers or policies.

Many studies covering topics such as presidential election campaigns,
the Vietnam War, and local news conclude that the news media are not
biased *systematically* toward a particular person, party, or ideology, as measured in the amount or favorability of coverage.[43] In the same vein, after six
years as President Reagan's press secretary, Larry Speakes concluded that
the news media had generally given the administration "a fair shake" and
that "they probably gave us a longer honeymoon than we deserved."[44]

This discussion of the general neutrality of news coverage in the mass
media pertains most directly to television, newspaper, and radio reporting.
Columnists, commentators, and editorial writers usually cannot even pretend
to be neutral. Typical newspaper endorsements for presidential candidates
overwhelmingly favor Republicans (1992 was an exception).[45] Newsmagazines are generally less neutral than newspapers or television because they
often adopt a point of view in their stories.

Restraints on Bias   A number of factors help to explain why most mass-media news coverage is not biased systematically toward a particular person, party, or ideology. Reporters tend not to be partisan or strong ideologues; nor are they politically aligned or holders of strong political beliefs. Journalists are typically not intellectuals or deeply concerned with public policy. Moreover, they share journalism's professional norm of objectivity. The organizational processes of story selection and editing also provide opportunities for softening reporters' judgments. The rotation of assignments and rewards for objective news gathering are further protections against bias. Local television station owners and newspaper publishers are in a position to apply pressure regarding the presentation of the news, and, although they rarely do so, their potential to act may restrain reporters.

Self-interest also plays a role in constraining bias. Individual reporters may earn a poor reputation if others view them as biased. The television networks, newspapers, newsmagazines, and wire services, which provide most of the Washington news for newspapers, have a direct financial stake in attracting viewers and subscribers and do not want to lose their audience by appearing biased, especially when multiple versions of the same story are available to major news outlets. Slander and libel laws and the "political attack" rule, providing those personally criticized on the electronic media with an opportunity to respond, are formal limitations on bias.

Distortion   To conclude that the news contains little explicit partisan or ideological bias is not to argue that it does not distort reality in its coverage. Even under the best of conditions, some distortion is inevitable as a result of simple error or such factors as lack of careful checking of facts, the efforts of the news source to deceive, and short deadlines.

We have already seen that the news is fundamentally superficial and oversimplified and is often overblown, all of which provides the public with a distorted view of, among other things, presidential activities, statements, policies, and options. The emphasis on action and the deviant (and therefore "newsworthy" items) rather than on patterns of behavior and the implication that most stories represent more general themes of national significance contribute further to this distortion. Personalizing the news downplays structural and other impersonal factors, which may be far more important in understanding the economy, for example, than individual political actors.

Themes   We have also seen that the press prefers to frame the news in themes and story lines, which both simplify complex issues and events and provide continuity of persons, institutions, and issues. Once these themes and story lines have been established, the press tends to maintain them in subsequent coverage and stories that dovetail with the theme are more likely to be in the news. Of necessity, framing the news in this fashion emphasizes some information at the expense of other data, often determining what information is most relevant to news coverage and the context in which it is presented.

George Bush's privileged background gave rise to a greatly distorting media theme of isolation from the realities of everyday life in the United States. Thus, a story that he expressed amazement at scanners commonly used at supermarket checkout lines was widely reported as further evidence of his isolation—even though the story was incorrect. Similarly, once the theme of Bill Clinton's weak political and ethical moorings had been established, even the most outrageous tabloid claims of his past misbehavior received media attention, while stories about his policy stances frequently focused on whether or not he was displaying backbone.

Once a president is typecast by the press, his image is repeatedly reinforced by news coverage and late-night comedians and will be difficult to overcome. For example, after a stereotype of President Ford as a "bumbler" had been established, his every stumble was magnified as the press emphasized behavior that fit the mold. Ford was repeatedly forced to defend his intelligence, and many of his acts and statements were reported as efforts to "act" presidential.[46] The same thing happened to Vice President Dan Quayle, and as a result, after he misspelled "potato" during the 1992 presidential campaign, it became a widely reported story.

In 1992 the press's predominant theme regarding the presidency was that President Bush was in trouble, so it focused on information that would illustrate the theme. Bush received overwhelmingly negative coverage during the year. Indeed, the television networks' portrayal of the economy became more negative even as the economy actually improved! Similar themes were established for President Carter in 1980 and President Ford in 1976.[47]

Media Activism   Some people may equate objectivity with passivity and feel that the press should do no more than report what others present to it. This simple conveying of news is what occurs much of the time, and it is a fundamental reason for the superficiality of news coverage. If the press is passive, however, it can be more easily manipulated and even made to represent fiction as fact. Sometimes reporters feel the necessity of setting the story in a meaningful context. The construction of such a context may entail reporting what was *not* said as well as what was said; what had occurred before; and what political implications may be involved in a statement, policy, or event. More than in the past, reporters today actively and aggressively interpret stories for viewers and readers. They no longer depend on those whom they interview to set the tone of their stories.[48]

Negativity One of the most important trends of press coverage of the presidency is the increase in emphasis on the negative, although the negative stories are typically presented in a seemingly neutral manner. Seemingly "objective" reporting can be misleading, however, as the following excerpt from Jimmy Carter's diary regarding a visit to Panama in 1978 illustrates:

> I told the Army troops that I was in the Navy for eleven years, and they booed. I told them that we depended on the Army to keep the Canal open, and they cheered. Later, the news reports said that there were boos and cheers during my speech.[49]

Similarly, an emphasis on scandals in an administration, even if the stories are presented in an even-handed manner, rarely helps the White House. (The coverage of the Monica Lewinsky story seems to be an exception, as President Clinton benefited, at least for most of 1998, from a backlash against media intrusiveness into his private life.)

In the 1980 election campaign, the press portrayed President Carter as mean and Ronald Reagan as imprecise rather than Carter as precise and Reagan as nice. The emphasis, in other words, was on the candidates' negative qualities. In recent campaigns presidential candidates have received more bad news than good news—a notable change from the past.[50] President Clinton has received mostly negative coverage during his tenure in office, with a ratio of negative to positive comments on network television of about two to one.[51]

Some observers feel that the press is biased against whomever holds office at the moment and that reporters want to expose them in the media. Reporters, they argue, hold disparaging views of most politicians and public officials, whom they find self-serving, dishonest, incompetent, hypocritical, and preoccupied with reelection. Thus, it is not surprising that, as part of the "watchdog" function of the press, journalists see a need to expose and debunk them. This orientation to analytical coverage may be characterized as neither liberal nor conservative, but reformist.[52]

White House reporters are always looking to expose conflicts of interest and other shady behavior of public officials. Moreover, many of their inquiries revolve around the question of whether the official is up to the job. Reporters who are confined in the White House all day may attempt to make up for their lack of investigative reporting with sarcastic and accusatory questioning. Moreover, the desire to keep the public interested and the need for continuous coverage may create in the press a subconscious bias against the presidency that leads to critical stories.

On the other hand, one could argue that the press is biased *toward* the White House. Reporters' general respect for the presidency may be transferred to individual presidents. Framed at a respectful distance by the television camera, the president is typically portrayed with an aura of dignity and as working in a context of rationality and coherence on activities benefiting the public. The press's word selection often reflects this orientation as well. It has only been in recent years that journalists stopped following conventions that protected politicians and public officials from revelations of private misconduct.

The White House enjoys a great deal of positive coverage in newspapers, magazines, and network news. The most favorable coverage comes in the first year of a president's term, before there is a record to criticize or critics for reporters to interview. Coverage focuses on human interest stories of the president and on his appointees and their personalities, goals, and plans. The president is pictured in a positive light as a policy maker dealing with problems. Controversies over solutions typically arise later.[53] President Clinton was not as fortunate in his first year because of especially active congressional critics; his own partisans, who clamored for policies they had been denied during twelve years of Republican presidencies; an inability of the White House to keep its internal dissensions to itself; and the poor performance of the White House public relations staff.

Ultimately, the issue of bias may hang on questions of nuance. As public affairs analyst and former presidential press secretary Bill Moyers put it, "Depending on who is looking and writing, the White House is brisk or brusque, assured or arrogant, casual or sloppy, frank or brutal, warm or corny, cautious or timid, compassionate or condescending, reserved or callous."[54] Given the limitations of language and the lack of agreement on the exact nature of reality, it is almost impossible for the media to please everyone.

MEDIA EFFECTS

The most significant question about the substance of media coverage, of course, is about the impact it has on public opinion. Most studies on media effects have focused on attitude changes, especially in voting for presidential candidates, and have typically found little or no evidence of influence. Reinforcement of existing attitudes and opinions was said to be the strongest effect of the media.[55] In the words of one expert: "Most media stories are promptly forgotten. Stories that become part of an individual's fund of knowledge tend to reinforce existing beliefs and feelings. Acquisition of new knowledge or changes in attitude are the exception rather than the rule."[56] There are other ways to analyze media effects, however.

Media Priming

The concept of media priming is premised on the fact that most of the time the cognitive burdens are too great for people to reach judgments or decisions based on comprehensive, integrated information. Instead, the public takes short cuts or uses cues by relying heavily on the mass media.

The media are more likely to influence perceptions than attitudes. The press can influence the perceptions of what public figures stand for and what their personalities are like, what issues are important, and what is at stake. If the media raise certain issues or personal characteristics to prominence, the significance of attitudes that people already hold may change and thus alter their evaluations of, say, presidential performance, without their attitudes themselves changing. In other words, the media can influence the criteria by which the president is judged.

People with only marginal concern for politics may be especially susceptible to the impact of the media because they have few alternative sources of information and less-developed political allegiances. Thus, they have fewer strongly held attitudes to overcome. Similarly, coverage of new issues that are removed from the experiences of people and their political convictions is more likely to influence public opinion than coverage of continuing issues.

Setting the Public's Agenda

The public's familiarity with political matters is closely related to the attention they receive in the mass media,[57] especially in foreign affairs. The media also have a strong influence on the issues the public views as important.[58] "Many people readily adopt the media's agenda of importance, often without being aware of it."[59] Moreover, when the media cover events, politicians comment on them and take action, reinforcing the perceived importance of these events and ensuring more public attention to them.

During the 1979–1980 Iranian hostage crisis, in which several dozen Americans were held hostage, ABC originated a nightly program entitled *America Held Hostage,* Walter Cronkite provided a "countdown" of the number of days of the crisis at the end of each evening's news on CBS television, countless feature stories on the hostages and their families were reported in all the media, and the press gave complete coverage to "demonstrations" held in front of the U.S. embassy in Tehran (often artificially created by demonstrators for consumption by Americans). This crisis dominated American politics for more than a year and gave President Carter's approval rating a tremendous, albeit short-term, boost. In the longer term, however, the coverage destroyed his leadership image. Conversely, when the American ship *Pueblo* was captured by North Korea, there were many more American captives and they were held for almost as long as the hostages in Tehran, but there were also no television cameras and few reporters to cover the situation. Thus, the incident played a much smaller role in American politics.

Evaluations of the President

Media coverage of issues also increases their importance in the public's evaluation of political figures such as the president. In the words of a leading authority on the impact of television news on public opinion: "The themes and issues that are repeated in television news coverage become the priorities of viewers. Issues and events highlighted by television news become especially influential as criteria for evaluating public officials."[60] There is also evidence that presidential approval is strongly affected by elite opinion, as brought to the public's attention in the mass media.[61]

When the media began covering the Iran-Contra affair, Ronald Reagan's public approval took an immediate and severe dip as the public applied new criteria of evaluation.[62] The role of assessments of George Bush's economic performance in overall evaluations of him decreased substantially after the Gulf War began, and it is reasonable to conclude that media priming effects caused a shift of attention to his performance on war-related criteria.[63]

When the press gave substantial coverage to President Ford's misstatement about Soviet domination of Eastern Europe, this coverage had an impact on the public. Polls show that most people did not realize the president had made an error until they were told so by the press. Afterwards, pro-Ford evaluations of the debate declined noticeably as voters' concerns for competence in foreign policy making became salient.[64] A somewhat similar switch occurred after the first debate between Walter Mondale and Ronald Reagan in 1984.[65]

The public's information on and criteria for evaluating presidential candidates parallel what is presented in the media.[66] However, the press probably has the greatest effect on public perceptions of individuals and issues between election campaigns, when people are less likely to activate their partisan defenses. The prominent coverage of Gerald Ford's alleged physical clumsiness was naturally translated into suggestions of mental ineptitude. In the president's own words:

> Every time I stumbled or bumped my head or fell in the snow, reporters zeroed in on that to the exclusion of almost everything else. The news coverage was harmful, but even more damaging was the fact that Johnny Carson and Chevy Chase used my "missteps" for their jokes. Their antics—and I'll admit that I laughed at them myself—helped create the public perception of me as a stumbler. And that wasn't funny.[67]

Once such an image is established in the mass media, it is very difficult to change, as reporters continue to emphasize behavior that is consistent with their previously established themes.

Moreover, the extraordinary attention that the press devotes to presidents magnifies their flaws. Even completely unsubstantiated charges against them may make the news because of their prominence (see the Hot-Button Issue box). Familiarity may not breed contempt, but it certainly may diminish the aura of grandeur around the chief executive.

Limiting the President's Options

If the media affect mass attitudes about the importance of issues and president's handling of them, the president has a strong incentive to address

---

☼ HOT- BUTTON ISSUE

The Rush to Judgment

In the past, criticism of presidents was restrained by the reluctance of many editors to publish analyses sharply divergent from the president's position without direct confirmation from an authoritative source who would be willing to go on the record in opposition to the president. During the famous investigation of the Watergate scandal, the *Washington Post* verified all information attributed to an unnamed source with at least one other independent source. It also did not print information from other media outlets unless its reporters could independently verify that information.[68] Things have changed, however.

When the story broke about charges that President Clinton had sexual relations with a young White House intern named Monica Lewinsky, virtually all elements of the mass media went into a feeding frenzy,[69] relying as much on analysis, opinion, and speculation as on confirmed facts. Even the most prominent news outlets carried unsubstantiated reports about charges that had not received independent verification by those carrying the story. If another news outlet carried a charge, it was soon picked up by most of the rest, which did not want to be scooped. For example, unsubstantiated charges that Ms. Lewinsky had a dress stained with the president's semen were widely reported, as was the charge that members of the Secret Service had found the president and Ms. Lewinsky in a compromising position. Such reporting helped sensationalize the story, keeping it alive and undermining the president's efforts to focus the public's attention on matters of public policy.

those issues—to put them on his agenda. Analysts B. Dan Wood and Jeffrey S. Peake, in a surprising finding, concluded that even in foreign policy it is the media that influences the president's agenda rather than the other way around.[70] Former secretary of state James Baker argued that media coverage of issues creates powerful new imperatives for prompt action, making it more difficult for the president to selectively engage in world affairs.[71] This pressure may force presidents to state policies or send troops when they would prefer to let situations develop or encourage other nations to deal with a problem. Bill Clinton complained that television coverage of Bosnia was "trying to force me to get America into a war."[72]

Colin Powell recalled, "The world had a dozen other running sores that fall [1992], but television hovered over Somalia and wrenched our hearts, night after night, with images of people starving to death before our eyes." Scenes of children starving in Somalia pressured the United States to send in armed forces to maintain peace and deliver food to the hungry. Things changed after eighteen soldiers were killed in Somalia, however. When scenes of an American soldier being dragged through the streets of Mogadishu were shown on television, Powell reflected, "We had been drawn into this place by television images, now we were being repelled by them." Television coverage now forced President Clinton to begin a troop withdrawal.[73]

Television coverage may limit the president's options even during a crisis. Pictures of Iraqi troops retreating from Kuwait on the "Highway of Death" created an impression of a bloodbath and thus influenced President Bush's decision to end the Gulf War. Bush himself described the "undesirable public and political baggage [that came from] all those scenes of carnage" appearing on television.[74] Similarly, during the 1990 invasion of Panama, the press noticed that a radio tower was standing near the center of Panama City. Reports of the tower led policy makers to order its destruction, although it had no value to the enemy.[75]

Undermining the President

Presidents need public understanding of the difficulty of their job and the nature of the problems they face. The role of the press here can be critical. Watching television news seems to do little to inform viewers about public affairs; reading the printed media is more useful. This may be because reading requires more active cognitive processing of information than watching television and because more information is presented in the newspapers.

We have seen that press coverage of the president is often superficial, oversimplified, and overblown, thus providing the public a distorted picture of White House activities. This trivialization of the news drowns out the coverage of more important matters, often leaving the public ill-informed about matters with which the president must deal (ranging from the negotiations over international trade to funding Social Security benefits). The underlying problems, which the president must confront, may be largely ignored. The preoccupation of the press with personality, drama, and the results of policies does little to help the public appreciate the complexity of presidential decision making, the trade-offs involved in policy choices, and the broad trends outside the president's control. Instead, illustrations of international conflict—scenes of combat or demonstrations, for example— may become the essence of the issue in the public's mind.

In Chapter 4 we saw that the president's access to the media is at least a potential advantage in influencing public opinion. However, the president has to compete with other media priorities while attempting to lead the public. The television networks created distractions during President Clinton's 1997 State of the Union message when they delivered the news of the verdict in the civil suit against O.J. Simpson, and the front page of the *Washington Post* the next day led with the story on Simpson, not the story on the president.

Press focus on the president has disadvantages as well. It inevitably leaves the impression that the president *is* the federal government and is crucial to our prosperity and happiness. This naturally encourages the public to focus its expectations on the White House. Another problem arises from the national frame of reference provided by a truly mass media and the media's penchant for linking coverage of even small matters with responses from the president or presidential spokespersons.

Commentary following presidential speeches and press conferences may influence what viewers remember and may affect their opinions.[76] Although the impact of commentary on presidential addresses and press conferences is unclear, it is probably safe to argue that it is a constraint on the president's ability to lead public opinion. In the words of observers David L. Paletz and Robert M. Entman:

> Critical instant analysis undermines presidential authority by transforming him from presentor to protagonist. . . . Credible, familiar, apparently disinterested newsmen and—women—experts too, usually agreeing with each other, comment on the self-interested performance of a politician. Usually the president's rhetoric is deflated, the mood he has striven to create dissipated.[77]

The increasing negativism of news coverage of the presidents parallels the increasingly low opinions voters have of them. The media impugns the motives of presidents and presidential candidates and portrays them as playing a "game" in which strategy and maneuvers, rather than the substance of public policy, are the crucial elements. This fosters public cynicism and encourages citizens to view presidents and other political leaders in negative terms.[78]

Limits on Media Effects

While reviewing evidence of the impact of the media on public opinion concerning the president, it is important to keep in mind the significant limitations on this influence. Characteristics of readers and viewers—including short attention spans, lack of reading ability, selective perception (especially for those who have well-developed political views), general lack of interest in politics, lack of attentiveness to the media when exposed to them, and forgetfulness—limit the impact of the media. Another limitation depends on the ability of people to reject or ignore evaluations (implicit or explicit) in stories.[79]

The nature of the news message also affects the impact of the media, and the factors constraining its influence are many: the great volume of information available in the news; the limited time available in which to absorb it (especially for television viewers); the superficial coverage of people, events, and policies; the presentation of the news on television and in most newspapers in disconnected snippets; and the lack of guidance through the complexities of politics. As a result, people often do not understand the news and actually learn little in the way of specifics from it. The lack of credibility of news sources among some readers and viewers further limits the impact of the media.

Visuals may also distract from verbal messages. For example, Leslie Stahl of *CBS News* did a long report on Ronald Reagan during the 1984 presidential campaign in which she criticized him for deceiving the American people with public relations tactics. Instead of the complaints she expected from the White House, however, she received thanks. Reagan's press aides appreciated the pictures of the president campaigning and were not concerned with the journalist's scathing remarks.[80]

CONCLUSION

The mass media play a prominent role in the public presidency, providing the public with most of its information about the White House and mediating the president's communications with constituents. Presidents need the press in order to reach the public, and relations with the press are an important complement to the chief executive's efforts at leading public opinion. Through attempts to coordinate news, press conferences, and the provision of a wide range of services for the press, the White House tries to influence its portrayal in the news.

The president's press relations pose many obstacles to efforts to obtain and maintain public support. Although it is probably not true that press coverage of the White House is biased along partisan or ideological lines or toward or against a particular president, it frequently presents a distorted picture to the public and fails to impart an appropriate perspective from which to view and evaluate complex events. Moreover, presidents are continuously harassed by leaks to the press and faced with superficial, oversimplified coverage that devotes little attention to substantive discussions of policies and often focuses on trivial matters. This type of reporting undoubtedly affects public perceptions of the president, usually in a negative way. It is no wonder that chief executives generally see the press as a hindrance to their efforts to develop appreciation for their performance and policies in the public.

It is clear that in relation to the press, presidents are facilitators rather than directors. They engage in a constant struggle with the press and cannot depend on it to stress what they feel is most important about their administration or provide favorable coverage in the stories it produces. Presidents vary in their success in using the media to promote their goals, but all are limited in doing so by the nature and independence of this "fourth branch of government."

Before ending this chapter, we feel it is important to put the subject in perspective. Americans benefit greatly from a free press, a fact that should not be forgotten as we examine the media's flaws. The same press that provides superficial coverage of the presidency also alerts people to abuses of authority and attempts to mislead public opinion. Moreover, it is much less biased than the heavily partisan newspapers that were typical early in the nation's history. Clearly, the press is an essential pillar in the structure of a free society.

Moreover, perhaps the fundamental reason that press coverage is much less than its critics would like it to be is that it must appeal to the general public. If the public, or a sizable segment thereof, demands more of the mass media, it undoubtedly will receive better coverage. In short, although mass-media coverage of the presidency is often poor, it could be much worse and it is probably more or less what the public desires. Thus, the media reflect, as well as influence, American society.

DISCUSSION QUESTIONS

1. It is common to criticize the media for providing the American people with superficial coverage of presidents and their policies. What should the balance be between "hard news" on public policy and human inter-

est stories such as scandals and personal conflicts? Can the media educate a public that prefers superficial coverage?

2. Has the media been biased in covering the various charges of misdeed that that have been levied against President Clinton? How can we identify bias when we see it?

3. Journalists have become more active in interpreting stories for their viewers and readers rather than depending on those they interview to set the tone for their stories. Is the public better served by this approach to journalism?

WEB EXERCISES

1. Read some White House press releases and the president's press secretary's briefing for reporters. Notice the give and take between the press secretary and the journalists. You can also subscribe and have the White House send you these releases and briefings every day. Go to <http://www.whitehouse.gov/WH/html/briefroom.html>.

2. The Pew Center for the People and the Press regularly surveys people about which news events they follow most closely. Examine the list of stories since the mid-1980s. Which type of stories do people follow most closely? How much interest do people have in the *typical* issue with which the president deals? Go to <http://www.people-press.org/database.htm>.

SELECTED READING

Braestrup, Peter. *Big Story*. Garden City, N.Y.: Anchor, 1978.

Edwards, George C., III. *The Public Presidency*. New York: St. Martin's, 1983.

Grossman, Michael Baruch, and Martha Joynt Kumar. *Portraying the President: The White House and the News Media*. Baltimore: Johns Hopkins University Press, 1981.

Hallin, Daniel C. "The Media, the War in Vietnam, and Political Support." *Journal of Politics* 46 (February 1984): 2–24.

Iyengar, Shanto. *Is Anyone Responsible?* Chicago: University of Chicago Press, 1991.

Iyengar, Shanto, and Donald R. Kinder. *News That Matters*. Chicago: University of Chicago Press, 1987.

Kerbel, Matthew Robert. *Edited for Television*. Boulder, Colo.: Westview, 1994.

Krosnick, Jon A., and Laura A. Brannon. "The Impact of the Gulf War on the Ingredients of Presidential Evaluations: Multidimensional Effects of

Political Involvement." *American Political Science Review* 87 (December 1993): 963–975.

Krosnick, Jon A., and Donald R. Kinder. "Altering the Foundations of Support for the President through Priming." *American Political Science Review* 84 (June 1990): 497–512.

Kurtz, Howard. *Spin Cycle.* New York: Free Press, 1998.

Patterson, Thomas E. *Out of Order.* New York: Knopf, 1993.

Robinson, Michael Jay, and Margaret A. Sheehan. *Over the Wire and on TV: CBS and UPI in Campaign '80.* New York: Russell Sage Foundation, 1983.

Steeper, Frederick T. "Public Response to Gerald Ford's Statements on Eastern Europe in the Second Debate." In George F. Bishop, Robert G. Meadow, and Marilyn Jackson-Beeck, eds., *The Presidential Debates: Media, Electoral, and Public Perspectives.* New York: Praeger, 1978.

Notes

1. Martha Joynt Kumar, "The White House Beat at the Century Mark," *Press/Politics* 2 (Summer 1997): 10–30.
2. Doris A. Graber, *Mass Media and American Politics,* 5th ed. (Washington, D.C.: Congressional Quarterly Press, 1993), pp. 270–272; Elmer E. Cornwell, Jr., "Presidential News: The Expanding Public Image," *Journalism Quarterly* 36 (Summer 1959): 275–283; Alan P. Balutis, "The Presidency and the Press: The Expanding Presidential Image," *Presidential Studies Quarterly* 7 (Fall 1977): 244–251; *Media Monitor,* July/August 1994, pp. 1–2; *Media Monitor,* September/October 1994, pp. 1–2; *Media Monitor,* May/June 1995, pp. 1–2.
3. Richard Harris, "The Presidency and the Press," *New Yorker,* October 1, 1973, p. 122; Dom Bonafede, "Powell and the Press: A New Mood in the White House," *National Journal,* June 25, 1977, p. 981.
4. Quoted in Harris, "The Presidency and the Press," p. 122; and Peter Forbath and Carey Winfrey, *The Adversaries: The President and the Press* (Cleveland: Regal Books, 1974), p. 5.
5. Quoted in Joseph P. Berry, Jr., *John F. Kennedy and the Media: The First Television President* (Lanham, Md., 1987), p. 66.
6. Quoted in Jann S. Wenner and William Greider, "President Clinton," *Rolling Stone,* December 9, 1993, p. 81.
7. Marlin Fitzwater, *Call the Briefing* (New York: Times Books, 1995), p. 4.
8. Quoted in "Press Secretaries Explore White House News Strategies," *APIP Report* 1 (January 1991), p. 2.
9. Quoted in Bob Woodward, *The Agenda: Inside the Clinton White House* (New York: Simon and Schuster, 1994), p. 313.
10. Graber, *Mass Media and American Politics,* pp. 286–287.
11. Michael Baruch Grossman and Martha Joynt Kumar, *Portraying the President: The White House and the News Media* (Baltimore: Johns Hopkins University Press, 1981), pp. 59–60, 63–64, 280–281.
12. Mark J. Rozell, "Presidential Image-Makers on the Limits of Spin Control," *Presidential Studies Quarterly* 25 (Winter 1995): 77.
13. Interview by author with Peter Jennings, New York, October 18, 1987.
14. Paul Brace and Barbara Hinckley, *Follow the Leader: Opinion Polls and the Modern Presidents* (New York: Basic Books, 1992), chap. 3.
15. Dom Bonafede, "The Washington Press: It Magnifies the President's Flaws and Blemishes," *National Journal,* May 1, 1982, pp. 267–271.
16. Graber, *Mass Media and American Politics,* p. 281.
17. Quoted in David L. Paletz and Robert M. Entman, *Media-Power-Politics* (New York: Free Press, 1981), pp. 55–56.

18. Howard Kurtz, *Spin Cycle* (New York: Free Press, 1998), p. 134.
19. William Safire, *Before the Fall: An Inside View of the Pre-Watergate White House* (New York: Doubleday, 1975), p. 373; Henry Kissinger, *Years of Upheaval* (Boston: Little, Brown, 1981), p. 116.
20. Lyndon Johnson quoted in George Christian, *The President Steps Down: A Personal Memoir of the Transfer of Power* (New York: Macmillan, 1970), p. 203.
21. Gerald S. Strober and Deborah H. Strober, *"Let Us Begin Anew"* (New York: HarperCollins, 1993), p. 156.
22. "The U.S. vs. William Colby," *Newsweek*, September 28, 1981, p. 30.
23. "The Tattletale White House," *Newsweek*, February 25, 1980, p. 21.
24. Robert T. Hartmann, *Palace Politics: An Inside Account of the Ford Years* (New York: McGraw-Hill, 1980), p. 38.
25. William J. Lanouette, "The Washington Press Corps: Is It All That Powerful?" *National Journal*, June 2, 1979, p. 898.
26. Kurtz, *Spin Cycle*, p. 92.
27. "Power Couple," *Newsweek*, October 31, 1994, p. 6.
28. James A. Baker III, *The Politics of Diplomacy* (New York: Putnam, 1995), p. 520; see also pp. 34, 154.
29. Dick Morris, *Behind the Oval Office* (New York: Random House, 1997), pp. 101–102.
30. Lou Cannon, *President Reagan: The Role of a Lifetime* (New York: Simon and Schuster, 1991), p. 452.
31. Donald T. Regan, *For the Record: From Wall Street to Washington* (San Diego, Calif.: Harcourt Brace Jovanovich, 1988), p. xiv.
32. Morris, *Behind the Oval Office*, p. 122.
33. Woodrow Wilson quoted in William Small, *To Kill a Messenger: Television News and the Real World* (New York: Hastings, 1970), p. 221.
34. President Carter, quoted in Michael Baruch Grossman and Martha Joynt Kumar, "Carter, Reagan, and the Media: Have the Rules Really Changed or the Poles of the Spectrum of Success?" (paper presented at the Annual Meeting of the American Political Science Association, New York, September 3–6, 1981), p. 8.
35. Dan Rather, quoted in Hoyt Purvis, ed., *The Presidency and the Press* (Austin, Tex.: Lyndon B. Johnson School of Public Affairs, 1976), p. 56.
36. See *Media Monitor*, May/June 1998 and June/July 1998.
37. See George C. Edwards III, *The Public Presidency* (New York: St. Martin's, 1983), p. 149, and sources cited therein. See also Bruce Buchanan, *Electing a President* (Austin: University of Texas Press, 1991), chap. 4; Graber, *Mass Media and American Politics*, pp. 210–211; Thomas E. Patterson, "The Press and Its Missed Assignment," in Michael Nelson, ed., *Elections of 1988* (Washington, D.C.: Congressional Quarterly Press, 1989); Thomas E. Patterson, *Out of Order* (New York: Knopf, 1993), chaps. 2, 4; Matthew Robert Kerbel, *Edited for Television* (Boulder, Colo.: Westview, 1994), chaps. 2, 4; Guido Stempel and John Windhauser, ed., *The Media in the 1984 and 1988 Presidential Campaigns* (Westport, Conn.: Greenwood Press, 1991); S. Robert Lichter and Richard E. Noyes, *Good Intentions Make Bad News*, 2nd ed. (Lanham, Md.: Rowman and Littlefield, 1996), chaps. 4, 8, postscript.
38. Kathleen Hall Jamieson and Joseph N. Capella, "The Role of the Press in the Health Care Reform Debate of 1993–1994," in Doris Graber, Denis McQuail, and Pippa Norris, eds., *The Politics of News, The News of Politics* (Washington, D.C.: Congressional Quarterly Press, 1998), pp. 118–119.
39. Quoted in Grossman and Kumar, *Portraying the President*, p. 43.
40. Quoted in Grossman and Kumar, *Portraying the President*, p. 26.
41. Sam Donaldson, quoted in "Washington Press Corps," *Newsweek*, May 25, 1981, p. 90.
42. Sam Donaldson, *Hold On, Mr. President* (New York: Random House, 1987), pp. 196–197.
43. See Edwards, *The Public Presidency*, p. 156, and sources cited therein.
44. Larry Speakes, quoted in Eleanor Randolph, "Speakes Aims Final Salvos at White House Practices," *Washington Post*, January 31, 1987, p. A3.
45. John P. Robinson, "The Press as King-Maker: What Surveys from Last Five Campaigns Show," *Journalism Quarterly* 51 (Winter 1974): 587–594, 606.
46. See Mark J. Rozell, *The Press and the Ford Presidency* (Ann Arbor: University of Michigan Press, 1992).

47. Patterson, *Out of Order*, chap. 3; Kerbel, *Edited for Television*, pp. 60–64, 88; Lichter and Noyes, *Good Intentions Make Bad News*, chaps. 6–7.

48. Patterson, *Out of Order*, pp. 113–115; Kerbel, *Edited for Television*, pp. 111–112; Kevin G. Barnhurst and Catherine A. Steele, "Image-Bite News: The Visual Coverage of Elections on U.S. Television, 1968–1992," *Press/Politics* 2, no. 1 (1997): 40–58, Lichter and Noyes, *Good Intentions Make Bad News*, pp. 116–126.

49. Jimmy Carter, *Keeping Faith: Memoirs of a President* (New York: Bantam, 1982), pp. 179–180.

50. Patterson, *Out of Order*, pp. 3–27; "Clinton's the One," *Media Monitor* 6 (November 1992): 3–5; Lichter and Noyes, *Good Intentions Make Bad News*, chaps. 6–7, esp. pp. 288–299.

51. *Media Monitor*, May/June 1995, pp. 2–5; Thomas E. Patterson, "Legitimate Beef: The Presidency and a Carnivorous Press," *Media Studies Journal* 8 (Spring 1994): 21–26. However, compare Andras Szanto, "In Our Opinion . . . : Editorial Page Views of Clinton's First Year," *Media Studies Journal* 8 (Spring 1994): 97–105; Lichter and Noyes, *Good Intentions Make Bad News*, p. 214.

52. See Edward Jay Epstein, *News from Nowhere: Television and the News* (New York: Vintage, 1973), pp. 215–220; Herbert J. Gans, *Deciding What's News* (New York: Vintage, 1979), pp. 68–69, 187; Stephen Hess, *The Washington Reporters* (Washington, D.C.: Brookings Institution, 1981), p. 88; Patterson, *Out of Order*, chap. 2; and Kerbel, *Edited for Television*, p. 116.

53. Grossman and Kumar, *Portraying the President*, pp. 255–259, 270–271, 274–279; Grossman and Kumar, "Carter, Reagan, and the Media," p. 13; Hess, *The Washington Reporters*, p. 98.

54. Bill D. Moyers, "The Press and Government: Who's Telling the Truth?" in Warren K. Agee, ed., *Mass Media in a Free Society* (Lawrence: University Press of Kansas, 1969), p. 19.

55. For an overview, see Cliff Zukin, "Mass Communication and Public Opinion," in Dan D. Nimmo and Keith R. Sanders, eds., *Handbook of Political Communication* (Beverly Hills, Calif.: Sage, 1981), pp. 359–390. See also Diana C. Mutz and Joe Soss, "Reading Public Opinion: The Influence of News Coverage on Perceptions of Public Sentiment," *Public Opinion Quarterly* 61 (Fall 1997): 431–451. However, compare Russell J. Dalton, Paul A. Beck, and Robert Huckfeldt, "Partisan Cues and the Media: Information Flows in the 1992 Presidential Election," *American Political Science Review* 92 (March 1980): 111–126.

56. Graber, *Mass Media and American Politics*, pp. 194–195.

57. Benjamin I. Page and Robert Y. Shapiro, *The Rational Public* (Chicago: University of Chicago Press, 1992), pp. 12–13.

58. Shanto Iyengar, Mark D. Peters, and Donald R. Kinder, "Experimental Demonstrations of the 'Not-So-Minimal' Consequences of Television News Programs," *American Political Science Review* 76 (December 1982): 848–858; James P. Winter and Chaim H. Eyal, "Agenda-Setting for the Civil Rights Issue," *Public Opinion Quarterly* 45 (Fall 1981): 376–383; Michael Bruce MacKuen and Steven Lane Coombs, *More Than News* (Beverly Hills, Calif.: Sage 1981), chaps. 3–4; Fay Lomax Cook, Tom R. Tyler, and Edward G. Goetz, "Media and Agenda-Setting: Effects on the Public, Interest Group Leaders, Policy Makers, and Policy," *Public Opinion Quarterly* 47 (Spring 1983): 16–35; David L. Portess and Maxwell McCombs, eds., *Agenda Setting: Readings on Media, Public Opinion, and Policymaking* (Hillsdale, N.Y.: Lawrence Erlbaum Associates, 1991); Doris A. Graber, "Agenda-Setting: Are There Women's Perspectives?" in *Women and the News*, ed. Laurily Epstein (New York: Hastings House, 1978), pp. 15–37; James W. Dearing and Everett M. Rogers, *Agenda Setting* (Thousand Oaks, Calif.: Sage, 1996); William Gonzenbach, *The Media, the President, and Public Opinion: A Longitudinal Analysis of the Drug Issue, 1984–1991* (Mahwah, N.J.: Lawrence Erlbaum Associates, 1996); Maxwell McCombs and George Estrada, "The News Media and the Pictures in Our Heads," in Shanto Iyengar and Richard Reeves, eds., *Do the Media Govern? Politicians, Voters, and Reporters in America* (Thousand Oaks, Calif.: Sage, 1997); Maxwell McCombs, and Donald Shaw, "The Evolution of Agenda Setting Research: Twenty-five Years in the Marketplace of Ideas," *Journal of Communication* 43, no. 2 (1993): 58–67.

59. Graber, *Mass Media and American Politics*, p. 201.

60. Shanto Iyengar, *Is Anyone Responsible?* (Chicago: University of Chicago Press, 1991), p. 2. See also Iyengar, Peters, and Kinder, "Experimental Demonstrations of the 'Not-So-Minimal' Consequences of Television News Programs"; and Larry M. Bartels, "Messages Received: The Political Impact of Media Exposure," *American Political Science Review* 87 (June 1993): 267–285.

61. Richard A. Brody, *Assessing the President* (Stanford, Calif.: Stanford University Press, 1991).

62. Jon A. Krosnick and Donald R. Kinder, "Altering the Foundations of Support for the President through Priming," *American Political Science Review* 84 (June 1990): 497–512; Iyengar, *Is Anyone Responsible?* chap. 8.

63. Jon A. Krosnick and Laura A. Brannon, "The Impact of the Gulf War on the Ingredients of Presidential Evaluations: Multidimensional Effects of Political Involvement," *American Political Science Review* 87 (December 1993): 963–975. See also Shanto Iyengar and Adam Simon, "News Coverage of the Gulf Crisis and Public Opinion," in W. Lance Bennett and David L. Paletz, eds., *Taken by Storm* (Chicago: University of Chicago Press, 1994).

64. Frederick T. Steeper, "Public Response to Gerald Ford's Statements on Eastern Europe in the Second Debate," in George F. Bishop, Robert G. Meadow, and Marilyn Jackson-Beeck, eds., *The Presidential Debates: Media, Electoral, and Public Perspectives* (New York: Praeger, 1978), pp. 81–101.

65. Michael J. Robinson, "News Media Myths and Realities," in Kay Lehman Schlozman, ed., *Elections in America* (Boston: Allen and Unwin, 1987), p. 149.

66. Thomas E. Patterson, *The Mass Media Election: How Americans Choose Their President* (New York: Praeger, 1980), pp. 84–86, 98–100, 105, chap. 2; Doris A. Graber, "Personal Qualities in Presidential Images: The Contribution of the Press," *Midwest Journal of Political Science* 16 (February 1972): 295; Graber, *Mass Media and American Politics*, pp. 257–260.

67. Gerald R. Ford, *A Time to Heal: The Autobiography of Gerald R. Ford* (New York: Harper and Row, 1979), p. 289; see also pp. 343–344.

68. Katherine Graham, *Personal History* (New York: Vintage, 1998).

69. See, for example, *Media Monitor*, June/July 1998.

70. B. Dan Wood and Jeffrey S. Peake, "The Dynamics of Foreign Policy Agenda Setting," *American Political Science Review* 92 (March 1998): 173–184.

71. Baker, *Politics of Diplomacy*, p. 103.

72. Quoted in Morris, *Behind the Oval Office*, pp. 197, 245.

73. Colin Powell, *My American Journey* (New York: Ballentine, 1995), pp. 550, 573.

74. Quoted in Powell, *My American Journey*, p. 507.

75. Powell, *My American Journey*, p. 418.

76. Dwight F. Davis, Lynda Lee Kaid, and Donald L. Singleton, "Information Effects of Political Commentary," *Experimental Study of Politics* 6 (June 1977): 45–68; Lynda Lee Kaid, Donald L. Singleton, and Dwight F. Davis, "Instant Analysis of Televised Political Addresses: The Speaker versus the Commentator," in Brent D. Ruben, ed., *Communication Yearbook I* (New Brunswick, N.J.: Transaction Books, 1977), pp. 453–464; John Havick, "The Impact of a Televised State of the Union Message and the Instant Analysis: An Experiment" (unpublished paper, Georgia Institute of Technology, 1980).

77. Paletz and Entman, *Media-Power-Politics*, p. 70.

78. Patterson, *Out of Order*, p. 22, chap. 2.

79. Doris A. Graber, *Processing the News*, 2nd ed. (New York: Longman), pp. 90–93.

80. Interview by author with Leslie Stahl, West Point, N.Y., 1986.

6

THE PRESIDENT'S OFFICE

THE MANY AND VARIED TASKS EXPECTED *of contemporary presidents are too complex for any one person to perform. Presidents thus need help in making, promoting, and implementing their decisions. They need help in attending to the symbolic and ceremonial functions of the office. They need help in articulating their beliefs, communicating their policy, and discerning and responding to public moods, opinions, and expectations.*

The executive departments and agencies were obviously intended to provide such help, but they alone have not been sufficient. Their interests, needs, and ongoing responsibilities have not been synonymous with the president's all the time—or even most of the time. Besides, they serve a number of masters. In addition to the chief executive, they must look to Congress for their programs and budgets and to their clientele for policy requests and political support. With an increasing number of issues overlapping departmental jurisdictions and an increasing number of matters requiring presidential attention, presidents need their own advisory bodies and institutional structures for assistance.

They need them for three principal reasons: to obtain information on people and policies; to maintain linkage to the constituencies, within and outside the government, with whom they must interact; and to ensure that their priorities are clear, their decisions are implemented, and their interests are protected. Only if these needs are satisfied can presidents exercise effective leadership.

Although presidents cannot lead alone, their dependence on others creates potential problems for them. The information they receive on people or policy can be incorrect, biased, or simply too narrow. Their link to the community can be severed or overloaded by too little—or too much—activity. Overzealous behavior by their staff can result in a loss of perspective, a failure to consider all options or consult with a range of people, and unwise or even illegal behavior. None of this serves the president's interests. In short, presidents need good staff support. But good staff support, in turn, requires telling presidents what they may not want to hear; being sensitive to diverse and often critical political forces; and operating according to recognized and accepted rules, procedures, and public norms and doing so under the microscope of press attention.

In this chapter we will examine the institutional components of presidential leadership and their operation within the governmental system: the cabinet, the Executive Office, and the president's personal office, the White House. Beginning with the oldest of these advisory bodies, the cabinet, we briefly describe its creation, evolution, and its demise. We then explore the institutionalization of advisory responsibilities in the Executive Office. Here the emphasis is on the growth of this "bureaucracy within a bureaucracy" and its impact on the president and the performance of presidential responsibilities. After a historical sketch of the evolution of the White House, we examine patterns of staffing and their relationship to the style and objectives of the president. In the final section we assess the increasing importance of the vice presidential office and also the president's spouse.

ORGANIZING EXECUTIVE ADVICE

The Evolution of the Cabinet

The Constitution did not create a separate advisory council for the president. The framers had discussed the idea but rejected it largely out of the fear that presidents might try to sidestep responsibility for their decisions and actions by using their council as a foil. In order to avoid the fiction, popular in England at the time, that the king could do no wrong, that any harmful action he committed was always the result of poor or even pernicious advice from his counselors, the Constitution designated that presidents could demand written opinions of their subordinates. Having these in writing, it was hoped, would pinpoint responsibility.

Although presidents had been expected to use their department secretaries in both administrative and advisory capacities, there was no expectation that the secretaries would function as the principal body of advisers. However, in 1791, when George Washington prepared to leave the capital city, he authorized his vice president, secretaries of state, treasury, and war, and the chief justice to consult with each other on governmental matters during his absence. The following year, Washington began to meet more frequently with the heads of the executive departments. During the undeclared naval war with France, these meetings became even more frequent. It was James Madison who referred to this group as the president's cabinet. The name stuck. Jefferson's resignation as secretary of state in 1794 in protest over the administration's policies fixed the partisan nature of the group. Members were expected to provide counsel as well as support.

For the next 140 years, the cabinet functioned as the president's principal advisory body for both foreign and domestic affairs. Administrative positions on controversial proposals were often thrashed out at cabinet meetings. Presidents also turned to their cabinets for help in supporting them on Capitol Hill. The personal relationships between the individual secretaries and members of Congress frequently put the cabinet officials in a better position than the president to obtain this support. Strong cabinets and weak presidents characterized executive advisory relationships during most of the nineteenth century.

The president's influence began to increase in the twentieth century. The ability to shape public opinion and mobilize partisan support, evident during the administrations of Theodore Roosevelt and Woodrow Wilson, strengthened the chief executive's hand in dealing with Congress and with department heads. Beginning in 1921, the power to affect executive branch decision making through the budget process also contributed to a stronger presidency.

As a consequence of these changes, cabinet meetings became more of a forum for discussion than a mechanism for making decisions and building support for them. Franklin Roosevelt even trivialized the forum. His practice was to go around the table asking each participant what was on his or her mind. Frequently after the session, several secretaries remained to discuss their important business with him without other secretaries in attendance. Truman continued Roosevelt's emphasis on one-to-one relationships with his secretaries rather than calling on them collectively as a group.

The cabinet enjoyed a resurgence under Eisenhower, meeting some 230 times during his eight years in office. The president personally presided over most of these meetings and used his presence to achieve consensus on policy. The sessions themselves often featured elaborate presentations of proposals by individual department heads and their staffs. These presentations, replete with visual aids and supporting materials, were the prelude to final decisions on the administration's legislative program prior to its presentation to Congress.

After Eisenhower's presidency, the cabinet functioned less and less as a policy-making or advisory body. Presidents continued to meet with their cabinets in part because they were expected to do so, but the meetings decreased in frequency over the course of their administration and were not the subject of important policy discussions. Labor Secretary Robert Reich described (with considerable literary license) Clinton's first cabinet meeting:

> The purpose of this meeting, it seems, is to come up with symbolic ways to show taxpayers we intend to do government on the cheap. The deficit continues to haunt all discussion. Bill asks for suggestions.
> "I've reduced our fleet of limousines from five to two," says one proud member of the cabinet.

"I've got rid of them all," says another, trumping the first.

"I've closed the executive dining room," says a third. Damn, that was what I was going to brag about.

Ideas are flying. It's an orgy of austerity.

"I've cut my entertainment allowance by half." The comment is greeted by murmurs of approval. I hadn't even known that we had entertainment allowances.

"We should not use government airplanes unless absolutely necessary." Everyone nods, more murmurs of approval. . . .

My turn[:] . . ."I think we should fly coach."

Silence. It's as if I had suggested that we wear sackcloth and sleep on nails.

"*Coach?*" sniffs [Treasury Secretary Lloyd] Bentsen, finally breaking the silence. "I don't believe *that* would be appropriate."

I grope for a way to rescue myself. "It's not a problem for me," I explain with a lame smile. "I don't need the legroom."[1]

The cabinet's decline in importance has been caused by the increasingly technical nature of policy making and the need for highly specialized information, which makes it difficult for secretaries to be sufficiently versed in the intricacies of issues outside their own areas. At best, this has limited participation at cabinet meetings to the few individuals who were informed and competent; at worst, it reduced the level of the discussion and extended the time of debate. Increasing pressure from outside groups has also forced secretaries to assume more of an advocacy role for their respective departments (referred to as "going native"), particularly when they had to go on the record, but even in closed sessions that could be leaked to the press. Besides, secretaries prefer meeting with the president in private settings, not forums where others could learn their plans.

These factors help explain why presidents since Eisenhower have tended to meet with their cabinets less often over time, particularly in the last years of their administrations.[2] They also suggest why presidents have increasingly differentiated among their secretaries in seeking advice. The heads of certain departments have tended to have closer and more collaborative relationships with the president. These tend to be the most influential secretaries, who comprise the so-called inner cabinet: State, Treasury, Justice, and Defense.[3]

In contrast, the other secretaries, who are considered members of the outer cabinet, tend to have a more distant relationship with the president because of the nature of their departments and clientele. According to political scientist Thomas E. Cronin, "These departments experience heavy and often conflicting pressures from clientele groups, from congressional interests, and from state and local governments, pressures that often run counter to presidential priorities."[4] The need to advocate departmental interests and exercise administrative responsibilities makes it more difficult for secretaries to perceive problems from the president's perspective and recommend solutions that accord with the president's needs rather than their own.

Table 6–1 lists the departmental components of the contemporary cabinet. In addition to the secretaries, other individuals who may attend include the vice president, senior White House aides, and other executive officials of cabinet rank.

The Development of Cabinet Councils

The departmental orientation of the cabinet has given presidents little choice but to develop their own councils and personal staffs. The continued need for internal coordination within the executive has been met by cabinet councils organized on the basis of broad issue areas and consisting of departmental and White House policy makers. These councils have assumed various organizational forms and operating procedures in different administrations, but all have performed similar functions. They deliberate policy, make recommendations to the president, and help coordinate the implementation of key presidential decisions.

Since the mid-1970s, cabinet councils have operated in the domestic, economic, and national security areas. In addition, other, more specialized councils have focused on science, technology, space exploration, competitiveness, and the environment. In general, the councils of two-term presidents have been more active in the first term, when the administration is designing and coordinating its policy proposals, rather than in the second term, when generally it is implementing them. A cabinet secretary, based in the White House, oversees the operation of the councils and provides them with staff support.

The cabinet council system facilitates a president's desire to stay deeply involved in policy issues if the executive chooses to do so. Clinton chose to stay involved; Reagan did not. The latter's councils served more as a debate forum prior to the president's making his final policy decisions.

Although a council system can enhance the president's influence and promote interagency cooperation, it may not always assume a presidential perspective. For that, presidents need their own aides, advisers, and intermediaries—in short, their own office.

The Creation of a Presidential Bureaucracy

The Executive Office of the President (EOP) was established by executive order in 1939. Its title, however, is a misnomer: Its functions are not pri-

TABLE 6–1. The Cabinet, 1999

Department*	Year Created	President	Discretionary Budget Authority (1999)	Proposed Number of Civilian Personnel (1999)
State	1789	Washington	13	10
Treasury	1789	Washington	10	3
Interior	1849	Polk	12	6
Agriculture	1862	Lincoln	9	5
Justice	1870	Grant	7	4
Commerce (formerly part of Department of Commerce and Labor, 1903)	1913	Wilson	14	9
Labor (formerly part of Department of Commerce and Labor, 1903)	1913	Wilson	11	11
Defense (consolidated Department of War, 1789, and Department of Navy, 1798)	1947	Truman	1	1
Housing and Urban Development	1965	Johnson	5	13
Transportation	1966	Johnson	2	7
Energy	1977	Carter	8	12
Health and Human Services† (formerly part of Department of Health, Education, and Welfare, 1953)	1980	Carter	3	8
Education (formerly part of Department of Health, Education, and Welfare, 1953)	1980	Carter	4	14
Veterans Affairs	1988	Reagan	6	2

*President Clinton has proposed to Congress that the Environmental Protection Agency be elevated to cabinet status but Congress has not acted on this proposal.

†No longer includes Social Security, which became a separate agency on March 31, 1995.

marily executive, nor is it a single office. The staffers in the EOP do work for a single client, however—the president.

The principal objective of the EOP has always been to help presidents perform central, nondelegable tasks, including those involved in their expanded policy-making roles. The various offices in the EOP have not taken over the ongoing responsibilities of the departments and agencies, although they have helped to integrate some interagency projects and enable the administration to speak with a single voice.

However, the Executive Office is not a monolith. Instead, it has always consisted of a number of specialized staffs. The first EOP was composed of five separate units, including the Bureau of the Budget and the White House, and over the years many different boards, offices, and councils have been placed within its purview. Today the EOP consists of twelve offices, two executive residences, a staff of almost 1,800, and a budget of $253 million.[5] Figure 6–1 lists the current units, authorized personnel, and budget allocations of the EOP.

While the EOP has evolved in size and function, it has not done so in a systematic, carefully planned way. Rather, its development has been a product of historical accident, the needs of different administrations, and the goals of different presidents. Most chief executives have changed the Executive Office in some way, whether adding to or deleting from it. Some have attempted to overhaul it entirely. In fact, the most extensive reorganization occurred during the first term of the Nixon presidency.

Feeling unhappy with the piecemeal expansion of the executive branch that had occurred prior to 1968, President Nixon centralized power and streamlined the executive branch in an attempt to make it more responsive to his political needs. He created more appointive positions and then filled them with Republicans who were loyal to his political and policy goals.

The politicization of the executive branch reduced the role and influence of civil servants on priority policy making and shifted power from the departments and agencies to the presidency. Political appointees in the upper echelon of the White House and the Office of Management and Budget (OMB) dominated activities, ran the processes, provided advice, and made sure that the president's wishes were carried out.

Criticism of the hierarchical structure of the Nixon presidency, the heavy-handed tactics of his principal aides, and the inaccessibility of the president to others in the executive branch and Congress led to a moderating effect and less-centralized control during the Ford and Carter presidencies. However, the Reagan administration subsequently recentralized power in the White House and the Office of Management and Budget, where it has remained ever since.

Consequences of Structural Change

The evolution of the EOP has made the structure of that office more consistent with the personal styles of individual presidents. This stylistic consistency has resulted in short-term advantages for the president but long-term

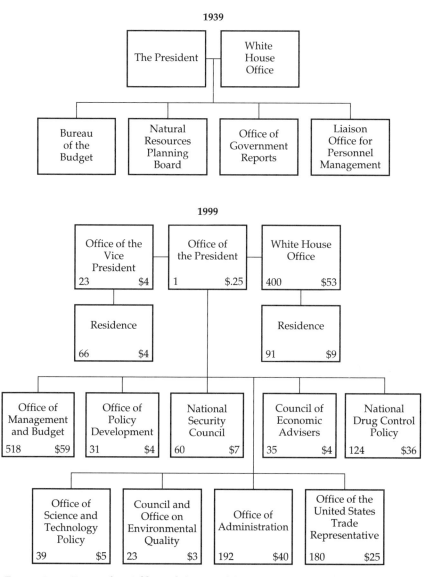

FIGURE 6–1. Executive Office of the President at Its Inception and Today

Note: Numbers on left indicate full-time personnel. Dollar amounts (in millions) indicate proposed budget authority for the 1999 fiscal year.

Source: *Budget of the United States Government, Fiscal Year 1999.* Washington, D.C.: Government Printing Office, 1998.

disadvantages for the presidency. The structural changes in the EOP have produced instability in organization, irregularity in operations, turnover in personnel, and continuing uncertainty in the relations between the president and executive branch agencies. Transitions between administrations, particularly those of different parties, have been made more arduous. In effect, the wheel has had to be perpetually reinvented. The slowness of the appointment process has contributed to the problem.[6]

Despite the initial objectives of the office—to help the president oversee the operational responsibilities and policy-making efforts of the executive departments and agencies, not to substitute for them—separate policy-making units have been firmly established either in or near the White House. Moreover, despite the initial desire to staff the EOP with civil servants, political appointees have increased in number and in influence. Finally, despite the initial goal—to keep the Executive Office small in size and general in scope and capabilities—the office has become a larger, more highly specialized presidential bureaucracy.

The growth, differentiation, and politicization of the EOP have worked at cross-purposes. On one hand, they have increased the political sensitivity of the president and the ability of the White House to exercise centralized control over the rest of the executive branch; on the other, they may have decreased the president's capacity to obtain neutral policy advice. Discontinuities in policy between, and even within, administrations have resulted.

There is another problem: Politicization has caused the presidency's institutional memory to fade. Turnover within the EOP has increased, often placing the president's people at a competitive disadvantage when dealing substantively with officials from the departments and agencies. Nevertheless, the politicization of the executive branch has helped presidents to achieve their policy objectives by maintaining as much centralized control as possible.[7]

Although the establishment of a presidential bureaucracy has increased the presidency's discretion and influence, it has also generated internal rivalry and competition. Senior presidential aides enjoy status by virtue of their access to, and interaction with, the president. They also exercise considerable authority within their functional areas. Their status and authority have contributed to tension between department and agency heads and the White House, which, in turn, has increased the difficulty of maintaining loyalty and mobilizing support within an administration. Clinton's first labor secretary, Robert Reich, embellished such an incident to illustrate this friction and his obvious frustration.

Aide: "The White House wants you to go to Cleveland."
Reich: "Why?"
Aide: "Because we're hitting the first hundred days of the Clinton administration and the President along with his entire cabinet are fanning out

across America to celebrate, because Ohio is important, because there are a lot of blue-collar voters out there, and because you haven't been to Ohio yet." . . .

Reich: "Who wants me to go . . . ?"

Aide: "The White House. They called this morning."

Reich: "Houses don't make phone calls. *Who* called?"

Aide: "I don't know. Somebody from Cabinet Affairs. Steve somebody."

Reich: "How old is Steve? . . . I bet he's under thirty."

Aide: "He is probably under thirty. A large portion of the American population is under thirty? So what?"

Reich: "Don't you see? Here I am, a member of the president's cabinet, confirmed by the Senate, the head of an entire government department with eighteen thousand employees, responsible for implementing a huge number of laws and rules, charged with helping people get better jobs, and *who is telling me what to do?* . . . Some *twerp* in the White House who has *no clue* what I'm doing in this job. Screw him. I won't go." . . .

Aide: "You'll go to Cleveland. The President is going to New Orleans, other cabinet members are going to other major cities. You're in Cleveland."

Reich: "I'll go *this* time. . . . But I'll be damned if I'm going to let them run my life."[8]

Reich's feelings are not unique. Senior departmental officials often resent White House aides telling them what to do, particularly if those aides are young, middle- or low-level staffers.

While the establishment of an institutional mechanism within the presidency has increased the president's ability to meet the multiple demands of the office, it has also helped perpetuate those demands. Bureaucracies—even presidential bureaucracies—have a self-perpetuating character. By performing functions and meeting expectations, these structures encourage those expectations to persist. Presidents who do not meet them are criticized.

Finally, the development of the institutionalized presidency has enhanced the presidency's power, but it may also have made it more difficult for individual presidents to exert personal influence on that institution. There are now more people to supervise, all of whom make decisions and request information in the president's name; more bureaucratic layers to cut through; and more sign-offs to obtain. All this has increased the burdens on an activist president and the dangers for a passive one.

Most chief executives find themselves with two undesirable options. The first is to immerse themselves in the details of administration in order to make themselves less dependent on their staff aides. This consumes their valuable time and energy, makes it more difficult to discern the big picture, and increases the likelihood that the president will be blamed for problems that may emerge.

The second option is to delegate responsibility to others. If they choose this course, as all presidents have to do to some extent, they then face the danger of letting key operational and policy decisions be shaped by others acting on their behalf. Ronald Reagan fell victim to the dangers of overdelegation, and Jimmy Carter and Bill Clinton (particularly in the latter's first two years in office) were guilty of underdelegation. All three presidents suffered as a consequence.

PROVIDING A PRESIDENTIAL STAFFING SYSTEM

In addition to the support the institution requires, presidents need assistants to help them perform their personal duties and responsibilities. Until the creation of an official White House staff in 1939, that help was mainly clerical and was frequently in short supply.

The Early Years

For the first seventy years, Congress did not even provide the president with secretarial support. Early presidents were expected to write their own speeches and answer their own correspondence. Most employed a few aides and paid them out of their own salary. These assistants tended to be young and undistinguished. Frequently, they were related to the president. They were paid low wages and generally performed menial tasks.

In 1857 Congress enacted a separate appropriation for a personal secretary, but the position did not assume great importance or even much potential at the time. If anything, the quality of the secretaries actually employed by presidents declined. Andrew Johnson's aide, his son Robert, was an alcoholic; Grant's secretary, General Orville E. Babcock, was indicted for fraud; Hayes's assistant, William Rogers, was generally regarded as incompetent.[9]

The presidential secretary's role began to expand with the administration of Chester Arthur and has continued to expand in the twentieth century. Theodore Roosevelt's principal aide, William Loeb, Jr., began to deal with the press on a regular basis. Wilson's secretary, Joseph Tumulty, controlled access to the Oval Office and functioned as an appointments secretary, political adviser, administrative manager, and public relations aide.

The number of presidential assistants also began to increase during this period. Whereas Benjamin Harrison could house his entire staff on the second floor of the White House, near his own living quarters, during McKinley's administration a separate group of offices had to be constructed outside the mansion for the president's staff. When the West Wing was completed in 1909, the president's aides came to occupy an even larger space near the president's office.

Hoover doubled the number of his administrative aides from two to four and was also helped by more than forty others: clerks, typists, messengers, and so on. However, it was during Franklin Roosevelt's administration that a separate White House Office was created as part of the Executive Office.

The Personalized White House, 1939 to 1960

Franklin Roosevelt designed a highly personal staff system in his White House. Six key administrative aides performed action-forcing assignments for the president, assignments dictated by Roosevelt's immediate needs and activities. The president ran the staff operation himself, making assignments, receiving reports, and generally coordinating activities. Presidential assistants, who were expected to work beyond the scene, were given general responsibilities. No one exercised exclusive jurisdiction over a particular function or program. In fact, Roosevelt purposely blurred the lines of authority and overlapped assignments, encouraging competition among his aides in order to maximize his information and extend his influence. According to Professor Richard E. Neustadt, Roosevelt enjoyed "bruised egos."[10] The organization of Roosevelt's White House was a prescription for personal control that satisfied Roosevelt's needs. It was not, however, a model his successors could easily follow.

The White Houses of Truman and Eisenhower were more hierarchial in form and more carefully differentiated in function than Roosevelt's, although senior aides in both administrations continued to cooperate with each other with a great deal of informality and enjoyed easy access to the president. Of the two staffs, Eisenhower's was the larger, more formal, and more clearly differentiated. As a career soldier, Eisenhower had a penchant for organization and adopted a system along the lines of the one he experienced in the military. A chief of staff oversaw the operation and also regulated the flow of visitors and memoranda to the Oval Office. Unlike Roosevelt and Truman, who desired to maximize their information and involvement, Eisenhower preferred a system that relieved him of numerous detailed decisions. He desired to set general policy and then work behind the scenes to build political support for it. Consequently, he used his staff as a shield to enhance his own flexibility.

While the Roosevelt, Truman, and Eisenhower operations differed somewhat in size, structure, and style, they had much in common. By contemporary standards, they were relatively small and operated more as a personal extension of the president than an institutional extension of the presidency. With the exception of Sherman Adams, Eisenhower's chief of staff, presidential aides did not possess the status and clout of department secretaries. Instead, their influence stemmed from their mediating role, their ability to obtain information, and their proximity to the president. When the White House called, the president's personal interests were usually the reason.

The Institutionalized White House, 1960 to the Present

Changes began to occur in the White House in the 1960s. They had a profound effect, not only on how the White House was structured and how it operated, but on the operation of the entire executive branch itself. Presidential aides became better known, exercised more power, and tended to monopolize the president's attention and time. The White House grew in size, specialization, and responsibilities. Today it has approximately 400 people on its budget plus another 100 to 150 detailed to it for specific assignments and a budget of $53 million for the fiscal year 1999. (See Figure 6–2 for the organization of the contemporary White House.)

The most notable change during the Kennedy-Johnson period was the institutionalization of policy-making functions by, and in, the White House, with senior aides becoming the principal policy advisers. They supervised their own staffs, which were based in the Executive Office and competed with the departments and agencies for influence.

The institutionalization of policy making in the White House had three major effects: (1) It gave presidents more discretion and allowed them to take more personal credit for policy developed by their administration; (2) it gave the presidency a capacity to formulate policy distinct from, and independent of, the departments and agencies; and (3) it accelerated the shift of power from the departments and agencies to the White House. The status of cabinet secretaries declined, and that of the president's assistants increased.

The growth of the White House distanced presidents from their aides, particularly those at the middle and lower levels of the White House staff structure. The larger number of people made personal interaction with all but a few senior aides more difficult and less frequent. Perquisites, such as office location, mess privileges, and parking (especially portal-to-portal limousine service), began to differentiate aides and their status in the White House hierarchy. The president's time became an even more precious and closely guarded commodity.

How presidents related to their senior aides was still a matter of personal style. Kennedy consciously attempted to emulate Franklin Roosevelt's model, but without the internal competition that Roosevelt generated. Senior Kennedy staffers, many of whom had worked together on the 1960 election campaign, were a close-knit group and operated in an ad hoc, collegial manner. Lyndon Johnson did little initially to change Kennedy's staffing, but over time Johnson replaced his predecessor's personnel and

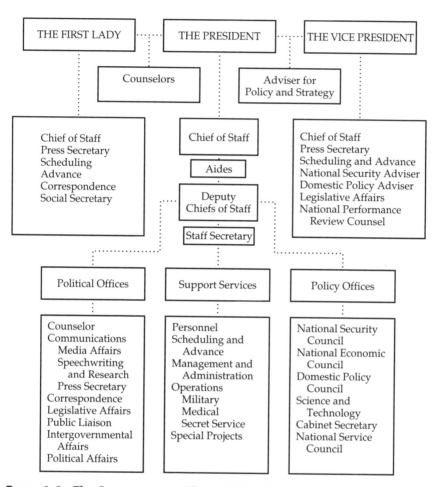

FIGURE 6–2. The Contemporary Clinton White House

staffing structure with his own. Johnson's policy advisers, in particular, exercised considerable influence.

Nixon gave his senior aides even greater power. His White House was structured like a pyramid and managed by a chief of staff and two principal policy aides. It had clear lines of authority and vertical patterns of decision making. From a centralized managerial perspective, it operated smoothly, but from a political perspective, it created problems that impeded the president's ability to make and implement policy. The system insulated Nixon from the departments and agencies, members of Congress, and even many on his own staff. Access to the president was limited to a few top aides. The difficulty of communicating with Nixon produced dissatisfaction with White House decision-making procedures, although in the short run it also enhanced the clout of the White House aides, who coordinated the processes and saw the president on a regular basis.

After his reelection in 1972, Nixon sought to expand White House influence by transferring trusted aides to the departments and agencies. However, the events of Watergate aborted the plan, immobilized the White House, and raised doubts about the wisdom of having so many presidential aides whose blind loyalty to the president impaired their judgment and his.

Ford and Carter both reacted to the Nixon experience by organizing their White House staff like the spokes of a wheel, with the president at the hub. In addition to flattening their staff structure and abandoning the position of chief of staff, both presidents cut down on the number of White Houses aides. But their systems did not work well. Turf battles quickly erupted within the White House and between it and other executive agencies. Each administration had difficulty establishing and articulating its priorities. Presidential interests were not always protected or promoted. Eventually, a more efficient operating structure, headed by a chief of staff, emerged in each administration, which brought about improved coordination between the White House and the departments by the end of their terms in office.

The lessons of the Ford and Carter experiences were not lost on their successors. First, the White House had grown too large and too specialized during the 1970s to operate effectively without a tighter administrative structure and more efficient operating procedures. Second, while considerable autonomy was necessary for those engaged in policy making and consensus building, the White House offices that dealt with these activities had to be coordinated if the administration wished to speak with a single voice and act in a unified manner. Third, although White House involvement in a host of presidential activities could not be easily reduced, the activities and initiatives of the president could be more carefully marshaled and focused.

Ronald Reagan's approach at the start of his presidency was to maintain a large, structurally differentiated White House, even expansion of the staff to include more outreach efforts. A more centralized management orientation was imposed, with the cabinet council system used to coordinate the input of departments into the policy-making process. The system operated smoothly during Reagan's first term and at the end of his second, largely because of the personal interaction of the senior aides, who oversaw the operation of the White House and linked its staff to the president. Reagan delegated considerable responsibility to his staff.

Personnel changes at the beginning of Reagan's second term, however, produced a very different environment for White House decision making. Chief of Staff Donald Regan dominated all aspects of White House activity.

Instead of having the president speak out on a variety of issues, Regan designated an administration spokesperson to take over that burden. The result was a White House operation that eased the president's load as it shielded him from external opinions and limited his contact with the outside world. The machinations of several members of the national security staff that culminated in the Iran-Contra affair, as well as the president's unprepared and disengaged reaction to the affair, illustrate the dangers for presidents of delegating too much power to others and then providing them with too much autonomy.

The early Bush White House followed the strong chief of staff model. Former New Hampshire governor John Sununu was put in charge, and for the most part, senior staff aides reported through Sununu to the president. But again, overreliance on a single individual hurt the president. Sununu's abrasive manner and controlling personality, his strong ideological perspective, and his penchant for publicity all got him into trouble, decreased his usefulness to the president, and eventually forced him to resign from office.[11] For most of the remainder of his presidential term, Bush's White House operated with much less internal discipline and central control.

During its early years in office, the Clinton White House made many of the same mistakes as the Carter and Ford administrations. Lines of authority were unclear; staff meetings were large, long, and discursive; there were frequent leaks of pending or proposed decisions; and access to the president was not sufficiently limited, nor was effective use made of his time. Poor staff work resulted in a slow and sloppy appointment process, inadequate communication and consultation with members of Congress, mixed messages sent to the public, and revelations of embarrassing presidential activities. These blunders contributed to low public approval ratings for the president.

It took more than two years and considerable personnel and organizational change to improve the situation. New chiefs of staff, first Leon Panetta, then Erskine Bowles, and later John Podesta, centralized authority under their direction. They focused the White House more on presidential priorities and coordinated the various units in the White House and departments to speak with a single voice, rather than the many voices that had characterized the early Clinton administration. A new press secretary, Michael McCurry, dealt more effectively with the White House press corps, while two deputy chiefs of staff orchestrated the outreach activities and policy-making councils.

Finding the right people with the right skills for the right job had proved difficult for Clinton and cost him valuable time and political capital in his first term. However, by the second term the president was reaping the benefits of effective staff work (see The Clinton Presidency box).

THE CLINTON PRESIDENCY

Staffing Trials and Tribulations

The first two years of the Clinton presidency were marked by confusion and indecision in policy making, confrontation with Congress (both Republicans and Democrats) and powerful interest groups, and complexity and contradictions in its communications to the public. The White House was largely responsible for these shortcomings. Its inexperience in executive management, in the ways of Washington, and in getting started created a nightmarish situation in which the new president was embarrassed by poor staff work, lack of coordination, and ineffective short- and long-term planning.

The absence of a White House transition in which careful thought was given to personnel, processes, and priorities contributed to the problem. The president made several poor personnel selections among his senior aides. Instead of compensating for his lack of national government experience with a seasoned staff that had worked in Washington and had good political connections, Clinton chose outsiders from his campaign, acquaintances from Arkansas, and "friends of Bill," people he had befriended throughout his political career, to serve in most of the top positions in his presidency. The few insiders who were selected, such as congressional liaison chief, Howard Pastor, were regularly circumvented by Clinton loyalists.

Compounding the problem was the president's choice of Thomas "Mack" McLarty as chief of staff. A long-time friend but not a strong manager, McLarty failed to exercise tight control over the White House and was sometimes unaware of internal presidential recommendations and decisions. Nor was he able to control the revolving door into and out of the Oval Office.

There was also the problem of the president's own work style: his tendency to get involved in a myriad of policy and personnel matters, often in great detail and for considerable periods of time, at the expense of maintaining a tight schedule, focusing on the big picture, and distancing himself from the internal bickering and battles that occur in most administrations. Clinton's involvement in detailed discussions, frequently in the early stages of policy formulation, created the appearance of indecision and inconsistency as the president changed his mind in response to additional information and expertise. Moreover, Clinton's tendency to think out loud and float ideas in public also got him into trouble.

Complicating Clinton's public relations was the way in which the administration initially tried to deal with the Washington press corps—circumventing it whenever possible by going directly to local media. Without a steady flow of White House–sponsored pictures and news, members of the White House press corps set their own agenda and got their own information, which frequently was critical of the new administration.

Two incidents, both occurring in spring 1993, shaped the tone of this news coverage and became the metaphors for an amateurish White House operation. The first was the firing of the personnel in the White House Travel Office, which makes the arrangements and provides the creature comforts for members of the press who travel with the president. Seeking to place its own political appointees in this office as well as steer the White House's travel business to friends of the administration, the head of the administration unit in the White House, David Watson, fired the personnel who had been there in previous administrations. As the cause, he alleged lax and improper accounting procedures and accused the head of the office of embezzling government funds. Pressure was placed on the FBI to conduct an investigation on the embezzlement charges. The administration's heavy-handed tactics, including the role of Hillary Rodham Clinton in the firings, became an object of media attention and criticism and, later (after the Republicans gained control of Congress), a subject of a congressional investigation.

The other incident, which seems trivial by comparison, involved a $200 haircut the president received from a fashionable hair stylist onboard his plane, *Air Force One,* while standing on a runway at Los Angeles International Airport. Not only did the cost of the cut embarrass the Democratic president, who had made much of his humble beginnings and his ability to empathize with average Americans, but the press reported that the styling delayed hundreds of travelers flying to Los Angeles, whose planes could not land for reasons of security while the president's plane was on the ground. Although the report of a delay proved to be inaccurate, it nonetheless cast the president's judgment, and that of the advisers who accompanied him, in a very unfavorable light.

These incidents, along with the defeat of the administration's major legislative initiative in spring 1993, its economic stimulus bill, and the president's precipitous decline in public approval ratings, led Clinton to institute a major staffing change in the White House after only four months in office.

Two deputy chiefs of staff were hired to help McLarty, one to run the White House and the other to coordinate public outreach activities. To sharpen the administration's policy focus, improve its relations with the Washington community and the news media, and recast the president's public image, David Gergen, who had served in the Nixon and Reagan White Houses as a speech writer and, later, as head of communications, joined the White House as a senior adviser.

The shift in personnel helped restore confidence in the administration. Combined with Democratic legislative successes in Congress, it improved the president's standing with the American public and the press coverage Clinton received during the fall of 1993. However, the gain was only short-lived.

Tensions developed within the White House on how to react to the Whitewater allegations in early 1994 and eventually led to Gergen's resignation, a new round of senior staff turmoil and, ultimately, additional staff turnover. Chief of staff McLarty was "elevated" to counselor and replaced by Leon Panetta, Clinton's director of the Office of Management and Budget. Panetta wanted Michael McCurry, the State Department's press spokesman, to replace Dee Dee Myers (the first woman to hold the White House press secretary's job but not an insider in the Clinton entourage). Myers, however, did not want to be forced out and appealed to Mrs. Clinton, who persuaded the president to retain her. Eventually

Panetta hired McCurry, but not before his initial request had been thwarted. Changes in the legislative liaison staff, communications office, and policy councils followed. By the end of his first term, Clinton had replaced most of his senior aides and even some of their replacements. His White House had two chiefs of staff, five deputy chiefs of staff, four counsels, three legislative liaison heads, three communication directors, two press secretaries, three political directors, and two staff secretaries—all in his first four years in office.

Panetta did bring discipline and stability to the White House. Under his leadership, the White House began to operate more smoothly, with clearer lines of authority and areas of responsibility. Panetta also tried to funnel the flow of people and papers to the president, but Clinton's operating style, penchant for calling aides and associates day or night, and desire to involve himself deeply in policy and political matters made it difficult for the chief of staff to exercise tight control.

Panetta also tried to focus the White House's public persona more clearly. He became a principal spokesman for the president, both in Congress and, even, on the Sunday morning talk shows. Press secretary Michael McCurry performed a similar function in the White House.

The changing political environment—beginning in fall 1994 with the Democrats' devastating loss in the midterm elections, continuing with the president's confrontation with the Republican Congress, and culminating in the planning for his reelection effort—prompted new changes in White House personnel and decision-making circles, which upset senior staff and generated internal frictions in the process.

Clinton, who felt blindsided by the magnitude of the Democrats' loss in 1994, wanted a political strategist to help position him for reelection. He turned to Dick Morris, a campaign consultant who had helped Clinton win reelection as governor of Arkansas in 1982 after being defeated in his quest for reelection two years earlier. Morris, who had direct access to the president, recommended that Clinton take centrist, moderate positions on a range of contentious issues currently before Congress, including support for a balanced budget. Moreover, he urged that Clinton's reelection committee undertake an advertising campaign to reinforce these positions in the minds of the voters.

Some of Clinton's principal advisers disagreed strongly with Morris's advice, policy recommendations, and expenditure of $2.5 million of preconvention campaign funds on the advertising campaign, which was launched almost a year and a half before the presidential election. They also objected strongly to Morris's ability to circumvent the White House advisory process in giving his recommendations directly to the president and getting his ideas into Clinton's speeches without the senior staff reviewing them.

By winter 1994–1995, the president's senior aides were essentially split into two warring camps: one headed by chief of staff Leon Panetta and his top aides, and the other by Morris and the consultants he had brought into the White House. To try to reconcile this factional division within his own house, the president initiated weekly political strategy sessions beginning in winter 1995.

Meeting in the living quarters of the White House in the evening, the sessions were attended by almost two dozen people including the president, the vice president, a few cabinet secretaries, White House senior staff, and the outside political consultants—but not Mrs. Clinton, as it was feared that the first lady's presence would fuel criticism from those who felt she was overstepping her role. The group discussed the political environment and advised the president on how to deal with it. The latest polls, political developments, and Republican campaign activity were assessed and recommendations were made to Clinton on how he should position himself on a range of issues and priorities.

The rise in the president's public standing in winter 1995 and spring and summer 1996 provided some evidence that Morris's strategy was working; it also provided incentive for the White House and political strategists to work together, creating, in the words of *Washington Post* reporter Bob Woodward, "an uneasy equilibrium," between them.[12] One indication of the effectiveness of president's staff was that Clinton campaigned for reelection without appearing to do so. The White House choreographed his activities in such a way as to maximize his image as president and minimize it as candidate.

Although occasional embarrassments continued to occur, such as the discovery of FBI files of prominent Republicans stashed in the security office of the White House and Morris's resignation after a tabloid revealed his relationship with a Washington, D.C., prostitute, they did not seem to affect the president's public image as much as previous incidents. Nor did Panetta's resignation adversely impact on White House operations. His replacement by Erskine Bowles, Panetta's former deputy chief of staff, and the selection of White House insiders for the top staff positions in the second term kept the Clinton White House functioning smoothly and focusing directly on the president's political needs. By projecting Clinton as an active, caring president bent on doing the people's business, the staff was able to counter the negative news that a partisan scandal (Democratic campaign fund-raising) and personal allegations about the president's sexual improprieties had generated at least until the report of the independent counsel on Clinton's behavior reached Congress.

The Clinton experience suggests that the White House is not a good place for on-the-job training. It requires knowledge, experience, and political savvy to work there. A staff that demonstrates these criteria can be a critical asset to a president and a major component for the exercise of that president's leadership skills. It can make a detached and passive person, such as Ronald Reagan, *appear* to be a strong, determined, and confident leader, and a partisan, pragmatic person, such as Bill Clinton, whose honesty, integrity, and moral values were mistrusted by a majority of the populace, *appear* to a statesman, a unifying figure, and a caring, hard-working, people-oriented president (see Figure 6–2).

Trends in White House Staffing

Since its creation, the White House has undergone significant growth and increasing specialization. Greater presidential needs and responsibilities have resulted in a larger and more functionally differentiated office, and most recent presidents have added to that structure. Eisenhower established a congressional liaison office, Kennedy created a national security adviser and staff, Johnson instituted a domestic counterpart, and Nixon expanded both policy staffs, as well as the press and communications offices. Ford added an economic assistant and a modest public liaison operation, Carter vastly enlarged the public liaison function and also created an office for intergovernmental affairs, and Reagan added a political affairs office and a secretariat for cabinet administration, in addition to a short-lived Office of Planning and Evaluation. Clinton created a National Economic Council to coordinate economic policy making and eventually appointed two deputy chiefs of staff to coordinate outreach and reelection activities as well as his major policy initiatives. Although the number of full-time staff budgeted to the White House has been slightly reduced since the Nixon administration (largely for reasons of politics and public relations), the functions and capabilities of the office are as broad as ever.

The institutional components reflect these functions, and there is little that presidents can do to alter them as long as the expectations and obligations they inherit remain great. They may tinker with the structure, but they cannot radically change it.

Over time, the White House has become more important to the president. The need for a more centrally managed and efficiently run staff has become obvious, in large part because presidents now find that they depend increasingly on their assistants for information, advice, and liaison activities. To the extent that these activities are now subject to full public view (see the Hot-Button Issue box), that dependency may lessen. It did during independent counsel Kenneth Starr's inquiry into the president's relationship with White House intern Monica Lewinsky. White House aides, fearful that they might have to testify before a grand jury about their conversations with the president avoided discussing the matter with him.[13] According to Howard Kurtz, even press secretary Mike McCurry ". . . never asked Clinton whether the allegations were true." Kurtz added, [a]s always, he [McCurry] had to stay away from fact gathering, had to leave that to the lawyers, or he could be subpoenaed next in the Paula Jones case."[14] Vice President Gore even went so far as to bring his own attorney with him to the first White House staff meeting that was held to discuss the charges after they initially became public. Thus, Clinton was left increasingly alone, having only his lawyers and wife with whom to confide and strategize.

☼ HOT- BUTTON ISSUE

The Privacy of Internal Communications

Presidents and their aides need to be able to communicate with each other freely, candidly, and easily. Anything that inhibits this communication threatens to disrupt the information flow to and from the president, which is vital for decision making and implementation.

However, in a democratic society the public also has a right to know what decisions government officials make and why. This right is particularly important whenever there is suspicion of possible criminal activities.

Several times in the last three decades these rights have clashed: when Richard Nixon refused to release tapes of conversations he had in the Oval Office concerning the Watergate burglary, when the Reagan and Bush administrations wished to delete the hard drives of their computers on leaving office, and when the Clinton administration argued that presidential aides and secret service personnel should not be required to testify in the investigation of the president's relationship to a White House intern.

In each of these incidents, the courts had to intervene—and in each case, the president's claim that the information was privileged and its release would impair internal White House communications was rejected. The Supreme Court held, in *United States v. Nixon*, 418 U.S. 683 (1974), that President Nixon could not use the claim of *executive privilege* to refuse to comply with a congressional subpoena for taped conversations that contained information of possible criminal activity in the Watergate affair. Similarly, after computer backup files revealed incriminating E-mail sent between members of the president's National Security Council staff, the courts held that E-mail, like other written communications, was part of the public record and could not be destroyed after an administration left office. In the dispute between the independent counsel who was investing President Clinton's relations, conversations, and activities with various women, the courts stated that White House aides had to testify about personal conversations with the president and that secret service officers had to testify as well. Clearly, these decisions indicate the judiciary's strong belief that no public official, especially the president, can be considered above the law.

However, the impact on the presidency may be considerable. Aides may now communicate with the public record in mind. Will they be as candid as they were in the past? Will they be as willing to take unpopular positions or use "colorful" language to get the president's attention and make their point? Finally, will they think twice about accepting a White House position knowing that they may have to incur huge legal expenses if they are called to testify on any aspect of their White House work?

Nonetheless, the president had no choice but to use the White House as his fortress and the staff in his defense. Even without knowing the facts, the staff was expected to help the president combat the charges. Chief of Staff Erskine Bowles, Mike McCurry, and various other senior aides orchestrated a public relations campaign in which the president was seen doing the people's business: he visited Africa, China, Russia, and Ireland to meet with foreign leaders; he offered hope and promised help to those Americans hurt by natural disasters, terrorist attacks, or human tragedies such as school shootings; and he attended scheduled events around the country to promote his policy agenda. During the bombing attack on a terrorist training area in Afghanistan and a pharmaceutical factory in Sudan thought to be producing the ingredients for chemical weapons, he was seen at the helm of state and with congressional leaders.

In addition to focusing public attention on Clinton's presidential activities, the White House also responded to attacks from by the president's critics and leaks from the independent counsel's office with attacks and leaks of their own. And after the independent counsel submitted his report to Congress, the president's lawyers delivered two detailed responses while the White House developed a public relations strategy for dealing with the crisis and began to mobilize support on the president's behalf against impeachment. Clinton played an active role in the planning and staging of his own defense.

Evaluating the Staffing System: Spokes of the Wheel versus Central Management

Spokes of the Wheel	**Central Management**
Pro:	Pro:
easy interaction among senior aides	clear lines of authority
greater presidential discretion	efficient operating system
loyalty of aides to president	wide range of information and options to president

Spokes of the Wheel	Central Management
Con:	Con:
danger of groupthink mentality	chief of staff may exercise too
staff can become captive of	much control
presidential perspective	president can become captive of
overinvolvement of the president	staff system and isolated from
too early in the decisional process	reality

What staffing system is best? The answer depends on the kinds of decisions that need to be made and the president's personal style of decision making. In general, those presidents who wish to maximize their involvement, discretion, and influence will benefit from a more fluid staffing arrangement. On the other hand, those who prefer to make the final decision themselves while leaving the burden of soliciting, collecting, and coordinating advice to others are better served by a more formal, hierarchial structure. The styles of Kennedy, Johnson, Carter, and Clinton fall into the first category and those of Eisenhower, Nixon, and Reagan into the second; Ford and Bush lie somewhere in between. In each case, either too much fluidity or too much structure can be dangerous.

Presidents who wish to depart from existing policy, particularly policy based on strong outside interests, will tend to gain most from the flexible advisory arrangement. The less formal the structure, the more quickly it can respond to changing conditions and the more easily it can produce innovative policy. Kennedy is an example of a president who desired new and creative policy, and Johnson is another. Nixon and Carter, in contrast, were less interested in innovation and more interested in obtaining the careful analysis that a well-staffed White House policy operation could produce.

THE GROWTH OF THE VICE PRESIDENCY

Presidential support has been supplemented in recent years by the activities of the vice president and his staff. These activities range from providing policy advice and making political appeals to performing a variety of ceremonial functions. However, the vice president's role has changed over time.

For years the vice presidency was regarded as a position of little importance, and it was the butt of jokes and laments. The nation's first vice president, John Adams, complained, "My country has in its wisdom contrived for me the most insignificant office that ever the invention of man contrived or his imagination conceived."[15] Thomas Jefferson, the second person to hold the office, was not quite as critical. Describing his job as "honorable and easy," he added, "I am unable to decide whether I would rather have it or not have it."[16]

Throughout most of the nineteenth century, the vice president performed very limited functions. Other than succeeding to the presidency, the holder of this position had only one designated constitutional responsibility—to preside over the Senate and vote in case of a tie. Nor did presidents enlarge these responsibilities very much. Vice presidents played only a peripheral role within their respective administrations, so much so that when Professor Woodrow Wilson wrote his treatise on American government in the 1880s, he devoted only one paragraph to the vice president. "The chief embarrassment in . . . explaining how little there is to be said about it," Wilson concluded, is that "one has evidently said all there is to say."[17] John Nance Garner, Franklin Roosevelt's first vice president, offered perhaps the most earthy refrain in his much-quoted comment that the office was "hardly worth a pitcher of spit."[18]

Were Adams, Jefferson, and Garner alive today, they would have to reevaluate their assessments as the position has increased enormously in importance. Roosevelt's sudden death, Eisenhower's illness, and Kennedy's assassination cast attention on the vice president and generated support for clarifying succession during presidential disability and filling the vice presidency should the position become vacant. These events also contributed to the enhancement of the office by encouraging presidents to do more to prepare their vice president for the number one job.

Eisenhower was the first of the modern presidents to upgrade the vice president's role. He invited Richard Nixon, his vice president, to attend cabinet, National Security Council (NSC), and legislative strategy meetings, and during his illness, Nixon presided over these sessions.[19] In addition, as vice president Nixon was sent on a number of well-publicized trips for the administration.

Lyndon Johnson was also involved in a variety of activities as John Kennedy's vice president. He helped coordinate administration efforts to eliminate racial discrimination and promote exploration of outer space, participated in legislative lobbying efforts, joining Kennedy at the White House breakfasts for congressional leaders, and he also traveled abroad on behalf of the administration. Still, however, Johnson was not enamored with the job. To biographer Doris Kearns he stated:

> Every time I came into John Kennedy's presence, I felt like a goddamn raven hovering over his shoulder. Away from the Oval Office, it was even worse. The Vice Presidency is filled with trips around the world, chauffeurs, men saluting, people clapping, chairmanships of councils, but in the end, it is nothing. I detested every minute of it."[20]

Despite their own experiences, neither Johnson nor Nixon added new responsibilities to the office, even though both continued to have their vice presidents perform a variety of ceremonial, diplomatic, and political roles such as chairing committees, making speeches, and representing the administration at international and national events. Hubert Humphrey, Johnson's vice president, and Spiro Agnew, Nixon's vice president, were not influential presidential advisers. Humphrey was not invited to the Tuesday lunch group-strategy sessions held concerning the Vietnam War, and Agnew found his access to the president increasingly limited as the term progressed. Aides joked that Nixon kept the vice president under "house arrest" in the old Executive Office Building even before Agnew was forced to resign for accepting kickbacks from Maryland contractors and failing to pay taxes on this illegal supplementary income. Neither Humphrey nor Agnew exercised major influence on the formulation of important policy initiatives within their administrations.

Nelson Rockefeller, Gerald Ford's vice president, had the opportunity to exercise influence when he was given an important policy-making role by President Ford—to oversee the development of domestic programs. Quickly, however, Rockefeller's priorities clashed with those of other Republicans within the administration and Congress. Coming under increasing criticism from fellow partisans, Rockefeller announced his intention not to seek the vice presidency in 1976 and subsequently removed himself from an active policy-making and advisory role.

Whereas Rockefeller failed to realize the vice president's potential as a presidential adviser, Walter Mondale did not. He was the first vice president to have an office in the West Wing of the White House, and his staff was integrated with that of the presidents.

Mondale saw Carter on a regular basis. While he had no ongoing administrative responsibilities, he was given *carte blanche* to attend any conference, see any paper, and participate in any study he wished. Carter wrote in his memoirs that Mondale "received the same security briefings I got, was automatically invited to participate in all my official meetings, and helped to plan strategy for domestic programs, diplomacy, and defense."[21]

Carter provided opportunities for Mondale to shape policy, and he improved congressional relations for the administration. Mondale headed a priority-setting mechanism; he facilitated administration lobbying on key bills; he helped to establish a public liaison operation in the White House; and used his own political connections with labor and minority groups outside the government to foster coalition building for the president.

When President Reagan wished to demonstrate his concern with crisis management, drug enforcement, and government relations, he appointed Vice President Bush to head committees studying these issues. Bush also served as a personal envoy of the president by visiting North Atlantic Treaty Organization (NATO) countries, making a fact-finding trip to Lebanon, and attending the funerals of several foreign policy leaders. When he was in

Washington, he attended key White House meetings with the president, had a one-on-one lunch with Reagan on a weekly basis, and was kept in the loop on major administrative policy decisions.[22] However, Bush was not considered an influential Reagan adviser, nor was he outspoken at the policy meetings he attended.

Dan Quayle played a role in the Bush administration similar to the one that Bush played in the Reagan administration, but Quayle attracted more public attention. As vice president, Quayle was sent on a number of fact-finding and morale-boosting trips for the administration, chaired the committee overseeing space exploration (as Lyndon Johnson had done during the Kennedy administration), and served as a liaison to conservative groups and members of Congress. His most important policy-making role was as head of a business-oriented group known as the Council of Competitiveness. In this capacity, Quayle engineered the delay, reduction, or elimination of regulations that threatened to have an adverse effect on business. Although he was an active participant in internal discussions within the administration, as with his predecessor, he was not perceived as an influential presidential adviser.

Vice President Al Gore has had considerably more policy and personal influence within the Clinton administration than Quayle did with George Bush. He participated in the personnel selection process for cabinet and subcabinet appointments at the beginning of the administration, reviewed the drafts of presidential speeches, and, in his most important role, directed the National Performance Review Project, which was the administration's effort to "reinvent government" by making it more efficient and less costly.

As an important Clinton adviser, Gore lunches regularly with the president, attends political strategy sessions, and has had regular input into most major policy decisions. In such areas as the environment, high technology, and matters of science, he has had the most influence. A principal link to organized labor, Senate Democrats, and the Democratic party in general, Vice President Gore has also played a prominent role in foreign affairs as a personal representative of the president. Valuing his vice president's advice, Clinton usually does not make a major policy decision without informing Gore and getting his reaction to it.

Gore has also been charged with overseeing the coordination of regulatory priorities and agendas. A key legislative lobbyist, he cast the tie-breaking vote in the Senate on the 1993 deficit reduction bill. Additionally, he has performed the traditional vice presidential roles of engaging in political fund-raising and public outreach—but not without considerable controversy.[23]

One reason for the increased influence of contemporary vice presidents has been their willingness to exercise power behind the scenes and avoid stealing the spotlight or taking credit from the president. Being a loyal and energetic team player is an essential quality of a person whose position, reputation, and political future are inevitably tied to those of the president. Thus, the relationship between the vice president and the president can be a source of either strength or weakness. If the administration is perceived as successful, the vice president will benefit, as Bush did in 1988; if it is not, the vice president will suffer, as Mondale did in 1984. Vice presidents cannot cut the umbilical cord to the president, nor can they easily establish leadership in the number two position.

The growth of the vice presidency has not only helped the vice president, it has also worked to the advantage of the presidency by providing the institution with additional resources for the performance of ceremonial and symbolic functions.

THE PRESIDENT'S SPOUSE

The president's spouse has the potential to become an important component or point of controversy in the contemporary presidency. Although the Constitution does not acknowledge a spousal responsibility, presidential spouses have performed social and ceremonial functions from the time the government began to operate. Initially and throughout the nineteenth century, they avoided involvement in policy matters and, to a slightly lesser extent, in politics. Even though they were expected to stay out of the limelight, some became controversial. Rachel Jackson and Mary Todd Lincoln in particular became objects of ridicule by their husbands' political opponents.

In the twentieth century, and with the development of a White House press corps, spouses became more visible, but not necessarily more influential in matters of state. The earliest exception was Edith Wilson, whose husband was felled by a major stroke in 1919. While President Wilson was recuperating, the first lady allegedly made decisions in his name, may have forged his signature to legal documents including legislation, and shielded him from Washington politicians, the press, and the public.

Eleanor Roosevelt established an important communications link between her husband, who had been crippled by polio and moved with great difficulty, and the American people. She traveled across the country, monitored public opinion, and reported the country mood to the president. She also wrote a column, entitled "My Day," which appeared in newspapers around the country.

Jacqueline Bouvier Kennedy and "Lady Bird" Johnson supplemented the policy interests of their husband's respective administrations by their concerns with history, culture, and landscaping. Mrs. Kennedy was instrumental in the restoration of the Lafayette Park area across from the White House and the preservation and restoration of the White House interior.

Mrs. Johnson cared deeply about the environment and worked to enhance the beautification of Washington.

Betty Ford and Rosalyn Carter spoke out on health care issues and other family-related concerns, and Mrs. Carter was the first spouse to attend a cabinet meeting. Nancy Reagan played a spokesperson role in her husband's administration's antidrug policy by spearheading the "Just Say No" campaign. In addition, Mrs. Reagan was involved in internal personal and personnel matters, particularly as they pertained to the staffing and travel of her husband. She was also instrumental in the removal of several key aides who, she believed, were serving President Reagan poorly. Barbara Bush served as an advocate for literacy, and Hillary Rodham Clinton has spoken out for universal health care, human rights, and family values.

Mrs. Clinton's role with the administration's health care proposal, however, went well beyond advocacy. In fact, she was its chief architect and proponent. Her role in policy making and coalition building inevitably embroiled her in politics, which has contributed to the controversy surrounding her participation in her husband's administration.

Hillary Clinton is the first spouse since Eleanor Roosevelt to become a partisan figure. Her alleged involvement in the firing of personnel in the White House Travel Office, combined with the disappearance of some of her legal records (Mrs. Clinton was the first presidential spouse to be subpoenaed to testify about her activities before a federal grand jury) has added fuel to the fire and contributed to her reputation as a liberal activist and partisan Democrat.

What is a proper spousal role? Some believe that Mrs. Clinton has set the course that others will most likely follow and laud this as natural outgrowth of the education and professionalization of women and the development of two-career families.

Supporters of the Eleanor Roosevelt–Hillary Rodham Clinton model of the first lady see her as a valuable partner who can help the president perform a multitude of tasks, from ceremonial duties to policy making and political leadership. In fact, a spouse may be in a unique position to tell the president what the president does not want to hear—and other advisers might be fearful of saying.

Besides, in an age of gender equality, preventing a spouse from performing a voluntary role may itself be discriminatory. By law, no member of the president's immediate family may hold an appointive position within the federal government.

Some observers, however, are concerned about the unique relationship that the president's spouse enjoys with the president. The fact that spouses cannot be fired although they can be divorced makes them less vulnerable to the usual constraints on presidential advisers. Moreover, it places them in a position to impose their own views on the president and those close advisers. They may also be able to prevent others from reaching the president. These dangers, however, may be partially offset by sensitivity to this position being exercised by all concerned: the president, the news media, and the spouse.

Except for the public's reaction to health care, Mrs. Clinton has received favorable approval ratings and a positive press. Significant partisan, gender, and generational differences, however, have been evident in the public's evaluation of her as first lady. Democrats, women, and younger people have been consistently more approving of her performance than have Republicans, men, and older people.

The controversy over the spousal role and the partisan cleavages over performance in office are likely to continue as long as presidential spouses involve themselves in political matters and contentious policy issues.

CONCLUSION

Today the tasks of contemporary presidents are far too numerous, require too much knowledge, and may be fraught with too many obstacles to be undertaken alone. Presidents need information and advice from others, they need to build and maintain political alliances, and they need to increase the credit and reduce the blame for their actions. All these needs are serviced by the staff in the Executive Office, including the vice president and, in recent years, the president's spouse.

The founders undoubtedly would have been surprised, and probably dismayed, by the growth and institutionalization of the presidential office. They conceived of presidents in narrower terms, as chief executives with subsidiary responsibilities. They also envisioned their need for subordinates and advisers. Still, nothing in their deliberations suggests an institution as large, complex, and influential as the presidency is today.

Most of this growth has occurred in the twentieth century, much of it since the 1960s. Not only has the office become larger, it has become more specialized, more policy-oriented, and more politicized. It has developed an independent capacity to advise and inform the president, to formulate and prioritized policy, to orchestrate and oversee department and agency input, and to build public and congressional support.

As a result of this growth, senior presidential aides have become more important, prestigious, and visible—and subject to more press scrutiny and criticism. Such aides now occupy more of the president's time. In contrast, the department secretaries have lost some of their notoriety and status, access to the president, and formerly exclusive influence over policy.

The creation and maintenance of a presidential office has occurred, not only at the expense of the departments and agencies, but also at some cost to the president. While the influence of the presidency and its capacity to affect policy have been enhanced, the president's personal ability to oversee staff on an ongoing basis has not. In fact, oversight has been made more difficult by the growth in the size of the office and the number of functional responsibilities it performs.

This evolution confronts contemporary presidents with a dilemma: They need a large, functionally differentiated staff to exercise leadership, yet their leadership ability is frequently at the mercy of that staff. Thus, the expansion of the presidency has been a mixed blessing. Although created to meet increased expectations, the presidential office has generated new ones. Designed to coordinate and facilitate executive branch decision making, it has produced serious tensions between the White House and the departments. Tailored to systematize advice to the president, it has proliferated that advice, and sometimes has worked to isolate presidents from their advisers.

However, the expansion has obviously been necessary. It has been both a cause and effect of the growth of government, the executive branch, and the president's leadership responsibilities.

DISCUSSION QUESTIONS

1. Has the institutionalization of the presidency contributed to or detracted from the president's personal power and accountability? Explain the impact of institutionalization and give examples from recent presidencies.

2. Pretend that you are an expert on the presidency and have been asked by a presidential candidate to write a memo on staffing the White House. Write a memo in which you suggest the structure and functions for this candidate's White House, the type of people who should be appointed to the top positions, and the kinds of problems that may be encountered. Also indicate the strengths and weaknesses of your proposal.

3. George Reedy, in an analysis titled, *Twilight of the Presidency* (New York: New American Library, 1987), suggested that the White House inevitably elevates and isolates a president. Do you feel that Reedy is correct? If correct, explain how these problems can be avoided. If incorrect, give your reasons.

WEB EXERCISES

1. Go to the White House Web site at <http://www.whitehouse.gov> and identify all of the ways in which the White House is attempting to build a coalition on a pending issue on which the president has taken a position. Indicate whether you think this coalition will be effectively mobilized and able to help the presidency achieve its objectives.
2. Go to the Web site of the Office of Management and Budget at <http://www.eop/omb/gov> and look at that office's structure and functions. Illustrate the work of as many of the office's principal units as possible by downloading memos, circulars, and clearance, budget, and management documents.

SELECTED READING

Blanton, Tom, ed. *White House E-Mail*. New York: New Press, 1995.

Buchanan, Bruce. "Constrained Diversity: The Organizational Demands of the Presidency." *Presidential Studies Quarterly* XX (1990): 791–822.

Cohen, Jeffrey E. *The Politics of the U.S. Cabinet: Representation in the Executive Branch, 1789–1984*. Pittsburgh: University of Pittsburgh Press, 1988.

Ellis, Richard J. *Presidential Lightning Rods: The Politics of Blame Avoidance*. Lawrence: University of Kansas Press, 1995.

Hart, John. *The Presidential Branch: From Washington to Clinton*. 2nd ed. Chatham, N.J.: Chatham House, 1995.

Light, Paul C. *Vice Presidential Power*. Baltimore: Johns Hopkins University Press, 1984.

Moe, Terry M. "The Politicized Presidency." In John E. Chubb and Paul E. Petersen, eds., *The New Direction in American Politics*, pp. 235–271. Washington, D.C.: Brookings Institution, 1985.

Patterson, Bradley H., Jr. *The Ring of Power*. New York: Basic Books, 1988.

Pfiffner, James P., ed. *The Managerial Presidency*. Belmont, Calif.: Brooks/Cole, 1991.

Reedy, George. *The Twilight of the Presidency*. New York: New American Library, 1987.

Reich, Robert. *Locked in the Cabinet*. New York: Alfred A. Knopf, 1997.

Walcott, Charles, and Karen M. Hult. *Governing the White House: From Hoover Through LBJ*. Lawrence: University of Kansas Press, 1995.

Weko, Thomas J. *The Politicizing Presidency: The White House Personnel Office, 1948–1994*. Lawrence: University of Kansas Press, 1995.

Notes

1. Reich is four feet, ten inches tall. (Robert Reich, *Locked in the Cabinet* [New York: Alfred A. Knopf, 1997]) p. 78.
2. The need to develop a team approach and produce new policy is most acute at the beginning of an administration. This is when cabinet input is desired. Toward the end of the term, the implementation of that policy, which is often the prerogative of a single department, consumes more time. The increasing constraints on a president's time resulting from periods of extended foreign travel or the quest for reelection also make it difficult to continue to meet with the cabinet on a regular basis.
3. As president-elect, Bill Clinton acknowledged the importance of these particular secretaries when he announced his intention to name a woman to one of these top four positions. After nominating and then withdrawing the name of Zoe Baird for attorney general and then proposing Kimba Wood, Clinton nominated, and the Senate confirmed, Janet Reno as attorney general, making her the first woman to hold this office.
4. Thomas E. Cronin, *The State of the Presidency* (Boston: Little, Brown, 1980), p. 283.
5. The EOP budget is supplemented by other executive departments that provide services for the president and his staff. These include units of the Department of Defense—the White House Communications Agency (secure communications), the air force (air transportation), the army (explosive detection and ground transportation), and the navy (helicopter transportation, marine guards, food, and medical facilities)—the General Services Administration (buildings and grounds), National Park Service (visitors and the fine arts collection), National Archives (custody of official documents), Secret Service (protection of the president, vice president, and their families as well as those of former presidents), and the State Department (official visits and receptions for foreign dignitaries).
6. The appointment process has become progressively slower. The average amount of time from designation of a nominee by the president to confirmation by the Senate and assumption of his or her designated position within the government was 2.4 months during the first year of the Kennedy administration, 3.4 during Nixon's first year, 4.6 during Carter's, 5.3 during Reagan's, 8.1 during Bush's, and 8.5 during Clinton's. *Obstacle Course: Report of the Twentieth Century Fund Task Force on the Presidential Appointment Process* (New York: Twentieth Century Fund, 1996), p. 72.
7. For the case for centralization and politicization, see Terry M. Moe, "The Politicized Presidency," in John E. Chubb and Paul E. Peterson, eds., *The New Direction in American Politics* (Washington, D.C.: Brookings Institution, 1985), pp. 235–271.
8. Reich, *Locked in the Cabinet*, pp. 108–109.
9. William C. Spragens, "White House Staffs, 1789–1974," in Bradley D. Nash et al., eds., *Organizing and Staffing the Presidency* (New York: Center for the Study of the Presidency, 1980), pp. 20–21.
10. Richard E. Neustadt, "Approaches to Staffing the Presidency," *American Political Science Review* 54 (December 1963): 857.
11. Charged with ethical violations that included the personal use of White House air and ground transportation, Sununu soon found himself the object of ridicule fueled by negative criticism, both from Republicans in the Congress and from the executive branch staffers whom he had offended.
12. Bob Woodward, *The Choice* (New York: Simon and Schuster, 1996), p. 417.
13. And the staff's concerns were justified. In one of the potentially impeachable indictments against the president, the independent counsel alleged that Clinton has purposely obstructed justice by lying to senior aides whom he knew would be called to testify about their conversations with the president.
14. Howard Kurtz, *Spin Cycle* (New York: Free Press, 1998) p. 327.
15. John Adams, *The Works of John Adams*, vol. 1, ed. C. F. Adams (Boston: Little, Brown, 1850), p. 289.
16. Thomas Jefferson, *The Writings of Thomas Jefferson*, vol. 1, ed. P. L. Ford (New York: Putnam, 1896), pp. 98–99.
17. Woodrow Wilson, *Congressional Government* (New York: Meridian Books, 1956; originally printed in 1885), p. 162.

18. Whether Garner actually used the word "spit" or an even more objectionable word (a colloquial expression for urine) is subject to some controversy.
19. According to Bradley H. Patterson, Jr.:

> Nixon was present at over 171 Cabinet meetings and chaired at least 20 of them in Ike's [Eisenhower's] absence. He attended more than 217 NSC meetings and presided at some 26 of those, joined 173 legislative leaders' meetings, chairing two of them. The Cabinet and the National Security Council papers were sent to Nixon; his policy assistant attended both the post-Cabinet debriefings at the White House and the meetings of the NSC Planning Board. Eisenhower's privileged daily Staff Notes information memoranda were also taken to the vice president. (Bradley H. Patterson, Jr. *The Ring of Power* [New York: Basic Books, 1988], p. 287)

20. Lyndon Johnson quoted in Doris Kearns, *Lyndon Johnson and the American Dream* (New York: Harper and Row, 1976), p. 164.
21. Jimmy Carter, *Keeping Faith* (New York: Bantam Books, 1982), p. 39.
22. His attendance at these meetings got him into trouble when the Iran-Contra affair became public. When he was accused of knowing of the plan and being part of the group that had approved it, Bush denied his involvement, claiming that he could not even remember the discussion of it at key White House meetings. One week before the 1992 election, however, the independent counsel, who was investigating the planning and execution of the operation, indicated that he believed that Bush had attended the critical meetings in which the plan was discussed and thus knew about it. This charge severely damaged Bush's credibility and undercut the issue of trust, which he had raised during the campaign.
23. Gore was accused of making telephone calls to solicit money for the Democratic party from his office in the White House and visiting a Buddhist temple to accept political contributions, both actions that, Republicans charged, were illegal under current law. The money collected from the temple was later returned by the Democratic party. He was also accused of having known that some of the money he raised was being diverted by the party into its federal account while other donations were funneled to the states.

7

Presidential Decision Making

THE ESSENCE OF THE PRESIDENT'S JOB IS MAKING DECISIONS—about foreign affairs, economic policy, and literally hundreds of other important matters. The task is a difficult one, and there are many obstacles to making rational decisions. Leadership in the area of decision making is of a different nature than in the other arenas of presidential activity examined in this book. Presidents need to ensure that they have before them a full range of options and the appropriate information necessary for evaluating them.

The president's leadership in decision making requires the establishment of a working relationship with subordinates and an organization in the White House that serves presidential decision-making needs. Often presidents have to persuade their own appointees in the White House and the bureaucracy to provide the options and information that they require. However, these appointees have many incentives not to do so. Lack of time to consider decisions and previous commitments of the government may constrain a president's decision making, as may the president's own personal experiences and personality.

Director presidents will have a full range of options and information at their disposal and will be relatively unencumbered by environmental constraints on their range of choices. On the other hand, being more subject to the influence of contextual factors, facilitator presidents will be more dependent on their environment for options and information and hence more constrained in their decision making.

Figure 7–1 is a graphical representation of the influences on presidential decision making. In the outer circles are the broad contexts in which decisions take place; in the inner circles are the more immediate influences. In this chapter we examine the influence of the factors represented in the outer five rings on presidential decision making. In the following chapter we consider the impact of the president's personal characteristics.

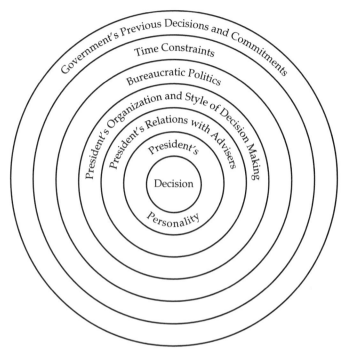

Figure 7–1. Influences on Presidential Decision Making

PREVIOUS COMMITMENTS

The first step in understanding presidential decision making is to recognize that presidents operate under severe constraints in their decision making, no matter what their approaches to making decisions. As Kennedy aide Theodore Sorensen observed:

> We assume that the President makes decisions. . . . Presidents rarely, if ever make decisions . . . in the sense of writing their conclusions largely on a clean slate. They make choices. They select options. They exercise judgments. But the basic decisions, which confine their choices, have all too often been previously made by past events or circumstances, by other nations, by pressures or predecessors or even subordinates.[1]

Thus, the president's decisions usually fall within parameters set by prior commitments of the government that obligate it to spend money, defend allies, maintain services, or protect rights.[2]

For example, when Bill Clinton took office in January 1993, the American people were in general agreement that the federal deficit was the most important matter for the new president to tackle. Clinton was not able to start from scratch and consider how best to allocate federal expenditures, however. As we discuss in Chapter 13, almost the entire federal budget was already committed before Clinton took the oath of office. A president could propose to save money by, say, eliminating the navy or ending the provision of health care for the indigent, but such solutions would receive little support. Thus, Clinton's decision making was restricted to marginal changes in the budget.

The president is also constrained by the institutional capabilities of the executive branch, which are also products of past decisions. For example, the option of airlifting aid to a country experiencing famine is a viable one because the air force has a well-established airlift capability. However, rapidly allocating federal police officers to a city experiencing a crime wave is not feasible because the national government does not have a large police force.

TIME CONSTRAINTS

The diverse obligations of the president and his top aides impose severe constraints on the amount of time they can devote to generating and evaluating options and information. According to a Carter aide, "When the President asks to see all the potential alternatives, it is an impossible request [because] . . . it involves too much time."[3]

Overloaded advisers may rely on others, who may be equally overloaded, to bring crucial information to the attention of the president. Several of President Truman's advisers believed there would be a serious danger of Chinese intervention in the Korean War if the president attempted to reunite all of Korea under a noncommunist government. However, no one went to him to argue that he should reverse his decision allowing General Douglas MacArthur to invade communist North Korea. Each person thought that someone else would do it.[4]

The president and his advisers rarely have the luxury of anticipating new issues. According to Jim Baker, secretary of state for President Bush, due to the demise of the Soviet empire, the unification of Germany, the 1989 massacre in Tiananmen Square in Beijing, the Middle East peace process, and the civil wars in Central America, the administration paid little attention to Iraq prior to the invasion of Kuwait.[5]

Sometimes deadlines make it necessary for the president and his aides to cease the consideration of information and options and make a decision. In the words of President Reagan's budget director, David Stockman:

> I just wish that there were more hours in the day or that we didn't have to do this so fast. I have these stacks of briefing books and I've got to make decisions

about specific options. . . . I don't have time, trying to put this whole package together in three weeks, so you just start making snap judgments.[6]

Because of such time limits, the less controversial parts of elaborate policies often receive inadequate attention.

If a study about an issue is not available when policy makers must make a decision, the report will go unread. Therefore, if the report is required by a certain date and more than one person has been engaged to produce it, there is an incentive for the participants to "soften" their views in order to reach a consensus. This, in turn, can mask problems that are inherent in the policies they recommend. Moreover, the pressure of hammering together a report under a strict deadline may reduce its coherence.

ORGANIZATION AND STYLE OF DECISION MAKING

Each president is unique and has broad discretion in structuring his decision making in the White House. There are many ways to do this, and each has consequences for the effectiveness of the advisory system. In this section we explore the ways in which the organization and style of the presidential advisory process can affect the president's consideration of options and information.

White House Organization

Many commentators on the presidency stress the formal aspects of White House organization, but these may be overemphasized, at least as they relate to presidential decision making. As Kennedy aide Theodore Sorensen commented, "To be preoccupied with form and structure—to ascribe to . . . form and structure a capacity to end bad decisions—is too often to overlook the more dynamic and fluid forces on which presidential decisions are based."[7]

Virtually all observers of the presidency agree that there is no ideal organization for the White House that is appropriate for every president. After analyzing sources of decisional problems in foreign policy, political scientist Alexander George came to this conclusion: "There appears to be no single structural formula by which the chief executive and his staff can convert the functional expertise and diversity of viewpoints of the many offices concerned with international affairs into consistently effective policies and decisions."[8] We may confidently add that this is also true for domestic policy decisions.

The organization of the White House will inevitably reflect the personality and work habits of the incumbent. (For a discussion of the impact of personal style on presidential performance, see Chapter 8.) Moreover, the chief executive's personal style will dominate any organizational scheme, no what the organizational charts may say. If presidents have a penchant for acting without adequate study, they will defeat any advisory system they may have established in the White House. According to an experienced presidential aide, "The nature of the man is absolutely crucial and decisive, altogether overriding the issue of organization."[9] Henry Kissinger added that the influence of a presidential assistant "derives almost exclusively from the confidence of the President, not from administrative arrangements."[10]

Presidents may simultaneously use several approaches to organizing their decision making, depending on their level of interest in a policy area, their policy priorities, and the strengths and limitations of their principal advisers in each policy area. For example, President Ford employed a hierarchical model of centralized management for foreign policy, whereby he concentrated responsibility in Henry Kissinger's hands. In economic policy, he employed a managed multiple advocacy system in which collegial discussions among a wider range of advisers occurred. In the area of domestic policy, where he did not want to undertake policy initiatives, he delegated responsibility to Vice President Rockefeller and dealt with issues on an ad hoc basis.[11] George Bush employed much the same structure in each of these policy areas.

On the other hand, organization does indeed make a difference. As explained in Chapter 6, the two most common White House organizational schemes are the hierarchical and the "spokes of the wheel." Even presidents like Ford, Carter, and Clinton, who began their tenures trying to employ the latter approach, had to alter their organizational schemes to establish more hierarchical systems headed by a chief of staff to coordinate the flow of White House business (see The Clinton Presidency box). Someone has to be responsible for scheduling appointments, coordinating the paper flow, following up on decisions, and giving status reports on projects and policy development.[12]

Presidents need their staff to give them time to focus on priorities and reflect on questions of basic strategy. The president's staff also needs to screen issues so that only those requiring direct involvement by the chief executive will be presented. If attempts are made to solve all the problems that come to the White House, the president will spread his attention and that of his advisers too thinly, wasting time and scarce resources. In addition, the more the president does, the more problems will arise for which others will hold him accountable. Presidents Ford, Carter, and Clinton all tended to become involved in relatively minor matters and were criticized, in some cases even by their own aides, for lacking the appropriate breadth of vision and understanding that are necessary to shape and guide the government.

THE CLINTON PRESIDENCY

Getting a New Chief of Staff

Shortly after Bill Clinton took office, the White House was an organizational shambles. Unlike most presidents, Clinton had not chosen between the wheel-and-spokes and the hierarchical models of organizing the White House. Instead, he placed a boyhood friend, Mack McLarty, in the position of chief of staff but then refused to empower McLarty or anyone else to impose discipline on the White House.

As a result, the White House decision-making process ran in an ad hoc manner for most of Clinton's first two years in office. The president's predisposition for deliberation, inclination to listen sympathetically, and appetite for details led to endless informal meetings involving large numbers of participants in which there was much discussion but little structure and few clear decisions. Moreover, many of the decisions that were reached were shortly reopened in yet further discussions. Numerous aides felt free to simply drop in on the president. There was little structure to the decision-making process and weak coordination of policy groups, policy initiatives, and legislative efforts.

Finally, it became clear that something needed to be done. As one cabinet officer put it, "The President by nature wants to be exposed to a lot of views and a lot of issues, and therefore you need a disciplinarian in the White House, someone able to make decisions that need to be made and don't have to go to the President, and to control the place more."* Clinton therefore asked Leon Panetta, the director of the Office of Management and Budget and a former member of Congress, to replace McLarty as chief of staff.

It took Panetta a while to get control of the White House, but soon his influence was clear. There were fewer meetings, fewer people attended the meetings that were held, and the president was better prepared. Fewer people walked into the Oval Office unscheduled, and no decision papers went to Clinton without Panetta's review. Panetta ran meetings crisply, moved sessions along, and showed little tolerance for reopening previous decisions. Decisions were made, aides had clear responsibilities, and even the president became more disciplined.

These changes did not guarantee that good decisions would be made in the White House, but they do show the importance of organization in presidential decision making. Washington is a long way from Little Rock, and Clinton had to refine his style accordingly.

---

*Quoted in Elizabeth Drew, *On the Edge: The Clinton Presidency* (New York: Touchtone, 1994), p. 348.

Some presidents—Eisenhower, Nixon, Ford, and Reagan are examples—tend to want their advisers to reach a consensus on an issue and make a recommendation to them before it receives much consideration in the Oval Office. This does not mean they will accept the recommendation, however. As Gerald Ford put it, "I reserved the right to go behind that consensus to find out what the differing views were in the process."[13]

Hierarchical staff organizations save the president's time and promote thorough evaluation of the options, yet many observers of the presidency are concerned that a centrally managed system may aggravate the proclivity toward isolation that White Houses usually evidence over time. A hierarchy that screens information may also distort it and insulate the president and those around him from public as well as private criticism. Important decisions may also be made before they even reach the president. This occurred during Reagan's second term, when chief of staff Donald Reagan unduly restricted the flow of people and paper into the Oval Office and isolated the president. The risk is that sufficient weight will not be given to countervailing views, and bad policy decisions and poor political judgments can result.

We should not assume that presidential aides can easily "capture" the president, however. Even in the Nixon administration, which boasted a "palace guard" around the president, whatever isolation occurred in the Oval Office had the full concurrence and encouragement of the president. The president used his staff to serve his own needs and to keep out those individuals he did not want to see. As long-time presidential adviser Clark Clifford put it, "In the end, every President gets the advice—and the advisers—that, in his heart, he really wants."[14] Moreover, we lack systematic evidence that Nixon's chiefs of staff provided the president with a distorted view of the issues with which he dealt.

The Form of Advice

Different presidents prefer to receive advice in different forms. Presidents Nixon and Carter preferred to reach their decisions on the basis of written memoranda discussing the pros and cons of various options. In contrast, Presidents Eisenhower, Kennedy, Johnson, Ford, Bush, and Clinton used memos to focus the discussion but frequently explored the issues with advisers in relatively open settings. President Reagan had a more detached style, reading less than other recent presidents and instead talking directly to a small number of aides.

There are advantages and disadvantages of both the verbal and paper approaches. The latter requires that options that go to the president be thoroughly "staffed out"—that is, that relevant officials comment on them following a careful analysis. This analysis decreases the chances that verbal fluency will overwhelm cool analysis and that a fleeting and superficial consensus will leave crucial assumptions unexamined. It also makes it more likely that recommendations will be translated into specific operational terms and that advisers will rigorously evaluate the consequences of the options they present to decision makers.[15]

Reviewing advice on paper saves the president time and protects the confidentiality of communications. It may also provide an outlet for those who find it difficult to express themselves directly to the president in order to articulate their views. It is not unusual for the most vociferous critic out of the president's presence to become the meekest lamb when meeting the president personally. People's oral skills often desert them when in the Oval Office.

On the other hand, the requirement that communications to the president be written and thoroughly researched may deny the chief executive access to some useful information and ideas. Some aides simply resist writing memos, as did Jody Powell, one of President Carter's closest advisers. Face-to-face discussions with advisers may also provide the president with information that is not reflected in the written word. Direct confrontation between advocates of diverse positions allows the participants to pinpoint their critiques of each other's positions and raise relevant follow-up points. Oral discussions also provide opportunities for advisers to highlight the most important points and crucial nuances in arguments and for presidents to learn the intensity of officials' views and the confidence with which they hold them. This may alert the chief executive to the level of support he may expect from officials who oppose his ultimate decision. In addition, some ideas, especially those that are highly sensitive, can be best, or perhaps only, advanced personally and informally in the give-and-take of conversation, and some may not be ready for memoranda yet deserve mention so the president will be aware of the fullest range of options.

In order for face-to-face discussions among advisers and the chief executive to be useful, the president must be able to accommodate the interpersonal tensions inherent in an advisory system of close give-and-take. However, not all presidents possess this tolerance. Ronald Reagan hated conflict, as did Richard Nixon, whose personality was not amenable to dealing with oral confrontations. Thus, Nixon conducted as much business as possible by memos. In fact, his aversion to open disagreement both affected the quality of his decision-making process and led him to alter policy decisions to achieve consensus. According to national security adviser Henry Kissinger:

> So much time, effort, and ingenuity were spent in trying to organize a consensus of the senior advisers that there was too little left to consider the weaknesses in the plan or to impose discipline on the rest of the government. There was no role for a devil's advocate. At every meeting, to gain the acquiescence of the potential recalcitrant, Nixon would offer so many modifications that the complex plan he was seeking to promote was eventually consumed.[16]

The oral approach also carries the danger that the president will make a decision based on the last person talked to instead on a careful consideration of alternatives. President Ford sometimes did this, as happened when he agreed to support Secretary of Labor John Dunlap on a labor relations bill only to face the opposition of the rest of his cabinet and top advisers after the bill passed. The president then vetoed the bill amid embarrassing publicity on his policy reversal, thus angering labor interests, which felt betrayed, and undercutting his secretary of labor, who resigned over the matter.

Another requirement for reliance on oral communication to be effective is that the president must not dominate the discussion. If he does, he may not devote sufficient attention to the advice he receives and may influence that advice by his comments. According to Hamilton Jordan, Jimmy Carter's White House chief of staff:

> I had learned . . . that if I wanted to change his mind or challenge him on something that was important or complicated, it was best to do it in writing. If I went into his office to argue with him, armed with five reasons to do something, I would rarely get beyond point one before he was aggressively countering it. I seldom got to the second or third point.[17]

When personally confronted, President Carter may have gone on the defense; written differences of opinion were perhaps easier for him to accept.

Multiple Advocacy

Closely related to the form in which presidents receive advice is the range of options they receive and the effectiveness with which those options are presented. The president should not be dependent on a single channel of information, as occurred, for example, when the president and other high officials, including the Joint Chiefs of Staff, relied upon the CIA's estimates of the success of the 1961 invasion of Cuba at the Bay of Pigs. This occurred again in 1965 when the president relied on the American embassy in the Dominican Republic for the information that led to the U.S. invasion of the island. Moreover, the key assumptions of alternatives should be evaluated by officials who did not develop them and thus have no personal stake in them. Only the CIA evaluated the Bay of Pigs plan, with disastrous consequences.

Quality decision making requires more than simply presenting the president with a diversity of views. It is also necessary that each point of view be represented by an effective advocate. This is not always the case, however, because differences exist among advisers in persuasive skills, intellectual ability, policy expertise, power, status, standing with the president, and analytical staff support. These disparities may distort the decision-making process by giving some viewpoints an undue advantage. As Kennedy aide

Theodore Sorensen observed, "The most formidable debater is not necessarily the most informed, and the most reticent may sometimes be the wisest."[18]

Multiple advocacy also forces a larger number of issues to the top—that is, to the president. Debate and give-and-take on them require a substantial commitment of time on the part of both the president and his staff, and time is a scarce commodity in the White House. According to a Ford assistant: "Multiple advocacy is very nice on paper. It just can't work in the White House. We don't have time to make sure all the advisors have access to the President. This is not day-care; it is survival of the fittest."[19] In addition, the president may not be interested in all that his advisers have to offer on a policy about which he cares little.

Multiple advocacy also runs a considerable risk of increasing staff conflict. Presidents must engage in the delicate balancing act of being in firm control of the process of decision making while encouraging free and open discussion. This is difficult enough to accomplish while they are considering options. It is even more of a challenge after they decide on a course of action, because it is not uncommon for both winners and losers among presidential advisers to be less than gracious and turn to backstabbing and leaking information to the press.

Some political scientists have suggested that the president needs a process manager to balance the resources of his advisers and strengthen the weaker advocates, ensure that all options are articulated and have effective advocates, set up additional channels of information, arrange for independent evaluations of decisional premises and options when necessary, and generally monitor the decision-making process and identify and correct any malfunctions. This delicate role can easily be undermined if the custodian is also a policy adviser, presidential spokesperson, enforcer of decisions, administrative operator, or watchdog for the president's power stakes. He or she must remain an "honest broker" who is concerned with the process of advising the president. This adviser must also keep his or her own staff small so that it will not become specialized and circumvent established channels of advice.

In some decision-making situations an adviser may adopt the role of "devil's advocate" in order to provide a challenge to the dominant point of view. The devil's advocate may relieve some of the stress of decision making because officials feel they have considered all sides of an issue, and there may be some public relations benefits for publicizing the fact that the president considered a full range of views. Decision makers may also benefit from listening to and rebutting challenges to their course of action, and those who are least enthusiastic about a decision may be more willing to join in a consensus view if there was prior debate.

Nevertheless, the devil's advocate does not necessarily improve the quality of White House decision making. Since the devil's advocate is playing a role and is not a true dissenter, he or she is unlikely to persist in opposition or try to form coalitions or employ all resources to persuade others. Such an advocate is not really engaged in a truly competitive struggle. Moreover, officials may discount ahead of time the comments of someone who persistently plays the devil's advocate role. Nonetheless, if devil's advocacy is not routinized, there is no assurance that it will operate when needed to provide balance to an argument.

Even if presidents choose to consider a range of viewpoints, they may not benefit fully from them. For example, Gerald Ford was criticized for falling back on his experience as a legislator and reaching decisions by weighing the views of others and then leaning in the direction of the consensus opinion. Presidential authority is diluted when the chief executive bases decisions on the number of advisers on a side rather than his own informed judgment.

Presidential Involvement

In his classic study of presidential power, Richard Neustadt alerted future presidents that they would need information, including tangible details, to construct a necessary frame of reference for decision making.[20] Presidents cannot assume that any person or advisory system will provide them with the options and information they require, and thus they must reach out widely.

If a president fails to do so and is not able to actively oversee the decision-making system, the consequences may be profound. For example, Bill Clinton was blindsided by the negative congressional and public response to his proposal to lift the ban on homosexuals in the military. He saw the issue as one of discrimination, but many others saw it in other terms—as an issue of morality, of military readiness, or both. By not seeking other perspectives, the president subjected himself to a firestorm of criticism and had to backtrack on his policy.

Other presidents have faced similar problems. On January 17, 1986, President Ronald Reagan signed a document (technically called a "finding") that paved the way for the United States to sell arms secretly to Iran in hopes of obtaining the release of American hostages held in the Middle East. The finding also created the opportunity to generate profits on the arms sales, which then were diverted covertly to the contra rebels fighting the Nicaraguan government.

The finding was presented to the president by his national security adviser, Vice Admiral John Poindexter. It included a cover memo prepared by Lt. Col. Oliver North, which the president did not read. Although the memo pointed out that the plan was opposed by the secretaries of state and defense, it presented neither their opposing views nor justifications for its assertions of success. However, the president failed to insist that better staff work be done. Eleven days earlier, before the National Security Council meeting he had called to discuss the memo took place, the president had signed a similar finding, which also had not been fully staffed out, failing to realize that the paper was only a proposal for discussion. As he explained in his memoirs, "Because I was so concerned about getting the hostages home, I may not have asked enough questions about how the Iranian initiative was being conducted."[21]

The arms sale policy was a failure and undermined the nation's strongly asserted position of refusing to trade arms—or anything else—for hostages. When details of this policy decision began to emerge later in the year, there was a loud public outcry. The president's standing fell substantially in the polls, and his political clout was diminished. The situation became even worse when the diversion of funds to the contras came to light. At this point the president fired North, accepted the resignation of Poindexter, and had to endure a year of congressional hearings and a critical investigation by a special commission that he had to appoint to examine his handling of the matter.

A spate of books written by top officials in the Reagan administration (detractors term them "kiss and tell") has revealed that Ronald Reagan was a peculiarly detached decision maker. As noted in Chapter 6, he had strong views on the basic goals of public policy but left it to others to implement his broad vision. Aides prepared detailed scripts on index cards for his use in meetings. Reagan's detachment and lack of mastery of policy details hindered his evaluation of policy options, a process he left to others.

RELATIONSHIPS WITH ADVISERS

Presidents require the services of personal aides to carry out their duties. Since they must rely heavily on their aides and work closely with them, they naturally choose persons of similar attitudes and compatible personalities. Moreover, strong personalities, which typically characterize presidents, create environments to their liking and weed out irritations.

Disagreeing with the President

Many—perhaps most—people have found it difficult to stand up to a president and disagree with him. For example, several of President Reagan's top aides had doubts about his economic policies even in 1981 but did not relay them to the president until after the program was enacted. At times, advisers may be strong advocates of a position before a meeting with the president yet will completely switch their arguments during the meeting if they learn the president has accepted the opposite view. It was because of this phenomenon that President Kennedy often absented himself from meetings of his advisers during the Cuban missile crisis—he wanted the participants to feel free to speak their minds.

Sometimes advisers find it difficult to disagree with the president due to his strong, dynamic, or magnetic personality. These traits are certainly not unusual in successful politicians, especially presidents. For example, former White House assistant Chester Cooper wrote that President Johnson often polled his foreign policy advisers one at a time to hear their views on the Vietnam War. Each dutifully would respond, "I agree," even though Cooper, and undoubtedly others, did not. Cooper even dreamed of answering no, but he never did.[22] Other Johnson administration officials reported a similar tendency for those around the president to tell him what they thought he wanted to hear about the war rather than what they really thought.

Source: Drawing by H. Martin; Copyright © 1979 The New Yorker Magazine, Inc.

One reason for the reluctance of presidential aides to challenge the president is that they are completely dependent on him for their jobs, their advancement, and the gratification of their egos through his favor. Cabinet members are nearly as dependent, although they may also have support in Congress or from interest groups. Because aides usually desire to perpetuate their positions, they may refrain from giving the president "unpleasant" information or from fighting losing battles on behalf of their principles. Even Nixon's White House chief of staff, H. R. Haldeman, felt that in order to survive in his own job, he could not fight sufficiently to counter the dark side of the president's character.

Thus, presidents often find it difficult to evoke critical responses from staff members. Gerald Ford made this observation:

> Few people, with the possible exception of his wife, will ever tell a President that he is a fool. There's a majesty to the office that inhibits even your closest friends from saying what is really on their minds. They won't tell you that you just made a lousy speech or bungled a chance to get your point across. . . . You can tell them you want the blunt truth; you can leave instructions on every bulletin board, but the guarded response you get never varies.
>
> And yet the President—any President—needs to hear straight talk. He needs to be needled once in a while, if only to be brought down from the false pedestal that the office provides. He needs to be told that he is, after all, only another human being with the same virtues and weaknesses as anyone else. And he needs to be reminded of this constantly if he's going to keep his perspective.[23]

Discouraging Advice

The reluctance of advisers to disagree with the president may be reinforced by an executive who "punishes" those aides who present options or information he dislikes. Lyndon Johnson was such a person. He forced top aides and officials who dissented on Vietnam to leave his administration, and he went so far as to reduce contact with such key people as Secretaries of Defense Robert McNamara and Clark Clifford and Vice President Hubert Humphrey.

Johnson's press secretary, George Reedy, observed that the Johnson White House had an inner political life of its own. Consequently, the staff carefully studied the president's state of mind to gain and maintain access to him. They wanted to be around when there was good news to report and discreetly absent when the news was bad in hopes that someone else would receive the blame.[24] Naturally, this gamesmanship served to distort Johnson's view of reality.

Richard Nixon had little interest in hearing critiques of his weak points, and those who attempted to criticize him did not maintain their influence for long. Even as secure and personable a president as Franklin Roosevelt is reported to have permitted only staffers who would not challenge him. Bill Clinton is generally open to a range of views, but he has a hot temper, which he frequently unleashes at aides.

The dampening effect of behavior like that of Johnson, Nixon, or Clinton on discussions even outside the Oval Office can be substantial. Aides may be fearful of presidential punishment or tirades, and therefore remain silent lest they provoke the president to anger. Johnson's Office of Congressional Relations chief Lawrence O'Brien and Vice President Hubert Humphrey were in constant contact for months before they became aware of each other's views on Vietnam. Because President Johnson equated criticism with disloyalty, even the highest officials in the White House kept their dissent to themselves.

Strong presidents may also, in effect, tell their advisers what advice to offer them. Richard Nixon turned to Secretary of the Treasury John Connally for "tough" advice—for example, when he wanted someone to urge him to mine the harbor at Haiphong, North Vietnam. A Nixon aide once observed the president and Connally cruising down the Potomac on the presidential yacht, the *Sequoia*, as Nixon was trying to talk his adviser into recommending that he institute wage and price controls on the economy.

Presidents with heightened fears of security leaks may place loyalty above competence, independence, or openness as a criterion for evaluating and relying on their advisers. They may also control the information flow tightly and keep everyone, even insiders, in the dark. One of the reasons why President Johnson relied so heavily on a group of five or six high officials (called the "Tuesday lunch group") to advise him on the Vietnam War was that he felt the larger National Security Council leaked too much information. According to Secretary of State Dean Rusk: "The Tuesday luncheons were where the really important issues regarding Vietnam were discussed in great detail. This was where the real decisions were made. And everyone knew how to keep his mouth shut."[25]

Ironically, one inhibition on freedom of dissension in the White House and the upper levels of the bureaucracy is public opinion. If the president allows an open discussion of policy views, there will inevitably be disagreement, which then may be presented in the press as evidence that the president is not in control and the White House lacks a sense of direction. Thus, by being open, the president may lose some public support, but by being closed to options and information, he may make poor decisions.

Not all presidents discourage dissent, however. George Bush was a secure decision maker who was well informed, knowledgeable, experienced, and involved in decision making. He wanted to hear a wide range of options, and he worked at maintaining civility and openness in discussion. Similarly,

Dwight Eisenhower established an environment in which his advisers felt free to challenge his views.

Groupthink

Psychologist Irving Janis argued that another factor discouraging disagreement among presidential advisors is a psychological phenomenon he terms *groupthink*. Groupthink refers to the conformist thinking that may result when people are intensely involved in small, cohesive decision-making groups, such as are formed during crisis situations. What happens, according to Janis, is that the stress of a crisis generates a desire for unity among policy advisers which, in turn, reduces their uncertainty over the proper course of action. The advisers' desire for unanimity overrides their motivations to realistically appraise situations and policy alternatives. Critical opinions are suspended, and a consensus is produced.[26] A number of high-level administration decisions may have been influenced by the groupthink effect. The ill-fated decision by almost all President Kennedy's advisers to support an invasion of the Bay of Pigs in Cuba in 1961 is one illustration that Janis used to support his thesis. Other examples of conformist—and incorrect—decision making include the failure to anticipate the Japanese attack on Pearl Harbor and the North Korean attacks on South Korea that began World War II and the Korean War.

Staff Rivalries

Feuding and infighting for power and access to the president among ambitious aides are also obstacles to rational decision making. This rivalry takes several forms. One of the most common techniques is to attack rivals through leaking to the press that they are out of favor with the president or not competent to carry out their duties. Sometimes the leaks place competitors for power in a context that is favorable but will displease the president, who may prefer having credit and publicity for himself rather than his aides.

In recent years, the Nixon, Ford, and Reagan administrations stand out for the extent of their internal feuding and infighting. One high-level Reagan aide disclosed how he and other White House officials tried to undercut Secretary of State Alexander Haig: "In a classic case of Washington infighting, we threw virtually every booby trap in his way that we could, planted every story, egged the press on to get down on him."[27]

This widespread feuding encourages self-interested behavior by presidential advisers, which may distort their vision and cause them to overextend their arguments and present unbalanced discussions of options and their consequences to the president. There is also a tendency for competing advisers to seek to aggrandize influence and monopolize the counsel on which presidential decisions are based, thereby providing insufficient information, analysis, and deliberation for decisions. Staff rivalry also detracts from the efficiency of White House operations, as it wastes time and lowers morale. Moreover, feuding in the White House can embarrass the president if it is covered in the press (which it inevitably is).

High officials in Washington know that their ability to interact effectively with the bureaucracy depends on being known for their effectiveness with the president. Former Secretary of State Dean Rusk argued that "the real organization of government at higher echelons is . . . how confidence flows down from the President."[28] To maintain their reputations for effectiveness with the president, officials may not strongly advocate positions that they consider sound if they feel the president is unlikely to adopt their proposals. An official does not usually want to be known as someone whose advice the president rejected.

Loss of Perspective

An additional potential hindrance to sound advice for the president is the loss of perspective by White House aides. Because working in the White House is a unique experience, a narrowing of viewpoints can easily occur. Especially for top aides, the environment is luxurious, secure, and heady; the exercise of power is an everyday experience. The potential for isolation is real, and therefore the chief executive must fight these insulating tendencies. President Johnson was very sensitive about the risk that his aides might lose perspective, so he closely controlled the use of White House perks and stripped his staff of pretensions with a "merciless persistency."[29]

Role Conceptions

Advisers' conceptions of their jobs influence their delivery of information and options. President Eisenhower's secretaries of defense, Charles Wilson and Neil McElroy, considered themselves managers of the department and did not become heavily involved in disputes over foreign policy or strategic doctrine. By contrast, Secretary of Defense Robert McNamara adopted an aggressive stance as an adviser, yet McNamara's colleague, Secretary of State Dean Rusk, did not consider it his job to participate in policy disputes with his colleagues or the president. In fact, many observers thought that Rusk failed to effectively present State Department views on important foreign policy issues.

The impact of the decision-making process on the substance of one important policy is shown in the Hot-Button Issue box.

☼ HOT- BUTTON ISSUE

What Difference Does the Decision-Making Process Make?

Presidents Eisenhower and Johnson both faced the decision of military intervention in Vietnam (in 1954 and 1964–1965, respectively). Eisenhower chose not to intervene, while Johnson eventually sent more than a half million American troops. How did the two presidents' decision-making processes affect their decisions?

Eisenhower, who had headed organizations of enormous size and complexity as a military commander, was sensitive about the impact of the structure of advisory systems on the process of analyzing policies and making decisions. His system produced spirited, open debate; his aides would challenge the president, often tenaciously, even though he openly expressed his own opinions. He was exposed to diverse views (rather than "loaded" presentations of options), sharply focused alternatives, and advice separated from parochial interests. In addition, he supplemented his formal advisory system with an informal, fluid process of consultation that interacted with, and reinforced, the formal system.

Contrary to the conventional wisdom of the time, Eisenhower was clearly in charge and kept his options open. He reasoned explicitly about the means and ends, the trade-offs, and the consequences of options, and he thought strategically, viewing issues as parts of more comprehensive patterns. In this way, he set the tone for decision making in his administration.

Johnson, in contrast, was insensitive to the impact of advisory structures. His advisory system was organizationally chaotic, marked by an absence of regular meetings and routinized procedures, shifts in the membership of advisory and decision-making groups, a reliance on out-of-channel advocacy, weak staff work, and other impediments to rigorous policy analysis.

Johnson's heavy reliance on informal advising by a few people and a lack of systematized staff work left many policy disagreements unresolved and unexamined. Frequently, options were neither coherently assembled nor carefully considered, and there was a lack of broad strategic debate in which the underlying assumptions of policy could be questioned. Policy differences at all levels were typically not sharply stated or directly analyzed, and there was a lack of forums in which contradictory views could be clarified, studied, and debated. The views of most dissenters were not rejected after discussion; instead, they were simply not discussed. The lack of systematic policy analysis and the reliance on a few advisers left the upper and lower levels of the foreign policy community separated, and the impact of advice became more a function of skill and resources in bureaucratic politics than the logic of the argument.

In many ways, the president was his own worst enemy. He immersed himself in detail rather than focusing on broad policy questions, and he was insulated from confrontation with his advisers' views. Johnson failed to press for additional alternatives or question incisively the options presented to him. Continuing the pattern of his years in the Senate, he remained preoccupied with searching for consensus within, and probing for areas of agreement rather than disagreement. His personal interactions with his advisers encouraged a narrowing rather than a broadening of options, and his intolerance of disagreement had a chilling effect on the range of advice he received.

In sum, Eisenhower was a planner and conceptualizer, whereas Johnson was an individualistic political operator. Eisenhower was preoccupied with analyzing policy, and Johnson, with the politics of making it. Each constructed an advisory system to meet his needs. At least in the case of Vietnam, these advisory systems, as well as the people who composed them and the presidents themselves, made a difference in the options the president chose.[30]

BUREAUCRATIC POLITICS AND DECISION MAKING

A primary source of options and information for the president is the bureaucracy. However, this is not a neutral instrument. Individuals and the agencies they represent have interests of their own to advance and protect and may not necessarily view issues from the president's perspective. Moreover, the structure of the flow of information and the development of options in the White House may also hinder decision making.

Organizational Parochialism

Government agencies have a tendency toward inbreeding, as the selective recruitment of new staff serves to develop homogeneous attitudes. People who are attracted to work for government agencies are likely to support the policies carried out by those agencies, whether they be in the fields of social welfare, agriculture, or national defense. Naturally, agencies prefer hiring like-minded persons. Within each agency, the distribution of rewards creates further pressure to view things from the perspective of the status quo. Personnel who do not support established organizational goals and approaches to meeting them are unlikely to be promoted to important positions. Moreover, all but a few high-level policy makers spend their careers within a single agency or department. Since people want to believe in what they do for a living, this long association strongly influences the attitudes of bureaucrats.

Related to longtime service in an agency is the relatively narrow range of each agency's responsibilities. Officials in the Department of Education, for example, do not deal with the budget for the entire national government but only with the part that pertains to their programs. It is up to others to recommend to the president what is best allocated to education and what should go to national defense, health, or housing. With each bureaucratic unit focusing on its own programs, there are few people to view these programs from a wider, national perspective.

Influences from outside an agency also encourage parochial views among bureaucrats. When interest groups and congressional committees support an agency, they expect continued bureaucratic support in return. Since these outsiders generally favor the policies the bureaucracy has been carrying out all along (and which they probably helped initiate), what they really want is to perpetuate the status quo.

The combination of these factors results in a relatively uniform environment for policy making. Intraorganizational communications pass mainly among persons who share similar frames of reference and reinforce bureaucratic parochialism by their continued association.

The influence of parochialism is strong enough that even some presidential appointees, who are in office for only short periods of time, are "captured" and adopt the narrow views of their bureaucratic units. The dependence of such officials on their subordinates for information and advice, the need to maintain organizational morale by supporting established viewpoints, and pressures from their agencies' clienteles combine to discourage high-ranking officials from maintaining broad views of the public interest.

President Nixon observed that "it is inevitable when an individual has been in a Cabinet position or, for that matter, holds any position in Government, [that] after a certain length of time he becomes an advocate of the status quo; rather than running the bureaucracy, the bureaucracy runs him."[31] Thus, parochialism can lead officials to see different faces on the same issue.

When President Carter considered asking Congress for authorization for a 20 percent cutback in wheat acreage and the placing of several million tons of food and feed grains in reserve, there arose an intense internal debate, in which the Department of Agriculture, reacting to the demands of farmers, wanted an even bigger cutback; the Treasury Department and the

Council of Economic Advisers opposed any cutback out of concern for future consumer prices and the export potential of the United States should food shortages develop; and the State Department expressed concern about the proposal's effect on international negotiations regarding an international grain reserve. In other words, policy makers in different bureaucratic units with different responsibilities saw the same policy in a different light and reacted differently to it.

A president can benefit from a diversity of views among the organizational units, but the White House must recognize that each view is likely to be articulated from a biased perspective. It was to combat this parochialism that President Reagan went to considerable lengths to insulate his new cabinet appointees from the traditional agency arguments in defense of programs that the White House had slated for cuts. The appointees received their initial briefings from the president, the director of the Office of Management and Budget, and citizens groups rather than from the bureaucracy; they were often assigned deputies with close personal and ideological ties to the White House; and they were given little time to react to the president's proposals.

Maintaining the Organization

As a result of parochialism in the bureaucracy, career officials come to believe that the health of their organization and its programs is vital to the national interest. In their eyes, this well-being depends, in turn, on the ability of the organization to fulfill its missions, secure the necessary resources (personnel, money, and authority), and maintain its influence. Organizational personnel can pursue their personal quests for power and prestige, the goals of their organization, and the national interest simultaneously without perceiving any role conflicts. Moreover, policy makers in different organizational units are prone to see different faces on the same issues due to their different organizational needs.

The single-mindedness of policy makers who are attached to various agencies causes them to raise options and gather information that support the interests of their organization and avoid or oppose those which may challenge those interests. In this way, the goals of maintaining an organization may actually *displace* the goals of solving the problems for which the organization was created. As one former high White House official wrote, "For many cabinet officers, the important question was whether their department would have the principal responsibility for the new program— not the hard choices that lay hidden within it."[32]

Within most organizations, there is a dominant view of the *essence* of the organization's mission and of the attitudes, skills, and experience that employees should have to carry it out. Organizations usually propose options that they believe will build up and reinforce the essential aspects of their organizations. For example, during the Vietnam War, the air force lobbied for strategic bombing and deep interdiction, even though its bombing campaigns had not enjoyed unqualified success in previous wars. One way to promote this goal was to argue for bombing as a central feature of U.S. policy in order to show its utility. The lack of success only reinforced the air force's efforts to step up the bombing even further; its commanders never admitted that it was not accomplishing its objectives.

Organizations will also vigorously resist the efforts of others to take away, decrease, or share their essence and the resources deemed necessary to realize it. In their struggles over roles and missions, bureaucrats may distort the information and options that are provided to senior officials. For example, during the Vietnam War, the air force and navy were each concerned that the other might encroach on its bombing missions; the navy was also concerned about justifying the high cost of its aircraft carriers. Thus, the two branches competed in their efforts at air warfare. The aspect of this interservice competition that was most damaging to the accuracy of the perceptions of high-level decision makers concerning the degree of American success in the war was the battle over the relative effectiveness of each service's air warfare. Each service was concerned about future budgets and missions and felt it could not let the other get the upper hand. Thus, each branch exaggerated its own performance and expected the other to do likewise.

Budgets are another vital component of the strategies necessary to maintain an organization. This is true for grant-awarding agencies as well as for agencies with large operational capabilities like the military services and the Department of Agriculture. Because the staff within governmental organizations generally believe that their work is vital to the national interest, and because conventional wisdom stipulates that a larger budget enables an organization to perform its functions more effectively, units will normally request an increase in funding and fight any decreases. The size of a group's budget not only determines the resources available for its services but also serves as a sign of the importance that others attach to the organization's functions.

Agency personnel also examine any substantive proposal to ascertain its impact on the budget and will rarely suggest adding a new function to their responsibilities if it must be financed from monies already allocated for ongoing activities. Moreover, components of large organizations, like units in the military or the Department of Health and Human Services, are concerned about maintaining or increasing their percentage of the larger unit's budget.

An organization's staff members are likely to raise and support options that give them autonomy. In their view, they know best how to perform their essential mission. Consequently, they tend to resist options that would place control in the hands of higher officials or require close coordination with other organizations. This desire for autonomy helps explain why several agencies independently gather and evaluate national security intelligence from their own perspective. As Richard Nixon complained after being disappointed by the intelligence reports he received, "Those guys spend all their time fighting each other."[33]

Because organizations seek to create and maintain autonomous jurisdictions, they rarely oppose each other's projects. This self-imposed restraint reduces the conflict between organizations, and correspondingly reduces the options and information available to the president. In dealing with their superiors, the leaders of an organization often guard their autonomy by presenting only one option for a new program. The rationale is that if higher officials are not permitted to choose among options, they also cannot interfere with the organization's preference. Once an agency of government has responsibility for a program, however, it has a tendency to evaluate it positively.

Organizational and Personal Influence

To achieve the policies they desire, organizations and individuals seek influence. In pursuing power, officials often further distort the processes of generating options and gathering information for the president. One way for organizations to increase their influence is to defer to one another's expertise. The operations of all large-scale organizations, including governments, require a considerable degree of specialization and expertise. Those who possess this expertise, whether within executive agencies or on congressional committees, naturally believe that they know best about a subject in their field and therefore desire primary influence over the resolution of issues in their subject area. Because each set of experts has a stake in deference to expertise (each receives benefits from it), reciprocal deference to expertise becomes an important theme in policy making. One result of this reciprocity is that fewer challenges to expert views are aired than might otherwise be the case.

For several decades there was an implicit agreement between the Departments of State and Defense that each would stay out of the other's affairs. Thus, during the Vietnam War, the State Department often took no part in shaping war policies and refrained from airing many of its views. Contributing to this restraint was Secretary of Defense Robert McNamara's adamant belief that the State Department should not challenge the military's appraisal of the actual progress of the war. Once when the director of the State Department's Bureau of Intelligence and Research attempted to do so, McNamara forcefully elicited a promise from Secretary of State Dean

Rusk that such a challenge would not recur. He thus deliberately blocked the flow of information on the war. This meant that policy makers had to defer to Defense Department assessments, which were often inaccurate and biased toward military rather than political solutions.

Although deference to expertise is not always a satisfactory way of resolving conflicts in policy making, it is often the only possible course of action. Governmental agencies are the sole source of data and analysis on many issues. As their work becomes increasingly specialized, it becomes harder to check their information and evaluations. This problem is exacerbated by a need for secrecy on most national security policies, which makes it necessary to limit even further the number of participants in the policy-making process.

To take full advantage of deference to expertise and increase their influence further, organizations seek to prevent their own experts from disseminating conflicting information and options. Contrary information and evaluations are believed to undercut the credibility of a unit's position. Moreover, by presenting several real options, a unit increases the range of possible policy decisions, and commensurately decreases the probability that the option favored by the unit's leaders will be selected. Thus, the Joint Chiefs of Staff rarely disagree in their recommendations. Similarly, the relevant departments never presented President Carter with real options on welfare reform, in part because they were afraid he would select an alternative they opposed. No one would insist to the president that reform would be costly because they feared he would then reject their reform efforts.[34]

If disagreements exist among the experts in an organizational unit, efforts to produce an appearance of unanimity can reduce the experts' recommendations to broad generalizations. A record of agreement on the least disputed common denominators usually fails to mention many controversial points, which may be crucial to the ultimate success of the policy at issue. When compromise positions reach the president in a form that suggests a unified consensual judgment, they can give him a false sense of security because he may lack an awareness of the potential problems buried within the recommendations.

The imperative of consensus can also stifle innovative thinking. For example, the Bush administration launched a strategic review of foreign policy early in its first year. The papers were produced by bureaucratic units that had vested interests in established policy. As Secretary of State Jim Baker put it, "In the end what we received was mush," with potentially controversial and interesting ideas omitted in the name of bureaucratic consensus.[35]

For bureaucrats interested in their own careers, the prospect of a deferred promotion, or even dismissal, makes them reluctant to report information that undercuts the official stands of their organizations. The example of the Foreign Service officers who frankly (and accurately) reported on the strength of the communists in China during the late 1940s was not quickly forgotten in the bureaucracy. They were driven from the Foreign Service for allegedly holding procommunist sympathies. Over forty years later, in 1992, CIA Director Robert Gates announced that many within the CIA felt that intelligence reports were still being tailored to please superiors.

Some officials anticipate sanctions even when they are not exercised. One of the most embarrassing incidents of Jimmy Carter's early presidency was the scandal surrounding Bert Lance, his close friend and the director of the Office of Management and Budget. Lance eventually resigned under pressure after details of his business and personal financial dealings were made public. For our purposes, the question is why the president did not know of these problems.

At least a large part of the answer seems to be that officials responsible for reviewing Lance's background soft-pedaled the reports in an effort to cultivate the goodwill of the new administration. The deputy comptroller general (who was acting comptroller) later testified that he knew of Lance's problems but downplayed them to avoid losing his job. Indeed, he hoped to be appointed comptroller general. It also appears that the relevant U.S. attorney closed his investigation of Lance early, over the objections of several of his subordinates, in hopes of not irritating the new president. The attorney's priorities were to keep his job and qualify for a federal pension.

Experts can create an illusion of competition when they agree to compare their preferred action to unfeasible alternatives. Lyndon Johnson's advisers have been criticized for juxtaposing, in 1964, their favored option of bombing North Vietnam against two phony options: in effect, destroy the world or scuttle and run.

Bureaucratic Structure

The structure of administrative organizations is one of the factors that impedes the flow of options and information to higher-level decision makers.

Hierarchy   Most bureaucracies have a hierarchical structure, whereby the information on which decisions are based usually passes from bottom to top. At each step in this ladder of communication, personnel screen the information from the previous stage. Such screening is necessary because the people at the top—presidents—cannot absorb all the detailed information that exists on an issue and must have subordinates summarize and synthesize the information as it proceeds upward. The longer the communication chain, the greater is the chance that judgments will replace facts, nuances or caveats will be excluded, subordinates will paint a positive face on a situation to improve their own image or that of their organization, human error will distort the overall picture, and the speculations of "experts" will be reported as fact.

Screening, summarizing, and human error are not the only pitfalls in the transmission of information. When subordinates are asked to transmit information that can be used to evaluate their performance, they have a tendency to distort it in order to put themselves in the most favorable light. For example, many of the military's assessments of damage done to Iraqi forces and weaponry in the Gulf War turned out to be erroneous, having been inflated substantially by soldiers in the field.

Subordinates sometimes distort facts by not reporting those that indicate danger. President Kennedy was not apprised of the following problems with the contingency plan for the invasion of the Bay of Pigs: the men participating in the invasion had not been told to flee to the mountains should the invasion fail; between the beach and the mountains, which supposedly offered refuge, was a large swamp; there was no good evidence that the Cuban people would rise up to support the invasion; and only one-third of the men had received guerrilla training. Instead, he was simply informed that if the invasion failed, the troops would retreat to the mountains, where they would carry out guerrilla warfare and win the support of the Cuban people. At other times subordinates may exaggerate the evidence in support of their favored alternative in order to increase the probability that it will be chosen.

Even in the hierarchical executive branch, the president cannot depend that information will be centralized. There was a great deal of information pointing to the impending Japanese attack on Pearl Harbor, for example, but it was never fully organized. No one brings forward all the political, economic, social, military, and diplomatic considerations of a policy in a recognizable manner for the president's deliberation because the bureaucracy that is relevant to any policy is too decentralized and too large and produces too much information to coordinate it effectively.

The president may attempt to compensate for the problems of hierarchy by sending personal aides or outsiders to assess a situation directly and propose options. However, the person assigned to the task, more than the situation itself, may determine the nature of the resulting report. Moreover, the president cannot bypass senior officials very often without lowering their morale and undercutting their operational authority.

President Kennedy's chief White House national security adviser, McGeorge Bundy, ordered that cables to the State Department, the CIA, and the Pentagon be sent directly to the White House, and not just to the Washington headquarters of those departments where they could be summarized and analyzed for transmittal to the president. However, this practice did not correct any distortion that may have gone into the cables in the first place, and someone still had to summarize and synthesize the tremendous volume of information before it reached the president. President Bush discovered the same problems when he asked for direct information channels from the field.

Standard Operating Procedures   Organizations use routines or standard operating procedures (SOPs) to gather and process information in a methodical fashion. However, the character of the SOPs may delay the recognition of critical information, distort the quality of information, and limit the options presented to policy makers.

In the case of the Cuban missile crisis, several weeks before the president was aware of the missiles there was already a good deal of information in the U.S. intelligence system pointing to the missiles' presence. However, the time required by SOPs to sort out raw information and double-check it delayed recognition of the new situation. Organizational routines also masked signs forecasting the 1974 leftist coup in Portugal. Officials from the intelligence services of the CIA, the Defense Department, and the State Department testified after the event that their routines failed to focus much attention on Portugal and they could not shift personnel rapidly to a new area of concern.

SOPs affect, not only *if* and *when* information is collected, but also its substance. In Vietnam the military's concentration on the technical aspects of bombing caused it to substitute a set of short-run physical objectives for the ultimate political goals of the war. Military reports emphasized physical destruction per se rather than the political impact of such destruction. The enemy's capacity to recruit more men or rebuild a structure never seemed to enter into the calculations.

Standard operating procedures give disproportionate weight to information entering the system from regular channels. For example, the United States was highly dependent on the shah of Iran and Savak, the shah's secret police organization, for information about that nation. Up until a few months before the shah was deposed, they reported to the CIA and President Carter that there was no likelihood of revolution. The White House rejected more pessimistic reports from journalists and others outside the regular flow of information.

SOPs structure the process of decision making by preselecting those who will be asked for advice and predetermining when they will be asked. There are routine ways of invading foreign countries and determining agency budgets. Some persons will be involved at earlier stages than others, and some will be viewed as having more legitimate and expert voices in policy discussions. When Lyndon Johnson limited his circle of personal advisers on the Vietnam War to a half-dozen top officials, those at a lower rung in the foreign policy hierarchy found it harder to have their dissent heard. In addition, there was little opportunity for others in the cabinet to challenge the war policy because they were not located in the proper decision-making channels.

Purely analytic units often have problems in being heard. According to Henry Kissinger:

> I can think of no exception to the rule that advisers without a clear-cut area of responsibility eventually are pushed to the periphery by day-to-day operators. The other White House aides resent interference in their spheres. The schedulers become increasingly hesitant in finding time on the President's calendar.[35]

Thus, information is most likely to influence policy making if the position of those who have it ensures that they must be consulted before a decision is made.

Standard operating procedures also affect the nature of the alternatives proposed by bureaucratic units. Bureaucracies typically propose their standard ways of doing things rather than innovative solutions to problems. These standard policies may not be appropriate for the problem at hand, as when military commanders attempted to transplant to Indochina the operational methods of conventional warfare that had been successful in the European battle theaters of World War II, instead of developing a strategy more appropriate for fighting a counterinsurgency effort in the jungles of Vietnam.[36]

As a result of problems with established routines, presidents often create special task forces of "outside" experts to develop new programs, as President Clinton did with his health care proposal. Such bodies, when brought together for a new purpose, are less likely than established agencies to be blinded by SOPs.

Because only decision makers directly responsible for a policy are normally consulted on sensitive matters, fewer advisers contribute to secret deliberations than to debate on more open issues. This reduces the range of options that are considered in a secret decision and limits the analysis of the few options that are considered. For example, the secrecy of President Johnson's "Tuesday lunch group," which made the important decisions on the Vietnam War, prevented an advance agenda. Thus, decisions were made without a full prior review of the options. Secrecy also makes it easier for those directly involved to dismiss (intentionally or unintentionally) the dissenting or offbeat ideas of outsiders as the products of ignorance. This is unfortunate because secret information is often inaccurate or misleading. President Kennedy wished he had not been successful in persuading the *New York Times* not to publish the plans for the Bay of Pigs invasion as afterward, he felt that publicity might have elicited some useful critiques.

CONCLUSION

Presidents face an enormously difficult and complex task in making decisions on a wide range of issues. They must work within the parameters of the national government's prior commitments, and are further constrained by the limited time they can devote to considering options and information on any one policy. In addition, they face a number of other potential hazards in reaching decisions. The struggling facilitator, not the dominating director, is the description that generally matches the process of presidential decision making.

There are a variety of ways for presidents to organize the White House and acquire advice, but not all are equally useful in ensuring that presidents are presented with a full range of options, each supported with effective advocacy. Moreover, presidents may experience problems if their aides are reluctant to present candid advice, which may be aggravated by the aides' desire to increase their own influence and by the presidents themselves.

Bureaucratic politics also plays a role in determining the options and information that presidents receive and the forms in which these are presented. Agencies and their personnel inevitably have narrower perspectives than the White House and will desire to maintain and expand their programs, status, and influence. Those ambitions often bias the options and information presented to the White House. The ways in which bureaucratic units collect, process, and transmit options and information and the secrecy that sometimes accompanies the process may further distort what the president perceives.

It is important that presidents be sensitive to the many obstacles to effective decision making and attempt to avoid or compensate for them as well as possible, while realizing that perfectly rational decision making is unattainable.

DISCUSSION QUESTIONS

1. It is convenient to argue that the president should examine *all* the options regarding an important policy issue, yet is it really possible for presidents to evaluate a wide range of options on all the policy questions with which they must deal? What do you think presidents really do? Do conservative presidents, for example, often consider liberal options, and vice versa? Give examples of contemporary presidents to support your answers.
2. We have seen that organizational parochialism may bias the information that bureaucratic units provide to the president. Is there a solution to this problem? Is it possible for committed, expert managers to run government agencies and still take a broad view of public policy?

3. A critical step in presidents' decision making is evaluating the consequences of the various options before them. How well can the White House do this? Is it possible to predict the consequences of choices that have not yet been made, such as levying sanctions against a country or cutting taxes for certain groups?

WEB EXERCISES

1. Go to the "White House Briefing Room" Web site. Look at the wide range of issues on which the president must make a decision in just one week. How much can one person know about all these issues? Is there a way for presidents to be better informed? Go to <http://www.whitehouse.gov/WH/html/briefroom.html>.
2. Select an issue that interests you from the "White House Briefing Room." How might the president's decisions on the issue have been different had there been no previous commitments restraining him? Go to <http://www.whitehouse.gov/WH/html/briefroom.html>.

SELECTED READING

Allison, Graham. *Essence of Decision: Explaining the Cuban Missile Crisis.* Boston: Little, Brown, 1971.

Anderson, Paul A. "Decision Making by Objection and the Cuban Missile Crisis." *Administrative Science Quarterly* 28 (June 1983): 201–222.

Barilleaux, Ryan J. *The President and Foreign Affairs.* New York: Praeger, 1985.

Bendor, Jonathan, and Thomas H. Hammond. "Rethinking Allison's Models." *American Political Science Review* 86 (June 1992): 301–322.

Best, James J. "Who Talked to the President When?" *Political Science Quarterly* 103 (Fall 1988): 531–545.

Burke, John P. *The Institutional Presidency.* Baltimore: Johns Hopkins University Press, 1992.

Burke, John P., and Fred I. Greenstein. *How Presidents Test Reality: Decisions on Vietnam, 1954 and 1965.* New York: Russell Sage Foundation, 1989.

Downs, Anthony. *Inside Bureaucracy.* Boston: Little, Brown, 1967.

Gelb, Leslie H., with Richard K. Betts. *The Irony of Vietnam: The System Worked.* Washington, D.C.: Brookings Institution, 1979.

George, Alexander L. *Presidential Decisionmaking in Foreign Policy: The Effective Use of Information and Advice.* Boulder, Colo.: Westview Press, 1980.

Halperin, Morton H. *Bureaucratic Politics and Foreign Policy.* Washington, D.C.: Brookings Institution, 1974.

Hult, Karen. "Advising the President." In George C. Edwards III, John H. Kessel, and Bert A. Rockman, eds., *Researching the Presidency*. Pittsburgh: University of Pittsburgh Press, 1993.

Janis, Irving. *Groupthink*, 2nd ed. Boston: Houghton Mifflin, 1982.

Jones, Charles O. "Presidents and Agendas: Who Defines What for Whom?" In James P. Pfiffner, ed., *The Managerial Presidency*, pp. 197–213. Belmont, Calif.: Brooks/Cole, 1991.

Kessel, John H. "The Structures of the Reagan White House." *American Journal of Political Science* 28 (May 1984): 231–258.

Neustadt, Richard E. *Presidential Power and the Modern Presidents*. New York: Free Press, 1990.

Porter, Roger B. "Gerald R. Ford: A Healing Presidency." In Fred I. Greenstein, ed., *Leadership in the Modern Presidency*, pp. 199–227. Cambridge: Harvard University Press, 1988.

Wayne, Stephen J. "President Bush Goes to War: A Psychological Analysis from a Distance." In Stanley A. Renshon, ed., *The Political Psychology of the Gulf War: Leaders, Publics, and the Process of Conflict*. Pittsburgh: University of Pittsburgh Press, 1993.

Notes

1. Quoted in John C. Donovan, *The Politics of Poverty*, 2nd ed. (Indianapolis: Pegasus, 1973), p. 111.
2. On continuity in foreign policy despite changes in the occupant of the presidency, see William J. Dixon and Stephen M. Gardner, "Presidential Succession and the Cold War: An Analysis of Soviet-American Relations, 1948–1988," *Journal of Politics* 54 (February 1992): 156–175.
3. Quoted in Paul C. Light, *The President's Agenda: Domestic Policy Choice from Kennedy to Carter* (Baltimore: Johns Hopkins University Press, 1982), p. 179.
4. Richard E. Neustadt, *Presidential Power and the Modern Presidents* (New York: Free Press, 1990), pp. 121–122.
5. James A. Baker III, *The Politics of Diplomacy* (New York: Putnam, 1995), p. 263.
6. Quoted in William Greider, "The Education of David Stockman," *Atlantic*, December 1981, p. 34.
7. Theodore C. Sorensen, *Decision-Making in the White House: The Olive Branch or the Arrows?* (New York: Columbia University Press, 1963), p. 3. See also Patrick J. Haney, *Organizing for Foreign Policy Crises* (Ann Arbor: University of Michigan Press, 1997).
8. Alexander L. George, "The Case for Multiple Advocacy in Making Foreign Policy," *American Political Science Review* 66 (September 1972): 766.
9. Bryce Harlow quoted in Emmet John Hughes, *The Living Presidency: The Resources and Dilemmas of the American Presidential Office* (Baltimore: Penguin, 1973), p. 345.
10. Henry Kissinger, *White House Years* (Boston: Little, Brown, 1979), p. 47; see also p. 1455.
11. Roger B. Porter, "Gerald Ford: A Healing Presidency," in Fred I. Greenstein, ed., *Leadership in the Modern Presidency* (Cambridge: Harvard University Press, 1988), pp. 199–227.
12. President Ford wrote about this problem in *A Time to Heal: The Autobiography of Gerald R. Ford* (New York: Harper and Row, 1979), p. 147; see also p. 186.
13. Gerald R. Ford, "Imperiled, Not Imperial," *Time*, November 10, 1980, p. 31.
14. Clark Clifford, *Counsel to the President* (New York: Random House, 1991), p. 636.
15. See Kissinger, *White House Years*, pp. 40, 602.

16. Kissinger, *White House Years*, p. 996.
17. Hamilton Jordan, *Crisis: The Last Year of the Carter Presidency* (New York: Putnam, 1982), p. 42.
18. Sorensen, *Decision-Making in the White House*, p. 62.
19. Quoted in Light, *The President's Agenda*, p. 200.
20. Neustadt, *Presidential Power*, chaps. 6–7.
21. Ronald Reagan, *An American Life* (New York: Simon and Schuster, 1990), pp. 540–541.
22. Chester L. Cooper, *The Lost Crusade: America in Vietnam* (New York: Dodd, Mead, 1970), p. 223.
23. Ford, *A Time to Heal*, pp. 187–188; see also Reagan, *An American Life*, p. 536.
24. George E. Reedy, *The Twilight of the Presidency* (New York: New American Library, 1970).
25. Dean Rusk, quoted in Leon V. Sigal, *Reporters and Officials: The Organization and Politics of Newsmaking* (Lexington, Mass.: Heath, 1973), p. 147.
26. Irving Janis, *Groupthink*, 2nd ed. (Boston: Houghton Mifflin, 1982).
27. Larry Speakes, *Speaking Out* (New York: Scribner's, 1988), pp. 244–245.
28. "Mr. Secretary: On the Eve of Emeritus," *Life*, January 17, 1969, p. 62B.
29. Jack Valenti, *A Very Human President* (New York: Norton, 1975), pp. 115–116.
30. John P. Burke and Fred I. Greenstein, *How Presidents Test Reality: Decisions on Vietnam, 1954 and 1965* (New York: Russell Sage Foundation, 1989); Robert S. McNamara, *In Retrospect: The Tragedy and Lessons of Vietnam* (New York: Times Books, 1995).
31. Richard M. Nixon, *Public Papers of the Presidents: Richard Nixon, 1972* (Washington, D.C.: Government Printing Office, 1974), p. 1150.
32. Harry McPherson, *A Political Education* (Boston: Little, Brown, 1972), p. 298.
33. Quoted in H. R. Haldeman, *The Ends of Power* (New York: Times Books, 1978), p. 107.
34. Laurence E. Lynn, Jr., and David deF. Whitman, *The President as Policymaker: Jimmy Carter and Welfare Reform* (Philadelphia: Temple University Press, 1981), pp. 116, 269.
35. Baker, *The Politics of Diplomacy*, p. 68.
36. Henry Kissinger, *Years of Upheaval* (Boston: Little, Brown, 1982), p. 74.
37. Robert S. McNamara, *In Retrospect; The Tragedy and Lessons of Vietnam* (New York: Times Books, 1995), pp. 211–212; Andrew F. Krepinevich, Jr., *The Army and Vietnam* (Baltimore: Johns Hopkins University Press, 1986).

8

THE PSYCHOLOGICAL PRESIDENCY

IN CHAPTER 6 WE DISCUSSED THE OFFICE OF THE PRESIDENCY. The size of that office, its structures and modes of operation, and its patterns of communication, coordination, and interaction all affect what presidents do and how effectively they do it. Presidential decisions and actions are also influenced by the environment in which they occur. We focused on that environment in Chapter 7.

But presidents are not robots. They have choice and exercise it. It matters how skilled they are, how smart they are, and how quickly they absorb information and make decisions. Their attitudes and values, their view of their roles and tasks, and their long- and short-term goals can all affect their decisions and conduct in office. Moreover, how they feel on a particular day—whether they are sick or healthy, tired or rested, sad or happy, frustrated or content—may also have an impact. Beneath these feelings, their personality, cognitive skills, and interactive behavior will affect either directly or indirectly their perceptions, evaluations, and ultimately their judgments and actions as president.

The type of leadership role presidents desire and the one they usually pursue, whether they try to direct or facilitate change, follow in large part from their personal needs and abilities. Theodore Roosevelt needed to maintain a strong, public presence as president; Calvin Coolidge preferred to operate in a low-key manner outside of public view; Lyndon Johnson had to dominate personal relations; both he and Richard Nixon wanted to exercise strategic control; Ronald Reagan was more laid-back and willing to delegate; and Bill Clinton needs to be involved.

Whether presidents are successful in the leadership role they choose to pursue depends in large part on the fit between their personality and the public mood, on their capacity to influence people and shape events, and on their ability to make the right choices and avoid problems and decisions that can be dealt with by others. This chapter will discuss these personalized aspects of the presidency. After treating the purely formal, constitutional requirements for office, it will examine factors that affect presidents' preferences and, ultimately, their ability to lead: their social and political background, their physical attributes and general health, their psychological character and style of doing business, and their cognitive skills and perceptions. Additionally, patterns of interaction within the White House that directly or indirectly impinge on presidential priorities and their implementation will also be discussed. In this manner the chapter will address the critical question that the American electorate faces and must answer every four years: What difference does it make who is elected president?

QUALIFICATIONS FOR OFFICE

The framers of the Constitution were naturally aware that personal factors could and would affect presidential performance. Although they hoped that presidents would have altruistic motives and set exemplary standards in their public and private behavior, they could not predicate the powers and responsibilities of the office on this assumption. Rather, they had to take precautions against the potential abuse of power by the executive, abuses they believed they had experienced during the colonial period under the reign of George III.

Thus they devised a constitutional structure to constrain the president and other federal officials from exceeding their authority and provided a mechanism for removing them if they did. Moreover, they envisioned a selection process in the Electoral College with electors exercising an independent judgment as more likely to result in the choice of a highly qualified person without major character flaws than a direct election by the people. One of their fears about direct election was the type of candidates it would attract, those who thrived on popular support, perhaps even those who had demagogic tendencies.

Conceiving that character was more a product of personality than position, the delegates at the Philadelphia Convention did not impose a long list of qualifications for the office. On the contrary, they listed only three constitutional requirements. The president must be a natural-born citizen who has been a resident in the United States for fourteen years and is at least thirty-five years old. The citizenship and residence qualifications were designed to prevent those with allegiances to other countries, by virtue of their birth or residential preference, from becoming president and thereby being in a position to subvert the national interests of the United States. The age requirement was imposed because the delegates at the Philadelphia Convention believed that the presidency demanded a higher level of maturity than any other position in the U.S. government. The minimum age for the House of Representatives was set at twenty-five and for the Senate at thirty.

With the possible exception of age, these formal requirements have precluded few who might otherwise be considered qualified from seeking the presidency. However, a set of informal requirements, as noted in Chapter 2, has in practice restricted eligibility to a much smaller subset of the population. Despite the notion, so appealing in democratic theory, that the nation's highest office should be one to which any citizen can aspire and achieve, the fact is that presidents as a group have not represented a microcosm of American society.

SOCIAL AND POLITICAL BACKGROUND

To put it simply, American presidents have not been typical Americans. They have been advantaged by virtue of their wealth, the professional positions they have held, and the personal contacts they have made. Born into families of high social status and considerable economic means, they have benefited from greater educational and professional opportunities than their fellow citizens have enjoyed.

Despite the log cabin myth, perpetuated by Abraham Lincoln's rise to political prominence, most presidents have not had humble origins. In fact, Lincoln did not either. The early presidents in particular were men of high social class. Eight of our presidents were the product of only four families: John Adams and John Quincy Adams (father and son), William Henry Harrison and Benjamin Harrison (grandfather and grandson), Theodore Roosevelt and Franklin Roosevelt (first cousins), and James Madison and Zachary Taylor (common grandparents). At least half of those who have served in the White House during the twentieth century had backgrounds of social or political prominence. Only Calvin Coolidge, Richard Nixon, and Ronald Reagan might be said to have suffered from poverty in their youth. Bill Clinton's family was not wealthy, but by Arkansas standards they were probably middle class.[1]

The advantages that higher income and social status provide can be seen in the educational levels and professional activities that presidents as a group have attained. Most have been well educated: Of those who held office in the twentieth century, only Truman did not attend a university. Most, in fact, have undergraduate and graduate degrees (see Table 8–1).

Education has been used as a springboard for professional careers that have culminated in public service. Most presidents held elective office prior to being president. Eisenhower was the last not to have done so, although he did run and defeat Senator Robert A. Taft in the Republican presidential primaries. The increasing public dimensions of the office have also put a premium on communication skills, which contributed to actor Ronald Reagan's rise to political prominence and success in office.

Although social and political position give certain individuals an advantage in winning the presidency, it is much less clear whether they contribute to success in office.[2] Coming from an upper-class background did not help

Table 8–1. Social and Political Background of Twentieth-Century Presidents

Presidents	Years Served	Father's Occupation	Own Occupation	Undergraduate College
William McKinley	1897–1901	Businessman	Lawyer	Allegheny College
Theodore Roosevelt	1901–1909	Businessman	Lawyer	Harvard
William H. Taft	1909–1913	Lawyer	Lawyer	Yale
Woodrow Wilson	1913–1921	Minister	Educator	Princeton
Warren G. Harding	1921–1923	Physician	Journalist	Ohio Central
Calvin Coolidge	1923–1929	Storekeeper	Lawyer	Amherst
Herbert Hoover	1929–1933	Blacksmith	Engineer	Stanford
Franklin D. Roosevelt	1933–1945	Businessman	Lawyer	Harvard
Harry S Truman	1945–1953	Farmer	Businessman	None
Dwight D. Eisenhower	1953–1961	Mechanic	Military	U.S. Military Academy
John F. Kennedy	1961–1963	Businessman	Journalist	Harvard
Lyndon B. Johnson	1963–1969	Farmer	Educator	Southwest Texas Teachers College
Richard Nixon	1969–1974	Streetcar motorman	Lawyer	Whittier College
Gerald Ford	1974–1977	Businessman	Lawyer	University of Michigan
Jimmy Carter	1977–1981	Farmer	Farmer	U.S. Naval Academy
Ronald Reagan	1981–1989	Shoe salesman	Actor	Eureka College
George Bush	1989–1993	Businessman, politician	Businessman, politician	Yale
William Clinton	1993–	Salesman	Politician	Georgetown

George Bush. In fact, it contributed to the perception, especially during the economic recession, that he just did not understand the problems of the average American family. In contrast, Bill Clinton made much of his humble background during the 1992 presidential campaign, asserting that it enabled him to empathize with the plight of those in the lower and middle classes.[3]

PHYSICAL ATTRIBUTES AND GENERAL HEALTH

Although background and upbringing may be only indirectly related to presidential performance, other factors such as physical and mental health and personal attributes have a more direct effect. Take feelings, for example. Few would deny that people's feelings affect their job performance. For presidents, these feelings could increase or decrease their willingness to listen to options, their capacity to weigh alternatives and make the best decision, and their ability to persuade others to support their choice. They could also affect their energy level, their capacity to withstand the rigors of the office, their concentration, even their tolerance.

Despite the importance of health, information about the medical pathologies of presidents has been extremely limited. Even today, the medical diagnoses and treatments of presidents are presented in a sketchy way, particularly at the onset of a health problem. The principal reason that health problems are understated is that presidents and their advisers want to prevent precipitous public reactions to an illness or injury to the president and desire to maintain continuity of policy both within the government and between it and other governments.

Take the case of Lyndon Johnson. Professor Robert E. Gilbert described an incident that occurred just three days after the inauguration in 1964 when Johnson, who had suffered a major heart attack in 1955, awoke to chest pains and was rushed to the hospital at 2:26 A.M. Vice President Humphrey, who was in Minnesota at the time, was informed an hour later that Johnson was in the hospital but told to fulfill his schedule, "so that no one would think his [Johnson's] illness was serious." However, Humphrey was not given any information about the president's condition.[4] "It was an awesome prospect, a terrible shock," Humphrey later wrote in his memoirs, "compounded by not knowing what precisely was happening."[5]

Although Humphrey's treatment as vice president may have been exceptional, the temptation of presidents and their staffs to cover up or downplay health problems has been the rule. Thus, it was not revealed until weeks after Ronald Reagan left the hospital following the attempt on his life how close he had actually come to death. Even to this day, we do not know whether the onset of Alzheimer's disease occurred during his time in office. Similarly, the public was not informed of Grover Cleveland's two cancer operations, Woodrow Wilson's incapacity after a stroke, Franklin Roosevelt's worsening health, and John F. Kennedy's affliction with Addison's disease during their presidencies.

Given the magnitude of their tasks and the stress they are under, presidents need excellent and continuous medical care and get it. There is an official White House physician, typically a political appointee, who works with a team of doctors who are detailed to the White House usually from the military. However, even a group of doctors may not initially perceive a medical problem if the president does not tell them about it. Nor can they give the president a thorough examination every day.

Yet presidents have had their share of medical problems even with the best of care.[6] In the contemporary era, for example. Dwight Eisenhower had three major illnesses: coronary thrombosis in 1955, acute ileitis in 1956, and a minor stroke in 1957. Jack Kennedy had Addison's disease, for which he received shots of steroids and amphetamines, and he also aggravated a back problem, for which he took a cortisone-based medicine (which can have serious side effects).[7] Lyndon Johnson had both a gall bladder and a hernia operation while in office, and he caught pneumonia on at least one occasion. The burdens of Vietnam and Watergate put both Johnson and Richard Nixon under severe mental strain, although in general, Richard Nixon, Gerald Ford, and Jimmy Carter enjoyed relatively good health as president. Ronald Reagan had operations for the removal of malignant growths in his colon and on his face, as well as suffering serious injury during the assassination attempt in 1981. George Bush had Graves disease, a thyroid-related illness that often results in hyperactivity and severe mood swings. Bill Clinton has a chronic allergy problem that makes him congested and hoarse much of the time. His condition is treated by injections, throat sprays, drugs, and drinking large amounts of water.

Given the stress presidents are under, it is not surprising that they have had their share of illness.[8] There is no getting away from the presidency, not even on vacation. In his memoirs, titled *Mandate for Change*, President Eisenhower wrote:

> A President is President no matter what his location. For example, during eight weeks in Denver 1954 my staff and I worked every day other than Sundays, including six that I spent in the mountains at Fraser, Colorado. During those weeks I saw 225 visitors, not including my own immediate staff, made four official trips out of Denver, delivered six speeches, made three television appearances, attended five official luncheons or dinners, considered 513 bills from Congress, signing 488 into law and vetoing 25. Finally, I signed 420 other official papers or documents—all of the business of direct concern to the running of the Executive Branch.[9]

Lady Bird Johnson, Lyndon Johnson's wife, made the same complaint about her husband's so-called vacations on his ranch in Texas: "[R]est at the ranch is a complete misnomer to me. The airport stays busy, with planes disgorging Cabinet members with important, difficult decisions, budget estimates, crises. . . . Visitors pour in and news pours out. And these old walls are bursting at the seams."[10]

Medical studies link long hours, persistent pressures, and a stressful environment to the onset of a variety of physical and mental illnesses, including high blood pressure, cardiovascular disease, stroke, and, generally, lower resistance to communicable diseases. Perhaps this explains why presidents who have served more than four years in office have had more serious health problems and shorter life spans than those who completed one term or less. Similarly, presidents who are judged less successful and who, as a consequence, may have encountered more frustration and difficulty have lived shorter lives than those who were evaluated as more successful.

Of course, the effects of medical problems on presidential performance vary. In general, the more serious the illness or injury, the longer is the recovery period, the more removed the president becomes from the day-to-day functioning of the office, and the more likely it is that critical decisions will be delayed or delegated to others. What is more difficult to discern is how decision making is affected when presidents are not in optimal health or when their judgment is affected by medication or pain.

Health issues are also related to the aging process.[11] Presidents are older than most Americans: Their mean age on assuming office has been fifty-four. Reagan was the oldest, having first been elected at sixty-nine (although at that age he was four years younger than Robert Dole when the latter ran in 1996). Theodore Roosevelt and Kennedy have been the youngest, inaugurated at forty-three. Bill Clinton was forty-six.[12]

The onerous duties and awesome responsibilities of the office may aggravate these manifestations of the aging process. How many times have your heard the expression, look how much the president has aged in office and then seen before-and-after pictures that seem to show the toll on the president. Lyndon Johnson is a good example. Historian Eric Goldman, who worked in the Johnson White House, commented on the changes in Johnson's appearance during the five years that he was president:

> On March 31, 1968, I and the millions of others sat at our television sets for a speech of President Johnson's that he had labeled as especially important. I had not seen LBJ on television for quite a while and I was shocked. My mind went back over the changes in his appearance and manner during his five years in the White House. There were the days immediately after the assassination—the rangy, rugged figure, every antenna alert, trailed by edgy aides, looking around him with those hard, piercing eyes, always as if he were sniffing out a friend and foe, always as if he were remembering that a smile or a handshake might be needed here or there. . . .
>
> Now, in March 1968 an old, weary, battered man was on the television screen. The face was deeply lined and aging; the drawl occasionally cracked and wavered. His manner gave no intimation of FDR, and little of the LBJ of 1964. Rather it suggested a lecturish, querulous schoolmaster.[13]

Although the Johnson experience may not be typical, it is suggestive of the physical toll that the presidency can exact.

Statistics on the longevity of those who have served in the nation's highest office tend to support the "killing" nature of the job. As a group, presidents have had shorter life spans than their contemporaries. Excluding the four presidents who were assassinated at a relatively young age, the longevity of others is still shorter than that of their peers.[14]

PSYCHOLOGICAL ORIENTATION

Common sense suggests that personality affects behavior, but this is difficult to prove scientifically. Personality is not directly observable. Instead, it must be inferred from observable behavior. That inference, in and of itself, is likely to be based on unverifiable assumptions, such as those postulated by Sigmund Freud, Carl Jung, Alfred Adler, and more contemporary psychological theorists. The increasing emphasis given to personal character by the news media, candidates, and those in office demands that we examine personality as a critical component of political leadership.

There have been two basic types of studies that focus on the relationship between personality and performance. One, known as *psychobiography,* seeks to explain presidential behavior on the basis of a comprehensive psychological analysis of a president's life. Frequently beginning with youth, adolescence, and early political experiences, the study progresses through the president's career as a public official. Examples of presidential psychobiographies that have been frequently cited include Alexander George and Juliette L. George, *Woodrow Wilson and Colonel House*; Fawn Brodie, *Thomas Jefferson*; Doris Kearns, *Lyndon Johnson and the American Dream*; Bruce Mazlish, *In Search of Nixon*; Betty Glad, *Jimmy Carter: In Search of the Great White House,* and Stanley Renshon, *High Hopes* (a psychologically oriented assessment of Clinton's presidency).[15]

The other type of analysis, more comparative in scope, seeks to generalize about presidential behavior on the basis of certain of its psychological dimensions. It seeks to uncover the ways in which personality may affect seeking the presidency and then exercising power within it—how personality shapes, motivates, activates and conditions responses, and influences judgments. One of the most stimulating, influential, and controversial studies to address these questions is James David Barber's *The Presidential Character.*[16]

Presidential Character

Originally published in 1972, Barber's book seeks to explain and, under certain conditions, predict generalized reactions on the bases of several dimensions of personality. Barber's objective is to create a framework that can be used to categorize a president's psychological tendencies and then use that categorization as an explanatory and predictive tool. Of course, psychological orientation is not discernible to the naked eye: It must be inferred from observable behavior. Three manifestations of behavior are words, work, and personal interaction. Together, they provide clues to aspects of an individual's personality. Which of these aspects of personality are most relevant? From the standpoint of presidential performance, Barber suggests three: character, style, and worldview.

Character is the least discernible, but most basic, of the personality components. In Barber's words, it "is the way the President orients himself toward life"—how he views himself.[17] Self-esteem underlies character. Naturally, the better presidents feel about themselves, the more likely they will be able to accept criticism, think rationally, and learn on the job.

If character is the inner core, style is the outer garb. It constitutes the way a:

> President goes about doing what the office requires him to do—to speak, directly or through media, to large audiences; to deal face to face with other politicians, individually and in small, relatively private groups; and to read, write, and calculate by himself in order to manage the endless flow of details that stream onto his desk. No President can escape doing at least some of each.[18]

Style varies with the president and the times. It is important to consider because it is a predictable coping mechanism—a way of handling people, tasks, and communication.

The third component is worldview. Barber defines it as "how he [the president] sees the world and his lasting opinions about what he sees."[19] It consists of "his primary, politically relevant beliefs, particularly his conceptions of social causality, human nature, and the central moral conflicts of the time."[20]

According to Barber, these three psychological components form a pattern of motives, habits, and beliefs that result in behaviors that are evident throughout life. Moreover, these behaviors and the psychological foundation on which they rest are not easily changed. Once developed, they tend to persist. Thus, while politicians shift, and may even reverse, their stands on policy, usually to resonate better with changes in public opinion, their personality and its behavioral manifestations remain more stable; as a consequence, personality may be a better predictor of how people will perform in office than what they say they will do if elected. This makes the study of personality important, not only to those who wish to understand the "whys" of presidential behavior, but also to those who must decide which candidates have the temperament, style, and vision that is most likely to succeed in office. Helping the American electorate in its voting decisions is an important objective of Barber's work.

To provide some analytic tools that the average citizen can use to make this evaluation, Barber has developed a typology based on two observable behavioral dimensions: activity and affect. Activity is the level of energy that is devoted to the job—whether a person is basically active or passive. Affect concerns the level of satisfaction that is obtained from the work—whether a person's political life is a positive or negative experience. In Barber's words, "The activity baseline refers to what one does, the affect baseline to how one feels about what he does."[21] There are four possible combinations, which are summarized in Table 8–2.

Of these four character types, the active-positive is clearly the one Barber believes is best suited for the presidency. Such a person brings to the office the level of activity needed to sustain the multiplicity of roles and duties the president must assume. Moreover, the positive attitude toward work generates its own psychological and physical benefits: It contributes to energy level; it eases the inevitable interpersonal conflicts that result from competing perspectives, interests, policy goals, and ambitions; and it increases tolerance. Presidents who enjoy their work tend to be more eager to take on new and difficult challenges. Each of the other character types

TABLE 8–2. Presidential Character Types

Active-Positive	Active-Negative
This presidential type is characteristic of an energetic president who enjoys his work and who tends to be productive and capable of adjusting to new situations. Such a person generally feels confident and good about himself.	This type describes a president who works hard but does not gain much pleasure from it, and who tends to be intense, compulsive, and aggressive. He may pursue his public actions in a self-interested manner. Such a person generally feels insecure and uses his position to overcome feelings of inadequacy and even impotency.

Passive-Positive	Passive-Negative
This type describes a relatively receptive, laid-back individual who wants to gain agreement and mute dissent at all costs. Such a person is apt to feel pessimistic and unloved on a deep psychological level. As president, the passive-positive individual attempts to compensate for these feelings by being overly optimistic and by continually trying to elicit agreement and support from others.	This presidential type can be said to abhor politics and withdraw from interpersonal relationships. Such an individual is ill-suited for political office, much less the nation's highest post. He or she suffers from low self-esteem and a sense of uselessness and is apt to take refuge in generalized principles and standard procedures.

Source: Adapted from James David Barber, *The Presidential Character,* 4th ed. (Englewood Cliffs, N.J.: Prentice-Hall, 1992), pp. 9–10.

TABLE 8-3. The Personality Types of Contemporary Presidents

Active-Positive	Active-Negative
Franklin Roosevelt	Woodrow Wilson
Harry Truman	Herbert Hoover
John Kennedy	Lyndon Johnson
Gerald Ford	Richard Nixon
Jimmy Carter	
George Bush	

Passive-Positive	Passive-Negative
William Taft	Calvin Coolidge
Warren Harding	Dwight Eisenhower
Ronald Reagan	

Source: James David Barber, *The Presidential Character,* 4th ed. (Englewood Cliffs, N.J.: Prentice-Hall, 1992)

has built-in weaknesses that could impede the performance of their presidential duties—perhaps adversely affecting a president's vision, judgment, or actions.

Barber's model assumes that typecasting can provide a valuable clue to the potential difficulties that might develop in the presidency. Although Barber cannot predict these difficulties with certainty, or anticipate particular reactions to events, he believes that he can indicate general tendencies and reactions to which certain character types are prone.

One problem, however, with making electoral judgments on the basis of this type of analysis is the difficulty of judging character. Experts disagree, for example, whether Eisenhower is a passive-negative type, as Barber claims, or active-positive, as scholar Fred Greenstein concluded.[22] Moreover, even when there is agreement on the character categorization, it has not always followed that the active-positive presidents have turned out to be the most effective and the other types, the most ineffective or dangerous. Compare presidents Ford and Carter, both of whom are categorized by Barber as active-positive, and Woodrow Wilson and Abraham Lincoln, both seemingly active-negative.[23] Most would argue that the latter were outstanding presidents whereas the former were not. Two extremely popular presidents, Dwight Eisenhower and Ronald Reagan, were not active (and in Eisenhower's case, not positive either, according to Barber). Table 8-3 lists Barber's categorization of twentieth-century presidents, beginning with William Howard Taft.

What is the problem? Has Barber made a major methodological error or has he merely miscategorized some presidents? Much controversy has surrounded these and other questions. Barber's critics have alleged that his categories are too broad and ambiguous and that his activity and affect dimensions are too crude because they are dichotomous. Moreover, psychological tendencies themselves do not neatly fit a single box, an allegation that Barber admits although he believes that it is possible to identify a dominant tendency.

There is another difficulty with Barber's analysis. In addition to being reductionist—reducing the causes of very complex behavior to a single psychological explanation—Barber's argument also tends to be tautological. Categories are defined first by their characterological tendencies (active-positive, active-negative, and so on) rather than being derived from empirical evidence of how people behave; these definitions are then used to predict behavior. This generates self-fulfilling prophesies, according to political scientist Alexander George.[24] If they turn out to be correct, as they did in the case of Nixon, then Barber can claim that the psychological explanation is valid, but if the predictions are not realized, then he can assert that the environment was not ripe for the psychological tendencies to produce their expected reaction. None of these criticisms invalidates the model, but they do question its scope, application, and general utility as an explanatory and predictive tool.

In addition to the methodological difficulties, there may be another reason why psychological types and presidential success do not always mesh. Barber himself alluded to this reason when he discussed the interaction of personality, the power situation in which presidents find themselves, and the national climate of expectations. Presidents must make decisions and take actions within a potent and often rapidly changing political environment over which they have limited influence. Thus, although their character, style, and worldview are relatively constant, the power mix and public moods are not. An environment that allows one president to achieve policy objectives may prevent another from doing so. Active-positive presidents in particular are prone to circumvent existing structures and processes—often at their own peril—in attempting to achieve results.[25] Franklin Roosevelt's failed attempt to pack the Supreme Court is a case in point.[26] Bill Clinton's willingness to let his wife oversee the development of a comprehensive health care policy, largely behind closed doors, may be another.

The changing public mood, combined with the stability of personality structures, provides a potential future problem for many presidents. Having been selected in part because their personality may have coincided with the public mood at the time of the election, they may have difficulty adjusting when that mood changes. This happened to George Bush. After being elected to continue the policies of the Reagan administration, Bush was unable to alter his basic approach to the economy in the light of the recession that occurred in the final years of his presidency. His unwillingness to

☼ HOT- BUTTON ISSUE

How Important Is Character?

Does character really matter? Does it affect performance in office in a tangible way? If so, is it as influential on what and how presidents decide and when and how they act as the power situation in which they find themselves and the economic and social concerns they face?

The question of character has plagued Bill Clinton before and during his presidency and is likely to continue to be debated by historians after he leaves office. He has faced numerous allegations that have raised questions about his fitness for the job, his judgment when personal issues are involved, and his candor, integrity, and moral values. The principal allegations have been that he dodged the draft during the Vietnam War, smoked marijuana as a young man, was involved in a shady land deal when governor of Arkansas (Whitewater), made unwanted sexual advances to women, that he had a sexual relationship with a twenty-one-year-old White House intern and then suggested that she need not reveal it to a court-appointed independent counsel, and abused the perquisites of his office to raise money, some illegally, for the Democrats and his own reelection campaign.

How relevant have these allegations been to Clinton's presidency? Clinton's critics believe that they are very relevant—that they go to the core of what the position is all about. If the person holding the nation's highest office fails to exemplify Americans' highest ideals and values, then who will, they ask? At the very least, a chief executive cannot violate the Constitution and the nation's laws, which he has sworn to uphold. In a democracy, no one, least of the all the president, can be considered above the law, a judgment the Supreme Court reiterated in 1997 when it held that a sitting president is subject to civil suit.

Even if the law were not violated, these critics contend, presidents must still set a good example, be believable in what they say, and be above-board in what they do. Their integrity and candor are part and parcel of their persuasiveness in office, which affects their power and, in turn, their capacity to achieve their goals and be successful.

Other observers, however, see different character traits as more important, including energy, empathy, decisiveness, perseverance, resiliency, and flexibility, plus such attributes such as vision, creativity, intelligence, articulateness, and the ability to relate to others. Judged by these criteria, Clinton scores much higher.

There are still others who draw a distinction between the public and the private—between job performance and personal behavior. They judge presidents by their accomplishments. The peace and prosperity of the Clinton years suggest that the president has done a good job—at least that is what a majority of the people generally believed during much of the time when Bill Clinton was subject to many personal allegations about his behavior.

Much depends on the people's expectations of the president. If moral and ethical leadership are a major part of the job description, then personal character is obviously critical; if solving problems, improving conditions, making life better for more people, giving the impression that the country is on the right track—that the future will be better than the present and the present is better than the past—are the major part of the job description, then personal behavior and the character traits it suggests are less important than concrete results. Obviously, there are many points of view concerning the importance of character.

initially acknowledge the economic problem, to develop a plan to combat it, and to devise a strategy for getting Congress and the public to support him made Bush appear ill-suited for a job for which he had seemed so well suited earlier in his presidency. On the other hand, Bill Clinton, who was elected to fix the economy and change policy (particularly health care and welfare reform), overestimated the public's appetite for extensive policy change involving the national government. However, he was able to redirect his goals and realign them with the more moderate, incremental desires of the public in order to gain reelection and maintain his popularity (see The Clinton Presidency box).

The influence of a variety of factors on behavior point to the difficulties of using a psychological model to explain and anticipate presidential performance. Nonetheless, character is an important component of that behavior, and Barber's contribution has been to focus attention on it. His model, despite its methodological and substantive limitations, continues to frame much of the debate on whether and how character affects performance in office (see the Hot-Button Issue box).

THE CLINTON PRESIDENCY

The Impact of Personality Traits on Performance in Office

Bill Clinton's biological father died in an automobile accident before he was born. His mother, Virginia, remarried several years later. Bill's stepfather, Roger Clinton, was reputed to be a kind and generous man, but he was also an alcoholic. Under the influence of liquor, he tended to be abusive and violent toward his family, forcing the young Clinton to act as an intermediary.[27] Virginia and Roger Clinton eventually were divorced, but they remarried after Roger was found to be dying of cancer and at that time Bill reconciled with his stepfather.[28]

A traumatic childhood that also included being left for two years with his grandparents while his mother attended nursing school left an indelible mark on Clinton's psyche and helped forge the character that has shaped his political life. Four personality features—his limitless political ambition, his reckless personal behavior, his perseverance in the face of adversity, and his willingness to compromise in order to please and heal—have reappeared throughout his career, including his presidency.

Bill Clinton has always been goal oriented and has sought to achieve his goals through political activity. The goals represent steps on a ladder that led, in his own mind, toward the presidency, starting from the day when he shook hands with John F. Kennedy at the White House in 1963: band major in high school, president of his freshman and sophomore classes at college, Rhodes scholar, Yale Law School graduate, Arkansas attorney general at age thirty, and governor at thirty-two, making him the youngest governor in the country since Harold Stassen of Minnesota. After being defeated once, Clinton was reelected five times and achieved national prominence as leader of the National Governors' Association and head of the Democratic Leadership Conference prior to his election as president in 1992.

Clinton explained his nonstop political career as a kind of reaction to the death of his biological father and the precariousness of life as he saw it:

> For a long time I thought I would have to live for both of us in some ways. . . . I think that's one reason I was in such a hurry when I was younger. I used to be criticized by people who said, "Well, he's too ambitious," but to me, because I grew up sort of subconsciously on his timetable, I never knew how much time I would have. . . . It gave me an urgent sense to do everything I could in life as quickly as I could.[29]

Clinton's frantic pursuit has not been without its setbacks. After being elected two years in a row as undergraduate class president at Georgetown University, he was defeated in an attempt to be head of the school council; after being elected as the youngest governor in Arkansas history, he was defeated in his quest for reelection; and when asked to give the nominating speech for Michael Dukakis at the 1988 Democratic Convention, he bored delegates with a long-winded, passionless address. Then, after being acknowledged as the leading Democrat for his party's nomination in 1992, his campaign was rocked by charges of marital infidelity, draft dodging, and conflicts of interest while he was governor of Arkansas. Moreover, after promising new policy, an end to gridlock, and a higher moral and ethical standard for his administration, he suffered the defeat of two of his three principal policy initiatives in his first two years in office, saw his party lose control of both houses of Congress in 1994, and continued to be the object of numerous allegations of personal wrongdoing and illicit sexual relationships.

Nonetheless, he survived these hurdles that threatened to capsize his political career and destroy his presidency, his greatest challenge, when the independent counsel investigating his activities with a 21-year-old White House intern uncovered evidence suggesting that Clinton may have lied under oath and obstructed justice. The president was forced to admit that he had an improper relationship with the intern and later apologized for it. It was during this inquiry into his personal behavior that Clinton wrapped himself in presidential garb and performed his official roles, trying to demonstrate his determination to focus on his job as president.

The ability to persevere and survive despite adversity may be traceable to the events of his youth, which were reinforced by his personal experience in politics. After his biological father's death, Bill's mother also persevered under difficult circumstances: She sent her two-year-old son to live with her parents while she completed her nursing education. Her marriage to Roger Clinton improved the family's financial situation but also brought the alcohol-related problems of an abusive stepfather into the household. Later, Bill's stepbrother, Roger, would also experience serious drug abuse problems.

Early on, Bill Clinton developed an instinct to survive. He did so by adopting an interpersonal strategy as a "healer"—a compromiser and a peacemaker. Throughout his entire life, getting along for Bill Clinton has meant trying to please as many diverse, and often conflicting, interests as possible. Journalist Peter Applebome defined this strategy as a "compulsive need to please, to bring people together at some hazily defined, accommodating center—as if he [Clinton] were still re-enacting in politics the role he played at home."[30]

Both supporters and opponents have noted Clinton's passion to please. According to John Brummett, the editor of *Arkansas Times Magazine:* "He tries not to say no to anyone. He has an obsession to please. For years, I've seen legislators from different sides of the same question come out of his office, all thinking he's on their side."[31] Supporters see this as a desirable trait that is responsible for his political successes. Said Betsey Wright, his chief of staff for six years while he was governor of Arkansas, "Part of what attracted me to Bill is he's always been secure enough as a person to be able to listen, to be able to negotiate, to hear other points of view."[32]

Critics, however, see another side: the attempts of someone who is trying to please others primarily to further his own political ambitions and provide salve for his own ego. The appellation "Slick Willie," coined by Arkansas newspaper columnist Paul Greenberg, was intended to describe this aspect of Clinton's personality, which Greenberg termed "a tendency to tell people whatever it is they wanted to hear."[33]

Clinton does overpromise in public—concerning what he will do and how he will conduct himself—and this tendency has repeatedly gotten him into trouble. It has made him look weak, vacillating, and insincere, thereby reinforcing the "Slick Willie" image. Once in office, he found he could not obtain his policy goals unless he modified them. However, on altering his stance, he was accused of being unprincipled, inconsistent, even hesitant—of not standing for anything. The tendency to please has also led to another charge: that he compromises too easily and can be "rolled." It has frustrated members of Congress, particularly Democrats, and led one, Representative David Obey of Wisconsin, to complain during the 1995–1996 budget debate, "I think most of us learned some time ago, if you don't like the President's position on a particular issue, you simply need to wait a few weeks."[34]

Many of the difficulties Clinton has encountered as governor and as president can be traced in part to his haste, his desire and need for continual personal gratification, and his limitless ambition. He tries to do too much for too many too quickly, including himself, without considering the political realities and ramifications of his actions. Here are three examples (out of many), which show a pattern of behavior:

1. After rejection by the voters of Arkansas in 1981 and a precipitous decline in public approval during his first five months as president, Clinton adapted; he did what he needed to do to survive. He hired some new advisers, including a few older, experienced hands; consulted with his opponents; redefined his priorities; refocused his attention; articulated a simpler, clearer message; and moderated his programs by moving closer to the political center, where his skills as an energetic, intelligent compromiser would be most effective.

2. Clinton was rejected again a year and a half later. After suffering another sharp decline in his job approval—a consequence of the defeat of his health care legislation, the loss of Democratic control, continuing allegations over his involvement in the Whitewater land development affair and attempts by the White House to cover it up—Clinton rebounded by using the same strategy that had helped him in the past. Following the 1994 election, he took more centrist, moderate policy positions on legislation; he weighed public opinion more carefully; he extended an olive branch to the new Republican congressional leadership, promising to work with them on many of their key policy initiatives, from balancing the budget and reforming welfare to curbing the excesses of lobbyists. Moreover, he enhanced his presidential image by assuming a more active role as chief of state and foreign policy maker. These efforts were rewarded with increasing public approval and reelection.

3. Clinton was put on the defensive once again when allegations surfaced that he had committed sexual improprieties while in office. After initially denying the charges publicly and to family, friends, and aides, he admitted the improper relationship. But he still contended that technically he had not lied about it when he was questioned during a deposition for a civil suit that

had been filed against him, nor did he apologize for his actions. When his statement was not viewed as sufficiently contrite, he apologized again and again—all the while maintaining his presidential posture, duties, and responsibilities. In winter 1998, after the Monica Lewinsky scandal broke, he gave a well-received State of the Union address; he took many well-publicized trips abroad, to Africa, China, Russia, and Ireland; and he continued to speak out on important public issues and tried to broker a Middle East peace accord.

In other words, the pattern we see is initially resistance and even self-denial to the charges of improper behavior. If and when that defense fails, Clinton attempts to accommodate those whose support he needs to maintain his position. Once he obtains the support and survives, he moves on.

Ambition, entitlement, perseverance, and compromise are four character tendencies that have had a profound and continuing impact on Bill Clinton's entire political career. However, these tendencies frequently conflict with one another. Personal and policy ambitions have encouraged Clinton to attempt more than he has the political support to accomplish. He goes out on a limb or engages in reckless behavior and soon finds himself the target of increasing criticism and public disapproval. He then copes with this adversity by pulling himself back from the brink. In doing so, he perseveres, trying to please as many of those people who were disaffected by his leadership as he can. He tones down his rhetoric, moderates his policy, and more carefully and consciously orchestrates his behavior in line with public expectations. This behavioral pattern has become Bill Clinton's recipe for political survival.

From a psychological perspective, what Clinton tries to do (with the help of friends) is to discipline himself, which is not an easy task for someone with great ambition and desires. The self-imposed "corrective" can only be temporary, however, because Clinton's desire for personal gratification and political accomplishment soon takes over and again may need constraint. In short, ambition, perseverance, and compromise coexist in an uneasy alliance within Bill Clinton, constituting essential characterological ingredients that help explain both his political successes and his failures.

COGNITIVE DIMENSIONS

There is a link between personality dimensions and political perspectives. Beliefs are shaped by how individuals view themselves and others within their environment. Personal character traits and needs condition the processing of information, the consideration of options, and the making of judgments.

Impact of Worldviews

Presidents and their aides bring to office sets of beliefs about politics, policy, human nature, and social causality—in other words, beliefs about how and why the world works as it does. These beliefs serve public officials by providing a frame of reference for raising and evaluating policy options, for filtering information and giving it meaning, and for establishing potential boundaries of action. Beliefs also help busy officials cope with complex decisions to which they can devote limited time, and they predispose people to act in certain directions. Although sets of beliefs are inevitable and help to simplify the world, they can be dysfunctional as well.

Identifying Problems   First, they may distort the identification of a problem that requires attention. This is perhaps most dramatically illustrated in the case of surprise attacks by one country on another—unfortunately, not a rare occurrence.[35] The Bush White House was surprised when Iraq invaded Kuwait in 1990 even though it had obtained substantial evidence of a massive military build-up on the Kuwaiti border. As Secretary of State Jim Baker put it, no one believed that Saddam Hussein would attack because an attack made no sense from the perspective of those who calculated his interests.[36] Similarly, the Clinton administration was taken by surprise when India tested nuclear weapons in 1998, which undermined the United States' efforts to halt proliferation. Officials assumed that it would not be rational for India to carry out such tests, so no one paid attention to the signals that it indeed planned to do so.

Ronald Reagan had a clear and uncomplicated belief system. His strongly held opinion on the undesirability of government regulations on business led him to disregard or downplay mounting problems with the savings and loan associations in the 1980s, problems that resulted in numerous failures and cost the taxpayers over $500 billion.

Determining Objectives   Belief systems also influence the determination of the objectives of public policies. For example, decisions about U.S. participation in the Vietnam War were molded by the consensus of top officials that a non-communist Vietnam was important to the security and credibility of the United States; that the war-torn country was a critical testing ground for the ability of this country to counter communist support for wars of national liberation; that communism was a world conspiracy; that South Vietnam would fall to the North without American aid; and that if South Vietnam did fall to the communists, the rest of Southeast Asia would follow. When these views were coupled with President Johnson's more general premises that all problems were solvable and that the United States could do anything, this country's intervention became a foregone conclusion.

This doctrinal consensus on Vietnam made it difficult to challenge U.S. policy. Defining doctrine in terms of necessity foreclosed policy options. As a result, "no comprehensive and systematic examination of Vietnam's importance to the United States was ever undertaken within the executive branch. Debates revolved around how to do things better and whether they could be done, not whether they were worth doing."[37] Similarly, Robert McFarlane, President Reagan's former national security adviser, testified before the special congressional committee investigating the Iran-Contra affair that no government-wide analysis of American interests in Nicaragua was ever made. Answers to the most important questions were simply assumed.

Raising Options   The worldviews of top decision makers also affect the options they raise to deal with issues and the choices they make. Decision making regarding the Cuban missile crisis is often cited as an example of a deliberate, comprehensive consideration of alternatives, but President Kennedy precluded diplomatic and nonmilitary responses to the situation at the outset and actually considered a fairly narrow range of military options. He believed that the presence of Soviet missiles in Cuba greatly increased the threat to the national security of the United States and that the Soviet Union would remove the missiles only if forced to do so by the threat of American military sanctions. His decisions followed directly from those premises. Similarly, President Reagan believed that the Soviet Union would only enter into serious negotiations with the United States if it were facing an overwhelmingly powerful military force. Consequently, Reagan believed he had no choice but to vastly increase military spending, which he did.

In a crisis, a president's view of a problem and proposed response to it are especially likely to foreclose consideration of alternatives because there will be a premium on rapid and decisive action. For example, in the period directly preceding the actual fighting in the Gulf War, General Colin Powell, chairman of the Joint Chiefs of Staff, wanted to consider the option of continuing economic sanctions against Iraq. President Bush, however, told him there was not time to try such a strategy.[38]

Managing Inconsistency

The environment in which the president operates is complex and uncertain, characteristics with which the human mind is not comfortable. The mind has certain cognitive needs and prefers stable views to a continuous consideration of options. About a month before the commencement of hostilities in the Gulf War, George Bush told an interviewer: "I've got it boiled down very clearly to good and evil. And it helps if you can be that clear in your own mind."[39]

It does not follow that the president should not continue to consider options and information once a policy decision has been made. The decision may have been a poor one. Yet busy aides are typically reluctant to risk irritating an even busier president by attempting to reopen a question he thought was settled. It is especially difficult to review decisions regarding national security while fighting is taking place. Speaking from experience, Vice President Hubert Humphrey wrote: "Once a wartime decision has been made and men's lives have been lost, once resources are committed—and most dangerously, once a nation's honor has been committed—what you are doing becomes almost Holy Writ. Any division, dissension, or diversion is suspect."[40]

Presidents have to find a level of consistency with which they are comfortable and that is compatible with their intellectual capacities and psychological needs. This may be a difficult task. Decision makers often experience stress as they try to cope with the complexity of decisions, especially in times of crisis. Warren Harding and Ronald Reagan both had difficulty understanding complex policy issues.[41] They dealt with these difficulties by delegating to others much of the responsibility for sorting out the issues and presenting viable options. Second, they depended on developing clearcut (some would say "simplistic") cognitive frameworks for making decisions. These frameworks helped them simplify reality and gave their decisions the appearance of consistency. Once Reagan came to an "understanding" of an event, he did not want to deal with facts that challenged his understanding. As Secretary of State George Schultz put it, "no fact, no argument, no plea for reconsideration would change his mind."[42]

Presidents Carter and Clinton offer a contrast, as they both enjoy grappling with tough policy problems and synthesizing large amounts of data. An example is Clinton's formulation of his economic program. Even before taking office, he held a two-day forum with experts from business, labor, and academia. Then, as soon as he became president, he had in-depth discussions with a range of economic policy advisers; listened to the recommendations of his political consultants, Democratic party leaders, and members of Congress; attended lengthy sessions of the National Economic Council; and met frequently with Federal Reserve Board chairman Alan Greenspan. Out of these discussions, he developed his initial economic programs.

Clinton's elaborate study of the issue had a political downside, however. It took him longer than promised to design his legislative proposals, the proposals themselves were subject to continuing shifts in emphasis and content, and they were difficult to explain to the American people, which was necessary to build support for them in Washington. Moreover, throughout the process the president appeared indecisive and inconsistent.

Inference Mechanisms People often simplify reality to deal with the world's complexities and resolve uncertainty by ignoring or deemphasizing information that contradicts their existing beliefs. To do this, they employ inference mechanisms that operate unconsciously and that may have as great an influence on a person's judgments as objective evidence. Consequently, most policy makers remain unreceptive to any major revision of their beliefs in response to new information, especially if they have had success in the past with applying their general beliefs to specific decisions or have held their beliefs for a long time. Moreover, they are unlikely to search for information that challenges their views or options contrary to those they advocate. Instead, they tend to incorporate new information in ways that render it comprehensible within their existing frames of reference. In other words, they rationalize it to support their previously held beliefs.

This rationalization process, combined with the stake presidents have in their previous decisions, explains why it is so difficult for them to change policy or even for their advisers to get them to reconsider them unless circumstances force them to do so. A good example of this phenomenon can be seen in the Clinton administration's failure to consider the changing role of the American military in Somalia in 1993. It took a tragic confrontation between U.S. troops and Somalians backing a local warlord to force the administration to confront the issue and ultimately to terminate the mission. Unless presidents make it clear that they really want to hear criticism within their administration, they may not become aware of it until they see it on the news. Advisers find it extremely difficult to tell presidents what they do not wish to hear.

There are various devices that presidents use to manage inconsistency. One is to attach very negative consequences to alternatives, as President Johnson and his top aides did to the option of disengaging from the war in Vietnam. In concluding that the role of the United States in international relations would be seriously diminished by such action, decision makers preemptively dismissed an alternative that was widely advocated outside the government. Similarly, Ronald Reagan would never consider the option of negotiating about his Strategic Defense Initiative ("Star Wars"). Other presidents, such as Bill Clinton and George Bush, have been more flexible in their approaches to issues.

Officials may also employ selective information to make inferences that a particular situation could not possibly occur. If policy makers accept this inference of impossibility, there is no need for them to consider information pointing to the "impossible" situation, alternatives to prevent or respond to it, or what effect it would have on the alternatives that *are* being considered. Most officials believed that the Japanese could not attack Pearl Harbor. Because they were not expecting an attack, American officials did not notice the signs pointing toward it. Instead, they paid attention to signals supporting their current expectations of enemy behavior. Similar behavior inhibited policy makers from anticipating the North Korean attacks on South Korea in 1950 that precipitated the Korean War and the massive Tet invasion of South Vietnam by the North in 1968.

Another means of reducing inconsistency and thereby decreasing the pressure to consider alternatives is similar to what we commonly term "wishful thinking." Secretary of State George Shultz describes his boss, Ronald Reagan, as engaging in wishful thinking regarding issues and events, sometimes rearranging facts and allowing himself to be deceived—for example, when he insisted that he had not traded arms for hostages in the Iran-Contra affair.[43] Wishful thinking also played a prominent role in decision making about the ill-fated invasion of Cuba at the Bay of Pigs.

Another form of wishful thinking occurs when information inconsistent with ongoing policy is deemphasized and policy makers conclude that undesirable conditions are only temporary and will ameliorate in response to current policy. Officials used this type of reasoning to garner support for the continued escalation of the Vietnam War. All that was needed to force the enemy to succumb, they argued, was to keep up the pressure. More generally, in the face of contradictory or ambiguous indicators of the progress of the war, they listened most carefully to the optimistic rather than the pessimistic reports or the caveats to positive assessments and hoped for the best.

Reasoning by analogy is yet another means of resolving uncertainty and simplifying decision making. The conclusions supported by this type of reasoning seem to have strength independent of the available evidence, probably because the analogies simplify and provide a coherent framework for ambiguous and inconsistent information.

Metaphors and similes simplify a complex and ambiguous reality by relating it to a relatively simple and well-understood concept. If one is then used as the basis of an analogy, the possibilities for error are considerable. Part of the theoretical underpinning for the Vietnam War was often characterized as the "domino theory" of international relations, which held that the United States must prevent countries from falling to the communists because a chain reaction would occur and the countries would fall one after another, like falling dominoes. The simplistic nature of the metaphor indicates how much room exists for differences between that view and reality.

Discrediting the source of information and options is another means of reducing the complexity and resolving the contradictions with which policy makers must deal. At first, President Johnson handled the critics of his Vietnam policy quite well, inviting them to his office and talking to them for hours. However, as opposition increased and polls indicated a dip in his popularity, he responded to criticism by discrediting its source. He maintained that Senator William Fulbright (the chairman of the Senate Foreign Relations Committee) was upset at not being named secretary of state; the liberals in Congress were angry at him because he had not gone to Harvard, because the Great Society was more successful than Kennedy's New Frontier, and because he had blocked Robert Kennedy from the presidency; columnists were said to oppose him so as to make a bigger splash; and young people were hostile because they were ignorant.

At other times, presidents may simply avoid information they fear will force them to face disagreeable decisions that complicate their lives and produce additional stress. Richard Nixon is a classic example. In his memoirs he wrote of putting off a confrontation with his own attorney general, John Mitchell, because of Mitchell's hypersensitivity and his own desire to remain ignorant about Mitchell's involvement in Watergate in case it would prove unpleasant. Referring to Nixon's ability to engage in self-delusion and avoid unpleasant facts, White House Chief of Staff H. R. Haldeman argues that the "failure to face the irrefutable facts, even when it was absolutely clear that they were irrefutable, was one of our fatal flaws in handling Watergate at every step."[44]

Each of the cognitive processes that reduces uncertainty and complexity can be a reasonable response to a situation. The point is that people have a tendency to rely on them, not only by conscious choice, but because of their need for certainty and simplicity. In each of the examples cited above, the president and his advisers made use of an inference mechanism that diverted their attention from vital information and led them to ignore appropriate options. Potential actions that were considered disastrous would have been far less so than those that were taken, situations thought to be impossible actually occurred, hoped-for results from policies never materialized, inferences were based upon inappropriate analogies, and worthwhile criticism was rejected. Thus, the inference mechanisms that top decision makers employ to manage inconsistency may jeopardize rational decision making.

At the same time, it is important to recognize the interplay between motivation and cognition. Many people can tolerate at least some inconsistency, and there are other motives aside from consistency that drive behavior, including accuracy, fairness, efficiency, accountability, ideological biases, and time pressure. Consequently, presidents and their advisers have a variety of cognitive strategies available to them and may choose to face the facts rather than simplify if they have sufficient motivation. Understanding which motivations are operative in a given situation remains one of the most intriguing questions of presidential politics.

PRESIDENTIAL STYLE

Presidents set the tone for their White Houses. How they approach their job and interact with their aides, what they demand from their subordinates, and how much supervision they exercise over the aides have a lot to do with how the White House functions and how well they are served.

Stylistic differences are a product of personal needs and experience. Some presidents work constantly. Carter, Bush, and Clinton put in twelve- to fourteen-hour days on a regular basis. Eisenhower and Reagan had a more leisurely schedule, however. Reagan worked from 9 A.M. to 5 P.M., Monday through Thursday, and he would usually leave early Friday afternoon for the presidential retreat at Camp David in Maryland.

Some presidents feel the need to dominate relationships with their subordinates. Lyndon Johnson was a good example. He monopolized discussions and was unable to accept criticism. Others, such as Kennedy and Ford, have treated their senior staff almost as equals.

Some presidents need to operate in a very protective environment. Nixon saw only a few trusted aides and wanted all recommendations and advice written and presented as option papers. Carter and Clinton, although much more open than Nixon, also operated primarily off paper. Bush's style was mixed. Eisenhower and Reagan preferred oral briefings to written memoranda. Ford is said to have maintained a "revolving door" into and out of the Oval Office, as did Clinton at the beginning of his administration.

Some presidents need to be involved in almost everything. Johnson, Carter, Bush, and Clinton maintained a hands-on approach to decision making. Others, such as Eisenhower and Reagan, waited for decisions to reach them. Nixon and Ford were more active, but Nixon was uninvolved in the detailed, middle-level decisions, and so left much of the budget decision making to his budget director. Ford, on the other hand, was heavily involved in budget matters.

Presidents create the mood and condition the way their White House operates. In general, the more personable, accessible, and tolerant the president, the happier the staff will be. Efficiency, however, is not always promoted by the chief executive acting like a nice person.

Each White House has had its own style. During the Nixon years, the style was described as macho. Aides had to prove how tough they were, how long they worked, and how many sacrifices they were making for the job. In contrast, Presidents Ford and Carter permitted a looser operation. They were more tolerant, more open, and less imposing.[45]

The early Clinton White House is another good example of a fluid staff system; indeed, it was described by New York Times reporter Richard L. Berke as "controlled pandemonium."[46] Senior aides became involved in a variety of overlapping issues; meetings were frequent and attendance was open to all interested staff; and there was little discipline at any point in the chain of command. Everyone seemed to have a position on the principal issues. One Clinton staffer likened the individuals who held senior positions in the administration to a basketball team in which any one of the players could dribble down the court and shoot. In subsequent years, the style of the Clinton White House became less frantic. Senior aides were more sensitive to the political implications of the president's decisions and actions, and a more concerted effort was made to keep Clinton in sync with the public mood. With the exception of the White House chief of staff and press secretary, presidential aides tried to stay out of the media spotlight.

WHITE HOUSE STAFF RELATIONSHIPS

Character, worldviews, and style are not limited to the president. Aides also have orientations and feelings that affect their work. Moreover, their working environment conditions the decisions and actions that are made. For example, the long hours for which presidential assistants must work, the unrelenting pressures they are under, the complex issues with which they must deal, and the significant, and often long-term, implications of their decisions cannot help but affect how they interact and communicate with one another and how they perform their jobs.

The work is arduous and the hours, extensive. Aides usually arrive before the president and leave after he departs. For most, a sixty- to eighty-hour week is standard. Senior and middle-level aides arrive early in the morning and stay into the evening five days a week; they usually work a full day on Saturday and, frequently, a half-day on Sunday, whether in the office or at home.

Group pressures also serve to reinforce the White House work ethic. Members of the presidential staff tend to be conscious of how many hours others work. "There's always a customary desire to be around when the phone rings," was the way one Carter aide put it.[47] Similarly, a Clinton staffer likened the White House to "a campus full of overachievers—everybody wants to be the last one to turn out the lights."[48]

The long hours of work generate fatigue and, over time, lower people's stamina. They make doing a thorough job more burdensome, particularly as the term progresses. As a result, there is a tendency to circumvent those who might place obstacles in the way of decisions or actions. Thus, in the Reagan administration, the secretaries of defense and state were not included in many meetings on the Iran-Contra situation after it became clear that they opposed selling arms to the Iranian government. Similarly, during their first year in office, Clinton aides avoided consulting, and even communicating with, Republican members of Congress who opposed the president's economic and budget proposals.

In addition to the workload, the pressures of the deadlines, crises, and decisions that can have a major impact on the president's reputation are enormous. Combined with time constraints and high performance expectations, they contribute to a very stressful environment, which affects behavior on and off the job. William Clark, one of Reagan's national security advisers, had to leave his job after suffering from migraine headaches and nightmares.[49] A Ford legislative aide commented, "I could never have existed on this job without Valium."[50]

For years the White House has had a reputation as a "divorce mill." Stories of aides adopting unhealthy coping mechanisms, such as philandering and alcohol abuse, abound. One particularly tragic illustration of these pressures was the suicide of Vincent Foster, deputy counsel in the Clinton White House, who apparently took his own life after he and several others were named in a *Wall Street Journal* article criticizing the work of the counsel's office in the White House.

Not only is sufficient time to perform quality work often lacking, but the constant need to deal with a highly complex and politically divided governmental system further complicates the task and makes it very frustrating. Richard Cheney, Ford's chief of staff and Bush's defense secretary, summed it up this way:

> There is a tendency before you get to the White House or when you're just observing it from the outside to say, "Gee, that's a powerful position that person has." The fact of the matter is that while you're here trying to do things, you are far more aware of the constraints than you are of the power. You spend most of your time trying to overcome obstacles getting what the president wants done.[51]

Internal competition also tends to be heightened by these job-related pressures. The greater the work demands on staff, both in terms of quantity and quality, and the more severe the sanctions for shoddy or tardy performance, the more likely it is that the environment will promote self-interested, competitive behavior.

Internal rivalries are not generated solely by the White House environment, however. The nature of people who are attracted to jobs as presidential aides also contributes to their behavior. This is because the White House tends to draw very ambitious people with very large egos.

Staff competition, of course, does not always adversely affect the running of the White House (although it does tend to make working there less enjoyable). The Franklin Roosevelt White House, where a competitive staff structure reaped benefits for a president who was interested in maximizing his information, options, and influence, illustrates that some internal competition can be advantageous. On the other hand, infighting usually detracts from the efficiency of staff operations and lowers morale. Moreover, when carried into the public arena, it can cause political embarrassment for the president.

A competitive environment also encourages self-interested behavior, which can warp vision, overextend arguments, and lead to inaccurate or unbalanced presentations of issues and options and their consequences for the president. All this contributes to the dangers that Lyndon Johnson's former press secretary, George Reedy, described in his book, *The Twilight of the Presidency.*[52] Reedy was concerned with the isolation of presidents—with their making of decisions and taking of actions in an environment that did not accord with reality. He saw the deference paid to the president by his aides, the aides' propensity for telling the president what he wanted to hear, and an obsession with satisfying the president's every whim as contributing to this potential danger. To make good decisions, Reedy contended, the president needs accurate information, not pleasantries; wise recommendations, not self-motivated advocacy; and intelligent support, not blind loyalty.

All the pressures and deadlines, internal competition, and tendencies toward isolation cannot help but have an impact on the presidency. Presidents have no choice but to delegate, since their tasks exceed their time, energy, and, often, their expertise. How their aides interact with them, each other, and their executive and congressional counterparts affects presidential performance in a direct, and often immediate, way. Presidents themselves can influence this pattern of interaction, but they cannot control it. To some extent, all presidents are at the mercy of the organizational, operational, and personal proclivities of their staff. However, this is particularly a problem for presidents who wish to direct change, and thus tend to concentrate their advisory and decision-making structures in the White House staff.

CONCLUSION

Fundamentally, the type of person the president is does matter. Social background, physical well-being, presidential character, cognitive views, and personal style and staff interaction all condition the president's performance in office. How they affect that performance is difficult to measure with precision, but their impact must be considered when trying to explain presidential actions or predict presidential responses.

A case can also be made that some of these characteristics are better than others; that is, they are more desirable because they are more likely to lead to the president's achievement of his policy and political goals. James David Barber and others have argued that voters should take the character of the candidates into account when making their decisions on Election Day. They do attempt this, although most people lack the kind and amount of information that may be necessary to render an informed, astute, psychologically oriented judgment.

Nonetheless, if socialization, physical condition, and psychological orientation—which includes character, worldviews, and style—affect behavior, then they must have an impact on the president's capacity to lead. We have come to expect certain characteristics from those people who have demonstrated the most outstanding leadership skills in our society: that they have a wide range of personal experience, particularly on the issues with which they must deal as president; that they are physically and mentally healthy; that they are stable, independent, and self-assured; that they have a sophisticated understanding of domestic and international policy problems; and that they relate easily and effectively to those around them. Some presidents have obviously demonstrated many of these tendencies and characteristics, but a surprising number of them have not.

As a group, presidents have tended to come from the country's social and economic elite. Some have experienced serious health problems in office. Some have manifested psychological needs that seem to have influenced their desire for the nation's highest office as well as their conduct in it, and that energize or immobilize them in different kinds of situations. The perspectives of some of the most accomplished presidents have also been limited or skewed. In contrast, some of the less-accomplished presidents have had more humble origins, enjoyed better health, and been less burdened with psychological traits that made it difficult for them to separate their personal needs from their public policy decisions.

Our conclusion is that leadership is not only a consequence of who the leader is but of how that leader interacts with others in the changing social, economic, and political milieu of the presidency. Individuals who are better able to perceive change and adjust to it are apt to be more successful than those who cannot. Moreover, not only does a great leader require the capacity to exercise significant leadership skills, he or she also needs an environment in which those skills can be effectively exercised.

Returning to our distinction between two leadership types, we conclude that within the American political system, bad times, crises, or some cataclysmic event are probably necessary for a director-type leadership to win and rule, while prosperous times in a politics-as-usual environment makes it likely that the president will be pragmatic and incremental, a facilitator in the government.

DISCUSSION QUESTIONS

1. What are the principal criticisms of James David Barber's model of presidential character? Defend Barber for each criticism you have presented. Illustrate your criticism and defense with examples from recent presidencies.

2. Richard Nixon's actions in the Watergate affair have been explained largely on the basis of politics—his attempt to obtain valuable information about his opponents, keep them off guard, and cover up the dam-

aging activities of his aides to protect his 1972 reelection campaign, his reputation, and his power as president. Provide an alternate, psychologically oriented explanation for some of Nixon's actions in this affair. What aspects of President Nixon's personality might have influenced his judgment, his words, and his behavior? (You may have to do some research on Nixon to answer this question.)

3. Character, cognition, and decisional style can affect presidential judgments and contribute to the ability of an administration to make and execute sound policy judgments. Discuss the impact of these variables, singularly or together, on a major policy decision made in the Reagan, Bush, or Clinton administrations.

WEB EXERCISES

1. Go to the White House Web site <http://www.whitehouse.gov> and examine the transcript of a recent presidential news conference. Do you discern any patterns in the president's words that might suggest a character tendency, mind-set, or style of decision making that has affected his explanation or rationalization at that press conference for a decision he made, policy he articulated, or action he took?

2. Examine a confrontation between the president and another public official, a member of Congress, for example, by obtaining their statements about one another from the White House and another appropriate Web site. Does either or both parties impute a personality dimension of the other party? Does either or both use personality as an explanation for their or own position, decision, or action or that of their adversaries?

SELECTED READING

Barber, James David. *The Presidential Character.* 4th ed. Englewood Cliffs, N.J.: Prentice-Hall, 1992.

Birnbaum, Jeffrey. *Madhouse: The Private Turmoil of Working for the President.* New York: Times Books, 1996.

Burke, John R., and Fred I. Greenstein. "Presidential Personality and National Security Leadership: A Comparative Analysis of Vietnam Decision-making." *International Political Science Review* 10 (1989): 73–92.

George, Alexander. "Assessing Presidential Character." In Aaron Wildavsky, ed., *Perspectives on the Presidency,* pp. 91–134. Boston: Little Brown, 1975.

Gilbert, Robert E. *The Mortal Presidency.* New York: Basic Books, 1993.

Greenstein, Fred I. "The Presidential Leadership Style of Bill Clinton: An Early Appraisal." *Political Science Quarterly* 108 (Winter 1993–1994): 589–601.

Greenstein, Fred I. "There He Goes Again: The Alternating Political Style of Bill Clinton," *PS* 31 (1998): 179–181.

Hargrove, Erwin C. "Presidential Personality and Leadership Style." In George C. Edwards, John Kessel, and Burt Rockman, eds., *Researching the Presidency*, pp. 69–109. Pittsburgh: University of Pittsburgh Press, 1993.

Hermann, Margaret, and John Thomas Preston, "Presidents, Advisers, and Foreign Policy: The Effects of Leadership Style on Executive Agreements." *Political Psychology* 15 (1994): 111–142.

Post, Jerrold M., ed. "Symposium on Presidential Health." *Political Psychology* 16 (December 1995): 757–860.

Reedy, George E. *The Twilight of the Presidency*. Rev. ed. New York: New American Library, 1987.

Renshon, Stanley A. *High Hopes*. New York: New York University Press, 1996.

Renshon, Stanley A., ed. " The Psychology of the Clinton Presidency: Initial Appraisals." *Political Psychology* 15 (1994): 331–394.

Renshon, Stanley A., ed. *The Clinton Presidency: Campaigning and Governing, and the Psychology of Leadership*. Boulder, Colo.: Westview Press, 1995.

Notes

1. Said one of his neighbors, Rose Crane, who met Clinton in the third grade:

   > Compared to the kids he ran into at Georgetown and Oxford and Yale, he was poor as a church mouse. . . . But they were not poor, not in the sense of Arkansas poor. I was terribly envious of Bill, in a childhood sort of way, for three things he had that I thought would probably make the entire world okay, if I had them: One was that they had a big red Coca-Cola box in the garage, and the Coke truck came and filled it up. Two, they had a convertible. And three, Virginia [Bill's mother] always had all of the bones and all of the skin out of chicken and dumplings, and there were little tiny pieces of white meat in the chicken and dumplings. And if your mother would do that, and you had a convertible and a Coca-Cola box, it was a perfect world. (Rose Crane, quoted in James Morgan, "An Arkansas State of Mind," *Washington Post Magazine*, July 12, 1992, p. 17).

2. Two sociologists, E. Digby Baltzell and Howard G. Schneiderman, say they do contribute. Correlating the social class origins of presidents with recent evaluations by historians and political scientists of those who have served as president, Baltzell and Schneiderman found that presidents from higher social classes tended to be more favorably evaluated than those from lower social classes (Digby Baltzell and Howard G. Schneiderman, "Social Class in the Oval Office," *Society* 25 [September/October 1988]: 44).

3. Getting a $200 haircut from a well-known Los Angeles hair stylist damaged this image, which Clinton had worked hard to cultivate. Nonetheless, empathy has remained one of Clinton's most enduring traits as president, particularly in contrast to the conservative Republican leaders to whom he has been compared.

4. Robert E. Gilbert, "The Political Effects of Presidential Illness: The Case of Lyndon B. Johnson," *Political Psychology* 16 (December 1995): 763.

5. Hubert H. Humphrey, *The Education of a Public Man* (Garden City, N.Y.: Doubleday, 1976), p. 314.

6. George Washington had pneumonia, rheumatism, and a persistent back problem; Andrew Jackson was sick during much of his eight years as president; William Henry Harrison died in office after a bout with viral pneumonia, which he contracted on Inauguration Day; Zachary Taylor also died in office, succumbing to gastroenteritis early in his presidency; Abraham Lincoln suffered from headaches and depression, which may have been an indication that he suffered from Marfan syndrome, a genetic disease that affects joints and connective tissues; Woodrow Wilson had a debilitating stroke; Warren Harding had heart disease and a weak stomach and died from a misdiagnosed seizure; and James Garfield and William McKinley were shot and probably lost their lives from improper and inept medical treatment.

7. One such effect is that it results in feelings of euphoria for some people.

8. According to Dr. Lawrence C. Mohr, White House physician from 1987 to 1993:

> Of our 43 presidents at least 21 (almost 50%) have had significant illnesses or injuries while in office. Eight of our presidents (almost 20%) have died in office. Of that eight, four died from illness and four were assassinated. In addition, there have been five unsuccessful assassination attempts on our presidents. (Lawrence C. Mohr, "The White House Physician: Role, Responsibilities and Issues," *Political Psychology*, 16 [December 1995]: 778).

9. Dwight D. Eisenhower, *Mandate for Change* (New York: Doubleday, 1963), p. 267.

10. Lady Bird Johnson quoted in Gilbert, "The Political Effects of Presidential Illness," p. 763.

11. James E. Birren and K. Warner Schaie, *Handbook of The Psychology of Aging*, 2nd ed. (New York: Van Nostrand, 1985); James F. Fries and Lawrence M. Crapo, *Vitality and Aging* (San Francisco: Freeman, 1981); James N. Schubert, "Age and Active-Passive Leadership Style," *American Political Science Review* 82 (1988): 763–772.

12. The reason why the framers set a minimum age was their assumption that maturity, wisdom, and experience were products of age—but so is infirmity.

13. Eric Goldman, *The Tragedy of Lyndon Johnson* (New York: Knopf, 1969), pp. 511–512.

14. Robert E. Gilbert, "Personality, Stress and Achievement: Keys to Presidential Longevity," *Presidential Studies Quarterly* 15 (Winter 1985): 33–50.

15. Alexander George and Juliette L. George, *Woodrow Wilson and Colonel House* (New York: John Day, 1956); Fawn Brodie, *Thomas Jefferson* (New York: W. W. Norton, 1974); Doris Kearns, *Lyndon Johnson and the American Dream* (New York: Harper and Row, 1976); Bruce Mazlish, *In Search of Nixon* (New York: Basic Books, 1972); Betty Glad, *Jimmy Carter: In Search of the Great White House* (New York: W. W. Norton, 1980); Stanley Renshon, *High Hopes* (New York: New York University Press, 1996).

16. James David Barber, *The Presidential Character*, 4th ed. (Englewood Cliffs, N.J.: Prentice-Hall, 1992).

17. Barber, *The Presidential Character*, p. 5.

18. Barber, *The Presidential Character*, p. 5.

19. Barber, *The Presidential Character*, p. 5.

20. Barber, *The Presidential Character*, p. 5.

21. Barber, *The Presidential Character*, p. 9.

22. For a discussion of Eisenhower's activism, see Fred I. Greenstein, *The Hidden-Hand Presidency* (New York: Basic Books, 1982).

23. Barber does not classify Lincoln, but political scientist Jeffrey Tulis sees him as an active-negative. See Jeffrey Tulis, "On Presidential Character," in Joseph M. Bessette and Jeffrey Tulis, eds., *The Presidency in the Constitutional Order* (Baton Rouge: Louisiana State University Press, 1981), pp. 292–301.

24. Alexander George, "Assessing Presidential Character," in Aaron Wildavsky, ed., *Perspectives on the Presidency* (Boston: Little, Brown, 1975), pp. 110–111.

25. Barber, *The Presidential Character*, p. 426.

26. Barber, *The Presidential Character*, pp. 243–246.

27. On occasions when he was a teenager, Bill had to call for outside help to settle family disputes that threatened to become violent. In one incident a fourteen-year-old Clinton actually confronted his stepfather and warned him never to hit his mother or stepbrother again. "If you

want them, you'll have to go through me," he said. (William J. Clinton quoted in Peter Apple-bome, "Bill Clinton's Uncertain Journey," *New York Times Magazine,* March 8, 1992, p. 60).

28. While a student at Georgetown University, Bill recalled driving from Washington to Duke University Hospital to visit his stepfather. One particular trip, which occurred over Easter weekend, left an indelible mark on Clinton's memory. He recalled that he and his stepfather went to a religious service at Duke's chapel:

> It was, God, beautiful. I think he knew that I was coming down there just because I loved him. There was nothing else to fight over, nothing else to run from. It was a wonderful time in my life, and I think in his. (Applebome, "Bill Clinton's Uncertain Journey," p. 60)

29. William J. Clinton, quoted in David Maraniss, "Clinton's Life Shaped by Early Turmoil," *Washington Post,* January 26, 1992, pp. A1, A17.
30. Applebome, "Bill Clinton's Uncertain Journey," p. 60.
31. John Brummett quoted in "As Governor, Clinton Remade Arkansas in His Own Image," *New York Times,* March 31, 1992, p. A16.
32. Betsey Wright quoted in Bill McAllister and David Maraniss, "Clinton: An Instinctive Dealmaker," *Washington Post,* March 28, 1992, p. A12.
33. Paul Greenberg as quoted in Joel Brinkley, "Clinton Remade Home State in Own Image," *New York Times,* March 31, 1992, p. A16.
34. David Obey quoted in Elizabeth Drew, *Showdown* (New York: Simon and Schuster, 1996), p. 237.
35. Richard K. Betts, *Surprise Attack: Lessons for Defense Planning* (Washington, D.C.: Brookings Institution, 1982).
36. James A. Baker III, *The Politics of Diplomacy* (New York: Putnam, 1995), p. 274.
37. Leslie H. Gelb with Richard K. Betts, *The Irony of Vietnam: The System Worked* (Washington, D.C.: Brookings Institution, 1979), pp. 190, 353–354, 365–367; see also Robert S. McNamara, *In Retrospect: The Tragedy and Lessons of Vietnam* (New York: Times Books, 1995).
38. Bob Woodward, *The Commanders* (New York: Simon and Schuster, 1991), pp. 41–42, 299–302.
39. Quoted in Kenneth T. Walsh, "Commander in Chief," *U.S. News and World Report,* December 31, 1990–January 7, 1991, p. 24.
40. Hubert H. Humphrey quoted in Hamilton Jordan, *Crisis: The Last Year of the Carter Presidency* (New York: Putnam, 1991), p. 24.
41. Harding once complained to a friend:

> John, I can't make a damn thing out of this tax problem. I listen to one side and they seem right, and then God! I talk to the other side and they seem just as right, and there I am where I started. I know somewhere there is a book that would give me the truth, but hell, I couldn't read the book. I know somewhere there is an economist who knows the truth, but I don't know where to find him and haven't the sense to know him and trust him when I did find him. God, what a job! (Warren G. Harding quoted in William Allen White, *Masks in a Pageant* [New York: Macmillan, 1928], pp. 422–423).

42. George P. Schultz, *Turmoil and Triumph* (New York: Scribner's, 1993), pp. 263, 819.
43. Schultz, *Turmoil and Triumph,* pp. 263, 1133.
44. H. R. Haldeman, *The Ends of Power* (New York: Times Books, 1978), p. 34.
45. Stephen J. Wayne, "Working in the White House: Psychological Dimensions of the Job" (paper presented at the annual meeting of the Southern Political Science Association, New Orleans, November 1977).
46. Richard L. Berke, "Inside the White House: Long Days, Late Nights," *New York Times,* March 21, 1993, p. 1.
47. Wayne, "Working in the White House," pp. 9, 34.
48. Burt Solomon, "When the Potomac Becomes . . . a Turbulent River of No Return," *National Journal,* July 31, 1993, p. 1936.
49. Solomon, "When the Potomac Becomes . . . a Turbulent River," p. 1936.
50. Interview conducted by Stephen J. Wayne with a senior White House aide in the Ford administration.
51. Wayne, "Working in the White House," p. 35.
52. George Reedy, *The Twilight of the Presidency* (New York: New American Library, 1987).

9

THE PRESIDENT AND THE EXECUTIVE BRANCH

PUBLIC POLICIES ARE RARELY SELF-EXECUTING. They require a staff of experts who have an understanding of the substantive issues, institutional processes, and political implications involved in turning statutes, executive orders, and the like into services and benefits for the nation. These are the people who work in the executive branch. Some are civil servants, while others are political appointees, but both groups are charged with the implementation of public policy.

The president sits atop the executive branch, the organization of which is illustrated in Figure 9–1. As the title of chief executive implies, the president has responsibility for executing or implementing government policies. Implementation includes issuing and enforcing directives, disbursing funds, making loans, awarding grants, signing contracts, collecting data, disseminating information, analyzing problems, assigning and hiring personnel, creating organizational units, proposing alternatives, planning for the future, and negotiating with private citizens, businesses, interest groups, legislative committees, bureaucratic units, and even other countries.

In this chapter we examine presidents' efforts, in conjunction with their subordinates in the executive branch, to implement public policies. Presidents who are directors will be able to dominate this process and ensure that policies are executed as they wish; presidents who are facilitators will face just as great a challenge in leading the executive branch as in leading those who are not directly in their chain of command. We will find that, despite the unquestioned importance of implementation, it receives relatively low priority in the White House. We will also find that presidents face an uphill fight in implementing the policies for which they are responsible. Thus, we focus on the obstacles to effective policy implementation, including communication, resources, implementers' dispositions, bureaucratic structure, and executive follow-up, to better understand the difficulties the president faces.

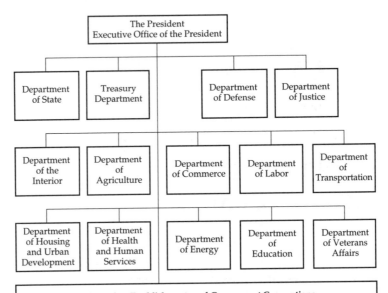

FIGURE 9–1. Organization of the Executive Branch

Source: Office of the Federal Register, *The United States Government Manual, 1997–98* (Washington, D.C.: Government Printing Office, 1997), 22.

Before we move on, we should clarify an important point. The president's role in implementation is not always as direct as it is in giving a speech, negotiating with Congress, or making decisions. Moreover, implementation typically occurs over an extended period of time and far from the confines of the White House. In addition, the implementation of federal policy usually requires the efforts of many people (often thousands) at the federal, state, and local levels and in the private sector. As a result, many observers of the presidency mistakenly restrict their discussions of the role of chief executive to actions the president personally takes in executing the law. To avoid this error we cast our view more broadly in order to understand the problems with which presidents must contend as they seek to carry out their responsibilities for implementing policies, including those that they initiate, those that were established in previous administrations, and those that were passed over their objections.

IMPLEMENTATION PROBLEMS

Since policy implementation is extremely complex, we should not expect it to be accomplished easily or exactly as a president desires. Indeed, experiences of the presidents in recent years would turn even the most optimistic observers into cynics. Once again we see the validity of Richard Neustadt's warning that presidents are rarely in a position to simply issue commands and have them obeyed.

All presidents face implementation troubles. During the Reagan presidency, a potentially severe gap in U.S. national defenses was created when several plants involved in producing the material for nuclear weapons had to be shut down after flaws in their design and operations endangered the public's health. Equally damaging was the Iran-Contra affair, in which some national security aides in the White House took foreign policy into their own hands and illegally funneled funds obtained from the sale of arms to Iran to those opposed to the Marxist government in Nicaragua.

Given the frustration that presidents experience, we should not be surprised that President Carter complained: "Before I became president, I realized and I was warned that dealing with the federal bureaucracy would be one of the worst problems I would have to face. It has been even worse than I had anticipated."[1]

LACK OF ATTENTION TO IMPLEMENTATION

Policy implementation has had a low priority in most administrations. Presidents have many obligations, of which implementing policy is only one. Policies must be developed, decisions made, legislation passed, controversies defused or contained, and the public courted, to name only the most obvious tasks. Moreover, presidents—even former governors—generally lack experience in administration on the scale of the federal government (the federal workforce is nearly twice the population of Arkansas) and tend to find other tasks more compatible with their skills and interests.

Foreign affairs are always a top priority of presidents because of their importance, the unique constitutional responsibilities of the president to deal with them, and the strong interest in international relations that many presidents bring to office. Besides, presidents often feel they can accomplish more in the international arena than at home, where they must wrestle over domestic issues with an unresponsive Congress or a recalcitrant executive branch. Ceremonial functions performed in the role of chief of state are traditions maintained by the president to broaden public support. For example, within six weeks of assuming office, George Bush had traveled to Canada, Japan, China, and Korea and had trips planned to Europe and other parts of the world. All these activities typically take priority over implementation.

In addition, the incentives to invest time in implementation are few. Presidents have only a short time in office, and in their first terms they must constantly think about reelection. This encourages a short-run view in the White House, whereby presidents are more likely to try to provide the public with immediate gratification through the passage of legislation or the giving of speeches than with efforts to manage the implementation of policies. As one Office of Management and Budget official put it:

> The people in the White House are there for such a short time. The pressure is on making some impact and getting some programs passed. There is not enough time or reward in thinking carefully about effectiveness and implementation. The emphasis is really on quantity, not quality. The President could never be reelected on the effectiveness theme. "We didn't do much, but it is all working very well." Do you think a President could win with that?[2]

Presidents know that they will receive little credit if policies are managed well because it is very difficult to attribute effective implementation to them personally. Moreover, to most people, the functioning of government is seldom visible. When they pay attention to government at all, both citizens and the press are most interested in controversial scandals, the passage of new policies, or ceremonial functions. Policies such as welfare reform or affirmative action, which can have a direct effect on people's lives, attract their attention, yet even here the press and public are mainly concerned with the enactment of policies, not the process of their implementation. Although implementation directly influences the final results, this seems insufficient to entice the mass public and the press that caters to it to turn their attention to policy implementation. As a result of these incentives, presidents devote a comparatively small amount of their time to policy implementation.

Similarly, too little consideration is given to problems of implementation in the formulation of policies.[3] Again, the proper incentives are missing. According to a Carter aide: "We all believe there should be more planning. The President has stressed the need for more caution. But when we fall behind, the President will impose a deadline. It is still a political system; and political systems are interested in results, not implementation."[4] As an aide to President Reagan commented: "It's unfortunately true that the management of the bureaucracy becomes one of the lowest priorities of almost every administration that comes to this city. Every administration pays a heavy price for it before it's over."[5]

Things may be changing, however, as the budget deficits of the 1980s and 1990s placed a premium on using scarce public funds efficiently. Early in his tenure, President Clinton launched a "National Performance Review" under Vice President Al Gore. In September 1993, the White House produced a report on "reinventing government" that emphasized cutting red tape, making government agencies more responsive to the needs of their clients, and cutting wasteful spending (see The Clinton Presidency box).[6] Streamlining government and improving its effectiveness are likely to be important themes in future presidential campaigns.

COMMUNICATION OF PRESIDENTIAL DECISIONS

The first requirement for the effective implementation of presidential decisions or policies for which the president is responsible is that the individuals who are to implement a decision must know what they are supposed to do. Policy decisions and implementation orders must be transmitted to the appropriate personnel before they can be followed. Naturally, these communications need to be accurate and their implementers must accurately perceive them. Implementation directives must also be clear. If they are not, implementers may be confused about what they should do and will have the discretion to impose their own views on the implementation of policies (views that may differ from those of the president). Consistency in the communication directives is also crucial. Contradictory decisions confuse and frustrate administrative staff and constrain their ability to implement policies effectively.

Transmission

Before subordinates can implement a presidential decision, they must be aware that the decision has been made and an order to implement it has been issued. This is not always as straightforward a process as it may seem.

THE CLINTON PRESIDENCY

The National Performance Review

The National Performance Review (NPR) grew out of the 1992 Clinton/Gore presidential campaign and the conviction that a reorienting of the executive branch bureaucracy was necessary. A decision was made during the 1992–1993 presidential transition to make management reform one of the key components of the initial Clinton policy agenda and to place the vice president in charge of the effort. The result was one of the most ambitious, far-reaching, and thoroughly prepared management reform efforts of the twentieth century.

The resulting report, entitled *Creating a Government That Works Better and Costs Less,* was presented to the president at a ceremony on the White House lawn with a backdrop of pallets of regulations and reports that symbolized the red tape the NPR was supposed to eliminate. The report contained 384 recommendations and was organized around the key principles of cutting red tape, putting customers first, empowering employees, and going back to basics. The following example, involving a simple ashtray, illustrates the problems NPR is designed to correct.

When the U.S. General Services Administration (GSA) buys ashtrays, which are better known to the GSA as "ash receivers, tobacco (desk type)," it has some very specific ideas on how they should be constructed. In March 1993, the GSA issued Regulation AA-A-701E: nine full pages of specifications and drawings detailing the precise dimensions, color, polish, and markings required for simple glass ashtrays that would pass U.S. government standards. A "Type I, glass, square, 4 1/2 inch (114.3 mm) ash receiver" had to include "a minimum of four cigarette rests, spaced equidistant around the periphery and aimed at the center of the receiver, molded into the top. The cigarette rests shall be sloped toward the center of the receiver or in each corner. . . . All surfaces shall be smooth."

Government ashtrays must be sturdy, too. To guard against the purchase of defective units, the GSA required that all ashtrays be tested.

> The test shall be made by placing the specimen on its base upon a solid support (a 1 3/4 inch, 44.5 mm maple plank), placing a steel center punch (point ground to a 60-degree included angle) in contact with the center of the inside surface of the bottom and striking with a hammer in successive blows of increasing severity until breakage occurs.

Then, according to paragraph 4.5.2.:

> The specimen should break into a small number of irregular shaped pieces not greater in number than 35, and it must not dice. . . . Any piece 1/4 inch (6.4mm) or more on any three of its adjacent edges (excluding the thickness dimension) shall be included in the number counted.

Ignorance or misunderstanding of decisions frequently occurs. Although the executive branch has established highly developed lines of communication throughout the bureaucracy, this does not guarantee that communications will be transmitted successfully. The Bay of Pigs fiasco illustrates this point. On April 17, 1961, a force of 1,200 Cuban refugees who had been recruited, trained, and supplied by the Central Intelligence Agency landed ninety miles south of Havana with the announced goal of overthrowing the Communist regime of Fidel Castro. Within three days the "invasion" had been crushed, inflicting a disastrous blow to American prestige, not to mention that of the new president, John F. Kennedy. The CIA told the leader of the brigade sent to invade Cuba only too late that the president had ordered the soldiers that if the invasion failed they must go to the mountains and fight a guerrilla war. The CIA disregarded the president's order, which it thought might weaken the brigade's resolve to fight or encourage it to retreat to the mountains too quickly.

Sometimes aides and other officials ignore presidential directives with which they disagree, primarily to avoid embarrassment for their chief. Such orders are generally given in anger and without proper consultation. For example, President Nixon especially liked to let off steam by issuing outrageous orders. At one time he instructed Secretary of State William Rogers to "fire everybody in Laos," and he often told aides to "go after" reporters. These and similar outbursts were ignored by White House Chief of Staff H. R. Haldeman and other aides close to Nixon, who knew the president would view things differently after he calmed down.[7]

In most instances, implementers have considerable discretion in interpreting their superiors' decisions and orders. Orders from the White House are rarely specific, and personnel at each rung in the bureaucratic ladder must use their judgment to expand and develop them. Obviously, this process invites the distortion of communications. Moreover, the further down in the bureaucracy presidential implementation directives go, the greater is the potential for distortion. Moreover, subordinates do not always interpret the communications of their superiors in a way that advances the goals of the president. Bureaucrats often use their discretion to further their personal interests and those of their agencies. Interest groups also take advantage of the discretion granted to bureaucrats by pushing for their own demands at intermediate and low decision-making levels. It is for these reasons that observers of the federal bureaucracy often recommend that presidents and other high officials make every attempt to commit their directives to writing (in detail where possible), use personalized communications where appropriate, and show persistence in attempting to accurately convey their orders to those who actually implement the policies.

In general, the more decentralized the implementation of a public policy, the less likely it is to be transmitted accurately to its ultimate implementers. Decentralization usually means that a decision must be communicated through several levels of authority before it reaches those who will carry it out. The more steps a communication must traverse from its original source, the weaker will be the signal that is ultimately received. Presidents can tell their secretary of state to go to another country and deliver a policy pronouncement to its prime minister with little concern that the message will be inaccurately transmitted. However, they cannot have the same confidence about messages aimed at caseworkers in a Social Security office or soldiers in the field. Here, the distance between the White House and the implementers is too great.

Moreover, the distance is increasing. Paul Light showed that a "thickening" of government has occurred over the past few decades. There are now more steps than ever through which information must flow to reach the individuals who actually implement a policy. (In the early Clinton administration, there were 507 deputy assistant secretaries alone.)[8] As one front-line manager put it recently, "By the time an idea gets down here, it has been translated, reworked, and bureaucratized to the point where we just can't do it."[9]

In late 1983 and early 1984, President Reagan ordered reconnaissance flights over Lebanon. By the time the troops in the Middle East who were to implement the orders received them through the chain of command, however, they had been changed—undermining U.S. efforts to negotiate peace. In fact, the Pentagon *canceled* the flights at the very time when U.S. policy was to stand firm in Lebanon, and then *resumed* the flights later, at a time when U.S. policy was to move toward withdrawal.[10]

At times, executives and their staffs prefer *not* to transmit policy directives personally; they would rather get others to communicate for them. President Johnson wanted Secretary of the Treasury Henry Fowler to apply "jawboning," or powerful persuasion, to try to lower interest rates. Because Fowler opposed such efforts, Johnson decided not to communicate his wishes to the secretary directly. Instead, he called House Banking Committee Chairman Wright Patman, a supporter of "jawboning," and asked him to pressure Fowler. However, any time a step is added to the chain of communication, the potential for distortion is increased. Those who speak for others will have their own styles, views, and motivations. Not even presidents can depend on other people to transmit directives exactly as they would desire.

Some presidents lack a personality that is suited to direct communication. Richard Nixon, who feared rejection and confrontation, adopted an indirect administrative style to avoid possible unpleasantness. He spoke elliptically to those who disagreed with him to avoid being rebuffed, and typically failed to issue unambiguous orders directly to his subordinates. He did not like to say no personally or to discipline recalcitrant officials. When he found opposition within his administration, he either tried to accomplish his objectives without his adversaries being aware or he had intermediaries deliver his adversaries either written or verbal orders. The president shunned personal efforts at persuading or inspiring subordinates.[11]

Nixon's unwillingness to communicate directly with his subordinates fostered an environment in which discipline and cohesion were often low. It also revealed a disunity in his administration that outsiders could exploit, further eroding cohesion. Officials in positions of power, such as Secretary of State William Rogers, could increase their discretion by implementing orders with which they disagreed only when transmitted personally to them by the president—which they rarely were.[12]

The press also may serve as a means of more straightforward presidential communication. Individuals in the White House often believe that since most high-level bureaucrats read the *New York Times* and the *Washington Post,* they can communicate with these officials about policy matters more rapidly through news stories than through normal channels. The White House also uses other media outlets, such as television, newsmagazines, and specialized publications, to send messages to government officials. Such messages may indicate a policy decision or position, or they may signal that an official White House statement was issued merely to appease special interests and should not be taken literally. On the other hand, the information provided in a story or as a response to a reporter's question is unlikely to be sufficient for guiding the implementation of a complex policy, and indeed, it may even be in error. However, it is to the nuances contained in such communications that ears in Washington are often most attuned.

Clarity

If policies are to be administered as presidents desire, their implementation directives must not only be received, they also must be clear. However, often the instructions transmitted to implementers are vague and do not specify when or how a program is to be carried out. Lack of clarity provides implementers with the leeway to give new meaning to policies, which sometimes inhibits the intended change or brings about unintended consequences.

The lack of clarity in many implementation orders can be attributed to several factors. Perhaps the most important is the sheer complexity of policy making. When they establish policy, neither presidents nor members of Congress have the time or expertise to develop and apply all the requisite details for how it will be carried out. They have to leave most (and sometimes all) of the details to subordinates (usually in the executive branch).

Thus, although it is the president's responsibility to implement the policies of the national government no matter who initiates them, much of this responsibility must be delegated to others.

The difficulty in reaching consensus on policy goals also inhibits clarity in implementation directives. In the United States we share wide agreement on the goals of avoidance of war, equal opportunity, and efficiency in government, but this consensus often dissolves when specific policy alternatives are under consideration. Lyndon Johnson once said, "If the full implications of any bill were known before its enactment, it would never get passed."[13]

Clearly, imprecise decisions make it easier for presidents to develop and maintain winning coalitions. Different people or groups can support the same policy for different reasons, as each may hold its own conception of the goal or goals the program is designed to achieve. Ambiguous goals also may make it less threatening for groups to be on the losing side of a policy conflict, which may reduce the intensity of their opposition.

The problems of starting up a new program may also produce confusion in the implementation instructions. Often, the passage of a new policy is followed by a period of administrative uncertainty in which a considerable time lag occurs before any information on the program is disseminated. This period is followed by a second phase in which rules are made but are then changed quickly as high-level officials attempt to deal with unforeseen problems of implementing the policy and of their own earlier directives.

A cynical, yet realistic, explanation for the lack of clarity in federal statutes is that Congress does not want them to be detailed. It would rather let the executive branch agencies provide the specifics, not because of the latter's expertise but because the agencies can later be assigned the blame for the rules that turn out to be unworkable or unpopular. One law affecting almost every college and university in the United States is Title IX of the Education Act Amendments of 1972, which states that "no person in the United States shall, on the basis of sex, be excluded from participation in, or be denied the benefits of, or be subject to discrimination under an education program or activity receiving Federal financial assistance." Such broad language allows Congress to sidestep many touchy questions and leave their resolution to the president and his appointees. Moreover, individual members of Congress can gain credit with their constituents by intervening on their behalf regarding the application of regulations. In addition, if the goals are not precise, Congress cannot be held accountable for the failure of its policies to achieve them. All this only adds to the president's burden in guiding the bureaucracy.

Sometimes Congress makes efforts to restrict the discretion of implementers. The Voting Rights Act reduced the discretion of local voting registrars by limiting the use of literacy tests and similar voter qualification devices. In some cases the administration of voting registration was physically taken over by federal officials so that local officials could not inhibit voter registration. Congress has also invested a great deal of time in specifying eligibility requirements for government benefits ranging from social services and agricultural subsidies to grants for state and local governments.

It is generally easier for the president to reduce the discretion of officials via orders to stop doing something rather than instructions to start something. For example, an absolute ban on providing funds for abortions for poor women is more likely to be unambiguous and to be noticed if it is violated than an order to begin implementing a new policy. The implementation of most policies, however, requires positive actions rather than prohibitions. Moreover, in general, a series of positive actions extending over a long period of time and involving the technical expertise of numerous persons throughout a bureaucratic hierarchy is necessary to implement a policy. The complexity of such policy making makes it very difficult for a president to communicate and enforce rules that effectively reduce the discretion available to most policy implementers.

Vague policy decisions often hinder effective implementation, but directives that are too specific may also adversely affect implementation. Implementers sometimes need the freedom to adapt policies to suit the situation at hand. A myriad of specific regulations can overwhelm and confuse personnel in the field and may make them reluctant to act for fear of breaking the rules. Apparently this is what occurred in the Federal Emergency Management Agency as it tried to help the victims of Hurricane Andrew in 1992. During spring and summer 1993, President Clinton gave the same agency clearer direction and a shorter time frame in which to provide emergency assistance to Midwest flood victims, and the agency responded with greater dispatch and efficiency.

Strict guidelines may also induce a type of goal displacement in which lower-level officials become more concerned with meeting specific requirements than with achieving the basic goals of the program. By rigidly adhering to the letter of a regulation, they may become so bogged down in red tape that the purpose of the rule is forgotten or defeated. Conversely, implementers sometimes simply ignore rigid regulations.

Consistency

Inconsistency as well as vagueness in guidance from the president may provide operating agencies with substantial discretion in the interpretation and implementation of policy, which may not be exercised when carrying out a policy's goals. For example, the Immigration and Naturalization Service is often confronted with inconsistencies: the agency is supposed to keep out illegal immigrants but allow necessary agricultural workers to enter the country; it must carefully screen foreigners seeking to enter the country but facilitate the entry of foreign tourists; and it must find and expel illegal aliens yet not break up families, impose hardships, violate civil rights, or deprive employers of low-paid workers. As James Q. Wilson pointed out, "No organization can accomplish all of these goals well, especially when advocates of each have the power to mount newspaper and congressional investigations of the agency's failures."[14] Similarly, the Forest Service is supposed to both help timber companies exploit the lumber potential in the national forests *and* preserve the natural environment.

Many of the factors that produce unclear communications are also responsible for inconsistent directives. The complexity of public policies, the difficulties in starting up new programs, and the multiple objectives of many policies all contribute to inconsistency in policy communications. Another reason why decisions are often inconsistent is that the president and top officials constantly attempt to satisfy a diverse set of interests that may represent views on both sides of an issue. Consequently, policies that are not of high priority to the president may simply be left to flounder in a sea of competing demands.

RESOURCES

Implementation orders may be clear, consistent, and accurately transmitted, but if the president lacks the resources necessary to carry out policies, whether established at his discretion or by Congress, implementation is likely to be ineffective. Important resources include money, staff of sufficient size and with the proper skills to carry out its assignments, and the information, authority, and facilities necessary to translate written proposals into functioning public services.

Money

Sometimes the problem the president faces in implementing policy and delivering services is simply a lack of money. President Clinton's efforts to provide increased access to education and training for Americans have been severely constrained by the lack of funds. Because of lack of funding, the popular Head Start program serves fewer than half the children who are theoretically eligible to participate. While secretary of the Department of Health, Education and Welfare, Elliot Richardson discovered that the funds that Congress had appropriated for the various programs permitted his department to reach only very small percentages of all who were eligible for the benefits. When his staff estimated the cost of having the department's service-delivery programs reach each eligible person, it turned out to exceed the entire federal budget for that year.

Staff

Certainly an essential resource in implementing policy is staff. In an era in which "big government" is under attack from all directions, it may seem surprising to learn that a principal source of implementation failure is inadequate staff. Although nearly 5 million military and civilian personnel work for the federal executive branch (see Table 9–1), and therefore for the president, there are still too few people with the requisite skills to do an effective job implementing many policies. We must evaluate the bureaucracy, not only in terms of absolute numbers, but also in terms of its capabilities to perform desired tasks.

The federal government provides a wide range of services—from national defense and immigration control to the maintenance of recreational facilities—through its own personnel. Each of these areas, and others like them, are labor intensive, and thus the services provided are directly related to the size and quality of the staff available to the relevant agencies over which the president presides. However, there is substantial evidence that many agencies and departments are woefully understaffed. For example:

+ A shortage of staff at the Federal Drug Administration has been responsible for delays in the testing of new drugs to combat AIDS.

+ The Federal Aviation Agency lacks the proper personnel to safely direct the nation's air traffic.

+ The Immigration and Naturalization Service lacks the resources even to identify, much less deport, more than 10 percent of the 200,000 convicted criminal aliens in the United States. It also lacks the personnel to open letters containing checks for application fees.

+ The Department of Education's lack of sufficient auditors prevented it from detecting fraud in the federal government's student-aid programs.

+ Some observers fear that the lack of maintenance of national parks will lead to permanent deterioration of such treasured American vacation spots as Yosemite and Yellowstone.

Although staff size can be critical for almost every policy, it is more critical for some than for others. Insufficient staff is especially critical to implementation when the policy involved imposes unwelcome constraints on people, whether the requirements be those of grant policies, regulatory

TABLE 9–1. **Federal Employment**

	Number of Employees[a]
Executive Departments	
Agriculture	99,000
Commerce	38,300
Defense (civilians in military functions)	731,000
Education	4,600
Energy	17,100
Health and Human Services	58,500
Housing and Urban Development	10,400
Interior	67,600
Justice	119,800
Labor	16,700
State	22,900
Transportation	64,900
Treasury	146,000
Veterans Affairs	206,000
Larger Independent Agencies	
Corps of Engineers	26,100
Environmental Protection Agency	18,100
General Services Administration	14,100
National Aeronautics and Space Administration	19,600
Social Security Administration	65,700
Tennessee Valley Authority	14,400
U.S. Information Agency	6,700
U.S. Postal Service	838,000
Armed Forces	
Army	488,000
Navy	386,900
Air Force	371,400
Marines	173,000
Reserves	886,100
Total	2,305,400

[a]Figures are for 1998.

Source: Office of Management and Budget, *Budget of the United States Government, Fiscal Year 1999: Analytical Perspectives* (Washington, D.C.: Government Printing Office, 1998), Tables 10–1, 10–3; Appendix.

policies, or criminal law. Since such policies generally involve highly decentralized activities, sufficient staff must be available to monitor this behavior. It is much easier for the chief executive to implement a policy, such as

Social Security, that distributes benefits that recipients desire. More person-nel are required to enforce limitations on people than to write checks to them.

However, the lack of staff makes compliance data difficult to obtain. Thus, the president and his subordinates often have to rely on information about compliance from those who are doing the complying. This occurs in a wide range of policies, including school desegregation, hospital care, and environmental protection. Quite naturally, this system of information raises questions about effective implementation. It should come as no sur-prise to us, then, when faulty welds are discovered in the trans-Alaskan pipeline, federal grants to state and local governments are misspent, or haz-ardous wastes are found to cause pollution.

The fear of creating a totalitarian bureaucratic monolith and the pres-sures to allocate personnel to more direct services, such as the provision of agricultural expertise to farmers, keep the staffs available to monitor imple-mentation small. In addition, the scarcity of payroll funds, coupled with the irresistible urges of policy makers to provide public services (at least in form), ensure that staff size will often be inadequate to implement the pro-grams. Moreover, in an age when "big government" is under attack, there are strong political incentives to downsize the bureaucracy. President Clinton was well received when he promised to reduce the size of the federal workforce by 272,900 persons over a five-year period, but the wisdom of such a policy remains to be seen.

Federal programs rely heavily on state agencies for their implementa-tion. This reliance, however, does not solve the president's problem of lack of staff at the federal level; it merely transfers the problem to the states. Since this shortage of personnel exists at every level of government, dele-gating the implementation of a policy to a lower level rarely alleviates the problem.

Sometimes presidents turn limited staff size to their advantage. For example, the Reagan administration actually decreased staff in areas such as antitrust, civil rights, and environmental protection in an effort to reduce enforcement activities to which it was opposed.[15] The Republican Congress that was elected in 1995 attempted a similar strategy regarding the Environmental Protection Agency. Such a strategy may be useful for stopping an activity, such as regulatory behavior, but it undermines efforts to take the positive actions that the administration may desire.[16]

In addition to numbers, skill is an important characteristic of imple-mentation staff. Personnel with substantive skills are also often in short supply in the executive branch. This is especially true when a government agency is carrying out or regulating highly technical activities. For example, inadequately trained inspectors for the Environmental Protection Agency were found to be missing more than half the serious violations in their inspections of facilities handling and storing hazardous waste.

Sometimes the necessary personnel are very difficult to hire because of the higher incomes and greater flexibility that they can enjoy by working in the private sector. As a case in point, the Federal Aviation Administration has had difficulty hiring personnel to manage the development of appropriate software for its computers because it cannot pay salaries to compete with private industry.

At other times, the needed staff may simply not exist, even in the private sector, and a government agency must invest in developing the expertise. The federal government's efforts to regulate energy prices and allocations in the 1970s illustrate both problems. No one really knew how to accomplish these tasks, and few people outside the energy companies had the background to understand the industry. Thus, employees of the Federal Energy Office relied on a sort of on-the-job training.

Staff skills are especially critical for new policies or those involving technical questions. Routine functions, such as dispersing funds, building roads, training troops, hiring typists, or purchasing goods, are relatively straightforward in their operation, and a wealth of information exists on how to carry them out. However, the implementers of policies such as controlling hospital costs or developing a jet fighter do not share these advantages: They are being asked to meet goals no one has ever met. Thus, it is one thing for Congress or the White House to mandate a change in policy, but something quite different for the executive branch officials who work for the president to figure out how to do it.

As a result, some responsibilities will simply not be met or else will not be met on time. Inefficiency is also likely to characterize the implementation of such policies. Some efforts will prove to be mistakes, and the implementers will have to try again. Moreover, regulations may be inappropriate, causing other government units or organizations in the private sector to purchase equipment, fill out forms, or stop certain activities unnecessarily. For example, ideally, before an agency acts to implement a law by ordering costly changes in an industry or its products (automobiles, for instance), the agency should be able to predict the effects of the change on the economic health of the industry in question. Such information, however, is frequently lacking, and the president may be severely criticized as a result.

Authority

Authority is often a critical resource in policy implementation. Surprising as it may seem, the president actually has relatively little direct authority over executive branch operations. Congress vests most of the authority in subordinate executive officials. Sometimes agency officials simply lack the authority, even on paper, to implement a policy properly. For example, the policy being implemented may provide no sanctions against those violating the law or the agency may lack authority to initiate administrative or judicial actions.

Many observers feel that the Federal Drug Administration (FDA) lacks adequate powers to protect the public from drugs and devices that may be potentially dangerous to some individuals, such as silicon breast implants or various sleeping pills and sedatives. The FDA does no testing of its own and must rely entirely on the test results submitted by manufacturers. However, it lacks the subpoena power to obtain drug company documents when its suspicions are aroused regarding the withholding of data about adverse drug reactions or fraudulent representation of test results. Often it even lacks access to potentially damaging company documents that reveal a manufacturer's involvement in product liability cases.

When formal authority does exist, observers frequently mistake it for effective authority. However, authority on paper is one thing; authority effectively exercised is quite another. Executive branch officials may be reluctant to exercise authority for a number of reasons. One of the potentially most effective sanctions is the withdrawal of funds from a program. Cutting off funds is a drastic action. It may be embarrassing to all involved and antagonize the implementers of a program whose active support is necessary for effective implementation. Cutting off federal funds from projects also alienates the members of Congress from the areas losing the money. Requiring states or cities to repay misspent funds can also have severe political consequences. In addition, terminating a project or withdrawing federal funds may hurt most those whom the policy is designed to aid. Schoolchildren, the elderly, or the poor are often the real victims of cutbacks. If a company loses federal contracts because of racial or sexual discrimination, it may be forced to lay off workers. Those with the least seniority may be the minorities the policy is trying to help. Similarly, cutting off federal funds for the educationally disadvantaged because of misallocation is most likely to hurt students from poor families.

The desire for self-preservation keeps many of the president's agencies from withdrawing funds. Agencies like the Federal Highway Administration and the Department of Education are primarily involved in channeling grants to other levels of government. To survive, they must give away money. If they fail to do so, they may look bad to Congress and superior executive officials. This may hurt them in their future quests for budgets and authority, resources of great significance for most bureaucrats. Thus, they may sacrifice the economic and social objectives of a program to the "maintenance" objectives of the bureaucratic unit.

Although executive officials often lack effective authority over other public officials, this lack of control is small compared with their lack of authority over private individuals, groups, and businesses, on whom the successful implementation of policies often depends. Therefore, they must

☼ HOT-BUTTON ISSUE

The Use of Executive Orders to Bypass Congress

It is common for presidents to see their legislative programs bogged down in Congress. It is also common for presidents to turn to the use of executive orders and other instructions to the executive branch to accomplish at least some of what they cannot win legislatively. The president's power is theoretically limited to the executive branch, and executive orders and other instructions to the departments are supposed to be based on existing authority under law. But presidents frequently test those boundaries.

In 1998, President Clinton, who was frustrated in his attempts to get Congress to pass a "patients bill of rights" that would regulate health care benefits, applied his own patients bill of rights to nine million federal employees and family members and 75 million people covered by Medicare, Medicaid, and other governmental health plans. In 1996, the president transformed 1.7 million acres in southern Utah into a national monument—something Congress would not do—using executive authority under the 1906 Antiquities Act.

Sometimes, however, the president overreaches. In 1995, certain that Republicans in Congress would kill any legislative effort to bar employers from replacing striking workers, the president attempted to impose his own labor policy on the executive branch through an executive order preventing federal agencies from entering into contracts with employers that permanently replaced striking workers. In this case, however, the order was overturned in the courts.

make their policies attractive to the private sector. As a result of these efforts, the enforcement of policies such as those dealing with safety in the workplace rarely results in serious penalties for noncompliance. Environmental pollution, however, is another matter, in which large settlements between alleged polluters and the Environmental Protection Agency (EPA) have been, and continue to be, negotiated. For a more dramatic exercise of executive authority, see the Hot-Button Issue box.

Facilities and Equipment

Physical facilities may also be critical resources in implementation. Without the necessary buildings, equipment, supplies, and even green space, implementation will not succeed. National parks are overcrowded; military equipment, ranging from rifles to spare parts for airplanes, has often been in short supply; and those patrolling our borders lack the appropriate ships and planes to prevent the smuggling of illegal drugs.

Frequently, there is also a shortage of sophisticated equipment. Computers are essential to the implementation of modern defense policy; they issue paychecks, assign personnel, navigate ships, and track missiles. Nevertheless, studies of the military's computers have found that the Defense Department has been saddled with thousands of obsolete machines (and the software that runs them), which leaves the military services ill-prepared for a modern war. Similar problems have beset other agencies. The Federal Aviation Administration's air traffic control centers across the nation depend on aging, outdated equipment in the effort to direct the nation's air traffic. Similarly, the Internal Revenue Service lacks the appropriate computer systems to integrate the dozens of databases that contain the information necessary to collect the $1.8 trillion in taxes that finance the federal government.

Although the president can request funds for new or additional facilities, both the White House and Congress hesitate to raise taxes to pay for them. Moreover, as was the case for staff, Congress often prefers to spread resources over many policies rather than to fund fewer programs adequately. Internal government procurement rules ("red tape") may add additional burdens to those trying to purchase expensive equipment such as computers.

DISPOSITIONS

We have seen in our discussion of communication that bureaucrats often operate with considerable discretion in their implementation of policy.[17] Ultimately, how they exercise this discretion depends on their dispositions about the policies and rules they administer. If the implementers are well disposed toward a particular policy, they are more likely to carry it out as the president intended. Other policies fall within a "zone of indifference." These policies will probably be implemented faithfully because implementers lack strong feelings about them.

When bureaucrats are asked to execute orders with which they do not agree, however, slippage between policy decisions and performance is inevitable. If policies are in direct conflict with the policy views or personal or organizational interests of the implementers, they may exercise their discretion, sometimes in subtle ways, to hinder implementation. President Ford offered this observation:

> There are bureaucratic fiefdoms out in the states or in various regions, and the people who occupy those pockets of power want to do things in their own way.

They are pros at it. They have been disregarding Presidents for years, both Democratic and Republican.[18]

Implementers may oppose a policy, and their opposition can prevent a policy option from even being tried. For some time there has been a policy debate over whether there should be a work requirement for those receiving welfare payments and able to work. During the Nixon administration, many top officials concluded that welfare administrators would not enforce a work requirement provision, even in the face of presidential exhortations and congressional demands. Thus, they turned to other alternatives, such as tax incentives, to encourage welfare recipients to work. On another occasion, Nixon ordered Secretary of Defense Melvin Laird to bomb a hideaway of Palestine Liberation Organization guerrillas, a move that Laird opposed. According to the secretary: "We had bad weather for forty-eight hours. The Secretary of Defense can always find a reason not to do something."[19] Thus, the president's order was stalled for days and eventually rescinded. President Reagan's national security assistant explained that the United States could not employ a strategy involving the selective use of force in order to support diplomatic efforts to keep peace in Lebanon because of the lack of cooperation between the Departments of State and Defense.[20]

The opposition of presidential subordinates to a policy may also defeat some of its immediate goals after it becomes law. For example, President Carter ordered federal agencies to discourage the development of low-lying areas that were in danger of damage from flooding. Twenty-five months later, however, only fifteen of the seventy-five agencies that had received the directive had issued regulations specifying how they were going to comply with the president's wishes. Forty-six of the agencies had not even taken the first step toward adopting the regulations. The primary reason for this lack of action was not bureaucratic indolence. Instead, it was the opposition of agencies to the substance of the president's order. Similarly, Ronald Reagan's efforts to build up special commando units for unconventional warfare and counterterrorist operations were hampered by the failure of the air force to provide adequate aircraft to deliver the forces and the army to provide the units with the proper equipment.

Differences in organizational viewpoints may also impede the cooperation between agencies that is so often necessary in policy implementation. The army requires aircraft, which belong to the air force (at its insistence), to transport troops. However, transporting troops is a low priority for the air force, which is more interested in flying strategic bombers and fighter planes. Thus, it typically does not fight for resources for troop transport planes or choose to allocate its scarce resources to that function, which undermines the ability of the army to carry out its own function.

There may also be differences in viewpoints between presidential subordinates with different program responsibilities within a single agency. There was intraagency conflict over the implementation of the National Environmental Policy Act. Secretaries of transportation, for example, had a difficult time getting development-oriented agencies in the department, such as the Federal Highway Administration, to consider seriously the environmental consequences of their projects.

Bureaucratic units also vigorously resist the efforts of others to take away or share the resources deemed necessary to accomplish their missions. Turf fights over jurisdiction are not unusual in the executive branch. According to Richard Nixon, when J. Edgar Hoover directed the FBI, he "totally distrusted the other intelligence agencies—and, whenever possible, resisted attempts to work in concert with them."[21] At one point the director cut off all liaison activities with the other intelligence agencies, including the Central Intelligence Agency, the Defense Intelligence Agency, and the National Security Agency.

Staffing the Bureaucracy

The dispositions of implementers may pose obstacles to policy implementation. The most straightforward response from the White House is to replace personnel who fail to implement policies the way the president desires with people who will cooperate. When presidents succeed in doing this, they can change the way in which a policy is implemented.[22] There are many limits on the use of such a strategy, however.

Appointments   The president has the authority to directly appoint about 650 top officials in the executive branch. This total includes the White House staff, between one and four dozen individuals in each of the cabinet-level departments, about ten persons in each of the major independent agencies (such as the National Aeronautics and Space Administration), the heads of some lesser agencies, and the commissioners of the independent regulatory agencies (as their terms expire).[23] Of the approximately 4.5 million employees in the executive branch, far less than 1 percent are appointed by the president and his designees (who appoint about 2,500 persons). Mid- and upper-level bureaucratic managers outnumber their political counterparts by almost 100 to 1, which places an obvious constraint on the ability of any administration to alter personnel.

After being elected, a president has less than three months to search for a new team to take over the government. Moreover, this must be done by the president-elect and the president's aides, all of whom will have been exhausted by the long, arduous election campaign and have many other demands on their time, such as preparing a budget and a legislative program. Members of the cabinet and other appointees usually have little advance notice of their selection and will be busy wrapping up their other responsibilities and doing preparation on the issues relevant to their new positions prior to their confirmation hearings. Thus, they also often resort to haphazard recruiting techniques when they make their appointments.

Presidents are also constrained politically in their appointments. Usually, they feel that such appointments must show a balance of geography, ideology, race, ethnicity, gender, and other demographic characteristics that are salient at the time. (President Clinton made it a high priority to have an administration "as diverse as America.") Thousands of persons seek appointments for themselves or are urged on an administration by members of Congress or people in the president's party. Few are qualified for the available jobs, yet due to political necessity, some will be appointed. Political favors may please political supporters, but they do not necessarily provide the basis for sound administration. Moreover, such appointments may result in incompatibilities with the president that lead to politically costly dismissals.

The interest groups that appointments are designed to please keep a watchful eye, throughout a president's tenure in office, on who is appointed to what position. Not only is "balance" important at the beginning of a new administration, but it remains a constraint on recruiting personnel. Thus, for example, in the middle of a term White House aides may be ordered to find a Chicano woman to serve as U.S. treasurer. A president may also desire to reward new groups. After the 1972 presidential election, Richard Nixon wanted his cabinet and subcabinet to represent more accurately his broadened electoral coalition. This led to a renewed emphasis on the demographic characteristics of appointees, delays in filling positions, and, most significantly, compromises in the quality of some appointees, such as many of the individuals who were placed in top positions in the Labor Department to please the president's new "hard hat" constituency. It also led to a humorous incident in which Claude Brinegar was selected as secretary of transportation partly on the basis of his purported Irish Catholic background. The White House was in error, however; Brinegar was really a German Protestant.

A different type of "political" constraint may arise if a strong member of an administration or a chair of the Senate committee that must clear a nomination opposes a person the president desires to appoint. Usually the president can overcome this opposition within the ranks, but sometimes the price may be too high. For example, in his second term, President Nixon wanted to appoint John Connally as secretary of state but did not do so because of the opposition of his chief adviser on national security matters, Henry Kissinger. Instead, Kissinger was named to the post.

A surprising, but nonetheless real, limitation on personnel selection is that presidents often do not know of individuals who are qualified for the positions they have to fill. Following his election in 1960, John F. Kennedy told an aide: "For the last four years I spent so much time getting to know people who could help me get elected President that I didn't have time to get to know people who could help me, after I was elected, to be a good President."[24] Thus, presidents often appoint persons they do not know to the highest positions in the federal government.

Early in their terms many presidents have not imposed their preferences for subcabinet-level officials on those whom they appoint to head the departments and agencies. The reason has partially been the lack of organization in the personnel system. In addition, however, there has been a concern that since top officials will be held accountable for the agencies' performances, they should be able to appoint subordinates whom they like and who will complement their own abilities and help them accomplish their jobs. Naturally, top officials generally request this freedom. High officials also fight to name their subordinates, because if they lose to the White House on personnel matters, their standing within their departments will drop.

The Reagan administration, on the other hand, insisted on White House clearance of all subcabinet appointments. Although there is disagreement about the quality of the personnel appointed to high-level executive branch positions during this period, there is consensus on the view that Reagan's appointees were unusually loyal to the president and committed to his conservative ideology.

The Bush administration reverted to the more common practice of giving department and agency heads discretion in making political appointments. It was more concerned with the competence and personal loyalty to the president of its political appointees than with their ideology. The Clinton White House clears subcabinet appointments and has put a high priority on recruiting minorities and women to high office. This process slowed the president's initial appointments, and, as a result, a large percentage of top departmental positions were still unfilled more than six months into his tenure.

As presidential terms extend from weeks into months and years, every White House experiences frustrating problems in policy implementation and tends to take a direct interest in personnel matters below the levels of department and agency heads. For example, in mid-1978 the Carter administration began a review of subcabinet officials with the object of weeding out those who were incompetent or disloyal. Tim Kraft was promoted to the position of assistant for political affairs *and* for personnel (indicating an appreciation for the linkage between the two), and Kraft and his staff began taking more interest in the appointees: "We have told the personnel people in the departments that we want to be consulted on all appointments, whether they are presidential appointments or appointments to high GS [civil service] positions."[25]

Despite its frequent use, political clearance is often a crude process. Many policy views fit under a party label. Democrats range from very liberal to very conservative, and the range for Republicans is nearly as great. Moreover, political appointees may be motivated by materialistic or selfish aims and not necessarily be responsive to the president. For example, a person may want the status of an ambassadorship, or a young lawyer may seek experience in the Justice Department or a regulatory agency in hope of cashing in on it later for a high-paying job in the private sector. Political appointees may also remain loyal to their home-state political organizations, interest group associations, or sponsors in Congress—rather than to the White House.

Civil Service   Most executive branch employees rank below appointed officials in the federal hierarchy. Almost all civilian employees are covered by the protection of personnel systems designed to fill positions on the basis of merit and protect employees against removal for partisan political reasons. The military has a separate personnel system designed to accomplish the same goals.

Political appointees often bring to office a distrust of the permanent bureaucracy; such suspicions were fueled by presidential election campaigns such as those of Jimmy Carter and Ronald Reagan, in which the winning candidate ran as a Washington outsider and engaged in "bureaucrat bashing." (George Bush and Bill Clinton, however, abstained from the temptation to criticize the bureaucracy in their campaigns, and both praised government employees.) Regardless of the attitudes they bring with them to government, before they leave office, most political appointees come to regard members of the civil service as both competent and responsive to their leadership.[26]

If the president or a presidential appointee finds that a civil servant is obstructing implementation of the president's policies, he or she has some potential remedies. Those at the top of the civil service—in the Senior Executive Service (SES)—may be transferred and may be demoted more easily than in the past. Although members of the SES compose only a small percentage of the civil service (there are about 9,000 members of the SES), they are among the most powerful members of the career bureaucracy and the most crucial to implementing the president's policies.

Those below the SES are more difficult to move. It is possible for an incompetent or recalcitrant civil service employee to be dismissed, but this rarely happens. It takes more time, expertise, and political capital to fire a civil servant than most officials have or are willing to invest in such an effort. Transferring unwanted personnel to less troublesome positions is one of the most common means of quieting obstructive bureaucrats. In President Carter's words, it is "easier to promote and transfer incompetent employees than to get rid of them."[27] Transferring unwanted personnel is much easier when the civil servants in question opt not to use the technicalities and protections of the civil service system or their allies in Congress and the interest groups. Ironically, these tend to be the type of person most likely to be dedicated to the notion of a civil service, and therefore an employee that an executive would probably least desire to replace. In addition, transferring personnel is not a panacea for the problems of implementers' dispositions because it does not solve problems, but simply relocates them.

As the size and scope of the federal government have grown since the 1960s, so has distrust, especially among Republican presidents and the general public. Over this period there has been a trend toward politicizing the bureaucracy and emphasizing the White House's operational control of the executive bureaucracy rather than traditional patronage. The number of political appointees at the top of the executive bureaucracy has increased substantially, as has the number of political appointees at lower ranks.[28] Employing a related technique (developed by his predecessors), President Reagan made efforts to place political appointees in career positions just before leaving office.

Politicizing the bureaucracy has drawbacks, however. It is difficult to recruit high-quality political appointees to some of the lower subcabinet positions, especially with the new financial reporting and divesting requirements and the visible and contentious nature of many confirmation hearings. No matter how loyal to the president the appointees are, they need to know what to do and how to do it once they obtain their positions. People with these capabilities are not easy to find. Moreover, the short tenure in the same job of typical political appointees (less than two years)[29] diminishes their ability to implement policy effectively. As administrative positions become more and more complex, both politically and substantively, it takes appointees more time to learn their jobs and forge the relationships that make effective implementation possible. Moreover, the more layers there are in a bureaucracy, the more complex the management job becomes.

In addition, layering political appointees at the top of bureaucratic units may separate the top executive from the bureaucracy and its services, thus decreasing the executive's opportunities to build personal support within the bureaucracy through communication, consultation, and access, and also undermining the motivation of the career service and closing off career options. The diffusion of responsibility that comes with a large number of decision points in a bureaucracy also increases the number of actors involved in policy implementation and, therefore, the costs of implementing presidential policy because the White House and the president's top appointees have to influence more people in the implementation chain. Having more political checkpoints means there are more obstacles to innovation and barriers to employee involvement, which makes it more difficult to give frontline employees the authority to solve problems.

The recent presidents have placed many persons who had favorable attitudes toward their administrations' policies in top career and politically appointed managerial positions. However, the number of vacancies they can fill remains limited. A study of the Nixon and Ford administrations found that after eight years in the White House, nearly 70 percent of the existing top career and political executives had assumed their positions before Nixon took office. (The figure for career executives alone was 85 percent.) Thus, filling vacancies is unlikely to be a sufficient strategy to alter the attitudes in the bureaucracy. The president must also influence those who are already holding their jobs.[30]

Incentives

Changing the personnel in government bureaucracies is difficult, and it does not ensure that the implementation process will proceed smoothly. Another potential technique that the president can use is to alter the dispositions of existing implementers through the manipulation of incentives. Since people generally act in their own interest, the manipulation of incentives by high-level policy makers may influence their subordinates' actions. Increasing the benefits or costs of a particular behavior may make implementers either more or less likely to choose it as a means of advancing their personal, organizational, or substantive policy interests.

The ability of top officials to exercise sanctions is severely limited. Rewards are the other side of the incentive coin, but they are even more difficult for executives to administer than penalties. Individual performance is difficult to reward with pay increases. President Carter once complained that "more than 99 percent of all federal employees got a so-called 'merit' rating."[31] Raises are almost always given across-the-board, with everyone in the same category of employment receiving a similar percentage increase in salary, regardless of differences in performance. The Civil Service Reform Act of 1978 created the potential for awarding merit pay increases or bonuses for many managers, supervisors, and top executives in the federal civil service, but Congress has appropriated little money for these raises and few civil servants have received them. Usually personal performance can be rewarded only by promotions, which are, necessarily, infrequent. There may not be room at the top for qualified bureaucrats. Unlike a typical private business, a government agency cannot expand simply because it is performing a service effectively and efficiently. In addition, presidential subordinates who oppose or are indifferent to a policy are unlikely to employ incentives to further its implementation.

In the absence of positive and negative incentives, the government relies heavily on rules to limit the discretion of implementers. As Vice President Al Gore explained in a report issued by the National Performance Review:

> Because we don't want politicians' families, friends, and supporters placed in "no-show" jobs, we have more than 100,000 pages of personnel rules and regulations defining in exquisite detail how to hire, promote, or fire federal employees. Because we don't want employees or private companies profiteering from federal contracts, we create procurement processes that require endless signatures and long months to buy almost anything. Because we don't want agencies using tax dollars for any unapproved purpose, we dictate precisely how much they can spend on everything from telephones to travel.[32]

Often these rules end up creating new obstacles to effective and efficient governing, however. For example, in fall 1990, as U.S. forces were streaming toward the Persian Gulf to liberate Kuwait from Iraq, the air force placed an emergency order for 6,000 Motorola commercial radio receivers. However, Motorola refused to do business with the air force because of a government requirement that the company set up separate accounting and cost-control systems to fill the order. Ironically, the only way the air force could acquire the much-needed receivers was for Japan to buy them and donate them to the United States!

THE BUREAUCRATIC STRUCTURE

Policy implementers may know what to do and have sufficient desire and resources to do it, but they may still be hampered in implementation by the structures of the organizations in which they serve. Two prominent characteristics of bureaucracies are standard operating procedures (SOPs) and fragmentation, both of which may hinder presidential policy implementation.

Standard Operating Procedures

Standard operating procedures (SOPs) are routines that enable public officials to make numerous everyday decisions. They have many benefits for the chief executive. For one thing, they save time, and time is valuable. If a Social Security caseworker had to invent a new rule for every potential client and have it cleared at higher levels, few clients would be served. Thus, detailed manuals are written to cover as many particular situations as officials can anticipate. The regulations elaborating the Internal Revenue Code compose the bible of an Internal Revenue Service (IRS) agent; similarly, a customs agent has binders filled with rules and regulations about what can and cannot be brought into the United States free of duty.

SOPs also bring uniformity to complex organizations. Justice is better served if rules are applied uniformly, as in the implementation of welfare policies that distribute benefits to the needy or the levying of fines for underpayment of taxes. Uniformity also makes personnel interchangeable. Soldiers, for example, can be transferred to any spot in the world yet still do their job by referring to the appropriate manual, which is a substantial advantage for the commander in chief.

Although they are designed to make implementing policies easier, at least in theory, SOPs may be inappropriate in some cases and even function as obstacles to action. Presidents have had many a plan thwarted by standard government practices. They certainly frustrated President Franklin D. Roosevelt, as he explained:

> The Treasury is so large and far-flung and ingrained in its practices that I find it is almost impossible to get the action and results I want. . . . But the Treasury is not to be compared with the State Department. You should go through the experience of trying to get any changes in the thinking, policy, and action of the career diplomats and then you'd know what a real problem was. But the Treasury and the State Department put together are nothing as compared with the Na-a-vy. . . . To change anything in the Na-a-vy is like punching a feather bed. You punch it with your right and you punch it with your left until you are finally exhausted, and then you find the damn bed just as it was before you started punching.[33]

Standard operating procedures may hinder policy implementation by inhibiting change. Because they are designed for typical situations, SOPs can be ineffective in new circumstances. For example, in 1962 the United States discovered the presence of Soviet missiles in Cuba and reacted by blockading the island. President John F. Kennedy was very concerned about the initial interception of Soviet ships, so he sent Secretary of Defense Robert McNamara to check with Chief of Naval Operations George Anderson on the procedures being followed. McNamara stressed to Anderson that the president did not want to follow the normal SOP, whereby a ship risked being sunk if it refused to submit to being boarded and searched. This was because Kennedy did not want to goad the Soviet Union into retaliation. However, Admiral Anderson was not cooperative. At one point in the discussion, he waved the *Manual of Naval Regulations* in the secretary's face and shouted, "It's all in here." To this McNamara replied: "I don't give a damn what John Paul Jones would have done. I want to know what you are going to do now."[34] The conversation ended after the admiral asked the secretary of defense to leave and let the navy run the blockade according to established procedures.

Sometimes SOPs cause organizations to take actions that superior officials do not desire, as the Cuban missile crisis dramatically illustrates. Despite President Kennedy's explicit order that the initial encounter with a Soviet ship not involve a Soviet submarine, the U.S. Navy, according to established procedure, used its "Hunter-Killer" antisubmarine warfare program to locate and float above Soviet submarines within 600 miles of the continental United States. Also following standard "Hunter-Killer" procedures, the navy forced several Soviet submarines to surface. Neither the president nor the secretary of defense ordered this drastic action. It came about because it was the programmed response to such a situation. The highest officials, who ostensibly had authority over the navy, never imagined that standard procedures would supplant their directives. Clearly, SOPs can become deeply embedded in an organization and be difficult to control, even in times of crisis.

New policies are the most likely to require a change in organizational behavior and are therefore the most likely to have their implementation hindered by SOPs. For example, in October 1983, 241 U.S. Marines were killed in their sleep during a terrorist attack on their barracks outside Beirut, Lebanon. A presidential commission appointed to examine the causes of the tragedy concluded that, among other factors contributing to the disaster, the marines in the peacekeeping force were "not trained, organized, staffed or supported to deal effectively with the terrorist threat."[35] In other words, they had not altered their SOPs regarding security (which are basic to any military unit) to meet the unique challenges of a terrorist attack.

Fragmentation

A second aspect of bureaucratic structure that may impede implementation is fragmentation—the dispersion of responsibility for a policy area among several organizational units.

The extent of governmental fragmentation is widespread. For example, the federal government has ninety-six agencies involved with the issue of nuclear proliferation. Similarly, in the field of welfare, ten different departments and agencies administer more than one hundred federal human services programs. The Department of Health and Human Services has responsibility for basic welfare grants to the states to aid families; the Department of Housing and Urban Development provides housing assistance for the poor; the Department of Agriculture runs the food stamp program; and the Department of Labor administers training programs and provides assistance in obtaining employment. Twelve agencies regulate food safety. For example, cheese pizzas are the responsibility of the Food and Drug Administration, but pizzas with pepperoni on top fall under the purview of the Department of Agriculture. As President Carter declared, "There are too many agencies doing too many things, overlapping too often, coordinating too rarely, wasting too much money—and doing too little to solve real problems."[36] The more actors and agencies are involved with a particular policy and the more interdependent are their decisions, the less is the probability of successful implementation.

Over the years Congress has created many separate agencies and has favored categorical grants that assign specific authority and funds to particular agencies in order to oversee more closely and intervene more easily in the administration of policies. Dispersing responsibility for a policy area also disperses "turf" to congressional committees. For example, in water resource policy, three committees in the House and three in the Senate have authority over the Army Corps of Engineers, the Soil Conservation Service, and the Bureau of Reclamation, respectively. None of these committees wants to relinquish its hold over these agencies, and therefore, the agencies and programs that deal with a common problem remain divided among three departments.

Like congressional committees, agencies are possessive about their jurisdictions. Usually department or agency heads will vigorously oppose executive branch reorganizations that encroach on their sphere of influence. For example, when President Carter requested that funds for state drug abuse programs be divided into single, consolidated grants for mental health, drug, and alcohol abuse services, Congress refused to consent to the proposal. Professionals in the alcohol and drug abuse programs feared that their programs would be downgraded if they lost their separate legislative identities and were combined with mental health programs, so as a result, they blocked the president's attempt to reduce program fragmentation. President Clinton proposed to merge the FBI with the Drug Enforcement Agency (DEA), both of which are units *within* the Justice Department. Nonetheless, DEA officials, who were fearful of losing their agency identity and, perhaps, their jobs, mobilized sympathetic members of Congress to oppose the move.

Interest groups are a third force supporting fragmentation. When Lyndon Johnson tried to move the Maritime Administration from the Department of Commerce to the Department of Transportation, a labor organization, the American Federation of Labor and Congress of Industrial Organizations (AFL-CIO) successfully opposed him. Although it made sense administratively to house the Maritime Administration with other transportation-related agencies, labor leaders feared that a bureaucratic reorganization would jeopardize their close relationship with the Maritime Administration. Groups also develop close working relationships with congressional committees and do not want to lose their special access in a reorganization of committee jurisdictions that might follow an executive branch reorganization.

Often a combination of interest groups and legislative committees oppose reorganization. The Department of Education, which was proposed by President Carter, is composed almost exclusively of education programs from the old Department of Health, Education and Welfare. Head Start, Native American education, the school lunch program, GI bill benefits, job training, and some vocational and rehabilitation education programs remained where they were because of opposition to their being moved. For example, the Senate Agriculture Committee opposed any change out of fear of losing oversight responsibility for child nutrition programs, whereas the American Food Service Association opposed any change because it feared nutrition would not be a high priority with educators.

The nature of public policy is also a factor in producing fragmentation. Broad policies, such as those dealing with environmental protection, are multidimensional and overlap with dimensions of other policies, such as agriculture, transportation, recreation, and energy. Thus, presidents cannot easily organize government agencies around a single policy area.

Fragmentation implies diffusion of responsibility, which makes the coordination of policies difficult. The resources and authority necessary for the president to attack a problem comprehensively are often distributed among many bureaucratic units. For example, President Bush found that his high-priority efforts to interdict illegal drugs at the country's borders required coordination among the Treasury Department's Customs Service; the Department of Justice's Drug Enforcement Agency, Federal Bureau of Investigation, and Border Patrol; and the Transportation Department's Coast Guard. During the invasion of Grenada, President Reagan learned that an army officer on the island had to use his credit card to place a call to North Carolina in order to speak to a ship just offshore! Clearly, the army and navy had not coordinated their communications systems.

Duplication in the provision of public services is another result of bureaucratic fragmentation. President Carter complained, "There are . . . at least 75 agencies and 164,000 Federal employees in police or investigative work. Many of them duplicate or overlap state and local law enforcement efforts unnecessarily."[37]

Implementation may result in two or more agencies working at cross-purposes. According to Richard Nixon:

One department's watershed project, for instance, threatens to slow the flow of water to another department's reclamation project downstream. One agency wants to develop an electric power project on a certain river while other agencies are working to keep the same area wild. Different departments follow different policies for timber production and conservation, for grazing, for fire prevention and for recreational activities on the federal lands they control, though the lands are often contiguous.[38]

Not only do such conflicts defeat the purposes of the programs involved, they also force the president's highest-level aides and departmental executives to spend great amounts of time and energy negotiating with one another. This is wasteful, and it may result in compromises representing the lowest common denominators of the officials' original positions. Unfortunately, bold and original ideas may be sacrificed for intragovernmental harmony.

Sometimes responsibility for a policy area is so fragmented that certain functions fall between the cracks. Some tasks do not fit neatly within an agency's formal authority. For example, a former intelligence official wrote of serving in a Scandinavian embassy and hiring someone to read the local communist literature. From this activity, a useful chart showing the hierarchy of the Communist party was developed. The project was cut from the budget, however, because although coverage of the communist movement was considered to be a CIA function, the CIA could not carry out this function because it was "overt" while the CIA was a clandestine organization.[39] Thus, the project fell between the divisions of organizational responsibility, and, as a result, useful information was not made available to the White House or others in government.

FOLLOW-UP

As a result of all the hindrances to effective policy implementation, it seems reasonable to suggest that implementation would be improved if presidents followed up on their decisions and orders to see that they have been properly implemented. An incident that occurred during the Nixon administration illustrates the importance of follow-up.

President Nixon ordered the CIA to destroy its stockpile of biological weapons. CIA Director Richard Helms relayed the president's order to the deputy director for plans (the head of the covert action division), who, in turn, relayed it to a subordinate. Five years later, however, two lethal toxins were discovered in a secret cache. A middle-level official had disobeyed the president's order and then retired, and his successor had assumed that the storage of the toxins had official approval. When called before Congress, Helms testified that he had undertaken no follow-up check on his own order, and when asked who told him the toxins had been destroyed, he replied, "I read it in the newspapers." Indeed, if the official who discovered the toxins had not received a directive from the new CIA director, William Colby, to be on the constant lookout for illegal action, he might not have checked on the legality of the toxins and the cache would still exist.[40]

The importance of follow-up was made apparent to Nixon at many other points in his administration. Once he ordered the demolition of two old Department of Defense buildings on the Mall near the White House, only to have it take more than a year to get them down. White House aide William Safire explained:

> Because the President of the United States took a continuing interest, because at least two of his aides were made to feel that its success was a crucial test of their ability and because the President kept prodding, issuing orders, refusing to be "reasonable," a few miserable buildings were finally knocked down and their occupants reassigned. . . . [After the demolition the president called together his aides, and, with] "pride, relief, and wonderment" [he told them,] "We have finally gotten something done."[41]

Thus, a president must constantly check up on his orders, yet most recent presidents, including Nixon himself, have not followed this advice. On the whole, follow-up has been haphazard. Presidents and their staffs have been too busy with crisis management, electoral politics, or encouraging the passage of legislation to delve into the details involved in monitoring policy implementation. Moreover, they lack systematic information about the performance of agencies, and finally, some presidents are philosophically opposed to engaging in much follow-up. For example, Ronald Reagan believed that the chief executive should set broad policy goals and general ground rules and then appoint good people to accomplish the goals. He did not believe presidents should constantly monitor their subordinates.[42]

One technique that presidents can use to increase their capacity to follow up on their decisions is to enlarge the size of their personal staffs. Certainly the executive staff is crucial to the president's ability to put his stamp on policy implementation. As Secretary of State George Shultz put it: "If the president's staff does not support a policy, the policy is not likely to succeed. The president by himself cannot make sure that a policy is being implemented, so the staff has to be brought along."[43]

Relying heavily on the White House staff for policy implementation can create additional burdens for the president, however—even if the staff supports a policy. Because chief executives can personally deal effectively with only a limited number of people, they are forced to relay implementation orders and receive feedback through additional layers of their own staffs. This, in turn, increases both the possibility of communication distortion and the burden of administration, which the staff is supposed to lighten.

The more authority is delegated to persons at the top of a hierarchy, the more possibilities there are for inadequate coordination, interoffice rivalries, communication gaps, and other typical administrative problems to arise. Moreover, having a large number of aides with limited access to a top official such as the president increases the chance that they may carry out a presidential order given in anger. Individuals with limited access will be less likely to know the executive well enough or have enough confidence to hold back on implementing their supervisor's instructions.

Having a large implementation staff for a president has another drawback: Only a few people can credibly speak for the president. If too many people begin giving orders in the president's name, for example, they will undermine the credibility of all those claiming to speak for him. This credibility is important for aides trying to help the president implement policies. As one Carter aide explained: "If you are perceived by people in a given agency as being close to the president because you have an office in the West Wing, your phone calls will be returned more rapidly and your requests for information or action will be taken more seriously."[44]

Presidential assistants carry the contingent authority of the president, which is essential to accomplish anything at all since under the law, presidential assistants have no authority of their own. However, presidential authority is undermined if numerous people attempt to exercise it.

Excessively vigorous staff involvement in implementation decisions may cause other problems. For example, some observers of recent presidential administrations have concluded that as larger numbers of bright, ambitious, energetic assistants probe into the activities of departments and agencies, they will bring for decision to the president more issues, which were formerly decided at lower levels in the bureaucracy. Bureaucrats will begin to pass the buck upward, and the White House must then make increasing numbers of decisions. This can easily make the Executive Office of the President top-heavy and slow. Involvement in the minutiae of government may also divert resources (including time) from the central objectives and major problems of a president's administration. In addition, if White House aides become intimately involved in the management of government programs, they may lose the objectivity necessary to evaluate new ideas regarding "their" programs.

Overcentralization of decision making at the highest levels may have other negative consequences: It may discourage capable people from serving in government posts where their authority is frequently undercut; it may lower morale and engender resentment and hostility in the bureaucracy, which may impede future cooperation; it may decrease respect for lower officials among their subordinates; it may reduce the time bureaucratic officials have for internal management because they must fight to maintain access to and support of the chief executive; and it may weaken the capability of agencies to streamline or revitalize their management. Similarly, too much monitoring of subordinates' behavior may elicit hostility or excessive caution and lack of imagination in administering policy.

Another factor inhibiting follow-up is secrecy. Secretly executed policies, such as those implemented by the CIA, require few reports to Congress or superiors in the executive branch. Consequently, such officials' actions are not routinely monitored. Since members of Congress risk criticism for violating national security if they make public any secret information, they are reluctant to do so and have incentives to forgo their responsibility for the oversight and follow-up of certain secret policies. For example, when President Johnson's fear of leaks regarding decisions on the Vietnam War led him to restrict his direct communications to a few top officials (the "Tuesday lunch group"), he did without a prearranged agenda or minutes of the meetings, which would have recorded decisions and made it possible to follow up on them.

The increasing number of management layers in government can also hamper follow-up. The thickening of government makes it more difficult to ascertain the locus of responsibility for policy implementation. Accountability is reduced when no one unit or individual can be held responsible for a lack of action or poor communication.

An organization's personnel may be aware of implementation problems yet fail to report them to the president or other administration officials. There are several reasons for this. An obvious one is that subordinates may fear that reporting implementation failures will reflect poorly on their own performance and also, possibly, anger their superiors. Additionally, employees may have a natural loyalty to their organization or to others in the organization who might be hurt by their negative reports. Further, the informal norms against reporting negative information may be very strong. Thus, employees may withhold information from their superiors to escape social ostracism in their peer groups. Finally, some bureaucrats may feel that the president is simply too busy to bother with matters of policy implementation.

Even when information indicating poor policy implementation is available to the president and other top executive officials, they may fail to use it. Information coming from the field is often fragmentary, circumstantial, inconsistent, ambiguous, and unrepresentative—in sum, it is very often unreliable. In addition, as noted in Chapter 7, such information may become lost in the huge volume of information circulating in the executive branch. It is very difficult for the president to have a clear idea of how a complex policy is actually implemented.

Organizations may fail to report problems in policy implementation for political reasons, such as the fear of losing public or legislative support for their programs. Also, within some organizations, rivalries between head-quarters and field personnel make the latter reluctant to expose themselves to negative reactions to their implementation efforts.

Although there are limitations on performing follow-up properly, this does not mean that follow-up cannot work. Moreover, there is substantial evidence that it needs to be done. For example, one study found that the Nixon administration's efforts to monitor and evaluate the actions of welfare caseworkers, and especially to review them for errors that allowed ineligible persons to receive funds under the Aid to Families with Dependent Children program, had a significant influence on reducing the number of persons receiving welfare. (Unfortunately, it appears that this approach also resulted in many eligible persons not receiving welfare payments.)[45]

The Reagan administration made headway in monitoring agency regulations when it required the Office of Management and Budget (OMB) to review all regulations proposed by executive agencies (see Chapter 6). This procedure allows the president to influence or block individual regulations more effectively than before. An additional requirement is that agencies must inform OMB of upcoming regulations, thus aiding the White House in preempting the proposal of regulations it opposes or influencing them before they are proposed (when the political costs of opposition are less). Finally, the White House requires agencies to provide cost-benefit analyses of their proposed regulations. Since this type of analysis is often as much art as it is science, ideological preferences may determine the conclusions, which in turn may be used to resist regulations to which the administration is opposed.[46]

CONCLUSION

The president faces many obstacles in implementing public policies. Although the president is the "chief executive," he or she is typically not in a position to command the bureaucracy within the executive branch. Moreover, the president operates in an environment of scarce resources and few incentives to devote time and energy to implementation, and will generally emerge from this process as a facilitator rather than a director.

Improving implementation is very difficult as the roots of most implementation problems are embedded deeply in the fabric of American government and politics. Moreover, as long as presidents remain more concerned with shaping legislation to pass in the Congress than with the implementation of the law after it is passed, persist in emphasizing public relations rather than policy, and allow "crisis" situations to continue to dominate their time, little progress is likely to be made in improving policy implementation. Moreover, until there are more political incentives for officials to devote more attention to policy implementation and to develop better administrative skills, these priorities will probably not change. Given both the low visibility of many policy implementation activities and the lack of interest in them, the prospects for a change in incentives are not very favorable.

DISCUSSION QUESTIONS

1. We have seen that many agencies are understaffed. We also know that there are strong budgetary pressures to reduce the size of the federal bureaucracy. How should a president deal with the dilemma of making trade-offs between saving money and providing high-quality public services?
2. Some presidents have emphasized bureaucratic responsiveness and made strong efforts to place administration loyalists throughout the bureaucracy. Other presidents have focused on efficiency and emphasized finding the most skilled persons to fill administrative positions. Which strategy do you feel is best for the country?
3. In the private sector, businesses and institutions use salary increases and bonuses to encourage effective job performance. Selective bonuses and substantial pay raises are relatively rare in the public sector, however. Should Congress appropriate more funds for the bureaucracy so that the president and his appointees can use economic incentives to make the bureaucracy more responsive to their policies?

WEB EXERCISES

1. The National Performance Review has been a visible and highly touted effort by the Clinton administration to "reinvent government." Go to their Web site and see what the effort is designed to accomplish and what accomplishments it claims. Think about whether this has made the bureaucracy more responsive to the president or the public. Go to <http://www.npr.gov>.
2. From the *United States Government Manual* you can obtain a good sense of how the executive branch is organized and some of the implications of implementing policy. For example, click on the Department of Agriculture. Note that in addition to supporting agricultural research and directly aiding farmers, the department has responsibilities in nutrition, food safety, housing, conservation, and international trade—areas also covered by other agencies and departments. Go to <http://www.access.gpo.gov/nara/browse-gm.html>.

SELECTED READING

Aberbach, Joel D., and Bert A. Rockman. "Clashing Beliefs within the Executive Branch: The Nixon Administration Bureaucracy." *American Political Science Review* 70 (June 1976): 456–468.

Allison, Graham. *Essence of Decision: Explaining the Cuban Missile Crisis.* Boston: Little, Brown, 1971.

Cole, Richard L., and David A. Caputo. "Presidential Control of the Senior Civil Service: Assessing the Strategies of the Nixon Years." *American Political Science Review* 73 (June 1979): 399–413.

Cooper, Joseph, and William W. West. "Presidential Power and Republican Government: The Theory and Practice of OMB Review of Agency Rules." *Journal of Politics* 50 (November 1988): 864–895.

Derthick, Martha. *Agency under Stress.* Washington, D.C.: Brookings Institution, 1990.

Diamond, Edwin. *White House to Your House: Media and Politics in Virtual America.* Cambridge, MA: MIT Press, 1997.

Durant, Robert F. *The Administrative Presidency Revisited.* Albany: State University of New York Press, 1992.

Edwards, George C., III. *Implementing Public Policy.* Washington, D.C.: Congressional Quarterly, 1980.

Heclo, Hugh. *A Government of Strangers: Executive Politics in Washington.* Washington, D.C.: Brookings Institution, 1977.

Kaufman, Herbert. *Administrative Feedback.* Washington, D.C.: Brookings Institution, 1973.

Light, Paul C. *Thickening Government.* Washington, D.C.: Brookings Institution, 1995.

Mackenzie, G. Calvin. *The In-and-Outers.* Baltimore: Johns Hopkins University Press, 1987.

Moe, Terry M. "The Politicized Presidency." In John E. Chubb and Paul E. Peterson, eds., *The New Directions in American Politics.* Washington, D.C.: Brookings Institution, 1985.

Nathan, Richard P. *The Administrative Presidency.* New York: Wiley, 1983.

Peterson, Paul E., Barry G. Rabe, and Kenneth K. Wong. *When Federalism Works.* Washington, D.C.: Brookings Institution, 1986.

Radin, Beryl A., and Willis D. Hawley. *The Politics of Federal Reorganization.* New York: Pergamon Press, 1988.

Waterman, Richard W. *Presidential Influence and the Administrative State.* Knoxville: University of Tennessee Press, 1989.

Weko, Thomas L. *The Politicizing Presidency: The White House Personnel Office, 1948–1994.* Lawrence: University Press of Kansas, 1995.

Wood, B. Dan, and Richard W. Waterman. *Bureaucratic Dynamics.* Boulder, Colo.: Westview, 1994.

Notes

1. President Carter quoted in G. Calvin Mackenzie, "Personnel Appointment Strategies in Post-War Presidential Administrations" (paper presented at the Annual Meeting of the Midwest Political Science Association, Chicago, April 1980), introductory page.

2. Quoted in Paul C. Light, *The President's Agenda: Domestic Policy Choice from Kennedy to Carter* (Baltimore: Johns Hopkins University Press, 1982), p. 145.

3. On this point see Martha Derthick, *Agency under Stress* (Washington, D.C.: Brookings Institution, 1990), esp. pp. 66, 184.

4. Quoted in Derthick, *Agency under Stress*, p. 152.

5. David Gergen quoted in "How Much Can Any Administration Do?" *Public Opinion,* December/January 1982, p. 56.

6. Al Gore, *From Red Tape to Results: Creating a Government That Works Better and Costs Less* (New York: Times Books, 1993).

7. See, for example, William Safire, *Before the Fall: An Inside View of the Pre-Watergate White House* (New York: Doubleday, 1975), pp. 112–113, 285–287, 353, 566–567; H. R. Haldeman, *The Ends of Power* (New York: Times Books, 1978), pp. 58–59, 111–112, 185–187.

8. Paul Light, "How Thick Is Government?" *American Enterprise,* November/December 1994, pp. 59–63.

9. Paul C. Light, *Thickening Government* (Washington, D.C.: Brookings Institution, 1995), p. 86.

10. George P. Shultz, *Turmoil and Triumph* (New York: Scribner's, 1993), pp. 228–229.

11. See, for example, Henry Kissinger, *White House Years* (Boston: Little, Brown, 1979), pp. 26, 28–29, 45–46, 48, 141–142, 158–159, 264, 482, 729, 806, 879, 887, 900, 909, 917, 994.

12. Kissinger, *White House Years*, pp. 28–29, 264, 900.

13. Lyndon Johnson quoted in Doris Kearns, *Lyndon Johnson and the American Dream* (New York: Harper and Row, 1976), p. 137.

14. James Q. Wilson, *Bureaucracy* (New York: Basic Books, 1989), p. 158.

15. See, for example, Dan B. Wood and James E. Anderson, "The Politics of U.S. Antitrust Regulation," *American Journal of Political Science* 37 (February 1993): 1–39; B. Dan Wood and Richard W. Waterman, *Bureaucratic Dynamics* (Boulder, Colo.: Westview, 1994), chap. 4; and Evan J. Ringquist, "Political Control and Policy Impact in EPA's Office of Water Quality," *American Journal of Political Science* 39 (May 1995): 336–363.

16. Robert F. Durant, *The Administrative Presidency Revisited* (Albany: State University of New York Press, 1992).

17. On administrative discretion, see Gary S. Bryner, *Bureaucratic Discretion* (New York: Pergamon Press, 1987).

18. Gerald R. Ford, "Imperiled, Not Imperial," *Time,* November 10, 1980, p. 30.

19. Melvin Laird quoted in Seymour M. Hersh, *The Price of Power: Kissinger in the Nixon White House* (New York: Summit, 1983), pp. 235–236.

20. Robert C. McFarlane, *Special Trust* (New York: Cadell and Davies, 1994), pp. 270–271.

21. Richard M. Nixon, *RN: The Memoirs of Richard Nixon* (New York: Grosset and Dunlap, 1978), pp. 472–473, 513.

22. See, for example, Wood and Waterman, *Bureaucratic Dynamics*, chap. 3; and Ringquist, "Political Control and Policy Impact."

23. There are also nominations for about 170 ambassadors, 94 U.S. attorneys, and 93 U.S. marshals.

24. John F. Kennedy quoted in Kenneth P. O'Donnell and David F. Powers, *Johnny, We Hardly Knew Ye: Memories of John Fitzgerald Kennedy* (New York: Pocket Books, 1972), p. 270.

25. Tim Kraft quoted in Dom Bonafede, "Carter Sounds Retreat from 'Cabinet Government,'" *National Journal,* November 18, 1978, pp. 1852–1857; see also "Rafshoon and Co.," *Newsweek,* January 29, 1979, p. 23.

26. James P. Pfiffner, *The Strategic Presidency* (Chicago: Dorsey, 1988), p. 98.

27. Jimmy Carter quoted in "Civil Service Reform," *Congressional Quarterly Weekly Report,* March 11, 1978, p. 660.

28. See Light, *Thickening Government*; and Terry M. Moe, "The Politicized Presidency," in John E. Chubb and Paul E. Peterson, eds., *The New Directions in American Politics* (Washington, D.C.: Brookings Institution, 1985).

29. See Hugh Heclo, *A Government of Strangers: Executive Politics in Washington* (Washington, D.C.: Brookings Institution, 1977); Carolyn Ban and Patricia Ingraham, "Short-Timers: Political Appointee Mobility and Its Impact on Political-Career Relations in the Reagan Administration," *Administration and Society 22* (May 1990): 106–124.

30. Richard L. Cole and David A. Caputo, "Presidential Control of the Senior Civil Service: Assessing the Strategies of the Nixon Years," *American Political Science Review* 73 (June 1979): 399–413.

31. Jimmy Carter quoted in "Press Conference Text," *Congressional Quarterly Weekly Report*, March 11, 1978, p. 655.

32. Gore, *From Red Tape to Results*, p. 11.

33. Franklin D. Roosevelt quoted in M. S. Eccles, *Beckoning Frontiers* (New York: Knopf, 1951), p. 336.

34. Robert McNamara quoted in Graham T. Allison, *Essence of Decision: Explaining the Cuban Missile Crisis* (Boston: Little, Brown, 1971), pp. 131–132.

35. *Report of the DOD Commission on Beirut International Airport Terrorist Act, October 23, 1983* (Washington, D.C.: Government Printing Office, December 20, 1983), p. 133.

36. Jimmy Carter quoted in "Carter Criticizes Federal Bureaucracy," *Congressional Quarterly Weekly Report*, June 3, 1978, p. 1421.

37. "Carter Criticizes Federal Bureaucracy," p. 1421.

38. Richard Nixon, "Government Reorganization—Message from the President," in Stanley Bach and George T. Sulzner, eds., *Perspectives on the Presidency: A Collection* (Lexington, Mass.: Heath, 1974), p. 257.

39. William Colby, *Honorable Men: My Life in the CIA* (New York: Norton, 1975), pp. 101–102.

40. Colby, *Honorable Men*, pp. 440–441; "Intelligence Failures, CIA Misdeeds Studied," *Congressional Quarterly Weekly Report*, September 20, 1975, p. 2025.

41. Safire, *Before the Fall*, pp. 250–260.

42. Ronald Reagan, *An American Life* (New York: Simon and Schuster, 1990), p. 161.

43. Shultz, *Turmoil and Triumph*, p. 166.

44. Quoted in Stephen J. Wayne, "Working in the White House: Psychological Dimensions of the Job" (paper presented at the annual meeting of the Southern Political Science Association, New Orleans, November 1977), pp. 16–17.

45. Ronald Randall, "Presidential Power versus Bureaucratic Intransigence: The Influence of the Nixon Administration on Welfare Policy," *American Political Science Review* 73 (September 1979): 795–810.

46. Joseph Cooper and William W. West, "Presidential Power and Republican Government: The Theory and Practice of OMB Review of Agency Rules," *Journal of Politics* 50 (November 1988): 864–895.

10

THE PRESIDENT AND CONGRESS

IF ONE WERE TO WRITE A JOB DESCRIPTION OF THE PRESIDENCY, near the top of the list of presidential responsibilities would be that of working with Congress. According to Lyndon Johnson, "There is only one way for a President to deal with Congress, and that is continuously, incessantly, and without interruption."[1] Since our system of separation of powers is really one of shared powers, presidents can rarely operate independently of Congress. Although they require the cooperation of Congress, they cannot depend on it. Thus, one of the president's most difficult and frustrating tasks is trying to persuade Congress to support his or her policies.

The differences in our contrasting views of presidential leadership are perhaps most clear in the area of executive-legislative relations. Director presidents will dominate Congress, reliably obtaining its support for their policies and precluding legislative initiatives to which they are opposed. Facilitators, on the other hand, will find the going much tougher. They will often fail to achieve their legislative goals and almost always have to struggle to win at all. Congress may pass major legislation over their opposition, and frustration and stalemate may characterize such a presidency much of the time.

In this chapter we examine the president's leadership of Congress. Because it is important to understand the context of presidential-congressional interaction, we begin with a discussion of the president's formal legislative powers and the inevitable sources of conflict between the two branches. We then move to an examination of the potential sources of presidential influence in Congress, including party leadership, public support, and legislative skills. In our discussion we emphasize both how presidents attempt to persuade members of Congress and the utility of each source of influence.

FORMAL LEGISLATIVE POWERS

Presidents today have a central role in the legislative process. They are expected to formulate and promote policies. They are expected to coordinate them within the executive branch, to introduce them to Congress, and to mobilize support for them on Capitol Hill and, increasingly, with the general public.

These expectations suggest a broad scope of legislative authority for the president. In actuality, however, the constitutional basis for this authority is quite limited. Only four duties and responsibilities were designated by Article 2: (1) to inform Congress from time to time on the state of the union; (2) to recommend necessary and expedient legislation; (3) to summon Congress into special session and adjourn it if the two houses cannot agree on adjournment; and (4) to exercise a qualified veto.

With the exception of the veto, these responsibilities stem primarily from the president's unique position within the political system—as the only official other than the vice president who was to have continuous tenure, a national perspective, and the ability to respond quickly and decisively to emergencies. As the framers of the Constitution saw it, these job-related qualifications placed the president in a unique position to inform Congress, recommend legislation, and summon Congress into session if necessary.

The rationale for the veto was different. Justified within the Constitutional Convention as a defensive weapon, the veto was proposed as a device by which the president could prevent executive powers from being usurped by the legislature. The founders feared that the institutional balance would become undone and that the Congress would be the likely perpetrator. The extent to which their fears were justified and the use of the veto as a political and constitutional weapon are examined later in this chapter.

Over the years presidents have used their legislative responsibilities to enlarge their congressional influence. The State of the Union address is a good example. In the nineteenth century it was a routine message dealing primarily with the actions of the executive departments and agencies for the previous year. Beginning with Jefferson and continuing through Theodore Roosevelt, the address was sent to the Congress to be read by the clerk of the House and then distributed to the members. Woodrow Wilson revived the practice of the first two presidents and delivered the speech himself. Subsequently, however, presidents have timed the address to maximize its public exposure, and today it is an important vehicle by which presidents can articulate the legislative goals of their administrations, recite their accomplishments, present their agendas, and try to mobilize support for their programs.

Similarly, presidents have transformed their responsibility to recommend necessary and expedient legislation into an annual agenda-setting function. Although nineteenth-century presidents formulated some legislative proposals and even drafted bills in the White House, it was not until the twentieth century that the practice of presidential programming developed on a regular basis. Wilson and Franklin Roosevelt submitted comprehensive legislative proposals to Congress. Truman packaged them in the State of the Union address. With the exception of Eisenhower in his first year in office, every subsequent president has followed the Truman tradition.

To some extent, the Congress has found the president's legislative initiatives advantageous, and in some cases it has insisted on them. For example, the 1921 Budget and Accounting Act, the 1946 Employment Act, and the 1974 Budget Act require the president to provide Congress with annual reports and an annual executive budget.

The calling of special sessions by the president has fallen into disuse. The length of the current legislative year, combined with changes in the calendar, has made this function largely obsolete. The last special session occurred in 1948. In the past, however, presidents frequently would call special sessions after their inauguration to gain support for their objectives and to initiate "their" Congress. Until the passage of the Twentieth Amendment in 1933, Congress began its session on or about December 1. This made every other session of Congress "a lame duck" session and forced a newly elected president to wait nine months for the newly elected Congress. Between the Lincoln and Franklin Roosevelt administrations, there were nineteen special sessions.[2]

SOURCES OF CONFLICT BETWEEN THE EXECUTIVE AND LEGISLATIVE BRANCHES

Presidents must influence Congress because they generally cannot act without its consent. Under the constitutional system of separation of powers, Congress must pass legislation and can override vetoes, and the Senate must ratify treaties and confirm presidential appointments to the cabinet, the federal courts, regulatory commissions, and other high offices. However, these overlapping powers do not explain the president's need to influence Congress. Theoretically, the two branches could be in agreement. In fact, the president and some members of Congress will always disagree because of their personalities or past histories, yet these differences are not the source of systematic conflict. Rather, the source lies in the structure and processes of American politics.

Constituencies

In "The Federalist, No. 46," James Madison focused on the greatest source of conflict between the president and Congress—their different constituencies:

> The members of the federal legislature will likely attach themselves too much to local objects. . . . Measures will too often be decided according to their probable

effect, not on the national prosperity and happiness, but on the prejudices, interests, and pursuits of the governments and the people of the individual states.[3]

Only presidents (and their vice presidential running mates) are chosen in a national election. Each member of Congress is elected by only a fraction of the populace. Inevitably, presidents must form a broader electoral coalition in order to win their office than any member of Congress. Moreover, two-thirds of the senators are not elected at the same time as the president, and the remaining senators and all the House members seem to be increasingly insulated from the causes of presidential victories. In addition, the Senate overrepresents rural states because each state has two senators regardless of its population. Thus, the whole that the president represents is different from the sum of the parts represented by each legislator. Each member of Congress will give special access to the interests that he or she represents, but Congress as a body has more difficulty in representing the nation as a whole.

Internal Structures

The internal structures of the executive and legislative branches also cause differences between the president and Congress. The executive branch is hierarchically organized, which aids the president in examining a broad range of viewpoints on an issue and then weighing and balancing various interests. This structure also helps the president to view the trade-offs among various policies. He or she must take a comprehensive view of those policies and support all the major initiatives emanating from the executive branch.

On the other hand, each house of Congress is highly decentralized. The party structure is usually not a unifying force within the U.S. legislature. Committee memberships are frequently unrepresentative of each chamber, and members of each committee may defer to members of the other committees. Thus, members representing special interests have a disproportionate say over policy regarding those interests.

One of the functions of decentralizing power and responsibility in Congress is to allow for specialization in various policy areas. However, because of specialization, legislators tend to rely on the cues of party leaders, state party delegations, relevant committee leaders of their party, and other colleagues to decide how to vote. These cue givers, however, are chosen because they represent constituencies or ideologies that are similar to those of the member who is consulting them. They do not represent a cross section of viewpoints.[4]

Members of Congress are not generally in a position to make trade-offs between policies. Because of its decentralization, Congress usually considers policies serially—that is, without reference to other policies. Without an integrating mechanism, members have few means by which to set and enforce priorities and emphasize the policies with which the president is most concerned, particularly when the opposition party controls Congress. In addition, Congress has little capability, except within the context of the budget, to examine two policies, such as education and health care, in relation to each other. Through not knowing that giving up something on one policy will result in a greater return on another policy, members have little incentive to engage in trade-offs. Congress is also poorly organized to deal comprehensively with major policy domains as it distributes its workload among committees with jurisdictions that often do not cover entire policy areas, such as welfare, national security, or economic stability.

Thus, although the structure of Congress ensures that a diversity of views will be heard and that many interests will have access to the legislative process, it does not follow that *each* member will hear all the views and see the proponents of each interest. Indeed, the decentralization of Congress almost guarantees that the information available to it as a whole is not a synthesis of the information available to each legislator. The Congress as a whole does not ask questions; individual members do. Thus, not all its members receive the answers.

The hierarchical structure of the executive branch, with the president at the pinnacle, forces the president to take responsibility for the entire executive branch. Moreover, when the president exercises power, it is clear who is acting and who should be held accountable. Congress, on the other hand, is not responsible for implementing policies, and each member is relatively obscure compared to the president. Since Congress is so decentralized, any member can disclaim responsibility for policies or their consequences. Members of Congress, therefore, can, and do, make irresponsible or self-serving decisions and then let the president take the blame.

All this can be very frustrating to the president. Gerald Ford, who spent most of his adult life in Congress, wrote the following after leaving the White House:

> When I was in the Congress myself, I thought it fulfilled its constitutional obligations in a very responsible way, but after I became President, my perspective changed. It seemed to me that Congress was beginning to disintegrate as an organized legislative body. It wasn't answering the nation's challenges domestically because it was too fragmented. It responded too often to single-issue special interest groups and it therefore wound up dealing with minutiae instead of attacking serious problems in a coherent way.[5]

Information and Expertise

Another source of conflict between the president and Congress is the difference in information and expertise available to them. There has been a substantial increase in congressional staff in the past few decades (although this trend was reversed under the Republican majority in 1995), including the services of the General Accounting Office, the Congressional Research Service in the Library of Congress, and the Congressional Budget Office. Nevertheless, members of Congress usually do not have access to the same quantity and quality of expertise as that available to the president.

Aside from the fact that the executive branch includes nearly 5 million civilian and military employees plus hundreds of advisory committees, while Congress employs only a few thousand persons (many of whom work in supporting agencies, including the Library of Congress), the expertise of the two branches differs. Members of Congress tend to hire generalists, even on committee staffs. Some individuals develop great expertise in a particular field, but others may only be amateurs compared with their counterparts in the executive branch. Many are selected to serve legislators' needs and desires, which have little to do with policy analysis, and neither house has a merit system, a tenured career service, or a central facility for recruiting the best available talent.

Because the president and Congress have different information and expertise available to them, they may well see issues from different perspectives. The president's views will generally be buttressed with more data and handled more expertly, inevitably giving the chief executive different views and more confidence in those views.

We have seen that the structure of American government exerts strong pressure on the two branches to represent different sets of interests and to view policies differently. This, in turn, sets the stage for conflict and virtually compels a president to try to influence Congress.

PARTY LEADERSHIP

"What the Constitution separates our political parties do not combine."[6] Richard Neustadt wrote these words nearly four decades ago to help explain why presidents could not simply assume support from the members of their party in Congress. The challenge of presidential party leadership in Congress remains just as great and is just as important today as it was when Neustadt wrote his famous treatise on presidential power.

Party Support of the President

Representatives and senators of the president's party are almost always the nucleus of coalitions supporting the president's programs. As one White House aide put it: "You turn to your party members first. If we couldn't move our own people, we felt the opportunities were pretty slim."[7] No matter what other resources presidents may have, without seats in Congress held by their party, they will usually find it very difficult to move their legislative programs through Congress. Thus, leading their party in Congress is the principal task of all presidents as they seek to counter the tendencies of the executive and legislative branches toward conflict inherent in the system of checks and balances.

Tables 10–1 and 10–2 show the support given presidents by members of each party on roll-call votes on which the presidents took a stand. Clearly, there is a substantial difference between the levels of support presidents receive from members of the two parties, with the gap generally exceeding 30 percentage points. Although the presidents of each party varied considerably in their policies, personalities, and political environments, their fellow partisans in Congress gave them considerably more support than they gave presidents of the opposition party.

With a president of their own in the White House, party members in Congress may alter their voting tendencies.[8] For example, Republicans have a tendency to be more supportive of internationalist foreign policies and are more likely to accept governmental economic activity when a Republican is president. Democrats, on the other hand, have a tendency to move in the opposite direction when there is a Republican in the White House. In 1981, with a conservative Republican as president, many Republicans in Congress shifted to supporting foreign aid and increasing the national debt ceiling, even though they had opposed these policies under the previous Democratic administration of Jimmy Carter. Similarly, many members of the president's party who voted for a bill when it was originally passed will switch and vote against the same legislation if their party leader vetoes it.

Although the president receives more support from members of his party than from the opposition, this is not necessarily the result of party affiliation. It is difficult to tell whether a member of the president's party votes for the president's policies because of shared party affiliation, basic agreement with those policies, or some other factor. Undoubtedly, members of the same party share many policy preferences and have similar electoral coalitions supporting them. For example, in 1981 President Reagan won several crucial votes in Congress on his taxing and spending proposals. He was immediately credited with extraordinary party leadership because nearly 100 percent of the Republicans in Congress supported his programs. If we examine voting on budget resolutions under Democrat Jimmy Carter,

TABLE 10-1. Presidential Support by Party, 1953–1996 (in percentages)*

		House		Senate	
Year	President's Party	Democrats	Republicans	Democrats	Republicans
1953	R	45%	70%	42%	66%
1954	R	34	74	36	74
1955	R	42	52	37	70
1956	R	38	72	35	69
1957	R	48	52	44	69
1958	R	52	55	37	66
1959	R	34	72	28	73
1960	R	46	64	41	66
1961	D	73	26	68	31
1962	D	72	30	64	31
1963	D	75	21	63	37
1964	D	78	26	63	56
1965	D	75	24	64	44
1966	D	67	20	53	35
1967	D	70	28	56	42
1968	D	63	36	46	41
1969	R	48	57	42	65
1970	R	41	60	35	63
1971	R	41	71	33	65
1972	R	46	68	34	66
1973	R	31	65	24	64
1974	R	38	59	31	53
1975	R	37	68	36	67
1976	R	32	67	29	62
1977	D	61	32	62	39
1978	D	65	34	64	36
1979	D	64	26	67	39
1980	D	63	31	60	38
1981	R	39	72	33	81
1982	R	30	61	35	72
1983	R	28	71	39	73
1984	R	32	66	31	74
1985	R	28	68	27	76
1986	R	23	72	26	80
1987	R	26	75	27	70
1988	R	24	70	29	68
1989	R	34	71	36	77
1990	R	25	72	31	69
1991	R	26	76	28	78
1992	R	23	73	20	75
1993	D	75	34	86	19

continued

TABLE 10–1. Presidential Support by Party, 1953–1996 (in percentages)*
continued

		House		Senate	
Year	President's Party	Democrats	Republicans	Democrats	Republicans
1994	D	70	36	82	28
1995	D	75	15	84	19
1996	D	71	25	78	24

*On roll-call votes on which the winning side was supported by fewer than 80 percent of those voting.

†R = Republican, D = Democrat.

Source: George C. Edwards III, *At the Margins: Presidential Leadership of Congress* (New Haven: Yale University Press, 1989), Table 3.1; updated by author.

TABLE 10–2. Partisan Support for Presidents, 1953–1996 (in percentages)*

	House		Senate	
	President		President	
	Democratic	Republican	Democratic	Republican
Democrats	70%	35%	66%	33%
Republicans	28	67	35	70
Difference†	42	32	31	37

*On roll-call votes on which the winning side was supported by fewer than 80 percent of those voting.

†Differences expressed as percentage points.

Source: George C. Edwards III, *At the Margins: Presidential Leadership of Congress* (New Haven: Yale University Press, 1989), Table 3.3; updated by author.

however, we find nearly the same degree of Republican party unity in the House. Thus, we should not necessarily ascribe Reagan's success to party loyalty. Republican members of the House had been voting a conservative line well before Ronald Reagan came to Washington, and they have continued it through the Clinton administration.

Despite the proclivity of members of Congress to support presidents of their party, the White House may also experience substantial slippage in party cohesion in Congress. Table 10–2 shows that presidents can count on their own party members for support only two-thirds of the time (this is also true on key votes). This forces them to adopt an activist orientation toward party leadership and devote as much effort to converting party members to support them as to mobilizing members of their party who already agree with them.

Leading the Party

That members of the president's own party are more open to presidential influence is clear. Members of the president's party typically have personal loyalties or emotional commitments to their party and their party leader, which the president can often translate into votes when necessary. Thus, members of the president's party vote with him when they can, thus giving him the benefit of the doubt, especially if their own opinion on an issue is weak. Moreover, this proclivity for supporting the president increases the effectiveness of other sources of party influence.

One of these sources is the desire of members of the presidential party to avoid embarrassing "their" administration. This attitude stems from two motivations. The first is related to the sentiments already discussed, but the second is more utilitarian. Members of the president's party have an incentive to make the president look good because his standing in the public may influence their own chances for reelection. They also want a record of legislative success to take to the voters. In 1993, the need to end gridlock between the president and Congress was a unifying force among Democrats in both the House and the Senate, thus motivating them to support President Clinton.

Presidents may also find it easier to obtain party unity behind their programs if their party regains control of one or both houses of Congress at the time of their election. Many new members may feel a sense of gratification for the president's coattails. Moreover, the prospect of exercising the power to govern may provide a catalyst for party loyalty, while the loss of power may temporarily demoralize the opposition party. All the motivations to support the president are, of course, buttressed by a basic distrust of the opposition party.

Working with Congressional Leaders   Each party has a set of floor and committee leaders in the House and Senate who, in theory, should be a valuable resource for their party's leader in the White House. The president needs both their advice and their resources for making head counts and other administrative chores. Because of their role perceptions, because their reputations for passing legislation give them a clear stake in the president's success, and because they are susceptible to the same sentiments and pressures toward party loyalty as are other members of Congress, floor leaders of the president's party in Congress are usually very supportive of the White House. For example, in the month before Ronald Reagan's inauguration, the new

Senate majority leader, Howard Baker, declared, "I intend to try to help Ronald Reagan [carry out] the commitments he made during the campaign."[9]

Committee leaders of the president's party usually have a similar orientation. Representative Daniel Rostenkowski, chair of the House Ways and Means Committee, told President Clinton, "You send the proposals, and I'll be the quarterback." Senator Daniel Patrick Moynihan, the chair of the Senate Finance Committee, declared, "The most important thing for me coming to the job . . . is that I want to get the president's agenda through."[10]

However, party floor leaders are not always dependable supporters, and they certainly are not simply extensions of the White House. House Majority Leader Richard Gephardt and House Majority Whip David Bonior broke with President Clinton over several important trade bills and led the opposition to them. There is little the White House can do in such a situation. Presidents do not lobby for candidates for congressional party leadership positions, and they virtually always remain neutral during the selection process. They have no desire to alienate important members of Congress whose support they will need.

Similarly, committee chairpersons and ranking minority members are usually determined by seniority. Furthermore, the chairpersons always come from the majority party in the chamber, which often is not that of the president. For all practical purposes, the president plays no role at all in determining the holders of these important positions. Moreover, the norm of supporting a president of one's party is weaker for committee leaders than for floor leaders.

Presidents and their staff typically work closely with their party's legislative leaders, meeting regularly for breakfast when Congress is in session. (Sometimes these meetings include the leaders of the opposition party as well.) These gatherings provide opportunities for an exchange of views and for the president to keep communication channels open and maintain morale. The significance of these efforts has varied, however. On one extreme, Nixon's meetings were often pro forma, serving more as a symbolic ritual than a mechanism for leadership. On the other, Johnson used them as strategy sessions to integrate congressional leaders into the White House legislative liaison operation.

Equally as important as the congressional party leaders' relations with the president are their relations with their party colleagues in Congress. Major changes have occurred over the past few decades that have weakened the ability of party leaders to produce votes for the president. According to Gerald Ford:

> Today a President really does not have the kind of clout with the Congress that he had 30 years ago, even in matters that affect national security. There is not

the kind of teamwork that existed in the '50s, even if the President and a majority of the Congress belong to the same party. The main reason for this change is the erosion of the leadership in the Congress. Party leaders have lost the power to tell their troops that something is really significant and to get them to respond accordingly. The days of Sam Rayburn, Lyndon Johnson, and Everett Dirksen are gone. That has adversely affected the Congress's ability to do things even in very difficult circumstances involving the national interest.[11]

With both houses of Congress under the control of the Democrats for forty-two years preceding 1995 (with the exception of the Senate in 1981 through 1986), power became widely dispersed. Seniority was no longer an automatic path to committee or subcommittee chairs, and chairpersons had to be more responsive to the desires of committee members. There were also more subcommittees and more subcommittee chairpersons, and the subcommittees had a more important role in handling legislation. Members of both parties had larger personal, committee, and subcommittee staffs at their disposal, as well as new service adjuncts such as the Congressional Budget Office. The new freedom and additional resources, combined with more opportunities to amend legislation, made it easier for members of Congress to challenge the White House and the congressional leadership and to provide alternatives to the president's policies.

The president's program also became subject to more crosscutting demands within Congress as a result of split and joint committee referrals for some legislation. This further complicated the task of influencing members of Congress, because it is difficult to lobby several committees at once with the limited resources available to the president. Similarly, more than a quarter of the members of Congress sit on committees that raise, budget, or appropriate funds. Thus, it is not surprising that presidents have had trouble getting their budgets passed.

Yet other reforms have increased the leaders' burden. The increased number of roll-call votes and, thus, the increased visibility of representatives' voting behavior, generated more pressure on House members to abandon party loyalty, which made it more difficult for the president to gain passage of legislation. Reforms that opened committee and subcommittee hearings to the public had the same effect. There has also been a heavy turnover in the congressional personnel in recent years, and new members have brought with them new approaches to legislating. They are less likely to adopt the norms of apprenticeship and specialization than were their predecessors in their first terms. Instead, they have eagerly taken an active role in all legislation. They place a heavy emphasis on individualism, and usually much less on party regularity.

Thus, congressional party leaders now had more decision makers to influence. They could no longer rely on dealing with the congressional aristocracy and expect the rest of the members to follow. According to one Johnson assistant:

> In 1965, there were maybe ten or twelve people who you needed to corral in the House and Senate. Without those people, you were in for a tough time. Now, I'd put that figure upwards of one hundred. Believe it, there are so many people who have a shot at derailing a bill that the President has to double his effort for even routine decisions.[12]

Things seemed to change in 1995, however. With the Republican takeover of the House, Speaker Newt Gingrich quickly centralized power in the hands of the party leadership. He made committee chairs less powerful by limiting their terms to six years and placed them on notice that to maintain their positions they had to support the party program. He ignored seniority in several instances and named his allies as chairs, and he played the predominant role in selecting members to the committees. In addition, to write major legislation, he frequently displaced committees with ad hoc task forces of his choosing, he eliminated proxy voting, which had given committee chairs the power to cast the votes for absent members, and he reduced committee staffs. Gingrich reduced the power of subcommittees by reestablishing the power of committee chairs—who were now responsive to him—over them.

Of course, none of this helped Democrat Bill Clinton pass his program. It only made opposition to him more effective as Republicans dominated the agenda-setting process in Congress, and the president suffered the lowest level of success in winning votes in Congress in modern history. By 1997, however, the Speaker's power within his own party was fraying. He even had to put down a Republican revolt. It remains to be seen whether any Speaker can maintain a centralization of power and be able to use it on behalf of a president's program.

Although the party leadership, at least in theory, possesses sanctions that it can exercise to enforce party discipline (including exercising discretion on committee assignments, patronage, campaign funds, trips abroad, and aid with members' pet bills), in reality, this discretion exists primarily on paper. Most rewards are considered a matter of right, and it is the leadership's job to see that they are distributed equitably. Party leaders usually do not dare to withhold benefits because they fear being overturned by the rank and file. (Senate Majority Leader Robert Dole sometimes termed his position that of "majority pleader".) Threats of sanctions in such a situation are unconvincing and thus rarely occur. Even Newt Gingrich has been constrained. When he removed a recalcitrant member from a committee, many Republicans rebelled and the Speaker had to compensate the member with a prestigious committee assignment. In addition, few representatives were impressed when Gingrich refused to campaign for those who had failed to provide him reliable support.

Obstacles to Party Unity   The primary obstacle to party cohesion in support of the president is lack of a consensus among members of the president's party on policies, especially if the president happens to be a Democrat. This diversity of views often reflects the diversity of constituencies represented by party members. The frequent defection from support of Democratic presidents by the conservative southern Democrats, or "boll weevils," is one of the most prominent features of American politics. Republican presidents often lack stable coalitions as well. Ronald Reagan received nearly unanimous support from his party on his 1981 proposals to reduce taxes and expenditures, but the next year, when he proposed legislation to increase taxes, to restrict abortions and forced busing for integration, and to allow school prayer, things were different. Republicans were in the forefront of the opposition to these policies.

Although in recent years the parties in Congress have become more homogeneous (as conservative constituencies increasingly elect Republicans, especially in the House),[13] there is still a substantial range of opinion within each party. When constituency opinion and the president's proposals conflict, members of Congress are more likely to vote with their constituencies, to whom they must return for reelection. For example, Bill Clinton has found it very difficult to obtain party support for policies designed to encourage international trade because of the opposition of blue-collar interests, the traditional base of the Democratic party.

A shift in the status of party members may present another obstacle to party unity. Just as regaining power may encourage party unity, having to share it may strain intraparty relations. When a party that has had a majority in Congress regains the White House, the committee and floor leaders of that party will typically become less influential because they will be expected to take their lead on major issues from the president. This may cause tensions within the party and make party discipline more difficult.

Yet other obstacles may confront a president trying to mobilize his party in Congress. If the president's party has just regained the presidency but remains a minority in Congress, its members need to adjust from their past stance as the opposition minority to one of a "governing" minority. This is not always easily done, however, as Richard Nixon found when he sought Republican votes for budget deficits.

Further difficulties may stem from the fact that the winning presidential candidate may not be the natural leader of the party. Indeed, as in the case of Jimmy Carter and, to a lesser extent, Bill Clinton, some presidents campaign against the party establishment and are not identified with the Democratic party program as it exists at the time. Naturally, when a new president arrives in Washington under these conditions, intraparty harmony is not likely to materialize overnight and appeals for party loyalty may fall on less than receptive ears.

Midterm Election Campaigning   Members of Congress who are of the president's party are more likely to support the president than are members of the opposition party, and presidents do their best to exploit this potential of partisan support. Nevertheless, such actions are inevitably at the margins of coalition building because they take place within the confines of the partisan balance of the Congress. To fully exploit the benefits of party leadership, presidents need as many of their fellow partisans in Congress as possible. Once members of Congress have been elected, however, they rarely change their party affiliation, and the few instances when they have changed have not resulted from presidential persuasion. (Indeed, under Democrat Bill Clinton, five members of the House and two in the Senate switched from Democrat to Republican.) Thus, if presidents are to alter the party composition of Congress, they must help to elect additional members of their party. One way to try to accomplish this goal is to campaign for candidates in midterm congressional elections.

There are a number of limitations to such a strategy, however. Sometimes presidents are so unpopular that the candidates of their party do not want their support. For example, President Johnson adopted a low profile during the 1966 campaign because of his lack of public support (below 50 percent in the Gallup Poll). Similarly, in 1974, before he resigned, President Nixon wanted invitations to campaign for Republicans to prove that he was not political poison, but he received few offers as the Watergate crisis reached a head. Some candidates asked Ronald Reagan to stay away because of the recession in 1982, with which many voters identified him, and in 1994, opposition to Bill Clinton was a primary cause of the Democrats' loss of both houses of Congress.

Nevertheless, modern presidents have often taken an active role in midterm congressional elections. Typically, however, they are disappointed in the results of their efforts.[14] As Table 10–3 shows, a recurring feature of American politics is the decrease in representation of the president's party in Congress in midterm congressional elections. We can trace this phenomena back further in U.S. history, as in Woodrow Wilson's midterm campaigning in 1918, which was rewarded by the loss of both houses of Congress. (Even George Washington's Federalists lost seats in the House in the first midterm election, in 1790.)

Presidential Coattails   Another potential way in which presidents may influence the partisan composition of Congress is through their coattails. Presidential coattails are part of the lore of American politics. Politicians

TABLE 10–3. **Changes in Congressional Representation of the President's Party in Midterm Elections**

Year	President	House	Senate
1954	Eisenhower	−18	−1
1958	Eisenhower	−47	−3
1962	Kennedy	−4	+3
1966	Johnson	−47	−4
1970	Nixon	−12	+2
1974	Ford	−47	−5
1978	Carter	−15	−3
1982	Reagan	−26	0
1986	Reagan	−5	−8
1990	Bush	−9	−1
1994	Clinton	−52	−8
1998	Clinton	+5	0

project them in their calculations, journalists attribute them in their reporting, historians recount them, and political scientists analyze them. However, we have limited understanding of how they affect the outcomes in congressional elections. (A coattail victory is a victory for a representative of the president's party in which presidential coattail votes provide the increment of the vote necessary to win the seat.)

Coattail victories, whether they bring in new members or preserve the seats of incumbents, can have significant payoffs for the president in terms of support for the administration's programs. Those members of the president's party who won close elections may provide an extra increment of support out of a sense of gratitude for the votes they perceive were received due to presidential coattails or out of a sense of responsiveness to their constituents' support for the president.

However, research has found that the outcomes of very few congressional races are determined by presidential coattails.[15] For example, in 1988 George Bush won election while his party actually lost seats in both houses of Congress. Similarly, the Democrats lost ten seats in the House and gained none in the Senate when Bill Clinton won election in 1992, and they lost two seats in the Senate when he won reelection in 1996. (Clinton ran behind all but a handful of members of Congress in their states or districts in both elections.) This is nothing new: In 1792, George Washington easily won reelection, but the opposition Democrat-Republicans captured the House of Representatives. The results of elections over the past forty years are shown in Table 10–4. Most House seats are too safe for a party, and especially for an incumbent, to have the election outcome affected by the presidential election. Senate elections are more affected by the president's

TABLE 10–4. Changes in Congressional Representation of the President's Party in Presidential Election Years

Year	President	House	Senate
1952	Eisenhower	+22	+1
1956	Eisenhower	−2	−1
1960	Kennedy	−22	−2
1964	Johnson	+37	+1
1968	Nixon	+5	+6
1972	Nixon	+12	−2
1976	Carter	+1	0
1980	Reagan	+34	+12
1984	Reagan	+14	−2
1988	Bush	−3	−1
1992	Clinton	−10	0
1996	Clinton	+9	−2

standing with the public, but the president's party typically gains no seats at all in a presidential election year.[16]

Thus, presidents cannot expect personally to carry like-minded running mates into office to provide additional support for their programs. On the contrary, rather than being amenable to voting for the president's policies due to shared convictions, representatives are free to focus on parochial matters and respond to narrow constituency interests. Similarly, although we cannot know the extent to which representatives have felt gratitude to presidents for their coattails, and thus have given them additional legislative support in the past, we do know that any such gratitude is rarely warranted. The more representatives are aware of the independence of their elections from that of the president, the less likely they are to feel that they must "thank" the president with an additional increment of support.

Bipartisanship   On July 27, 1981, President Reagan delivered an exceptionally important and effective televised address to the nation seeking the public's support for his tax-cut bill and going to great lengths to present his plan as "bipartisan." It was crucial that he convince the public that this controversial legislation was supported by members of both parties and was therefore, by implication, fair. Thus he described it as "bipartisan" a full eleven times in the span of a few minutes. No one was to miss the point. The president required the votes of Democrats in the House to pass his bill, and he wanted their constituents to apply pressure to them to support it.

Despite the advantage that presidents have in dealing with members of their party in Congress, they are often forced to solicit bipartisan support. There are several reasons for this. First, the opposition party may control one or both houses of Congress. Thus, even if all members of the president's party supported the administration on its key initiatives, that would not be sufficient. Between 1953 and 1992, Republican presidents faced a Democratic House of Representatives for twenty-six years and a Democratic Senate for twenty years. President Clinton has faced a Republican House and Senate since 1995. Without Republican support, he would not have obtained passage of the NAFTA and GATT trade agreements or the line-item veto.

A second reason for bipartisanship is that presidents cannot depend on all the members of their party to support them on all issues. Tables 10–1 and 10–2 showed clearly that members of the president's own party frequently oppose the president. As Jimmy Carter wrote, "I learned the hard way that there was no party loyalty or discipline when a complicated or controversial issue was at stake—none."[17] Southern Democrats support Democratic presidents less consistently than do Northern Democrats.

Not only do partisan strategies often fail, but they also may provoke the other party into a more unified posture of opposition. Where there is confrontation there can be no consensus, and consensus is often required to legislate changes on important issues. Presidents are also inhibited in their partisanship by pressures to be "president of all the people" rather than a highly partisan figure. This role expectation of being somewhat above the political fray undoubtedly constrains presidents in their role as party leader.

Despite the frequent necessity of a bipartisan strategy, it is not without costs. Bipartisanship often creates a strain with the extremes within the president's party as a Republican president tries to appeal to the left for Democratic votes and a Democratic president to the right for Republican votes. Although it is true that the Republican right wing and Democratic left wing may find it difficult to forge a coalition in favor of alternatives to their own president's policies, it is not true that they must therefore support their president. Instead, they may complicate a president's strategy by joining those who oppose administration policies.

The ultimate limitation on a bipartisan strategy is that, as Tables 10–1 and 10–2 demonstrate, the opposition party is generally not a fertile ground for obtaining policy support. Democratic presidents have often been frustrated in their efforts to deal with Republicans. President Clinton has faced virtually unanimous Republican opposition to his economic, budget, and health care proposals. Republican presidents also face obstacles to obtaining bipartisan support. Only twenty-three House Democrats supported Ronald Reagan on both the important budget and tax votes in 1981, despite the president's persuasive efforts, the perception that the president had a mandate, and the pull of ideology. Nevertheless, presidents cannot ignore the opposition party and even a few votes may be enough to bring them a majority.

PUBLIC SUPPORT

Although congressional seats held by members of the president's party may be a necessary condition for presidential success in Congress, they are not a sufficient one: The president needs public support as well. In the words of Eisenhower aide and presidential authority Emmet John Hughes, "Beyond all tricks of history and all quirks of Presidents, there would appear to be one unchallengeable truth: the dependence of Presidential authority on popular support."[18]

Public Approval

In his memoirs, President Johnson wrote, "Presidential popularity is a major source of strength in gaining cooperation from Congress."[19] Thus, following his landslide electoral victory, he assembled the congressional liaison officials from the various departments and told them that his victory at the polls "might be more of a loophole than a mandate," and, moreover, that since his popularity could decrease rapidly, they would have to use it to their advantage while it lasted.[20]

President Carter's aides were quite explicit about the importance of public approval in their efforts to influence Congress. One stated that the "only way to keep those guys [Congress] honest is to keep our popularity high."[21] The president's legislative liaison officials generally agreed that their effectiveness with Congress ultimately depended on the president's ability to influence public opinion. As one of them said, "When you go up to the Hill and the latest polls show Carter isn't doing well, there isn't much reason for a member to go along with him. There's little we can do if the member isn't persuaded on the issue."[22] The Reagan administration was especially sensitive to the president's public approval levels. According to one top aide, "Everything here is built on the idea that the president's success depends on grassroots support."[23]

Why is presidential approval or popularity such an important source of influence in Congress? According to a senior aide to President Carter:

> When the President is low in public opinion polls, the Members of Congress see little hazard in bucking him. . . . After all, very few Congressmen examine an issue solely on its merits; they are politicians and they think politically. I'm not saying they make only politically expedient choices. But they read the polls and from that they feel secure in turning their backs on the President with political impunity. Unquestionably, the success of the President's policies bears a tremendous relationship to his popularity in the polls.[24]

The public's evaluations of the president may be taken as indicators of broader opinions on politics and policy. Moreover, members of Congress must anticipate the public's reactions to their support for, or opposition to, the president and his policies. They may choose to be either close to or independent from the president, depending on his public standing, in order to increase their chances of reelection. Presidential approval often has a strong impact on voting for members of Congress.[25] For example, people who support President Clinton also voted for his party's candidates for the House and Senate, and vice versa. In the 1994 elections, the votes of about 83 percent of voters for members of the House were consistent with voters' approval or disapproval of President Clinton's performance in office.[26]

Members of Congress may also use the president's standing in the polls as an indicator of his ability to mobilize public opinion against his opponents. As Richard Nixon put it, "An even greater incentive for members [of Congress to support the president] is the fear that a popular president may oppose them in the next election."[27]

Public approval operates mostly in the background and sets the limits of what Congress will do for, or to, the president. Widespread support gives a president leeway and weakens resistance to the administration's policies. Moreover, it provides a cover for members of Congress to cast votes to which their constituents might otherwise object, as they can defend their votes as support for the president rather than on substantive policy grounds alone.

Lack of public support strengthens the resolve of those who are inclined to oppose the president and narrows the range in which he receives the benefit of the doubt, as Bill Clinton discovered when his approval ratings dipped into the 35 percent range in mid-1993. In addition, low ratings in the polls may create incentives to attack the president, further eroding an already weakened position. For example, after the arms sales to Iran and the diversion of funds to the contras became a cause célèbre in late 1986, it became more acceptable in Congress and in the press to raise questions about Ronald Reagan's capacities as president. Disillusionment is a dangerous phenomenon for the White House. As a chief of the White House congressional relations office put it, "When the president's approval is low, it's advantageous and even fun to kick him around."[28]

The impact of presidential approval on presidential support occurs at the margins of coalition building, within the confines of other influences. No matter how low a president's standing in public polls or how close it is to the next election, he or she will still receive support from a substantial number of senators and representatives. Similarly, no matter how high approval levels climb or how large a president's winning percentage of the vote, a significant portion of the Congress may still oppose his or her policies. Members of Congress are unlikely to vote against the clear interests of their constituents or the firm tenets of their ideology, even out of deference to a widely supported chief executive. Thus, widespread support should give presidents leeway and weaken resistance to their policies, giving them, at best, leverage but not control. On the other hand, when presidents lack popular support, their options are reduced, their opportunities are diminished, and their room for maneuver is checked.

As the most volatile leadership resource, public approval is the factor most likely to determine whether an opportunity for policy change exists. Public approval makes other resources more efficacious. If the chief executive is high in public esteem, the president's party is more likely to be responsive, the public is more easily moved, and legislative skills become more effective. Thus, public approval is the resource that has the most potential to turn a typical situation into one favorable for change, which provides a strong incentive for the president to try to gain popular support. However, presidential approval cannot be easily manipulated.

Thus, public approval is a necessary, but not a sufficient, source of influence in Congress. It is most useful in combination with party supporters in each house. If either approval or seats are lacking, the president's legislative program will be in for rough going.[29]

Mandates

Another indicator of the public's opinion of the president is seen in the results of the presidential election. Electoral mandates can be powerful symbols in American politics, as they accord added legitimacy and credibility to the newly elected president's proposals. Moreover, concerns for both representation and political survival will encourage members of Congress to support the president if they feel the people have spoken.

More important, mandates change the premises of decisions. Following the 1932 election, the essential question became *how* government should act to fight the Depression rather than *whether* it should act. Similarly, following the 1964 election, the dominant question in Congress was not whether to pass new social programs but, rather, how many to pass and how much to increase spending. In 1981, however, the tables were turned. Ronald Reagan's victory placed a stigma on big government and exalted the unregulated marketplace and large defense efforts. Reagan had won a major victory even before the first congressional vote.

Although presidential elections can structure choices for Congress, merely winning an election does not give a president a mandate. Every election produces a winner, but mandates are much less common. Even large electoral victories such as Richard Nixon's in 1972 and Ronald Reagan's in 1984 carry no guarantee that Congress will interpret the results as mandates from the people to support the president's programs, especially if the voters also elect majorities in Congress from the other party.

The winners in presidential elections usually claim to have been accorded a mandate, of course, but in the absence of certain conditions, few observers accept these assertions at face value. Conditions that promote the perception of a mandate include a large margin of victory, the impression of long coattails, hyperbole in the press analyses of the election results that exaggerates the one-sidedness of the victory, a surprisingly large victory accompanying a change in parties in the White House, a campaign oriented around a major change in public policy, or consistency of the new president's program with the prevailing tides of opinion in both the country and his party.

Since it is unusual for these conditions to be met, perceptions of mandates are rarely strong. Presidents can do little about these perceptions. Some are simply elected under more favorable conditions for legislative leadership than are others. When mandates do occur or are effectively claimed, the issue becomes one of exploiting the special opportunities they provide.

PRESIDENTIAL LEGISLATIVE SKILLS

In this section of our discussion of presidential influence in Congress, we examine other White House efforts to persuade members of Congress to support the president's legislative proposals. Some of these activities are aimed at building goodwill in the long run, and others at obtaining votes from individual members of Congress on specific issues. Whatever the immediate goal, the nature of the legislative process in America demands that presidents apply their legislative skills in a wide range of situations. In the words of one presidential aide:

> Senator A might come with us if Senator B, an admired friend, could be persuaded to talk to him. Senator C wanted a major project out of Chairman D's committee; maybe D, a supporter of our bill, would release it in exchange for C's commitment. Senator E might be reached through people in his home state. If Senator F could not vote with us on final passage, could he vote with us on key amendments? Could G take a trip? Would the President call Senator H?[30]

Congressional Liaison

Although the Constitution establishes separate institutions, the operation of the government requires those institutions to work together. Presidents are expected to propose legislation and to get it enacted into law. Clearly, they need all the help they can get. To assist them in these efforts as well as with their other ongoing legislative responsibilities, a congressional liaison staff, based in the White House, has operated since 1953. The size of this staff and the duties it performs have expanded significantly in recent years.

The growth of the president's liaison mechanism has occurred in three stages. In its initial phase, during the Eisenhower administration, the congressional relations office was small in size, adopted a low profile, and utilized a bipartisan approach in dealing with Congress. Wary of infringing on the legislature's prerogatives or of operating on its turf, the president's agents worked by telephone from the White House rather than in the halls of Congress; communicated mainly with, and through, the legislative leadership; and used gentle persuasion rather than arm-twisting to achieve their goals. Eisenhower himself was not heavily involved in the details of legislation, although he did have contact with members of Congress, especially with the Republican leaders.

The congressional relations office assumed a more aggressive posture in its second phase, which occurred during the Kennedy-Johnson years. With a larger and more comprehensive legislative agenda to advocate, the staff expanded its size and functions. In addition to pushing for major White House policy initiatives, the president's liaison team began funneling legislative views into the executive decision-making process. From a congressional perspective, the increasing development of policy by the White House made this input desirable.

Presidential assistants involved in legislation became more numerous, visible, and partisan. Attempts were made to organize executive department and agency liaison staffs more effectively behind the president's major priorities. Pressures were exerted on committee chairs, informal legislative groups, and, in general, on more members concerning more issues, and rewards were also more generously bestowed. "The White House certainly remembers who its friends are," Lawrence F. O'Brien, head of the office, both warned and promised legislators early in the Kennedy administration.[31]

In an effort to improve the atmosphere for the administration on Capitol Hill and to meet an increasing need of Congress, the White House began providing casework services for members and their staffs. This "care and feeding" operation soon became a congressional expectation that subsequent White Houses could not shirk. Social lobbying, such as inviting members of Congress to accompany the president on *Air Force One* or attend a state dinner at the White House, increased as well.

By the end of the 1960s, certain functions had come to be regarded as traditional liaison activities. In addition to catering to the constituency needs of members of Congress, these included gathering intelligence, tracking legislation, coordinating department and agency efforts, and working with the leadership on priority programs. These functions continue to be performed today, but the level of White House involvement and the scope of its activities have expanded even further. The principal reason for that expansion is the difficulty contemporary presidents have had in mobilizing majority coalitions in support of their policy proposals.

Phase three in the evolution of the presidency's liaison mechanism began in the Carter administration. Frustrated by its inability to get Congress to enact its policy recommendations in the first year and a half of the administration, the Carter White House began to broaden its interaction with Congress and utilize outside forces to help build legislative support. The president increased the size of his congressional relations office despite his highly publicized claim of reducing White House personnel in the aftermath of the Watergate scandal. Internal task forces on key initiatives were formed to coordinate the administration's congressional activities, and a mechanism for setting priorities for highly visible issues was established. In addition, more sophisticated information retrieval systems and computerized mail logs were developed to process congressional mail and assess voting patterns, and even President Carter, who was a private person by nature, began to interact more regularly with members of Congress, particularly the leadership.

In conjunction with these changes, other presidential offices became more involved with Congress and the legislative process. Although it did not solicit congressional views, the president's domestic policy staff became more receptive to them. Members of Congress and their staffs were given opportunities to affect the development of proposed legislation *before* it was sent to Congress. Moreover, a public liaison office was established to organize outside groups and community leaders into coalitions behind the administration's proposals.[32] Once established, these coalitions, which were orchestrated by the White House, mounted grassroots efforts, which they directed toward Congress. They identified the positions of members on key issues, targeted those who were wavering, and had them contacted by group representatives from their own constituencies, and supplemented these activities by organizing mass letter-writing and telephoning campaigns. These constituency-based pressures were designed to make it easier for members of Congress to vote with the president, regardless of their party affiliation, by providing them political cover.

During the Reagan presidency (especially the first term), a legislative strategy group consisting of senior presidential aides operated out of the chief of staff's office to coordinate these outreach efforts and tie them to administrative lobbying on Capitol Hill. Other White House offices, in addition to congressional relations and public liaison, also became involved in congressional affairs. A newly constituted political office handled patronage and other party-related matters, while an intergovernmental affairs office orchestrated state and local officials behind other administration initiatives.

The Bush and Clinton administrations did not orchestrate their congressional liaison operations as precisely or effectively as did the Reagan administration. There was no legislative strategy group, and instead, key White House staff were given responsibility for negotiating and lobbying major legislative initiatives. Both legislative operations ran into trouble, especially with members of the opposition party. Clinton in particular failed to deal effectively with the Republicans in his first term. Turnover in the office and the appointment of other senior administrative staffers to handle key issues such as health care, international trade, the budget, the debt ceiling, welfare reform, fast-track authority, and Medicare and Medicaid complicated the president's task. Clinton's legislative relations improved marginally in his second term, but after allegations of sexual improprieties, the president's focus turned elsewhere.

In summary, congressional liaison has developed and expanded because it serves the needs of both the executive and legislative branches. For Congress, it helps integrate legislative views into executive policy making, services constituency needs, forces presidents to indicate their legislative priorities, provides channels for reaching compromises, and helps the leadership to form majority coalitions. For presidents, it enables them to gain a congressional perspective, communicate their views to Congress, mobilize support for their programs, and reach accommodations with the legislature. Such efforts to bridge the constitutional separation have helped to overcome some of the hurdles in the formulation of public policy.

We now turn from institutionalized efforts to deal with Congress to the particular legislative techniques that presidents and their liaison aides must utilize in their efforts to win support for the administration's proposals on Capitol Hill.

Personal Appeals

A special aspect of presidential involvement in the legislative process is the personal appeal for votes. According to presidential scholar Richard Neustadt, "When the chips are down, there is no substitute for the President's own footwork, his personal negotiation, his direct appeal, his voice and no other's on the telephone."[33] Members of Congress are as subject to flattery as other people, and they are equally impressed when the president calls.

Calls from the president must be relatively rare to maintain their usefulness, and will have less impact if they are made too often. Moreover, members might begin to expect calls, for which the president has limited time, or they might resent too much high-level pressure being applied to them. On the other hand, they might exploit a call by saying they are uncertain about an issue in order to extract a favor from the president.

Presidents become intensely involved only after the long process of lining up votes is almost done and their calls are needed to win on an important issue (a situation that arises only a few times a year). A good example occurred on the House vote on the budget reconciliation bill in 1993. President Clinton focused on key members of Congress, whose votes served as cues for other members, and on members who were uncommitted or weakly committed in either direction. These members were identified by studying the head counts prepared by the White House congressional liaison office and the congressional party whips. The president was able to garner a few votes and thus eked out a narrow victory.

Despite the prestige of their office, their invocations of national interest, and their persuasiveness, presidents often fail in their personal appeals. For example, President Eisenhower liked to depend heavily on charm and reason. In 1953 he tried to persuade Republican chairman Daniel Reed of the House Ways and Means Committee to support the continuance of the excess profits tax and to oppose a tax cut. "I used every possible reason, argument, and device, and every kind of personal and indirect contact," he wrote, "to bring Chairman Reed to my way of thinking." Nonetheless, he failed.[34] Similarly, Lyndon Johnson was renowned for his persuasiveness but nevertheless failed on many issues, ranging from civil rights and education to Medicare and the Panama uprising. "No matter how many times I told Congress to do something," he wrote, "I could never force it to act."[35] If Eisenhower and Johnson often failed in their efforts at persuasion, we should not be surprised that other presidents have failed as well.

Bargaining

It is part of the conventional wisdom that the White House regularly "buys" votes through bargains struck with members of Congress. There can be no question that many bargains occur and that they take a variety of forms. Reagan's budget director, David Stockman, recalled that "the last 10 or 20 percent of the votes needed for a majority of both houses [on the 1981 tax cut] had to be bought, period." The concessions for members of Congress included special breaks for oil-lease holders, real estate tax shelters, and generous tax loopholes for corporations. "The hogs were really feeding," he declared. "The greed level, the level of opportunism, just got out of control."[36] Nevertheless, bargaining, in the form of trading support on two or more policies or providing specific benefits for representatives and senators, occurs less often and plays a less critical role in the creation of presidential coalitions in Congress than one might think. For obvious reasons, the White House does not want to encourage the type of bargaining Stockman described.

The president cannot bargain with Congress as a whole because it is too large and decentralized for one bargain to satisfy everyone. In addition, the president's time is limited, as are the administration's resources—only a certain number of appointive jobs is available, and the federal budget is limited. Moreover, funding for public works projects is in the hands of Congress. Thus, most of the bargains that are reached are implicit. The lack of respectability surrounding bargaining also encourages implicitness.

In addition, if many direct bargains are struck, word will rapidly spread, everyone will want to trade, and persuasive efforts will fail. A good example occurred in 1993 when President Clinton proposed to increase user fees for grazing and mineral rights on federal land. Following protests from Western senators, whose votes he needed for his budget, the president told them he would remove the fees from his budget and deal with them separately in a bill later in the session. His decision opened a Pandora's box because it signaled to every interest group in Washington that he would cave in to pressure. He was quickly inundated with requests to change his budget in other ways. The word was out that the president could be "rolled."

Fortunately for the president, bargaining with everyone in Congress is not necessary. Except on vetoes and treaties, only a simple majority of those voting is needed, and thus a large part of Congress can be "written off" on any given vote. Moreover, presidents generally start with a substantial core of party supporters and then add to this number those of the other party who agree with their views on ideological or policy grounds. Others may provide support on the basis of goodwill that a president has generated through White House services, constituency interest, or high levels of public support. Thus, the president needs to bargain only if all these groups fail to provide a majority for crucial votes, and bargaining is needed only with enough people to provide that majority.

Since resources are scarce, presidents will usually try to use them for bargaining with powerful members of Congress, such as committee chairs or those whose votes are most important. There is no guarantee that a tendered bargain will be accepted, however. The members may not desire what the president offers, or they may be able to obtain what they want on their own. This is, of course, particularly true of the most powerful members, whose support the president needs most. Sometimes, members of Congress do not want to trade at all because of constituency opinion or personal views. At other times, the president may be unwilling to bargain.

Most of the pressure for bargaining actually comes from Capitol Hill. When the White House calls and asks for support, representatives and senators frequently raise a question regarding some request that they have made. In the words of a presidential aide, "Every time we make a special appeal to a Congressman to change his position, he eventually comes back with a request for a favor ranging in importance from one of the President's packages of matches to a judgeship or cabinet appointment for a 'worthy constituent.'"[37]

More general bargains also take place. In the words of Nixon's chief congressional aide, William Timmons: "I think they [members of Congress] knew that we would try our best to help them on all kinds of requests if they supported the President, and we did. It kind of goes without saying." His successor in the Ford administration, Max Friedersdorf, added his assurance that people who want things want to be in the position of supporting the president. This implicit trading on "accounts" is more common than explicit bargaining.[38]

For the White House, a member of Congress indebted to the president is easier to approach and ask for a vote. For the member, previous support increases the chances of a request being honored. Thus, officeholders at both ends of Pennsylvania Avenue want to be in each other's favor. The degree of debt determines the strategy used in presidential requests for support. Although services and favors increase the president's chances of obtaining support, they are not usually exchanged for votes directly. They are strategic, not tactical, weapons.

Services and Amenities

Since a member of Congress who is indebted to the president is easier to approach to ask for a vote, the White House provides many services and amenities for representatives and senators. Although these favors may be bestowed on any member of Congress, they actually go disproportionately to members of the president's party. Personal amenities used to create goodwill include social contact with the president, flattery, rides on *Air Force One*, visits to Camp David, birthday greetings, theater tickets for the presidential box at the Kennedy Center, invitations to bill-signing ceremonies, pictures with the president, briefings, and a plethora of others, the number and variety of which are limited only by the imagination of the president and his staff.

In addition, the White House often helps members of Congress with their constituents. A wide range of services is offered, including greetings to elderly and other "worthy" constituents, signed presidential photographs, presidential tie clasps and other White House memorabilia, reprints of speeches, information about government programs, White House pressure on agencies in favor of constituents, passing the nominations of constituents on to agencies, influence on local editorial writers, ceremonial appointments to commissions, meetings with the president, and arguments to be used to explain votes to constituents. The president may also help members of Congress please constituents through patronage, pork-barrel projects and government contracts, and aid with legislation that is of special interest to particular constituencies.

Campaign aid is yet another service that the White House can provide to party members, and the president may dangle it before them to entice support. This aid may come in various forms, including campaign speeches by the president and executive officials for congressional candidates, funds and advice from the party national committees, presidential endorsements, pictures with the president, and letters of appreciation from the president. Bill Clinton has been especially active in directly raising funds for Democratic candidates.

All administrations are not equally active in providing services and amenities for members of Congress. The Johnson and Reagan White Houses fall at the "active" end of this spectrum, while the Nixon and Carter presidencies fall at the other end. However, any such differences are relatively small in comparison with the efforts made by every recent administration to develop goodwill among its party members in Congress. Although this activity is to the advantage of all presidents and may earn them a fair hearing and the benefit of the doubt in some instances, party members consider it their right to receive benefits from the White House and are unlikely to be especially responsive to the president as a result.

Pressure

Just as presidents can offer the carrot, they can also wield the stick. Moreover, the increased resources available to the White House in recent years provide increased opportunities to levy sanctions in the form of the withholding of favors. As the deputy chairman of the Republican National Committee said, there is more money than ever "to play hardball with. We're loaded for bear."[39] The threats of such actions are effective primarily with members of the president's party, of course, because members of the opposition party do not expect to receive many favors from the president.

Although sanctions or threats of sanctions are far from an everyday occurrence, they do happen. These may take the form of excluding a member from White House social events, denying routine requests for White House tour tickets, or shutting off access to the president. Each of these personal slights sends a signal of presidential displeasure. More dramatically, after Senator Richard Shelby complained about President Clinton's budget package, the White House announced that it was moving the management team for a space shuttle contract from Alabama to Texas, which constituted a loss of jobs for the senator's state. To add insult to injury, Senator Shelby was given only one ticket to the White House ceremony honoring the University of Alabama football team; Senator Howell Heflin, Alabama's other senator, was given eleven.

Heavy-handed arm-twisting is unusual, however (the White House backtracked on moving the National Aeronautics and Space Administration [NASA] team from Alabama, and Senator Shelby later switched parties and became a Republican). More typical is the orchestration of pressure by others. The Reagan White House was especially effective in this regard. By operating through party channels, its Political Affairs Office, and its Office of Public Liaison, the administration was able to generate pressure from party members' constituents, campaign contributors, political activists, business leaders, state officials, interest groups, party officials, and, of course, cabinet members. (The Clinton administration has tried the same strategy but with much less success.)

Despite the resources available to presidents, if members of Congress wish to oppose them, there is little the White House can do to stop them. This is true for those in the president's party as well as those in the opposition. The primary reason is that the parties are highly decentralized, and thus national party leaders do not control those aspects of politics that are of vital concern to members of Congress: nominations and elections. Members of Congress are largely self-recruited, gain their party's nominations by their own efforts and not those of the party, and provide most of the money and organizational support needed for their elections. Presidents can do little to influence the results of these activities; usually, they do not even try. As President Kennedy said in 1962: "Party loyalty or responsibility means damn little. They've got to take care of themselves first. They [House members] all have to run this year—I don't and I couldn't hurt most of them if I wanted to."[40]

Consultation

Consulting with members of Congress on legislation can be advantageous for the White House. Members of Congress appreciate advance warning of presidential proposals, especially those that affect their constituencies directly. No official, especially an elected one, wants to be blindsided. Politicians quite naturally want to be prepared to take credit or avoid blame. Moreover, when a policy fails, members of Congress are unlikely to support the president in the perilous landing of the policy if they are not involved in the take-off.

Consultation before announcing a bill may also be useful in anticipating congressional objections. It may, in fact, be possible to preempt some of the opposition with strategic compromises and to garner some advance commitments. At the very least, members of Congress will feel they have had an opportunity to be heard. They take pride in their work and may be offended if they feel the White House has not taken them seriously.

Despite these advantages, presidential consultation with Congress has often played a modest role in presidential-congressional relations.[41] Consultation is not easy to accomplish. Arriving at a common position within the executive branch may tax the resources and patience of the White House, particularly at a time when other exigencies press on the president and senior staff. Extending the negotiations to the legislature (and thus the public) and broadening the conflict may render the process of policy formulation unmanageable and increase its costs significantly. White House officials often are also concerned with the nature of Congress, which they often view as parochial, sieve-like, and prone to transform important matters of state into pork-barrel issues.

An additional challenge is determining with whom the White House should consult. The decentralization of power within Congress presents a substantial burden to executive branch officials wishing to consult with all the relevant members, especially on jurisdictionally complex matters. In some cases, even identifying the appropriate senators and representatives is difficult.

Time is an ever-present factor in White House operations, and it influences consultation with Congress as well. If severe deadlines are imposed on the production of a presidential initiative (such as the 1977 energy proposal), consultation may be difficult. For example, at least fifty congressional staff members of Democratic members of Congress participated in President Clinton's task force on health care, which took eight months to formulate. In contrast, few members were consulted on the president's earlier economic stimulus package or his original budget proposal, which were introduced in the early months of the administration. In addition, a president with an extensive legislative agenda may send a large number of bills to Congress, restricting the time officials can devote to consulting on any one of them.

A president with firm ideas on policy is unlikely to relish consulting with Congress in order to make compromises to satisfy congressional desires. In addition, some presidential proposals are designed by the White House to assuage constituency groups or fulfill campaign promises, which significantly constrains the possibilities of modifying these bills in response to congressional consultation.

Some observers propose that the White House involve relevant members of Congress in the process of developing the president's legislative program, the rationale being that those who have been involved in formulating a bill are more likely to support it after it is sent to the Hill. This process is not typical, however, because chief executives have found it too cumbersome to include members of Congress, especially those of the opposition party, in writing legislation, and most members of Congress prefer to protect their status as members of an independent branch. Speaker Tom Foley told President Clinton that he did not want Congress to help develop the president's economic program, as this was the responsibility of the White House.

Setting Priorities

An important aspect of a president's legislative strategy can be establishing priorities among legislative proposals. The goal of this effort is to set the congressional agenda. If the president is not able to focus the attention of Congress on his priority programs, these bills may become lost in the complex and overloaded legislative process. Congress needs time to digest what the president sends, to come up with independent analysis, and to schedule hearings and markups of bills. Unless the president gives some indication of what is most important, Congress will simply put the proposals in a queue where they will compete with each other for attention, often with disastrous results for the president.

This is especially likely to be a problem if much of the president's program must go through a single committee, as was the case for Jimmy Carter and the House Ways and Means Committee in 1977. Thus, it is wise to spread legislative proposals among several committees so that they can work on different parts of the president's agenda at the same time.

Setting priorities is also important because presidents and their staff can lobby effectively for only a few bills at once. Moreover, the president's political capital is inevitably limited, so it is sensible to focus it on the issues the administration cares about most. In 1977, Jimmy Carter spent his political capital on ending pork-barrel water projects, which was not one of his priority items. Similarly, in 1993 Bill Clinton risked losing focus on his economic and health care programs by proposing a host of controversial policies on abortion, homosexuals in the military, campaign reform, and environmental protection, among others. Many of these policies were initiated in response to pressures from segments of his party for action following twelve years of Republican presidents. Clinton did not repeat this mistake in 1997. In fact, he was criticized for proposing too few major initiatives.

It is particularly important that priorities be clearly established in the first year in office, when presidential influence in Congress is likely to be greatest. After the transition period, more items are likely to be on the agenda. For example, in 1981 Ronald Reagan focused attention on his priority programs and obtained passage of a large tax cut, a substantial increase in defense expenditures, and sizable decreases in the rate of spending increases for domestic policies. By 1982, however, the honeymoon was over and the legislative agenda was crowded.

The White House can put off dealing with the full spectrum of national issues for a period of months at the beginning of the term of a new president, but it cannot do so indefinitely. Eventually it must decide on them. By the second year, the agenda is full and more policies are in the pipeline as the administration attempts to satisfy its constituencies and responds to unanticipated, or simply overlooked, problems. Presidents with large legislative agendas and more diverse political constituencies, like Bill Clinton, find it more difficult to set priorities than those, like Ronald Reagan, with only a small number of proposals and relatively homogeneous supporters.

Moreover, presidents themselves may distract from their own legislative priorities. The more the White House tries to do, the more difficult it is to focus the country's attention on a few priority items. Presidents have so many demands to speak and decide on issues that it is impossible for White House planners to organize their schedules to focus the attention of Congress and the public for an extended period of time on their major goals.

Success in focusing attention on a few priority items will also be determined by the degree to which issues, including international crises, impose themselves on the president's schedule and divert attention, energy, and resources from his own agenda. As Clinton White House Communications Director George Stephanopolous put it: "On the campaign trail, you can just change the subject. But you can't just change the subject as President. You can't wish Bosnia away. You can't wish David Koresh away. You can't just ignore them and change the subject."[42]

Congress is also quite capable of setting its own agenda, which provides competition for the president's proposals. Of the thirteen major legislative actions (as defined by *Congressional Quarterly*) of the Ninety-Ninth Congress (1985–1986), the White House took the lead on only one. In 1987, President Reagan found Congress already working on the two primary domestic policy initiatives for his last two years in office, catastrophic health insurance and welfare reform. After the Republican victory in the 1994 midterm elections, President Clinton was reduced to a largely reactive posture as the Republicans set the agenda for Congress.

Moving Fast

The president must move quickly to exploit the honeymoon atmosphere that typically characterizes the early months of a new administration. First-year proposals have a better chance of passing Congress than do those sent to the Hill later in an administration. Lyndon Johnson explained, "You've got to give it all you can in that first year. . . . You've got just one year when they treat you right."[43]

The danger, of course, is in proposing a policy without thorough analysis in order to exploit this favorable political climate. This appears to have occurred with the budget cuts that Reagan proposed in early 1981. In this case, the departments, including cabinet members, and their expertise were kept at a distance in the executive decision-making process. Although taking time to draft proposals does not guarantee that they will be well conceived, it is by no means clear that the rapid drafting of legislation is in the best interests of the nation.

It is easier for a president who has a small agenda with an essentially negative character, such as Ronald Reagan's agenda of cutting taxes or domestic spending, to move rapidly to exploit the honeymoon. It is much more difficult to draft complex legislation rapidly, a problem Jimmy Carter faced in his first year when he tried to deal with issues such as energy, welfare reform, and the containment of health costs. Bill Clinton faced similar problems with his health care reform program. On the other hand, Kennedy and Johnson had the advantage of a party program that had been building up during the 1950s when the Democrats were not in the White House.

Structuring Choice

Framing issues in ways that favor the president's programs may set the terms of the debate and, thus, the premises on which members of Congress cast their votes. The key vote on Ronald Reagan's budget cuts in 1981 was on the rule determining whether there would be a single vote of yea or nay in the House. Once the rule was adopted, the White House could frame the issue as a vote for or against the popular president, and the broad nature of the reconciliation bill shifted the debate from the losses of individual programs to the benefits of the package as a whole. Although Reagan could not win an important individual vote on cutting a social welfare program, by structuring the choice facing Congress he was required only to win one vote and could avoid much of the potential criticism for specific reductions in spending.

Portraying policies in terms of criteria on which there is a consensus and playing down divisive issues are often at the core of efforts to structure choices for Congress. For example, federal aid to education had been a divisive issue for years before President Johnson proposed the Elementary and Secondary Education Act in 1965. To blunt opposition, he successfully changed the focus of debate from teachers' salaries and classroom shortages to fighting poverty, and from the separation of church and state to aiding children. This change in the premises of congressional decision making eased the path for the bill.

Although the structuring of choices can be a useful tool for the president, there is no guarantee that it will succeed, and opponents of the president's policies are unlikely to defer to an administration's attempts to structure choices on the issues. For example, President Bush wanted the debate over his proposal to cut taxes on capital gains to focus on economic growth and jobs. However, congressional Democrats were successful in framing the questions as being for or against giving benefits to the wealthy.

The Clinton administration has been beset with similar problems, as shown in The Clinton Presidency box.

THE CLINTON PRESIDENCY

Bill Clinton Tries to Define Himself

Bill Clinton is one of the most rhetorically skilled presidents of this century, yet he has found it difficult to effectively structure choice for the public and Congress on his priority issues. This has left him fighting an uphill battle to generate support for his policies and rendered him vulnerable to the vicissitudes of events and the definitions of his opponents.

On the president's first major legislative proposal—his fiscal stimulus package—Republicans succeeded in defining his economic program in terms of pork barrel instead of increasing employment. In response to his first budget, the Republicans focused public debate on tax increases rather than economic growth or deficit reduction. Clinton tried to present the issue of taxes as one of fairness, but there is little evidence that this perception was widely shared. When he said that his own proposal lacked sufficient spending cuts and challenged anyone to find more, the discussion focused on whether there were enough cuts rather than on economic stimulus or deficit reduction.

Clinton articulated six principles as the foundation for his health care plan— "security, simplicity, savings, choice, quality, and responsibility," with the emphasis on security. This was an attempt to set the terms of debate over health care and to depict the plan in comforting, affordable terms. His opponents did not simply submit, however. They launched an aggressive advertising campaign that characterized the president's plan as expensive, experimental, providing lower quality and rationed care, costing jobs, and bringing a lot more government and red tape to health care. The bill's complexity made it difficult to explain, and the dominant public response to the plan was confusion, which was heightened by competing plans in Congress. Instead of revolving around a central theme, public debate focused on the reform's pitfalls. Ultimately, the president was unable to structure the debate on health care, and the bill became his most notable legislative failure.

In 1997–1998, the president vocally supported a bill that would tax and regulate cigarettes and would reach a settlement with tobacco companies on their liability for smoking-related health problems. The president wished to portray the bill in terms of discouraging smoking, especially among teenagers, but his opponents spent millions of dollars on television ads portraying the bill as an example of big government and taxation of the working class (whose members are more likely to be smokers). In the end, the opponents prevailed in structuring the choice, and the bill died without a vote on passage.

The president's difficulty in defining himself and his policies has frustrated him. As Clinton reflected on the *Larry King Live* television show: "The thing that has surprised me most is how difficult it is . . . to really keep communicating what you're about to the American people."[44]

The Context of Influence

In our discussion of the president's legislative skills, it is important to keep in mind the general context in which a president is forced to operate today—a period characterized by congressional assertiveness. The diminished deference to the president by individual members of Congress and the institution as a whole naturally makes presidential influence more problematic.

Current presidents also have the misfortune to preside during a period of scarce government resources, whereas the Kennedy-Johnson years were characterized by stable prices, sustained economic growth, and expansive government. The prosperity of the 1960s provided the federal government with the funds for implementing new policies at little risk. Taxes did not have to be raised and sacrifices did not have to be made in order to help the underprivileged. Since the late 1970s, however, government resources have been more limited, in part because of the continuing cost of the programs enacted in the 1960s. This makes the passage of expensive new programs more difficult today. When resources are scarce, presidents are faced with internal competition for them and the breakdown of supporting coalitions. They must choose between policies rather than building coalitions for several policies through logrolling.

Under these circumstances, it is not surprising that the relations of recent presidents with Congress have often been characterized by stalemate. Clearly, the environment for presidential influence has been deteriorating.

The Impact of Legislative Skills

In general, presidential legislative skills must compete, as does public support, with other, more stable factors that affect voting in Congress, including party, ideology, personal views and commitments on specific policies, and constituency interests. By the time a president tries to exercise influence on a vote, most members of Congress have made up their minds on the basis of these other factors.

Systematic quantitative studies have found that, once we control for the status of their party in Congress and their standing with the public, presidents renowned for their legislative skills (such as Lyndon Johnson) are generally no more successful in winning votes (even close ones) or obtaining congressional support than those (such as Jimmy Carter) who are considered to have been less adept in dealing with Congress.[45] Even skilled presidents cannot change the contours of the political landscape and create opportunities for change very much. However, they can recognize favorable configurations of political forces, such as those that existed in 1933, 1965, and 1981, which they can effectively exploit to embark on major shifts in public policy. Franklin D. Roosevelt, Lyndon Johnson, and Ronald Reagan were particularly effective in exploiting their resources in their early years in office; Jimmy Carter and Bill Clinton were not.

THE VETO

Sometimes presidents not only fail to win passage of their proposals, but Congress also passes legislation to which they are strongly opposed. Since all bills and joint resolutions except those proposing constitutional amendments must be presented to the president for approval, he or she has another opportunity to influence legislation: the veto.

When Congress passes an item that must be submitted to the president, he or she has several options. Within ten days (Sundays excepted) of its presentation, the president may (1) sign the measure, in which case it becomes the law of the land; (2) not sign the measure and return it to the house in which it originated with a message stating the reasons for withholding approval; or (3) do nothing.

A bill or joint resolution that the president returns to Congress has been vetoed. It can then become law only if each house of Congress repasses it by a two-thirds majority of those present. Congress may override the presidential veto at any time before it adjourns sine die (that is, before the end of that particular Congress).

Early presidents exercised their veto power sparingly and ostensibly for the purpose of voiding legislation they deemed to be unconstitutional in its content or sloppy and improper in design. The first six presidents vetoed a total of eight bills; the seventh president, Andrew Jackson, vetoed twelve. However, Jackson used his negative to prevent legislation he opposed from becoming law, and others have followed his example.

The president can veto only an entire bill. Unlike most state governors, presidents do not have an item veto, which would allow them to veto specific provisions of a bill. As a result of this constraint, members of Congress use a number of strategies to avoid a possible veto of a particular proposal. For example, Congress may add increased appropriations or riders (i.e., nongermane provisions) that the White House might not want to bills that it otherwise desires, thus forcing the president to decide whether to accept these unattractive provisions in order to gain the legislation. In most such cases, presidents desist from using their vetoes. For example, after President Carter vetoed a bill providing for increased salaries for Public Health Service physicians, Congress added the pay raise to mental health services legislation, a pet project of First Lady Rosalyn Carter, and the president signed the bill.

In 1987 Congress passed the entire discretionary budget of the federal government in one omnibus bill. Consequently, the president had to accept the whole package or else lose appropriations for the entire government. President Reagan frequently called for a constitutional amendment giving the president an item veto, and Presidents Bush and Clinton followed his example. They argued that an item veto would allow the president to stop unnecessary spending within massive appropriations bills and thus help to bring the budget under control, and in 1996, Congress heeded their call (see the Hot-Button Issue box).

If the president does nothing after receiving a measure from Congress, it becomes law after ten days (Sundays excepted) provided Congress remains in session. If it has adjourned during the ten-day period, thus preventing the president from returning the bill to the house of its origination, the bill is *pocket vetoed*. A pocket veto kills a piece of legislation just as a regular veto does. Historically, somewhat fewer than half of all vetoes have been pocket vetoes. Table 10–5 presents data on the vetoes by recent presidents.

Presidents have sometimes attempted to use the pocket veto by taking no action on measures sent to them just before Congress went into a temporary recess, and claiming that the recess prevented them from returning their veto for congressional consideration. (In 1964 President Johnson pocket vetoed a bill during a congressional recess and then recalled and signed it.) However, in 1976, after the Nixon and Ford White Houses had lost litigation on the issue, the Ford administration promised that the president would not use the pocket veto during congressional recesses as long as an official of Congress was designated to be on hand to receive his vetoes. Since Congress is in session nearly all year, most people thought that only an adjournment *sine die* would provide the opportunity for a pocket veto.

Ronald Reagan used the pocket veto during a recess at the end of the 1981 session without apparent problems, but thirty-three House Democrats filed suit in federal court to challenge his pocket veto during the congressional recess at the end of 1983 of a bill making aid to El Salvador dependent on human rights progress. As a result, in 1984 a federal appeals court ruled against the president. President Bush also claimed to have pocket vetoed some bills during congressional recesses, but Congress treated them like regular vetoes.

The last column in Table 10–5 indicates that vetoes are infrequently used. Not only are the absolute numbers low, but fewer than 1 percent of the bills passed by Congress (which typically number several hundred per session) are vetoed. The table also shows that presidents who face Congresses controlled by the opposition party (Eisenhower, Nixon, Ford, Reagan, and Bush) used more vetoes, as we would expect. These presidents were more likely to be presented with legislation that they opposed. President Clinton vetoed no bills until the Republicans won majorities in Congress in the 1994 elections.

☀ HOT-BUTTON ISSUE

The Line-Item Veto

In April 1996, President Clinton signed into law the line-item veto act (PL 104–130). This bill created an elaborate mechanism for the president to veto specific items in legislation. After the president signed a bill into law, he had five days to cancel any of three types of specific items: discretionary spending, new entitlement spending, or limited tax benefits (defined as provisions that help one hundred or fewer taxpayers or new "transition rules" that help ten or fewer).

The president's cancellation would stand unless Congress overturned it within thirty calendar days. To do so, Congress had to clear a disapproval bill, passage of which requires only simple majorities in each house. However, the president could use the traditional veto to kill the disapproval bill, whereupon Congress could override it only by obtaining the support of two-thirds of those voting in each chamber.

In his first budget season of wielding the historic line-item veto power, the President Clinton canceled items that created $1.9 billion in savings over five years. Although this is a substantial amount of money, it is only a tiny fraction—about 0.02 percent—of the $9 trillion the federal government would spend over the period.

The president cast eighty-two line-item vetoes, thirty-eight of which were for military construction projects. The pace slowed substantially after that, as the White House discovered blunders in deciding which programs to cut. (It had to admit that some of its decisions were based on faulty information.) This more sparing use of the line-item authority prompted some conservatives—such as Senator John McCain of Arizona, who had fought for years to give the president the line-item veto power—to complain that the president did not use the veto often enough.

More important, the line-item veto was challenged in the courts. Opponents charged that under Article 1 of the Constitution, all legislative power is vested with Congress; the president can only accept or reject bills in their entirety. The new veto, the lawsuits argued, gave the president the power to change a law—or amend it—after he has signed it. In 1998, the Supreme Court agreed, finding the bill to be unconstitutional in *Clinton v. New York City.*

TABLE 10–5. Regular and Pocket Vetoes

President	Regular Vetoes	Pocket Vetoes	Total Vetoes
Eisenhower	73	108	181
Kennedy	12	9	21
Johnson	16	14	30
Nixon	26	17	43
Ford	48	18	66
Carter	13	18	31
Reagan	39	39	78
Bush	31	15	46
Clinton*	25	0	25

*Through 1998.

Table 10–6 illustrates another important fact about vetoes—their tendency to be overridden. Regular vetoes are generally sustained, but overriding does occur, especially when the president's party is in the minority in Congress. Some very important legislation has been passed over the president's veto. In the post–World War II era, such legislation includes the Taft-Hartley Labor Relations Act (1947), the McCarran-Walter Immigration Act (1952), the McCarran-Wood Internal Security Act (1950), and the War Powers Resolution (1973).

Sometimes presidents choose not to veto a bill, either because they feel that the good in it outweighs the bad or because they do not want their veto to be overridden. Thus, when Congress passed an amendment to a foreign aid authorization bill imposing new sanctions on China by such large margins that it was impossible to sustain a veto, President Bush, who was opposed to it, nonetheless reluctantly signed the measure.

TABLE 10–6. Vetoes Overridden

President	Regular Vetoes	Vetoes Overriden	Percentage of Vetoes Overriden
Eisenhower	73	2	3
Kennedy	12	0	0
Johnson	16	0	0
Nixon	26	7	27
Ford	48	12	25
Carter	13	2	15
Reagan	39	9	23
Bush	31	1	3
Clinton*	25	2	8

*Through 1998.

When a bill is introduced in either house of Congress, the chamber's parliamentarian classifies it as public or private. Generally, public bills relate to public matters and deal with individuals by classifications or categories, such as college students or the elderly. A private bill, on the other hand, names a particular individual or entity who is to receive relief, such as through payment of a pension or a claim against the government or the granting of citizenship. Up until 1969, presidents usually vetoed more private than public bills. Recent presidents have vetoed very few private bills, however.

The veto is an inherently negative element in the president's arsenal, but sometimes it may be used to shape legislation. Presidents frequently veto or threaten to veto bills unless certain provisions are removed or altered. For example, George Bush, a Republican facing large Democratic majorities in Congress, repeatedly made strategic use of the veto to move Congress in his direction. In a typical example, he vetoed a substantial increase in the federal minimum wage in 1989. This encouraged Congress to pass a more modest increase, which was acceptable to the president. President Clinton threatened to veto a large transportation bill in 1998 because it violated his 1997 budget agreement with Congress. Clinton's threatened veto gave leverage to members of Congress who wanted to trim the legislation, and they were successful. In a more unusual situation, in 1987 President Reagan threatened to veto the omnibus appropriations bill, which contained the money necessary for running the government for the following year, if Congress did not include certain provisions that he favored. Fearing a shutdown of the government, Congress acquiesced. Bill Clinton followed a similar strategy in 1998.

Once exercised, the veto's usefulness as a threat ends and the chances of the president obtaining positive action from Congress are substantially diminished. For example, in 1988 Reagan vetoed the defense authorization bill because he objected to some funding provisions and restrictions on his discretion in procurement and arms control. Angered because it felt the president had violated an agreement on the bill and was grandstanding to aid George Bush's presidential campaign, Congress repassed the bill with essentially cosmetic changes. Moreover, the veto threat must be exercised with caution lest it be used too often and be too easily overcome. Thus, although a president's vetoes are normally successful in stopping legislation, they are less effective when used as inducements to pass legislation that the White House desires, and they are utilized in this way only in exceptional cases.

CONCLUSION

Presidents face an uphill battle in dealing with Congress. Their formal powers of recommending legislation and vetoing bills help set the legislature's agenda and prevent some legislation from passing. However, these prerogatives are of only marginal help in obtaining what they want. Conflict between the executive and legislative branches is inherent in the U.S. system of government. The overlapping powers of the two branches, their representation of different constituencies, and the contrast of the hierarchical, expert nature of the executive and the decentralized, generalist Congress guarantee that, except in extraordinary circumstances, conflict between them will remain a central feature of American politics.

The chief executive's assets in dealing with Congress are unimpressive. Party leadership is a potential source of influence in Congress, and presidents receive considerably more support from members of their party than from the opposition. Much, or even most, of this support is the result of members of the same party sharing similar policy views rather than the influence of the president's party leadership. Nevertheless, presidents work closely with their party and its leaders in Congress and tend to gain some increment of support as a result of party loyalty. Party support is undependable, however, as constituency interests, a lack of policy consensus, and other factors intervene and diminish the importance of the party label. Congressional party leaders are typically in weak positions to move their troops in the president's direction. Ideally, presidents could influence the election of members of their party to Congress, but presidential coattails are very short and midterm campaigning seems to have limited payoffs. Thus, presidents generally have to seek support from opposition party members, but their efforts at bipartisanship, although necessary, may strain relations with the less moderate wing of their own party.

Presidents are more likely to receive support in Congress when they have the public's approval than when they sit low in the polls. Unfortunately (as seen in Chapter 4), they cannot depend on the public's support, nor can they be sure of being able to mobilize new support. Moreover, public approval is usually a necessary, but not a sufficient, source of influence. Even when presidents are high in the polls, they will find it difficult to pass their programs if their party lacks a majority of congressional seats.

The White House engages in a large-scale legislative liaison effort to create goodwill and influence votes on a more personal level. Bargains are consummated, services and amenities are provided, arms are twisted, presidential phone calls are made, and advance consultation takes place. However, there are severe limits on a president's time and resources. Presidents can increase the chances of their success by moving programs early in their tenure and not letting those programs clog the legislative process. However, many find it difficult or impossible to control the congressional agenda so neatly. Although presidential legislative skills are crucial in winning some votes, their importance is often exaggerated. Thus, presidents must constantly struggle to succeed in having their policies enacted into law.

Presidential leadership of Congress is at the margins most of the time. In general, successful presidential leadership of Congress has not been the result of the dominant chief executive of political folklore, who reshapes the contours of the political landscape to pave the way for change. Rather than creating the conditions for important shifts in public policy, the effective president is the less heroic figure of the facilitator, who works at the margins building coalitions to recognize and exploit opportunities presented by a favorable configuration of political forces.

The president remains an important influence on Congress but rarely dominates it. Ronald Reagan was considered a strong chief executive and began with a string of victories in Congress. However, after the Democrats won control of the Senate in the 1986 elections and his approval ratings plummeted in the wake of the Iran-Contra scandal, he was successful only 44 percent of the time in 1987 and 47 percent in 1988 in getting passage of the measures that he supported. Budgeting was one of his principal tools for affecting public policy, yet the budgets he proposed to Congress were typically pronounced "DOA"—dead on arrival. George Bush reached record levels of public approval in the wake of the Gulf War in 1991, but his domestic legislative program remained stalled. Bill Clinton was unable to win passage of two of his three highest legislative priorities—economic stimulus and health care reform—and had to compromise extensively to gain the other— deficit reduction. After the Republicans won majorities in both houses of Congress in 1994, he was occupied with thwarting their initiatives, and had little chance of passing his own. Thus, members of Congress truly compose an independent branch and in recent years have more often taken the lead in initiating major changes in public policy than the president.

DISCUSSION QUESTIONS

1. Some argue that members of the president's party in Congress should simply vote their consciences and pay little attention to party loyalty to their leader. Others say that the only way that election promises can be implemented, and thus be made meaningful to the majority of voters, is for the party to stick together and pass legislation. When should members of Congress defer to the president?

2. Many people seem to think that divided government is good for the country because it prevents the president from concentrating too much power in the executive branch. Others view divided government as an obstacle to bringing about change because different parties control the

Congress and the White House. What do you think? Is it good for people to split their tickets and vote for a president of one party and members of the House or Senate from the other party? What are the advantages and costs of divided government?

3. Why has President Clinton had such a difficult time obtaining support in Congress for his major legislation? What can he do to overcome congressional resistance? Which of the president's legislative activities have been most successful, and why were they?

WEB EXERCISES

1. Look at the items President Clinton vetoed with the line-item veto. Did these vetoes make an important contribution to public policy? Do you agree with the Supreme Court's decision in *Clinton v. New York City* (1998) that Congress had delegated power to the president unconstitutionally? Go to <http://www.access.gpo.gov/nara/nara004.html>.
2. The 1990 budget agreement was both contentious and precedent setting. It laid the groundwork for the balanced budget of today, but it also may have cost President Bush his chance for reelection. Look at the many factors affecting the outcome of the decision, ranging from the current budgetary situation and partisan politics to the Iraqi invasion of Kuwait. You can also search through relevant documents for the president's view of the negotiations. Go to <http://www.csdl.tamu.edu/bushlib/demo/budget.html>.

SELECTED READING

Campbell, James E. *The Presidential Pulse of Congressional Elections.* Lexington: University Press of Kentucky, 1993.

Edwards, George C., III. *At the Margins: Presidential Leadership of Congress.* New Haven: Yale University Press, 1989.

Edwards, George C., III, Andrew Barrett, and Jeffrey Peake, "The Legislative Impact of Divided Government." *American Journal of Political Science* 41 (May 1997): 545–563.

Fisher, Louis. *Constitutional Conflicts between Congress and the President.* 4th ed., rev. Lawrence: University Press of Kansas, 1997.

Jones, Charles O. *The Presidency in a Separated System.* Washington, D.C.: Brookings Institution, 1994.

Neustadt, Richard E. *Presidential Power and the Modern Presidents.* New York: Free Press, 1990.

Peterson, Mark A. *Legislating Together.* Cambridge: Harvard University Press, 1990.

Spitzer, Robert J. *The Presidential Veto*. Albany: State University of New York Press, 1988.

Wayne, Stephen J. *The Legislative Presidency*. New York: Harper and Row, 1978.

West, Darrell M. "Activists and Economic Policymaking in Congress." *American Journal of Political Science* 32 (August 1988): 662–680.

Notes

1. Lyndon Johnson quoted in Doris Kearns, *Lyndon Johnson and the American Dream* (New York: Harper and Row, 1976), p. 226.
2. Occasionally Congress may continue its session after the elections. The 103rd Congress did that in 1994 in order to consider the General Agreement on Tariffs and Trade (GATT), which the president supported, but on which members of Congress did not wish to vote until after the midterm elections. Special sessions occur only after Congress has adjourned.
3. James Madison, "The Federalist, No. 46," in *The Federalist* (New York: Modern Library, 1937), p. 307.
4. See, for example, John W. Kingdon, *Congressmen's Voting Decisions,* 3rd ed. (Ann Arbor: University of Michigan Press, 1989); Donald R. Matthews and James A. Stimson, *Yeas and Nays* (New York: Wiley, 1975).
5. Gerald R. Ford, *A Time to Heal: The Autobiography of Gerald R. Ford* (New York: Harper and Row, 1979), p. 150.
6. Richard E. Neustadt, *Presidential Power and the Modern Presidents* (New York: Free Press, 1990), p. 29.
7. Quoted in Paul C. Light, *The President's Agenda: Domestic Policy Choice from Kennedy to Carter* (Baltimore: Johns Hopkins University Press, 1982), p. 135.
8. See Terry Sullivan, "Bargaining with the President: A Simple Game and New Evidence," *American Political Science Review* 84 (December 1990): 1167–1196, concerning party members switching to support the president when needed.
9. Howard Baker quoted in James L. Sundquist, *The Decline and Resurgence of Congress* (Washington, D.C.: Brookings Institution, 1981), p. 402.
10. Moynihan quoted in "Recasting Senate Finance: Moynihan to Take Helm," *Congressional Quarterly Weekly Report*, December 12, 1992, p. 3796.
11. Gerald R. Ford, "Imperiled, Not Imperial," *Time*, November 10, 1980, p. 30.
12. Quoted in Light, *The President's Agenda*, p. 211.
13. David W. Rohde, *Parties and Leaders in the Postreform House* (Chicago: University of Chicago Press, 1991).
14. See Jeffrey E. Cohen, Michael A. Krassa, and John A. Hamman, "The Impact of Presidential Campaigning on Midterm U.S. Senate Elections," *American Political Science Review* 85 (March 1991): 165–180.
15. George C. Edwards III, *The Public Presidency* (New York: St. Martin's, 1983), pp. 83–93; Gregory N. Flemming, "Presidential Coattails in Open-Seat Elections, *Legislative Studies Quarterly* 20 (May 1995): 197–212.
16. James E. Campbell and Joe A. Sumners, "Presidential Coattails in Senate Elections," *American Political Science Review* 84 (June 1990): 513–524; Alan I. Abramowitz and Jeffrey A. Segal, *Senate Elections* (Ann Arbor: University of Michigan Press, 1992), pp. 121, 233, 238.
17. Jimmy Carter, *Keeping Faith: Memoirs of a President* (New York: Bantam, 1982), p. 80.
18. Emmet John Hughes, *The Living Presidency* (Baltimore: Penguin, 1974), p. 68.
19. Lyndon B. Johnson, *The Vantage Point: Perspectives of the Presidency, 1963–1969* (New York: Popular Library, 1971), p. 443.
20. Johnson, *The Vantage Point*, p. 323.
21. Quoted in "Run, Run, Run," *Newsweek,* May 2, 1977, p. 38.
22. Quoted in "Carter Seeks More Effective Use of Departmental Lobbyists' Skills," *Congressional Quarterly Weekly Report*, March 4, 1978, p. 585.

23. Quoted in Sidney Blumenthal, "Marketing the President," *The New York Times Magazine,* September 13, 1981, p. 110.

24. Dom Bonafede, "The Strained Relationship," *National Journal,* May 19, 1979, p. 830.

25. See, for example, Lonna Rae Atkeson and Randall W. Partin, "Economic and Referendum Voting: A Comparison of Gubernatorial and Senatorial Elections," *American Political Science Review* 89 (March 1995): 99–107.

26. 1994 Voter News Service exit poll.

27. Richard M. Nixon, *In the Arena: A Memoir of Victory, Defeat and Renewal* (New York: Simon and Schuster, 1990), p. 282.

28. Memorandum from William E. Timmons to Richard Nixon, December 31, 1973, p. 3.

29. Light, *The President's Agenda,* pp. 28–31.

30. Harry McPherson, *A Political Education* (Boston: Little, Brown, 1972), p. 192.

31. Lawrence F. O'Brien, quoted in Neil McNeil, *Forge of Democracy* (New York: McKay, 1963), p. 260.

32. On the office's organization of outside groups, see Mark A. Peterson, "The Presidency and Organized Interests: White House Patterns of Interest Group Liaison," *American Political Science Review* 86 (September 1992): 612–625.

33. Richard E. Neustadt, "Presidency and Legislation: Planning the President's Program," in Aaron Wildavsky, ed., *The Presidency* (Boston: Little, Brown, 1969), p. 596.

34. Dwight D. Eisenhower, *Mandate for Change, 1953–1956* (New York: Signet, 1963), pp. 254–255.

35. Johnson, *The Vantage Point,* p. 40.

36. David Stockman, *The Triumph of Politics* (New York: Harper and Row, 1986), pp. 251, 253, 260–261, 264–265; see also William Greider, "The Education of David Stockman," *Atlantic Monthly,* December 1981, p. 51.

37. Gary W. Reichard, *The Reaffirmation of Republicanism: Eisenhower and the Eighty-Third Congress* (Knoxville: University of Tennessee Press, 1975), p. 173.

38. William Timmons and Max Friedersdorf quoted in "Turning Screws: Winning Votes in Congress," *Congressional Quarterly Weekly Report,* April 24, 1976, pp. 952–953.

39. Quoted in "Turning Screws," pp. 952–953.

40. John Kennedy quoted in Theodore Sorensen, *Kennedy* (New York: Bantam, 1966), p. 387.

41. See Mark A. Peterson, *Legislating Together* (Cambridge: Harvard University Press, 1990).

42. Stephanopolous quoted in Thomas L. Friedman and Maureen Dowd, "Amid Setbacks, Clinton Team Seeks to Shake Off the Blues," *New York Times,* April 25, 1993, sect. 1, p. 12.

43. Lyndon Johnson, quoted in McPherson, *A Political Education,* p. 268.

44. Clinton quoted in Bob Woodward, *The Agenda: Inside the Clinton White House* (New York: Simon and Schuster, 1994), p. 313.

45. George C. Edwards III, *At the Margins: Presidential Leadership of Congress* (New Haven: Yale University Press, 1989), chap. 9. See also Jon R. Bond and Richard Fleisher, *The President in the Legislative Agenda* (Chicago: University of Chicago Press, 1990), chap. 8.

11

THE PRESIDENT AND THE JUDICIARY

THE PRESIDENT'S INTERACTIONS WITH THE CONGRESS and the bureau-cracy are constant, and they receive considerable attention. Relations with the third branch of government, the judiciary, however, are in many ways more inter-mittent and less visible. Nevertheless, chief executives have important relation-ships with the courts, and it is through this channel—through their nominations to the bench—that they have opportunities to influence public policy for years to come. The executive branch, operating through the solicitor general's office, is also a frequent litigant in the federal courts, especially at the Supreme Court level. Such litigation provides another opportunity for the president to influence judi-cial decisions.

In addition, presidents may end up with responsibility for enforcing court decisions even though they were not directly involved in them. Sometimes enforc-ing the law actually means complying with decisions directed at the White House. Although such instances are not common, they may provide moments of high political drama and have important consequences for our political system. Finally, the Constitution gives the president the right to exercise some judicial powers directly through the granting of pardons, amnesty, and clemency for indi-viduals who are accused or convicted of federal crimes.

The distinction between the director and facilitator presidential types is less clear in relationships with the judiciary than with Congress. Although both presi-dential types will be able to take advantage of the opportunity to nominate com-patible judges to the federal bench, those who are directors will be able to mold the courts more, moving them to reach decisions of which they approve and to overturn previous decisions that they oppose. Facilitators will be more con-strained in placing their first choices on the bench and will not dominate their judicial decision making. Their victories will result from the views of the judges they nominate to the bench rather than their influence over these judges once they don their judicial robes.

369

JUDICIAL SELECTION

The president's primary means of exercising leadership of the judicial branch is through the nomination of federal judges. In this section we examine the process of judicial selection for the federal courts and the types of persons who become federal judges.

Selection of Lower-Court Judges

We begin with the federal district courts and the courts of appeals, which include most federal judges and handle most federal cases. The president nominates persons to fill these slots for lifetime service, and the Senate must confirm each nomination by a majority vote. Because of the Senate's role, the president's discretion ends up being much less than it appears.

Senatorial courtesy is the customary manner in which the Senate disposes of state-level federal nominations for such positions as judgeships and U.S. attorneys. Under this unwritten tradition, nominations for these positions are not confirmed when opposed by a senator from the state in which the nominee is to serve (all states have at least one federal district court) or, in the case of courts of appeals judges, the state of the nominee's residence if the senator is of the same party as the president. To invoke the right of senatorial courtesy, the relevant senator usually simply states a general reason for opposing a nomination. The other senators will then honor their colleague's views and oppose the nomination regardless of their personal views or the candidate's merits.

The first instance of senatorial courtesy occurred in 1789, when President George Washington failed to have Benjamin Fishbourn confirmed as naval officer of the port of Savannah because of the opposition of Georgia's two senators, and since that time, senatorial courtesy has become better and better established. By 1840, senators were virtually naming federal district court judges. In addition, at times senatorial courtesy has been successfully invoked by a senator not of the president's party.

When a president fails to heed the tradition of senatorial courtesy, the results can be embarrassing. On April 1, 1976, President Ford nominated William B. Poff to a federal judgeship in Virginia even though Virginia's Republican senator, William Scott, had previously given notice of his opposition to Poff and of his support for another candidate, Glenn Williams. It is important to note that Scott himself agreed that Poff was qualified for the position. He simply felt that Williams's philosophy was closer to his own. Thus, on April 15, Scott formally announced his opposition to Poff's nomination in a letter to the Senate Judiciary Committee, where he simply termed Poff "unacceptable." On May 5 the committee chairman, Senator

James Eastland, moved to table the nomination, which was tabled without objection.

Presidents are not without assets in such a situation, but they rarely will find it worthwhile to fight a senator over a district court judgeship. These judges seldom interfere with their policies. If they desire to do so, presidents can refuse to appoint anyone to the position in an attempt to pressure a senator into supporting their nominee in order to avoid a backlog of federal cases in the state. Alternately, they may make an appointment during a congressional recess at the end of a session. Although the nominee must still be confirmed in the next session of Congress, by then he or she may have had an opportunity to demonstrate such exemplary capabilities on the bench that the Senate will look more favorably on the appointment.

Because of the strength of these informal practices, presidents usually check carefully with the relevant senator or senators ahead of time to avoid making a nomination that will fail to be confirmed. In many instances this is tantamount to giving the power of nomination to these senators. Typically, when there is a vacancy for a federal judgeship, the senator (or senators) of the president's party from the state where the judge will serve will suggest one or more names to the attorney general and the president. If neither senator is of the president's party, the state's representatives of the president's party or other state party leaders may make suggestions. Then the Department of Justice and the Federal Bureau of Investigation conduct competency and background checks on these persons, and the president usually selects a nominee from those who survive the screening process. It is very difficult for the president to reject the recommendation of a senator of his party in favor of someone else if the recommended person clears the hurdles of professional standing and integrity. Thus, the Constitution is turned on its head and the Senate ends up making nominations, which the president then approves.

The attorney general typically asks the Standing Committee on the Federal Judiciary of the American Bar Association (ABA) for its evaluation of potential nominees. Other individuals have input in judicial selection as well. The ABA committee or the Department of Justice may ask sitting judges, usually at the federal level, to evaluate prospective nominees. Sitting judges may also initiate recommendations to advance or retard someone's chances of being nominated. In addition, candidates for the nomination are often active on their own behalf. They have to alert the relevant parties that they desire the position and orchestrate a campaign of support for themselves. As one appellate judge observed: "People don't get judgeships without seeking them. Anybody who thinks judicial office seeks the man is mistaken. There's not a man on the court who didn't do what he thought needed to be done."[1]

Presidents usually have more influence in the selection of judges to the federal courts of appeals than to federal district courts. Since the decisions of appellate courts are generally more significant than those of lower courts, the president naturally takes a greater interest in appointments to the former. At the same time, individual senators are in a weaker position to determine who the nominee will be because the jurisdiction of an appeals court encompasses several states. Although custom and pragmatic politics require that these judgeships be apportioned among the states, the president has discretion in how this is done, and therefore has a greater role in recruiting appellate judges than district court judges. Even here, however, senators from the state in which the candidate resides may be able to veto a nomination.

George Bush experienced an especially difficult time obtaining the confirmation of lower-court judges from the Democratically controlled Senate during the second half of his term. Bill Clinton has experienced similar frustrations with the Republican Senate since 1995. As a result, he has had to negotiate agreements with Republican senators, giving some of them a role in the selection of judges equivalent to that of his fellow Democrats. As the next presidential election nears, the party that controls the Senate has an incentive to delay confirmations in the hope that it will gain control of the White House.

Backgrounds of Lower-Court Judges

What type of individual is selected as a judge through this process? The data in Tables 11–1 and 11–2 show that federal judges are not a representative sample of the American people. They are all lawyers (although this is not a constitutional requirement), and they are overwhelmingly white and male. Only Bill Clinton, George Bush, and Jimmy Carter have appointed a substantial number of women to the federal bench, and Clinton and Carter are the only presidents to have appointed a significant percentage of minority group members.

Federal judges have also typically held office as a judge or prosecutor, and often they have been involved in partisan politics. This involvement is generally what brings them to the attention of senators and the Department of Justice when they seek nominees for judgeships. As Griffin Bell, a former U.S. attorney general and circuit court judge, once remarked:

> For me, becoming a federal judge wasn't very difficult. I managed John F. Kennedy's presidential campaign in Georgia. Two of my oldest and closest friends were two senators from Georgia. And I was campaign manager and special, unpaid counsel for the governor.[2]

Perhaps the most striking finding in Tables 11–1 and 11–2 is the fact that presidents rarely appoint someone to a judgeship who does not share their party affiliation. Merit considerations obviously occur after partisan screening. Judgeships are patronage plums that may serve as rewards for political service to either the president or senators of the president's party, as consolation prizes for unsuccessful candidates, or even to "kick upstairs" an official in order to remove him or her from an executive branch post. When presidents nominate someone of the other party for a judgeship, it is

TABLE 11–1. Backgrounds of Recent Federal Appeals Court Judges

Characteristic	Clinton*	Bush	Reagan	Carter
		Administration		
Total number of nominees	29	37	78	56
Occupation (%)				
Politics/government	3	11	6	5
Judiciary	59	60	55	47
Large law firm	17	16	13	11
Moderate size firm	10	11	10	16
Solo or small firm	—	—	1	5
Professor of law	10	3	13	14
Other	—	—	1	2
Experience (%)				
Judicial	69	62	60	54
Prosecutorial	38	30	28	32
Neither one	21	32	35	38
Party (%)				
Democrat	86	5	—	82
Republican	3	89	97	7
Independent	10	5	1	11
Past party activism (%)	48	70	69	73
Ethnicity or race (%)				
White	72	89	97	79
African-American	14	5	1	16
Hispanic	10	5	1	4
Asian	3	—	—	2
Gender (%)				
Male	69	81	95	80
Female	31	19	5	20
Average age	51	49	50	52

*First term.

Source: Adapted from Sheldon Goldman and Elliot Slotnick, "Clinton's First-Term Judiciary: Many Bridges to Cross," *Judicature* 80, no. 6 (1997): 269.

TABLE 11-2. Backgrounds of Recent Federal District Court Judges

Characteristic	Administration			
	Clinton*	Bush	Reagan	Carter
Total number of nominees	169	148	290	202
Occupation (%)				
Politics/government	11	11	13	4
Judiciary	44	42	37	40
Large law firm	17	26	18	14
Moderate size firm	17	15	19	20
Solo or small firm	8	5	10	14
Professor of law	2	1	2	3
Other	1	1	1	1
Experience (%)				
Judicial	50	47	47	55
Prosecutorial	38	39	44	39
Neither one	31	32	28	28
Party (%)				
Democrat	91	5	5	93
Republican	2	89	93	4
Independent	7	6	2	3
Past party activism (%)	54	61	59	61
Ethnicity or race (%)				
White	72	90	92	79
African-American	20	7	2	14
Hispanic	7	4	5	7
Asian	1	—	1	1
Gender (%)				
Male	70	80	92	86
Female	30	20	8	14
Average age	49	48	49	50

*First term.

Source: Adapted from Sheldon Goldman and Elliot Slotnick, "Clinton's First-Term Judiciary: Many Bridges to Cross," *Judicature* 80, no. 6 (1997): 261.

usually because of ideological congruity with the nominee or to obtain support in a state where their party is weak.

Partisanship also plays a role in the creation of judgeships. Because of their keen interest in them, members of Congress are reluctant to create judicial positions to be filled by a president of the minority party in Congress.[3] For example, Democrats in Congress rejected President Eisenhower's efforts to create new judgeships in every year of his second term (1957–1960), even though he offered to name Democrats to half the new positions. In 1962, however, a similar bill easily passed Congress with Democrat John Kennedy in the White House. This partisan behavior was nothing new. In 1801 the newly elected Jeffersonians repealed a law creating separate judges for the circuit courts of appeal that had been passed by the outgoing Federalists a few months earlier.

There is no doubt that various women's, racial, ethnic, and religious groups desire to have as many of their members as possible appointed to the federal bench. At the very least, judgeships have symbolic importance for them. Thus, presidents face many of the same pressures for representativeness in selecting judges that they experience in naming their cabinet.

What is less clear is what policy differences result from presidents' appointing persons with different backgrounds to judgeships. The number of female and minority group judges has been too few and their service too recent to serve as a basis for generalizations about their decisions. Many members of each party have been appointed, of course, and it appears that Republican judges are, in general, somewhat more conservative than Democratic judges. Moreover, former prosecutors have tended to be less sympathetic toward defendants' rights than other judges. It seems, then, that background does make some difference.[4]

Selection of Supreme Court Justices

Like lower-court judges, justices of the Supreme Court must be approved by a majority of those voting in the Senate. There have been no recess appointments to the Court since the Senate voiced its disapproval of the practice in 1960. When the chief justice's position becomes vacant, the president may either nominate someone already on the Court or someone from outside it to fill the position. Usually presidents choose the latter course in order to widen their range of options, but if they decide to elevate a sitting associate justice, as President Reagan did with William Rehnquist in 1986, he or she must go through a new confirmation by the Senate.

The president operates under many constraints in selecting persons to serve on the lower federal courts, especially the district courts. Although many of the same actors are present in the case of Supreme Court nominations, their influence is typically quite different. The president is vitally interested in the Court because of the importance of its work, which includes making decisions on the scope of presidential powers, and will generally be intimately involved in the recruitment process.

Unlike the case of federal judges, presidents have been personally acquainted with many of the people they have nominated to the Court (reflecting their involvement in the selection process), and it is not unusual for an administration official to receive a nomination. Presidents also often rely on the attorney general and the Justice Department to identify and screen candidates for the Court.

There are few matters as important to justices on the Supreme Court as the ideology, competence, and compatibility of their colleagues, and thus it is not surprising that they (especially chief justices), often try to influence nominations to the Court. Chief Justice William Howard Taft, who was a former president, was especially active during his tenure in the 1920s, and Warren Burger played a prominent role in the Nixon administration. Nevertheless, although presidents will listen to recommendations from justices, they feel no obligation to follow them.

Senators play a much less prominent role in the recruitment of Supreme Court justices than in the selection of lower-court judges, especially for the district courts. No senator can claim that the jurisdiction of the Supreme Court falls within the realm of his or her special expertise, interest, or sphere of influence. Thus, presidents typically consult with senators from the state of residence of a nominee after they have decided whom to select. At this point senators are unlikely to oppose a nomination because they like having their state receive the honor and are well aware that should they reject the nominee, the president can simply select someone from another state.

Candidates for nomination are also much less likely to play a significant role in the recruitment process. Although there have been exceptions, most notably William Howard Taft, people seldom campaign for a position on the Court. Little can be accomplished through such activity, and because of the Court's standing, it might offend those who do play important roles in selecting nominees.

The American Bar Association's Standing Committee on the Federal Judiciary has played a varied, but typically more modest, role at the Supreme Court level than for nominations to lower courts. Usually the committee is asked to evaluate candidates for the Supreme Court only after the president has nominated them. The committee prefers to screen potential nominees before they are nominated, however, so it will not risk opposing the president's choice. Indeed, it has never found a nominee unqualified to serve on the Court.

Through 1998, there have been 148 nominations to the Supreme Court and 108 persons have served (4 people were nominated and confirmed twice, 8 declined appointments or died before beginning service on the Court, and 28 failed to secure Senate confirmation). Presidents, then, have failed 20 percent of the time to appoint the nominees of their choice to the Court—a percentage much higher than that for any other federal position.

Thus, although home-state senators do not play prominent roles in the selection process for the Court, the Senate as a whole does. In fact, through its Judiciary Committee it may probe a nominee's judicial philosophy in great detail.

For most of the twentieth century, Supreme Court nominations were routine affairs. Of the seven nominees that failed to receive Senate confirmation in this century (see Table 11–3), six have occurred since the presidency of John F. Kennedy. The 1960s were tumultuous times, which bred ideological conflict. Although Kennedy had no trouble with his two nominations to the Court (Byron White and Arthur Goldberg), his successor, Lyndon Johnson, was not so fortunate. He had to withdraw his nomination of Abe Fortas (already serving on the Court) to serve as chief justice, and therefore the Senate never voted on Homer Thornberry, Johnson's nominee to replace Fortas as an associate justice. Richard Nixon, the next president, had two nominees rejected in a row following bruising battles in the Senate.

The difficulties of these presidents are instructive. Liberal and civil rights groups opposed John J. Parker, Clement Haynsworth, and G. Harrold Carswell, and organized labor mounted active opposition against the first two men as well. Abe Fortas (who was already on the Court and had been nominated as chief justice) was opposed by conservative interests and charged with ethical violations, as was Haynsworth. Carswell was the only one of this group whose competence was seriously questioned. Haynsworth's and Carswell's troubles were compounded because they were Republican appointees facing a Democrat-controlled Senate, whereas Fortas was nominated at the end of President Johnson's term and Senate Republicans refused to confirm him in the hope that a Republican president would be elected and have the opportunity to nominate a new chief justice.

The last two failed nominations occurred in 1987. On June 26, Justice Lewis Powell announced his retirement from the Supreme Court. President Reagan had already been able to elevate Justice William Rehnquist to be

TABLE 11–3. Twentieth-Century Senate Rejections of Supreme Court Nominees

Nominee	Year	President
John J. Parker	1930	Hoover
Abe Fortas*	1968	Johnson
Homer Thornberry†	1968	Johnson
Clement F. Haynsworth, Jr.	1969	Nixon
G. Harrold Carswell	1970	Nixon
Robert H. Bork	1987	Reagan
Douglas H. Ginsburg*	1987	Reagan

*Nominations were withdrawn. (Fortas was serving on the Court as an associate justice and was nominated to be chief justice.)

†The Senate took no action on Thornberry's nomination.

chief justice and also had appointed Sandra Day O'Connor and Antonin Scalia. With yet another appointee, he would have a solid bloc of conservative votes on the Court for years to come.

Reagan nominated Judge Robert H. Bork to fill the vacancy. Everyone agreed that Bork was an intelligent and serious legal scholar, and he had also served in the Justice Department. (He was the individual who had fired special prosecutor Archibald Cox in the famous "Saturday Night Massacre" of Watergate fame.) At this point, agreement on his qualifications ended, however.

Bork testified before the Senate Judiciary Committee for twenty-three hours. At the end, his supporters portrayed him as a distinguished scholar who would practice "judicial restraint," deferring to Congress and the state legislatures and adhering to the precedents of the Supreme Court. Conversely, his opponents saw him as an extreme judicial activist who would use the Supreme Court to achieve conservative political ends, thus reversing decades of court decisions. A wide range of interest groups entered the fray, mostly in opposition to the nominee, and in the end, following a bitter floor debate, the Senate rejected the president's nomination by a vote of 58 to 42.

Six days after the Senate vote on Bork, the president nominated Douglas H. Ginsburg to the high court. Just nine days later, however, Ginsburg withdrew his nomination following disclosures that he had smoked marijuana at parties while a law professor at Harvard. Not until spring 1988 did Reagan finally succeed in filling the vacancy, with Anthony Kennedy.

In June 1991, at the end of the Supreme Court's term, Associate Justice Thurgood Marshall announced his retirement from the Court. Shortly thereafter, President Bush announced his nomination of another African American, federal appeals judge Clarence Thomas, to replace Marshall. Since Thomas was a conservative, this decision was consistent with the Bush administration's emphasis on placing conservative judges on the federal bench.

The president claimed that he was not employing quotas when he chose another African American to replace the only African American ever to sit on the Supreme Court, and argued that Thomas was simply the most qualified person for the job. This placed liberals in a dilemma. On the one hand, they favored having a minority group member serving on the nation's highest court. On the other hand, however, Thomas was unlikely to vote the same way as Thurgood Marshall. Instead, the new justice presented the prospect of strengthening the conservative trend in the Court's decisions. In the end, this ambivalence inhibited spirited opposition to Thomas, who was circumspect about his judicial philosophy in his appearances before the Senate Judiciary Committee, which sent his nomination to the Senate floor on a split vote.

Just as the Senate was about to vote on the nomination, however, charges of sexual harassment leveled against Thomas by University of Oklahoma law professor Anita Hill were made public. Hearings were reopened on the charges in response to criticism that the Senate was sexist for not seriously considering them in the first place. For several days, citizens sat transfixed before their television sets as Professor Hill calmly and graphically described her recollections of Thomas's behavior. Thomas then emphatically denied any such behavior and charged the Senate with racism for raising the issue. Ultimately, public opinion polls showed that most people believed Thomas, and he was confirmed by a vote of 52 to 48, the closest vote on a Supreme Court nomination in more than a century.

The Senate's treatment of President Clinton's nominees harkens back to the Kennedy era. Neither Ruth Bader Ginsburg nor Stephen Breyer caused much controversy. The Clinton administration undertook detailed background checks of potential nominees and floated several names to test public reaction prior to the president's announcements of his choices.[5] Whether the days of deference to the president on Supreme Court nominations have returned remains to be seen, especially now that the Republicans have a majority in the upper chamber.

The examples of recent failed nominations indicate that presidents are most likely to run into trouble under certain conditions. Presidents whose parties are in the minority in the Senate or who make a nomination at the end of their term face a greatly increased probability of substantial opposition. This is also the case for those who have the opportunity to nominate a justice whose confirmation would result in important shifts in the coalitions on the Court, and thus affect policy outcomes. Equally important, opponents of a nomination usually must be able to question a nominee's competence or ethics in order to defeat a nomination. Opposition based on a nominee's ideology is generally not considered a valid reason to vote against confirmation, as the case of Chief Justice William Rehnquist (who was strongly opposed by liberals) illustrates. Questions of the legal competence and ethics of nominees must usually be raised by their opponents in order to attract moderate senators to their side and make ideological protests seem less partisan.[6] A charge of scandal will weaken support for a nomination among the president's copartisans and galvanize the opposition.

Characteristics of Justices

Competence and ethical behavior are important to presidents for reasons beyond merely obtaining Senate confirmation of their nominees to the Court. Skilled and honorable justices reflect well on the president and will likely do so for many years. Moreover, they are more effective advocates, and thus can better serve the president's interests. In addition, presidents usually have enough respect for the Court and its work that they do not want to saddle it with a mediocre justice. Although the criteria of competence and character screen out some possible candidates, there is still a wide field from which the president may choose. Other characteristics then play prominent roles.

Like their colleagues on the lower federal courts, Supreme Court justices share many characteristics that are quite unlike those of the typical American. All have been lawyers, and all but four (Thurgood Marshall, nominated in 1967, Sandra Day O'Connor, nominated in 1981, Clarence Thomas, nominated in 1991, and Ruth Bader Ginsburg, nominated in 1993) have been white males. Most have been in their fifties and sixties when they took office, from the upper-middle to upper class, and Protestants.[7] (See Table 11–4 for some background information on the current Supreme Court.)

Race and gender have become more salient criteria in recent years. In the 1980 presidential campaign, Ronald Reagan promised to appoint a woman to a vacancy on the Court should he be elected. Geography once was a prominent criterion for selection to the Court but is no longer very important. Presidents do like to spread the slots around, however, as when Richard Nixon decided that he wanted to nominate a Southerner. At various times there have been what some have termed a "Jewish seat" and a "Catholic seat" on the Court, but these are not binding on the president. For example, after a half-century of having a Jewish justice, there was none between 1969 and 1993, until President Clinton nominated Ruth Bader Ginsburg to the Court.

Although presidents have often selected Supreme Court justices at least in part for their symbolic appeal to geographic, gender, racial, and religious

Table 11–4. Supreme Court Justices, 1999

	Year of Birth	Previous Position	Nominating President	Year of Appointment
William H. Rehnquist*	1924	Assistant U.S. Attorney General	Nixon	1971
John Paul Stevens	1920	U.S. Court of Appeals	Ford	1975
Sandra Day O'Connor	1930	State Court of Appeals	Reagan	1981
Antonin Scalia	1936	U.S. Court of Appeals	Reagan	1986
Anthony M. Kennedy	1936	U.S. Court of Appeals	Reagan	1988
David H. Souter	1939	U.S. Court of Appeals	Bush	1990
Clarence Thomas	1948	U.S. Court of Appeals	Bush	1991
Ruth Bader Ginsburg	1933	U.S. Court of Appeals	Clinton	1993
Stephen G. Breyer	1938	U.S. Court of Appeals	Clinton	1994

*William Rehnquist was promoted from associate justice to chief justice by President Reagan in 1986.

interests, such appointees may not actually provide these groups with much policy representation. There is evidence that most symbolic appointees do not vote for their own group's policy attitudes any more than do other members of the Court.[8]

Partisanship remains an important influence on the selection of justices; only 13 of 108 members were nominated by presidents of a different party. Moreover, many of the 13 exceptions were actually close to the president in ideology, as was the case in Richard Nixon's appointment of Lewis Powell. Herbert Hoover's nomination of Benjamin Cardozo seems to be one of the few cases where partisanship was completely subjugated to merit as a criterion for selection. However, usually over 90 percent of a president's judicial nominations are of members of his own party.

The role of partisanship is not really surprising even at the level of the highest court. Most of the presidents' acquaintances are in their own party, and there is usually a certain congruity between party and political views. The president may also use Supreme Court nominations as a reward, as when President Eisenhower nominated Earl Warren as chief justice. As leader of the California delegation to the 1952 Republican convention, Warren had played a crucial role in Eisenhower's obtaining of the Republican nomination for president. Many justices at one time were active partisans, which gave them visibility and helped them obtain the positions from which they moved to the Court.

Typically, justices have held high administrative or judicial positions before moving to the Supreme Court. Most have had some experience as a judge, often at the appellate level, and many have worked for the Department of Justice. Some have held high elected office, and a few have had no government service but rather have been distinguished attorneys. The fact that not all justices, including many of the most distinguished ones, have had previous judicial experience may seem surprising, but the unique work and environment of the Court renders this background much less important than it might be for other appellate courts.

PRESIDENT–SUPREME COURT RELATIONS

At the top of two complex branches of government stand the president and the Supreme Court. Each has significant powers. In a system of shared powers such as ours, it is not surprising that the president is interested in influencing the Court. In this section we examine efforts of the White House to mold the Court through filling vacancies, setting its agenda, and influencing and enforcing its decisions. We also look at interbranch relations that involve advising and other services.

Molding the Court

One of the most significant powers of the president lies in molding the Supreme Court through nominations. In effect, all presidents try to "pack" the courts. They want more than "justice"; they want policies with which they agree. Since justices serve for life, the impact of a president's selections will generally be felt long after that president has left office. As a result, the White House typically makes substantial efforts to ascertain the policy preferences of candidates for the Supreme Court.

Presidential aides survey candidates' decisions (if they have served on a lower court),[9] speeches, political stands, writings, and other expressions of opinion. They also turn to people who know the candidates well for information. Although it is considered improper to question judicial candidates about upcoming court cases, it is appropriate to discuss broader questions of political and judicial philosophy. The Reagan administration was especially concerned about such matters and had each potential nominee (for all judicial vacancies) fill out a lengthy questionnaire and be interviewed by a special committee in the Department of Justice.[10] The Bush administration, which was also attentive to nominating conservative judges, continued this practice.[11] Bill Clinton has been less concerned with the ideology of his nominees, at least partly to avoid costly confirmation fights. Instead, he has focused on identifying persons with strong legal credentials, especially women and minorities.

As a result of all this effort, presidents are generally satisfied with the actions of their nominees, especially those who had prior judicial experience to examine.[12] Liberalism and conservatism have several dimensions, including freedom, equality, and economic regulation, but the point is that policy preferences matter in judicial decision making, especially on the nation's highest court.[13] Thus, the right nominations can reinforce, slow, or alter trends in the Court's decisions. Franklin Roosevelt's nominees substantially liberalized the Court, while Richard Nixon's choices turned it in a basically conservative direction.

Nevertheless, it is not always easy to identify the policy inclinations of candidates, and presidents have been disappointed in their selections about a quarter of the time. President Eisenhower, for example, was displeased with the liberal decisions of both Earl Warren and William Brennan. Once when asked whether he had made any mistakes as president, he replied, "Yes, two, and they are both sitting on the Supreme Court."[14] Earlier, Woodrow Wilson was shocked by the very conservative positions of one of his nominees, James McReynolds. On a more limited scale, Richard Nixon was certainly disappointed when his nominee for chief justice, Warren Burger, authored the Court's decision calling for immediate desegregation of the nation's schools shortly after his confirmation. This did little for the president's "Southern strategy."

Presidents make what in their views are errors in nominations to the Court for several possible reasons, among them that they and their aides may have done a poor job of probing the views of candidates. Moreover, once on the Court, justices may change their attitudes and values over time because of new insights gained in their position, the normal process of aging, or the influence of other members of the Court. (Virtually all justices between 1801 and 1835 were strongly affected by Chief Justice John Marshall.) Justices are also often constrained by their obligation to follow precedents (when they are clear).

Some presidents have been relatively unconcerned with ideology in their nominations (see The Clinton Presidency box). In periods of relative political and social calm or when there is a solid majority on the Court that shares their views and likely to persist for several years, presidents might give less weight to policy preferences than to other criteria in choosing justices.

THE CLINTON PRESIDENCY

Clinton Decides Not to Pack the Courts

When Bill Clinton took office, many supporters were hoping he would quickly begin undoing a major legacy from twelve years of Republican control of the White House: a federal judiciary populated with conservative judges. These expectations have not been met, however. Although Clinton has nominated a record number of women and minorities to the federal bench, he has had little interest in ensuring that his nominees have been ideologically liberal.

The president was unwilling to spend political capital to win Senate confirmation for nominees labeled as liberal, especially after the Republicans took control of Congress following the 1994 congressional elections. As a result, Clinton's judges have been decidedly less liberal than those of other modern Democratic presidents.

In addition, the president has gone to extraordinary lengths to demonstrate his displeasure with some liberal decisions. Presiding over a drug case in February 1996, Judge Harold Baer, Jr., of the federal district court in Manhattan suppressed evidence of a videotaped confession and eighty pounds of cocaine and heroin found in the car of a confessed drug courier. The judge concluded that the police lacked reasonable suspicion for pulling the driver over. Although Judge Baer was one of Clinton's own nominees, the White House took the very unusual step of suggesting that if the judge did not change his mind, President Clinton might seek his resignation. Although some commentators criticized the president for violating the independence of the judiciary, Clinton stood his ground, and a few weeks later the judge reversed his decision.

Presidents cannot have much impact on the Court unless they have vacancies to fill, of course. Although, on the average, there has been an opening on the Supreme Court every two years, there is a substantial variance around this mean.[15] Franklin D. Roosevelt had to wait five years before he could nominate a justice, all the while being faced with a Court that found much of his New Deal legislation unconstitutional. In more recent years Jimmy Carter was never able to nominate a justice; indeed, between 1972 and 1984 there were only two vacancies on the Court. On the other hand, Richard Nixon was able to nominate four justices in his first three years in office.

Sometimes unusual steps are taken to enhance or limit a president's ability to fill vacancies. The size of the Supreme Court was altered many times between 1801 and 1869. In 1866 Congress reduced the size of the Court from ten to eight members so that Andrew Johnson could not nominate any new justices. When President Grant took office, Congress increased the number to nine since it had confidence he would nominate members to its liking. This number has remained unchanged since then, and it now seems inviolate. Franklin D. Roosevelt attempted to "pack" the court in 1937, when he proposed to add a justice to the Court for every justice currently serving who was over age seventy and had served ten years. This proposal was an obvious attempt to change the direction of Court decisions on his economic policies and, after a prolonged political battle, Congress refused to approve it. The refusal, however, was given only after the Court made a strategic reversal and began approving liberal legislation. Thus, Roosevelt lost the battle but won the war.

The president's role in Supreme Court judicial selection is not limited to the nomination of justices; it extends to the creation of positions as well. Justices are typically not prone to retirement, but presidents are sometimes frustrated enough at Court decisions to attempt to accelerate the creation of vacancies. Thomas Jefferson and his supporters tried to use impeachment to remove justices and thus gain control of the judiciary, which was largely Federalist (and thus anti-Jefferson). This strategy was abandoned, however, when, in 1805, the Senate failed to convict Justice Samuel Chase, who had made himself vulnerable with his partisan activities off the bench and injudicious remarks on it.

More often, presidents have relied on indirect pressure. Theodore Roosevelt resorted to leaks in the press in an unsuccessful effort to induce two justices to resign. More recently, the Nixon administration orchestrated a campaign to force liberal justice Abe Fortas to resign after he was accused of financial improprieties.

Justices also play the game of politics, of course, and may try to time their retirements so that a president with compatible views will choose their successor.[16] This is one reason why justices remain on the Court for so long, even when they are clearly infirm. William Brennan and Thurgood Marshall, the most senior justices on the Court in the 1980s, stayed through the Reagan years because their liberal views contrasted sharply with those of the president. William Howard Taft, a rigid conservative, even feared a successor being named by conservative Republican Herbert Hoover.

Such tactics do not always succeed. In 1968 Chief Justice Earl Warren submitted his resignation to President Johnson, whom he felt would select an acceptable successor. When Johnson's choice of Abe Fortas failed to win confirmation, however, the opportunity to nominate the new chief justice passed to Warren's old California political rival, newly elected president Richard Nixon.

Arguments in the Courts

The president may influence what cases the courts hear as well as who hears them. The solicitor general is a presidential appointee who must be confirmed by the Senate and serves in the Department of Justice.[17] It is he or she (not the attorney general) who supervises the litigation of the federal executive branch. In this position the solicitor general plays a major role in determining the agenda of federal appellate courts. Although able to exercise wide discretion, the solicitor general is subject to the direction of the attorney general and the president, with the latter playing a role in major cases.

The solicitor general decides which of the cases lost by the federal government in the federal district courts or the courts of appeal will be appealed to the next higher court. The courts of appeal must hear properly appealed cases, but the Supreme Court, for all practical purposes, has complete control over its own docket. Thus it is significant that the Court is far more likely to accept cases that the solicitor general wants to have heard than those from any other party.[18] Moreover, the amount of litigation involved is quite large. In recent years, the federal government has been a party to about half the cases heard in federal courts of appeals and the Supreme Court.

The executive branch also participates in cases to which it is not directly a party. The solicitor general files *amicus curiae* (friend of the court) briefs supporting or opposing the efforts of other parties before the Court. These cases range from school busing for racial integration and abortion rights to equal pay for women. Once again, the Court usually grants the government's request to participate in this way.

When a case reaches the Supreme Court, the solicitor general supervises the preparation of the government's arguments in support of its position, whether it is a direct party or an *amicus*. These arguments are often reflected

*"Do you ever have one of those days when every-
thing seems un-Constitutional?"*

Source: Drawing by Jow Mirachi. Copyright © 1974 The New Yorker Magazine, Inc.

in Court decisions and thus become the law of the land. Since the government has participated in almost every major controversy decided by the courts in the past fifty years, the potential influence of the executive branch on public policy through the courts is substantial. Moreover, both as a direct party and as an *amicus,* the federal government wins a clear majority of the time.[19]

The government's success is due to several factors. The solicitor general builds credibility with the Court by not making frivolous appeals and, in a few instances, even by telling the Court that the government should not have won cases in lower courts. Equally important, the solicitor general and his or her staff (again, not the attorney general) develop more expertise in dealing with the Court than anyone else since they appear before it more frequently, and they will provide the Court with high-quality briefs.

On a very rare occasion the president may directly attempt to influence a Court decision. For example, in a very unusual move in 1969, Department of Justice officials visited Justice Brennan and Chief Justice Warren to alert them that the administration was worried about the outcomes of some wiretapping cases on the Court's agenda. The administration was concerned that the Court's decisions would force the discontinuance of its surveillance of embassies or its prosecutions based on the information obtained from them. According to Warren, this visit had no influence on the Court's decision making.[20]

Enforcing Court Decisions

Another important relationship between the judicial and executive branches involves the enforcement of court decisions. Although the executive branch provides the federal courts with United States marshals, they are too few and lack sufficient authority to be of systematic aid, especially if a court order is directed against a coordinate branch of government. Thus, the courts must often rely on the president to enforce their decisions, especially their more controversial ones.

The Constitution is, not surprisingly, ambiguous as to the president's responsibility for aiding the judicial branch. Although it never explicitly discusses the point, it does assign the president the responsibility to "take care that the laws be faithfully executed." Typically, presidents have responded to support the courts or, at least, the rule of law. On several occasions, such as during the efforts of Presidents Eisenhower and Kennedy to integrate educational institutions, presidents have gone so far as to deploy federal troops to ensure compliance with court orders.

Presidents may use the carrot as well as the stick to encourage others to comply with Court decisions. One of the most significant and controversial Supreme Court decisions of this century was *Brown v. Board of Education* (347 U.S. 483, 1954), which called for an end to segregation in the public schools. Compliance with this decision was a long and tortuous process, but it was aided by the passage of laws that provide federal aid only for school districts that do not segregate and that provide schools with extra funds to help ease the process of desegregation.

There have been exceptions to presidential cooperation, however. In *Worcester v. Georgia* (6 Peters 515, 1832), the Court found that the state of Georgia had no authority over Cherokee Indian lands and that missionaries arrested there by the state should be released. The Court also implied that it was the president's responsibility to enforce its decision. Georgia refused to comply with the decision, however, and President Andrew Jackson took no actions to enforce it. He is reputed to have stated, "Well, [Chief Justice] John Marshall has made his decision, now let him enforce it."

Other Relationships

In the earliest years of our nation, the line of separation between the executive and judicial branches was vague and was often crossed. President George Washington consulted with the chief justice on a range of matters and received written advisory opinions on matters of law. Washington even used the first two chief justices as diplomats to negotiate with other countries. The chief justice was also placed on a commission to manage the fund for paying off the national debt.

This interbranch cooperation did not last long, however. The diplomatic efforts of justices were criticized by many, the Court decided against providing further advisory opinions, and the frequency of informal consultation between the White House and justices declined. The Court also refused to examine pension claims for the secretary of the treasury. The years of Jefferson's presidency were marked by hostility between the president and the judiciary, which was populated primarily by his Federalist political enemies.

In recent decades, the most notable formal exceptions to a strict separation between the two branches have been Justice Robert Jackson's service as chief American prosecutor at the Nuremberg trials of Nazi leaders following World War II and Chief Justice Earl Warren's chairmanship of the commission investigating the assassination of President Kennedy. Abe Fortas received a great deal of criticism for his activities as an informal adviser to President Johnson on a wide range of issues. In the words of one biographer, while on the Court, "Fortas served as political advisor, speechwriter, crisis manager, administration headhunter, legal expert, war counselor, or just plain cheerleader."[21]

This type of relationship has occurred from time to time, however (principally between justices and the presidents who appointed them), continuing a pattern established before the justice reached the Court. Felix Frankfurter continued to advise Franklin D. Roosevelt after he took his seat on the court, as did Louis Brandeis for Wilson,[22] Chief Justice Fred Vinson for Truman,[23] and a number of others throughout our history.

More striking perhaps is the fact that Chief Justice Warren Burger appears to have discussed the Court's internal activities and issues pending before it with President Nixon and other top administration officials.[24] This would seem to be a breach of the separation of powers. Burger also appears to have asked Nixon to use his influence with congressional Republicans to discourage them from proceeding with their attempt to impeach Justice William O. Douglas.

COMPLYING WITH THE COURT

It is one thing for the White House to enforce a court decision against someone else, and something quite different for it to comply with an order directed at the president after he has lost a case in the Supreme Court. At that point, interesting constitutional questions arise that have the potential for substantial interbranch conflict. However, presidents typically do comply with court orders, a task that is made easier by the general deference of the courts to the chief executive.

Presidential Compliance

The Constitution is ambiguous about which branch shall have the final say in interpreting it. The Supreme Court made some progress in resolving this question in *Marbury v. Madison* (1 Cranch 137, 1803), in which it voided an act of Congress for the first time and asserted its right to make the final judgment on the constitutionality of actions of the other branches of government. *Marbury* did not really settle the question of the president's obligation to accept and follow the Court's interpretation of the Constitution, however, because the president could argue that the law the Court had voided actually pertained directly only to the Court's own branch, the judiciary. It was not until *Dred Scott v. Sanford* (19 Howard 393, 1857) that the Court again declared an act of Congress unconstitutional, and this time, the law was not directly related to the judiciary.

Several presidents, including Jefferson, Lincoln, and Franklin D. Roosevelt, have threatened privately to disobey Court decisions that went against them, but in each case defiance was unnecessary because the Court supported them. The most blatant instance of a president's threatening to disobey a Court order occurred in a case in which the Court was asked to enjoin President Andrew Johnson from administering military governments in Southern states following the Civil War. In oral argument before the Court, the president, speaking through his attorney general, let it be known that he would not comply with a decision enjoining him from implementing the laws. The Court, in turn, found in *Mississippi v. Johnson* (4 Wallace 475, 1867) that it lacked jurisdiction to stop the president from performing official duties that required executive discretion; consequently, the issue failed to come to a head. We should also note that Johnson had vetoed these bills when Congress passed them, yet once they were passed, the president faced impeachment if he failed to execute them.

Presidents typically have obeyed Court decisions even when it has been costly to do so. There are two prominent examples of this in recent years. First, near the end of President Truman's tenure and during the Korean War, the United Steelworkers of America gave notice of an industrywide strike. Concerned about steel production during wartime, the president ordered the secretary of commerce to seize and operate the steel mills. The steel companies then asked the courts to find the president's actions unconstitutional and, in *Youngstown Sheet and Tube Co. v. Sawyer* (343 U.S. 579, 1952), the Supreme Court did so. It found that the president lacked inherent power under the Constitution to seize the steel mills and that Congress had chosen not to give him statutory power to do so. Thus, in a rare occurrence, the president was ordered to reverse his actions, and Truman immediately complied.

The Watergate scandal produced another important case involving presidential prerogatives. The special prosecutor, Leon Jaworski, subpoenaed tapes and documents relating to sixty-four conversations of President Nixon with his aides and advisers. Jaworski needed the material for the prosecution of Nixon administration officials, but the president claimed that executive privilege protected his private conversations with his assistants and refused to produce the subpoenaed material. Thus, the case worked its way quickly to the Supreme Court.

In *United States v. Nixon* (418 U.S. 683, 1974), the Court unanimously ordered the president to turn the subpoenaed material over to the special prosecutor. Although Nixon had threatened not to comply with anything less than a "definitive" decision, he obeyed the Court. The Court held that a claim of executive privilege unrelated to military, diplomatic, or national security matters cannot be absolute and in this case must give way to considerations of due process of law in criminal proceedings. Moreover, the justices reaffirmed that it was they, and not the president, who must be the final judge in such matters. Nixon resigned the presidency about two weeks later.[25] For a more recent case on presidential prerogatives, see the Hot-Button Issue box.

Presidents have not always been responsive to court orders, however. For example, in *United States v. Burr* (25 Fed. Cas. 187, No. 14,964, 1807), President Jefferson was subpoenaed to appear at the treason trial of Aaron Burr and to produce a certain letter. Jefferson refused to appear at the trial

---

☀ HOT-BUTTON ISSUE

Is the President Immune from Private Lawsuits?

Paula Jones sued Bill Clinton over "abhorrent" sexual advances that she claimed he made to her while he was governor of Arkansas and over punishment that she claimed she received from her supervisors in her state job after she rejected the governor's advances. The White House, fearing a media circus surrounding the embarrassing charges, claimed that while in office, the president was immune from private civil litigation arising out of events that occurred before he took office. The Supreme Court saw things differently and, in *Clinton v. Jones* (1997) the Court held that the president enjoyed no such immunity. Preparations for the trial went forward, but the presiding judge dismissed the case as frivolous shortly before it was scheduled to begin in 1998.

but he did provide the document, while stressing that he did so voluntarily and not because of judicial writ. Similarly, President James Monroe was subpoenaed as a witness in a trial, but he sent a written response instead.

The Civil War raised many difficult constitutional questions for the Court and the president. One set of cases found President Abraham Lincoln simply ignoring court orders. The president had suspended the writ of habeas corpus, which requires the government to explain why a person has been detained, and in the most famous of these cases, a citizen held prisoner by the military sued for his freedom. Chief Justice Roger Taney ordered his release, but Lincoln refused to give him up to the U.S. marshal sent to bring him into court. The chief justice (on circuit court duty) then held, in *Ex parte Merryman* (17 Fed. Cas. 144, No. 9,487, 1861), that the president had exceeded his constitutional authority (the Constitution seems to give only Congress the power to suspend habeas corpus), but Lincoln simply ignored the decision and Merryman remained under arrest. Lincoln argued that he had not violated the Constitution, but that in any case, it would be better for the president to violate a single provision to a limited extent than to incur anarchy because of failure to suppress the rebellion in the South.

Another aspect of presidential compliance with Court decisions is the administration of laws that the Court has approved and that the president opposes. This issue has arisen most directly with the claims of some presidents to the right to decide not to execute laws that they view as unconstitutional, even if they have received court approval. Jefferson's opposition to the Alien and Sedition acts, which were passed under his predecessor John Adams and upheld by the courts, led him to stop all prosecutions and pardon all those who had been convicted under these laws when he took office. Similarly, Andrew Jackson dismantled the Bank of the United States although the Court had approved it as constitutional.

This issue has never been really resolved, and presidents have often been lax in administering laws that they oppose. George Bush declared sections of bills that he had signed into law to be unconstitutional and therefore unenforceable, but the administration's actions did not result in court battles.[26] The Nixon administration was ordered by federal courts to more strictly enforce laws to eliminate segregation and sex discrimination in public educational institutions. Such court orders are rare, however.

If presidents are dissatisfied with Supreme Court decisions, their first thought is usually directed toward appointing new members with views similar to theirs. There are some other options, however. They may join in congressional efforts to remove certain types of cases from the Court's appellate jurisdiction.[27] Alternatively, they might support efforts to pass a constitutional amendment to overturn a Court interpretation of the Constitution, as George Bush did when the Court held that the burning of the

American flag was a form of protected speech. President Reagan supported amendments to allow prayer in public schools and to prohibit abortions. Such efforts rarely succeed, however, and Reagan's and Bush's attempts did not. On the other hand, when the Court has made a statutory interpretation in which it interprets an act of Congress, its decision can be reversed simply by changing the law to clarify the intentions of those supporting the policy.[28] In a notable example, in 1953 President Eisenhower supported legislation that deeded federal mineral rights on offshore lands to the states even though the Court had held in 1951 that the federal government owned the rights.

Deference to the President

A principal reason why complying with judicial decisions has rarely posed a problem for the president is the small number of instances in which the courts have held presidential actions to be in violation of the Constitution. Rarely have even these decisions interfered significantly with the president's policies (the *Youngstown* case being a major exception). More typically, these cases have dealt with matters such as presidential instructions to customs officials or the suspension of the writ of habeas corpus.

Most presidential actions are not based on the president's prerogatives under the Constitution and therefore do not lend themselves to constitutional adjudication. Effective opposition to most presidential policies must focus on the broader political arena. Moreover, it is especially difficult to prevent the president from acting. Most challenges occur only after the fact. On some occasions it is possible to oppose the president by challenging the constitutionality of laws he supported and Congress passed. Such efforts are rarely successful, but they were important during the early years of the New Deal. In the end, however, President Roosevelt prevailed.

In the area of foreign and defense policy, the Court has interpreted the Constitution and statutes so as to give the president broad discretion to act. In general, the history of litigation regarding challenges to the president's actions in the field of national security policy has been one of avoidance, postponement of action, or deference to the chief executive, particularly during the time frame in which the action occurs. The judiciary has been content to find that discretionary actions of the executive branch were beyond its competence to adjudicate.[29]

Since the Civil War, presidents have been allowed especially broad powers in wartime. In that conflict the Supreme Court approved President Lincoln's deployment of troops during hostilities in the absence of a declaration of war and gave the chief executive discretion to determine the extent of force the crisis demanded and when an emergency existed. Similarly, it upheld the president's blockade of the South, the expansion of the army and navy beyond statutory limits, the calling out of the militia, and most of his suspensions of habeas corpus. He spent public funds without appropriations, declared martial law in various areas, ordered people arrested without warrant, tried civilians in military courts, closed the use of the Post Office for "treasonable" correspondence, seized property, and emancipated slaves—all without interference from the courts.[30]

During World War I, Congress delegated President Woodrow Wilson broad authority to regulate commissions, transportation, and the economy; to draft soldiers; and even to censor criticism—all with the approval of the Court. Franklin D. Roosevelt exercised even broader economic powers during World War II: He relocated Japanese Americans from the West Coast to relocation centers and confiscated their property, and he bypassed the courts to establish special military commissions to try Nazi saboteurs, again with the Court's approval.

During the period of U.S. military involvement in Vietnam, no declaration or other formal congressional authorization for the war was ever issued. Many people, including many legal authorities, felt that this country's participation in the war without a formal declaration by Congress was unconstitutional, and several dozen cases were brought in federal court by opponents of the war to challenge various aspects of its legality. However, the Supreme Court simply refused to hear all but one of these cases and never issued a written opinion regarding the war. A combination of deference to the president and pragmatic politics (one wonders what would have happened had the war been declared unconstitutional while troops were engaged in combat) rendered the Court irrelevant to the issue.[31]

Similarly, a district court refused to hear a suit brought by several members of Congress that challenged George Bush's expansion of U.S. forces in the Persian Gulf in 1991 as a prelude to war. In this case the court simply found that the country was not yet at war, and thus there was no basis for the suit. Another court also found the military to be within its rights to inoculate members of the armed forces against biological weapons, even without their permission, so as to facilitate the preparation for war in the Gulf.

It is interesting that in times in which presidents are most likely to stretch their power (that is, in wartime), the courts are the least likely to intervene. When they finally do, the war may already be over. For example, following both the Civil War and World War II, the Supreme Court held that military tribunals could not try civilians while the civilian courts were open. In each case, however, the president at whom the decision was directed was no longer living.

During peacetime, the courts have found that presidents also have substantial discretion to act in the areas of foreign affairs and defense. They have broad prerogatives to act in negotiating and executing international agreements, withholding state secrets from the public, allocating international airline routes, terminating treaties, making executive agreements, recognizing foreign governments, using military activities to protect American interests abroad, punishing foreign adversaries, and acquiring and divesting foreign territory.

In the domestic sphere the president's prerogatives are closely linked to maintaining order. Thus, presidents have discretion to declare and terminate national emergencies and even martial law. They may also call out the militia or the regular armed forces to control internal friction and keep the peace.

Of course, a president does not always receive supportive decisions from the courts. President Clinton was not allowed to invoke executive privilege to prevent his aides from answering questions posed by Independent Counsel Kenneth Starr before a grand jury. Similarly, President Nixon was told that he could not impound funds appropriated by Congress, engage in electronic surveillance without a search warrant, or prevent the publication of the *Pentagon Papers*. He also was forced to turn over the Watergate tapes. However, Nixon's presidency was atypical, and most presidents operate under few constraints from the courts.

It is not unusual for actions of executive branch officials to be found in violation of statutes passed by Congress, usually for exceeding the discretionary limits in the law. In these situations the judiciary generally finds that the law, not the Constitution, must be changed (or perhaps just clarified) before the president's agents can take certain actions. Depending on the prevailing view in Congress, this may pose little problem for the president. At any rate, rarely are the issues involved central to his program.

JUDICIAL POWERS

In addition to enforcing court orders, presidents have some judicial instruments of their own. For example, they can issue pardons, grant clemency, and proclaim amnesty. These powers are exclusively theirs.

Over the years the exercise of this judicial authority by presidents has sparked controversy. Gerald Ford's unconditional pardon of his predecessor, Richard Nixon, in 1974 became a major political issue that adversely affected Ford's electability two years later. Issued prior to a conviction or even an indictment of the former president, the pardon, "for all offenses against the United States which Richard Nixon has committed or may have committed or taken part in during the period from January 20, 1969, through August 9, 1974," precluded any criminal prosecution. Although Ford was accused of subverting the legal process, his power to issue the pardon was not disputed.[32] Whether Nixon's acceptance of it amounted to an admission of guilt is also unclear.

In addition to the issuance of unconditional pardons, presidents may grant conditional reprieves. In 1954 the Supreme Court upheld President Eisenhower's commutation of a death sentence provided that the individual never be paroled, and in 1972 President Nixon granted executive clemency to former labor leader James Hoffa on the condition that he refrain from further union activities.

Presidents may also issue general amnesty to those who have impeded war efforts. President Lincoln exercised this authority in 1863 in an effort to persuade Southern deserters to return to the Union. In order to heal the wounds of the Civil War, his successor, Andrew Johnson, in 1868 granted universal amnesty to all those who had participated in the insurrection. Twentieth-century presidents have used this power to pardon those individuals who were convicted of crimes and subsequently served in the military and to prevent the imposition of wartime penalties (still on the books) on those who failed to register for the draft during peacetime.

The most sweeping and controversial amnesty proclamation in recent times occurred in 1977 when, implementing one of his campaign promises, President Carter pardoned all Vietnam draft resisters and asked the Defense Department to consider, on an individual basis, the cases of military deserters during that war. Congress attempted to undercut Carter's general pardon by prohibiting the use of funds to execute his order, but was unsuccessful because the president's directive to the Justice Department did not require a separate appropriation.

CONCLUSION

Presidents are involved in vital relationships with the judicial branch, especially the Supreme Court. They attempt to influence its decisions through the process of selecting judges and justices and through the arguments of their subordinates before the courts. There are strong congressional constraints on them in the selection of judges, however, and presidents sometimes err in their choice of nominees. Although the executive branch has skilled litigators before the federal appellate courts and a clear record of success, the chief executive is ultimately dependent on the judgment of members of a branch of government that is much more autonomous than the legislature. The president is once again a facilitator, not a director, of change.

A judicial decision does not end a president's relationship with the courts on an issue, as in the capacity as chief executive, a president may be obliged to enforce judicial decisions (a responsibility that sometimes conflicts with policy goals). Moreover, although the judiciary is generally deferential to presidents, the courts may order a president to comply with a holding against a presidential action. Such decisions fail to affect most of what presidents do, but in some instances they do hamper their actions. Thus, the president's relations with the courts are characterized both by conflict and by harmony, and influencing judicial decisions remains an important, but at times frustrating, priority for the White House.

DISCUSSION QUESTIONS

1. President Clinton is facing considerable opposition to his judicial nominees. What should be the role of the Senate in the confirmation process? Should an opposition-controlled Senate oppose nominees who share the president's views, or should the Senate simply be a check on the nominees' basic qualifications?
2. What criteria should the president employ when choosing judicial nominees? Should racial, gender, and partisan criteria be used? What is the role of ideological considerations, such as whether a nominee believes in judicial activism or restraint?
3. Should the president be immune from civil lawsuits from private individuals while serving in office? Was the Supreme Court correct to state that such suits would not be a drain on the president's time and energy and that there would not be many frivolous suits? Did the Paula Jones suit distract President Clinton or encourage him to be more presidential in behavior?

WEB EXERCISES

1. Listen to the oral arguments before the Supreme Court in the case of *Clinton v. Jones* (1987). You can also read the transcript of the argument. Go to <http://court.it-services.nwu.edu/oyez/support/cases/844/argument.html>.
2. Read the Supreme Court's decision in *United States v. Nixon* (1974). Note how the Court denied the president's claim of executive privilege while at the same time establishing the principle of executive privilege for the first time in a Supreme Court case. Go to <http://court.it-services.nwu.edu/oyez/cases/case.pl?case_id=410&mode=show>.

SELECTED READING

Abraham, Henry J. *Justices and Presidents: A Political History of Appointments to the Supreme Court,* 3rd ed. New York: Oxford University Press, 1992.

Bond, Jon R. "The Politics of Court Structure: The Addition of New Federal Judges, 1949–1978." *Law and Policy Quarterly* 2 (April 1980): 181–188.

Caplan, Lincoln. *The Tenth Justice: The Solicitor General and the Rule of Law.* New York: Random House, 1987.

Ducat, Craig R., and Robert L. Dudley. "Federal District Judges and Presidential Power during the Postwar Era." *Journal of Politics* 51 (February 1989): 98–118.

Goldman, Sheldon. *Picking Federal Judges.* New Haven, Conn.: Yale University Press, 1997.

Maltese, John Anthony. *The Selling of Supreme Court Nominees.* Baltimore: Johns Hopkins University Press, 1995.

Murphy, Bruce Allen. *Fortas.* New York: William Morrow, 1988.

O'Brien, David M. "The Reagan Judges: His Most Enduring Legacy?" In Charles O. Jones, ed., *The Reagan Legacy,* pp. 60–101. Chatham, N.J.: Chatham House, 1988.

Rowland, C. K., Robert A. Carp, and Ronald Stidham. "Judges' Policy Choices and the Value Basis of Judicial Appointments." *Journal of Politics* 46 (August 1984): 886–902.

Rowland, C. K., and Bridget Jeffery Todd. "Where You Stand Depends on Who Sits: Platform Promises and Judicial Gatekeeping in the Federal District Courts." *Journal of Politics* 53 (February 1991): 175–185.

Schmidhauser, John R. *Judges and Justices: The Federal Appellate Judiciary.* Boston: Little, Brown, 1979.

Scigliano, Robert. *The Supreme Court and the Presidency.* New York: Free Press, 1971.

Stidham, Ronald, Robert A. Carp, and C. K. Rowland. "Patterns of Presidential Influence on the Federal District Courts: An Analysis of the Appointment Process." *Presidential Studies Quarterly* 14 (Fall 1984): 548–560.

Walker, Thomas G., and Deborah J. Barrow. "The Diversification of the Federal Bench: Policy and Process Ramifications." *Journal of Politics* 47 (May 1985): 596–617.

Notes

1. Quoted in J. Woodford Howard, Jr., *Courts of Appeals in the Federal Judicial System: A Study of the Second, Fifth, and District of Columbia Circuits* (Princeton: Princeton University Press, 1981), p. 101.

2. Griffin Bell quoted in Nina Totenberg, "Will Judges Be Chosen Rationally?" *Judicature* 60 (August/September 1976): 93.

3. See Jon R. Bond, "The Politics of Court Structure: The Addition of New Federal Judges, 1949–1978," *Law and Policy Quarterly* 2 (April 1980): 181–188.

4. On the impact of the background of members of the judiciary, see Robert A. Carp and C. K. Rowland, *Policymaking and Politics in the Federal District Courts* (Knoxville: University of Tennessee Press, 1983); C. Neal Tate, "Personal Attribute Models of the Voting Behavior of United States Supreme Court Justices: Liberalism in Civil Liberties and Economics Decisions, 1946–1978," *American Political Science Review* 75 (June 1981): 355–367; C. K. Rowland, Robert A. Carp, and Ronald Stidham, "Judges' Policy Choices and the Value Basis of Judicial Appointments," *Journal of Politics* 46 (August 1984): 886–902; Ronald Stidham, Robert A. Carp, and C. K. Rowland, "Patterns of Presidential Influence on the Federal District Courts: An Analysis of the Appointment Process," *Presidential Studies Quarterly* 14 (Fall 1984): 548–560; C. K. Rowland, Donald R. Songer, and Robert A. Carp, "Presidential Effects on Criminal Justice in the Lower Federal Courts: The Reagan Judges," *Law and Society Review* 22, no. 1 (1988): 191–200; John Gottschall, "Reagan Appointments to the United States Court of Appeals: The Continuation of a Judicial Revolution," *Judicature* (June/July 1986): 48–54; Timothy B. Tomasi and Jess A. Velona, "All the President's Men? A Study of Ronald Reagan's Appointments to the U.S. Courts of Appeals," *Columbia Law Review* 87 (May 1987): 766–793; C. K. Rowland and Bridget Jeffery Todd, "Where You Stand Depends on Who Sits: Platform Promises and Judicial Gatekeeping in the Federal District Courts," *Journal of Politics* 53 (February 1991): 175–185; and Robert A. Carp, Donald Songer, C. K. Rowland, Ronald Stidham, and Lisa Richey-Tracy, "The Voting Behavior of Judges Appointed by President Bush," *Judicature* 76 (April/May 1993): 298–302. On the impact of female and minority judges, see Thomas G. Walker and Deborah J. Barrow, "The Diversification of the Federal Bench: Policy and Process Ramifications," *Journal of Politics* 47 (May 1985): 596–617.

5. See John Anthony Maltese, *The Selling of Supreme Court Nominees* (Baltimore: Johns Hopkins University Press, 1995).

6. See John Massaro, *Supremely Political* (Albany: State University of New York Press, 1992); Charles M. Cameron, Albert D. Cover, and Jeffrey A. Segal, "Senate Voting on Supreme Court Nominees: A Neoinstitutional Model," *American Political Science Review* 84 (June 1990): 525–534; Jeffrey Segal, "Senate Confirmation of Supreme Court Justices: Partisan and Institutional Politics," *Journal of Politics* 49 (November 1987): 998–1015; and P. S. Ruckman, Jr., "The Supreme Court, Critical Nominations, and the Senate Confirmation Process," *Journal of Politics* 55 (August 1993): 793–805.

7. On the background of justices, see John R. Schmidhauser, *Judges and Justices: The Federal Appellate Judiciary* (Boston: Little, Brown, 1979).

8. Thomas R. Marshall, "Symbolic versus Policy Representation on the U.S. Supreme Court," *Journal of Politics* 55 (February 1993): 140–150.

9. One study found, however, that judicial experience is not related to the congruence of presidential preferences and the justices' decisions on racial equality cases. See John Gates and Jeffrey Cohen, "Presidents, Supreme Court Justices, and Racial Equality Cases: 1954–1984," *Political Behavior* 10, no. 1 (1988): 22–35.

10. David M. O'Brien, "The Reagan Judges: His Most Enduring Legacy?" in Charles O. Jones, ed., *The Reagan Legacy* (Chatham, NJ: Chatham House, 1988), pp. 60–101.

11. Sheldon Goldman, "The Bush Imprint on the Judiciary: Carrying on a Tradition," *Judicature* 74 (April/May 1991): 294–306.

12. Robert Scigliano, *The Supreme Court and the Presidency* (New York: Free Press, 1971).

13. See, for example, David W. Rohde and Harold J. Spaeth, *Supreme Court Decision Making* (San Francisco: W. H. Freeman, 1976); Jeffrey A. Segal and Albert O. Cover, "Ideological Values and the Votes of U.S. Supreme Court Justices," *American Political Science Review* 83 (June 1989): 557–566; and Tracey E. George and Lee Epstein, "On the Nature of Supreme Court Decision Making," *American Political Science Review* 86 (June 1992): 323–337.

14. Dwight Eisenhower quoted in Henry J. Abraham, *Justices and Presidents: A Political History of Appointments to the Supreme Court*, 3rd ed. (New York: Oxford University Press, 1992), p. 266.

15. See Gary King, "Presidential Appointments to the Supreme Court: Adding Systematic Explanation to Probabilistic Description," *American Politics Quarterly* 15 (July 1987): 373–386.

16. On the importance of ideology and partisanship considerations in judicial retirement and resignation decisions, see Deborah J. Barrow and Gary Zuk, "An Institutional Analysis of Turnover in the Lower Federal Courts, 1900–1987," *Journal of Politics* 52 (May 1990): 457–476; and Gary Zuk, Gerard S. Gryski, and Deborah J. Barrow, "Partisan Transformation of the Federal Judiciary, 1869–1992," *American Politics Quarterly* 21 (October 1993): 439–457.

17. See Rebecca Mae Salokar, *The Solicitor General* (Philadelphia: Temple University Press, 1992); and Lincoln Caplan, *The Tenth Justice: The Solicitor General and the Rule of Law* (New York: Random House, 1987).

18. On the Court's acceptance of cases, see H. W. Perry, Jr., *Deciding to Decide: Agenda Setting in the United States Supreme Court* (Cambridge: Harvard University Press, 1991); Doris Marie Provine, *Case Selection in the United States Supreme Court* (Chicago: University of Chicago Press, 1980); and Stuart H. Teger and Douglas Kosinski, "The Cue Theory of Supreme Court Certiorari Jurisdiction: A Reconsideration," *Journal of Politics* 42 (August 1980): 834–846.

19. On the solicitor general's success, see Jeffrey A. Segal, "Courts, Executives, and Legislatures," in John B. Gates and Charles A. Johnson, eds., *The American Courts* (Washington, D.C.: Congressional Quarterly Press, 1991), pp. 376–382.

20. Earl Warren, *The Memoirs of Chief Justice Earl Warren* (Garden City, N.Y.: Doubleday, 1971), pp. 337–342.

21. Bruce Allen Murphy, *Fortas* (New York: William Morrow, 1988), p. 235. Murphy chronicles the Johnson-Fortas relationship in great detail. See also Joseph A. Califano, Jr., *The Triumph and Tragedy of Lyndon Johnson* (New York: Simon and Schuster, 1991), pp. 95–96, 118, 120, 153–154, 161–163, 189, 191, 205, 213–218, 298, 306, 312–315.

22. Bruce Allen Murphy, *The Brandeis/Frankfurter Connection: The Secret Political Activities of Two Supreme Court Justices* (New York: Oxford University Press, 1982).

23. See Clark Clifford, *Counsel to the President* (New York: Random House, 1991), p. 215; and David McCullough, *Truman* (New York: Simon and Schuster, 1992), p. 897.

24. John Ehrlichman, *Witness to Power: The Nixon Years* (New York: Simon and Schuster, 1982), p. 133.

25. In a more recent case involving privileged information, President Clinton initially refused to turn over to a Senate committee the notes from a White House meeting in which lawyers for the president met with senior aides. When the Senate threatened to subpoena the notes, however, the president yielded.

26. Charles Tiefer, *The Semi-Sovereign Presidency* (Boulder, Colo.: Westview, 1994), chap. 3.

27. Congress has succeeded in such an action only once, however—on jurisdiction to hear appeals on certain writ of habeas corpus cases following the Civil War—and in this case, the president supported the Court.

28. William N. Eskridge, "Overriding Supreme Court Statutory Interpretation Decisions," *Yale Law Journal* 101 (1991): 331–455; Joseph Ignagni and James Meernik, "Explaining Congressional Attempts to Reverse Supreme Court Decisions," *Political Research Quarterly* 10 (June 1994): 353–372. See also R. Shep Melnick, *Between the Lines: Interpreting Welfare Rights* (Washington, D.C.: Brookings Institution, 1994).

29. See, for example, Craig R. Ducat and Robert L. Dudley, "Federal District Judges and Presidential Power during the Postwar Era," *Journal of Politics* 51 (February 1989): 98–118.

30. Forrest McDonald, *The American Presidency: An Intellectual History* (Lawrence: University Press of Kansas, 1994), pp. 398–402.

31. Anthony A. D'Amato and Robert M. O'Neil, *The Judiciary and Vietnam* (New York: St. Martin's, 1972).

32. There were many allegations of a deal between the two men, and some observers even accused Ford of having agreed to the pardon in exchange for his nomination as vice president by Nixon. However, in sworn testimony before the House Judiciary Committee in 1974, Ford vehemently denied that such an agreement had been made.

12

Domestic Policy Making

THE FRAMERS OF THE CONSTITUTION GAVE PRESIDENTS a policy role, but they did not expect them to dominate that policy. Yet that is precisely what has occurred. Seizing on the initiative that the Constitution provides—and which their central perspective, institutional structure, and political support facilitate—presidents have become chief policy makers. Today, the public expects presidents to propose and achieve national goals. They are expected to redeem campaign promises, to respond to policy emergencies, and to propose solutions to the country's social, economic, and political ills on a regular basis. Failure to address critical issues and rectify national problems will likely result in public criticism and perhaps even electoral defeat should unsatisfactory conditions persist.

The problem that presidents face in performing their leadership role is that public expectations often exceed their ability to meet them. They have at their disposal significant policy expertise, but the experts are not always in agreement on what to do or how to do it. They have considerable institutional resources in their presidential office and the executive branch, but they cannot control the behavior of those in other branches of government, much less those outside the government who affect that behavior. They have difficulty even overseeing the actions of those who are presumably subordinate to them. Finally, they have political clout, but that clout varies with time and circumstances and they cannot always exercise it effectively. Thus, the president's policy role is not an easy one, but it is a critical one for success in office. This chapter will focus on presidential leadership of domestic public policy.

The president's domestic policy role did not evolve gradually; it developed in response to policy problems during the twentieth century. To begin the chapter, we describe those responses and chronicle the growth of the president's role. Next we discuss the mechanism and processes that have been established to help meet these enlarged responsibilities. Initially we focus on the work of the Office of Management and Budget (known as the Bureau of the Budget prior to 1970) in the clearance and coordination of policy initiatives and regulations emanating from the executive departments and agencies. We then turn to the White House and the development of a domestic policy office from Johnson to Clinton. Finally, we look at policy-making strategies and the questions of how external forces can be accommodated and internal agendas be constructed and accomplished. We place particular emphasis on the politics of agenda building—the content, packaging, and timing of domestic policy proposals.

THE DEVELOPMENT OF A POLICY ROLE

The framers of the Constitution did not envision the president as chief domestic policy maker. They did, however, anticipate that the institution would have a policy-making role. Within the framework of the separation of powers, the president was given the duty to recommend necessary and expedient legislation and latitude in the execution of the law. Taken together, this duty and that discretion provided the constitutional basis upon which a substantial policy-making role could be built.

For the first one hundred years, presidents recommended measures, took positions, and occasionally even drafted bills, but they did not formulate domestic policy on a regular basis. Beginning with Theodore Roosevelt and continuing with Woodrow Wilson, presidential participation in the policy-making process expanded. Theodore Roosevelt developed a close relationship with Speaker of the House Joseph Cannon. The two consulted frequently on major policy initiatives. Cannon's power as Speaker and party leader enabled him to gain support for proposals that Roosevelt initiated or favored.

Woodrow Wilson expanded the president's role even further. Seeing his responsibilities as analogous to the British prime minister—to propose an integrated set of measures that addressed social and economic problems and then to utilize personal and political influence to get them enacted—Wilson became the first president since John Adams to use the State of the Union address to articulate his goals directly to Congress.

Wilson's program, which was known as the New Freedom, included labor measures, tariff reform, and consumer protection. He also introduced legislation that led to the creation of the Federal Reserve system. Working primarily with the leaders of his party on Capitol Hill, he secured the passage of many of his domestic proposals, including the Adamson Act (which provided an eight-hour day for railroad workers), the Clayton Antitrust Act, and the legislation that established the Federal Trade Commission.

Wilson's Republican successors (Harding, Coolidge, and Hoover) did not expand the presidency's policy-making responsibilities. Their conservative philosophy undoubtedly influenced their conception of a more limited presidential role. From the perspective of the 1920s, the Republican interlude was a return to "normalcy," as Warren Harding termed it, where Congress proposed and the president disposed. From today's perspective, it was a brief respite in the evolution of the president's domestic role.

Institutionalizing Presidential Initiatives

Franklin Roosevelt, more than any other president, enlarged the domestic role and shaped contemporary expectations of the presidency. Coming into office in the throes of the Great Depression, Roosevelt believed it was absolutely essential for the president to take the policy initiative. In his first inaugural address, he stated:

> I am prepared under my constitutional duty to recommend the measures that a stricken Nation in the midst of a stricken world may require. These measures or such other measures as Congress may build out of its experience and wisdom, I shall seek within my constitutional authority to bring to speedy adoption.[1]

Having a sizable Democratic majority that was inclined to support his initiatives, and being the kind of person who was not averse to using his personal influence to get them adopted, Roosevelt quickly and dramatically became deeply involved in the policy process. Moreover, he stayed involved throughout his presidency.

During the first one hundred days of the New Deal, Roosevelt and his aides formulated a series of measures to address the nation's most pressing economic problems. Designed to regulate and stimulate financial, agricultural, and business sectors, these proposals, which Congress enacted into law, also created new executive and regulatory agencies. The agencies expanded the bureaucracy, but they did not necessarily improve the president's ability to oversee the implementation of "his" laws.

In the period from 1934 to 1936, another series of programs, fashioned by the president and his aides, was subsequently passed by Congress. Known as the second phase of the New Deal, these proposals included labor reform, Social Security, soil conservation, and various public works projects. New administrative structures were also established to administer these programs.

By the end of the Roosevelt era, the president's role as domestic policy maker was firmly established. In fact, when Harry S Truman, Roosevelt's successor, asked Congress for legislation to combat inflation, he was criticized by the Republican majority for not presenting a draft bill. When Dwight D. Eisenhower failed to propose a legislative program during his first year as president, he was criticized from both sides of the aisle. "Don't expect us to start from scratch on what you people want," an irate member of the House Foreign Affairs Committee told an Eisenhower official. "That's not the way we do things here. You draft the bills and we work them over."[2]

Whereas Roosevelt extended presidential initiatives primarily into the economic sphere, Presidents Kennedy and Johnson expanded them to include social welfare and civil rights measures.[3] Medical aid to the elderly, public housing, community health, minimum wages, and conservation and education programs, plus a variety of civil rights policies, were crafted during their administrations. By the end of the 1960s, the domestic policy initiative was firmly focused in the White House.

Presidents were expected to set their policy agendas and determine the contours of legislative debate; they were expected to draft legislation and to work for its enactment. As time went on, they were also expected to mobilize public coalitions in support of their legislative proposals. Moreover, when Congress was slow in acting or obstructionist in its response, presidents were expected to find other ways of fulfilling their policy promises. Executive orders and other administrative actions became vehicles by which they could accomplish some of their policy goals. In particular, Republican presidents, when confronted by Democratic Congresses, resorted to their executive powers to achieve their policy goals.

Changing Policy Environment

That the decade of the 1960s was a period of unbridled prosperity, replete with low inflation and high employment, permitted the expansion of government services, and most elements of the society benefited. Presidents reaped political advantage from their policy-making role. As chief providers, they were charged with finding solutions to the country's domestic ills. These solutions took the form of federal programs to the disadvantaged. However, the weakening of the economy in the 1970s and early 1980s, combined with the persistence of social problems that the 1960s legislation was intended to ameliorate, cast doubt about the efficacy of these programmatic solutions. It also placed increasing burdens on presidents in the performance of their policy-making role.

Higher inflation, greater unemployment, declining productivity, increasing foreign competition, and decreasing natural resources limited the capacity of the federal government to respond to economic and social ills. Beginning with the Nixon administration and continuing through the Clinton years, presidents attempted to slow and, in some cases, even reverse the federal government's involvement in the domestic sector. President Nixon initiated a program of New Federalism in which the national government's revenues were to be shared with the states in exchange for a larger state and local role in providing social services. President Reagan carried this initiative one step further; he proposed a swap in which the states would take over the welfare and food stamp programs while the federal government would run the Medicare program. Nixon's revenue-sharing policy was enacted; the Reagan program was not. However, during the Reagan administration, the revenue-sharing program was ended and the national government's share of domestic programs declined. It was during the first Clinton administration that the national government welfare entitlement was terminated.

In addition to the devolution of federal responsibilities to the states, presidents, beginning with Carter, proposed reductions or elimination of other domestic programs. However, the big entitlement programs, such as Social Security, Medicare, and veterans' benefits, were not cut for the most part.

Contemporary presidents have also reduced the government's regulatory activity. The Carter administration successfully pushed for the deregulation of the airline, railroad, and trucking industries. The Reagan administration relaxed the enforcement of many regulations, particularly in the areas of consumer protection, worker safety, and the environment. Bush stopped the issuance of new regulations in the last year of his term, but Clinton resumed them.

The persistence of large budget deficits, declining public confidence in the national government, and congressional opposition to increase federal spending also constrained the Clinton administration, even when the Democrats controlled Congress. The president's program to have government provide inoculations for all children, increased funding for the Head Start program for preschoolers, and give grants to college students in exchange for national service were all scaled back by a Democratic Congress to meet contemporary fiscal realities and the public perception that the federal government is neither an effective nor an economical provider of social services. Similarly, Clinton's major initiative to reform the health care system was not enacted.

When the Republicans took control of Congress in 1995, they made a concerted effort to reduce the size and reach of the federal government still further. Pursuing the policy objectives in their "Contract with America," the Republicans proposed legislation to balance the budget; eliminate federal entitlements in welfare, Medicaid, and farm subsidies; and devolve responsibilities for these social needs to the states (initially funding them with a bloc grant). The president lost his ability to set the policy agenda and had to resort to his veto to prevent programs that he supported from being reduced too much or eliminated entirely.

The struggle between a Democratic president and a Republican Congress persisted, with some key Republican initiatives, notably welfare reform and the reduction of agricultural subsidies, enacted into law but others, such as Medicaid reform and supplementary Social Security payments to legal immigrants, failing because of the president's opposition to them. Similarly, measures that the administration wanted, such as a comprehensive tobacco settlement, a patient's bill of rights, and campaign finance reform, were also not enacted. The problems between the congressional Republican majority and the Democratic White House has not only involved a clash of differing ideologies and visions. The ambivalence of the general public, which favors limiting federal spending but opposes specific spending cuts in "their" programs, combined with the power of organized groups to protect "their" interests, has made it difficult to reduce government programs, expenditures, and regulations. Divisions within the parties that reflect representation from diverse constituencies, the increasing ability of groups to mobilize their members and sympathizers, and the absence of a policy consensus have created powerful tendencies toward the maintenance of the status quo, tendencies which policy initiators in the White House and Congress must overcome if public policy is to be changed.

The tendency of the system to resist change conflicts with contemporary public expectations that government address pressing national needs. This has produced a policy leadership dilemma, one that has fallen primarily on the president's shoulders, but as the 1995–1998 period of congressional initiatives attest, Congress often assumes this burden as well.

How can public needs be satisfied with existing economic resources and large budget deficits? How can elected government officials build political support for programs that lack organized national constituencies? How can they maintain their electoral and governing coalitions without being captive of those within these coalitions? These problems led one astute observer, Paul C. Light, to conclude that domestic policy making places the policy makers, in most cases the president, in a no-win situation: "The cost of presidential policy has grown, while the President's ability to influence outcomes has declined."[4]

How can this policy leadership dilemma be overcome? In the next section we will explore this question by examining the mechanisms and processes that have been developed to aid the president in this increasingly difficult task.

THE OFFICE OF MANAGEMENT AND BUDGET AND THE EXECUTIVE BRANCH

Presidents cannot make policy alone. They need others to provide them with information and expertise, coordinate and implement their decisions and actions, articulate their positions publicly and privately, and build coalitions in support of them on Capitol Hill and within the executive branch. Initially, many of these functions were performed by the Bureau of the Budget, working in conjunction with a small White House staff.

Exercising Central Clearance

The Bureau of the Budget was originally established in 1921 to help the president prepare an annual budget and submit it to Congress. In performing this function, the budget agency annually reviewed the requests for funds of the executive departments and agencies. Beginning in the 1930s, this centralized clearance process was extended to include all executive branch requests for legislation, regardless of whether money would be expended. In each case, the budget officials had to decide whether the proposal was in accord with the president's program, consistent with the president's objectives, or at the very least, not opposed by the president. Any proposal that the Bureau of the Budget believed conflicted with presidential policy could not be advanced by the departments or agencies.

In making their judgments, the analysts in the Budget Bureau used presidential campaign statements, major addresses and reports, and special messages to Congress. If the Budget Bureau was uncertain how the president's program applied or what the program actually was in regard to a major issue, the White House would be consulted. This situation was rare, however, and as a consequence, the Budget Bureau's decision was usually final. Although an appeal could be made to the White House by the departments and agencies, the practice was not encouraged and was rarely successful. Presidents wanted the clearance procedure to work, and it did. In fact, they extended it to include the positions that departments and agencies take on legislation and the testimony their officials present to Congress, a body that also found the process useful. Indeed, beginning in 1947, standing committees of both houses requested that the Bureau of the Budget indicate the president's position on legislation that did not originate in the executive departments and agencies.

From the president's perspective, the central clearance process offered a number of benefits: (1) It provided a mechanism for imprinting a presidential seal of approval on those proposals that the administration supported and withholding it from those it opposed; (2) it made the departments and agencies more aware of each other's views; and (3) it helped resolve interagency disputes and promote interagency coordination. One of its most important functions was the resolution of conflict. Rather than kill a proposal, the Budget Bureau tried to have the objectionable parts removed and to mediate the differences between the agencies. From the department's perspective, however, the clearance requirement was seen as a constraint and the Bureau of the Budget as the policing agency. The civil servants who worked in the budget agency were regarded as the people who said "no."

The central clearance process continues to operate today in much the same manner as it did in the past. However, it has become more politicized in the sense that civil servants play a less important role and political appointees a more important one in making key clearance decisions. It is a behind-the-scenes operation, but occasionally it engenders public controversy. A case in point occurred in May 1989 when the Office of Management and Budget (the successor to the Bureau of the Budget), altered the congressional testimony of Dr. James E. Hansen, director of NASA's Goddard Institute for Space Studies, to weaken his conclusion that man-made gases were primarily responsible for the so-called "greenhouse effect"—the warming of the earth's atmosphere by depletion of the ozone layer. When congressional leaders found out about the change (after it was reported in the *New York Times*), they criticized the administration for trying to suppress scientific evidence that conflicted with its policy.

The controversy points to the increasing political role of the Office of Management and Budget (OMB). It is the political appointees in the OMB and in the White House who make the critical decisions on what does or does not accord with the program of the president. In the greenhouse effect controversy, it was White House and cabinet officials, in addition to staff in the OMB, who participated in the decision.

Coordinating Executive Advice

In addition to applying the president's position on the policy proposals and stands of the executive agencies, the Office of Management and Budget performs another coordinating function: It solicits and summarizes recommendations on enrolled bills, which is legislation that has passed both houses of Congress and is awaiting presidential action.

After Congress has enacted the legislation, the Office of Management and Budget circulates copies of it to all executive branch units that have been involved in its development, would be involved in its implementation, or have a substantive interest in the program itself. The departments and agencies have forty-eight hours in which to make a recommendation to the president. Their recommendations, accompanied by supporting arguments and, frequently, by drafts of signing and veto statements, are then summarized by the OMB, which adds a recommendation of its own and sends the entire file to the White House (usually within the first five days of the ten-day period granted to the president to approve or disapprove the legislation). A similar process, which was designed to solicit the views of key White House aides, was also begun in 1965. A diagram of the central clearances and enrolled bill processes is shown in Figure 12–1.

Today, when presidents are ready to make decisions on pending legislation, they have the benefit of the advice of a large number of executive officials. Moreover, because they have limited time and expertise of their own,

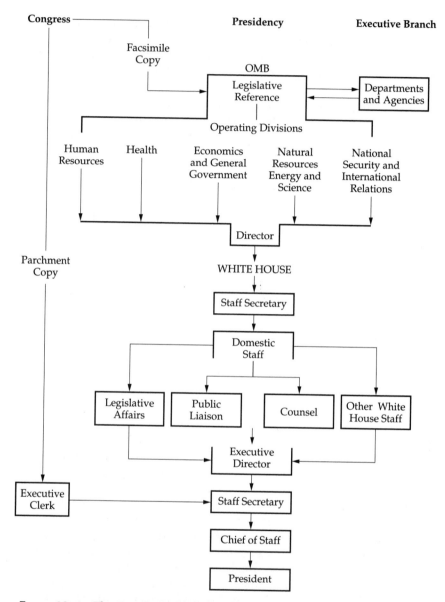

Figure 12–1. The Enrolled Bill Process

they tend to follow it. Of all the executive participants in the enrolled bill process, presidents seem to be most influenced by the OMB, and secondarily by the principal agency into whose jurisdiction the legislation falls. An

OMB recommendation to approve a bill is almost always accepted. As the agency that says "no" most often, its advice to the president to approve legislation seems to be regarded by the White House as an all-clear signal. On the other hand, the OMB's advice to veto may be ignored if there is significant political pressure in favor of the legislation.

A study by Richard L. Cole and Stephen J. Wayne of executive recommendations and presidential actions on enrolled bills from the beginning of the Johnson administration in 1963 to 1982 found that the OMB's recommendation to veto was followed only a little more than half the time.[5] When other executive agencies also urged the president to disapprove the legislation, the chances of a veto increased to 64 percent. In general, the more unified the advice given to the president, the more likely it was to be taken.

Reviewing Agency Regulations

The role of the OMB as policy overseer was extended at the end of the 1970s by the enactment of the Paperwork Reduction Act. A new unit was established in the OMB, the Office of Information and Regulatory Affairs, to administer the legislation. Initially, its principal task was to ensure that excessive reporting requirements were not imposed by agencies of the federal government. Within one month of assuming office, however, President Reagan enlarged the charter of this office to include a review of all pending executive regulations to implement new or existing legislation in order to make sure that they were necessary and, if issued, would be cost-effective. In 1985 he further extended its scope—to include all pre–rule-making activities of the executive departments and agencies—and its charge—to decide whether the pending rules unduly interfered with the private sector, families, or state and local government responsibilities.

In order to conform to the new guidelines and protect their own autonomy, executive branch agencies decreased the volume of the new rules they promulgated during the Reagan administration. This decline was consistent with that administration's philosophy to reduce the role of the national government within the domestic arena and its campaign promise to try to eliminate governmental burdens on the private sector.

During the Bush administration, however, the number of regulations began to increase. To counter conservative criticism that the government was becoming more intrusive, Bush placed a moratorium on the issuance of new regulations in fall 1991, as he readied his reelection campaign.

The Clinton administration has continued to use this OMB office to monitor agency regulations. However, the procedures for reviewing agency regulations were modified by an executive order issued by the president on September 30, 1993. Intended to open up the regulatory review process, the order requires federal officials to disclose their contacts with interest group representatives and requires the groups to submit their opinion in writing on pending regulations. The requirement has proved onerous and in practice has been circumvented. A timely schedule for the review process has also been established. To discourage needless and costly regulations, federal agencies are now obligated to analyze the costs, benefits, and cumulative impact of all significant regulations, defined as those whose annual effect is $100 million or more on the economy. The administration charged Vice President Gore with coordinating its regulatory priorities and agendas.

As a consequence of this regulatory oversight, the presidency, through its surrogate, the OMB, has extended influence over executive branch activities. Not only have departments and agencies been discouraged from issuing new regulations, but those that have been issued are now subject to clearance and, if necessary, to modification.

Moreover, the OMB's stature with outside groups has also been enhanced. Business and professional organizations can now appeal directly to the budget agency to remove or modify regulations if they are thwarted by the issuing department or agency. This appeals process also works to increase the OMB's influence at the expense of the departments and agencies and also at the expense of Congress. It circumvents the "iron triangle" relationship that has traditionally existed among the executive branch agencies, the congressional committees that oversee them, and outside interest groups, putting the OMB in a position to negate or modify the political compromises that may have been made among these parties.

Presenting an Annual Program

Since 1948, presidents have developed an annual legislative program and presented it to Congress in the form of special and required messages and addresses. During the Truman and Eisenhower administrations, the Bureau of the Budget coordinated the process as part of its annual budget review. When departments and agencies were asked to submit their budgets for the next fiscal year, they were also asked to submit ideas for new proposals that would require funding. The Budget Bureau collected these ideas and forwarded them to the White House, which decided which of them to include in the president's program. The State of the Union address became the vehicle for presenting these policy proposals to Congress.

This departmental orientation to policy making ended in the 1960s. The desire of Presidents Kennedy and Johnson to generate new initiatives, combined with their view of the bureaucracy as a pretty conservative place where innovative ideas were not likely to originate, resulted in a shift of focus from inside the executive branch to outside the government. In the words of President Johnson:

I had watched this programming process for years, and I was convinced that it did not encourage enough fresh or creative ideas. The bureaucracy of the government is too preoccupied with day to day operations, and there is strong bureaucratic inertia dedicated to preserving the status quo. As a result, only the most powerful ideas can survive. Moreover, the cumbersome organization of government is simply not equipped to solve complex problems that cut across departmental jurisdictions.[6]

To generate new ideas, both Kennedy and Johnson set up task forces composed of campaign supporters, academicians, and business and labor leaders to investigate problems and present options to the president.[7] The large number of task forces forced an expansion in the White House personnel who regularly dealt with domestic policy matters. By the mid-1960s, a separate White House staff was created to systematize the programming operation.

As a consequence of the growing White House role in policy making, the status and influence of the departments and agencies and the people who ran them declined. A two-track programming system eventually emerged with the departments and agencies on the second track. While they continued to submit proposals with their annual budget estimates, these submissions had less of an impact on the president's major domestic objectives. As power shifted to the White House, the Budget Bureau's influence in determining major presidential priorities also declined.

THE DOMESTIC POLICY OFFICE
AND THE WHITE HOUSE

The first domestic policy office was organized by the White House in 1965 to coordinate Lyndon Johnson's Great Society program. Charged with staffing Johnson's task forces and then reviewing their recommendations, the office developed policy initiatives and then converted them into a legislative format, an executive order, or a departmental regulation.

President Nixon enlarged and institutionalized this White House policy-making operation. In 1970 he created a Domestic Council composed of his domestic cabinet secretaries and a supporting staff. Organized as a separate unit in the Executive Office of the President and directed by a senior White House aide, the staff quickly dominated the process. It created and coordinated internal task forces, composed of departmental representatives, to examine issues, conduct studies, prepare recommendations for the president, and coordinate the implementation of his decisions.[8] The council as such met infrequently. In fact, cabinet secretaries had difficulty even communicating with the president on an individual basis, much less as a group.

The Nixon system was modified in 1972 when senior White House staff were reassigned to the executive departments and agencies, a thinly veiled attempt by the president to rein in the executive bureaucracy.[9] However, the events of Watergate ended these efforts and subsequently, the Nixon presidency.

A domestic policy office has continued to function in each subsequent administration. Although its title has changed and its influence has varied, its principal functions have remained essentially the same—the development and coordination of major domestic policy initiatives for the president. During the Ford presidency, it did not play a major role; during the Carter presidency, it did. Ronald Reagan's penchant for turning to his department secretaries individually and collectively in their cabinet councils for advice and his opposition to new and costly domestic programs reduced the clout of the White House's domestic policy staff. It provided institutional support for the cabinet councils and handled more perfunctory policy matters such as messages to Congress, liaison with interest groups, and policy-oriented speeches. Under Bush, the office maintained a lower profile and operated according to a system in which cabinet secretaries were policy advocates for their departmental interests but were encouraged to reach a consensus on policy issues through negotiation.

The Clinton administration's initial focus on economic issues, which were within the purview of its National Economic Council, left lower priority issues to the domestic staff in Clinton's first two years in office. After the Republicans took control of Congress, it was the domestic council's job to develop responses to the GOP's Contract with America and then help reposition the administration on a range of policy issues from crime to welfare to agricultural subsidies, as the president prepared for reelection. During Clinton's second term, the staff designed a series of policy initiatives in areas of health and education which the president announced in his 1988 State of the Union address. However, the personal scandals that plagued the White House, combined with different Republican legislative priorities, left these new Clinton initiatives dangling and largely unfulfilled and forced the staff into a reactive mode, countering the congressional Republicans on policy matters. Throughout his presidency, Clinton has stayed heavily involved in formulation and, to a somewhat lesser extent, in negotiations with Congress.

In summary, domestic policy staffs have functioned since the Johnson administration. The size of these staffs has varied from a high of approximately eighty, at the end of Nixon's first term, to about thirty to forty, in other administrations. A senior presidential assistant, based in the White House, has headed the office. In the course of its operation, the White House domestic policy staff has worked to develop priority policy and responses to key congressional initiatives while the OMB has cleared, coordinated, and reviewed less important, departmental-initiated policy as well as budget and appropriations matters. Conflict and cooperation have alternately characterized relations between these and other presidential staffs. From time to time, turf battles have also erupted between those who are responsible for economic advice and those who are charged with domestic policy making.

Structural Orientation

The relationship between the domestic policy staff and the executive departments and agencies has been critical to the success of the president's policy efforts. While most presidents-elect ritually promise to institute a cabinet government on taking office, they often find this undesirable and do not follow through on this promise.

In general, contemporary presidents have adopted one of two approaches to policy making. They have either assumed a White House orientation in which their senior aides dominate the process or adopted a cabinet-orientation system in which department secretaries exercise greater influence. The Nixon, Clinton, and, to a lesser extent, Carter presidencies illustrate the first approach, and the Reagan and Bush presidencies exemplify the latter.

In the White House approach, strong, influential domestic advisers funnel recommendations to the president. They filter and broker ideas, and thus their influence stems primarily from their control over the information flow to and from the president and the analytic network on which that information rests.

The senior advisers tend to be advocates as well as mediators. Presidents rely on them for advice, which enhances their status and provides them with greater influence, not only with the president but also with others who wish to affect the president's policy judgments. In contrast, the cabinet approach is less centralized. Cabinet secretaries, individually and collectively, have a greater impact. The White House policy office functions as a liaison and secretariat rather than as a policy initiator. It coordinates executive branch activity rather than dominates it. Thus, the senior adviser is more of a broker than an advocate.

Presidents Reagan and Bush utilized this approach in their cabinet council system. The councils, which are organized on the basis of substantive issue areas, provided a forum for the discussion of policy issues that crossed departmental lines. The system, which was patterned on a model that Ronald Reagan had used as governor of California, involved the president when final policy decisions were to be made. It provided a setting in which Reagan could hear the issues debated, have points clarified, and then retire to make a decision.[10]

Reagan wanted his cabinet councils to generate broad discussion, help develop consensus, and provide a mechanism for implementing administration decisions in accordance with his wishes. To work, end runs had to be avoided, an administrative structure tied to the White House had to be established, and decisions had to be made that were consistent with the general ideological perspective of the administration. Consequently, secretaries could not simply be departmental advocates. These conditions were more prevalent during Reagan's first term than during his second.

Any policy-making apparatus has its limitations, and a council system is no exception. It requires many hours of meetings and group discussions. It is prone to leaks and may also be subject to a groupthink mentality. In Reagan's second term and during Bush's presidency, these structural limitations, the changes in personnel, and the absence of clear and urgent policy objectives effectively reduced the influence of the cabinet councils.

Stylistic Differences

In addition to the structural orientations presidents have adopted, their policy goals and personal styles have also affected White House policy making. The desire for innovative policy, which was particularly evident during the Kennedy, Johnson, and Clinton presidencies, spurred the development of new sources for ideas and programs. All three presidents turned to individuals and groups outside the government to supplement the input they received from those inside their administrations. In contrast, the goals of retrenchment and consolidation, which were particularly evident during the Reagan administration, turned the focus back to executive officials appointed by the president who shared the executive's ideological and policy perspectives.

While Kennedy and Johnson did not believe the bureaucracy could develop innovative policy, they were confident that civil servants would be able and willing to implement that policy once it had been initiated. Bush and Clinton also were willing to defer to the bureaucracy once policy had been formulated. However, Reagan lacked that confidence. He did not think that career bureaucrats could be trusted to execute the demise of their own programs.

STRATEGIES FOR POLICY MAKING

The organizational component is only one aspect of policy making. Presidents obviously need a mechanism to help them design and coordinate their program, but that mechanism alone cannot ensure their program's success. Policy must be strategically accomplished. External interests must be accommodated; agendas must be artfully constructed and packaged; and long-term national objectives must be maintained, despite the persistence of parochial perspectives and short-term goals.

Accommodating External Forces

Changes within the political and institutional environment, the decentralization of power in Congress, the growth of single-issue groups, and the weakening of partisan coalitions have increased and diversified pressures on the presidency. This has affected the policy-making process in two principal ways: It has made it more sensitive to outside interests, and it has required that presidents devote more personal and institutional resources to the achievement of their domestic policy goals within the public arena.

Prior to the 1970s, the Bureau of the Budget and, to a lesser extent, the White House were relatively invulnerable to external groups seeking to influence their decisions. The Budget Bureau considered itself to have only one principal client—the president. Civil servants, not political appointees, ran the process and made most of the decisions. They were expected to do so within the framework of the president's objectives but also on the basis of the merits of the issue.

Taking political factors into account was the job of senior presidential aides in the White House, who operated in a relatively closed environment. While leaders of the president's party, influential supporters, and friends could gain access, the general public, including most organized groups, were excluded. Congress and the bureaucracy were the principal turfs on which groups fought their political battles with the Bureau of the Budget and the White House distanced from the fray.

This began to change in the 1970s. The reorganization of the Budget Bureau into the Office of Management and Budget and the creation of a number of political positions to oversee its operation, the increase in the size of the policy staffs in the White House and their growth in power and influence, and the need to mobilize interest groups behind the president's program all contributed to the increased receptivity to outside views and sensitivity to outside pressures. The reaction of Presidents Ford and Carter to Watergate—particularly to Nixon's closed presidency—provided further impetus to open the White House to public view and political influence.

Lobbyists, who themselves were rapidly increasing in number, began to contact administration officials directly in the OMB and the White House to try to affect their policy judgments. The White House, in turn, began to utilize interest group and community leaders in building coalitions for its programs. By the mid-1970s, a separate office within the White House, the Office of Public Liaison, had been established to link the administration with interest group and community leaders.

Initially, the office functioned as a conduit, providing access for those outside the government and public relations opportunities for the president. Literally thousands of group representatives and community leaders have been invited to the White House to meet administration officials and hear them promote their programs. Presidents have used interest groups to legitimize their position in office, to improve their political status, to build coalitions for their policy, and to extend representation and access to a broad spectrum of groups operating within the political environment.[11]

The strategies presidents have used to guide their relations with interest groups have varied with their particular goals. According to Mark Peterson, who studied the White House–interest group connection, Roosevelt mobilized groups to support his program; Johnson was more concerned with building a broad-based public consensus; and Carter at first reached out to those who lacked effective representation, but later toward groups that could more effectively help him get his policy initiatives through Congress. The Reagan administration appealed to both sympathetic and nonsympathetic groups in order to cast the president in a more favorable light and meet increasing group expectations of access to the administration and service from it.[12]

Clinton has had mixed success in mobilizing outside groups to support his interest. In the fight for the North Atlantic Free Trade Agreement (NAFTA), the administration worked closely with business lobbyists. During the period when Congress was considering the agreement, White House officials met weekly with a coalition of business groups to coordinate actions in support of it. The U.S. Chamber of Commerce also participated in the campaign to rally its members to support the free trade zone. Labor unions, however, parted company with the administration by actively opposing the agreement.

Whereas NAFTA succeeded in large part because of the support it received from the business community, the president's health care reforms failed because of opposition from the private sector. Graham K. Wilson attributed this failure to the administration's exclusion of prominent medical groups in the task forces that formulated the plan, the attacks against the insurance and pharmaceutical industries by Hillary Rodham Clinton and other senior officials, and the inability of the White House to coordinate an inside-the-Beltway coalition of lobbyists as it had for NAFTA. Groups who anticipated that the legislation would hurt them financially or restrict their freedom to conduct business or practice medicine opposed the legislation. A multimillion dollar advertising campaign was conducted by the Health Insurance Association of America in opposition to the Clinton plan (see The Clinton Presidency box).[13]

The expansion of group representatives in Washington and their involvement in a range of policy issues has forced the White House to

THE CLINTON PRESIDENCY

The Health Care Fiasco

This is a story of domestic policy making, of formulating one of President Clinton's top legislative priorities during his first term, health care reform. It is also a story of how the process affected the product, and how both adversely affected the legislative outcome.

The story begins well before the congressional debate in 1994. When Bill Clinton took office in 1992, over 37 million Americans were uninsured or under-insured, and their numbers were steadily rising. Millions of others feared that their health insurance would not cover a catastrophic illness. Medical costs had been increasing by 10 percent per year, far more than the rate of inflation. Although a majority of Americans expressed satisfaction with the quality of the health care they personally received, they also believed that the system itself was too expensive and inefficient, that it was broke and needed fixing.

Five days after he took office, the president met with senior White House staff, cabinet officials, and the first lady to discuss the health care issue and a procedure for designing legislation to fix it. The meeting ended with Clinton announcing the formation of a presidential task force on national health reform to prepare the necessary legislative proposal. To demonstrate his resolve, the president asked his wife, Hillary Rodham Clinton, to oversee the task force's effort.

By creating a presidential task force and putting Mrs. Clinton in charge of it, the president raised the political ante for himself and for his administration. Being a policy "wonk," President Clinton wanted to keep control of this major initiative, not farm it out to the executive branch where turf fights, clientele pressures, and bureaucratic thinking could compromise the president's objectives. Clinton also wanted to prevent leaks from torpedoing the proposal.

The original plan was to assemble a relatively small group of policy experts, primarily from outside the government, to design an innovative system that addressed two primary concerns: cost and coverage. However, the number of participants mushroomed when Democratic members of Congress and department secretaries, who were anxious to get in on the action, volunteered their staffs. Eventually the number working on the task force exceeded 600, an extraordinarily large figure considering that maintaining control, preventing leaks, and constraining outside pressures were three of the principal rationales for setting up a presidential operation in the first place.[14] Leaks did occur, and the secret meetings themselves became an issue. Republican members of Congress, whose staffs were not invited to join the group, objected to the closed-door sessions. They instituted a legal challenge on the grounds that officials on government salary were participating, and therefore the public had a right to know what was transpiring. A federal court agreed, forcing the task forces to open their doors.

Eight teams organized around issue clusters examined the problems and costs and proposed solutions. In trying to meet the president's self-imposed deadline of one hundred days, participants adhered to a very tight and arduous schedule. Working papers on different components of the issue were reviewed and critiqued by a small group of senior advisers, who made the final recommendations to the president.

The large task force group officially disbanded on May 31, 1993, but it was not until early September that the health care group reported to the president. The delay was caused by two factors: the comprehensiveness and complexity of the health care proposal itself and the administration's need, during summer 1993, to focus its efforts on deficit reduction. Health care had to be postponed until the deficit reduction issue was resolved.

Prior to making his final decisions on the plan, the president met with his senior policy advisers and cabinet secretaries. Several had serious objections, as they believed the proposal to be too ambitious, comprehensive, costly, and bureaucratic. Treasury Secretary Lloyd Bentsen even sent the president a private, thirty-eight-page memo detailing his department's criticism of the plan.[15]

On September 22, 1993, over two hundred days after the administration took office, the president finally delivered his health care address to a joint session of Congress. Even now, however, the delivery was marred by difficulties. The wrong speech appeared on Clinton's teleprompter. As the president's aides scurried to correct the problem, Clinton, who had not brought his reading glasses with him, had to depend on the written text, which was not even typed in large letters.

The address was a call to action. "This health care system is badly broken and we need to fix it," the president said. "We must make this our most urgent priority." Despite the appeal to urgency, it was more than another month before the actual bill was introduced—all 1,342 pages of it.

The rest of the story is well known. The bill was so large and comprehensive that it went to five separate committees in the House and Senate. In addition, several members of Congress, both Republican and Democratic, introduced their own plans.

As Congress considered the health care issue, numerous interest groups, which had initially been reluctant to criticize the president's proposals and Mrs. Clinton's defense of them, sprung into action and raised objections to almost every aspect of the plan. Small businesses opposed the bill's requirement that employers pay the health insurance costs of their employees; private insurers criticized the health care alliances that employers and employees had to join; and health care providers, fearful of cost control, opposed any attempt by the government or a special commission to set prices.

Many of the groups that were active in the health care debate mounted extensive public relations campaigns to reinforce their congressional lobbying. Most effective of these efforts were the "Harry and Louise" ads sponsored by the Health Insurance Association of America, in which a typically middle-class couple expressed fear that the administration's proposals would limit their choice of doctors and health care providers, bankrupt the federal treasury, and create another huge government bureaucracy. Their objections became the principal criticisms of the Clinton plan.

In the face of these criticisms, public opinion began to turn against the administration. Within months, opponents outnumbered supporters. The shift in public sentiment naturally affected members of Congress, who responded to the competing interests and demands of their constituents.

Diverted by other issues, defensive about its own proposal, and encountering increasing opposition from within its own party, the administration was unable to mount an effective counterattack. The plan was too comprehensive to explain easily to the American people, and the universality of the coverage added costs that the public seemed unwilling to shoulder. Moreover, the managed care provision to control costs involved more government, regulation, and potential red tape at a time when the public was displaying increasing frustration and mistrust of the national government. Health care reform, which had held much promise in 1992, gradually died of its own weight in Congress.

It was a bitter loss for the president, the Congress, and its Democratic majority. The president had failed to achieve his principal legislative priority. In doing so, he lost prestige and political power. He also lost most of his other legislative proposals, which were delayed because of the focus on health care. Moreover, it was a loss that, in retrospect, might have been avoided.

The administration made several critical misjudgments in formulating its health care policy. The appointment of a presidential task force circumscribed the political system in which executive branch officials, operating in their capacity as departmental representatives and supported by outside groups, debate policy options and try to reach a consensus on what is and is not politically feasible. The White House orientation also inhibited the coalition building that is essential to gain public support and congressional backing. By placing responsibility for health care in the White House and putting his wife in charge of it, the president put himself in the position of assuming the blame should the proposal fail—which it did.

Health care became the metaphor for a failed presidency, weak and ineffective leadership, and a policy proposal that was too grandiose and costly for the times. In response, the public took its wrath out on Clinton and the Democrats in the 1994 midterm elections.

devote considerable time, energy, and staff to this important and potent political constituency. One potentially pernicious effect of the expansion of presidential–interest group activities has been the extension of "revolving-door politics"—the practice of public officials leaving the government, obtaining jobs in the private sector, and cashing in on their political contacts. The key to interest group influence is access. Those individuals who, by virtue of their personal acquaintances, knowledge, and experiences, can provide such access are extremely valuable to interest groups and are well compensated for their ability to open doors, present positions, and influence policy making. Senior White House officials fall into this category. In one celebrated case, Michael Deaver, deputy chief of staff to Reagan during his first term, left the administration to form his own consulting–public relations firm. He was subsequently accused of violating a federal conflict-of-interest law that restricts the contacts former public officials may have with those with whom they worked for one year and prohibits forever their involvement on issues on which they worked while in government. Deaver was subsequently convicted of perjury after testifying about his private activities before Congress.

To avoid any appearance of impropriety, President Clinton requested that his appointees take a pledge not to have contacts with those with whom they worked in the government for a period of five years after they leave public service. According to the Clinton pledge, those officials who deal with foreign policy issues, such as trade, can never represent a foreign government or corporation after they leave the federal government. Yet the first two senior White House officials who left his administration took jobs with public relations firms that had extensive dealings with government although both claimed that they had not and would not violate their pledge. Subsequently, other Clinton officials have also moved into the private sector to work in the area of government relations.

In addition to group outreach activities, the White House has expanded its communication with state and local governments and with party officials and political leaders around the country. A larger, more sophisticated White House communications operation has been created to market the president and his policy objectives more effectively with the general population. Beginning in the 1980s, more than one-third of the people who work in the White House have been involved in public relations activities of one type or another.

Building a Policy Agenda

The changing institutional and political environment for policy has also affected the content of agendas. In recent years the scope of these agendas has become more modest, while the policies within them have become more complex. Moreover, their promotion has become more closely tied to the cycle of presidential influence.

In the past, agendas tended to be laundry lists of proposals designed to appeal to as broad a segment of electoral supporters as possible. Franklin Roosevelt's New Deal, Truman's Fair Deal, Kennedy's New Frontier, Johnson's Great Society, and even Nixon's New Federalism programs fit into this category. The depressed American economy of the 1930s, the increasing social consciousness of the 1960s, the democratizing of the nomination process in the 1970s, and the expansion of the electoral period during the past decade have all contributed to the demands for a large and diverse policy agenda.

The way in which presidents have formulated their domestic programs also contributed to the same end. By soliciting proposals from a variety of sources and established interests, presidents have generated multiple pressures on their own programs. The most effective way to deal with these pressures has been to accommodate them in packages that included something for almost everyone.

While these pressures have persisted and even increased, the president's ability to achieve them has diminished. Resources have become scarce; a huge national debt and budget deficits into the late 1990s limited the amount of money to fund such programs. Moreover, the system has become more pluralistic, with the result that it takes a greater effort to mobilize a majority coalition. This has increased the costs of domestic policy making for the president.

One consequence of increasing costs and decreasing resources has been the need to limit items, particularly high-cost items, in the domestic agenda, prioritizing them more clearly and cycling them more effectively over the congressional calendar rather than overwhelming Congress with too many proposals too quickly. Another has been the need to package and promote the proposals in such a way as to maximize their public appeal and minimize their initial cost. A third imperative for contemporary presidents is to avoid excessive involvement in policy which causes them to lose sight of a broader and longer-term national perspective.

Limiting the Items   The expansion of governmental activities has generated more groups with a stake in public policy. Today, there are more opinions to hear, interests to balance, more agendas to combine, producing in the words of Hugh Heclo, "policy congestion."[16] It has also increased the complexity of many issues with which contemporary administrations must deal. One policy decision affects another. Spheres of jurisdiction overlap. Distinctions between domestic and international concerns are no longer clear-cut.

The task for presidents and their aides is to sort out the relationships among the competing interests and complex issues and to integrate them into a comprehensive administrative policy. One way to do this has already been discussed: Use an institutional mechanism that imposes a presidential perspective such as the Bureau of the Budget did prior to 1965 and the White House has done since then. Another tactic is to reduce the agenda to fewer critical items and bind them together in some fashion. The Reagan administration employed this latter strategy quite successfully in its first two years in office; Clinton tried to do so as well but was not nearly as successful.

Upon taking office, both presidents tried to convert their campaign promises into carefully defined policy agendas. Reagan had two basic legislative initiatives: budget reform and tax reform; Clinton had three: economic stimulus, budget reduction, and health care reform. However, Clinton also proposed a number of other programs, such as national service, child immunization, lobbying reform, and campaign finance reform, programs that diverted focus from his principal priorities at a time when he needed to mobilize public support for them.

Limiting items helps presidents set the pace and tone of public debate. It helps them direct public attention to certain presidential activities, thereby contributing to the perception that they are in command. It also enables them to concentrate resources behind their administration's priorities rather than have them dissipated in accordance with numerous wish lists that emanate from the Congress or the executive departments and agencies.

There is, of course, a negative side to limiting the agenda too much. Some people's expectations will not be satisfied. For the Reagan administration it was the social objectives of the conservatives that were largely abandoned in the legislature. For the Clinton administration both liberal and conservative Democrats accused the administration of tilting against them. Another problem with limiting the agenda is that defeats will appear that much more serious if one or two of only a few priorities are derailed, as it was for Clinton when he failed to get his economic stimulus and health care proposals enacted into law.

Cycling Political Issues   Another strategic consequence of the increased costs of domestic policy making is that an administration's priorities must be cycled over the course of the congressional calendar. Presidents cannot wait several months before making their initial proposals nor should they inundate Congress with them.

Moving quickly on the most controversial items is important for two reasons. Electoral cycles, department pressures, and public moods tend to decrease presidential influence over time. As members of Congress position themselves for the next election, as bureaucrats and their clientele begin to assert their claims on political appointees, as segments of the winning coalition become disillusioned, as the outparty begins to coalesce in opposition to the incumbent, it is more difficult for a president to achieve domestic policy goals. Moreover, presidential reputations are built early and tend to persist longer than does their ability to achieve policy successes.[17]

Carter found this out the hard way. He used his first six months in office to develop policies to implement his election promises. By the time these proposals were readied for Congress, his honeymoon had ended and his policies got stuck in a legislative labyrinth.

The same thing happened to Clinton in his first two years in office. He delayed his health care proposals until September to avoid overwhelming Congress with too many complex issues and thereby diluting his administration's efforts to get its deficit reduction plan through Congress. But when health care was introduced, it consumed the congressional agenda, delaying consideration of other administration initiatives. And when it failed, there was not sufficient time nor did the president have sufficient clout to deal with most of these issues.

In contrast, the Reagan administration had its agenda in place prior to taking office. Seizing on his unexpectedly large electoral victory in 1980, Reagan claimed a mandate for his economic program and then moved quickly to obtain its enactment. Proposals that were developed later in the administration, such as the New Federalism and urban enterprise zone plans, met with considerably more congressional resistance. In general Reagan was less successful as his administration progressed. His congressional support declined even as his popularity increased.

The dilemma presidents often face is that their influence tends to be greatest when their knowledge of substantive policy issues and how to win support for them is least. Not only do they not have sufficient time to educate themselves before making critical policy judgments, but they may not have time to develop innovative policy at all. According to Paul C. Light, declining influence requires presidents to look for available alternatives among existing options and take the first acceptable one.[18]

Declining influence may also require presidents to take advantage of items carried over on the legislative agenda from one Congress to the next. Backing proposals that already have garnered support in Congress and with the general public can enhance an administration's early legislative record, although it obviously limits a president's personal impact on this legislation and the credit received from its enactment; it may also divert Congress and the public from other items that are higher priorities for the new president. Nonetheless, the opportunities for quick victories, the need to redeem campaign promises or platform planks on these pending, unresolved legislative issues, and the desire of a new president to placate groups in Congress who support the legislation are all inducements for the president to pursue this strategy rather than wipe the slate clean and begin anew. Thus, Clinton announced that he supported and would approve legislation that the previous Congress had enacted but his predecessor had vetoed—legislation requiring employers to provide for parental leave, requiring states to ease voter registration procedures, and permitting federal workers to become more involved in political activities. The enactment of this legislation contributed to his early legislative record. Similarly, in his second term, Clinton pursued policy he had been unable to obtain in his first four years such as campaign finance reform and legislation aimed at curbing teen smoking (see the Hot-Button Issue box).

The degree to which the ongoing legislative agenda limits the president's ability to set the public agenda for the country has been the subject of debate among political scientists. Charles O. Jones argued that a variety of factors affects presidential discretion: the election campaign, the range of policy alternatives being considered, and the political environment in which a president has to operate. Jones went on to conclude that the greater the congruity between the president's agenda and that of Congress, the greater the likelihood for achieving major legislative successes. Jones points to the elections of 1964 and 1980 and to their legislative consequences to illustrate his point.[19]

Presidential discretion also varies with the type of issue, according to a study by Fengyan Shi. She postulated that presidents have more discretion on long-term issues than short-term ones and on ordinary, ongoing issues than on crisis and newly emergent ones.[20] Presidents usually have more discretion when they replace a president of the opposite party than when they succeed one of their own party.

Packaging and Promoting Legislative Priorities In addition to setting the agenda by deciding which items to include and when to include them, it is necessary to package them artfully. Presenting a few key proposals rather than a comprehensive set of policies reduces the number of instances in which supporters of the president can disagree, and presenting them as an either/or proposition may lessen the chances that the president's proposal will be modified by others. The Reagan and Clinton experiences are instructive here. In 1981 Reagan presented Congress with a "take it or leave it" budget reconciliation plan. In 1993 Clinton gave Congress a third option with his budget reconciliation plan, declaring that if legislators did not like his proposed combination of spending cuts and tax increases, they could change them. They did, jettisoning the president's proposed energy tax and increasing cuts in domestic spending in the process. Moreover, Clinton's willingness to accept changes encouraged members of Congress to bargain with the president, whereas the Reagan strategy did not. Whether Clinton could have achieved a substantial deficit reduction plan had he not indicated his willingness to compromise, however, is questionable.

The fewer the roll-call votes on a legislative proposal, the easier it is for a president to concentrate resources and mobilize winning coalitions. Reagan successfully pursued this strategy in his 1981 and 1982 budget battles with the Democrats in Congress. Similarly, the packaging of the large personal and corporate income tax cut in 1981, the Social Security compromise in 1983, and the tax reform program in 1986 were key to the enactment of

☼ HOT-BUTTON ISSUE

The President's Tobacco Plan Goes Up in Smoke

President Clinton had a problem in spring 1998: He needed to pursue more major domestic policy initiatives. For one thing, throughout his reelection campaign and the year following, the press had accused him of abdicating his policy-making responsibilities for a more public, ceremonial presidential role. Clinton also needed to placate his liberal Democratic constituency, which was upset by his move to the center, his approval of Republican legislation that ended the federal entitlement for welfare and decreased and, ultimately, eliminated farm subsidies, and a balanced budget agreement that made substantial cuts in domestic spending. Third, he needed to take the offensive with congressional Republicans rather than simply use his veto to thwart them. The ongoing investigation of Democratic fund-raising activities, another ongoing investigation by an independent counsel on the president's own activities before and during his presidency (Whitewater, FBI files, and the Monica Lewinsky affair), and the civil suit initiated by Paula Jones charging him with sexual harassment made taking this presidential initiative all the more important.

The tobacco settlement offered an opportunity for the president to lead. In an agreement between the tobacco industry and forty state attorney generals, the industry had agreed to pay $368.5 billion over five years in exchange for immunity from class-action suits and a cap on the amount of punitive damages they would be liable to pay in any one year. Congress, however, had to approve the settlement.

The president urged the legislature to do so. In his 1998 budget proposals, Clinton recommended that a major part of the money from the settlement be used to fund health and educational programs, bolster medical research on tobacco-related illness, and mount a public relations campaign against teenage smoking.

The Senate Commerce, Science and Transportation Committee, chaired by Seantor John McCain (Republican from Arizona), held hearings that resulted in settlement legislation removing the class-action immunity against the tobacco companies and adding a $1.10 tax increase per pack of cigarettes over a five-year period (to discourage teen smoking). Republicans, many of whom had received substantial contributions and support from the tobacco industry in their election campaigns, opposed the McCain bill, as did the tobacco industry, which launched a $40 million public relations campaign against the legislation.

The administration announced its support for the McCain bill, but Republican senators proceeded to introduce a series of amendments that made the legislation less palatable to its supporters. They voted to remove liability caps on the industry, cap attorney fees, and direct the revenue from the settlements to drug interdiction efforts and a tax cut. As the debate continued, unsuccessful attempts were made by McCain and his supporters to invoke cloture. After these attempts failed, Senate Majority Leader Trent Lott pulled the bill from the floor so that the Senate could continue with other business.

Comprehensive tobacco legislation was dead for 1998, and the president and his Democratic supporters had suffered a major defeat, indicating once again how difficult it is for presidents to influence Congress—particularly Congresses controlled by the opposite party.

each of these proposals into legislation. Clinton adopted a similar strategy in 1993, but again he was less successful.

One of the reasons why the Reagan administration was perceived to be so effective was the president's ability to promote his priorities within the Congress and among the general public. To gain congressional support, it is necessary to convince members of Congress that the proposed legislation is supported within their constituencies. Generating a constituency-based response with a primetime television appeal is one way to achieve that objective. Showing an economic benefit for a particular area or group is another. In an effort to gain the support of New Jersey Senator Frank Lautenberg, up for reelection in 1994, President Clinton announced that his budget legislation would create 75,000 new jobs in New Jersey; to gain the support of Senator Dennis DeConcini of Arizona, a state with a large elderly population, the president agreed to limit increased taxes on Social Security benefits. Presidents normally invite members of Congress to the White House prior to a critical vote on legislation.

Discerning the Forest from the Trees   Constraints on time and energy suggest another lesson for contemporary presidents. They should not involve themselves too deeply in the details of decision making, although they must provide general policy guidance. Jimmy Carter is a case in point. Finding it difficult to delegate to others, he spent considerable time becoming an expert on the various policy issues in which he was interested or which came to his attention. At the beginning of his administration, he read around four hundred pages of papers and memos a day! James Fallows, a former Carter speechwriter, described his boss as "the perfectionist accustomed to thinking that to do a job right you must do it yourself." Fallows illustrated his point:

> He [Carter] would leave for a weekend at Camp David laden with thick briefing books, would pore over budget tables to check the arithmetic, and during his first six months in office, would personally review all requests to use the White House tennis court. . . . After six months had passed, Carter learned that this was ridiculous, as he learned about other details he would have to pass by if he was to use his time well. But his preference was still to try to do it all.[21]

Naturally, this prodigious effort took its toll, and Carter was eventually forced to cut back. Bill Clinton evidenced similar tendencies, getting involved in detailed policy decisions and personally making mid-level personnel selections. When problems resulted from these decisions or selections, the president received most of the criticism. He could not easily shift blame to his staff.

In contrast to Carter and Clinton, Reagan took the opposite tack. While he articulated a strong ideological perspective, he left most of the details to senior White House and cabinet officials. This exposed him to the charge that he was manipulated by his staff and that he was overly dependent on key White House aides for the decisions he had to make, the time frame in which he had to make them, and the range of options from which he had to choose. It also left him prey to his staff's misperceptions.

Sustaining a National Perspective   Reagan's ideological perspective helped him tackle another policy-making problem that often besets contemporary presidents: how to sustain a national perspective in the light of continuous parochial pressures that are exerted on almost every policy issue. A strong, consistent ideological orientation provides a rationale for including (and excluding) certain items in a policy agenda and linking them to one another in a way that makes sense to partisan supporters. It helps transform an electoral coalition into a policy one. It is also useful in overcoming the tendencies that frequently lead executive officials to adopt views and advocate interests that are at variance with those of the president.

The Reagan administration employed ideology in converting electoral promises into tangible policy goals. It also used ideology as a criterion for appointment. Cabinet and subcabinet officials were nominated in part because they shared the president's views. They were expected to impose those views on their agencies rather than the other way around.

Ideology or a set of coherent policy views, in short, can be a unifying tool. They can build support by simplifying and focusing. They can also give people a sense of where the president is coming from and going to. But ideology is not without its dangers. Rigid adherence to a certain perspective or issue position makes compromise difficult. As it unites supporters so too can it unify opponents, thereby polarizing the political environment and blinding adherents to the nuances of proposals and the need for adjustment and change. The budget debate between Clinton and the Republican Congress in 1995–1996 is a good example of how two sides digging in their heels can lead to stalemate and inaction rather than compromise.

On the other hand, lack of an overarching policy framework can produce the same problem within an administration. Critics have contended that policy inconsistencies in the Carter administration were due in part to this problem. Again, as James Fallows observed:

> I came to think that Carter believes fifty things, but no one thing. He holds explicit, thorough positions on every issue under the sun, but he has no large view of the relations between them, no line indicating which goals (reducing unemployment? human rights?) will take precedence over which (inflation control? a SALT [Strategic Arms Limitation Talks] treaty?) when the goals conflict.[22]

The same criticism was directed at Clinton, especially during his first two years in office.

Maintaining a Long-Range View   Another problem related to promoting policy consistency is maintaining a long-range perspective. In making policy, everyday emergencies tend to drive out future planning. This limits the outlook of those involved in policy making to the short term and rarely beyond the next election.

Contemporary White Houses have attempted to design a longer-range domestic planning capability, but without much success. In 1975 President Ford asked Vice President Rockefeller to provide leadership and direction for the establishment of social goals. However, Rockefeller's decision not to run for office one year later abruptly ended this effort. The Reagan administration's attempt to create a long-range policy-making capability in the form of a new office of planning and evaluation met with a similar fate. Charged with developing strategic plans for the president's agenda and schedule, the office fashioned a series of early blueprints that consisted of possible responses to international and national crises. As the administration got underway and confronted changing external conditions and public moods, the office's futuristic planning became less relevant to day-to-day decisions that had to be made, and it was disbanded within two years.

CONCLUSION

Presidents have become national policy makers. This role developed primarily in the twentieth century and largely as a consequence of social, economic, and political problems that required solutions by the federal government. With a national perspective, a large staff structure, and the ability to focus public attention and mobilize support, presidents have been placed in a position to propose policy and get it adopted. The electoral process has provided them with further incentives to do so. Congress, the executive, and the public frequently look to them for leadership.

The mechanism necessary to accomplish this leadership took form over two decades. Initially the Budget Bureau provided the resources and managed the processes, with its senior civil servants working closely with the White House to develop, coordinate, and clear policy proposals emanating from the departments and agencies. Once presidents turned from departments and agencies to other sources for policy ideas, however, the budget agency's influence declined and the White House's increased.

Since the mid-1960s, the president's chief policy aides have dominated the policy-making process. They in turn have depended on their assistants to monitor and integrate the input of other members of the administration. The White House has become the focal point for building support for these priorities. These developments have enhanced the presidency's influence but not necessarily that of individual presidents, who have become increasingly dependent on their staff for deciding when they should become involved, what options they should consider, and how those options are presented, articulated, and promoted, both within and outside the government.

Changes within the political system have made the president's tasks more burdensome. Competing demands, complex issues, and confrontational politics have made it more difficult to design programs and obtain support for them. The dilemma presidents face is that expectations of their performance usually exceed resources at their disposal. This has affected strategies for policy making.

To exert policy leadership today, presidents must accommodate external forces and mobilize them into a policy coalition. They must limit their priorities, cycling and carefully packaging and promoting them over the course of their administration. Finally, they must work to establish and maintain a long-term national perspective. It is important that they develop and move key parts of their legislative agenda early in their administration, not only because their chances for legislative success are better but because early successes enhance their reputation and increase the political capital they can use later on in their presidency. Addressing the national policy needs and contributing to the administration's political needs also serve the president's leadership needs.

These tasks are not easy. They require skillful personal and institutional leadership. Presidents cannot dictate policy outcomes, but they can affect them. Their reputation, their subsequent achievements, and, ultimately, the fate of their presidency may hinge on how well they do so.

DISCUSSION QUESTIONS

1. What are the principal limitations on a president's ability to affect domestic policy? Discuss these limitations and indicate their impact on the past three presidencies.
2. In recent years the White House has been forced to devote increasing attention to consensus building to achieve the president's policy goals. Explain the institutional mechanisms and practices that have been developed to build policy majorities. Assess the success of recent presidencies in utilizing these instruments.
3. Every president tries to leave an imprint on the nation, and Bill Clinton has been no exception. Discuss Clinton's domestic policy legacy. In your discussion indicate his primary objectives during his presidency and the success he has had in achieving them.

WEB EXERCISES

1. Go to the White House Web site <http://www.whitehouse.gov>. Indicate the principal policy positions the president has taken on recent issues and the ways in which he has tried to gain public attention and support for these positions (via his announcements, meetings, and ceremonies).
2. Go to the White House Web site <http://www.whitehouse.gov> and access the president's last State of the Union address. From the address, list the president's principal domestic priorities. Then search the White House and Congressional Web sites <http://www.thomas.loc.gov> to see which of these priorities have been enacted into law, which are still pending in Congress, and which have failed to become public policy.

SELECTED READING

Cohen, Jeffrey E. *Presidential Responsiveness and Public Policy Making: The Publics and the Policies that Presidents Choose.* Ann Arbor: University of Michigan Press, 1997.

Fett, Patrick J. "Truth in Advertising: The Revelation of Presidential Legislative Priorities. *Western Political Quarterly* (Winter 1992): 895–920.

Fuhrman, Susan H. "Clinton's Education Policy and Intergovernmental Relations in the 1990s, *Publius* 24 (1994): 83–97.

Jones, Charles O. *The Presidency in a Separated System*. Washington, D.C.: Brookings Institution, 1994.

LeLoup, Lance T., and Steven A. Shull. *Congress and the President: The Policy Connection*. Belmont, Calif.: Wadsworth, 1993.

Light, Paul C. *The President's Agenda*, rev. ed. Baltimore: Johns Hopkins University Press, 1991.

Peterson, Mark A. "The Presidency and Organized Interests: White House Patterns of Interest Group Liaison." *American Political Science Review* 86 (September 1992): 612–625.

Quirk, Paul J., and Joseph Hinchliffe, "Domestic Policy: The Trials of a Centrist Democrat," in Colin Campbell and Bert A. Rockman, eds., *The Clinton Presidency: First Appraisals*. Chatham, N.J.: Chatham House, 1996, pp. 262–289.

Riddlesperger, James W., Jr., and Donald W. Jackson, eds. *Presidential Leadership and Civil Rights Policy*. Westport, Conn.: Greenwood Press, 1995.

Steger, Wayne. "Presidential Policy Initiation and the Politics of Agenda Control, *Congress and the Presidency*. 24 (1997): 17–36.

Warshaw, Shirley Anne. *The Domestic Presidency: Policy Making in the White House*. Boston: Allyn and Bacon, 1997.

Wayne, Stephen J. *The Legislative Presidency*. New York: Harper and Row, 1978.

Wilson, Graham K., "The Clinton Administration and Interest Groups," in Campbell and Rockman, *The Clinton Presidency: First Appraisals*, pp. 212–233. Chatham, N.J.: Chatham House, 1996.

Notes

1. Franklin D. Roosevelt, "First Inaugural Address," March 4, 1933," *Congressional Record*, 73rd Congress, Special Session, pp. 5–26.
2. Quoted in Richard E. Neustadt, "Presidency and Legislation: Planning the President's Program," *American Political Science Review* 49 (December 1955): 1015.
3. The one major exception was the creation of the Social Security program during Roosevelt's presidency.
4. Paul C. Light, *The President's Agenda* (Baltimore: Johns Hopkins University Press, 1982), p. 217.
5. Richard L. Cole and Stephen J. Wayne, unpublished research.
6. Lyndon B. Johnson, *The Vantage Point: Perspectives of the Presidency 1963–1969* (New York: Holt, Rinehart and Winston, 1971), pp. 326–327.
7. Under Johnson, the number of task forces increased but their composition and recommendations were secret. The purpose of the secrecy was to enable the president to take credit for ideas he liked but at the same time avoid being burdened by those he did not. The secrecy also permitted the president to ascertain the opinions of influential members of Congress without embarrassment on either side. The Johnson aide who communicated with individuals in Congress would normally preface his remarks with the question, "The president hasn't decided to do this, but if he did, how would you respond?"
8. The Domestic Council staff member who presided over the group had to make certain that recommendations to the president were in conformity with Nixon's basic goals and that the

options he selected were properly converted into legislative proposals or executive actions. In this way, a White House orientation was imposed on the policy-making process.

9. Richard P. Nathan, *The Plot That Failed* (New York: Wiley, 1975).

10. Ralph Bledsoe, executive secretary to the Domestic Affairs Council during most of Reagan's second term, described how the councils worked in the Reagan administration:

> Interagency working groups are still the primary means by which policy issues are identified and scoped. Working groups and task forces are responsible for preparation of the issues and options papers to be discussed by the councils. As with the cabinet councils, issues are usually discussed in one or more council meetings without the President in attendance. When an issue is ready to be forwarded to the President for discussion and/or a decision, the council directs that a paper be prepared reflecting the council's views. If the President is being asked for a policy decision, the paper is in decision memorandum format, usually including a statement of the issue, background information, a discussion of decision options with advantages and disadvantages of each, and a recommendation, if appropriate. Following a meeting with the President, at which council members present their advice and views, the President will usually make a decision that is then communicated to the appropriate departments and agencies for implementation. (Ralph C. Bledsoe, "Policy Management in the Reagan Administration," in James P. Pfiffner and R. Gordon Hoxie, eds., *The Presidency in Transition* [New York: Center for the Study of the Presidency, 1989], pp. 60–61.)

11. Mark A. Peterson, "The Presidency and Organized Interests: White House Patterns of Interest Group Liaison," *American Political Science Review* 86 (September 1992): 612–616.

12. Peterson, "The Presidency and Organized Interests," pp. 617–620.

13. Graham K. Wilson, "The Clinton Administration and Interest Groups," in Colin Campbell and Bert A. Rockman, eds., *The Clinton Presidency: First Appraisals* (Chatham, N.J.: Chatham House, 1996), pp. 225–230.

14. According to *Washington Post* reporter, Dana Priest:

> They would not let documents out of the room. They numbered each copy of certain memos. They wouldn't even let the staff have phone numbers of other staff members, because they didn't want us to be phoning in to people. (Dana Priest quoted in Haynes Johnson and David S. Broder, *The System* [Boston: Little, Brown, 1996], p. 142.)

15. Johnson and Broder, *The System*, pp. 161–163.

16. Hugh Heclo, "One Executive Branch or Many?" in Anthony King, ed., *Both Ends of the Avenue* (Washington, D.C.: American Enterprise Institute, 1983), p. 32.

17. For a discussion of what strategies presidents should pursue to achieve their legislative policy objectives, see Mark A. Peterson, "Developing the President's Program: The President as a Strategic Player" (paper presented at the annual meeting of the Midwest Political Science Association, Chicago, March 1990); Cary Covington and Rhonda Kinney, "Presidential Agenda Setting Power, Attitudes toward Risk, and Congressional Contexts: Accounting for Differences in Rates of Presidential Success in Congress" (paper presented at the annual meeting of the American Political Science Association, Washington, D.C., September 1991); and Patrick J. Fett, "Truth in Advertising: The Revelation of Presidential Legislative Priorities," *Western Political Quarterly* (Winter 1992): 895–920.

18. Light, *The President's Agenda*, p. 219.

19. Charles O. Jones, "Presidents and Agendas: Who Defines What for Whom?" in James P. Pfiffner, ed., *The Managerial Presidency* (Pacific Grove, Calif.: Brooks/Cole, 1991), pp. 197–213.

20. Fengyan Shi, "Agenda Setting: What Influence Do Presidents Actually Have?" (paper presented at the annual meeting of the American Political Science Association, Washington, D.C., September 1993).

21. James Fallows, "The Passionless Presidency," *Atlantic* ccxxxxiii (May 1979): p. 38.

22. Fallows, "The Passionless Presidency," p. 42.

13

BUDGETARY AND ECONOMIC POLICY MAKING

PRESIDENTS HAVE ALWAYS BEEN CONCERNED with the costs of government, and the state of the economy, but that concern has never been greater than it is today. With a budget of over $1.7 trillion, with a national debt of over $5.3 trillion, with federal revenues tied to economic conditions and interest rates, with the private sector sensitive to public expenditures, almost any substantive policy decision a president makes has significant budgetary and economic implications as well as important political consequences.

Moreover, budgetary and economic decisions are interrelated. Budgetary problems are magnified by a weak economy and diminished by a strong one. Large and continuing budget and trade deficits can have both long- and short-term effects on the economy, as can a surplus in either of these accounts.

These factors make budgetary and economic policy making one of the most critical, complex, and persistent spheres for the exercise of presidential leadership. Like it or not, most things that presidents want and need to do cost money. Without sufficient financial resources, they will be unable to achieve many of their most important policy objectives. But ironically their budgets are not theirs alone, nor can they be. Hampered by the commitments of their predecessors and previous Congresses; obligated to pay interest on the national debt and meet the statutory requirements of other ongoing legislative programs, particularly those that entitle people to benefits; pressured to respond to natural disasters with emergency aid; and constrained by the need to maintain payrolls, continue research and development, and ensure the production of items, particularly in the area of defense, that are vital to the national security, presidents today exercise limited influence over how their budgets will be allocated. To make matters worse, the influence that they do exert is subject to congressional modification in the form of budget resolutions and reconciliations. Similarly, the revenue side is also conditioned by previous and current legislation and also fluctuates with the economy. And all of these constraints have significant political consequences that further condition the behavior of elected officials, including the president.

So presidents are confronted by a dilemma. They are expected to redeem their campaign pledges, meet the country's changing needs, and do so in a manner that is both economical and efficient. Yet they often lack the resources to achieve these objectives and the discretion to obtain those resources. Directing change under these circumstances is extremely difficult although it is not impossible, as Franklin Roosevelt and Ronald Reagan demonstrated at the outset of their administrations. Nonetheless, being a facilitator rather than a director tends to be the order of the day as far as budget and economic policy making are concerned, and even in the facilitator role, the president's task is not easy.

This chapter will explore the president's leadership dilemma in a sphere that has become associated with presidential popularity, reelectability, reputation, and, ultimately, the exercise of presidential power: the federal budget and the national economy. Beginning with a historic overview of the executive budget, we will look at the development of a presidential role in budgeting. The involvement of executive branch and Congress in budgetary decision making is also examined. Similarly, we explore the evolution of economic policy making and the participation of presidential and other executive branch offices in decision making within this sphere. Throughout we describe the forces that affect presidential action and limit presidential discretion. The concluding section summarizes the recent trends in budget and economic policy making.

THE FEDERAL BUDGET

The budget is a document that forecasts revenue and estimates expenditures of the federal government. It does so for a fiscal year—a twelve-month period beginning October 1 and continuing through the following September 30. Since the primary purpose of the budget is to allocate limited funds, that allocation is, by definition, highly political. Competition for limited resources is inevitable. Priorities have to be established. The budget is an instrument that reflects those priorities in a very concrete way.

A presidential budget has been required since 1921. Prior to that time departments and agencies went directly to Congress for their appropriations. Their requests were compiled in a "Book of Estimates," but neither the president nor the treasury secretary made any systematic attempt to coordinate total revenues, although they occasionally did modify some of the requests.[1] However, with revenues (primarily from custom duties) exceeding expenditures during most of the nineteenth century, the lack of centralized planning was not perceived to be much of a problem.

Expenditures rose at the end of the century and the beginning of the next, and modest surpluses turned into deficits. Concerned about them,

Congress enacted legislation in 1905 to ensure that the government spent money prudently. It gave the president the statutory responsibility and authority to prevent the unwise and unnecessary expenditures of government funds.[2] The costs of World War I, however, vastly increased federal government expenditures, produced sizable budget deficits, and encouraged Congress to give the president budget authority. The Budget and Accounting Act of 1921 made the president responsible for an annual executive branch budget and established a bureau within the Department of the Treasury to handle these new presidential duties. Acting as a surrogate for the president, this bureau organized and ran a process that solicited yearly expenditure estimates from the departments and agencies, evaluated and adjusted them according to the president's goals, and finally combined them in a comprehensive executive budget. This budget review cycle has continued through the years, although Congress's consideration of the budget has undergone significant change.

The federal budget, however, has also changed dramatically since the 1920s.[3] In its early years it was relatively small by contemporary standards, oriented toward the executive agencies, and utilized primarily as a vehicle for controlling federal spending. Since the primary object of the budget was to make the national government more economical, to eliminate the deficits, and to keep a lid on spending, federal outlays were substantially reduced during the initial period of 1921–1930.[4]

Total government expenditures were in the range of $2 billion to $3 billion. Most of the money went directly to the departments and agencies for the costs of running the government. There were relatively few public works projects that required direct funding.

The Great Depression of the 1930s had a major effect on the character of the budget. Increased demands for government intervention in the economy culminated in Franklin Roosevelt's New Deal programs. Followed by World War II and the Cold War, this larger governmental role greatly accelerated spending in domestic and defense areas. Fortunately, the economic recovery, beginning in the late 1940s and continuing through the 1950s, provided increased revenues for these greater expenditures. These developments not only expanded the size of the budget but also moved it into an incremental phase, one in which existing programs continued to be maintained with a budget that included an increment to cover increased costs.

During this phase, which reached its zenith in the 1960s, the budget highlighted new programs and supported existing ones. Agencies assumed that the costs of their ongoing programs would be met in addition to whatever priority legislation the president wished to introduce.

Although the departments continued to administer their programs, more and more of the outlays went to third parties. Programs designed to help the invalid and the poor, senior citizens, veterans, and others provided direct payments to individuals from the treasury. Since the 1970s, these so-called entitlement programs have consumed an ever-increasing proportion of government expenditures, expenditures that are not easily subject to presidential control. Today they constitute more than half of the total budget (see Figures 13–1 and 13–2).

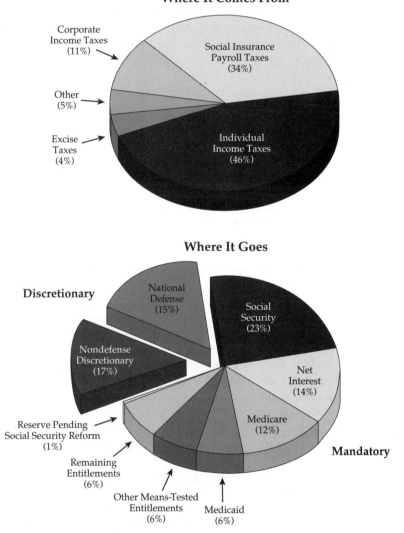

Where It Comes From

Corporate Income Taxes (11%)

Social Insurance Payroll Taxes (34%)

Other (5%)

Excise Taxes (4%)

Individual Income Taxes (46%)

Where It Goes

Discretionary

National Defense (15%)

Social Security (23%)

Nondefense Discretionary (17%)

Net Interest (14%)

Medicare (12%)

Mandatory

Reserve Pending Social Security Reform (1%)

Remaining Entitlements (6%)

Other Means-Tested Entitlements (6%)

Medicaid (6%)

FIGURE 13–1. The Federal Budget for Fiscal Year 1999

Source: *A Citizen's Guide to the Federal Budget, Fiscal 1999* (Washington, D.C.: Government Printing Office, 1998).

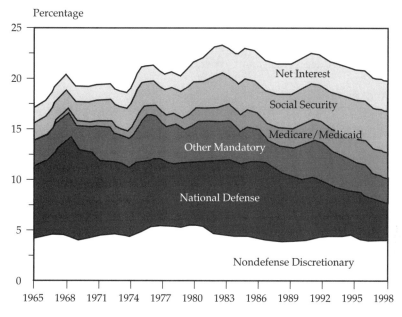

FIGURE 13–2. The Growth of Mandatory Expenditures, 1965–1998 (percentage of the gross domestic product)

Source: *A Citizen's Guide to the Federal Budget, Fiscal 1999* (Washington, D.C.: Government Printing Office, 1998).

The reason why entitlements are not under the president's control is that these programs and others like them legally entitle individuals to benefits as long as they meet stated eligibility requirements (age, income, or military service). These entitlements are independent of specific appropriations by Congress. In 1974, Congress decided to peg Social Security payments to the Consumer Price Index, forsaking decision making even on the levels of benefits. The president also does not have the authority to change these payments; only an act of Congress can do so.[5]

From the president's perspective, the sad fact is that a relatively small proportion of the total budget is subject to presidential control. Interest on the national debt, which constitutes about 15 percent of the total budget, must be met. Payments for agricultural commodities and government support programs were also required until Congress in 1996 voted to phase out farm price supports for some crops.

Even within the so-called discretionary part of the budget—that is, the part of the budget for which annual appropriations are required—many of the expenditures are for big-ticket items, such as personnel, military weapons systems, and government construction projects, items that cannot be reduced or eliminated without basic changes in policy and/or significant cost to the taxpayer. When these expenditures and the entitlement programs are considered, the result is that presidents can exercise only limited discretion over less than 25 percent of the total budget. Thus, presidents who wish to reduce government expenditures substantially have little leverage to do so.

And there is another problem. Recent legislation has placed limits, referred to as *caps,* on discretionary spending. It is only within these caps that the president and Congress can exercise discretion. In addition, the law requires that increases in spending be offset by decreases in other parts of the budget. This *pay-as-you-go* rule, intended to limit deficit spending, also limits what the president and Congress can effectively do.

The political ramifications of the budget constrain public officials as well. Instead of primarily affecting departments and agencies, the budget now has a direct impact on many outside the government. As a consequence, constituencies composed of veterans, senior citizens, industry representatives, labor, and others have organized to protect and extend their benefits. The pressure they exert also reduces the range of acceptable options for those in power. The 1995–1996 budget debate over Medicare cuts is a good example. When the Republican Congress tried to increase Medicare premiums and decrease anticipated expenditures, the public response was so negative that they were forced to abandon this proposal.

The regular involvement of interest groups on budgetary politics has made it more difficult for the president and Congress to use the budget as a device for controlling spending. By the late 1970s, the budget demonstrated more of the presidency's weaknesses than its strengths; presidents were responsible for it yet controlled little of it.

In the 1980s the primary objective of presidential budgeting began to change. Seeds of this change were sown in the economic problems of the previous decade: the decline in the nation's productivity and its industrial competitiveness and the rise in inflation and unemployment, especially during the 1970s. These factors, along with a steadily increasing national debt and sizable deficits, led those inside and outside the government to question the wisdom of ever-increasing government expenditures within the domestic sphere, particularly when the economy was weak.

Upon taking office, President Reagan took the lead in reordering national priorities and used the budget to achieve his objectives. Incremental increases gave way to decremental adjustments, which have actually lowered spending in parts of the budget when inflation is taken into account. The proportion of the budget devoted to domestic discretionary spending was cut, entitlement programs such as Social Security were adjusted, and money for defense was increased.

These changes affected the budget's orientation more than they affected overall outlays. Instead of distributing an expanding base of resources, the budget redistributed a declining one. This redistribution increased the competition and division among the agencies and outside groups concerned with "their" expenditures. With different interests and groups vying to protect and promote their own programs, a consensus supporting the budget was harder to achieve. Congress found it more difficult to enact budgetary policy, spending more time on budget matters and taking more votes on budget questions than it did in previous eras. Consideration of the budget drove other issues off the legislative calendar. This preoccupation has continued, reaching new heights in the 104th Congress when the battle to achieve a balanced budget literally closed the government for almost a month.

Presidents, like Congress, have also had to devote more time and energy to their budget activities, not merely to formulating the budget but to obtaining congressional approval for it. As principal policy makers and coalition builders, they had little option.

The Battle of the Budget: President versus Congress

Differing budget priorities, policy proposals, and partisan politics characterized presidential-congressional relations during the last six years of the Reagan presidency, all of the Bush presidency, and much of Clinton's as well. President Reagan and, to a lesser extent, President Bush wanted to maintain a relatively high level of defense expenditures and continue the level of personal and corporate income taxes that had been established in the early 1980s. To keep the budget more in balance, both presidents hoped to cut expenditures for domestic programs. Congress, however, was unwilling to do so, approving the bulk of their defense budgets but refusing to cut many of their proposals for decreasing domestic spending. Without a major increase in revenue, the result was readily predictable—a growing federal deficit. By the end of the Reagan administration, the yearly deficits had almost tripled the national debt. During the four years of the Bush administration, they continued to rise at a rapid rate. When George Bush left office in 1992, the national debt exceeded $4 trillion, having quadrupled over a twelve-year period (1980–1992), and the deficit had reached $290 billion (see Table 13–1). In the process, the United States moved from being the world's greatest creditor nation to the world's largest debtor nation.

In the 1980s Congress attempted, but failed, to impose discipline on government spending by enacting legislation that automatically triggered cuts if expenditures exceeded revenues by a certain amount. The first of these legislative acts, the Balanced Budget and Emergency Deficit Control Act of 1985—known by the names of three of its sponsors, Senators Phil Gramm, Warren Rudman, and Ernest Hollings—required a balanced budget within five years of its passage (subsequently extended to 1993), set specific

Table 13–1. The National Debt and Budget Deficit or Surplus, 1997–2003 (in billions of dollars)

	Actual			Estimate			
	1997	1998	1999	2000	2001	2002	2003
Federal government financing:							
Budget deficit or surplus	−22	−10	10	9	28	90	83
Other means of financing	−16	−16	−20	−13	−15	−14	−13
Borrowing from the public	38	26	10	4	−13	−76	−70
Federal government debt:							
Debt held by the public	3,771	3,797	3,807	3,812	3,798	3,722	3,652
Debt held by government accounts	1,599	1,747	1,931	2,104	2,281	2,482	2,684
Gross federal debt	5,370	5,544	5,738	5,916	6,079	6,204	6,336
Debt subject to legal limit	5,328	5,506	5,701	5,880	6,044	6,170	6,305

Note: Numbers may not add to the totals because of rounding.

Source: *A Citizen's Guide to the Federal Budget, Fiscal 1999* (Washington, D.C.: Government Printing Office, 1998).

deficit targets to be met over this period, and authorized automatic cuts in some domestic and most defense programs (except primarily those involving personnel) to bring the deficit to the required levels if the targets were not met.[6] By authorizing automatic cuts, Congress acknowledged its own inability to make tough and potentially unpopular political decisions.

The legislation, however, did not achieve its objective. To stay within the targets prescribed by the law but not suffer political retribution for making steep cuts in popular programs, Congress and the president devised a variety of accounting and reporting techniques that technically met the goals but actually evaded them. These included overly optimistic forecasts of revenue, underestimation of automatic government payments, the extension of expenditures into the next fiscal year, the pulling of revenues into the current year from the next one, and the enactment of supplemental spending bills not included in the Gramm-Rudman targets. The government even sold some of its assets to stay within the guidelines of the legislation. The need to bail out the savings and loan associations at the end of the 1980s further aggravated the problem.

As a result, real deficits continued to soar throughout the 1980s and were projected to exceed $320 billion by the early 1990s. These large deficits created pressure on Congress and the president to try again to fix the problem. (Figure 13–3 lists real and projected deficits from 1940 through 2003.)

Dollars in Billions

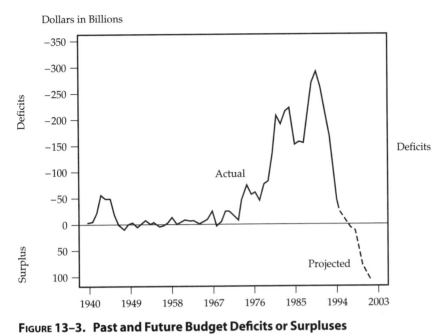

FIGURE 13-3. Past and Future Budget Deficits or Surpluses

Source: *A Citizen's Guide to the Federal Budget, Fiscal 1999* (Washington, D.C.: Government Printing Office, 1998).

After an extended series of meetings between representatives of the president and congressional leaders held behind closed doors in the spring of 1990, an agreement was reached to raise additional revenue and impose constraints on future government spending. The Budget Enforcement Act of 1990 was designed to reduce the deficit by making Congress and the president more responsible for those parts of the budget they could control directly. It placed specific limits on discretionary spending and set overall spending targets within three broad categories: defense, international affairs, and domestic programs. There was also a pay-as-you-go provision that required Congress to pay for the cost of any new program by obtaining savings from existing programs and to pay for any new tax reductions by obtaining additional revenues. The legislation shifted more enforcement responsibility from the Congress to the OMB and the president and also altered the schedule for the executive development and legislative consideration of the budget (see Tables 13–2 and 13–3).

Despite these efforts, however, deficits persisted. One problem with the 1990 act was that it exempted unpredictable and uncontrollable expenditures such as foreign debt forgiveness, increases in U.S. contributions to the International Monetary Fund, and the expenses resulting from the Persian

Table 13–2. The Executive Budgetary Process

There are four principal stages in the executive phase of the process. In the first, the overall guidelines of the budget are established. They are conditioned by the objectives of the president, the state of the economy, and the commitments of legislation, past and present. In the second stage, the departments and agencies prepare their estimates in accordance with these guidelines. Personnel from the Office of Management and Budget examine these estimates in a formal review process in the third stage. The fourth stage begins with the president being briefed by the budget director, hearing appeals from the department and agency heads, and making the final decisions. The budget is then printed and sent to Congress by the first Monday in February.

These stages of the budgetary process are detailed below.

APPROXIMATE TIMES	ACTIONS
	BUDGET POLICY DEVELOPMENT
February–March, 1st year	Senior economic advisers review the outlook for the current and future fiscal years; they predict effects on revenues and spending programs and report to the president.
April–June	The OMB conducts spring planning review sessions, exploring funding implications of major issues or programs that will be considered in the fall budget review. The OMB sets overall guidelines for the executive agency budget submissions and sends these, along with instructions on preparing their proposed budgets, to the agencies.
	AGENCIES' PREPARATION OF PROPOSED BUDGET
July–August	Agencies develop their proposed budgets.
September	Agencies send their proposed budgets to the OMB by September 1 for the fiscal year that begins thirteen months later. Other executive branch agencies not subject to the OMB review process submit their budgets later in the fall.
	OMB REVIEW
September–October	The OMB staff analyzes proposed budgets and holds hearings with agencies.
October–November	Economic advisers again review the outlook for the fiscal year that begins the next October. The director holds agency-by-agency reviews at which agency requests and staff recommendations are considered and recommendations are made to the president. The legislative branch and the judiciary submit budget requests to the OMB. The OMB transmits the proposed budget and economic advisers' findings to the president. The OMB gives agencies their recommended budget levels—also known as "the mark."

continued

TABLE 13–2. The Executive Budgetary Process *continued*

APPROXIMATE TIMES	ACTIONS
	PRESIDENTIAL DECISION
December	The president reviews OMB recommendations and decides on totals for agencies and programs. Possible appeals by agencies to the president are made. The OMB prepares budget documents for transmittal to Congress.
February, 1st Monday, 2nd year	The president delivers a proposed budget to Congress. The OMB sends an "allowance letter" to each agency giving its total within the president's budget and also transmitting "planning numbers" for the next two fiscal years.

Source: The Office of Management and Budget, as amended and updated by the author.

Gulf War. Additionally, the economic recession of 1991–1992 resulted in a shortfall of government revenues. With health care costs, including those for government programs of Medicare, Medicaid, and veterans benefits, continuing to rise more rapidly than predicted, still more money required to bail out the savings and loan industry, and other national emergencies cropping up—such as Hurricane Andrew which devastated South Florida in 1991—large, unbalanced budgets remained a problem and became a major issue during the 1992 presidential election.

After the election, Clinton, who promised that deficit reduction would be a major priority of his administration, proposed a deficit reduction plan to cut government spending and increase taxes. The proposal also extended the caps on discretionary spending to 1998 and the pay-as-you-go rules. The Democratic Congress modified Clinton's plan, increasing spending cuts and decreasing tax increases, and then enacted it into law by the barest of margins. The legislation, along with the end of the recession, had the desired effect, substantially reducing the deficit but not eliminating it.

Pressure to balance the budget persisted. When the Republicans won control of Congress in the 1994 midterm election, they made a constitutional amendment to require a balanced budget their principal priority. The amendment, however, failed by a single vote in Senate, prolonging the deficit debate.

Throughout the fall of 1995 and into the winter of 1996, Congress and the president battled over these budget issues. The president agreed to a balanced budget in seven years but only so long as it would provide adequate funding for Medicare, Medicaid, education, agriculture, national defense, veterans, and the environment. Both sides could not agree on a level of adequate funding. The Republicans contended that the president's

Table 13–3. The Congressional Budgetary Process

The congressional phase of the process begins with the budget committees of each house considering the president's request. In stage two the committees report their targets for revenue and expenditures and Congress enacts an advisory budget resolution. During the third stage the authorization and appropriation committees begin to draft their legislation within the guidelines of the budget resolution. In the final stage Congress enacts a second budget resolution and has the power, if it desires, to reconcile differences among its revenue, appropriations, and budget committees.

These stages of the process are enumerated below:

February	The first Monday of the month is the deadline for Congress to receive the president's budget. The Congressional Budget Office reports to budget committees on the president's budget. Budget committees hold hearings as background for a concurrent resolution.
March	Each standing committee sends its budget estimates to House and Senate budget committees.
April 1	The budget committees report a budget resolution to Congress.
April 15	Congress revises and enacts a concurrent resolution in which the House and Senate agree on budget targets for receipts, budget authorities, and outlays.
May 15	The House may consider individual appropriation bills.
June 30	The House completes action on annual appropriation bills. The Senate must complete action by October 1.
July 15	The president sends Congress a mid-session review of the budget that was submitted in February.
June–September	Authorization and appropriation bills are considered and adopted by both chambers of Congress. Congress must *reconcile* any changes in legislation it has enacted with its budget targets.
August	The OMB provides a "snapshot" of projected deficits or surpluses. By August 15, the CBO issues its initial report on the projected deficit or surplus. By August 20, the OMB issues its initial report on the projected deficit or surplus. If there is a deficit, and the president responds by issuing a sequestration order that reduces spending by the required amount to coincide with the budgetary spending limits.
October 1	The fiscal year begins. If Congress has not enacted appropriation bills, it must enact a resolution to continue spending at the current rate or some other rate that coincides with the budget. Failure to do so will deny money to the government and eventually force its closure. By October 15, the president issues his final sequestration order, which is effective immediately. The comptroller general issues a compliance report within thirty days of the president's order.

plan would not balance the budget, while Clinton claimed that the Republican proposal was too harsh and extreme. He vetoed the congressional budget as well as those appropriation bills that did not provide sufficient money for the programs he desired. As a consequence of this struggle, the government was forced to shut down twice, furloughing nonessential workers in agencies for which Congress had failed to enact appropriations, the first time for six days and the second, for three weeks. Public opinion turned against the Republican Congress for closing the government, forcing the GOP to back down. After enacting several temporary spending measures, Congress passed a comprehensive bill to fund the government for the reminder of the 1996 fiscal year.

Another election intervened with Democratic and Republican candidates echoing a similar refrain—their desire to balance revenues and expenditures, but not by raising taxes or savaging popular programs. It was the buoyant economy that allowed them to do so in 1997. With the Congressional Budget Office making a larger projection of revenue than previously anticipated, there were sufficient funds for both sides to claim that they accomplished their objectives *and* balanced the budget at the same time. For Clinton and the Democrats, it was a balanced budget with sufficient funding retained for programs in education, health, and the environment; for congressional Republicans, it was a balanced budget, lower government spending, and tax cuts (see the Hot-Button Issue box).

The difficulties which contemporary presidents have encountered in formulating their budgets and getting Congress to adopt them explains why the budget is not a very effective instrument of presidential power. Not only are presidents and Congress constrained by previous commitments, existing legislation, and their campaign promises, but they are also subject to strong clientele and constituency pressures as well as to fluctuations in the economy that may prevent them from doing what they desire. Negotiation and compromise, not dictation and domination, describes the relationship between the presidency and Congress on budgetary matters most of the time.

THE BUDGET MAKERS

The President

Presidents bear the primary responsibility for the executive phase of the budget and play a major role in the legislative phase as well. In each area, they have limited influence, but in neither can they easily or effectively dictate the outcome.

There are various ways presidents can affect the executive budget. Their goals dictate its priorities and shape its initial guidelines; their policies

☼ HOT-BUTTON ISSUE

What Should Be Done with the Budget Surplus?

After 30 years of deficits, who would have thought that the surplus would have become a problem? But it has in 1998, and if current projections of future revenue are correct, it will continue to be one in future years.

Although the problem may be new, the issues are not. Familiar divisions over philosophies, priorities, and partisanship have emerged. President Clinton, a moderate Democrat, wants to save the surplus for Social Security until its trust fund can be restructured to ensure that money will be available when future generations retire. The latest projections by the trustees of the system indicate that the fund will start depleting in 2013 and be out of money entirely by 2034. Liberal Democrats, while supporting the Social Security system and wanting to keep it viable for the future, also see current economic and social needs on which they believe some of the current surplus should be spent. But conservative Republicans are dead-set against new domestic spending. They are also dubious about whether Social Security can and should be preserved. These Republicans want to use the surplus to lower taxes, reduce the national debt, or increase defense spending.

The problem is compounded by different projections of revenue and expenditures from economic forecasters in the government and the private sector, differing estimates of the impact of a tax cut on future economic growth, and differing views of which policy decision would be more beneficial to Republicans and Democrats in the next round of elections. In the absence of a budget reconciliation agreement which eliminates the surplus by cutting taxes or increasing spending or by directing how the surplus is to be used, the issue is not likely to be easily or quickly resolved, even though the pressure to do so will be great.

determine the new big-ticket expenditures in their administrations and those that follow; their decisions resolve interagency disputes. They hear last-minute appeals and make final judgments on them. The budget presented to the Congress must meet with their approval.

In shaping the budget, presidents can get involved in detailed decision making, if they desire. Some have done so. Ford and Carter spent considerable time on budget matters; Nixon and Reagan did not. Nixon took little interest in the budget and delegated considerable authority to his budget director, while Reagan took a slightly different tack. Interested in setting broad budget policy, he was content to establish priorities and make decisions on items brought to his attention. By leaving the detailed evaluation of agency estimates to officials in the Office of Management and Budget, and by avoiding details, Reagan distanced himself from internal and external pressures to spend. This made it easier for him to propose budgets with substantial cuts in domestic spending, but not easier to mobilize support for those cuts in Congress.

George Bush and Bill Clinton were forced to assume a more active involvement in budget matters, particularly in the congressional phase of the process. Clinton has done so continuously. Upon taking office, he substantially altered the budget outline his predecessor prepared and during the next several years had adjusted his budget in the light of congressional reactions. Toward the end, he proposed tackling the big entitlement programs, Social Security and Medicare, so as to ensure their future viability.

The Office of Management and Budget

The Office of Management and Budget (OMB) is the president's principal institutional entity that oversees the budgetary process. It was created as the Bureau of the Budget (BOB) in 1921 to "assemble, correlate, revise, reduce, or increase the estimates of the several departments or establishments."[7] Originally located in the Treasury Department, it was moved to the newly created Executive Office of the President in 1939, where it has remained ever since, although in 1970 its title was changed to the Office of Management and Budget and its functions broadened to include management responsibilities.

Despite the fact that the Budget Bureau was housed in the Treasury Department for its first eighteen years, it functioned as an important, powerful, and independent presidential agency. During this early phase of its existence, the bureau exercised central oversight over the budget. It operated according to a standard rule that departmental estimates equal to or less than those of the previous year were automatically approved, while estimates for more money had to receive the authorization of the budget director and, in some cases, even the president.

The objectives of promoting economical government and controlling spending contributed to the bureau's power. Since most of the outlays prior to the mid-1930s went to the executive departments and agencies, there was little interest in the budget outside the government. The lack of public visibility and external pressure worked to the bureau's advantage. Its decisions were final unless overruled by the president, an infrequent practice in those days. Executive agencies were forbidden to circumvent the process by going directly to Congress for funds.

As the budget expanded, so did the size and functions of the budget agency and the interest in its decisions. In the 1920s and the 1930s, the bureau consisted of fewer than forty-five employees.[8] New responsibilities generated by World War II and the clearance of legislative policy matters enlarged the staff to more than 500 by 1949 and created an institutional memory upon which the White House grew increasingly to depend.[9] The budget for fiscal year 1999 provides for a staff size of 518 for the Office of Management and Budget and funding of $59 million.

Most of the people who worked in the bureau were civil servants. Initially, there were only two political appointees, the director and the deputy director. The latter, by tradition, was chosen from the ranks of the professionals who had worked their way up in the agency. As a consequence of its nonpartisan character, the Budget Bureau was particularly well suited to provide the president with "advice on the merits" as opposed to "advice on the politics." Moreover, its invulnerability to outside pressures, relative invisibility to the press, and accessibility to the president and his senior aides heightened its mystique and enhanced its clout.

Changes in the organization, influence, and roles of the Budget Bureau began to occur in the 1960s. These changes were a consequence of the increasing size of the White House staff, the increasing number of initiatives that emanated from it, and the increasing suspicion of the political loyalties of civil servants by new presidents and their staffs. Singularly and together, these factors decreased the agency's influence within the executive branch from 1961 through 1968. While it continued to run the budget review process and decide on routine budget matters, key issues became the more-or-less exclusive province of senior White House aides.

Changes in the character of the budget also worked to affect the bureau's role and ultimately its power. With less emphasis placed on limiting expenditures and more on highlighting programs, political policy makers, not career budget analysts, became the key players. With more requests emanating from the departments and agencies, budget review focused on the size of their increments rather than the merits of their existing programs. With an increasing percentage of the budget consisting of nondiscretionary spending, the Budget Bureau was limited in what it could cut and how much it could save. As a consequence of all these factors, the budget agency's influence declined while expenditures continued to expand. In the words of Allen Schick:

> Agencies became more vigorous (and successful) in pressing their claims for larger budget shares. The relationship [between the Budget Bureau and the executive agencies] became more a matter of bargaining, and less one in which high authority decided the outcome.[10]

Executive agencies acquired new allies and new bargaining chips in their efforts to maintain and increase spending. Outside groups, which benefited from the programs, supported agency requests on Capitol Hill, thereby creating an environment that made it difficult for the president to sustain cuts in these programs. Prior to the 1970s, these external political pressures were felt indirectly by the bureau. After 1970, the budget agency itself became more directly subject to outside influences. Changes in the organization and orientation of the agency were primarily responsible for its increased sensitivity to political matters.

A reorganization in July 1970 gave the Budget Bureau its new name, Office of Management and Budget, a new structure, and more political appointees. Civil servants who had previously exercised policy judgments on budgetary and legislative matters were relegated to positions of lesser importance in the organizational hierarchy.

The politicization of the OMB has continued under Presidents Carter, Reagan, and Clinton. Each of them added additional political positions and staffed them with people who shared their beliefs and perspectives. Today there are approximately two dozen senior political appointees in the top policy positions of the OMB.

The functions of the office also expanded during this period. Nixon and Ford used it to improve management techniques and evaluate existing programs. Carter set up a division within the agency to oversee reorganization efforts; Reagan used that office to increase oversight of executive regulations. He also used the OMB to achieve sizable cuts in domestic programs and to institute a series of management reforms. Bush gave his budget director, Richard Darman, considerable authority to negotiate agreements with Congress. Leon Panetta and Alice Rivlin, Clinton's first and second budget directors, were major lobbyists for the administration's deficit reduction plan during summer 1993 and negotiations with the Republican Congress in the 1995–1996 budget battles, while Franklin Raines was a prime negotiator in the balanced budget agreement that the Clinton administration reached with congressional leaders in 1997.

In recent times, the OMB's political sensitivities and its expanded functions have contributed to its influence. The willingness of presidents to use the agency to promote their objectives has worked to the same end. The OMB's clout in the process has increased, allowing it (in conjunction with the White House) to shift major allocations from agency to agency in accordance with the president's budget priorities. The extent to which executive budgeting has become a top-down rather than bottom-up process has further contributed to the OMB's influence, particularly that of its top political appointees.

The OMB's ability to effect change does vary, however, over the course of an administration. In the beginning, its institutional resources, particularly its access to information and expertise, are most valuable in overcoming departmental interests and congressional opposition to achieve new presidential goals. In the end its nay-saying abilities are apt to be most effective in maintaining the president's course.

How the Reagan administration obtained its 1981 budget cuts illustrates the advantage the OMB can give a president in his first year in office. In January 1981, before many of the departments were fully staffed and their secretaries had been fully briefed about their budget needs, the OMB proposed major reductions in domestic programs. Almost immediately, budget working groups were established. Composed of key White House personnel, budget officials, and appropriate department secretaries and their aides, the groups reviewed the proposed cuts and made recommendations to the president. In most cases the recommendations supported the cuts. This was because Reagan had stated his goals, the OMB had a near-monopoly over budget information, and the composition of the groups was stacked against the departments. The secretaries were not in a position to advocate their departments' interests even if they wanted to do so.[11] The OMB also exerted considerable influence on policy making at the beginning of the Bush and Clinton administrations.

Over time, however, the advantages that the OMB can give a president decline. The inevitability of pressure to maintain existing benefits, the relatively small amount of discretionary spending, and the tendency of departments to develop their own constituency-oriented programs limit the OMB's ability to effect major change over the course of an administration.

The Executive Departments and Agencies

While the OMB is the principal participant in the executive phase of the budgetary process, it is not the only one. In one way or another, every executive agency has an impact on the budget, mostly on its own.

Departments and agencies are asked to submit yearly estimates for their programs and operational costs. They are expected to defend these estimates before the OMB and the Congress. They may also have to appeal to the president if funding for a particular program is threatened.

Most agencies have a division that coordinates their budget preparation and another that facilitates their legislative activity. In deciding how much to request, agencies have limited discretion. A large percentage of their budget is required by existing legislation, either by formulas written into the law or by long-term commitments. Even within the discretionary portion there are presidential guidelines to follow, ceilings that cannot be exceeded, and administrative costs that must be met.

Nonetheless, the agencies have leeway when estimating their needs. They generally tend to request funds within an acceptable range but toward the top of that range, anticipating that the OMB will revise these requests downward as will the Congress. This expectation, in turn, contributes to their tendency to pad their estimates and the OMB's inclination to cut them. In general, the agencies that are most aggressive in requesting funds for their programs enjoy the greatest political support (which permits them to act this way).

Budget decisions of an agency frequently have impact beyond that agency. In the 1980s, the large increase in defense expenditures came at the expense of discretionary domestic programs. Even within the Department of Defense, the intense rivalry among the army, navy, and air force has had a major impact on how that department allocates its requests. In the 1990s the pressure on domestic spending has continued to generate interdepartmental rivalries for funds.

The president and his advisers establish the guidelines, the departments and agencies make their estimates, and the OMB evaluates those estimates; but Congress must appropriate the money. Table 13–2 indicates the major steps in the executive phase of the budgetary process.

The Congress

The Constitution requires that Congress appropriate all funds that the government spends and raise all revenues that it collects. Congress meets this requirement by the passage of thirteen annual appropriation bills and revenue measures. Prior to the Civil War, one committee of each house drafted the legislation that raised and appropriated money. As the demands of government became greater, separate policy committees in each house handled their own appropriation. There was no comprehensive national budget, budget committees, or overall budget authority.

Following the passage of the Budget and Accounting Act of 1921, in which Congress required the president to present such a budget, the legislature centralized its own spending power in two appropriation committees, although it did permit its policy committees some authority to borrow, contract, and authorize legislation that obligated the government to additional expenditures.[12] The appropriation committees, however, did not consider the budget as a whole. Rather, using the president's executive estimates as guidelines, they drafted individual bills for the separate departments. In many instances, congressional appropriations did not match the president's budget estimates. Supplemental money bills passed during the year also magnified the difference between the president's requests and the appropriations made by Congress. The legislature's consideration of the budget was fragmented and highly political. Members could publicly support the president's goals yet push for exceptions for their own pet projects.

After several abortive attempts to pass a comprehensive budget rather than simply separate appropriation bills, Congress enacted legislation in

1974 that enabled it to do so. The Budget and Impoundment Control Act of that year established a congressional budget process, two congressional committees, and a Congressional Budget Office (CBO) to provide it with a budget capacity that rivaled the president's. The process set up a timetable for considering the budget; the committees were charged with drafting advisory and binding budget resolutions that the Congress could not exceed; and the CBO provided staff support for revenue and expenditure estimates.

Although the Budget and Impoundment Control Act improved the capacity of Congress to consider a comprehensive budget, it did not force the legislature to abide by its own budget decisions. Separate appropriation bills still determined the actual expenditures; separate tax bills still determined the actual revenues. Thus, a gap between budget goals and appropriation and revenue measures was still possible—even probable. The 1974 act, however, did provide a procedure known as *reconciliation,* by which Congress could direct its committees to legislate within the guidelines of its budget decisions. It was used for the first time in 1980 and has continued to be employed from time to time since then.

Ronald Reagan took advantage of reconciliation in 1981 and 1982 by getting the Democratic House of Representatives to agree to a vote without amendments on a binding budget resolution that reconciled the differences between its budget estimates, appropriation bills, and revenue measures. In this way he was able to achieve many of his policy objectives through the mechanism of a single vote on the budget.

Today, a reconciliation provision is normally part of the binding budget resolution, which Congress is supposed to enact in the spring of every year. It was the reconciliation compromise of August 1993 that finalized the deficit reduction legislation that Clinton initiated after he took office; a reconciliation proposal by the Republicans in December 1995 that he vetoed, causing a three-week closure of nonessential government services; and two reconciliation proposals in 1997, one that cut taxes and the other that reduced spending, that put the balanced budget agreement into legislative format.

The legislation on the budget enacted since the 1980s has increased the importance of presidential involvement in the congressional phase of the budgetary process. The president's critical assessments of the economy and the administration's targets for funding continue to provide the basis for initial deliberations by Congress. Over the course of the legislature's budget hearings, markup, and floor debate, presidents must adjust their projections and may modify requests. In fact, Congress requires a midyear report in July. At each stage, presidential influence is important if the president's budget proposals are to prevail. Finally, if the deficit targets are not met, the sequestration process is triggered, and the president is forced to make cuts in many key federal programs.

The budget legislation, in short, has reinstituted a joint process in which both the president and Congress have important roles to play. The process involves many people, requires many reports, and extends many months over the course of the legislative calendar. It is a difficult one, highly political and public, dependent on the need for compromise.

The need for institutional cooperation but the difficulty of obtaining it explains why presidents in recent times have been more successful in designing their budgets than in getting them accepted without major modifications by Congress.[13] Both institutions have their own agendas and constituencies. Even when the same party controls both institutions, these agendas and constituencies do not always or usually coincide, as Clinton discovered in 1993 when he pursued his own deficit reduction plan only to meet opposition from conservatives within his own party as well as from his partisan political opponents.

With over half the Senate and a quarter of the House serving on budget, appropriations, or revenue committees, the task of achieving a consensus is often herculean. It requires a great allocation of time and significant political and legislative skills, although these skills in and of themselves may not be sufficient (see Table 13–3).

PRESIDENTIAL LEADERSHIP AND THE BUDGET

Presidents have a leadership problem when it comes to the budget. That problem has been magnified in recent times by the persistence (until recently) of deficits and the accumulation of a huge national debt. To reduce or eliminate the deficit and prevent the debt from getting larger requires tough decisions that may be unpopular with large groups. Were presidents to be able to make these decisions on their own, they might have the courage and will to do so and be able to survive politically. However, they cannot do so because budgetary power is not centralized, budgetary responsibilities are shared with Congress, and budgetary commitments have already been made by previous legislative and executive actions.

All this would not be so bad were it not for the expectation that presidents lead, particularly when their party controls Congress. However, with limited political power to use against recalcitrant members of their own party and practically none to use against their opponents, with limited persuasive power in the absence of a consensus or a crisis, and with limited time, energy, and knowledge to devote to this perennial problem, they are at the mercy of a variety of forces.

Under the circumstances, for most presidents the budgetary process becomes a necessary evil. It is the rare president who can use it to direct change. When this does occur, it is usually during the first year, following a change of administrations, and after an election in which economic and budgetary problems were the principal issues. The more likely result, however, is to use the budget as an instrument of incremental change to facilitate political compromises and economic decisions that inevitably result from the give-and-take in a highly diverse representative system.

Whereas the legislation of the last two decades has increased the president's need to be an active participant in congressional consideration of the budget, it has also reduced the executive's powers to control spending deemed unwise or uneconomical. The 1974 Budget and Impoundment Control Act limited the president's impoundment authority—that is, the ability to defer or rescind spending without congressional consent. Under terms of the statute, a temporary deferral of spending could have been overturned by either house of Congress; a permanent deferral, known as a rescission, required the approval of both houses. The Supreme Court subsequently ruled that a one-house veto was unconstitutional; the action of both legislative branches was necessary. After President Reagan tried to use the deferral authority in the absence of legislation, Congress enacted a law that limits presidential deferrals to routine managerial decisions.

In the light of contemporary deficit problems and the difficulty that Congress and the president have had resolving them, Congress enacted a line-item veto in 1996 which permitted the president to delete individual items in revenue and appropriation bills after approving the legislation. The law permitted Congress to disapprove of the president's actions, but if the president vetoed the disapproval, Congress had to override that veto in the usual fashion. During the first and only year in which the line-item veto provision was in effect, President Clinton used it eighty-two times, of which thirty-eight, all on military construction projects, were overridden by Congress. The president achieved a savings of $869 million with the line-item vetoes that were not overridden.

The constitutionality of the law was immediately challenged, first by a group of members of Congress who had opposed the legislation and second by those who were adversely affected by Clinton's vetoes. The Supreme Court held that the first group did not have standing but the second group did. In its decision the Supreme Court held that the law violated the veto provision of the Constitution. The president's use of the line-item veto which irritated some members of Congress, the surplus which reduces pressure to cut spending, and the political and legal arguments against Congress delegating its power to the president make the reenactment of some type of line-item legislation unlikely.

DOMESTIC ECONOMIC POLICY MAKING

Presidents have been involved in the budget process since 1921, but not until the administration of Franklin Roosevelt in the 1930s have they been concerned on a regular basis with economic policy making. Prior to that time presidential activities were generally limited to initiating or supporting proposals to correct specific problems that had arisen within the economy. Theodore Roosevelt's trust busting and Woodrow Wilson's labor reforms are two examples of these early forms of presidential involvement.

The depth of the 1930s Depression, the degree of public panic, and Herbert Hoover's resounding election defeat signaled the beginning of a more comprehensive presidential role in the economy. No longer could presidents enjoy the luxury of standing on the sidelines. Franklin Roosevelt's activism became the model for his Democratic successors. Even Republicans found that there was no turning back.

Congress expected and even required this involvement. The Employment Act of 1946 obligated the president to prime the economy to maximize employment and production. The Taft-Hartley Act of 1947 gave the president the power to intervene in labor-management disputes that threatened the nation's security and well-being. In each case Congress not only acknowledged an expanded presidential role but created mechanisms to help the executive fulfill it.

Every president since Roosevelt has strived to meet these expanded expectations. They have done so not only because they are required to do so, but because their popularity, reelectability, and even their legacy is thought to be closely related to their perceived economic success. A strong economy is good news for a president; a weak economy is not although it may be good news for a presidential challenger.[14]

The economic policies of presidents have varied. Truman, Kennedy, and Reagan desired to lower taxes to stimulate economic growth. Clinton advocated increased productivity through investment tax credits to encourage business to modernize and expand and education tax credits to allow more people to get a higher education or more advanced job training. Key to his economic proposals was a reduction in the size of the budget deficit. Eisenhower and Ford tried to achieve savings by cutting government spending, while Bush tried to do so in a less painful way by cutting projected growth. Johnson obtained a surtax to help pay for the costs of the Vietnam War and his Great Society programs, while Nixon implemented wage and price controls to reduce inflation and stabilize the economy. Carter tried a variety of revenue and budget measures to deal with the high inflation and stagnant economy that plagued his presidency.

Differing fiscal approaches lay at the core of these presidential policies.

A fiscal strategy is a plan to manipulate government revenue and expenditures to influence economic conditions. In contrast, a monetary approach regulates the supply of money to affect change. Presidents cannot affect monetary policy, generally the prerogative of the Federal Reserve Board, nearly as much as they can influence fiscal policy. However, even with fiscal policy, as pointed out previously, it is the Congress that enacts appropriations and revenue bills. Although presidents can influence the legislature's actions, they cannot control them.

Until the mid-1970s, fiscal strategies were predicated on the economic theories of John Maynard Keynes, the eminent British economist. Keynes argued that increases in government spending and reductions in government taxes would stimulate demand and invigorate the economy during periods of sluggish activity. The only drawback with such a policy was that it also resulted in budget deficits. Keynes was not worried about these deficits, however, because he believed that in the long run a vibrant economy would generate greater revenues, reducing or eliminating the difference between expenditures and income. With the exception of Eisenhower, presidents Truman through Nixon subscribed to this belief.

An expanding economy coupled with relatively low unemployment and inflation during most of the 1950s and 1960s seemed to confirm the merits of the Keynesian approach. By the beginning of the 1970s, however, economic conditions began to change. Budget deficits increased, the rate of growth declined, and inflation rose dramatically throughout the decade. Keynesian economics did not contain satisfactory answers. Other theories began to command attention.

The monetarists, led by Professor Milton Friedman of the University of Chicago, contended that the supply of money was the key to sound economic growth, particularly to control the ravages of inflation. Increasing interest rates would reduce the amount of money in circulation, decreasing inflationary pressures and cooling the economy. Lowering interest rates, on the other hand, would have the opposite effect, stimulating demand and output by making borrowing cheaper and more money available. In periods of high inflation and an overheated economy, a tight money policy made sense. But when inflation was high and the economy stagnant, it did not. It was precisely this condition in the late 1970s that gave credence to still another economic strategy—supply-side economics.

The supply-side philosophy combined the Keynesian approach to generating demand with the monetarist's desire to regulate currency. Tax cuts stimulate spending, while money supply controls inflation. Ronald Reagan, an advocate of this approach (and the first president to have majored in economics in college), sought to implement the fiscal component of this strategy as president. He proposed budgets that increased defense expenditures, cut domestic programs, and substantially reduced corporate and personal federal income taxes. Congress enacted the bulk of his requests to increase defense spending and cut taxes, but not to cut domestic spending, during his first two years in office, although he was forced to modify his tax stand in 1982 because of the need for additional revenues and the desirability of closing tax loopholes. Reagan pursued his supply-side policies throughout his presidency.

George Bush took a more pragmatic approach; he continued the general thrust of the Reagan program but moderated it where events and politics dictated. Like Reagan, Bush wished to minimize governmental interference in the private sector, maintain a strong defense, and keep taxes low. His desire to control the large budget deficit and have funds for domestic programs, however, forced him to accept a revenue increase as part of a compromise with congressional Democrats in 1990.

Bill Clinton advocated policies that require a more active government role to stimulate the economy, spur investment, and shift priorities to the domestic sector. A key component of his 1993 economic program to reduce the deficit was raising taxes on the wealthy, but he also accepted steep cuts in government spending, declaring in his 1996 State of the Union address, "the era of big government is over."

The impact of a president's policy on the economy is difficult to discern. So many factors that affect the economy and impact on the society lie beyond the president's control. Yet, presidents are held responsible for the state of economic affairs during their presidency. Carter's defeat in 1980 and, especially, Bush's defeat in 1992 can be attributed to their perceived failure as economic policy makers, while Reagan's victory in 1984 and Clinton's victory in 1996 can be attributed to their successful policy.

FOREIGN ECONOMIC POLICY MAKING

In recent years, increasing attention has been focused on international economic policy making, and specifically on agreements that promote freer and less encumbered trade between countries. The Clinton administration has concluded two such agreements—one with Mexico and Canada, the North American Free Trade Agreement (NAFTA), and one with major trading countries in the world, the General Agreement on Tariffs and Trade (GATT)—and initiated cooperative efforts that it hopes will lead to other regional trading agreements as well as bilateral arrangements. A key element of Clinton's foreign policy has been to position the United States at the center of the international economic community.

Clinton is not the first president to promote international economic cooperation. Ever since the United States emerged as a major power, presidents, beginning with Woodrow Wilson, have sought to lower the barriers to international commerce for American industry. Presidents Reagan and

Bush both argued against artificial impediments to free trade and worked to secure international agreements to protect the free flow of goods and services into and out of the United States. Clinton's trade policy continued and expanded these initiatives.

There has been persistent opposition to freer trade, however. Much of it stems from organized labor which fears the loss of American jobs to lower-paid foreign workers and from small businesses who fear lower-price foreign competition. Although tariffs and subsidies have traditionally been used to protect and promote American industries, the benefits of free trade have pressured Congress in recent years to support presidential initiatives in the international economic arena.

Realizing its own institutional limitations to making and judging deals, Congress has given the president more discretion to act in these matters, retaining for itself the authority to say "no." The Trade Act of 1974 gave the president authority to negotiate agreements as well as to impose sanctions against countries that violated them. Since that time, presidents have used or threatened to use these sanctions to prevent countries from engaging in unfair trading practices against the United States. In 1995 President Clinton indicated that he would institute a high tariff on imported Japanese luxury cars if Japan did not open its domestic market to American automobile manufacturers. It subsequently did so. Similarly, the president threatened sanctions against China if that country failed to respect U.S. copyrights and intellectual property of U.S. firms.

Congress has also authorized the president to recommend which countries should be given trading status as a "most favored nation." This status entitles a country to the lowest tariff charged for a particular commodity. The granting of such status, however, has become a political football which members of Congress regularly kick to the president when they are unhappy about the policy of a particular country—for example, China's treatment of political dissenters.

The most contentious battles concerning free trade are those that require congressional approval of new trade agreements. Controversy stems from the diverse pressures exerted by groups within the political environment, which stand to benefit or fear that they will be hurt by the legislation. Organized labor, older manufacturing industries, environmentalists, even consumer advocates opposed NAFTA and GATT, while big businesses, particularly those engaged in international commerce, high-tech companies, service industries, and most economists and investors supported them. These agreements, though enacted into law in 1993 and 1994, have continued to generate political debate. In the 1996 presidential campaign, Pat Buchanan, Ross Perot, and even Ralph Nader rallied against these agreements and the adverse impact they purported to have on the economy, environment, and safety standards in the United States. Their opposition has continued, as has labor's, making it difficult for a Democratic president to convince Democratic members of Congress to support a renewal of fast-track authority in which the president negotiates treaties subject to an up-or-down vote in Congress.

Not only do presidents have to contend with public pressures directed at Congress and the executive branch, they also must deal with the policies and actions of state governments as they vigorously compete with one another to promote their products abroad and solicit foreign tourism, capital, and industry for their states. Moreover, they must also review the actions of independent regulatory agencies, such as the U.S. International Trade Commission, which hears complaints by American companies of unfair trading practices against them by firms in other countries, and make recommendations for redress, which are subject to presidential and, often, congressional approval.

The multiple pressures, both foreign and domestic, on economic policy making have forced presidents to assemble and depend on large advisory and administrative staffs as they formulate and implement policy. These staffs, which are housed in the Executive Office and the executive departments, differ in their orientation, clientele, and substantive expertise. Coordinating them is a major task. It is to that economic policy mechanism that we now turn.

ECONOMIC POLICY MAKERS

The Department of the Treasury

Most of the president's economic advisory structure was established by Congress. The Treasury Department was the first executive branch agency to play a major role in the financial affairs of government. Originally charged with responsibility for collecting and dispersing federal funds, its functions have gradually expanded to include debt financing, import controls, and drug enforcement.

Representing the financial community, this department has exercised a conservative influence throughout the years on matters of economic policy. Its orientation is to promote stability and long-term growth.

The secretary's role as an economic adviser to the president has been enhanced in recent years by the emergence of international and domestic problems of particular concern to the department, such as stabilizing the value of the dollar as well as other foreign currencies (such as the Mexican peso and the Japanese yen) in international financial markets, overseeing foreign investments of the United States, and conducting negotiations on the repayments of international loans. Similarly, within the domestic arena, tax policy and savings bank failures thrust the Treasury Department into the center of political controversy. With no other presidential office or White House official charged with handling these matters, the secretary of the treasury took the lead as adviser, coordinator, lobbyist, and spokesperson for the president. In this capacity the treasury secretary chaired the councils that fashioned and implemented major economic priorities in the Reagan and Bush administrations, but not in the Clinton administration (although treasury secretaries Lloyd Bentsen and Robert Rubin were prominent spokespersons, advisers, and advocates for the president's economic program).

The Federal Reserve Board

The second oldest government agency concerned with economic policy is the Federal Reserve Board (known as the "Fed"). However, it is not a presidential agency. Created by legislation in 1913, its principal function is to regulate monetary policy. It does so by adjusting the discount rate that commercial banks must pay when they borrow money from one of the member banks in the Federal Reserve System. The percentage of deposits that commercial banks must maintain is also regulated by the Fed. A third way the Federal Reserve Board can affect the money supply is by requesting its regional banks to buy or sell government securities on the open market. It also intervenes on the international market to increase or decrease the value of the dollar in accordance with the needs of the American economy.

In theory, the Fed operates with considerable autonomy from the president and Congress. Its members, who are nominated by the president and appointed with the advice and consent of the Senate, serve for fourteen years. Its chair, designated by the president from members of the board of governors, has a four-year term that does not coincide with that of the president, which serves to increase the chair's independence.

However, the Fed does not operate in a vacuum. It must be concerned with the impact that the fiscal policies of the president and Congress have on the economy. The Fed regularly exchanges information about the nation's economy with other executive branch units, notably the Council of Economic Advisers and the Department of the Treasury.[15] Being sensitive to political pressures, the Fed has tended to refrain from making visible policy decisions in election years. In contrast, the decisions to raise interest rates, which are obviously less popular than those to lower them, are made more frequently in nonelection years.[16]

The Council of Economic Advisers

The principal economic advisory units within the Executive Office of the President are the Council of Economic Advisers (CEA) and the Office of Management and Budget, both of which were established by statute. The

Employment Act of 1946 created the CEA and charged it with advising the president on macroeconomic policy. Its functions include analyzing economic conditions, forecasting trends, and preparing the president's annual economic report to Congress. In addition to providing the president with long-term advice, the council has become increasingly involved in short-term microeconomic issues such as trade policy, deregulation, and even credit and housing programs. It has tried to avoid operational responsibilities and has, for the most part, succeeded.[17]

The council is small and specialized. It is composed of three members appointed by the president with the advice and consent of the Senate, who serve at the president's discretion. The council's chair, who is the principal link to the White House and the president's other economic advisers, participates in high-level economic policy meetings, supervises the operation of the CEA and the preparation of its annual economic report, and occasionally has acted as an administration spokesperson on economic affairs.

The council is supported by a small staff comprising approximately ten to fifteen professionals, mostly economists, who come primarily from the academic community and stay for a few years before returning to their academic institutions. The constant turnover of professional staff on the council infuses it with new ideas but limits its institutional memory and organizational clout.[18] Members of the council are also drawn from academia and frequently have worked on the council's staff prior to their appointment. Most of the council chairs have been university professors.

The academic orientation of the council has made it less subject to outside pressures than are other economic advisory units. As a consequence, when strong political pressures are exerted, the chair of the council can take a longer-term, less partisan perspective than can some of the president's other advisers. This was particularly evident during the third and fourth years of the Reagan presidency, when council chairman Martin Feldstein frequently disagreed with the administration's public position on interest rates and the deficit. After two years in office, Feldstein returned to his academic position and there was some question whether another chair would be appointed. Reagan waited until after his 1984 reelection to do so.

In general, the council has declined in importance as economic policy has become more political and as the number of economic advisers to the president has proliferated. Nonetheless, the personal relationship of the chair and the president remains the key to the council's impact on economic policy making. Arthur Burns (Eisenhower), Walter Heller (Kennedy), and Alan Greenspan (Ford) were three chairmen who had their president's confidence and were able to exercise considerable influence on economic decisions. Others have not been as fortunate.

No longer enjoying the information advantage that it had when there were fewer economic policy units within the government and fewer economists to run them, the council's voice today is one among many. It has tended to deal primarily with microeconomic issues.

The Office of Management and Budget

The OMB also performs economic advisory functions for the president. Not only does its director participate in the initial forecasts for revenue and expenditures as budget planning gets underway, but the director, deputy, and program associate directors continually analyze and evaluate the merits of department and agency requests. Revisions of the initial budget forecasts are also the responsibility of the OMB. Since the orientation of the budget director is toward the bottom line—the differences between expenditures and revenues—the director must be concerned with tax policy and other revenue-producing measures. The director regularly meets with the president's senior economic advisers.

International Economic Advisers

The Office of the U.S. Trade Representative, which was established by Congress during the Carter administration, was created to centralize trade policy in the presidency. It is a relatively large office with a staff of over 180 and a budget of $25 million. The head of the office has cabinet rank, the only EOP head to have such status.

The principal tasks of the trade representative are to formulate and coordinate policy and to monitor its implementation. Often an advocate for the administration, the trade representative is also its primary negotiator on trade issues. This office, however, is not the only one in the executive branch that is involved in matters of international commerce and trade.

Naturally, the State Department is also interested in the foreign policy impact and international implications of trade policy. State's charge—to promote diplomacy and maintain ongoing, multifaceted relations with other countries—orients it against protectionism and toward freer and easier trade.

In addition to the State Department, almost every other executive department has some interest and involvement in international trade. The Commerce Department, for example, represents and promotes business interests abroad. Its secretaries frequently lead trade delegations composed of executives from the private sector on missions to expand U.S. markets. It was on one of these trade missions, in Croatia in 1996, that Commerce Secretary Ron Brown, his staff, and the business leaders who accompanied him, lost their lives in a plane crash.

The Labor Department looks at the impact of trading issues from the perspective of the U.S. workforce, while the Department of Agriculture is concerned about the farm exports of large agribusinesses and also the viability of the family farm; the Transportation Department has to consider how trade will be conveyed and on whose carriers; the Energy Department deals with a variety of export/import issues from strategic stockpiles and oil availability and cost to nuclear technology, the storage of nuclear waste materials, and other energy sources; Defense is involved with a variety of national security matters that pertain to trade, including the sale of sophisticated U.S. technology, military aid and arms sales, and the proliferation of nuclear weapons; the Environmental Protection Agency focuses on environmental matters from acid rain to global warming to water pollution, and emission standards for imported automobiles and trucks; and the list goes on.

THE COORDINATION OF ECONOMIC ADVICE

In addition to using the Treasury Department, the Council of Economic Advisers, and the OMB in an advisory capacity, presidents have also concocted a number of other institutional arrangements for soliciting and coordinating recommendations and advice. The origins and organizations of these groups have varied.

Two political scientists, Erwin Hargrove and Michael Nelson, suggest that the pattern of economic advising since World War II can be described in stages.[19] In the first, 1946 to 1960, a broad, relatively unstructured relationship existed among the chair of the Council of Economic Advisers, the director of the Bureau of the Budget, and the secretaries of the treasury, commerce, and agriculture. These experts, both collectively and individually, provided the president with advice, advocacy, and administration within the economic sphere.

Beginning in 1960 and continuing through the end of the Nixon administration, relationships among the president's primary economic advisers became more structured in this second stage. A troika, consisting of the heads of three major advisory bodies—the Treasury Department, the OMB, and the CEA—met on a regular basis to coordinate policy. Within the group, a rough division of authority emerged with the Secretary of the Treasury becoming the major spokesperson and revenue adviser, the chair of the council the principal forecaster and analyst, and the budget director the chief overseer of expenditures. Other cabinet secretaries, who had previously rendered economic advice, were generally excluded. This had the effect of reducing the impact of outside forces on the group and maximizing the range of presidential decisions.

The third stage of economic advising commenced in the 1970s. It has been characterized by more participants, more external influences on policy judgments, and more formal advisory structures. With national economies more interdependent, foreign, defense, and national security affairs have greater impact on economic decisions and vice versa. As a consequence, the secretaries of state and defense, the president's national security adviser, and the president's special representative for trade negotiations all have legitimate concerns about the country's economic policy. Similarly, the explosion of federal programs in the 1960s, particularly entitlement programs, has created a large public constituency interested in and affected by economic decisions.

To cope with a policy-making process that has become more fragmentary, pluralistic, and political, recent administrations have had to devise council mechanisms, consistent with their presidents' particular styles of decision making, that not only permit a range of views to be presented and interests to be accommodated, but also work to coordinate these concerns, to promote consensus, to maximize the president's discretion, and to ensure the effective implementation of major decisions and actions.

Nixon initially appointed a Cabinet Committee on Economic Policy, with himself as its chair. He quickly found, however, that the meetings consumed too much of his time and were not productive. Within a year he had abandoned this arrangement in favor of an advisory system in which he depended on a single aide—his treasury secretary—for information, expertise, and public relations.

Gerald Ford, who came to the presidency after spending many years in Congress, was more comfortable with a group of advisers debating policy. He established an Economic Policy Board (EPB), consisting of practically the entire cabinet. During the Carter presidency, a more informal economic policy group and advisory process emerged. While the group's composition was similar to Ford's EPB, Carter's organization lacked a staff backup and a regular meeting schedule, as had existed during the Ford administration. Friction among its members produced acrimonious debate and made coordination and consensus difficult. Over time, Carter turned to key White House personnel, particularly domestic aide Stuart Eizenstat, for economic advice.

Presidents Reagan and Bush reverted to the Ford model. Their Cabinet Council on Economic Affairs provided a forum for discussion, a mechanism for providing recommendations, and an institution for implementing presidential decisions. Reagan depended more on his cabinet council than did Bush, who turned increasingly to his budget director and treasury secretary during the 1991–1992 recession.

Clinton created a National Economic Council to develop, coordinate, lobby, and oversee the implementation of his economic program. The council, which met frequently during the administration's first two years, fashioned the president's economic stimulus package and deficit reduction plan. Later it developed responses to the initiatives of the Republican Congress.

Presidents have considerable flexibility in establishing their own economic advisory system. How they do so relates to their personal style, their interest in economic matters, and the extent to which they wish to immerse themselves in the details of policy and make middle-level decisions. The advantage of the more formal advisory arrangement, such as adopted by Nixon, Ford, and Reagan, is that it relieved them of day-to-day decision making but still permitted them the opportunity to establish broad policy guidelines. In contrast, the more fluid systems that Carter and, to a lesser extent, Clinton used maximize personal involvement but also place greater decisional responsibilities on the president's shoulders.

THE POLITICS OF ECONOMIC POLICY MAKING

Economic policy making has become more political, more pragmatic, and less stable. These changes have affected the advice that presidents receive as well as the accommodations they must make. They have also affected presidential involvement in economic matters.

The recommendation process is more sensitive to outside pressures from Congress, the bureaucracy, and organized interest groups, each of which has its own interests to protect and its own political axes to grind. Members of Congress must consider the economic impact on their constituencies, while department and agency heads must be responsive to their clientele, and organized groups must placate their supporters. To the extent that economic decisions require coalition building to become public policy, presidents must take these varied interests into account as Clinton did in 1993 (see The Clinton Presidency box).

The politicization of economic decision making has made long-range planning more difficult. The election cycle must be considered when calculating the effect of policy change. Policy makers key recoveries to their own political benefit whenever possible.

Not only do short-run considerations such as elections tend to drive economic decisions, but they also enhance the pragmatic character of the decisions themselves. Presidents are more inclined to strive for what is politically feasible rather than what may be theoretically optimal or ideologically desirable. Perhaps this explains why they are more apt to pursue a policy of selective involvement in economic matters rather than to become a macromanager of the economy. This strategy has allowed them to claim credit for economic successes and share or, better still, avoid, blame for economic failures.

The experience of the Reagan administration is a case in point. Coming into office with clear-cut views of how it wished to stimulate the economy, the administration was forced to compromise its initial budget and tax proposals in order to get them enacted into law.[21] The compromises became more extensive as the next presidential election approached and presidential

THE CLINTON PRESIDENCY

Economic Decision Making in 1993

Bill Clinton faced major economic and budgetary problems when he entered the presidency, but they came as no surprise: He had talked about them during his campaign. He held a public seminar to discuss them as president-elect. He spoke about them during his first address to Congress and throughout his first six months in office—but he did not realize how difficult they would be to solve.

The basic issue was simple enough. The economy was in recession, and Clinton had promised to fix it. The federal budget was out of balance, and Clinton had promised to reduce it. How could he simultaneously stimulate the economy and reduce the federal budget deficit?

The policy solution was complicated by promises made during the presidential campaign. One promise that Clinton had often repeated in an effort to gain votes was to cut the income taxes of the hard-pressed middle class. However, cutting middle-class taxes would reduce government revenues, thereby aggravating the deficit problem. The president had also promised to propose legislation to encourage savings and investment. One way to do this was by providing tax incentives, which would also decrease revenues for government, at least in the short run. Finally, the president was under pressure from his Democratic constituency and some members of Congress to increase spending for a variety of domestic programs that had not fared well during the Reagan-Bush years. Increased government spending adds to the federal deficit and the accumulated national debt.

The dilemma, then, was how to stimulate the economy, reduce the federal deficit, and meet the needs of his political constituency. There were no easy answers.

Three groups vied for the president's attention with proposals designed to placate their supporters. Clinton's political advisers, most of whom had been active in his campaign, urged him to pursue a populist policy in which economic stimulation would be the primary objective and reduced middle-class taxes a principal stimulator. They also recommended that the president create job programs and extend unemployment benefits. To pay for these programs they argued for higher taxes on the rich and a reduction of business subsidies.

The president's economic advisers, however, cautioned against decreased taxes, increased spending, and any programs that increased burdens of American business. They saw the deficit as the primary issue and believed that only through substantial cuts in government expenditures plus some increase in revenue could this issue be satisfactorily addressed. And it needed to be addressed if confidence in the American economy was to be restored and long-term interest rates lowered.

To stimulate the economy or reduce the deficit, Congress would have to be involved. Congressional sentiment was divided, largely along partisan lines. The Republican minority in 1993 was dead set against any increase in taxes after what had happened to George Bush when he supported a tax increase in 1990;

they wanted deficit reduction to be achieved through massive government spending cuts.

The Democrats were much less united, with liberal members of Congress, particularly those from urban areas, wanting the president to create more jobs. Not only did they support increased government spending, they opposed reductions to programs that benefited their traditional political constituencies. Moderate and conservative Democrats, primarily those from the South, were more sympathetic to spending cuts, more opposed to new taxes, and more desirous of reducing the deficit.

Over the first four months of his administration, Bill Clinton vacillated among these three positions. A politician who desired to please, he struggled to find a consensus that would meet with some approval from each of these groups. In doing so, he made decisions and then was forced to reverse some of them after new information became available. Moreover, his decision making was also affected by leaks of potential policy options to the news media. These leaks embarrassed the president and limited his discretion, forcing him to back off proposals and engendering a strongly negative public reaction. The leaks also contributed to mixed messages that emanated from the White House.

Delay and indecision followed. The news media described a presidency in disarray with little leadership from the top. All this lowered public confidence in Clinton and weakened his already weak political position (he had received only 43 percent of the vote) during the so-called honeymoon period, the first one hundred days of his administration.

In the end Clinton proposed a $16 billion economic stimulus package as his number-one priority. It was enacted by the House of Representatives but defeated in the Senate by a Republican-led filibuster. The second priority, a deficit-reduction bill, was substantially modified by Congress, which eliminated a proposed energy tax and made more cuts in government spending, before it was enacted by the barest of margins. In the process the president was forced to make a number of highly publicized compromises, which were essential to the bill's legislative success but undercut his leadership image.

In August 1993, the president got a deficit reduction plan through Congress. He had finally achieved a major administration priority, but his reputation as a decision maker, legislative leader, and communicator in chief suffered in the process. His political capital had been depleted. His first six months in office had been rough, but his difficulties were characteristic of economic policy making in the modern presidency.[20]

influence in Congress declined. Pragmatic considerations, in short, muted the administration's ideological perspective but at the same time enhanced the chances for the passage of its legislative proposals. The Clinton administration provides another illustration of the need to be flexible, pragmatic, and willing to compromise on a continuing series of economic and budget proposals that the president and Congress negotiated.

The impact of politics on economic policy decisions has had another effect. It has made those decisions less stable over time. Unanticipated events and unintended consequences have frequently forced presidents to adjust their economic programs. President Ford was forced to abandon his Whip Inflation Now (WIN) program as economic conditions deteriorated and the country fell into a recession. President Carter had to recant a promise to provide taxpayers with a fifty-dollar rebate as the budget deficit soared. President Reagan had to support a large revenue increase one year after getting his massive tax cut through Congress. President Bush violated his "no new taxes" pledge in 1990, and President Clinton was not able to keep his 1992 campaign promise to cut middle-class taxes. The hopes and promises of candidates and the realities of governing often clash.

Another factor that contributes to fluctuations in economic policy is the economy itself. Although presidents are ritually blamed for unfavorable conditions and expected to improve them, many events and situations lie beyond their immediate control. Existing laws establish levels of revenue and high percentages of expenditures. Interest rates dictate the cost of government borrowing while cost-of-living adjustments (COLAs) automatically raise federal outlays. Presidents must meet these obligations. Over time they can try to change them, but change is not easy.

Similarly, international forces and events affect the American economy in ways that they did not prior to World War II. The rise in the price of imported oil in the mid-1970s contributed to the inflation in the United States at the end of the decade. The reindustrialization of Germany and Japan and the growth of new industries in Asia adversely affected American competition in steel, shipbuilding, textiles, and automobile manufacturing. On the other hand, the weakening of the Asian economies in the late 1990s initially reduced inflation pressure in the United States by making imported goods from that part of the world available at lower prices. The weakness or strength of the dollar affect the flow of trade and tourism, the stability of financial markets, and the ability of countries to meet their foreign debts, all of which have short- and long-term economic consequences that interfere with presidents' ability to manipulate the economy along the lines they desire. Nonetheless, the chief executive is ritually blamed for the economy's poor performance and lauded for its success.

These external factors also affect the process of making economic decisions. They have made that process more complex. Because they have produced more people inside and outside the government who are interested in economic policy, more interests must be balanced, more coordination is necessary, and more time must be devoted to economic affairs. The burdens on presidents and their advisers are greater, and economic issues have more political impact, yet presidential control is more difficult to achieve. In no other policy area (except possibly the budget) are presidential limits more discernible. The increased complexity of the economic decision-making process compounds the president's leadership problem.

CONCLUSION

Presidential responsibility has been enlarged in budgetary and economic spheres. That enlargement has been a product of need, statute, and precedent. Acknowledging its inability to fashion comprehensive budget and economic policy, Congress has required the president to do so. This requirement, coupled with the expanded role of the federal government, has forced presidents and their staffs to devote increasing resources to these activities.

The task has not been easy. Expectations of presidential performance have grown, but the president's capacity to affect budgetary and economic matters has not kept pace. Much of the budget is dictated by existing law and policy commitments. Presidents can affect discretionary funding, but even here, political pressures and congressional opposition often undercut their efforts to reorder spending priorities and revenue measures. Similarly, within the economic sphere, a myriad of forces from within the country and abroad challenge the president's control. These factors mute presidential efforts to stimulate the economy yet, at the same time, make those efforts more important.

To help the president fulfill expectations of leadership within these areas, advisory mechanisms have developed and decision-making processes have evolved. The OMB continues to be the principal presidential office called on to provide budget advice and oversee spending requests. However, the needs of the departments and agencies, the concerns of the House and Senate, the interests of organized groups, and more generalized public pressure have involved many additional participants in the budgetary and economic policy-making processes. This involvement has increased the complexity of these processes and has made them more political and less easily subject to presidential control. In both areas, power is decentralized and responsibility is more difficult to pinpoint.

For presidents, this has meant that they must devote more attention to economic matters (including the budget), weigh more factors in making critical judgments, and use more skills in articulating and shaping an administration position and negotiating with Congress. For the presidency, these changes have placed greater stress on the organizational mechanism that coordinates and integrates the policy decisions and builds support for them both within and outside the government. For budgetary policy, they have made it more difficult to use the budget as an instrument of presidential power. For economic policy, they have produced a short-term perspective with more variation within and between administrations, which places the emphasis on political feasibility.

In short, presidential roles have increased within the budgetary and economic spheres, but presidential influence has declined. Leadership is more difficult to exert. Presidents have less ability to control the factors that affect their judgments. However, those judgments are increasingly expected to solve national problems and promote national prosperity. Directing change under normal conditions is difficult. Presidents need crises as action-forcing and coalition-building mechanisms to do so. This need raises the stakes, delays solutions, and frequently shortens the time frame in which those solutions are developed and implemented. In general, the best presidents can do is facilitate. To do so effectively, they must devote more time to budgetary matters and must selectively involve themselves in economic issues. They must coordinate support within the executive branch, build coalitions within Congress, balance interests, and maintain the confidence of the general public—a tall order, to be sure.

DISCUSSION QUESTIONS

1. Can the contemporary budget be used as an instrument of presidential power with Congress and/or the executive branch departments and agencies? Explain why or why not, and illustrate the scope and limits of the president's budgetary power.
2. Ever since Franklin Roosevelt's administration, the president has been expected to be manager of the economy. Can the president really perform this role? What are some of the ways in which presidents can affect the economy, and some of the limits to the president's managerial role?
3. What were the most important economic and budgetary decisions made by President Clinton during his presidency? Indicate why these decisions were important, what impact they had, and how they affected other policy decisions during the Clinton presidency.

WEB EXERCISES

1. Go to the OMB Web site <http://www.whitehouse.gov/WH/EOP/omb/html> to access the budget for the current or future fiscal year. You can also access it via the Government Printing Office <http://www.gpo.ucop.edu/search/budget--.html>. In the two dashes, put the last two years of the budget that you want. Indicate how much money the president has requested for his office, the Executive Office of the President,

and compare that to the amount requested for the operation of the Congress and for the operation of the federal judiciary. Are you surprised by the results?

2. Access the Congressional Budget Office (CBO) <http://www.cbo.gov>. Compare its projections for spending and revenue for the next fiscal year with those found in the president's budget. What explains the difference in the projections? Which do you think may be more accurate, and why?

SELECTED READING

Carroll, Richard J. *An Economic Record of Presidential Performance: From Truman to Bush.* Westport, Conn.: Praeger, 1995.

Drew, Elizabeth. *Showdown.* New York: Simon and Schuster, 1994.

Frendreis, John, and Raymond Tatalovich. *The Modern Presidency and Economic Policy.* Itasca, Ill.: F. E. Peacock, 1994.

Ippolito, Daniel. *Uncertain Legacies: Federal Budget Policy from Roosevelt through Reagan.* Charlottesville: University of Virginia Press, 1990.

Kettl, Donald. *Deficit Politics.* New York: Macmillan, 1992.

Porter, Roger. "The President, Congress, and Trade Policy." *Congress and the Presidency* 15 (Autumn 1988): 165–184.

Porter, Roger. *Presidential Decision Making: The Economic Policy Board.* Cambridge: Cambridge University Press, 1980.

Rowan, Hobart. *Self-Inflicted Wounds: From LBJ's Guns and Butter to Reagan's Voodoo Economics.* New York: Times Books, 1994.

Schick, Allen. *The Capacity to Budget.* Washington, D.C.: Urban Institute Press, 1990.

Schick, Allen. *The Federal Budget: Politics, Policy, Process.* Washington, D.C.: Brookings Institution, 1994.

Stein, Herbert. "Presidents and Economics." *American Enterprise* 5 (January/February 1994): 6–10.

Stockman, David. *The Triumph of Politics.* New York: Harper and Row, 1986.

Tomkin, Shelley Lynne. *Inside the OMB.* New York: M. E. Sharpe, 1998.

Weatherford, M. Stephen. "The Interplay of Ideology and Advice in Economic Policymaking: The Case of Political Business Cycles." *Journal of Politics* 49 (1987): 925–952.

Weatherford, M. Stephen, and Lorraine M. McDonnell, "Clinton and the Economy: The Paradox of Policy Success and Political Mishap." *Political Science Quarterly* 111 (1996): 403–436.

Wlezien, Christopher. "The President, Congress, and Appropriations, 1951–1985." *American Politics Quarterly* 24 (January 1996): 43–67.

Woodward, Bob. *The Agenda.* New York: Simon and Schuster, 1994.

Notes

1. For a discussion of the budgetary process during this early period, see Louis Fisher, *The Politics of Shared Power: Congress and the Executive* (Washington, D.C.: Congressional Quarterly, 1992), pp. 177–178.
2. The legislation, known as the Anti-Deficiency Act of 1905, has been cited as the statutory basis of the president's impoundment authority—that is, the president's power not to spend money appropriated by Congress if that expenditure would not be wise or prudent.
3. Our description of the evolution of the budget is based primarily on Allen Schick's discussion and analysis in his paper, "The Politics of Budgeting: Can Incrementalism Survive in a Decremental Age?" (paper presented at the Annual Meeting of the American Political Science Association, Denver, Colorado, September 1982).
4. In 1920, federal expenditures totaled $6.357 billion. By 1930 they had been reduced to $3.320 billion.
5. The size of the cost of living adjustment (COLA) is determined by the Bureau of Labor Statistics on an annual basis. The bureau's calculation has been subject to some controversy in recent years. Some economists believe that the COLA has been overestimating inflation by approximately .5 percent per year. One proposal, made by Senator Daniel Patrick Moynihan during the perennial budget battles between the president and Congress, was to readjust the COLA, thus saving the government billions of dollars.
6. The General Accounting Office (GAO) was originally given the responsibility to determine the size of these cuts after receiving estimates from the Office of Management and Budget (OMB) and the Congressional Budget Office (CBO). However, the Supreme Court determined that the GAO's role violated the constitutional principle of separation of powers by involving a congressional agency in executive decisions.
7. Louis Fisher, *Presidential Spending Power* (Princeton, N.J.: Princeton University Press, 1975), p. 35.
8. Larry Berman, *The Office of Management and Budget and the Presidency, 1921–1979* (Princeton, N.J.: Princeton University Press, 1979), p. 8.
9. Berman, *The Office of Management and Budget*, p. 102.
10. Schick, "The Politics of Budgeting," p. 7.
11. William Greider, "The Education of David Stockman, *Atlantic*, December 1981, pp. 33–34.
12. Fisher, *The Politics of Shared Power*, p. 183.
13. Christopher Wlezien, "The President, Congress, and Appropriations 1951–1985," *American Politics Quarterly* 24 (January 1996): p. 43.
14. See, for example, Stephen E. Haynes, "Electoral and Partisan Cycles between U.S. Economic Performance and Presidential Popularity," *Applied Economics* 27 (January 1995): 95–106.
15. James E. Anderson, "The President and Economic Policy: A Comparative View of Advisory Arrangements" (paper presented at the Annual Meeting of the American Political Science Association, Washington, D.C., August–September, 1991), p. 10.
16. John T. Woolley, *Monetary Politics: The Federal Reserve and the Politics of Monetary Policy* (New York: Cambridge University Press, 1984).
17. Political scientist James E. Anderson described two instances, one during the Johnson administration and the other during the Carter administration, when the Council of Economic Advisers became involved in the implementation of policies. In both cases it did so because the department and agencies were unable or unwilling to do so (Anderson, "The President and Economic Policy," p. 5).
18. Anderson, "The President and Economic Policy," p. 5.
19. Erwin C. Hargrove and Michael Nelson, *Presidents, Politics and Policy* (New York: Knopf, 1984), pp. 186–189.
20. Stephen J. Wayne, G. Calvin Mackenzie, David M. O'Brien, and Richard L. Cole, *The Politics of American Government* (New York: St. Martin's Press, 1998), pp. 463–464.
21. Hugh Heclo and Rudolph G. Penner, "Fiscal and Political Strategy in the Reagan Administration," in Fred I. Greenstein, ed., *The Reagan Presidency* (Baltimore: Johns Hopkins University Press, 1983); Alan Schick, "How the Budget Was Won and Lost," in Norman J. Ornstein, ed., *President and Congress* (Washington, D.C.: American Enterprise Institute, 1982).

14

FOREIGN AND DEFENSE POLICY MAKING

FEW WOULD QUESTION THE OBLIGATION OF PRESIDENTS to preserve and protect the nation. Few would deny them the constitutional and statutory authority to do so. Few would dispute their need to perform a variety of roles with the help of a responsive, supporting staff. Still, the extent of presidents' powers, the scope of their roles, and the nature of their advisory systems have been subject to controversy.

These powers, roles, and advising systems all contribute to the president's leadership capacities. Powers are essential. Traditionally, executives have enjoyed a broad prerogative in foreign affairs, a prerogative that expands during crises that threaten the interests and security of the country. That expansion, however, is limited in scope and time. One critical aspect of presidential leadership is how those limits are defined, both in legal and political terms.

Other components of the leadership equation in foreign affairs are the multiple roles presidents assume and the multiple forces that affect them. The roles derive from the Constitution, from statutes, and from precedent. They have been more expansive in foreign affairs than in the domestic arena, but the president's leadership problem stems from the same basic root: Presidents do not control the environment in which they must operate, nor do they exercise their responsibilities exclusively. Moreover, there are additional components in the international arena—nation-states, regional alliances, and world organizations—that operate independently and are not responsive to the internal political forces that condition policy making in the United States.

Congress is empowered to act in foreign affairs; an increasing array of interest groups, plus professional lobbyists who represent foreign corporations and governments, seek to influence foreign policy decisions, most of which have domestic implications. The news media regularly report on, and evaluate, presidential actions in foreign affairs. Within the international arena, the United States is one player among many. Its economy, its resources, and its political and

473

military positions are more interdependent with others than ever before. More-over, presidents must deal with an increasing number of their own advisers, who represent and present differing perspectives, organizations, and interests.

How all of these factors affect the president's capacity to lead in foreign affairs and shape foreign policy will be the subject of this chapter. We first describe the president's formal authority in theory and in practice. We then turn to the expansion of the president's policy-making role, identifying the factors that have contributed to that expansion and the success presidents have had in achiev-ing their policy goals. Changes in the international and domestic environment, particularly within the last decade, have complicated the president's task. We dis-cuss those changes and their impact on presidential policy making within the con-text of the "two presidencies" thesis and then go on to describe and evaluate the advisory mechanisms that have been created to help the president coordinate, formulate, articulate, and implement foreign and defense policy. We conclude with a statement of how these factors, singularly and together, contribute to the kind of leadership a president can exert.

CONSTITUTIONAL AND STATUTORY AUTHORITY

The Original Design

The president's powers in foreign affairs and national defense have expanded significantly beyond their original design. The framers of the Constitution anticipated a foreign policy-making role for the president, but they did not want the executive alone to dominate that role. On the con-trary, their fear that a president might pursue self-interests at the expense of the nation's welfare led them to divide and share foreign policy-making responsibilities, just as they had in the domestic and economic arenas. Whether to go to war was to be the decision of Congress. The president had discretion to react in times of emergency to repel attacks, but presumably not to initiate hostilities or in any other way establish permanent war pol-icy. The expectation was that the Congress would do so. The president could, however, terminate hostilities.

Short of war, the executive was given considerable latitude. The presi-dent could initiate treaties in conjunction with the Senate; their approval required the concurrence of two-thirds of the upper chamber. Similarly, the president could appoint ambassadors, but that too required the advice and consent of the Senate. The performance of the ceremonial duties of a head of state and the conduct of foreign policy were seen as executive responsi-bilities.

In performing these functions, presidents would inevitably make deci-sions that had policy implications. The framers did not fear this. They anticipated that Congress, by virtue of its power to appropriate money, authorize programs, and regulate commerce, would establish the contours of that policy and be able to check presidential initiatives adequately.

The Exercise of Powers

Treaty Making Treaty making was to be jointly exercised with the Senate. An incident that occurred early in the Washington administration, however, soured this arrangement and presaged the difficulties that the president would have in dealing with the upper chamber as both an advisory and consenting body. In August 1789, President Washington came to the Senate to request its advice on a treaty with Native Americans in western Georgia. Armed with thirteen questions prepared by his secretary of war, General Henry Knox, Washington desired the Senate's guidance in the negotiations. Instead, he was treated to a long, discursive discussion that reached no conclusion. Forced to return two days later for what turned out to be insipid advice, Washington did not personally go back to the Senate for its counsel. Instead, he and his successors turned to their principal department heads for advice, and to the Senate primarily for its consent, as required by the Constitution.

Washington's experience had a profound effect on presidential-senatorial relations. It discouraged the president from involving the Senate in the negotiation phase of treaty making. While some consultation continued, presidents began to do more on their own. Woodrow Wilson's refusal to consider senatorial opinion in the negotiations on the Treaty of Versailles represents one of the most flagrant and unsuccessful examples of a chief executive going it alone.

Historically, the Senate has approved without modification about 70 percent of the approximately 1,600 treaties that have been submitted to it by the president since 1789. Only 20 of those that have come to a vote have been voted down (the most famous probably being the Treaty of Versailles, which ended World War I and established the League of Nations). However, many other proposed treaties have been withdrawn by the president because of opposition in the Senate, and thus have never come up for a vote. About 150 have been withdrawn since World War II, including the SALT (Strategic Arms Limitation Talks) II treaty proposed by President Carter and withdrawn to protest the Soviet Union's armed presence in Afghanistan.[1]

Not only can the Senate approve treaties without modification, as it did with the Intermediate Range Nuclear Forces Treaty (INF) with the Soviet Union in 1988 and the Chemical Weapons Treaty in 1997, or reject them outright; it can also approve them with reservations or with amendments, thereby requiring changes or deletions. In early 1978 the Senate consented to two treaties dealing with the Panama Canal. It added a reservation to one of them stating that the United States had a right to use military force, if necessary, to keep the canal open. Sometimes these reservations, voiced in advance, can lead to modifications or side agreements in the negotiations on the treaty itself, as they did with the North American Free Trade Agreement (NAFTA), which the Bush and Clinton administrations negotiated with Canada and Mexico.

From time to time the House of Representatives has also attempted to impose itself in the treaty-making process, but usually without success. Arguing that the Congress as a body is empowered to deal with foreign commerce, military affairs, war, and international policy, it has proposed legislation and used its appropriations authority to this end. Both the president and the Senate have resisted the lower chamber's intrusion into their exclusive domain, however. When treaties require authorizing legislation or appropriations to be implemented—as in the case of North Atlantic Free Trade Agreement (NAFTA) and the General Agreement on Tariffs and Trade (GATT)—then the House will be involved as a coequal legislative body.

Whereas Senate consent is necessary for the ratification of treaties, it has not been considered essential for their termination. When President Carter ended a long-standing defense treaty with the Chinese Nationalists on Taiwan, he did not request the approval of the Senate. The legality of Carter's action, which was challenged by Senator Barry Goldwater, was upheld by a federal appellate court. The Supreme Court also concurred, although the justices split in their reasons for upholding the appellate court's decision.[2]

Presidents also have some discretion in their interpretation and reinterpretation of treaties. However, they cannot digress from the interpretation that they or their predecessors represented to the Senate during the treaty's ratification hearings. When debating the Intermediate Range Nuclear Forces Treaty in 1988, the Senate declared that any digression from the "common understanding" of the treaty at the time of ratification would require joint action by Congress and the president by statute or by treaty.[3]

Formulating Executive Agreements The need to obtain the Senate's consent has encouraged recent presidents to enter into executive agreements in order to avoid the formal treaty ratification process. The number of such agreements has mushroomed in recent years, as indicated in Table 14–1.

An executive agreement is concluded by the president on behalf of the United States with the head of government of another country. Unlike a treaty, it does not require a two-thirds vote of the Senate. Thus, when President John Tyler failed to get the Senate to approve a treaty annexing Texas, he entered into an executive agreement to do so. Most executive agree-

TABLE 14–1. **Treaties and Executive Agreements Approved by the United States, 1789–1997**

Year	Number of Treaties	Number of Executive Agreements
1789–1839	60	27
1839–1889	215	238
1889–1929	382	763
1930–1932	49	41
1933–1944 (F. Roosevelt)	131	369
1945–1952 (Truman)	132	1,324
1953–1960 (Eisenhower)	89	1,834
1961–1963 (Kennedy)	36	813
1964–1968 (Johnson)	67	1,083
1969–1974 (Nixon)	93	1,317
1975–1976 (Ford)	26	666
1977–1980 (Carter)	79	1,476
1981–1988 (Reagan)	125	2,840
1989–1992 (Bush)	67	1,371
1993–1997 (Clinton)	80	1,269

Note: Varying definitions of what comprises an executive agreement and its entry-into-force date make the above numbers approximate.

Source: Harold W. Stanley and Richard G. Niemi, *Vital Statistics on American Politics,* 4th ed. (Washington: Congressional Quarterly, 1994), p. 280. Clinton data supplied by the Treaty Office, U.S. Department of State.

ments do not even need formal congressional approval, although some may require legislation to implement them. Such legislation is subject to a simple majority vote of both houses.

Even when Congress does not have a legislative responsibility, it does have a right to know about them. In 1969 and 1970, the Senate Foreign Relations Committee discovered that Presidents Johnson and Nixon had covertly entered into a number of secret agreements with South Vietnam, South Korea, Thailand, Laos, Ethiopia, Spain, and other countries. In response to these actions Congress passed legislation in 1972 which requires the secretary of state to transmit to Congress within sixty days the text of any international agreement other than treaties to which the United States is a party. If presidents feel publication of an agreement would jeopardize national security, they may transmit the text only to members of the Senate Foreign Relations and House Foreign Affairs committees under an injunction of secrecy that only they (or their successors) may remove.

Presidents Nixon and Ford did not fully comply with this legislation, however. Some agreements were not submitted to Congress and others were submitted after the sixty-day period. Consequently, in 1977 Congress passed legislation requiring any department or agency of the U.S. government that enters into any international agreement on behalf of the country to transmit the text to the State Department within twenty days of its signing. Neither of these two laws actually limits the president's power to act without Congress in defense and foreign affairs. Yet their passage indicates that Congress is increasingly unwilling to defer blindly to the president's judgment.

Unlike treaties, executive agreements do not supersede statutes. Otherwise, they are just as binding as treaties and have been used for such famous compacts as the destroyer-bases deal with Great Britain in 1940, the Yalta and Potsdam agreements in 1945, and the Vietnam peace agreement of 1973.

Presidents have been careful in their choice of instruments for making international agreements. In recent years treaties have dealt with such diverse subjects as shrimp, the protection of Mexican archaeological artifacts, the dumping of wastes at sea, and the maintenance of lights in the Red Sea; executive agreements have also been used to end wars and to establish or expand military bases in other countries. In 1972, as a result of SALT, President Nixon signed a treaty limiting the defensive weapons of the Soviet Union and the United States and an executive agreement limiting the offensive weapons of each country. President Clinton negotiated an agreement with Japan to open Japanese markets to U.S. automobiles and with China to prevent the pirating of patented and copyright material.

Although most executive agreements are routine and deal with noncontroversial subjects such as food deliveries or customs enforcement, some implement important and controversial policies. The U.S. loan to Mexico in 1995 is an example. After it became apparent that Congress would not enact legislation to bolster the falling value of the peso, the president used his discretionary authority to do so by entering into an agreement with the Mexican government.

In addition to concluding a formal agreement, presidents have also engaged in a form of diplomacy that recognizes "understandings" with other countries. A case in point is the SALT II treaty. Although the Senate never approved it, the Reagan administration abided by most of its provisions (as did the Soviet Union). Similarly, the Carter administration continued to observe the SALT I treaty for three years after it expired. Short of enacting legislation that requires a specific action, Congress can do little to prevent the president from making a unilateral policy declaration in concert with the leaders of other governments.[4]

Recognizing and Not Recognizing Countries   In addition to negotiating treaties and formulating executive agreements and understandings, presidents can initiate or terminate relations with other countries. The right of recognition has traditionally been considered a presidential responsibility. Although there is evidence to suggest that the framers intended this power to be purely ministerial, presidents have exercised their discretion when using their recognition authority.[5] George Washington was the first to do so when he received the representative of the new French Republic in 1789, Citizen Genet.

Presidents have gone so far as to recognize a government that has been removed from power and to acknowledge the rights of a people who lack a state. Following the signing of an agreement between Israel and the Palestine Liberation Organization (PLO) at the White House in 1993, President Clinton indicated that the United States might grant formal recognition to the PLO if it renounced terrorism and recognized Israel's right to exist. The Senate has no role in this recognition process other than to consent to the choice of an American ambassador.

Recognizing countries can be controversial. In 1933 Franklin D. Roosevelt recognized the government of the Soviet Union, fifteen years after it was constituted and functioning. In 1979 Jimmy Carter extended recognition to the People's Republic of China following a period of thirty years of nonrecognition. In 1984 Ronald Reagan announced the resumption of formal diplomatic relations with the Vatican. After approving a private visit to the United States by the president of Taiwan in 1995, an island over which China claims sovereignty, the Clinton administration went to great lengths to indicate to the Chinese that the visit did not imply or portend recognition. Each of these actions provoked criticism about the merits of presidents' judgments, but not about their right to make them.

Presidents can also end relations. Before war ensues, it is customary to sever relations with the adversaries. Similarly, events short of war can also result in a disruption of diplomatic activity. The revolutionary activities of Cuba and Iran led Presidents Eisenhower and Carter to cut formal ties with these countries. However, some contact was maintained by an "interests section," which operated out of the embassy of a friendly country.

There are other actions that presidents can take to register their disapproval of the policies of other countries. Recalling an ambassador, instituting a trade embargo, and reducing economic or military assistance are all devices that contemporary presidents have employed to sanction the actions of others. The Clinton administration labeled Sudan a terrorist country in 1993 after discovering a tie between two of its representatives at the United Nations and the terrorists who bombed the World Trade Center in New York City. Such designation denies a country economic and military assistance or trade status as a most favored nation. Clinton had also been under pressure not to renew China's most favored nation trade status because of that country's abuses of human rights, pressure to which he did not yield.

Making War   The Constitution gives Congress the sole power to declare war, a power it has exercised only five times (in 1812, 1846, 1898, 1917, and 1941). Full-scale wars, such as those in Korea, Vietnam, and the Persian Gulf, were not officially declared by Congress. In addition, presidents have employed a more limited use of force abroad without a declaration of war or statutory authority more than one hundred thirty times. This presidential involvement of armed forces presents a conflict between constitutional theory and practice.

The roles as commander in chief, head of state, and head of government have undoubtedly contributed to the capacity of presidents to commit the nation to battle. Armed with a near-monopoly on firsthand information, a potential for engaging public support, and an oath to provide for the common defense, they have used their prerogatives to broaden their constitutional powers. Jefferson ordered the navy and marines to retaliate against the Barbary pirates, who threatened American shipping. Polk ordered the army into disputed territory with Mexico to protect a claim by Texas to its borders. Lincoln instituted a blockade of the South and imposed other sanctions to put down the southern insurrection. Recent instances include the orders of President Eisenhower to send armed forces to Lebanon in 1958; of President Kennedy to blockade Cuba in 1962; of President Johnson to dispatch troops to the Dominican Republic in 1965; and of President Nixon to bomb Cambodia in 1970. They also include the orders of President Ford to attack Cambodia in order to rescue the crew of the *Mayaguez* (a U.S. merchant ship seized by Cambodia in 1975); of President Carter to rescue the American hostages in Iran in 1980; of President Reagan to send an armed force to the Caribbean island of Grenada and marines to Lebanon in 1983 and to bomb Libya in 1986; of President Bush to send military forces to Panama in 1989 and the Persian Gulf in 1990–1991; and of President Clinton to bomb Iraq, to increase the size and armaments of American forces in Somalia before withdrawing them, and to send 20,000 American troops to Bosnia to help enforce a peace treaty among the warring factions in that country's civil war, even ordering the bombing of two suspected terrorist sites in 1998, one for training in Afghanistan and the other a factory that allegedly produced ingredients for chemical warfare in Sudan.

Theoretically, Congress could have resisted many of these executive actions. In practice it has been unable and unwilling to do so. The House of Representatives condemned Polk, but only after the Mexican War had been concluded. Congress forced Nixon to end bombing in Cambodia, but only after that action had been carried on for more than two years. During periods of crisis, Congress finds it difficult, if not impossible, to oppose the president.

The Vietnam War, which stirred up deep dissent at home, was the last straw. In 1973 Congress passed the War Powers Resolution over President

Nixon's veto. It requires that the president consult with Congress "in every possible instance" involving the use of American troops in hostile or potentially hostile situations. The president must report to Congress in writing within forty-eight hours after ordering U.S. armed forces into hostilities. More significantly, the military action must stop sixty days after the submission of this report unless Congress declares war, authorizes the use of force, extends the sixty-day period, or is unable to meet because of an attack upon the United States. At any time Congress can end the use of American armed forces by passing a concurrent resolution (which is not subject to a presidential veto).[6] The president may extend the use of force for thirty additional days if deemed necessary to protect departing American forces.

The law has aroused considerable debate about just what consultation means and whether the president could, in sixty days of hostilities, place the United States in a position from which Congress could not extract it. These issues were not resolved by the applications of the War Powers Resolution since its passage: the evacuations from Southeast Asia in April 1975, the rescue of the *Mayaquez* from Cambodia in May 1975, the attempted rescue of the hostages from Iran in 1980, the Grenada invasion of 1983, and the use of armed forces in the Persian Gulf in 1991.

In practically every administration there have been instances that could have fallen under the purview of the act but were not reported to Congress in accordance with its provisions. Why? What is the problem?

The issue is a constitutional one: Which institution, the presidency or Congress, has the right to commit armed forces to potential conflict? Presidents have believed that the War Powers Resolution unconstitutionally constricts their obligation to provide for the common defense by constraining their powers as commander in chief. Although they have not challenged the constitutionality of the legislation in court, they have narrowly interpreted its provisions, particularly its consultation and reporting requirements. Although President Bush claimed that he did not need Congress's approval to commit American troops in the Gulf, he did seek and receive congressional authorization to do so. In approving the legislation that Congress enacted authorizing the use of force in the Gulf, Bush said:

> As I made clear to congressional leaders at the outset, my request for congressional support did not, and my signing this resolution does not, constitute any change in the long-standing positions of the executive branch on either the President's constitutional authority to use the Armed Forces to defend vital U.S. interests or the constitutionality of the War Powers Resolution.[7]

Although Congress obviously disagreed with the interpretation that Bush and other presidents have given to the constitutionality of the War Powers Resolution, as a legislative body, it has been reticent to impose the act's requirements on the president, much less start the clock running on the time limits contained in the legislation. Individual members, however, have raised and debated those issues with respect to specific presidential actions. In December 1990, fifty-four members of Congress took legal action against President Bush to require him to gain congressional approval before committing U.S. armed forces in the Persian Gulf.[8] Although the federal district court declared the request inappropriate because the president had not at that point committed troops to battle, the judge who heard the case rejected the broad claims of executive power that the administration put forth in arguing its position.[9]

Nonetheless, when President Clinton ordered troops to Haiti and Bosnia, both essentially in peacekeeping operations, he too maintained that Congressional approval was not required. The Haitian operation was not even put to a congressional test; Bosnia was. Although Congress enacted a resolution supporting the troops, it went on record as not supporting the policy that put them there.

Is the War Powers Resolution unworkable? Perhaps. Is it irrelevant? No. In theory it reasserts congressional authority while acknowledging expanded presidential powers; in practice, it does not prevent presidential initiatives but forces the president to consider the possibility that Congress, through action or inaction, could terminate those initiatives. This consideration presumably acts as a constraint on potentially unpopular presidential actions. However, the principal type of presidential initiatives that the War Powers Resolution seems designed to prevent is the long-term conventional limited wars similar to Korea and Vietnam. The public has opposed such an encounter since the mid-1970s. If the public mood were to change, however, the propensity of Congress to support military action begun by the president would probably increase as well. In general, the shorter the time frame and the quicker the needed response, the less Congress can play an effective role.

Although Congress is not likely to oppose presidential involvement in emergency situations that threaten the national security or adversely affect American interests abroad, its propensity for influencing presidential policy in nonemergency situations has increased. Congressional power to authorize conscription or maintain an all-volunteer military, to appropriate money for defense, even to affect the sales of arms has been greater in peacetime. Since the Vietnam War, presidents can no longer count on bipartisan support for all military actions, alliances, and aid. In 1981 President Reagan had to use all of his persuasive powers to keep Congress from preventing a sale of special reconnaissance aircraft known as AWACS (for Airborne Warning and Control Systems) to Saudi Arabia. Later in his presidency, he was forced to modify or abandon other arms deals because they faced certain defeat in Congress.

Commanding the Military   The powers of the president as commander in chief have also been expanded. The initial concept of this role was unclear. Did the framers of the Constitution vest the president with a title, "civilian head of the military" or empower the office with operational authority? Over the years, presidents began to behave as if they had operational authority. Lincoln used the crisis of the Civil War to institute a series of military actions including a blockade of the South, the arrest of suspected traitors, activation of the state militia, establishment of military courts in areas of civil insurrection, and suspension of the writ of habeas corpus. Lincoln also got involved in the conduct of the war and the selection of field commanders.

Other presidents have also expanded the operational component of their commander in chief responsibilities. Franklin Roosevelt ordered the internment of persons of Japanese ancestry on the West Coast, chose the principal theaters of operations and points of invasion, and established a map room in the White House to keep abreast of developments during World War II. Harry Truman ordered the use of atomic weapons in that war, forbade American planes to cross the Chinese border during the Korean War, and dismissed his Pacific commander, Douglas MacArthur. John Kennedy personally monitored the Bay of Pigs invasion and the blockade of Cuba during the missile crisis. Lyndon Johnson approved strategic and tactical military decisions in Vietnam, including the bombing of targets and mining of ports, while Richard Nixon extended the bombing to Cambodia.

Ronald Reagan was a particularly active military commander. In addition to committing American forces in Lebanon and Grenada and approving their military actions, he ordered the bombing of military targets in Libya, sent United States warships and personnel to Central America, and dispatched a naval force to the Persian Gulf. He was the first president in twenty-five years to review a war game conducted by the Defense Department and national security staff.

George Bush made crucial policy decisions to commit U.S. forces in Panama and the Gulf, approved the plans of action submitted by the Joint Chiefs of Staff, declared certain targets to be off-limits, and indicated when hostilities should begin and end. He left combat strategy to his military commanders, however, and did not get involved in day-to-day tactical decisions. Similarly, Bill Clinton made the decision to bomb Iraq twice, once in retaliation for an attempt on the life of George Bush, when the former president was visiting Kuwait, and the other time, when Iraqi troops aided one of the Kurdish factions vying for power in Northern Iraq. He also ordered a military force to Haiti to maintain order and return power to the democratically elected government (see The Clinton Presidency box) and a buildup of U.S. forces in the Persian Gulf after Iraq threatened to prohibit inspection of their weapons facilities by UN inspectors.

THE CLINTON PRESIDENCY

Dispatching U.S. Forces to Haiti

Accusations of human rights abuses in Haiti preceded the Clinton presidency. In fact, it was candidate Clinton who, in 1992, criticized the Bush administration for its refusal to allow refugees from that country into the United States. Clinton called Bush's repatriation policy of Haitian boat people, "cruel, inhuman, and morally wrong."[10] Nonetheless, when Clinton took office, he, too, was forced to adopt a similar policy after public officials in Florida warned him that the state could not absorb another massive influx of refugees.

The administration's policy, however, met with strong opposition from members of the African American community, who regarded it as racist. With the congressional black caucus threatening to withhold its support for the administration's domestic policy initiatives and Randall Robinson, a prominent African American leader, staging a hunger strike to protest U.S. policy, Clinton was caught in a political cross fire and ultimately had to modify his policy. He announced that victims of political persecution would be offered temporary asylum, but in a Latin American country, not the United States. His policy pleased no one, including people in those countries, such as Panama, which had been pressured to take the refugees.

It soon became clear to the administration that only the restoration of the democratically elected government of Jean-Bertrand Aristide would provide a satisfactory solution to the refugee problem. However, considerable opposition to Aristide's return emerged within the United States as well as among the Haitian military leaders who had seized power. The CIA considered Aristide an unreliable ally and mounted a clandestine campaign against him, that included even questioning his emotional stability. Republican members of Congress also saw him as a weak and unpredictable leader. Although an agreement had been negotiated among the various Haitian factions by representatives of the United States and the United Nations to pave the way for a redemocratization of the country, the military leaders refused to honor it. This left President Clinton with few alternatives.

With diplomatic efforts stymied, economic sanctions unsuccessful, and political persecutions mounting in Haiti, the president threatened to send U.S. military forces to free the country from its oppressors and put Aristide back in power. However, the threat could not be an idle one, as a U.S. naval ship with a small military contingent on board had already been turned away by armed Haitians ostensibly under the direction of the military government.

Moreover, Clinton had another problem: Clearly, the scars of the Vietnam War had not healed. Polls indicated that a sizable majority of the American people opposed sending U.S. troops to Haiti; officials in the defense and intelligence communities also questioned the invasion plan. The problem, as they saw it, was not so much achieving the military objective, but getting out. How long would U.S. forces have to remain in Haiti to restore and maintain civil order and a democratic government?

Nonetheless, the president proceeded with the invasion plan. He ordered U.S. forces to Haiti, while, at the same time, he tried a last-ditch effort for peace. He accepted an offer from former president Jimmy Carter to try to mediate the transition to civilian rule. To reinforce U.S. resolve, Clinton asked former chairman of the Joint Chiefs of Staff Colin Powell and chairman of the Senate Armed Services Committee Sam Nunn to join the negotiating team. At the last moment, with troops on the way, and perhaps because they were en route, Carter and his team were successful in persuading the military junta to leave. Thus, what might have been a hostile invasion turned into a peaceful operation.

The president had gambled and won. Foreign policy was one area where he could command, but it clearly involved great risks to his country, his popularity, and, ultimately, his exercise of political power.

The destructiveness of nuclear weapons combined with their rapid deployment and delivery suggests that presidents can no longer leave war making solely to their military commanders. As head of state and chief foreign policy maker, they must decide when and how to involve themselves. Although it is usually the international situation that dictates a military response, domestic pressures can also force the president's hand, particularly when Americans are attacked abroad.[11] And the ultimate responsibility for that response rests with the civilian commander, the president.

THE EXPANSION OF A POLICY-MAKING ROLE

Incentives for Presidential Leadership

The growth of the president's authority in foreign and military affairs has been the consequence of several factors: the increasing involvement of the United States within the international community; the public's desire for strong, personal leadership to direct that involvement; and the political ramifications of that leadership on the administration and its policy goals.

Since the end of World War II, the United States has been a dominant economic, military, and political power. It has tried to shape international developments, aiding its allies and resisting its adversaries, building its defenses yet promoting peaceful coexistence, fostering its interests yet supporting international cooperation. The industrial capacity, technological skills, and resource base of the United States were essential to the revitalization of the economies of countries in Western Europe and Asia in the aftermath of World War II. The economic strength of the United States has also been an important source of technical, financial, and agricultural aid to developing nations, which need the products and skills of an advanced technological society. The United States, in turn, has become increasingly dependent on the markets and resources of other countries. Today the economies of many nations, rich and poor, are more interdependent than ever before.

Resource dependency and economic interdependency have contributed to the incentives for American involvement as well as limited the control presidents have over foreign affairs. No longer can the United States afford to adopt an isolationist policy, nor can the president avoid international policy, at least not for long. Held accountable for the performance of the domestic economy, a president has no choice but to tackle international problems as well.

The technological advances in armaments, particularly nuclear weapons, and the conflict situations in which the United States finds itself around the world have forced presidents to be continuously concerned about military preparedness, strategic planning, alliance building, and arms control. The vulnerability of all nations, the proliferation of nuclear weapons, the threat of terrorism at home and abroad, and the persistence of armed conflict require the president to promote the common defense and peaceful coexistence at the same time. The end of the Cold War has actually complicated the president's task. It has reduced public perceptions of a national security threat but at the same time increased instability and unleashed the forces of ethnic, nationalistic, and religious violence around the world.

Not only have world events forced the president to emphasize foreign and military affairs, but domestic political forces have done so as well. The public looks to the president for leadership in times of crisis. A unifying figure, the president is the personification of the state and the person around whom the country can rally.[12]

In the short run, crisis situations may increase the public's approval of the president. When American hostages were seized in Iran in 1979, public approval of Carter's performance rose. However, over time, after he proved unable to obtain their release, his approval level declined. This suggests that in the long run the persistence of the crisis, combined with the failure to resolve it successfully, works to the president's disadvantage. The use of force in a crisis situation, such as the Persian Gulf War enhances the president's popularity, but the use of force in a noncrisis, such as Clinton's sending of 20,000 troops to Bosnia in 1996, does not.[13]

In addition to the short-run support that crises can generate, foreign policy leadership benefits the president in other respects. It contributes to the image of a strong national figure. This is particularly useful during reelection campaigns, when strength, assertiveness, will, and direction are seen as the most desirable presidential attributes. The public wants to feel secure. People look to the president to satisfy that feeling. The nation's security in modern times has been a source of continuous concern and a recurring campaign issue, although not since the Cold War ended.

The difficulties faced by presidents in formulating a policy agenda and in developing a consensus for it are not usually as arduous in foreign and military affairs as they are in domestic ones. Although partisanship has been increasingly evident in foreign and defense policy making, presidential dependence on legislative enactments is still not nearly as great as in the domestic area. Nor is the legislature's ability to impose its will on the president. Moreover, as the president's ability to effect domestic change decreases, the incentive to get involved in foreign affairs increases. Bill Clinton provides a good example. Elected in 1992 to stimulate the economy, reduce the budget deficit, and reform health care, he did not devote nearly as much time and energy to foreign policy issues as he did to domestic policy during his first two years in office. In fact, when the president had to spend more time on foreign affairs in 1993, the White House released a computerized analysis of Clinton's schedule during this period to show that he was not overdoing it.

Clinton's failure to pay sufficient attention to U.S. policy in the international arena resulted in several blunders and policy inconsistencies. In Somalia, the administration allowed the military's role to change from providing humanitarian aid to democratization but did not change its force structure or weaponry. It was only after the loss of American lives and prestige that Clinton reconsidered the policy and ultimately changed it. According to Elizabeth Drew:

> The Clinton administration had come to this pass via a series of casually made decisions. There was never a Principals meeting on the subject of Somalia until after Mogadishu. More of the work had been done in the Deputies Committee—composed of deputies of the Principals—and when it came to the higher-ups, decisions were made informally and without a lot of thought as to the consequences.[14]

Similarly, after reports of atrocities in Bosnia, the United States publicly threatened to use air power against the aggressors, much to the consternation of America's European allies. Later, after appropriate consultation, air power was used with European support, but since 1994, it has been another story. Unable to dominate domestic policy making with the Republicans in control of Congress, Clinton turned to foreign affairs, attending summits, visiting foreign countries, and meeting with the leaders of other countries in Washington. This activity boosted Clinton's presidential image for his reelection campaign and later helped divert the focus from the Democratic fund-raising scandal following the 1996 election and the allegations of sexual improprieties, until the independent counsel, Kenneth Starr issued his report to Congress.

Policy Goals and Presidential Success:
The Two Presidencies Thesis

Are presidents more apt to be successful in crafting foreign policy than domestic policy? According to the late political scientist Aaron Wildavsky, they have tended to be, particularly in the period from 1948 to 1964. In examining congressional action on presidential proposals during this period, Wildavsky found that presidents had significantly better records in foreign and defense policy than in domestic affairs. He gave several reasons for the president's dominance:

1. Presidents have had more constitutional and statutory authority in foreign affairs and more expertise available to them.

2. By tradition, presidents have assumed a more active role in foreign affairs.

3. Presidents can act more quickly and decisively than Congress.

4. Since there are fewer interest groups active in the foreign policy arena, presidents have more discretion to act as national spokespersons and leaders.

Wildavsky concluded that there were actually two presidencies, one in foreign affairs and one in the domestic arena.[15]

Wildavsky wrote his analysis in the mid-1960s after an era of bipartisanship in foreign affairs. He wrote after the emergence of the United States as a world power—after Presidents Roosevelt, Truman, Eisenhower, and Kennedy had established America's position as a leader of the Western world, container of communism, and promoter of international cooperation. He wrote before the Vietnam War.

The unpopularity of that war led to recriminations against the presidents who directed that effort and against the presidency itself. In an effort to deter future presidential action that lacked popular and congressional support, Congress passed a series of statutes, such as the War Powers Resolution, designed to constrain executive discretion in hostile or potentially hostile situations. As a consequence, presidents today still retain the policy initiative, but Congress has improved its capacity to modify and oppose that initiative.

Political and institutional changes during the 1970s have contributed to a more assertive posture in foreign affairs by Congress. The domestic impact of foreign policy has become more pronounced, blurring the old distinction between foreign and domestic affairs and creating new incentives for legislative involvement. In fact, a new term, *intermestic,* has been coined to describe policy that has both foreign and domestic implications. Additionally, the increasing importance of such economic considerations as the budget deficit, corporate tax structure, and the value of the dollar on foreign policy issues and of such foreign policy issues as tariffs, trade, and immigration on domestic affairs have encouraged Congress to get more involved and have made foreign policy subject to many of the same partisan pressures as domestic politics. The old adage that "politics stops at the water's edge" is no longer applicable for noncrisis situations.

With more committees and subcommittees dealing with international issues, more staff and better information facilities at their disposal, more foreign travel by legislators and their aides, more groups, governments, and individuals trying to affect policy judgments, members of Congress, individually and collectively, have become less disposed to acquiesce to the president's initiatives within the international arena.

Congress affects foreign policy in a variety of ways. Its direct impact may be exercised through legislation. In addition to the Senate's confirmation of ambassadors and ratification of treaties, Congress enacts laws that regulate foreign commerce, military affairs, and international environmental matters. Although presidents usually take the initiative in proposing these laws, Congress can, and does, imprint its stamp. It passed laws that constrained President Reagan in support of the Contras in Nicaragua; imposed sanctions against the white, apartheid government of South Africa against the wishes of the Reagan administration; and enacted legislation that required the president to impose economic sanctions against countries that test nuclear weapons such as India and Pakistan did in 1998.

A legislative policy solution, however, is a clumsy and difficult tool for Congress to use. As political scientist James M. Lindsay wrote:

> Legislation almost by necessity is rigid, but diplomacy frequently requires flexibility. Congress acts slowly, but issues can change rapidly. In some cases, resorting to legislation may mean taking a sledgehammer to a problem that requires a scalpel. . . . In short, legislators often do not want to win, because they believe that legislated solutions will prove unwise or unworkable in practice.[16]

Thus, Congress has generally delegated to the president in foreign affairs because of its institutional incapacity to exercise its authority with the same dispatch, consistency, and national perspective as the president. On the other hand, Congress has retained a check on how the president uses delegated authority. The Omnibus Trade and Competitiveness Act of 1988 gave the president discretion to initiate a so-called fast-track procedure for trade negotiations so long as neither the House nor Senate disapproved within ninety days (see the Hot-Button Issue box). Similarly, Congress institutionalized numerous reporting requirements into law, obligating the executive to inform Congress of actions or proposed actions that departments and agencies are considering. The CIA, for example, is required to inform the appropriate congressional committees of its covert operations.

In addition to these statutory requirements, Congress can also use the public arena to criticize presidential policy and try to change it. When President Reagan continued to back Philippine president Ferdinand Marcos after an election in which there were widespread allegations of fraud by his government, Senator Richard Lugar, chairman of the Senate Foreign Relations Committee and an observer of the elections, went on the Sunday morning television talk shows to present the case against Marcos. He claimed the president was misinformed, and the administration subsequently backed off its position.[17]

American policy toward Haiti during the Clinton administration provides another illustration of how domestic pressures can affect foreign affairs (see The Clinton Presidency box). Here too, members of Congress initiated much of the debate and affected the president's policy decisions.

Greater congressional scrutiny of, and involvement in, foreign policy making have led scholars to reexamine Wildavsky's two presidencies thesis. In general, political scientists have found that presidents are still more likely to prevail on foreign affairs than on domestic issues, but they are also more likely to have Congress modify their proposals than in the past. One study of congressional compliance with presidential requests in foreign affairs found that Congress gave presidents all or part of what they wanted 65 percent of the time.[18]

Partisanship is also a factor that affects presidential success in Congress. Party unity in congressional roll calls has increased and partisan divisions have become more evident on foreign policy issues.[19] Although these factors suggest that the two presidencies thesis may still be valid, they also indicate that the days of a bipartisan consensus on U.S. foreign policy are over.

The disintegration of this consensus places presidents in a leadership dilemma. They can no longer take public support for granted. They must build and maintain that support. Moreover, congressional involvement in foreign affairs has placed increasing burdens on presidential leadership and encouraged or forced chief executives to go it alone.

Why do presidents tend to get their way? Professor Paul Peterson argues that the international system requires them to be in charge.

> The role played by the executive in foreign affairs is not due to transient factors such as the vagaries of public opinion or the momentary absence of interest group pressures. Instead, it is rooted in the requirements imposed on the nation-state by the potentially anarchic quality of the international system. . . .

☼ HOT-BUTTON ISSUE

Fast Track Derailed

Congress has given it to every president since Gerald Ford. It is call *fast-track authority*, and it enables the president to negotiate international agreements and then present them to Congress for an up-or-down vote. Congress cannot amend the agreement; it can just say 'yes' or 'no' to it.

Although President Clinton's fast-track authority had expired in 1994, it was not until 1997 that he sought to get it back. In his State of the Union message, delivered in February of that year, Clinton urged Congress to reauthorize the fast-track authority, but he did not send the reauthorizing legislation up to the Hill until the following September. The seven-month delay was caused in large part by the administration's decision to disengage the free trade issue from that of granting most favored nation trading status to China.

During the period following the president's request, but before the actual proposal reached Congress, opponents of fast track (environmental groups, organized labor, and organizations concerned with product and worker safety), mounted a concerted effort to convince Democratic members of Congress to oppose the legislation. In contrast, groups such as trade associations and large multinational corporations, which were likely supporters of the legislation, waited to see the president's specific draft proposal before they determined their position and organized their lobbying efforts. Thus, the president started in a disadvantaged position, with the opposition far more united and active than the backers.

But Bill Clinton had also started behind with the North American Free Trade Agreement (NAFTA) and, nevertheless, won congressional support for that treaty in 1993. The odds, however, were different in 1997. The Republicans controlled Congress, which was an advantage for Clinton since the congressional leadership and a majority of the Republican members of Congress supported free trade and procedures, such as fast-track authority, that facilitate it. On the other hand, Democratic opposition to free trade in general, and fast track in particular, had hardened. Some members of Congress felt that the benefits from NAFTA had not been realized and the promises that the administration had made to reduce that treaty's harmful effects on jobs, the environment, and product safety had not been kept.

The political situation had also changed. The Democrats who remained in Congress were, by and large, a more liberal group than their predecessors. These survivors of the 1994 midterm election, in which the Republicans gained power, represented urban, blue-collar districts, and thus were more sympathetic to, and dependent on, labor support. Exacerbating the split between congressional Democrats and the White House was the rivalry between House Minority Leader Richard Gephardt, an opponent of fast-track authority, and Vice President Al Gore, a supporter.

Nor was the president in as strong a political position as he had been before the 1996 election. Even though he had easily been reelected and his job approval remained high, many Democrats believed that the price he had paid for his political rebirth and resurrection had been too great; the moderate, centrist policy positions he had had to advocate and the compromises he had had to make, especially those that reduced government spending and ended the welfare entitlement, undermined his influence within his own party.

Complicating Clinton's problem was the 1996 campaign fund-raising scandal and his own lame duck status, both of which reduced the rewards he could offer to fellow Democrats and the sanctions he could impose on them.

The issue of fast-track authority also worked against the president. It was not the approval of a negotiated treaty, like NAFTA, that was at issue; it was the expansion of presidential powers. Getting Congress to transfer some of its authority to the president is always difficult. It usually takes a crisis or a serious and persistent problem for Congress to give the president increased power to deal with the situation, and no such crisis or problem existed at that time. In fact, the persistence of large trade deficits, which some attributed to restrictions placed on U.S. exports by major trading partners such as Japan, China, and Brazil, was itself a problem that worked against giving the president this added authority.

Under the circumstances, what could the president do? He began his campaign for fast-track authority by lobbying individual Democratic members of Congress. But he did so behind closed doors which made it more difficult for him to use his popularity as leverage. When he did go public, it was the week before the vote, too short a period to mobilize the broad-based support he needed. Moreover, Clinton complicated his own persuasive task by calling the issue a "no-brainer" and suggesting that those members of Congress who opposed the fast track did so out of fear of electoral retaliation by labor and environmental groups, not because of their personal conscience or constituency concerns.

When the dust had settled, the president could only convince forty-two Democrats to back fast-track authority, which was not enough to ensure passage of the legislation. Rather than suffer a major defeat on the floor of the House of Representatives, the president asked the Speaker to withdraw the legislation. One year later it was defeated when it came to a vote. Only 29 of the 207 Democrats supported giving their Democratic president this authority. The president had lost the battle for fast-track authority *within his own party.*

The failure of Bill Clinton to adopt one of his key legislative priorities in 1997, fast-track authority, illustrates the obstacles to presidential leadership within his own party, within Congress, and even within the area of foreign policy—an area in which the party, the Congress, and the public usually expect the president to take the lead. In this case, however, the President was neither a leader nor a facilitator.

Policy takes precedence over politics because the international system both severely limits the sensible choices a country can make and shapes the processes by which these decisions are reached.[20]

Obviously, presidents need all the help they can get to meet their multiple tasks of formulating and articulating policy, building a public consensus, lobbying Congress to obtain the necessary legislation, and overseeing its implementation. It is to their advisory and administrative national security structure that we now turn.

THE DEVELOPMENT OF AN ADVISORY SYSTEM

The Executive Departments

Throughout the nineteenth century and well into the twentieth, the secretary of state was the president's principal foreign policy adviser, providing information and advice as well as implementing policy decisions. In performing this role, the secretary was assisted by a staff of career officials, who were organized primarily on the basis of five regional bureaus.

Over the years, the State Department has become more specialized. Functional divisions dealing with economics and business, international organization, environmental and scientific affairs, and public and congressional relations have supplemented the political bureaus. Nonetheless, the department remains relatively small. Its 1999 budget of $5 billion pales by comparison to the Defense Department's $258 billion, as does the size of its authorized workforce (23,200 compared to DOD's 708,500 civilian employees). One reason why the State Department has not grown dramatically as

American involvement in world affairs has increased is that a variety of old and new agencies now also participate in international activities.

There is an intelligence community consisting of almost forty separate agencies, which is dominated by the Central Intelligence Agency, National Security Agency, and Defense Intelligence Agency. There is a United States Information Agency (USIA), which operates libraries; sponsors cultural, scientific, and educational programs; coordinates press relations; and runs the Voice of America, a worldwide radio network, and Worldnet, its television affiliate. There is the special trade representative, an Arms Control and Disarmament Agency, and a National Aeronautics and Space Administration (NASA). Many of the principal executive departments also have international divisions and ongoing interests in international affairs. The State Department no longer enjoys a monopoly.

As noted in Chapter 13, a growing concern with international economic matters has hastened the development of an economic complex, a set of institutions and individuals with interests and expertise in international economics.[21] These include the Departments of Treasury, State, Commerce, Agriculture, and Energy, the Office of the Trade Representative, the Council of Economic Advisers, the OMB, and the Federal Reserve (Fed). Congressional committees that regulate commerce, banking, agriculture, and foreign affairs are also part of this complex.

The proliferation of agencies with international activities has presented problems: how to balance competing perspectives and interests within an administration; how to coordinate and integrate policy advice; how to articulate policy with a single voice; and how to do all of this within a political time frame that does not jeopardize presidential goals nor sacrifice discretion in the decision-making process. The resolution of these problems has proved difficult. Solutions have varied with the style and goals of individual presidents and with the institutional needs of their office.

President Franklin Roosevelt relied primarily on his White House staff to provide a liaison with the military and State Department, act as personal emissaries to other governments, and funnel information and advice to him. Partially in reaction to the ad hoc nature of Roosevelt's foreign policy advisory system and his reliance on personal aides rather than department heads, Congress enacted the National Security Act of 1947. This law, which combined the separate military departments into a single defense agency and established the Central Intelligence Agency, acknowledged presidential responsibilities within the national security sphere and provided a mechanism for meeting these responsibilities, the National Security Council (NSC).

The National Security Council

The National Security Council consists of four statutory members: the president, vice president, secretary of state, and secretary of defense. It also includes a number of advisory members such as the director of the CIA, the chairman of the Joint Chiefs of Staff, the director of the Arms Control and Disarmament Agency, and other advisers that presidents have added from time to time. Beginning with Truman, presidents provided it with staff support.

The council's charge is advisory but its mandate is broad: to help define goals and priorities; to coordinate and integrate domestic, foreign, and military policies; and to suggest specific courses of action—all within the national security sphere. During the Truman presidency, the council functioned as a forum for discussion and had an important advisory role during the Korean War. President Eisenhower converted the NSC into a policy-making body. It operated as a planning board for developing general policy positions. A White House secretariat, headed by a special assistant to the president for national security affairs, helped provide organizational support.

As an advisory body the council reached its zenith during the 1950s. Eisenhower's penchant for using formal organizations to establish broad objectives meshed well with the capacity of the National Security Council to provide an integrated set of policy recommendations. Beginning with Kennedy, however, the council's policy-making function was eliminated and its advisory role declined. Although it continued to meet, often for symbolic purposes, its principal responsibilities were assumed by a special assistant to the president for national security affairs who oversaw a national security staff.

The NSC enjoyed a mild resurgence during the Reagan and Bush administrations. Functioning within a cabinet council system, it helped coordinate policy among the various agencies involved in national security issues. A major component of that job was to oversee the implementation of key presidential decisions. In doing so its staff provided coordination at the working-group level for various departments and agencies. In the words of Colin Powell, the last national security adviser to hold office during the Reagan administration:

> We must make sure that all the relevant departments and agencies play their appropriate role in policy formulation. We must make sure that all pertinent facts and viewpoints are laid before the President. We must also make sure that no Cabinet official completes an "end run" around other NSC principals in pushing a policy line on which they too have legitimate concerns.[22]

The relative decline of the NSC's role as an advisory body has coincided with the development of a sizable staffing structure for the president's special assistant for national security affairs. Presidents have increasingly turned to that assistant for information, advice, and internal coordination.

The Special Assistant for National Security Affairs

Kennedy was the first president to create the position of special assistant for national security affairs. His goal was to integrate the growing diversity of executive branch perspectives and views, and to do so without the burden of a large staffing system. Kennedy's involvement in the management of foreign and defense policy enhanced the position of his national security adviser and staff at the expense of senior officials in the State and Defense departments. Power shifted from these departments to the White House, a shift that has continued and accelerated in subsequent administrations.

The national security office also grew, with its staff approaching 150 policy experts and supporting personnel by 1972. The reach of the president's national security assistant expanded accordingly. In addition, that assistant also acted as the president's personal representative, negotiator, and spokesperson, as Henry Kissinger did during the Nixon and Ford administrations and Zbigniew Brzezinski did during Carter's. This visible, public role for a presidential assistant created tension with the secretaries of state in both administrations.

Kissinger's personal relationships, particularly with President Nixon, prevented others from circumventing him. Moreover, Nixon and Kissinger's "closed" style of operating, combined with the president's penchant to consult primarily, sometimes exclusively, with his national security adviser, reduced the influence of Secretary of State William Rogers, who was not even informed of the president's China initiative until it was underway. For all intents and purposes, Kissinger had eclipsed the traditional policy functions of the secretary of state. After Rogers resigned in 1972, Nixon made it official. He appointed Kissinger to head the State Department yet allowed him to continue in his national security position.

Ford disengaged the positions in 1974, appointing Kissinger's principal assistant, General Brent Scowcroft, to replace him. With this disengagement came a reversion of the adviser's responsibilities to those that were performed during the Kennedy and Johnson periods. However, this reduced role was short-lived. The Kissinger model was restored during the Carter administration by one of Kissinger's former students, Zbigniew Brzezinski. Assuming functions of adviser, advocate, and sometimes spokesperson, Carter's assistant for national security affairs clashed repeatedly with Secretary of State Cyrus Vance. Of his role, Brzezinski wrote:

> I work very closely with the President. I'm his adviser in foreign policy and security matters. And I'm the coordinator for him of all the work that comes for his

decision from the State Department, from Defense and from the CIA. Finally, and expressly so, the President wishes me and my staff to help him play an innovative role, that is to say, to try to look beyond the problems of the immediate and help him define a larger and more distant sense of direction.[23]

In subsequent administrations the national security adviser has played a less visible role but has remained an influential presidential aide and confidant, focusing on those foreign and defense problems that the president must address. The adviser briefs the president in the morning, coordinating the administration's national security policy apparatus, and provides staff support for foreign travels and meetings with world leaders.

ASSESSING THE ADVISORY SYSTEM

During the Cold War, when national security matters were of prime concern, presidents tended to rely heavily on their national security advisers. This reliance allowed them to maximize their discretion, exercise more central control, act quickly and decisively, and do so in a manner that was consistent with their basic beliefs and their policy objectives. Naturally, presidents do not enjoy resistance to their policy from outside the administration, much less from within it (although the policy might benefit from such resistance). From presidents' perspectives, reliance on their advisers minimizes this resistance and provides a more supportive environment for the achievement of these objectives.

The reasons why presidents tend to look inward when seeking national security advice are much the same as the reasons for using their other White House aides as policy advisers. They know that these individuals will be loyal and have only the administration's best interests in mind. In contrast, their department secretaries will have several constituencies to consider: other governments, other departments, organized interest groups, and the department's own bureaucracy. Second, the national security assistant is more apt to be on the president's wavelength and have a staff of policy experts chosen in large part because of their acceptable political and ideological views. The secretaries are supported by a cadre of civil servants (and in the case of defense, career military officials), who have survived precisely because they do not enunciate partisan views or see the world primarily in ideological terms. The national security adviser and staff can be ideological and partisan; the secretary of state must be pragmatic and diplomatic. Moreover, the recommendations the national security staff make are apt to be more innovative and consist of fewer compromises than would result if a larger number of executive and legislative officials were involved.

In addition, the national security staff, which is unburdened by administrative responsibilities, can respond more rapidly and less visibly to presidential needs and requests, particularly emergencies. In contrast, department officials tend to move more slowly. They adhere to established procedures, utilize regular channels, and usually speak in carefully measured tones. Presidents often have become impatient with and distrustful of them. Being fearful of leaks, some presidents have even tried to avoid involving the departments entirely on very sensitive matters. But there are also disadvantages to a White House-centered foreign policy-making mechanism, disadvantages which were noted in a report prepared for President Bush by the National Academy of Public Administration. The report said, in part:

> The personal advice of the national security adviser, while not freighted with bureaucratic loads, is also less sensitive to the institutional apparatus necessary to build support and to implement policy decisions. Heavy reliance on informal processes may lead to inadequate communication and execution. . . . The departments provide greater institutional memory, continuity, professional experience, in-depth planning capability, and an orderly policy process. In negotiations with others, they also have the advantage of being once removed from the president so that mistakes are not likely to be as harmful, and changes of position can be made with less embarrassment to the president.[24]

As in other areas of policy, how presidents organize their national security advisory system ultimately depends on their own personality and style, policy goals, and institutional needs. Presidents have to be comfortable with the system and the system has to work for them. It needs to generate information and ideas, to organize and manage competing viewpoints, and to help define and achieve a president's basic goals. It should provide continuity in policy and promote the integration of policies. It should enable the president to exercise strong and steady leadership.

CONCLUSION

The role that the framers of the Constitution envisioned for the president in foreign and military affairs has been expanded significantly. Today, presidents are expected to take the policy-making initiative in both spheres. They are expected to oversee the conduct of war and diplomacy, and they are also expected to perform the symbolic duties of chief of state and commander in chief.

Although presidential expectations have increased, the ability of the president to meet these expectations has declined, particularly since the Vietnam War. That decline is a product of several factors: the interdependence of the United States on the economies, resources, and security of other countries; the increasing impact of foreign policy decisions on domestic affairs; the proliferation of groups and governments trying to affect policy decisions; the more assertive role that Congress has assumed; and the absence, since the end of the Cold War, of a foreign policy consensus. As a consequence, presidents have had to devote more time and increasing resources to the performance of their policy-making responsibilities. They have had to make greater efforts at coordination within the executive branch, at consensus building outside it, and at gaining and maintaining a congressional majority. In this sense, their needs in foreign and national security affairs are not much different than in the domestic arena, although expectations—their own, and those of the American public and foreign government leaders—seem to be greater, as are their constitutional and statutory authority and the precedent of strong presidential leadership in foreign affairs.

With the increasing importance of foreign and defense policy, presidents have turned increasingly to their national security staff for help. Established in 1960 and expanded in size and specialization since then, this internal White House mechanism has provided a cadre of loyal policy experts to help presidents with the everyday problems with which they have to deal. The national security staff functions primarily to inform and advise presidents and secondarily to handle their correspondence, speeches, and briefings. It has increased the information available to presidents, maximized their discretion, and created the capacity for rapid and decisive presidential responses. But, all of this has been achieved at some cost, and some administrations have experienced a great deal of tension between the White House and executive branch agencies.

Despite the increasing obstacles they face, presidents continue to emphasize foreign policy matters, particularly as their administrations progress. There are psychological, political, and policy reasons for doing so. As foreign policy leaders, they can act as unifying figures, overcome perceptions of partisanship, and work to achieve specific policy goals. Demonstrating leadership in this manner stands to increase their popularity, improve their reelectability, and enhance their place in history—all very desirable personal objectives. Moreover, as their congressional support declines, they have few other options. Finally, there is that intangible, yet real, desire to try to affect events, and particularly to promote peace among nations. In international affairs, American presidents want, and expect, to be more than facilitators. They want, and expect, to be world leaders.

DISCUSSION QUESTIONS

1. Over thirty years ago, a well-known political scientist, Aaron
   Wildavsky, argued that there were two presidencies: one in foreign

affairs, which usually got its way with Congress, and one in domestic affairs which was not as successful. Do you think Wildavsky's thesis was valid when he postulated it in 1966? Do you think it is accurate today? How can you find out the answers to these questions? Once you do so, give an explanation for the results you found.

2. Presidents are expected to be the chief foreign policy maker and chief diplomat. However, there are a number of obstacles that impede their ability to initiate and conduct foreign policy. Indicate some of these obstacles and illustrate how they have impeded recent presidents in the performance of their foreign policy role.

3. The good news is that presidents have many sources of information and expertise, which they need to formulate and execute national security policy. The bad news is that the sources do not always agree on what is going on, what is relevant, and what should be done about the problem. How have contemporary presidents handled the problem of information conflict and overload? What mechanisms have they established in their administrations to collect, coordinate, and evaluate this information, to make decisions on the basis of it; and to ensure that these decisions are carried out? Illustrate with examples from the most recent presidencies.

WEB EXERCISES

1. Go to the White House Web site <http://www.whitehouse.gov> and follow the president on a recent trip to another country. Look at the president's public statements and activities and indicate what point the president wishes to make to the citizens and government of the country he is visiting and what impression he wants the American people to have of this visit. Then access a public opinion poll, such as Gallup <http://www.gallup.com> to assess the short-term effect of the trip on the president's popularity.

2. Take any national security issue that is presently commanding public attention. Look at statements issued by the president and/or the press secretary at the White House Web site <http://www.whitehouse.gov>, a department official at the department's Web site, and the congressional leadership, including the chairs of the appropriate House and Senate committees, at their Web sites. Do these statements indicate a consensus or a conflict? Explain why.

SELECTED READING

Adler, David Gray. "The President's Recognition Power: Ministerial or Discretionary?" *Presidential Studies Quarterly* 25 (Spring 1995): 267–286.

Brzezinski, Zbigniew, Brent Scowcroft, and Richard Murphy. "Differentiated Containment." *Foreign Affairs* 76 (1997): 20–30.

Blanton, Tom, ed. *White House E–Mail: The Top-Secret Messages the Reagan/Bush White House Thought They Had Destroyed.* New York: New Press, 1995.

Dawson, Joseph G., III., ed. *Commanders in Chief: Presidential Leadership in Modern Wars.* Lawrence: University of Kansas Press, 1995.

Fisher, Louis. *Constitutional Conflicts between Congress and the President,* 3rd ed. Lawrence: University of Kansas Press, 1995.

Fisher, Louis. *Presidential War Power.* Lawrence: University of Kansas Press, 1995.

Haass, Richard N. "Fatal Distraction: Bill Clinton's Foreign Policy." *Foreign Policy,* no. 108 (1997): 112–123.

Kellerman, Barbara, and Ryan J. Barilleaux. *The President as World Leader.* New York: St. Martin's Press, 1991.

Koh, Harold Hongju. *The National Security Constitution: Sharing Power after the Iran-Contra Affair.* New Haven: Yale University Press, 1990.

Lindsay, James M. "Congress and Foreign Policy: Why the Hill Matters." *Political Science Quarterly* 107 (Winter 1992–1993): 607–628.

Lord, Carnes. *The Presidency and the Management of National Security.* New York: Free Press, 1988.

Mann, Thomas E., ed. *A Question of Balance: The President, the Congress, and Foreign Policy.* Washington, D.C.: Brookings Institution, 1990.

Meernik, James. "Presidential Support in Congress: Conflict and Consensus on Foreign and Defense Policy." *Journal of Politics* 55 (August 1993): 569–587.

Morley, Morris, and Chris McGillion. "'Disobedient' Generals and the Politics of Redemocratization." *Political Science Quarterly* 112 (1997): 363–384.

Peterson, Paul E. "The President's Dominance in Foreign Policy Making." *Political Science Quarterly* 109 (Summer 1994): 215–234.

Rose, Richard, and Robert J. Thompson. "The President in a Changing International System." *Presidential Studies Quarterly* 21 (Fall 1990): 751–770.

Shull, Steven A., ed. *The Two Presidencies.* Chicago: Nelson Hall, 1991.

Notes

1. Bill Clinton delayed even presenting the international treaty on global warming to the Senate in 1998 after the Republican leadership indicated that it would engender considerable opposition.
2. *Goldwater v. Carter*, 444 U.S. 996, 998 (1979).
3. Louis Fisher, *The Politics of Shared Power: Congress and the Executive* (Washington, D.C.: Congressional Quarterly, 1993), p. 156.
4. Fisher, *The Politics of Shared Power*, p. 157; Ryan J. Barilleaux, "Parallel Unilateral Policy Declarations: A New Device for Presidential Autonomy in Foreign Affairs," *Presidential Studies Quarterly* 17 (Winter 1987): 107–117.
5. David Gray Adler, "The President's Recognition Power: Ministerial or Discretionary?" *Presidential Studies Quarterly* 25 (Spring 1995): 267–286.
6. The Supreme Court's legislative veto decision, *Immigration and Naturalization Service v. Chadha*, 462 U.S. 919 (1983), calls into legal question the use of concurrent resolutions as a means of restricting executive activity. Nonetheless, Congress has continued to delegate authority to the president, subject to its approval or disapproval.
7. George Bush, *Weekly Compilation of Presidential Documents* 27 (January 14, 1991): 48.
8. *Dellums v. Bush*, 752 F. Supp. 1141 (D.D.C. 1990).
9. Fisher, *The Politics of Shared Power*, pp. 166–167.
10. Quoted in Ann Deroy and R. Jeffrey Smith, "Debate Over Risks Split Administration," *Washington Post*, September 25, 1994.
11. James Meernik, "Presidential Decision Making and the Political Use of Military Force," *International Studies Quarterly* 38 (March 1994): 121.
12. Fred I. Greenstein, "Popular Images of the President," *American Journal of Psychiatry* 22 (1965): 523–529.
13. Bradley, Lian, and John R. O'Neal, "Presidents, the Use of Military Force, and Public Opinion," *Journal of Conflict Resolution*, 37 (June 1993): 277.
14. Elizabeth Drew, *On the Edge: The Clinton Presidency* (New York: Touchstone, 1994), p. 319.
15. Aaron Wildavsky, "The Two Presidencies," in Steven A. Shull, ed., *The Two Presidencies: A Quarter-Century Assessment* (Chicago, Nelson-Hall, 1991), pp. 11–25.
16. James M. Lindsay, "Congress and Foreign Policy: Why the Hill Matters," *Political Science Quarterly*, 107 (Winter 1992/1993): 612.
17. Herrick Smith, *The Power Game* (New York: Ballantine Books, 1988), pp. 43–44.
18. Ralph G. Carter, "Congressional Foreign Policy Behavior: Persistent Patterns of the Postwar Period," *Presidential Studies Quarterly* 16 (Spring 1986): 333–334.
19. Quantitative studies of presidential success on roll-call votes in Congress lend support to this proposition. When the White House and Congress are controlled by separate parties, Republican presidents have done better on "conflictual" foreign policy than domestic policy, while Democratic presidents have not, according to a quantitative study by two political scientists, Richard Fleisher and Jon R. Bond. Richard Fleisher and Jon R. Bond, "Are There Two Presidencies? Yes, But Only for Republicans," *Journal of Politics* 50 [August 1988]: 747–767. See also Terry Sullivan, "A Matter of Fact: The 'Two Presidencies' Thesis Revitalized," in Steven A. Shull, ed., *The Two Presidencies* [Chicago: Nelson Hall, 1991], pp. 154–155.
20. Paul E. Peterson, "The President's Dominance in Foreign Policy Making," *Political Science Quarterly* 109 (Summer 1994): 232–233.
21. A good discussion of this complex and its components appears in I.M. Destler, "A Government Divided: The Security Complex and the Economic Complex," (paper presented at the annual meeting of the American Political Science Association, Washington, D.C., August 1991).
22. Colin L. Powell, "The NSC System in the Last Two Years of the Reagan Administration," *Presidential Studies Quarterly, Proceedings* 6 (1989): 206.
23. Zbigniew Brzezinski quoted in Dom Bonafede, "Brzezinski—Stepping Out of His Backstage Role," *National Journal*, 9 (October 15, 1977): 1596.
24. National Academy of Public Administration, *The Executive Presidency: Federal Management for the 1990s* (Washington, D.C.: National Academy of Public Administration, 1989), p. 10.

Studying the Presidency

Although many people consider the presidency the most fascinating aspect of American politics, unfortunately it is not easy to research. This overview of studying the presidency is designed to alert students to the implications, both positive and negative, of adopting particular research approaches and methodologies. Armed with this awareness, researchers should be able better to understand the advantages and limitations of various research designs. They can then more knowledgeably construct one that best suits their needs.

APPROACHES

There are many approaches to studying the presidency, ranging from concern with the constitutional authority of the office to dealing with the personality dynamics of a particular president. By *approaches* we mean orientations that guide researchers to ask certain questions and employ certain concepts rather than others. In this section we focus on four of the principal approaches employed by political scientists who study the presidency. The categories we use are neither mutually exclusive nor comprehensive. The goal here is not to create an ideal typology of scholarship on the presidency. Instead, it is to increase sensitivity to the implications of different approaches for what is studied, how a subject is investigated, and what types of conclusions may be reached. Similarly, our focus is on approaches per se rather than the works of individual authors or a comprehensive review of the literature.[1]

Legal

The oldest approach to studying the presidency, what we shall term the legal perspective, concerns the president's formal powers. Legal researchers analyze the Constitution, laws, treaties, and legal precedents to understand the sources, scope, and use of the president's formal powers, including their legal limitations.[2] Because these have changed over time, the legal approach has a historical orientation.

With its emphasis on the historical development of the office and the checks and balances in the Constitution, the legal perspective also lends itself to discussion of the president's place in our system of government, both as it is and as scholars think it ought to be. Thus there is often a clear prescriptive or normative element in these studies.

The range of issues involving presidential authority is great. Illustrations from the recent past include the constitutionality of the line-item veto and the right of the president to impound funds appropriated by Congress, to make long-term recess appointments, to issue executive orders and proclamations, to freeze federal hiring, and to use the pocket veto during brief congressional recesses. Other topics include the constitutionality of the legislative veto, the role of the comptroller general in triggering budget reductions, the president's claims of a partial veto of "unconstitutional" provisions of statutes, and numerous claims of executive privilege such as those proposed by President Clinton to prevent his senior aides from testifying in the probe of his relations with White House intern Monica Lewinsky. Foreign policy issues also have important legal dimensions. These include the conduct of the Vietnam War by Presidents Johnson and Nixon without explicit congressional authorization, the use of troops in invasions of Grenada by President Reagan and Panama by President Bush, the use of troops to occupy Haiti by President Clinton, President Carter's termination of a defense treaty with Taiwan and his settlement of the Iranian assets and hostage issues, and, more generally, the president's use of executive agreements as substitutes for treaties.

Although the legal perspective has a deservedly honored place among American political scientists—the United States prides itself on the rule of law—it also has its limitations. Most of what the president does cannot be explained through legal analysis. The Constitution, treaties, laws, and court decisions affect only a small portion of the president's behavior. Most of the president's relationships with the public, the Congress, the White House staff, and the bureaucracy do not easily fall within the purview of the legal perspective. Instead, this behavior can be understood primarily in terms of informal or extraconstitutional powers. Similarly, because the legal perspective is heavily government-centered, topics such as press coverage of the presidency, the public's evaluation of the president, and other relationships that involve nongovernmental actors are largely ignored.

It is equally significant that the legal perspective, although it requires rigorous analysis, does not lend itself to explanation of presidential behavior. Studies of the boundaries of appropriate behavior do not explain why actions occur within those boundaries or what their consequences are. Moreover, the heavy reliance on case studies by scholars employing this approach inevitably makes the basis of their generalizations somewhat tenuous.

Thus, although studies that adopt the legal perspective make important contributions to our understanding of American politics, they do not answer most of the questions that entice most people to study the presidency. For answers to these questions, we must turn to alternative approaches.

Institutional

A second basic approach to the study of the presidency focuses on it as an institution in which the president has certain roles and responsibilities and is involved in numerous structures and processes. Thus, the structure, functions, and operation of the presidency become the center of attention. These concerns are broad enough to include agencies such as the Office of Management and Budget and units in the White House such as the legislative liaison operation. Scholars following this approach can move beyond formal authority and investigate such topics as the formulation, coordination, promotion, and implementation of the president's legislative program, the president's relationships with the media and interest groups, or the president's decision-making processes.[3] Like the legal perspective, the institutional approach often traces the persistence and adaptation of organizations and processes over time. This gives much of the literature a historical perspective and also lends itself to evaluations of the success of institutional arrangements.

The institutional approach plays a crucial role in helping us to understand the presidency. Although at one time many institutional studies emphasized formal organizational structure and rules, such as organization charts of the White House or budgetary process procedures, in recent years the behavior of those involved in the operation of the presidency has received more attention. This has increased the utility of institutional research. It is, after all, necessary to collect empirical data about what political actors are doing before we can discuss the significance of their behavior, much less examine analytical questions of relationships such as those pertaining to influence. By seeking to identify patterns of behavior and studying interactions, such as those between the White House and the Congress, the OMB, or the media, institutional research tells us not only what happens but, more significantly, also helps us to understand *why* it happens. When scholars examine presidential efforts to influence the media, for example, they are looking at typical, and potentially significant, behavior that may explain patterns of media coverage of the White House.

The New Institutionalism has something to offer the institutional approach. It encourages students of the presidency to think of presidents in impersonal terms, as institutional actors whose incentives are structured in particular ways as a result of their institutional locations and who can thus be expected to behave in a characteristic manner—a presidential manner—regardless of who they are.[4] The goal of those applying this approach is to simplify the complexity of presidential studies and focus on one crucial factor influencing presidential behavior.

The institutional approach has two principal limitations. First, description is often emphasized at the expense of explanation. We know a great deal more about how presidents have organized their White House staffs, for example, than about how these arrangements have affected the kinds of advice they have received. In other words, we know more about the process than about its consequences. This in turn provides a tenuous basis for the prescriptive aspect of some institutional research. We cannot have confidence in recommendations about presidential advisory systems, for example, until we understand their effects.

The second limitation of some institutional studies is that they may downplay, or even ignore, the significance of political skills, ideology, and personality in their emphasis on organizations and processes. Indeed, the implicit assumption that underlies the often-extensive attention scholars devote to structures and processes is that they are very significant. However, this assumption may not always be justified. It may be that the worldview a president brings to the White House influences decisions more than the way the advisory system is organized. Similarly, ideology, party, and constituency views may be more important than the White House legislative liaison operation in influencing congressional votes on the president's program.

Political Power

In the political power approach to the study of the presidency, researchers examine not institutions but the people within them and their relationships with each other.[5] These researchers view power as a function of personal politics rather than formal authority or position. They find the president operating in a pluralistic environment in which there are numerous actors with independent power bases and perspectives different from his.

Thus the president must marshal resources to persuade others to do as he wishes; a president cannot rely on expanding the institution's legal authority or adjusting its support mechanisms.

The president's need to exercise influence in several arenas leads those who follow the power perspective to adopt an expansive view of presidential politics that includes both governmental actors, such as the Congress, bureaucracy, and White House staff, and those outside of government, such as the public, the press, and interest groups. The dependent variables in studying presidential interactions (what authors are trying to explain) are many and may include congressional or public support for the president, presidential decisions, press coverage of the White House, bureaucratic policy implementation, or a set of policy options prepared by the bureaucracy for the president.[6] Because this approach does not assume presidential success or the smooth functioning of the presidency, the influence of bureaucratic politics and other organizational factors in the executive branch is as important to investigate as behavior in more openly adversarial institutions such as Congress.

Power is a concept that involves relationships between people, so this approach forces researchers to try to explain behavior and to seek to develop generalizations about it. However, it also slights certain topics. The emphasis on relationships does not lead naturally to the investigation of the president's accountability, the limitations of the institution's legal powers, or the day-to-day operation of the presidency.

Some commentators are bothered by the top-down orientation of the power approach—that is, viewing the presidency from the perspective of the president.[7] They feel that this neglects the question of examining the presidency from the perspective of the American political system and that it carries the implicit assumption that the president should be the principal decision maker in American politics. These critics argue that such premises are too Machiavellian and that an evaluation of the goals and means of presidents must be added to analyses of power.

Other critics find exaggerated the depiction of the president's environment as basically confrontational, with conflicting interests of political actors creating centrifugal forces the president must try to overcome. Moreover, they claim that the heavy emphasis on power relationships may lead analysts to underestimate the importance of ideology or other influences on behavior.[8]

Psychological

Perhaps the most fascinating and popular studies of the presidency are those that approach the topic from the perspective of psychological analysis. Some of these take the form of psychobiographies of presidents;[9] others are attempts to categorize presidents on the basis of selected personality dimensions.[10] All are based on the premises that personality is a constant and that personality needs may be displaced onto political objects and become unconscious motivations for presidential behavior.

We need to take what goes on inside a person's head into account if we are to understand that person's behavior. A psychological perspective forces us to ask why presidents behave as they do and to look beyond external factors, such as advisers, Congress, the media, and interest groups, for answers. If individual presidents were not strongly affected by their personalities, they would neither be very important nor merit much attention.

Psychological analysis also has a broader application to the study of the presidency. Presidents and their staffs view the world through cognitive processes that affect their perceptions of why people and nations behave as they do, how power is distributed, how the economy functions, and what the appropriate roles of government, presidents, and advisers are. Cognitive processes also screen and organize an enormous volume of information about the complex and uncertain environment in which presidents function. Objective reality, intellectual abilities, and personal interests and experiences merge with psychological needs (such as those to manage inconsistency and maintain self-esteem) to influence the decisions and policies that emerge from the White House. Cognitive processes simplify decision making and lessen stress, especially on complex and controversial policies such as the Vietnam War. Group dynamics may also influence decision making, limiting the appraisal of alternatives by group members. Efforts to sort out the impact of these factors are only in their early stages, but there is little question that we cannot claim to understand presidential decision making until those efforts succeed.[11]

Although psychological studies can sensitize us to important personality traits that influence presidential behavior, they are probably the most widely criticized research on the presidency. A fundamental problem is that they often display a strong tendency toward reductionism; that is, they concentrate on personality to the exclusion of most other behavioral influences. As a result, they convey little information about the institution of the presidency or the relationships between psychological and institutional variables. Alternative explanations for behavior are rarely considered in psychological studies.

A related drawback is that psychological studies tend to stress the pathological aspects of a presidency. Scholars, like others, are drawn quite naturally to investigate problems. Their principal interest often becomes the relationship between the personality flaws of the president and what the author feels to be some of his most unfortunate actions in office. This reinforces the reductionist tendency because it is usually not difficult to find plausible parallels between psychological and decisional deficiencies.

The lack of systematic data is also a problem for psychological studies. It is difficult both to discern unconscious motivations or cognitive processes and to differentiate their effect from that of external factors. Often, authors must rely on biographical information of questionable validity about the behavior and environment of presidents, stretching back to their childhoods.

Summary

The legal, institutional, power, and psychological approaches have advantages and disadvantages for the researcher. Each concerns a different aspect of the presidency and concentrates on certain variables at the expense of others. Those thinking of doing research on the presidency should carefully determine what it is they want to investigate *before* selecting an approach, because not all approaches will be relevant to answering their questions. Although the power and psychological approaches are stronger in their concern for explanation, the legal and institutional orientations are better at providing broad perspectives on the presidency. Selecting an approach is not the only decision one must make in building a research strategy, however. Appropriate methods must also be chosen.

METHODS

Although political scientists have always been keenly interested in the American presidency, their progress in understanding it has been very slow. One reason is their reliance on methods that are either irrelevant or inappropriate to the task of examining the basic relationships in which the presidency is involved. This section examines some of the advantages and limitations of methods used by scholars to study the presidency. Throughout, we should remember that methods are not ends in themselves but techniques for examining research questions generated by the approaches discussed earlier.

Traditional Methods

Studies of the presidency typically describe events, behavior, and personalities. Many are written by journalists or former executive branch officials who rely on their personal experiences. Unfortunately, such anecdotal material, although it may be insightful, is generally subjective, fragmentary, and impressionistic. The commentary and reflections of insiders, whether participants or participant-observers, are limited by their own perspectives. For example, the memoirs of aides to Presidents Johnson and Nixon reveal very different perceptions of the president and his presidency. Henry Kissinger wrote this about the Nixon White House staff:

> It is a truism that none of us really knew the inner man. More significant, each member of his entourage was acquainted with a slightly different Nixon subtly adjusted to the President's judgment of the aide or to his assessment of his interlocutor's background.[12]

Similarly, Dick Morris's account of President Clinton's reelection suggests that the author called all or most of the shots—an account disputed by other White House insiders.[13]

Proximity to power may actually hinder, rather than enhance, an observer's perspective and breadth of view. The reflections of those who have served in government may be colored by the strong positions they advocated in office or a need to justify their decisions and behavior. Faulty memories further cloud such perceptions. Moreover, few insiders are trained to think in analytical terms of generalizations based on representative data and controls for alternative explanations. This is especially true of journalists.[14]

Several examples illustrate the problem. One of the crucial decision points in America's involvement in Vietnam occurred during July 1965, when President Johnson committed the United States to large-scale combat operations. In his memoirs, Johnson goes to considerable lengths to show he considered very carefully all the alternatives available at the time.[15] One of his aides' detailed account of the dialogue between Johnson and some of his advisers shows the president probing deeply for answers, challenging the premises and factual bases of options, and playing the devil's advocate.[16] Other participants and scholars have also concluded that Johnson kept an open mind regarding U.S. intervention in Vietnam during their period.[17] Yet, other scholars and participants have concluded that this "debate" was really a charade, staged by the president to lend legitimacy to the decision he had already made.[18]

Another useful example, this one focusing on attributions of influence, is President Johnson's efforts at obtaining the support or at least the neutrality of the Senate Finance Committee chairman, Harry Byrd of Virginia, on the 1964 tax cut. Hubert Humphrey reported in his memoirs that Johnson cajoled Byrd into letting the tax bill out of committee, relying on Lady Bird's charm, liquor, and his own famous "treatment."[19] Presidential aide Jack Valenti told a different story, however. He wrote that the president obtained the senator's cooperation by promising to hold the budget under $100 billion.[20] Thus, we have two eyewitnesses reporting on two different tactics employed by the president and each attributing Senator Byrd's response to the presidential behavior that he observed.

To confuse matters further, Henry Hall Wilson, one of the president's congressional liaison aides, indicated that both eyewitnesses were wrong. According to Wilson, when the president proudly told his chief congressional liaison aide, Lawrence O'Brien, about his obtaining Byrd's agreement to begin hearings on the tax cut on December 7, O'Brien replied: "You didn't get a thing. I already had a commitment for the seventh."[21] In other words, according to O'Brien, Johnson's efforts were irrelevant and both eyewitnesses were wrong in attributing influence to him.

Even tapes of conversations in the Oval Office may be misleading. As Henry Kissinger explains with respect to the Watergate tapes:

> Anyone familiar with Nixon's way of talking could have no doubt he was sitting on a time bomb. His random, elliptical, occasionally emotional manner of conversation was bound to shock, and mislead, the historian. Nixon's indirect style of operation simply could not be gauged by an outsider. There was no way of telling what Nixon had put forward to test his interlocutor and what he meant to be taken seriously; and no outsider could distinguish a command that was to be followed from an emotional outburst that one was at liberty to ignore—perhaps was even expected to ignore.[22]

Problems also arise in studies employing traditional methods when authors make assertions about the behavior of the public. They often fail to look at available systematic data. For example, numerous authors premise analyses of the Reagan administration on the president's enjoying substantial support among the public. In reality, as we saw in Chapter 4, Reagan's average approval level was a quite ordinary 52 percent.[23]

Although insider accounts have limitations, they often contain useful insights that may guide more rigorous research. They also provide invaluable records of the perceptions of participants in the events of the presidency. As long as the researcher understands the limitations of these works and accepts them as one among many perspectives, they can be of considerable use.

Not all studies of the presidency that employ traditional methods are written by insiders. Many are written by scholars[24] or journalists,[25] based primarily on the observations of others—who may be insiders. As one might expect, a common criticism of the traditional literature on the presidency is that it appears to be the same presentation, repeated in slightly different versions. Although such studies may be useful syntheses of the conventional wisdom or present provocative insights about the presidency, they are more likely to suffer from the limitations of their data and generally add little more than descriptive detail to our understanding of the presidency.

Quantitative Analyses

Research on the presidency, then, has often failed to meet the standards of contemporary political science, including the careful definition and measurement of concepts, the rigorous specification and testing of propositions, and the use of empirical theory to develop hypotheses and explain findings. This presents a striking irony: The single most important and powerful institution in American politics is the one that political scientists understand the least.

To increase our understanding of the presidency, we must move beyond the description of the institution and explain the behavior we observe, and we must seek to reach generalizations instead of being satisfied with discrete, often ad hoc analyses. Quantitative analysis can be an extremely useful tool in these endeavors.[26]

There have been three principal constraints on using quantitative analysis to study the presidency. The first, the frequent failure to pose analytical questions, has already been discussed. The second constraint has been the small number of presidents. Viewing the presidency as a set of relationships, however, helps to overcome this problem. Although the number of presidents may be few, many persons are involved in relationships with them, including the entire public, members of Congress, the federal bureaucracy, and world leaders. Because there are so many people interacting with the president, we are no longer inhibited by the small universe of presidents.

The third perceived constraint on the quantitative study of the presidency is lack of data. When we pose analytical questions, we are naturally led to search for data on the causes and consequences of presidential behavior. For example, we may ask what presidents want people to do. Among other things, they want support from the public, positive coverage from the media, votes for their programs from Congress, sound analysis from their advisers, and faithful policy implementation from the bureaucracy. Thus we can look for data on these political actors, whose behavior is usually the dependent variable in our hypotheses—that is, in what we are trying to explain. Similarly, we can seek data on independent variables—that is, on causes of behavior toward the president, such as the determinants of public opinion, congressional support, bureaucratic faithfulness, and judicial responsiveness.[27]

Considerable progress has been made in providing data for students of the presidency. For example, the White House is making a wide range of data available on its Web site. Ragsdale published a volume entitled *Vital Statistics on the Presidency.*[28] The Center for Presidential Studies at Texas A&M University created a Presidential Archive for data sets relevant to researching the presidency <www-bushschool.tamu.edu/prezindex.htm>.

The proper use of quantitative analysis, like any other type of analysis, is predicated upon a close linkage between the methods selected and the theoretical arguments that underlie the hypotheses being tested.[29] A statement that something causes something else to happen is an assertion, not a theoretical argument. A theoretical argument requires an emphasis on explanation—on why two variables are related. Quantitative analysis is not an end in itself. Instead, it is a means of rigorously analyzing theoretically meaningful explanations of behavior.

Despite its utility for investigating a wide range of questions, quantitative analysis is not equally useful for studying all areas of the presidency. It is least useful where there is little change in the variables under study. If the focus of research is just one president and the researcher is concerned not with the president's interactions with others but with how factors such as the president's personality, ideas, values, attitudes, and ideology have influenced his decisions, then quantitative analysis will be of little help. These independent variables are unlikely to vary much during a president's term. Similarly, important elements in the president's environment, such as the federal system or the basic capitalist structure of its economy, change little over time. It is therefore difficult to employ quantitative analysis to gauge their influence on the presidency.

Quantitative analysis is also unlikely to be useful for the legal approach to studying the presidency. There are well-established techniques for interpreting the law, and scholars with this interest will continue to apply them.[30]

Normative questions and arguments have always occupied a substantial percentage of the presidency literature, and rightly so. Can quantitative analysis aid scholars in addressing these concerns? The answer is, "partially." For example, to reach conclusions about whether the presidency is too powerful or not powerful enough (the central normative concern regarding the presidency) requires a three-part analysis. The first is an estimation of just how powerful the presidency is. Quantitative analysis can be of utility in measuring and explaining the power in the presidency in a wide range of relationships. For example, it can aid us in understanding the president's ability to influence Congress or the public.

The second step in answering the question of whether the presidency is too powerful or not powerful enough requires an analysis of the consequences of the power of the presidency. In other words, given the power of the presidency, what difference does it make? Are poor people likely to fare better under a weak or a powerful presidency, for example? Are civil rights and civil liberties more or less likely to be abused?

To answer rigorously these and similar questions requires that we correlate levels of power with policy consequences. This does not have to be done quantitatively, of course, but such analyses are likely to be more convincing if we have valid empirical measurements of economic welfare, school integration, wiretapping, military interventions, and other possible consequences of presidential power as well as measures of mediating variables.

Quantitative analyses will be much less useful in the third part of the analysis: Do we judge the consequences of presidential power to be good or bad? Our evaluation of these consequences will be determined, of course, by our values. Nevertheless, it is important to remember that quantitative analysis can be very useful in helping us to arrive at the point where our values dominate our conclusions.

In short, quantitative analysis leads us to examine theoretical relationships, and it has considerable utility in testing and refining them. The question remains, however, whether quantitative analysis is useful for developing theories themselves—that is, basic conceptions of the relationships between variables.

Although quantitative studies cannot replace the sparks of creativity that lie behind conceptualizations, they may produce findings upon which syntheses may be built. Conversely, quantitative analysis may also produce findings contrary to the conventional wisdom and thus prod scholars into challenging dominant viewpoints. To this extent, it may also be useful in theory building.

Quantitative analysis is not easy to do, nor is there consensus on appropriate methods or measures. Inevitably, some authors will employ indicators that lack validity and reliability and tests that are inappropriate. Their conclusions are likely to be incorrect. In addition, findings can and should be refined as our indicators and tests are improved. In essence, quantitative analysis poses methodological problems precisely because it attempts to measure concepts and to test for relationships carefully. Studies that do not involve such concerns avoid methodological questions, but often at the expense of analytical richness.

Case Studies

One of the most widely used methods for studying the presidency is the case study of an individual president, a presidential decision, or presidential involvement in a specific area of policy. The case study method offers the researcher several advantages. It is a manageable way to present a wide range of complex information about individual and collective behavior. Because scholars have typically found it difficult to generate quantitative data regarding the presidency, the narrative form often seems to be the only available choice.

Conversely, case studies are widely criticized on several grounds. First, they have been used more for descriptive than for analytical purposes, a failing not inherent in the case study. A more intractable problem is the idiosyncratic nature of case studies and the failure of authors to employ common analytical frameworks. This makes the accumulation of knowledge difficult because scholars often, in effect, talk past each other. In the words of a close student of case studies:

> The unique features of every case—personalities, external events and conditions, and organizational arrangements—virtually ensure that studies conducted without the use of an explicit analytical framework will not produce findings that can easily be related to existing knowledge or provide a basis for future studies.[31]

Naturally, reaching generalizations about the presidency on the basis of unrelated case studies is a hazardous task.

Despite these drawbacks, case studies can be very useful in increasing our understanding of the presidency. For example, analyzing case studies can serve as the basis for identifying problems in decision making[32] or in policy implementation.[33] These in turn may serve as the basis for recommendations to improve policy making. Case studies may also be used to test hypotheses or disconfirm theories, such as propositions about group dynamics drawn from social psychology.[34]

Some authors employ case studies to illustrate the importance of looking at aspects of the presidency that have received little scholarly attention, such as presidential influence over interest groups.[35] On a broader scale, Richard Neustadt used several case studies to explicate his influential model of presidential power,[36] and Graham Allison used a case study of the Cuban missile crisis to illustrate three models of policy making.[37]

Writing a case study that has strong analytical content is difficult to do.[38] It requires considerable skill, creativity, and rigor because it is very easy to slip into a descriptive rather than an analytical gear. It is especially important to have an analytical framework in mind before one begins—to provide direction to data gathering and the line of argument. Those who embark on preparing case studies are wise to remind themselves of the pitfalls.

CONCLUSION

Few topics in American politics are more interesting or more important to understand than the presidency. Researching the presidency is not a simple task, however. There are many reasons for this, including the small number of models to follow and the relative sparsity of research that has applied the approaches and methods of modern political science. But the obstacles to studying the presidency also present researchers with an opportunity. Few questions regarding the presidency are settled, and there is plenty of room for committed and creative researchers to make important contributions to our understanding. The prospects for success will be enhanced if researchers realize the implications of the approaches and methods they employ and choose those that are best suited to shed light on the questions they wish to investigate.

SELECTED READING

Edwards, George C., III, John H. Kessel, and Bert A. Rockman, eds. *Researching the Presidency*. Pittsburgh: University of Pittsburgh Press, 1993.

Edwards, George C., III, and Stephen J. Wayne, eds. *Studying the Presidency*. Knoxville: University of Tennessee Press, 1983.

Ragsdale, Lyn. *Vital Statistics on the Presidency*. Washington, D.C.: Congressional Quarterly Press, 1996.

Notes

1. For a more extensive discussion of approaches to studying the presidency, see Stephen J. Wayne, "Approaches," in George C. Edwards III and Stephen J. Wayne, eds., *Studying the Presidency* (Knoxville: University of Tennessee Press, 1983), pp. 17–49.

2. The classic work from the legal perspective is Edward S. Corwin's *The President: Office and Powers*, 4th rev. ed. (New York: New York University Press, 1957). More recent examples include Louis Fisher, *Constitutional Conflict between Congress and the President*, 4th rev. ed. (Lawrence: University Press of Kansas, 1997); Louis Fisher, *Presidential War Power* (Lawrence: University Press of Kansas, 1995); and Mark J. Rozell, *Executive Privilege* (Baltimore: Johns Hopkins University Press, 1994).

3. See, for example, Thomas J. Weko, *The Politicizing Presidency: The White House Personnel Office, 1948–1994* (Lawrence: University Press of Kansas, 1995); Stephen J. Wayne, *The Legislative Presidency* (New York: Harper and Row, 1978); Michael Baruch Grossman and Martha Joynt Kumar, *Portraying the President: The White House and the News Media* (Baltimore: Johns Hopkins University Press, 1981); Mark A. Peterson, "The Presidency and Organized Interests: White House Patterns of Interest Group Liaison," *American Political Science Review* 86 (September 1992): 612–625; John P. Burke and Fred I. Greenstein, *How Presidents Test Reality* (New York: Russell Sage Foundation, 1989); Joseph Cooper and William W. West, "Presidential Power and Republican Government: The Theory and Practice of OMB Review of Agency Rules," *Journal of Politics* 50 (November 1988): 864–895; Lawrence R. Jacobs and Robert Y. Shapiro, "The Rise of Presidential Polling: The Nixon White House in Historical Perspective," *Public Opinion Quarterly* 59 (Summer 1995): 163–195; Charles E. Walcott and Karen M. Hult, *Governing the White House* (Lawrence: University Press of Kansas, 1995); Paul C. Light, *The President's Agenda* (Johns Hopkins University Press, 1991); and Shirley Anne Warshaw, *The Domestic Presidency* (Boston: Allyn and Bacon, 1997).

4. See Terry Moe, "Presidents, Institutions, and Theory," in George C. Edwards III, Bert A. Rockman, and John H. Kessel, eds., *Researching the Presidency* (Pittsburgh: University of Pittsburgh Press, 1993), pp. 337–386.

5. The political power approach is best represented in Richard E. Neustadt, *Presidential Power and the Modern Presidents* (New York: Free Press, 1990). A very different, but provocative, work that focuses on the impact of the president is Stephen Skowronek, *The Politics Presidents Make* (Cambridge, Mass.: Harvard University Press, 1993).

6. See, for example, George C. Edwards III, *At the Margins: Presidential Leadership of Congress* (New Haven: Yale University Press, 1989); George C. Edwards III, *The Public Presidency* (New York: St. Martin's, 1983); and George C. Edwards III, *Implementing Public Policy* (Washington, D.C.: Congressional Quarterly Press, 1980). Other examples of the political power approach include Fred I. Greenstein, *The Hidden-Hand Presidency* (New York: Basic Books, 1982); Bert A. Rockman, *The*

Leadership Question (New York: Praeger, 1984); Terry M. Moe, "The Politicized Presidency," in John E. Chubb and Paul E. Peterson, eds., *The New Directions in American Politics* (Washington, D.C.: Brookings Institution, 1985); Jeffrey E. Cohen, "Presidential Rhetoric and the Public Agenda," *American Journal of Political Science* 39 (February 1995): 87–107; and Richard P. Nathan, *The Administrative Presidency* (Wiley, 1983).

7. See Bruce Miroff, "Beyond Washington," *Society* 17 (July/August 1980): 66–72.

8. See Peter W. Sperlich, "Bargaining and Overload: An Essay on Presidential Power," in Aaron Wildavsky, ed., *The Presidency* (Boston: Little, Brown, 1969), pp. 168–192.

9. See, for example, Alexander L. George and Juliette L. George, *Woodrow Wilson and Colonel House: A Personality Study* (New York: Dover, 1964); Robert Tucker, "The Georges' Wilson Reexamined: An Essay on Psychobiography," *American Political Science Review* 71 (June 1977): 606–618; and Stanley Renshon, *High Hopes* (New York: New York University Press, 1996).

10. The most notable example is James David Barber's *The Presidential Character: Predicting Performance in the White House*, 4th ed. (Englewood Cliffs, N.J.: Prentice-Hall, 1992). See also Alexander L. George and Juliette L. George, *Presidential Personality and Performance* (Boulder, Colo.: Westview, 1998), chap. 5.

11. Some relevant studies include Alexander L. George, *Presidential Decisionmaking in Foreign Policy: The Effective Use of Information and Advice* (Boulder, Colo.: Westview, 1980); Bruce Buchanan, *The Presidential Experience: What the Office Does to the Man* (Englewood Cliffs, N.J.: Prentice-Hall, 1978); John D. Steinbruner, *The Cybernetic Theory of Decision* (Princeton: Princeton University Press, 1974); Irving L. Janis, *Groupthink: Psychological Studies of Policy Decisions and Fiascoes,* 2nd ed. (Boston: Houghton Mifflin, 1982); and Richard E. Neustadt and Ernest R. May, *Thinking in Time* (New York: Free Press, 1986).

12. Henry Kissinger, *Years of Upheaval* (Boston: Little, Brown, 1982), p. 1182.

13. Dick Morris, *Behind the Oval Office* (New York: Random House, 1997).

14. Excellent studies of the misperceptions of participants in presidential policy making include Richard E. Neustadt, *Alliance Politics* (New York: Columbia University Press, 1970); and Fred I. Greenstein and Richard H. Immerman, "What Did Eisenhower Tell Kennedy about Indochina? The Politics of Misperception," *Journal of American History* 79 (September 1992): 568–587.

15. Lyndon B. Johnson, *The Vantage Point: Perspectives of the Presidency, 1963–1969* (New York: Popular Library, 1971), pp. 144–153.

16. Jack Valenti, *A Very Human President* (New York: Norton, 1975), pp. 317–319, 358.

17. See George W. Ball, *The Past Has Another Pattern* (New York: Norton, 1982), p. 399; and George McT. Kahin, *Intervention: How America Became Involved in Vietnam* (New York: Knopf, 1986), pp. 366–390.

18. Larry Berman, *Planning a Tragedy: The Americanization of the War in Vietnam* (New York: Norton, 1982), pp. 105–121; Chester Cooper, *The Lost Crusade: America in Vietnam* (Greenwich, Conn.: Dodd, Mead, 1970), pp. 284–285; U.S. Department of Defense, *United States–Vietnam Relations, 1945–1967,* vol. 3 (Washington, D.C.: Government Printing Office, 1971), p. 475.

19. Hubert H. Humphrey, *The Education of a Public Man: My Life and Politics* (Garden City, N.Y.: Doubleday, 1976), pp. 290–293.

20. Valenti, *A Very Human President,* pp. 196–197. See also Russell D. Renka, "Bargaining with Legislative Whales in the Kennedy and Johnson Administration" (paper presented at the annual meeting of the American Political Science Association, Washington, D.C., August 1980), p. 20.

21. Transcript, Henry Hall Wilson Oral History Interview, April 11, 1973, by Joe B. Frantz, p. 16, Lyndon B. Johnson Library, Austin, Texas.

22. Kissinger, *Years of Upheaval,* pp. 111–112. Recently, transcripts of tapes from several presidents have been published. These include Ernest R. May and Philip D. Zelikow, *The Kennedy Tapes* (Cambridge, Mass.: Belknap Press; 1997); Michael R. Beschloss, ed., *Taking Charge: The Johnson White House Tapes, 1963–1964* (New York: Simon and Schuster, 1997); and Stanley I. Kutler, ed., *Abuse of Power: The New Nixon Tapes* (New York: Free Press, 1997).

23. See George C. Edwards III, *Presidential Approval* (Baltimore: Johns Hopkins University Press, 1990), p. 175.

24. See, for example, Richard Tanner Johnson, *Managing the White House* (New York: Harper and Row, 1974).

25. A recent example is Bob Woodward, *The Agenda: Inside the Clinton White House* (New York: Simon and Schuster, 1994).

26. For a more extensive discussion of quantitative analysis of the presidency, see George C. Edwards III, "Quantitative Analysis," in George C. Edwards III and Stephen J. Wayne, eds., *Studying the Presidency* (Knoxville: University of Tennessee Press), pp. 99–124; and Gary King, "The Methodology of Presidency Research," in George C. Edwards III, Bert A. Rockman, and John H. Kessel, eds., *Researching the Presidency* (Pittsburgh: University of Pittsburgh Press, 1993), pp. 387–412.

27. Examples of quantitative studies of the presidency and the public include Jeffrey E. Cohen, *Presidential Responsiveness and Public Policy-Making* (Ann Arbor: University of Michigan Press, 1997); Edwards, *Presidential Approval*; Samuel Kernell, *Going Public*, 3rd ed. (Washington, D.C.: Congressional Quarterly Press, 1997); Jeffrey K. Tulis, *The Rhetorical Presidency* (Princeton: Princeton University Press, 1987); Lee Sigelman, "Gauging the Public Response to Presidential Leadership," *Presidential Studies Quarterly* 10 (Summer 1980): 427–433; Richard A. Brody, *Assessing the President: The Media, Elite Opinion, and Public Support* (Stanford, Calif.: Stanford University Press, 1991); Lyn Ragsdale, "The Politics of Presidential Speechmaking, 1949–1980," *American Political Science Review* 78 (December 1984): 971–984; Jon A. Krosnick and Donald R. Kinder, "Altering the Foundations of Support for the President through Priming," *American Political Science Review* 84 (June 1990): 497–512; Jon A. Krosnick and Laura A. Brannon, "The Impact of the Gulf War on the Ingredients of Presidential Evaluations: Multidimensional Effects of Political Involvement," *American Political Science Review* 87 (December 1993): 963–975; and George C. Edwards III, William Mitchell, and Reed Welch, "Explaining Presidential Approval: The Significance of Issue Salience," *American Journal of Political Science* (February 1995): 108–134.

   For quantitative studies of executive-legislative relations, see George C. Edwards III, Andrew Barrett, and Jeffrey Peake, "The Legislative Impact of Divided Government," *American Journal of Political Science* 41 (May 1997): 545–563; Edwards, *At the Margins*; Jon R. Bond and Richard Fleisher, *The President in the Legislative Arena* (Chicago: University of Chicago Press, 1990); Darrell M. West, "Activists and Economic Policymaking in Congress," *American Journal of Political Science* 32 (August 1988): 662–680; Terry Sullivan, "Bargaining with the President: A Simple Game and New Evidence," *American Political Science Review* 84 (December 1990): 1167–1195; and Terry Sullivan, "Headcounts, Expectations, and Presidential Coalitions in Congress," *American Journal of Political Science* 32 (August 1988): 567–589.

   On presidential-bureaucratic relations, see Joel D. Aberbach and Bert A. Rockman, "Clashing Beliefs within the Executive Branch: The Nixon Administration Bureaucracy," *American Political Science Review* 70 (March 1976): 456–468; B. Dan Wood and James E. Anderson, "The Politics of U.S. Antitrust Regulation," *American Journal of Political Science* 37 (February 1993): 1–39; B. Dan Wood and Richard W. Waterman, *Bureaucratic Dynamics* (Boulder, Colo.: Westview, 1994); and John H. Kessel, *Presidential Parties* (Homewood, Ill.: Dorsey, 1984), chaps. 4–5. On the president's impact on the judiciary, see Craig R. Ducat and Robert L. Dudley, "Federal District Judges and Presidential Power During the Postwar Era," *Journal of Politics* 51 (February 1989): 98–118.

28. Lyn Ragsdale, *Vital Statistics on the Presidency* (Washington, DC; Congressional Quarterly Press, 1996).

29. See George C. Edwards III, "Aligning Tests with Theory: Presidential Approval as a Source of Influence in Congress," *Congress and the Presidency* 24 (Fall 1997): 113–130.

30. For more on legal analysis of the presidency, see Louis Fisher, "Making Use of Legal Sources," in Edwards and Wayne, eds., *Studying the Presidency*, pp. 182–198.

31. Norman C. Thomas, "Case Studies," in Edwards and Wayne, eds., *Studying the Presidency*, p. 52.

32. See, for example, Alexander L. George, "The Case for Multiple Advocacy in Making Foreign Policy," *American Political Science Review* 66 (September 1972): 765–781; Burke and Greenstein, *How Presidents Test Reality*; and Ryan J. Barilleaux, *The President and Foreign Affairs* (New York: Praeger, 1985).

33. See, for example, Edwards, *Implementing Public Policy*.

34. See Janis, *Groupthink*.

35. See, for example, Bruce Miroff, "Presidential Leverage over Social Movements: The Johnson White House and Civil Rights," *Journal of Politics* 43 (February 1981): 2–23.

36. Neustadt, *Presidential Power*.

37. Graham T. Allison, *Essence of Decision: Explaining the Cuban Missile Crisis* (Boston: Little, Brown, 1971).

38. Recent examples of work focusing on a single president in an insightful and analytical fashion include Charles O. Jones, *The Trusteeship Presidency* (Baton Rouge: Louisiana State University Press, 1988); and Erwin C. Hargrove, *Jimmy Carter as President* (Baton Rouge: Louisiana State University Press, 1988); Lawrence R. Jacobs and Robert Y. Shapiro, "Issues, Candidate Image, and Priming: The Use of Private Polls in Kennedy's 1960 Presidential Campaign," *American Political Science Review* 88 (September 1994): 527–540; and Roger B. Porter, "Gerald R. Ford: A Healing Presidency," in Fred I. Greenstein, ed., *Leadership in the Modern Presidency* (Cambridge, Mass.: Harvard University Press, 1988), pp. 199–227.

Nonelectoral Succession, Removal, and Tenure

The Constitution and statutes provide for contingencies that might require the selection, removal, or replacement of a president outside the normal electoral process. In addition to the provisions of Article 1 ("Impeachment") and Article 2 ("Impeachment and Succession"), there have been three amendments (numbers 20, 22, and 25) and three laws concerning succession and term of office. This appendix will examine these contingency arrangements. It will also briefly describe the impeachment process and the two most serious attempts to remove a sitting president. The Constitution and statutes provide for methods of succession and removal.

SUCCESSION

The principal reason for creating the vice presidency was to have a position from which the presidency would automatically be filled by the second most qualified person should it become vacant. Death, resignation, and impeachment constitute clear-cut situations in which this succession mechanism would work. Eight presidents have died in office and one has resigned. In each of the nine instances, the vice president became president.

One contingency the founders did not consider was temporary or permanent disability while in office. On a number of occasions, presidents have become disabled and unable to perform their duties and responsibilities. James Garfield, who was shot by a disappointed job seeker, lingered for almost three months before he died. Ronald Reagan was hospitalized twice, the first time, following the attempt on his life and the other for an operation for cancer of the colon. During both hospital stays he was unconscious for several hours, and in both cases he was incapacitated for several months afterward. Other presidents have also been incapacitated. Wilson suffered a stroke that disabled him for much of his last year in office, while Eisenhower's heart attack, ileitis operation, and minor stroke severely limited his presidential activities in 1955, 1956, and 1957 (see Chapter 8).

During none of these periods did vice presidents officially take over. In fact, Chester Arthur and Thomas Marshall, Garfield's and Wilson's vice presidents, respectively, avoided even the appearance of performing presidential duties for fear that their actions would be wrongfully construed. Vice President Richard Nixon did preside at cabinet meetings during Eisenhower's absences, but did not assume the president's other responsibilities. Vice President George Bush, who was away from the capital at the time

Reagan was shot, flew back to Washington immediately to be available if needed. However, to avoid any appearance of impropriety, he had his helicopter land at the vice president's residence even though he was scheduled to meet at the White House with senior presidential aides. By prearrangement with the vice president, President Reagan passed his powers and duties to Bush during the period while he was under the influence of anesthesia during his colon operation in 1985. Reagan then reassumed his powers after he declared himself able to do so, several hours after his operation.

It was not until 1967 that procedures were established for the vice president to become acting president in the event of the president's disability. The Twenty-fifth Amendment to the Constitution permits the vice president to exercise the duties and powers of the presidency if the president declares in writing that he is unable to do so or if the vice president and a majority of the principal executive department heads reach that judgment. The president may resume office when he believes that he is capable unless the vice president and a majority of the principal executive department heads object. In that case, Congress must make the final determination. The procedures, however, are weighted in the president's favor. Unless Congress concurs in the judgment that the president is disabled, the president is entitled once again to exercise the duties and powers of the office.

Another important provision of this amendment provides for filling the vice presidency should it become vacant. Prior to 1967, it was vacant sixteen times. The procedures permit the president to nominate a new vice president, who takes office following confirmation by a majority of both houses of Congress. Gerald Ford and Nelson Rockefeller were the only two vice presidents who assumed office in this manner. Ford was nominated by President Nixon in 1973 following the resignation of Spiro T. Agnew, and after succeeding to the presidency following Nixon's resignation, Ford nominated Rockefeller.

Although the presidency and vice presidency have never been vacant at the same time, Congress has provided for such a contingency by establishing a line of succession. The most recent succession law, which was enacted in 1947, puts the Speaker of the House next in line, to be followed by the president pro tempore of the Senate and the department heads in order of the seniority of their departments, beginning with the secretary of state. The provision for appointing a new vice president, however, makes it less likely that legislative and executive officials would ever succeed to the presidency, barring a catastrophe or an unlikely set of events that resulted in a president's death before a new vice presidential nomination could be made and confirmed.

REMOVAL

In addition to providing for the president's replacement, the constitutional framers also thought it necessary to provide for the president's removal. They believed that it was too dangerous to wait for the electors' judgment should a president abuse the authority of the office. Impeachment was considered an extraordinary remedy, but one that could be used against executive officials, including the president and vice president, who violated the public trust.

Article 2, section 4, of the Constitution spells out the terms for removal. The president, vice president, and other executive officials can be removed from office for treason, bribery, or other "high Crimes and Misdemeanors." Precisely what actions would be considered impeachable offenses are left for Congress to determine.

The House of Representatives considers the charges against the president. If a majority of the House votes in favor of any of them, a trial is held in the Senate with the chief justice of the Supreme Court presiding. The House presents its case against the president, and the president, who may be represented by outside counsel, defends against the charges. A two-thirds vote of the Senate is required for conviction. A convicted president who is removed from office may still be subject to civil or criminal prosecution.

Only one president, Andrew Johnson, has ever been impeached. The incident that sparked his impeachment was Johnson's removal of Secretary of War Edwin Stanton. Congress had passed a law, over Johnson's veto, that required appointees to remain in office until the Senate approved their successor. Known as the Tenure of Office Act (1867), it permitted the president some discretion during a congressional recess but required the Senate's advice and consent after Congress reconvened. In the absence of senatorial approval, the office reverted to its previous occupant.

During a congressional recess, Johnson removed Stanton, but on its return, the Senate refused to concur in the removal. Under the law, Stanton was entitled to his old job. However, the president once again removed him. Following Stanton's removal for a second time, the House of Representatives passed a bill of impeachment against the president. The Senate trial lasted six weeks. In its first vote, the Senate fell one short of the required two-thirds needed to convict the president and remove him from office. A ten-day recess was called by those favoring Johnson's removal. Extensive lobbying ensued, but when the Senate reconvened, no one's vote changed, and Johnson was acquitted. The Tenure of Office Act was subsequently repealed during the Cleveland administration.

A second attempt to impeach a sitting president occurred in 1973. When Richard Nixon dismissed Archibald Cox, the special prosecutor who had been investigating charges of administration wrongdoing in the Watergate affair, members of Congress called for Nixon's removal. The Judiciary Committee of the House of Representatives began hearings on the president's impeachment. During the course of these hearings, the committee subpoenaed tapes of conversations that the president had held with aides in the White House, conversations that had been secretly recorded by the president. Claiming that these were privileged communications, Nixon refused to deliver the tapes, although he did send edited transcripts of them to the House committee. Not satisfied with this response, the House took its case to the Court and won. The Supreme Court ordered Nixon to release the tapes. When he did so, they revealed his early knowledge of the break-in and his participation in the cover-up. This information heightened calls for the president's ouster.

The House Judiciary Committee approved three articles of impeachment against Nixon. It looked as if the full House would vote to impeach him and that the Senate would vote to convict him. Faced with the prospect of a long trial and probable conviction, Nixon resigned on August 9, 1974.

A third attempt to impeach a sitting president was begun in September 1998 when the independent counsel investigating President Clinton's relationship with a White House intern reported to the House of Representatives that the president may have committed eleven possible impeachable offenses. (See Appendix D) The House sent the report and the White House's responses to it to its Judiciary committee which conducted hearings on whether to recommend that the House conduct an impeachment inquiry. By a straight party vote, the committee recommended an open-ended inquiry, one that would give it authority to investigate charges in the report as well as other matters which the independent counsel was currently investigating (the president's involvement in the firing of the White House travel office staff, the Whitewater land development deal in Arkansas, and the discovery of FBI files of prominent Republicans in the White House). The full House voted in October 1998 to authorize its Judiciary committee to conduct such an investigation after the 1998 midterm elections. Any report recommending impeachment, however, would have to be considered by the newly-elected members of the House after they convened in the 106th Congress.

TENURE

Electoral defeat and impeachment prematurely conclude a presidency—at least from the incumbent's perspective. Initially, the Constitution imposed no limit on the number of times a president could be elected. Indeed, reeligibility was seen as a motive to good behavior. Beginning with Washington, however, an unofficial two-term limit was established. Franklin Roosevelt ended this precedent in 1940 when he ran for a third term and won.

Partially in reaction to Roosevelt's twelve years and one month, as president, a Republican-controlled Congress passed, and the states ratified, the Twenty-Second Amendment to the Constitution. The amendment prevents any person from being elected to the office more than twice. Moreover, it limits to one election a president who has succeeded to the office and has served more than two years of his predecessor's term. Eisenhower was the first president to be subject to the provisions of the amendment; others have included Nixon, Reagan, and Clinton.

One of the consequences of the Twenty-Second Amendment is that it seems to weaken the president in the second term, particularly during the last two years in office. Not being able to run for the presidency again reduces a president's political power and lessens the capacity to mobilize public backing for the administration's programs and policies. On the other hand, it may improve the president's capacity to mobilize a bipartisan coalition because political motives may be less subject to suspicion if a president cannot seek reelection. This might result in a weaker domestic presidency but a stronger foreign policy one. It would certainly affect the incentives for policy making in each of these spheres.

Provisions of the Constitution of the United States That Relate to the Presidency

ARTICLE I

Section 2.

(3) [Representatives and direct Taxes[1] shall be apportioned among the several States which may be included within this Union, according to their respective Numbers, which shall be determined by adding to the whole Number of free Persons, including those bound to Service for a Term of Years, and excluding Indians not taxed, three fifths of all other Persons.][2] The actual Enumeration shall be made within three Years after the first Meeting of the Congress of the United States, and within every subsequent Term of ten Years, in such Manner as they shall by Law direct. The Number of Representatives shall not exceed one for every thirty Thousand, but each State shall have at Least one Representative; and until such enumeration shall be made, the State of New Hampshire shall be entitled to choose three, Massachusetts eight, Rhode-Island and Providence Plantations one, Connecticut five, New York six, New Jersey four, Pennsylvania eight, Delaware one, Maryland six, Virginia ten, North Carolina five, South Carolina five, and Georgia three.

(4) When vacancies happen in the Representation from any State, the Executive Authority thereof shall issue Writs of Election to fill such Vacancies.

(5) The House of Representatives shall choose their Speaker and other Officers; and shall have the sole Power of Impeachment.

Section 3.

(4) The Vice President of the United States shall be President of the Senate, but shall have no Vote, unless they be equally divided.

(5) The Senate shall choose their other Officers, and also a President pro tempore, in the Absence of the Vice President, or when he shall exercise the Office of President of the United States.

[1]The Sixteenth Amendment replaced this with respect to income taxes.
[2]Repealed by the Fourteenth Amendment.

(6) The Senate shall have the sole Power to try all Impeachments. When sitting for that Purpose, they shall be on Oath or Affirmation. When the President of the United States is tried, the Chief Justice shall preside: And no Person shall be convicted without the Concurrence of two thirds of the Members present.

(7) Judgment in Cases of Impeachment shall not extend further than to removal from Office, and disqualification to hold and enjoy any Office of honor, Trust or Profit under the United States: but the Party convicted shall nevertheless be liable and subject to Indictment, Trial, Judgment and Punishment according to Law.

Section 7.

(2) Every Bill which shall have passed the House of Representatives and the Senate, shall, before it become a Law, be presented to the President of the United States; If he approve he shall sign it, but if not he shall return it, with his Objections to that House in which it shall have originated, who shall enter the Objections at large on their Journal, and proceed to reconsider it. If after such Reconsideration two thirds of that House shall agree to pass the Bill, it shall be sent, together with Objections, to the other House, by which it shall likewise be reconsidered, and if approved by two thirds of that House, it shall become a Law. But in all such Cases the Votes of both Houses shall be determined by Yeas and Nays, and the Names of the Persons voting for and against the Bill shall be entered on the Journal of each House respectively. If any Bill shall not be returned by the President within ten Days (Sundays excepted) after it shall have been presented to him, the Same shall be a Law, in like Manner as if he had signed it, unless the Congress by their Adjournment prevent its Return, in which Case it shall not be a Law.

(3) Every Order, Resolution, or Vote to which the Concurrence of the Senate and House of Representatives may be necessary (except on a question of Adjournment) shall be presented to the President of the United States; and before the Same shall take Effect, shall be approved by him, or being disapproved by him, shall be repassed by two thirds of the Senate and House of Representatives, according to the Rules and Limitations prescribed in the Case of a Bill.

Section 9.

(2) The Privilege of the Writ of Habeas Corpus shall not be suspended, unless when in Cases of Rebellion or Invasion the public Safety may require it.

(8) No Title of Nobility shall be granted by the United States: And no Person holding any Office of Profit or Trust under them, shall, without the Consent of the Congress, accept of any present, Emolument, Office, or Title, of any kind whatever, from any King, Prince, or foreign State.

ARTICLE II

Section 1.

(1) The executive Power shall be vested in a President of the United States of America. He shall hold his Office during the Term of four Years, and, together with the Vice President, chosen for the same Term, be elected, as follows:

(2) Each State shall appoint, in such Manner as the Legislature thereof may direct, a Number of Electors, equal to the whole Number of Senators and Representatives to which the State may be entitled in the Congress, but no Senator or Representative, or

Person holding an Office of Trust or Profit under the United States, shall be appointed an Elector.

[The Electors shall meet in their respective States, and vote by Ballot for two persons, of whom one at least shall not be an Inhabitant of the same State with themselves. And they shall make a List of all the Persons voted for, and of the Number of Votes for each; which List they shall sign and certify, and transmit sealed to the Seat of the Government of the United States, directed to the President of the Senate. The President of the Senate shall, in the Presence of the Senate and House of Representatives, open all the Certificates, and the Votes shall then be counted. The Person having the greatest Number of Votes shall be the President, if such Number be a Majority of the whole Number of Electors appointed; and if there be more than one who have such Majority, and have an equal Number of Votes, then the House of Representatives shall immediately choose by Ballot one of them for President; and if no Person have a Majority, then from the five highest on the List the said House shall in like Manner choose the President. But in choosing the President, the Votes shall be taken by States, the Representation from each State having one Vote; A quorum for this purpose shall consist of a Member or Members from two thirds of the States, and a Majority of all the States shall be necessary to a Choice. In every Case, after the Choice of the President, the Person having the greatest Number of Votes of the Electors shall be the Vice President. But if there should remain two or more who have equal Votes, the Senate shall choose from them by Ballot the Vice President.][3]

(3) The Congress may determine the Time of choosing the Electors, and the Day on which they shall give their Votes; which Day shall be the same throughout the United States.

(4) No person except a natural born Citizen, or a Citizen of the United States, at the time of the Adoption of this Constitution, shall be eligible to the Office of President; neither shall any Person be eligible to that Office who shall not have attained to the Age of thirty-five Years, and been fourteen Years a Resident within the United States.

(5) In case of the Removal of the President from Office, or of his Death, Resignation, or Inability to discharge the Powers and Duties of the said Office, the same shall devolve on the Vice President, and the Congress may by Law provide for the Case of Removal, Death, Resignation or Inability; both of the President and Vice President, declaring what Officer shall then act as President, and such Officer shall act accordingly, until the Disability be removed, or a President shall be elected.[4]

(6) The President shall, at stated Times, receive for his Services, a Compensation, which shall neither be increased nor diminished during the Period for which he shall have been elected, and he shall not receive within that Period any other Emolument from the United States, or any of them.

(7) Before he enter on the Execution of his Office, he shall take the following Oath or Affirmation:—"I do solemnly swear (or affirm) that I will faithfully execute the Office of President of the United States, and will to the best of my Ability, preserve, protect and defend the Constitution of the United States."

Section 2.

(1) The President shall be Commander in Chief of the Army and Navy of the United States, and of the Militia of the several States, when called into the actual Service of the

---

[3]This paragraph was superseded in 1804 by the Twelfth Amendment.
[4]Changed by the Twenty-fifth Amendment.

United States; he may require the Opinion in writing, of the principal Officer in each of the executive Departments, upon any subject relating to the Duties of their respective Offices, and he shall have Power to Grant Reprieves and Pardons for Offenses against the United States, except in Cases of Impeachment.

(2) He shall have Power, by and with the Advice and Consent of the Senate, to make Treaties, provided two thirds of the Senators present concur; and he shall nominate, and by and with the Advice and Consent of the Senate, shall appoint Ambassadors, other public Ministers and Consuls, Judges of the supreme Court, and all other Officers of the United States, whose Appointments are not herein otherwise provided for, and which shall be established by Law: but the Congress may by Law vest the Appointment of such inferior Officers, as they think proper, in the President alone, in the Court of Law, or in the Heads of Departments.

(3) The President shall have Power to fill up all Vacancies that may happen during the Recess of the Senate, by granting Commissions which shall expire at the End of their next Session.

Section 3.

He shall from time to time give to the Congress Information of the State of the Union, and recommend to their Consideration such Measures as he shall judge necessary and expedient; he may, on extraordinary Occasions, convene both Houses, or either of them, and in Case of Disagreement between them, with Respect to the Time of Adjournment, he may adjourn them to such Time as he shall think proper; he shall receive Ambassadors and other public Ministers; he shall take Care that the Laws be faithfully executed, and shall Commission all the Officers of the United States.

Section 4.

The President, Vice President and all civil Officers of the United States, shall be removed from Office on Impeachment for, and Conviction of, Treason, Bribery, or other high Crimes and Misdemeanors.

ARTICLE IV

Section 4.

The United States shall guarantee to every State in this Union a Republican Form of Government, and shall protect each of them against Invasion; and on Application of the Legislature, or of the Executive (when the Legislature cannot be convened) against domestic Violence.

ARTICLE VI

(3) The Senators and Representatives before mentioned, and the Members of the several State Legislatures, and all executive and judicial Officers, both of the United States and of the several States, shall be bound by Oath or Affirmation, to support this Constitution; but no religious Test shall ever be required as a Qualification to any Office or public Trust under the United States.

AMENDMENT XII[5]

The Electors shall meet in their respective states and vote by ballot for President and Vice President, one of whom, at least, shall not be an inhabitant of the same state with themselves; they shall name in their ballots the person voted for as President, and in distinct ballots the person voted for as Vice President, and they shall make distinct lists of persons voted for as President, and of all persons voted for as Vice President, and of the number of votes for each, which lists they shall sign and certify, and transmit sealed to the seat of the government of the United States, directed to the President of the Senate;—The President of the Senate shall, in presence of the Senate and House of Representatives, open all the certificates and the votes shall then be counted;—The person having the greatest number of votes for President, shall be the President, if such number be a majority of the whole number of Electors appointed; and if no person have such majority, then from the persons having the highest numbers not exceeding three on the list of those voted for as President, the House of Representatives shall choose immediately, by ballot, the President. But in choosing the President, the votes shall be taken by states, the representation from each state having one vote; a quorum for this purpose shall consist of a member or members from two thirds of the states, and a majority of all the states shall be necessary to a choice. [And if the House of Representatives shall not choose a President whenever the right of choice shall devolve upon them, before the fourth day of March next following, then the Vice President shall act as President, as in the case of the death or other constitutional disability of the President.][6]—The person having the greatest number of votes as Vice President, shall be the Vice President, if such number be a majority of the whole number of Electors appointed, and if no person have a majority, then from the two highest numbers on the list, the Senate shall choose the Vice President; a quorum for the purpose shall consist of two thirds of the whole number of Senators, and a majority of the whole number shall be necessary to a choice. But no person constitutionally ineligible to the office of President shall be eligible to that of Vice President of the United States.

AMENDMENT XV[7]

Section 1.
The right of citizens of the United States to vote shall not be denied or abridged by the United States or by any State on account of race, color, or previous condition of servitude.

Section 2.
The Congress shall have power to enforce this article by appropriate legislation.

AMENDMENT XIX[8]

The right of citizens of the United States to vote shall not be denied or abridged by the United States or by any State on account of sex.

Congress shall have power to enforce this article by appropriate legislation.

[5]Adopted in 1804.
[6]Superseded by the Twentieth Amendment, section 3.
[7]Adopted in 1870.
[8]Adopted in 1920.

AMENDMENT XX[9]

Section 1.

The terms of the President and Vice President shall end at noon on the 20th day of January, and the terms of Senators and Representatives at noon on the 3rd day of January, of the years in which such terms would have ended if this article had not been ratified; and the terms of their successors shall then begin.

Section 2.

The Congress shall assemble at least once in every year, and such meeting shall begin at noon on the 3rd day of January, unless they shall by law appoint a different day.

Section 3.

If, at the time fixed for the beginning of the term of the President, the President elect shall have died, the Vice President elect shall become President. If a President shall not have been chosen before the time fixed for the beginning of his term, or if the President elect shall have failed to qualify, then the Vice President elect shall act as a President until a President shall have qualified; and the Congress may by law provide for the case wherein neither a President elect nor a Vice President elect shall have qualified, declaring who shall then act as President, or the manner in which one who is to act shall be selected, and such person shall act accordingly until a President or Vice President shall have qualified.

Section 4.

The Congress may by law provide for the case of the death of any of the persons from whom the House of Representatives may choose a President whenever the right of choice shall have devolved upon them, and for the case of the death of any of the persons from whom the Senate may choose a Vice President whenever the right of choice shall have devolved upon them.

Section 5.

Sections 1 and 2 shall take effect on the 15th day of October following the ratification of this article.

Section 6.

This article shall be inoperative unless it shall have been ratified as an amendment to the Constitution by the legislatures of three fourths of the several States within seven years from the date of its submission.

AMENDMENT XXII[10]

Section 1.

No person shall be elected to the office of the President more than twice, and no person who has held the office of President, or acted as President, for more than two years of a term to which some other person was elected President shall be elected to the office

---

[9]Adopted in 1933.
[10]Adopted in 1951.

of the President more than once. But this Article shall not apply to any person holding the office of President when this Article was proposed by the Congress, and shall not prevent any person who may be holding the office of President, or acting as President, during the term within which this Article becomes operative from holding the office of President or acting as President during the remainder of such term.

Section 2.
This article shall be inoperative unless it shall have been ratified as an amendment to the Constitution by the legislatures of three fourths of the several States within seven years from the date of its submission to the States by the Congress.

AMENDMENT XXIII[11]

Section 1.
The District constituting the seat of Government of the United States shall appoint in such manner as the Congress may direct:
A number of electors of President and Vice President equal to the whole number of Senators and Representatives in Congress to which the District would be entitled if it were a State, but in no event more than the least populous State; they shall be in addition to those appointed by the States, but they shall be considered, for the purposes of the election of President and Vice President, to be electors appointed by a State; and they shall meet in the District and perform such duties as provided by the twelfth article of amendment.

Section 2.
The Congress shall have power to enforce this article by appropriate legislation.

AMENDMENT XXIV[12]

Section 1.
The right of citizens of the United States to vote in any primary or other election for President or Vice President, for electors for President or Vice President, or for Senator or Representative in Congress, shall not be denied or abridged by the United States or any state by reasons of failure to pay any poll tax or other tax.

Section 2.
The Congress shall have power to enforce this article by appropriate legislation.

AMENDMENT XXV[13]

Section 1.
In case of the removal of the President from office or of his death or resignation, the Vice President shall become President.

[11]Adopted in 1961.
[12]Adopted in 1964.
[13]Adopted in 1967.

Section 2.

Whenever there is a vacancy in the office of the Vice President, the President shall nominate a Vice President who shall take office upon confirmation by a majority vote of both Houses of Congress.

Section 3.

Whenever the President transmits to the President pro tempore of the Senate and the Speaker of the House of Representatives his written declaration that he is unable to discharge the powers and duties of his office, and until he transmits to them a written declaration to the contrary, such powers and duties shall be discharged by the Vice President as Acting President.

Section 4.

Whenever the Vice President and a majority of either the principal officers of the Executive departments or of such other body as Congress may by law provide, transmit to the President pro tempore of the Senate and the Speaker of the House of Representatives their written declaration that the President is unable to discharge the powers and duties of his office, the Vice President shall immediately assume the powers and duties of the office as Acting President.

Thereafter, when the President transmits to the President pro tempore of the Senate and the Speaker of the House of Representatives his written declaration that no inability exists, he shall resume the powers and duties of his office unless the Vice President and a majority of either the principal officers of the executive departments or of such other body as Congress may by law provide, transmit within four days to the President pro tempore of the Senate and the Speaker of the House of Representatives their written declaration that the President is unable to discharge the powers and duties of his office. Thereupon Congress shall decide the issue, assembling within forty-eight hours for that purpose if not in session. If the Congress, within twenty-one days after receipt of the latter written declaration, or, if Congress is not in session, within twenty-one days after Congress is required to assemble, determines by two thirds vote of both houses that the President is unable to discharge the powers and duties of his office, the Vice President shall continue to discharge the same as Acting President; otherwise, the President shall resume the powers and duties of his office.

AMENDMENT XXVI[14]

Section 1.

The right of citizens of the United States, who are 18 years of age or older, to vote shall not be denied or abridged by the United States or any state on account of age.

Section 2.

The Congress shall have power to enforce this article by appropriate legislation.

[14]Adopted in 1971.

The Politics of Impeachment: Arguments for and against the Impeachment of William Jefferson Clinton

POSSIBLE GROUNDS FOR IMPEACHMENT: THE REPORT OF THE INDEPENDENT COUNSEL

1. President Clinton lied under oath in his civil case when he denied a sexual affair, a sexual relationship, or sexual relations with Monica Lewinsky.

2. President Clinton lied under oath to the grand jury about his sexual relationship with Ms. Lewinsky.

3. In his civil deposition, to support his false statement about the sexual relationship, President Clinton also lied under oath about being alone with Ms. Lewinsky and about the many gifts exchanged between Ms. Lewinsky and him.

4. President Clinton lied under oath in his civil deposition about his discussions with Ms. Lewinsky concerning her involvement in the Jones case.

5. During the Jones case, the President obscured justice and had an understanding with Ms. Lewinsky to jointly conceal the truth about their relationship by concealing gifts subpoenaed by Ms. Jones's attorneys.

6. During the Jones case, the President obstructed justice and had an understanding with Ms. Lewinsky to jointly conceal the truth of their relationship from the judicial process by a scheme that included the following means: (i) Both the President and Ms. Lewinsky understood that they would lie under oath in the Jones case about their sexual relationship; (ii) the President suggested to Ms. Lewinsky that she prepare an affidavit that, for the President's purposes, would memorialize her testimony under oath and could be used to prevent questioning of both of them about their relationship; (iii) Ms. Lewinsky signed and filed the false affidavit; (iv) the President used Ms. Lewinsky's false affidavit at his deposition in an attempt to head off questions about Ms. Lewinsky; and

(v) when that failed, the President lied under oath at his civil deposition about the relationship with Ms. Lewinsky.

7. President Clinton endeavored to obstruct justice by helping Ms. Lewinsky obtain a job in New York at a time when she would have been a witness harmful to him were she to tell the truth in the Jones case.

8. President Clinton lied under oath in his civil deposition about his discussions with Vernon Jordan concerning Ms. Lewinsky's involvement in the Jones case.

9. The President improperly tampered with a potential witness by attempting to corruptly influence the testimony of his personal secretary, Betty Currie, in the days after his civil deposition.

10. President Clinton endeavored to obstruct justice during the grand jury investigation by refusing to testify for seven months and lying to senior White House aides with knowledge that they would relay the President's false statements to the grand jury—and did thereby deceive, obstruct, and impede the grand jury.

11. President Clinton abused his constitutional authority by (i) lying to the public and the Congress in January 1998 about his relationship with Ms. Lewinsky (ii) promising at that time to cooperate fully with the grand jury investigation; (iii) later refusing six invitations to testify voluntarily to the grand jury; (iv) invoking Executive Privilege; (v) lying to the grand jury in August 1998; and (vi) lying again to the public and Congress on August 17, 1988—all as part of an effort to hinder, impede, and deflect possible inquiry by the Congress of the United States.

SUMMARY OF THE WHITE HOUSE RESPONSE

1. The president admitted that he committed a serious mistake, but that mistake does not amount to an impeachable offense. What he did was wrong but not a high crime or misdemeanor as required in the Constitution as grounds for impeachment. The framers intended impeachment to be used against wrongful *public* acts against the political system, not wrongful *personal* acts.

2. There was no perjury committed. The president answered questions around sexual relations according to his understanding of the term *sexual relations*, as used by the court.

The president gave narrow answers to ambiguous questions in his testimony during the Jones deposition and to the Grand Jury. He was under no obligation to do otherwise; a person accused of a crime is under no obligation to provide his accusers with information that could be used against him.

3. The president did not obstruct justice. He did not coach potential witnesses or ask anyone to lie. He never requested Ms. Lewinsky to return the gifts he gave her. The president did not try to get Ms. Lewinsky a job to influence her testimony. He did not facilitate her interview with Bill Richardson, U.S. Ambassador to the United Nations, nor did he ask his friend Vernon Jordan to make calls on Ms. Lewinsky's behalf.

4. The president's invocation of executive privilege is not an abuse of power. Nor did the president play any role in the Secret Service's legal attempt to prevent its agents from testifying.

5. The comments made by White House staff in the course of the independent counsel's investigation were not an abuse of presidential power nor did the president mislead

the White House staff in order to foil the investigation. He did admit, however, that he misled his family, staff, and friends, but misleading per se is not a criminal offense.

6. The actions of the White House attorneys were lawful. The president acted according to the legal advice that he received from them.

7. There was no perjury, no obstruction of justice, no abuse of power.

Figure 2–1: "The Cost of Politics: The 1996 Presidential Nomination." From "Revenues, Federal Election Commission, October 1996 Expenditures" from the *Washington Post,* April 18, 1996 and August 24, 1996, pp. A3 and A11, respectively. Copyright © 1996 Washington Post Writer's Group. Reprinted with permission.

Table 3-2: "Portrait of the American Electorate, 1984–1996 (in percentages)." From the *New York Times,* Nov. 10, 1996, p. 28. Copyright © 1996 by The New York Times Company. Reprinted by permission.

Box, page 146: "President Clinton Assesses the Press." By Jan Wenner and William Greider. From *Rolling Stone,* December 9, 1993. Straight Arrow Publishers, Inc., 1993. All Rights Reserved. Reprinted with permission.

Excerpts, pages 186–187, 192–193: From *Locked in the Cabinet* by Robert Reich. (New York: Alfred A. Knopf, Inc., 1997), pp. 78, 108–109. Reprinted with permission.

Box, page 466: "Economic Decision Making in 1993." Copyright © 1999. From *The Politics of American Government* by Stephen J. Wayne, G. Calvin Mackenzie, David M. O'Brien, and Richard L. Cole. Reprinted by permission of Bedford/St. Martin's.

Table 14-1: "Treaties and Executive Agreements Approved by the United States, 1789–1997." Data for 1789–1992 adapted from *Vital Statistics on American Politics,* 4th ed., by Harold W. Stanley and Richard G. Niemi. (Washington, D.C.: Congressional Quarterly Press, 1994), p. 280. Used with permission.

INDEX